OPERA NIGHTS

OPERA NIGHTS

By

ERNEST NEWMAN

PUTNAM

42 GREAT RUSSELL STREET
LONDON

First published September 1943
Reprinted August 1944
Reprinted October 1945
Reprinted April 1947
Reprinted September 1956

MADE AND PRINTED BY OFFSET IN GREAT BRITAIN BY
WILLIAM CLOWES AND SONS LIMITED, LONDON AND BECCLES

TO
VERA

CONTENTS

A*

ix

CONTENTS

x

OPERA NIGHTS

OVERTURE

Although a point of aesthetic is now and then touched upon in the following pages, I wish it to be understood at once that this is not a book of "musical criticism". Its object is severely practical —to help the listener to opera, whether in the theatre or by radio, to get more value out of his listening.

We are assured by the armchair aestheticians that a work of art ought to be its own sufficient explanation, and no doubt, in an ideal world, it would be. But we have the misfortune to live in a world constructed on anything but ideal principles; and the number of large-scale dramatic works that "explain themselves" beyond question in mere performance is smaller than we are inclined to think. Take, by way of simple illustration, the dialogue between Lorenzo and Jessica at the commencement of the fifth act of *The Merchant of Venice*. Will it be contended that these lines yield the same suggestiveness, the same beauty, to the man —supposing there to be such a man—who has never heard of Troilus and Cressida and Dido and Medea as they do to the man in whom the merest mention of these names at once floods the imagination with memories of emotions kindled in him by other great poems and dramas? Is there not something of Cervantes in us each time we listen to the *Don Quixote* of Strauss, something —however little—of Goethe present with us when we listen to *Faust* or *Mignon* in the opera house? Could we, if we tried, listen to Cornelius's Abul Hassan Ali Ebn Bekar without seeing him enveloped in the aura of that immortal ancestor of his whom we know from the pages of *The Thousand and One Nights?*

Most people know, from their own opera-going or concert-going, how large a part previous experiences of this kind play in the sum total of their pleasure in such works as those I have mentioned. By inference, therefore, they must be missing, in the case of many a work for their insight into which they are dependent wholly on what they see and hear on the stage, a good deal of rather vital stuff which the librettist and the composer intended

3

them to see and hear. This stuff was in the librettist and the composer when they conceived and executed the opera: without it their work would never have been just what it is: surely, then, it is necessary that it should be in us also when we see and listen, if our own imaginative apprehension of the work is to be as definite and as intense as theirs. Once more it is no use mumbling that "the work of art ought to explain itself". Notoriously it does not, in a thousand cases that could be cited. It can be asserted dogmatically that very few modern operas founded on a pre-existent novel, poem or play really explain themselves. In general, so much of the original has had to be omitted in the shaping of the libretto, so much inserted in the stead of what was omitted, so many episodes transposed in time or place, that the situations, the characters and the psychological states of the opera sometimes bear only a superficial resemblance to the work of art on which it was based.

"Quite so", it may be replied to this; "but does that alter the fact that the opera and the drama (or novel) in question are two completely different organisms, inhabiting each a world of its own, living each according to the laws of its own being? Should not the opera organism be complete in itself, self-consistent, self-sufficing? And is it not sufficient for us to listen to the opera just as it is and take it for just what it is, not troubling our heads as to its nearness to, or remoteness from, the drama or novel from which its subject was derived?" The answer to that would be, and could only be, precisely the one the questioner expects—but for one little fact which cannot be left out of consideration. No matter how much or how little of Anatole France's *Thaïs*, let us say, or of Prévost's *Manon Lescaut*, or of Gozzi's *Turandot* there may be in Massenet's *Thaïs* or *Manon* or in Puccini's *Turandot*, it still remains true that France's novel and Prévost's story and Gozzi's play were functioning in every brain cell of the opera poets and composers when they were fashioning *their* works. The infiltration of the original must have affected their own treatment of the subject in a thousand subtle ways. It is surely not superfluous, then, on the part of us listeners to go over again, in imagination, the ground they traversed so often before they reached their own goal.

If an opera invariably explained itself in performance there would be little need, of course, for books of the type of the present one. But operas, alas, are often far from explaining themselves, as we soon discover when we come to discuss this or that work with some one who has pursued it enthusiastically from theatre to theatre year after year but without ever having taken the trouble to read anything about it. People of this kind often have the quaintest ideas about a work which, they will assure us, they "adore". It was not until a valued friend of mine, who had seen Wagner's tetralogy each summer for several years, read at long last a "Story of the *Ring*" that she discovered that it was not merely an accident of the dressing room that the singer of Wotan had one eye obscured by a lock of his hair. She knew nothing of the legend that in days gone by Wotan had sacrificed one of his eyes to win Fricka's love, and that the seemingly truant lock of hair was intended to conceal the loss. My friend admitted that she had been struck by the frequency with which Wotan seemed to have a wisp of hair hanging down over one of his eyes; but so far as she had ever thought about it at all she had vaguely assumed that the god was perhaps a little careless in the matter of his coiffure, and no doubt she wondered why Fricka had not spoken to him about it.

It is not only with regard to episodes and motives that the plain opera-goer requires occasional guidance. There are many things also in connection with the music which he ought to know, but which he has little or no chance of getting to know merely by sitting in his seat and looking and listening. Probably a million people have heard *Der Rosenkavalier* since 1911. Of that million, how many, I wonder, have paid any particular attention to the little figure quoted as No. 2a in the following analysis? I do not mean when motive No. 2 is first heard as a whole in the orchestral prelude to the opera—no one can fail to be aware of it there—but some forty or fifty bars later, when it appears, in the condensed form of no more than just these three notes, as a counterpart to another theme. And even if the listener's attention does happen to have been caught by this fragment, how is he to know that Strauss has marked it "seufzend", thereby telling the student of the score in the plainest terms possible that he is expected to hear

in it the sigh of the Princess over the love that she is soon to lose
for ever? If I am told by the armchair aesthetician that Strauss
has no right to do such a thing, for by doing it he has violated the
primary law that "the work of art must be its own explanation",
my only reply is the humble one that Strauss *has* done it, openly,
unblushingly. The "seufzend" must have had considerable significance for him, or he would not have inserted it in his score. It
must surely, therefore, be of the same significance for us listeners.
No clarinettist can possibly make these three notes sound unmistakably like a sigh; indeed, precisely the same three notes coming
elsewhere in this or any other work might "mean" something
quite different. It is simply that these three notes in this particular
place were accompanied in Strauss's mind by a vision of the
Princess sighing her wounded heart out; and I submit that if it is
with that vision in his mind that the composer of the work listens
to the passage, it is with the same vision at the back of our minds
that *we* should listen to it. The question of aesthetic propriety or
impropriety is here of minor importance: all that matters is the
fact, and the inference to be drawn from the fact.

But these are not the only respects in which it is desirable,
indeed necessary, for us to listen to an opera with our memories
and our imagination co-operating with our eyes and ears. For
opera, alas, through no fault of its own, is rich in disappointments
and disillusionments for both eye and ear. Every musician can
recall orchestral performances by the dozen in the concert room
that came as near perfection as mortal man can achieve. But I
doubt whether any human being has ever heard a single perfect
performance of a single opera. Nature is so stupid: she has the most
unfortunate gift for placing the right voice in the wrong body, or
the wrong larynx underneath the right brains. No theatrical
manager would dream of casting an actor of the build of a Carnera
to play Slender in *The Merry Wives of Windsor*, or a stout young
woman with a high-pitched, piping voice to play Cassandra or
Medea. But the casting of the opera producer is a desperate matter
in which he has little choice. The main determining factor is the
kind of voice with which nature has endowed—if endowed is the
correct word in some instances—this singer or that. So long as
the actor whom the producer has in mind for Shakespeare's Ham-

let or Romeo is reasonably young, reasonably cultured and of a reasonably good figure, it does not make the slightest difference whether his voice is a baritone or a tenor, or whether its timbre is that of the clarinet or the oboe. But should an opera composer have made *his* Hamlet or Romeo a tenor, a particular singer might be ninety-nine per cent qualified for the part and yet be inexorably barred from it by the fact that nature has made him a bass. Singers of the most romantic appearance and irresistible romantic charm, who, had they been born tenors, would have made ideal Tristans or Belmontes or Des Grieux, have had to spend their theatrical lives grunting and spluttering in the depths of the Rhine as Alberichs or chalking a slate as Beckmessers, merely because nature has seen fit to pitch their vocal compass a fifth too low. We get a young woman fresh from the conservatoire whose monstrous bulk suggests to the spectator only what Ysaye used to call the Vénus de kilo. She looks like an ox; she moves like a cart horse; she stands like a haystack; she thinks, if she can be said to think at all, like a child whose mental development has been arrested at the age of twelve. Yet because nature has seen fit to give her a vocal organ of exceptional lightness, liquidity and capacity for coloratura, she is cast, as a matter of course, for some such flower-light, gem-bright creature as Lakmé, Violetta or Rosina.

Furthermore, even when the singer happens to be an artist of the first quality and his appearance is not too violently at variance with the character he is supposed to be representing, the most precious virtues of his voice may constitute an obstacle to his realising that character. Caruso was intelligent enough to see that the one vocal method, however perfect in itself, will not do for every dramatic part, and he knew that the timbre of the voice is to some extent the reflection of the mood of the moment. He knew that the surest way to make Otello *sound* different from Romeo was for the singer to *think* differently in each capacity; and he himself has told us that when he was due to sing one of the lighter tenor parts, such as Nemorino in *L'Elisir d'amore*, he would isolate himself, during the day, from everything that might have tended to make his spirit unduly serious in the evening. Yet even Caruso—or shall we say most of all Caruso?—could no more escape from the consequences of his own superb voice than he could have jumped over his own shadow. Take, as an illustration, his singing of "Ah! fuyez, douce image", (of which quite a good gramophone record exists). As singing, nothing could be more magnificent, more thrilling. But is this the Des Grieux of either Prévost or Massenet? Assuredly not! The tones, and the mentality at the back of the tones, are those not of the delicately-bred young French aristocrat that is Des Grieux but of the burly Italian man of the people that was Caruso. The latter's Des Grieux was necessarily no more like the real Des Grieux than Chaliapine's Pelléas, had Chaliapine been a tenor of the same calibre as Chaliapine's bass, would have been like the Pelléas of Maeterlinck and Debussy.

We are faced with the saddening paradox that first-rate singing, considered merely as singing, may sometimes be the worst possible kind of singing in a given part at a given moment of that part. This was the gist of Wagner's grievance against Albert Niemann, the Tannhäuser of the Paris production of 1861. There was a time, Wagner told him in effect, for a tenor to deploy the full splendour of his voice and a time when to do so would merely be to achieve dramatic nonsense. Niemann, being a Heldentenor, could think of nothing during the story of Tannhäuser's Pilgrimage but the effect he, Albert Niemann, wanted to make on the audience. He constantly turned the full resources of his powerful organ on to the part, whereas Wagner's conception of Tannhäuser at this stage of the opera was of a man exhausted by physical suffering and spiritually broken by remorse and despair. It was flat nonsense, he hinted to the tenor, to suppose that such a man would be expressing himself, after the hardships of his journey from Rome, with the vigour of tone, the brilliance of colour that would be appropriate to a character in the heyday of happy youth. But Wagner, of course, might as well have argued with a rhinoceros as with a vain young bumpkin of the Niemann type.

Not that the composers themselves are wholly free from blame for certain misfortunes that attend their works. Brooding over his characters in the quiet of his chamber, a composer is sometimes apt to lose touch with the realities of the theatre. Not many of them make so bad a mistake as Debussy, whose Pelléas proved to have been conceived, in great part, in terms not of any practicable male voice but of Debussy's own voice, which was a little

of everything and all of nothing. But instances abound of composers forgetting, in their enthusiastic absorption in their work,
some of the most elementary practical considerations. Several
famous operas need, for their ideal performance, a double or even
a triple casting of one of the leading parts. *Carmen,* for example,
demands one type of tenor in the first act and another in the
fourth; while in proportion as a Tristan can do all that Wagner
demands of him in the terrific third act he is likely to be incapable
of the delicacies of tone required of him in the greater part of the
second. Nor is it only in a comparatively simple matter of this
kind that the best composers, and those with the widest practical
experience of the theatre, miscalculate grievously at times. Wagner was so enchanted with the preliminary rehearsals for the first
Tristan production in the small Munich Residenz Theatre that he
begged King Ludwig to allow the performances to take place
there. One of the reasons for his enthusiasm was the fact that in
this small place every subtlety of facial expression on the part of
the actors was seizable by the spectators. Another reason was that
in the sectional rehearsals every finest thread of the orchestral
texture stood out clearly. But as the rehearsals developed and the
whole weight of the huge machine gradually came into operation
it became evident that the little theatre was over-resonant for
such a score; and Wagner himself had sorrowfully to request that
the performance should be given in the large Court Theatre,
where something indeed was gained, but much on which he had
set his heart was inevitably lost.

Sheridan is thought to have gone to the outermost edge of
extravaganza when he made the proud author of the tragedy of
The Spanish Armada expound to Mr. Dangle and Mr Sneer the
infinitude of meanings in Lord Burleigh's nod; but the musical
dramatist is constantly making demands on his audience's capacity
for seeing into the back of the beyond of things that would have
staggered Mr. Puff. Take, for instance, the case of the still living
composer, the story of which I had straight from the mouth of
the singer concerned in the affair. At the rehearsals of the opera
this singer found himself at one point alone on the stage for
several minutes, during which nothing whatever happened except
that the orchestra abandoned itself to an orgy of "symphonic

development." The singer, being an intelligent and conscientious man, and yearning to do all he could not merely for himself but for the work, one day asked the composer if he could suggest any "business" for him during this long musical standstill: alternatively, could he see his way to cutting out, or at any rate cutting down, the lengthy orchestral outpouring that was creating the difficulty? The composer was horrified at the suggestion. "It is impossible", he said, "to sacrifice a single bar of that music; it describes what is going on in the mind of So-and-So, *who comes on in the next act.*"

Here, if anywhere, was a case for thought-reading on the part of the audience! But even more experienced musical dramatists than the one of whom I have been speaking can be equally unreasonable in their demands on our gift of second sight when they come up against a snag in the construction of their work which there is no shifting and no getting round. In the last act of the *Götterdämmerung*, for instance, Siegfried lies dead on his bier. Surely now, the spectator says sadly to himself, there is nothing to prevent Hagen taking the Ring from his finger. What checks the villain in his wicked course? The dead man raises his hand, thus, so to speak, putting the fear of God in Hagen! Wagner's bland shirking of his problem at this point reminds us of the way of the Scotch parson with his congregation: "Here, my brethren, we come to a very deefficult passage, and having looked it bowldly in the face we will pass on."

In the Wagner case there is nothing for us to do but to put our standards of dramatic propriety in our pocket and pass on. In certain other less desperate cases we are given a little help "on the side" by the composer, who, all too worriedly aware that he has left a couple of important threads untied, makes a shame-faced attempt in a note in the text or the score to supply what ought to be, but assuredly is not, manifest in the stage action itself. I would cite, by way of illustration, the episode of the entry of the Princess in the last act of *Der Rosenkavalier*, a full discussion of which will be found in our analysis of that opera. Ask an ordinary theatregoer who has never seen the score or read the libretto how it comes about that this exceedingly aristocratic lady happens to turn up in the very dubious hostelry to which Ochs has taken

Mariandel, and he will confess his utter inability to tell you. For such knowledge as we have of the matter we are dependent upon a stage direction that has apparently been slipped in, *faute de mieux*, at the last moment. Even when we happen to be aware of this direction we are more than likely to miss, at a performance, the very thing Strauss wants us to notice—the approving look the Baron turns on his Body-servant; for it is not to either of these, but to the Princess, that the eyes of the whole house are irresistibly drawn at her entrance. Furthermore, even if the spectator does chance to intercept the exchange of looks between the Baron and the Body-servant, how can he be expected to read into them the precise significance that Strauss and Hofmannsthal intended them to carry? The librettist and the composer really seem at this point to be doing in all seriousness what Sheridan did only in gay burlesque.

I have said enough, I hope, to make the reader ask himself whether listening to opera is quite as simple a matter as he may have supposed it to be. Most people would maintain that while symphonies and so on require analytic exposition in order to render them fully accessible to the plain musical man, operas explain themselves by means of their words and their stage action. I make bold to say that precisely the reverse of this proposition is true. A good fugue, a good symphony, really explains itself, because, in the homogeneous medium in which he has been working, there has been nothing to prevent the composer from saying just what he set out to say; whereas in opera there are so many factors in operation that the chances are vastly against the perfect fusion of them all. I venture to repeat that listening to opera calls for the incessant reinforcement of eye and ear by memory, reflection and imagination. The primary object of the present volume is to stimulate these faculties in the listener in respect of the operas here treated, and so assist him to keener and more delighted listening.

I have not been able to use as many musical examples as I should have liked in the case of certain copyright works. The war having made it impossible to get into touch with foreign publishers, I have had to content myself with the limited amount of quotation sanctioned by international copyright law. I have to thank Messrs Boosey and Hawkes and the Universal Edition (London) for their kind acquiescence in the citations I have made from *Wozzeck* and from certain Russian operas.

Perhaps I ought to explain the principle—on the surface it may look like complete lack of principle—on which I have dealt with the titles of certain works. It may seem inconsistent to render the title into English in the case, say, of *Der Barbier von Bagdad* but not in the case of *Der Rosenkavalier*. My practice has been to refer to an opera by the title it receives in ordinary English or American usage. Both musicians and the man in the street speak of *Il Trovatore* and *La Traviata*, not of *The Troubadour* and *The Lost-and-lapsed Lady* (or something of that sort). Were we to speak of *The Troubadour*, some people might think we were referring to Mackenzie's opera of that name. For titles such as *La Traviata*, *Der Freischütz*, and *L'Heure espagnole* no satisfactory English equivalent can be found, which is one of the reasons why these works are always referred to among us by their original titles. If I were to tell a man I was going to Covent Garden or the Metropolitan to see *They All Do It* he would look at me in blank amazement: I should have to translate it back into *Così fan tutte* before he would understand. Even people without any knowledge of German speak of *Die Fledermaus*, not of *The Bat*. Difficulties of this kind multiply when we come to operas in what may be called the remoter languages, such as Russian or Czech. How many people would recognise *The Bartered Bride* in *Prodana Nevěsta?* And if we cannot call Smetana's opera by its native name, why call it, in a book intended for English and American readers, by its German one of *Die verkaufte Braut?*

It is considerations of this last order, again, that have made me omit the words from the musical illustrations in the case of three or four of the operas here discussed. To quote the Czech in the case of *The Bartered Bride*, or the Russian in the case of such a work as *Prince Igor*, would be useless, while no published English versions exist of most works of this sort. If I have made an exception in the case of *Boris Godounov*, it is because it is more than probable that if the reader possesses a score of this at all it will be the one with the English words of Mrs. Newmarch.

TURANDOT
Puccini (1858-1924)

PRINCIPAL CHARACTERS

TURANDOT	*Soprano*
ALTOUM	*Tenor*
TIMUR	*Bass*
THE UNKNOWN PRINCE	*Tenor*
LIÙ	*Soprano*
PING	*Baritone*
PANG	*Tenor*
PONG	*Tenor*

I

The reader who has seen Puccini's *Turandot* on the stage will remember three curious Chinese figures, bearing the perhaps not wholly authentic names of Ping, Pang and Pong, who seem to be always round and about the main action though rarely at the core of it, and who speak a musical language somewhat different from that of the leading characters. The explanation is that these three figures are descendants of the "masks" of the old Italian genre of improvised play, the commedia dell'arte.

Before Puccini's opera appeared, Richard Strauss and his librettist Hugo von Hofmannsthal had already made, in *Ariadne auf Naxos*, an attempt to combine these so-called masks organically with a serious dramatic action—an attempt which, on the whole, has to be written off as a failure, but at all events a noble failure. Puccini and his poets, Giuseppe Adami and Renato Simoni, have succeeded better in effecting this fusion in *Turandot*, partly because they have not ventured on the psychological subtleties and symbolisms so dear to the German mind, partly because excellent Italian models for the particular kind of fusion they desired lay ready to their hand. The master of this blend of serious drama and the commedia dell'arte was Count Carlo Gozzi (1720–1806), one of the last scions of a noble Venetian family that had become impoverished by the time of Carlo's birth. About the middle of the eighteenth century a new orientation had been given to the Venetian theatre by the "modern" plays of Goldoni and one or two other dramatists. Gozzi's passion for the ancient genre of improvised drama led him to associate himself with one of the still surviving companies of masks, and to write for them between 1761 and 1765, in a mixed genre of his own, ten plays which he called "Fiabe"— stories with a touch of unreality. The most famous of them all, perhaps, is *Turandot* (1762); but several of the others have also served as the basis for later plays or operas. The fiaba of *La donna serpente* was drawn upon by Wagner for his youthful opera *Die Feen*, and that of *L'amore delle tre melarance* by Prokofieff for an opera with the same title. The interesting central theme and the vivid incidents of *Turandot* have always made it a special favourite. In 1802 Schiller produced a German version of his own of Gozzi's play, for which Weber, seven years later, wrote an overture and some incidental music. Among modern operatic treatments of the subject the most notable are those of Busoni (1921) and Puccini (1926).

Gozzi seems to have derived his material mostly from a story in a Persian collection of tales which had been made known to Western Europe, in a French translation, towards the end of the seventeenth century. This version skilfully weaves into a unified tissue various motives that had been popular among story-tellers from time immemorial—that of the obstinately virgin princess who condemns her unsuccessful wooers to death, that of a trial for life or death by means of three enigmas, that of an Unknown who ripostes with an enigma of his own, and so on.

In Gozzi's five-act play, the kingdom of Astrakhan has been overcome by its enemies, and the old King (Timur), his queen, and his son (Calaf) driven into exile. Calaf, after enduring all kinds of privations and degradations for several years, finds himself at last in Pekin, where he comes upon another refugee from Astrakhan, the faithful Barach, who has settled down in Pekin under the name of Assan and there taken to himself a wife. Calaf learns from Barach that all China groans under the cruelty of the man-hating Princess Turandot,[1] who sets each of her would-be

---

[1] The correct pronunciation of the name is with the main accent on the first syllable and the final "t" sounded: Gozzi, indeed, sometimes spells it

lovers three enigmas to solve, and, on his failing to do so, remorselessly has him executed. The latest victim is the Prince of Samarcand, whose miniature of the lovely Turandot happens to come into Calaf's hands. He at once falls madly in love with her, and presents himself for the usual trial.

Everyone tries to dissuade the seeming madman, especially Turandot's father, the Emperor Altoum, who is sick of all this bloodshed and entirely out of sympathy with his daughter's whimsey, though he abides by his promise to her never to force her to marry under any other conditions than those she herself has laid down. At the public trial Calaf, to everyone's astonishment, solves all three enigmas. Turandot is furious, and, woman-like, at once demands a replay of the game, on the ground that the three enigmas solved by the Unknown were far too easy: owing to the trial having been sprung on her so suddenly, it appears, she has had insufficient time in which to think up three posers really worthy of her and of the occasion. Altoum refuses to listen to her: she herself had framed the rules of the game, she has lost, and she must now abide by the result. Thereupon Turandot tries a bit of characteristic feminine blackmail: if the Unknown Wooer and her cruel parent really insist on it she will go to the altar, but only to plunge a dagger into her heart when she gets there. Never, she swears, shall any man possess her.

The Unknown thereupon chivalrously gives her another chance. He wants her to come to him willingly, he says, or not at all. So he stakes not only his bride but his life on a last and supreme throw. *He* will set Turandot a single enigma: if by the next day she can discover his name and that of his father, she can have him slain like his predecessors. She accepts, and at once proceeds, of course, to do all she can to discover, by fair means or foul, the identity of this original and exceptionally audacious wooer. In this she succeeds, by a series of intrigues and accidents that need not be told in detail here. At the public divan next day she triumphantly announces the name—Calaf, son of Timur. But

as a four-syllable word—Turandotte. Singers, however, have found it convenient to omit the final "t", and so we arrive at "Turan*doh*" as the now customary pronunciation of the word. The strong accent, however, must still be on the first syllable, with the suspicion of a fainter one on the third.

alas, from the first sight of him she has felt secretly drawn towards him, and still more so since he made his generous gesture; and so she magnanimously spares his life, but bids him depart from Pekin for ever. In his despair at losing her he tries to kill himself. This certain proof of his disinterested love breaks down the last defence of her virgin pride, which had suffered a severe blow when, for the first time, her three enigmas had been solved. Confessing that he has conquered her, she voluntarily gives herself to him as his bride; and Gozzi's play ends with an assurance on her part that she deeply repents her former obstinacy and cruelty where the male sex was concerned.

2

The exigencies of a three-act opera necessitated some compression of Gozzi's five-act drama, the omission of several characters and scenes, the transformation of others, and the invention here and there of a new character or a new episode. Puccini and his poets, however, retain Gozzi's Italian masks in the Chinese milieu in principle, though, of course, with considerable modifications. In Gozzi there are four of these stock figures of the commedia dell'arte—Pantalone, Tartaglia, Brighella and Truffaldino. These he had to have, indeed, because the four male members of the Sacchi company of actors, with which the playwright was associated, specialised in them: the head of the troupe, Antonio Sacchi, was always the Truffaldino, Atanagio Zanoni the Brighella, Agostine Fiorelli the Tartaglia, and Cesare Darbes the Pantalone. In *Turandot* Gozzi elevated Pantalone to the post of the Emperor's Secretary, and Tartaglia to that of Grand Chancellor, in which exalted capacities, however, they still have only subsidiary parts to play. But Brighella, who is made Master of the Pages, and Truffaldino, who is at the head of Turandot's slaves, remain, in Gozzi's play, genuine figures of the commedia dell'arte. They take no part in the major events of the drama; they exist in a separate little world of their own, in which, as the tradition of the genre dictated, they *improvise* their lines (in dialect), and occasionally indulge in hearty popular humours.[1]

---

[1] Each of the Italian masks represented a familiar type. Harlequin was a nimble, extravagant, saucy rogue. The Captain was a swashbuckler and

Puccini, in his turn, finds the masks useful for moving incessantly about the fringes of the main action, supplying illuminating comment on it, and now and then furthering it a little. He makes Ping the Grand Chancellor, Pang the General Purveyor, and Pong the Chief Court Cook. The three invariably appear as a sort of tripartite entity, speaking, thinking and acting in concert; and their music is in a lighter, more everyday conversational style than that of the leading characters of the drama, whose terrific emotional tension demands a more exalted manner of speech.

The one really new character in the opera is the somewhat enigmatic little girl Liù, who, it appears, has been the guide and solace of old Timur during his miserable wanderings over the earth after the loss of his kingdom and the disappearance of his son. In a sense, she is superfluous so far as the essentials of the action are concerned, though she contributes very effectively to the emotional range of the music, and, near the end, helps to increase the tension of it considerably. The librettists seem to have dimly felt the necessity for reinforcing their text with a character corresponding in some degree to the Adelma of Gozzi's drama. This Adelma is a Tartar princess who, after the destruction of the royal house to which she belongs, has become the favourite slave of Turandot. In the days of her prosperity, however, she had felt a sympathetic interest in a young man, of whom no one knew anything, who used to perform menial tasks at the court of her father: this young man, of course, was the fugitive and anonymous Calaf. She recognises him again at the trial at the divan, realises that she loves him, becomes madly jealous of Turandot when she sees the possibility of the Unknown winning her, and, informing him that Turandot is plotting to have him killed, tries to induce him to flee with her. It is she who, partly by accident, partly by

braggart of the Ancient Pistol species. Pantaloon was an absurd old man, Scaramouche a gay roisterer, Tartaglia a ridiculous fat stutterer, Brighella a coward, boastful, dishonest and sycophantic, Truffaldino a universal butt; and so on. These general characteristics were of course susceptible to all kinds of nuance and modulation according to the subject and the milieu of each particular play. In the genuine commedia dell'arte the actors were provided only with a scenario of the action: their words and by-play were improvised. In Gozzi's *Turandot* this precedent is followed where Brighella and Truffaldino are concerned.

artifice, discovers Calaf's name and that of his father: these she discloses to Turandot, hoping in this way to ensure, to her own benefit, the failure of the Prince's wooing in that quarter.

Adami and Simoni having dispensed with Adelma, they transfer to Liù something of the motive—vital to Gozzi's play—of the former's love for Calaf. In the opera, it is clear, the Prince does not even know by sight this little companion of his father when he stumbles upon the forlorn couple in the square at Pekin. We learn that in the distant past he had chanced to smile, at his own court, on the humble little slave Liù, who, we gather, is still no more than a child at the period at which the action of the opera takes place—an important point which is generally obscured for the spectator in the theatre by the obvious physical maturity of the singer taking the part. This smile has remained ever since as a golden memory in the heart of the child. She loves Calaf in her simple way; and towards the close of the opera she makes the supreme sacrifice of her own life to him and to his passion for Turandot by refusing to reveal his identity to the myrmidons of the savage Princess, who is determined to have the name if everyone in Pekin has to perish in the quest of it. Naturally one expects, after this, Liù's self-immolation to have a vital bearing on the dénouement of the opera, especially when we remember how that dénouement is brought about in Gozzi's play by the somewhat parallel character of Adelma, who is also in love with Calaf. But whereas Adelma is directly instrumental in bringing about the conjuncture of events leading to Turandot's discovery of the name of the Unknown, and so to the ultimate unravelling of the tangled psychological threads, the heartrending self-sacrifice of little Liù is entirely without influence, or, indeed, bearing, on the dénouement of the opera. For Liù dies without having revealed the Prince's name, even under torture; and the final situation—in which Turandot, knowing the name at last, and, being able to revenge herself, if she wishes to do so, on the man who has humiliated her, decides that after all her new love is more potent than her old pride,—has to be brought about by the device of Calaf himself disclosing his name to her as the climax of his ecstatic bravado.

This ending is not without a certain ingenuity, but it has

neither the force nor the dramatic conviction of Gozzi's. Yet in the opera, after the death of Liù and the departure from the scene of the mourning Timur with the body, there remains nobody but the Prince to answer, for Turandot's benefit, his own enigma, and so bring the drama to its appointed end. We are left, then, wondering a little just *why* Liù has been allowed to play the relatively large part she does in the penultimate stage of the work. The answer seems to be that the horrible episode of the torture of Liù fascinated Puccini purely for its own sake. Strictly speaking, the opera could have managed, psychologically and dramatically, perfectly well without Liù. But episodes of super-suffering, and, at a pinch, of actual torture seem to have had a curious fascination for Puccini. We may conjecture that while the peculiarly pathetic character of Liù attracted him as a musician, the emotional appeal of this sympathetic little figure writhing under the crudest physical torture was simply irresistible. And so the child occupies an amount of space in the dramatic canvas of *Turandot* that is hardly justifiable on purely rational grounds.

3

After the completion of the triptych—*Il Tabarro, Suor Angelica* and *Gianni Schicchi*—in 1918, Puccini spent several months in an agonising search for a subject for a new opera. It was not until 1919 that Renato Simoni suggested looking for what he wanted in Gozzi. Oddly enough, Puccini seems to have made his first acquaintance with the story of Turandot through an Italian version, by Maffei, of Schiller's play. He soon realised that he had found his long-desired subject; but the way was long and dolorous before he and his poets could give it the shape he desired. His keen dramatic sense told him that two acts would be enough: but that plan seems to have been given up solely for reasons connected with the convenience of theatrical audiences.

The drafting of the first act presented few difficulties. But it was a long time before a satisfactory design for the remainder could be worked out; and Puccini had virtually completed the music for the first act before the words for the other two were ready. His letters show both his librettists and himself to have been in considerable and continuous perplexity as to the best way in which to end the opera; and one gathers, from a hint here and there, that it had not been the original intention to dispose of Liù after the fashion finally adopted in the opera. As late as November 1922 Puccini told Adami, "I think that Liù must be sacrificed to some sorrow, but I don't see how to do this unless we make her die under the torture. And why not? Her death could help to soften the heart of the Princess." This suggested psychological motive, however, is *not* incorporated in the libretto. When we read, indeed, of the long struggle of the composer and his poets against the difficulties of the last act we are not at all surprised at its showing a slight constructional weakness here and there.

Puccini's letters make it clear that he attached the utmost importance to the final duet between Turandot and Calaf. This was to be not only dramatically but musically the peak-point of the work: the music, we may surmise, was to elucidate triumphantly in its own way whatever might have been left a trifle unclear in the drama. By one of the bitterest ironies of fate under which any musician has ever suffered, he was destined never to complete this duet—the main outlines of the music of which he had long had in his head—because his poets failed to supply him with the necessary words in time. In the spring of 1924 a malady of the throat that had vaguely troubled Puccini from time to time became more insistent: though he was never allowed to know it, it was cancer. In the autumn of that year he consulted a Belgian specialist, and in October went to Brussels for an operation. This appeared, at first, to have been successful; but a couple of days later the heart failed unexpectedly, and on the 29th November Puccini was dead. Not long before the operation he said forebodingly to a friend: "The opera will be given incomplete, and some one will come to the front and say, 'At this point the Master died'." It happened precisely as he had foreseen. At the first performance, in the Scala Theatre, Milan, on the 25th April 1926, under Toscanini, an abrupt ending was made at the last page to be completed in the score by Puccini himself: and Toscanini, turning to the profoundly moved audience, said quietly, "At this point the Maestro laid down his pen." The work is always given now with an ending written by Franco Alfano, based on the composer's own sketches for the final scene.

4

The action of the opera takes place in Pekin, in legendary times. There is no orchestral prelude.

When the curtain rises we find ourselves in front of the great wall that surrounds the city, which glows in the distance in the rays of the evening sun. On the right a big bronze gong is suspended. Here and there on the wall are stakes on which are impaled the heads of some of Turandot's unsuccessful suitors. A vast crowd stands before the wall, silent and motionless.

The horror that broods over Pekin whenever Turandot is in one of her merciless moods is vividly suggested by the orchestra in the half-dozen bars that precede the rising of the curtain. The effect is mainly harmonic, with many reiterations of the type of chord shown in the following quotation:

and colouristic, with gong and xylophone breaking into the texture with barbaric tints and clangours of their own. At intervals there appears, above these harmonies, the melodic figure shown in the second bar of the above example. The crowd is listening to a mandarin reading, from the top of the wall, the latest decree: Turandot the Chaste will be the bride only of one of royal blood who shall solve the three enigmas she sets him; if he fails, he must lose his head. The Prince of Persia having lately tried and failed, he will die this day at the rising of the moon.

The mob, crazed with this incessant shedding of blood, cries out frantically to the executioner, Pu-Tin-Pao, to begin his work at once; and they make as if to storm the wall with a shout of "To the Palace!" The guards get to work among them with whips and drive them away, to a clamorous melody in the orchestra:

Above the shrieks of the frenzied crowd we hear the despairing voice of Liù, begging for help for the old man with her, who has been knocked down by the stampeding crowd. A youth among them bends over the old man and recognises him as his father. There is an affectionate scene between the two, accompanied throughout by No. 2. The youth—the Unknown Prince—entreats Timur not to call him publicly "My son", as the usurper of their throne pursues them implacably everywhere.

By this time the crowd has re-formed. It goes mad with excitement as the executioner's assistants, their garments stained with blood, appear on the wall with an enormous sword, which they begin to sharpen on a whetstone, singing a savage sadistic chorus in praise of their profession and of Turandot; wherever she may reign, they say, there will always be work for them to do! They gloat over the many victims, past and future; the enigmas are three, they repeat, but death is only one. Meanwhile we have learned from the old man's lips how, after the battle that had sealed the fate of his kingdom, little Liù had come to him and dragged him away. Since then she had been his guide and support in all his weary wanderings, comforting him, begging his bread for him. "Who art thou, Liù?" asks the Prince Calaf. "I am nothing, my lord—only a slave", the child replies. He asks her why she has taken on herself so great a burden of suffering. She returns the ecstatic answer, "Because one day, in the palace, you smiled on me!"

And that is all the light we get upon the antecedents and the mind of Liù, for now our attention is wholly taken up by the crowd once more. This has gradually re-gathered in front of the wall. Its lust for blood increases as the sky grows darker and the first pale rays of the moon begin to appear, heralding the death of the latest victim. The whole lighting of the scene gradually changes, and with it the colour and the harmonic texture of the music. At first the mob is almost calmed by the spectacle of the golden sun-gleam fading before the coming of the moon: then, as the sky becomes a livid silver, a monstrous cry of delight goes up from the crowd. "Pu-Tin-Pao! Pu-Tin-Pao!" they shout again and again, until from the distance comes the dirge of the children at the head of the approaching procession:

About this melody more will be said later.

Soon the procession comes into view along the wall—first the executioner's assistants, the priests with funeral offerings, various mandarins, and last of all the Prince of Persia, followed by the gigantic executioner. The Prince is so handsome and so young, his bearing so dignified, and his gentle eyes so full of his dream, so unheeding of everything around him, that at the sight of him the crowd's blood-lust dissolves into pity. A funeral march in the orchestra accompanies him on his slow way across the wall, and to the strains of this the crowd calls louder and louder on the Princess Turandot to show him mercy. The Unknown Prince joins in this appeal. At last he cries to the cruel one, "Oh, that I might see thee, that I might curse thee!" And at that moment Turandot herself appears on the imperial loggia to the right of the wall. The cold moonlight playing on her face seems to intensify the expression of proud indifference on it. The crowd, awed by the majesty and the conscious power that stream from this statuesque figure, falls on its face before her. On the wall there remain erect only the Persian Prince and the executioner; in the forefront of the stage only the Unknown Prince. At the sight of Turandot's beauty he has covered his dazzled eyes.

Even while the crowd is still murmuring its broken appeal for mercy, Turandot raises her hand in an imperious, conclusive

B

gesture. The executioner understands, and the cortège moves on
again and at last disappears, with the crowd following it. Turandot
slowly re-enters the palace, while the priests, to the last echoes of
the funeral march, offer up a prayer to great Kung-tze to receive
the soul of the man who is about to die. By now the light has
faded still further, and on the stage we see only the Unknown
Prince, Timur and Liù. Calaf has realised, at the sight of Turandot, that the hour of his destiny has struck. After a brief ecstatic
invocation to her beauty he stands absorbed in silent reflection,
until a word from Timur unlocks his lips again, only for him to
rave of the vision he has just seen. Timur, in terror at the sinister
enchantment that has fallen on his son, bids Liù take his hand: she
does so, urging him to come away with them, to where life is.
"Life is here, where Turandot is!" is his only reply. The name of
Turandot strikes upon our ears from afar also: it is the last invocation of the merciless beauty by the Prince of Persia as the axe
falls and the crowd gives a cry of horror.

Timur's appeals have no effect on Calaf, who moves towards
the great gong that is flashing in the moonlight. He is about to
strike it, thereby announcing himself as a new wooer of Turandot,
when three strange figures suddenly fling themselves across his
path. They are Ping, Pang and Pong. In urgent phrases they
advise him to go away from this door that leads only to butchery,
to return to the country whence he came and lose his head there
if he will, but not here, not here! Pekin and China are full enough
of fools who want to die: why should he add to their number?
And for what? For one who, when all is said, is merely a woman,
a thing of common flesh and blood. He can find elsewhere a
hundred wives if he wants them. Although the three masks speak
a musical language different from that of the tragic characters of
the opera, Puccini, here as elsewhere, succeeds in making them
all appear as part of the same dramatic milieu.

Ping, Pang and Pong are still gesticulating around the Unknown Prince and obstructing him, and he is making violent
efforts to get past them, when from the balustrade of the imperial
loggia comes a soft chorus of female voices—Turandot's maids,
bidding them all be silent, as their mistress is asleep. But the three
masks take no notice of them. They renew their entreaties to the

crazy Unknown to listen to reason. Turandot's enigmas, they
assure him, are all insoluble. But he hardly hears them, for now
there come to his ear, out of the darkness and the distance, not
voices but the mere shadows of voices. They are those of the dead
lovers of Turandot; they tell him to delay no longer but to call
on her of whom they still dream, and she will appear to him. As
the ghostly visions and voices fade from sight and sound, the
Unknown cries out that he alone loves Turandot. Again the
tolerant, cynical masks reason with the madman. All is illusion,
they say: nothing really exists, neither he nor Turandot, nor God,
nor man, nor the kings of this earth. As their last argument they
point to the gruesome spectacle now visible on the ramparts,
where the executioner is placing the head of the Prince of Persia
on a stake. The white moonlight beats down upon it; even so, say
Ping, Pang and Pong, will the moon one of these nights kiss
Calaf's face.

Timur, in a pathetic monologue, tries to recall his demented
son to the world of reality. Liù follows with a still more moving
appeal. She confesses that everywhere in her wanderings his
image has been in her heart, his name on her lips; if now he persists in his folly, old Timur will lose his son, and she will lose
"the shadow of a smile". She breaks down and weeps at the young
man's feet. He looks sadly and compassionately at the little
figure, and in a long monologue in which concern for Liù is
blended with a kind of pity for himself, he bids her remember that
smile of his of long ago of which she had spoken, and to devote
herself henceforth to old Timur, who now will need her more
than ever. The three masks, Timur and Liù unite in a last despairing appeal to Calaf, in a big ensemble that works up gradually
from the following theme:

to an outcry of the most frenzied kind. But appeals and force are alike unavailing. The gong once more gleams in the moonlight, and catches Calaf's eye. He tears himself loose from Ping, Pang and Pong. It is death, they tell him. "No! It is life!" he replies. In a sheer delirium of ecstasy he cries out three times the name of Turandot, seizes the hammer, and strikes three tremendous blows on the gong. The orchestra thunders out the majestic theme that symbolises Turandot (No. 3). Old Timur and Liù cling to each other in despair. The three masks fly in horror, leaving the madman to his fate. The curtain descends on Calaf standing before the gong, staring at it as if obsessed.

Puccini uses some genuine Chinese melodies in *Turandot*. That quoted as our example No. 3 is one of these: it will be found in the chapter on Chinese music in the *Travels in China* of John Barrow (London, 2nd ed., 1806), who had accompanied the Earl of Macartney in his mission to that country. According to Barrow, the tune was even at that time fairly familiar to the Western world, it having been arranged by one Mr. Hittner and published in London, but "with head and tail pieces, accompaniments, and all the refined arts of European music", says Barrow, "so that it ceases to be a specimen of the plain melody of China." He himself prints it in what he calls "its unadorned state, as sung and played by the Chinese":

The title of the song is "Moo-Lee-Wha". In 1862 the German historian of music Ambros quoted the melody in the chapter on Eastern music in the first volume of his great History. He condemned Chinese music in general as being "singular" and "unbeautiful", apparently never pausing to ask himself whether Chinese standards of beauty might not be different from those of the Western world. How completely he misconceived Chinese music in general and "Moo-Lee-Wha" in particular is shown by his harmonising the latter on the tonic-dominant-subdominant principles of European music, which are entirely alien to it. Some idea of the absurdity of Ambros' harmonisation may be had from the following quotation of the first four bars, and more especially from the "accompaniment" to the fourth bar:

It is strange that a writer of such learning should have failed to see that as the tune is one of those, so frequent in exotic or primitive music, that avoid the seventh of the scale, this "leading note" should also be avoided in any harmonisation of it, otherwise the whole character of the melody is changed. Puccini was perhaps no scholar; but he was a man of genius, and his intuition told him that if "Moo-Lee-Wha" was to sound at all Chinese in *Turandot* it would have to be harmonised with the "flat seventh",

i.e., with a whole tone, not a semitone, before the tonic. The
following quotation:

is from the big scene of the divan in the second act. It will be seen at a
glance how Puccini's method of harmonisation not merely preserves
unimpaired but heightens the non-European element in the melody,
which is utterly dissipated by Ambros' class-room harmonies.

<h2 style="text-align:center">5</h2>

The opening scene of the second act is given up entirely to
the masks, who once more illuminate the psychological situation
for us in a musical language of their own. We see the front
of a pavilion—a great curtain curiously decorated in the Chinese
style, with a door in the middle and one at each side. We seem,
for the moment, a long way from the tragedy of the first act when
Ping pops his head through the centre opening, and, turning first
to the right, then to the left, calls out Pang and Pong. Their entry
is formal enough—three servants follow them, each with a
different-coloured lantern, which they ceremoniously place on a
low table, round which are three stools, in the very middle of the
stage. The servants then retire to the background.

The three masks have met to discuss in their own fashion the
unpleasant situation created by the latest challenge to Turandot.
It will end, they foresee, in either a wedding or a funeral; and they
humorously profess to be prepared for either, whether it be a
gorgeous palanquin they will have to follow or a handsome
catafalque. They fall to musing on the China of old and the China
of their own day. For seven thousand centuries the country slept
the sleep of profound peace, everything proceeding tranquilly
according to ancient rule. Then came Turandot with her cursed

riddles and all that these have brought in their train—suitors, challenges, hopes, fears and beheadings in unending succession. They read out the melancholy record of deaths from three scrolls which the servants have left on the tables. And they are weary of it all, weary of being little more now than adjuncts to the executioner. Each of them is racked by a nostalgia of his own. Ping has a little house on a lake in Honan to which he longs to return and dream his life away: Pang thinks wistfully of his garden at Kiù: Pong has forests somewhere the grateful shade of which he has almost forgotten: and here they are in Pekin, all three of them wasting their lives poring over the sacred books, saddened by the interminable spectacle of human folly. Their weariness and their heart's longing are finally crystallised in an exquisite after-refrain in the orchestra:

Love and sweetness have vanished from the world: there is nothing but frenzy and decapitation: the end of China itself must surely be near:

Would that the day might come when it will fall to them to prepare the nuptial couch for Turandot, to escort the bride and groom with lanterns, and to sing in the garden until dawn of day of the coming back of love and light to spectre-ridden China!

From the dream in which they have gradually lost themselves more and more completely they are wakened by a volley of trumpets and trombones and drums from within the palace. For the town is alive again with the sound of people hastening to the great divan that is to be held that same day, at which yet another lover will try to vanquish the ice-cold Turandot. At a sign from Pong the servants remove the lanterns as ceremoniously as they had placed them on the tables, and with their hearts heavy within them the three masks go out to face the torture of the new trial.

When the curtain rises again it is on the huge square in front of the palace. An immense marble staircase with three landings stretches up from the centre of the stage. At the top of this stand the eight Wise Men, sages of great age and still greater dignity, if not, indeed, pomposity. Each has in his hand three sealed scrolls containing the solutions of Turandot's latest enigmas. Various officials and notables pass up and down, among them Ping, Pang and Pong, now in the yellow robes they wear only on important public occasions. At the foot of the staircase, on one side, is the Unknown Prince. On the other side are Timur and Liù, almost lost in the crowd. The people comment softly on it all, while the orchestra pours out a flood of ceremonial music, which increases in power and brilliance as the preparations for the divan advance towards their climax. This arrives when, the mists of incense having rolled away, the Emperor Altoum becomes visible on his throne at the highest central point of the scene, and the multitude greets him with a cry of "May you live ten thousand years!" and prostrates itself with its face to the ground. The Emperor is so old and venerable that he has the air more of an ageless religious symbol than of a mere human being.

Addressing the assembly in a thin blanched voice that betokens his years, he speaks of the oath by which he is bound to his daughter, but counsels the young Unknown to depart and so avoid the further shedding of blood. The Prince replies that he asks only to be put to the trial. In vain does old Altoum plead with him: the young man's resolution is immovable, and in the end there is nothing for it but for the Emperor to bid the trumpets sound and the ordeal that is certain to end in death begin. As it is essential that the Emperor's words shall be clearly heard, in spite of the weakness of his voice, Puccini makes him intone them without accompaniment; and as it would sound odd if the Prince's brief replies were delivered in another medium, these also are sung unaccompanied, the orchestra being restricted throughout the episode to an occasional interjection between the vocal phrases. The effect of it all is to concentrate our attention on the warnings and the challenge to an extent that could not have been achieved by any other means: the limitation imposed on the musician by the character of the old man's voice has been converted by Puccini into an instrument of extraordinary dramatic power.

A number of Turandot's women come out from the palace and take up a position on the staircase. They are followed by Turandot herself, beautiful, cold and aloof as usual. She throws a glance of proud indifference at the Unknown, who only by an effort at self-mastery can look at her with composure. To the accompaniment of the harmonies shown in No. 1, with a strong colouring of gong and xylophone as before, a mandarin recites the terms of the coming contest. A chorus of children in the distance intones once more the hymn in praise of Turandot (No. 3). Then, without any preamble, Turandot, from her place at the foot of the throne, begins her address to the Prince. She tells the story of how in that very palace, thousands of years ago, there lived in peace and purity the Princess Lo-u-ling, till one day the barbarian descended on China, the empire was lost, and Lo-u-ling slain in a night of atrocity by a man—a man such as the stranger who now braves Turandot. Long brooding on that story had bred in her a loathing of men and a consuming desire to avenge the innocent Lo-u-ling; never shall any man possess her, she cries, to one of the great themes of the opera:

Her own words working like an intoxicant on her as she utters them, her song rises to a climax of resentment against the man who now stands before her at the foot of the steps. "The enigmas are three", she cries, "death is one":

He answers her with "The enigmas are three, life is one", repeating her own melody higher in the scale, as if at once capping her words and confuting them. Then, at a still higher pitch, they repeat together their respective cries, each of them, as it were, bent on bearing down the other by sheer weight of asseveration.

The crowd urges Turandot to accept the challenge of this bold Unknown. The trumpets having imposed silence, she propounds her first enigma, the orchestra adding a tension and a poignancy of its own to the atmosphere of the scene:

Without a moment's hesitation the Prince replies: the thing that is born each night only to die next day is Hope. The eight Wise Men, having unrolled their scrolls, solemnly declare the answer to be correct. For a moment Turandot is abashed. Recovering her poise, she remarks menacingly that Hope flatters only to deceive; and to increase the terror of her next question she descends to the midway landing of the staircase, where, with her eyes burning into the Prince, she launches the second enigma. This is more difficult than the first one: the Unknown hesitates for a while, and both the Emperor and the crowd eagerly encourage him. But the solution comes to him in time: the thing that is like a flame yet is not a flame, that grows cold when life is lost and burns when life is won, is Blood. Once more the Wise Men confirm it from their scrolls.

The joyous cries of the crowd anger Turandot, who orders the guards to chastise them. She descends the remainder of the steps, halting in front of the Unknown, who sinks on his knees before her. A raging fury now, bending over him like a beast of prey, with her face almost touching his, she hurls at him the third enigma, and gloats ferociously over his seeming discomfiture. Suddenly a great light comes to him: he leaps to his feet to deliver his reply: this thing of ice that begets in him fire is TURANDOT.[1] Again the Wise Men pronounce him to be right, and the assembly gives out the typical Turandot melody (No. 3) in the form of No. 5, in a tremendous outburst of voices and orchestra, and to the words "Glory to the conqueror!"

Turandot refuses to accept defeat: she implores her father not to throw her into the arms of this stranger, and turning with a blaze of fresh hatred towards the Unknown she swears that neither he nor any man shall ever possess her. The Emperor's only reply is to declare that his oath is sacred: the crowd, too, is all on the side of the Unknown who has ventured and conquered where so many had failed, and lifted from the city the horror that has brooded over it so long. It is the Prince himself who offers Turandot a way out. He will release her from her bargain, he says, on one condition. Three enigmas she has propounded to him, and three he has solved. One only he will now put to her. She does not know who he is: if before dawn she can tell him his name, then at dawn he is willing to die. Turandot signifies by a gesture that she accepts:

11

Moderato sostenuto
espressivo

[1] Each of the enigmas has been condensed into as few words as possible for the purposes of this analysis.

Altoum and the crowd unite in singing the praises of this generous victor, and the curtain falls on a massive chorus of homage to the Emperor, to the melody of the Imperial Hymn.

6

The first scene of the third act shows us the great garden of the palace, with a pavilion on the right, which is supposed to lead into Turandot's chambers.

It is night. Turandot has lost no time in getting to work: all Pekin is being searched for some one able to give her the name of the Unknown. Mournful harmonies well up from the orchestra, conveying a sense of tension and of mystery, and we hear the voices of the heralds proclaiming that by command of Turandot no one in Pekin is to sleep that night. On pain of death for all, the name of the Unknown must be brought to her before dawn. From the far distances of the unhappy city come faint echoes of the heralds' words—"Nessun dorma! . . . Pena la morte!"

The "Nessun dorma" is taken up by the Unknown Prince, who all this while has been reclining on the steps of the pavilion, sunk in dreams and visions of his own. Softly—more softly than the average Italian tenor can generally manage to sing the passage—and reflectively, to some of the most beautiful music in the score, he sings, over harmonies of this type:

·12

Andante sostenuto

his message to Turandot. She, like the others, he says, shall not sleep. No one but himself knows his name; and from his lips alone shall she learn it at break of day, learn it in a kiss that will melt the frigid beauty and make her his. The orchestra repeats his final phrases in an ecstasy of passion; and it is remarkable with what perfect naturalness this tense strain merges into the lighter one that accompanies the irruption of the three masks into the scene, at the head of a number of dim figures that gradually define themselves, against the darkness, as the people of the town. They have come, with the masks at their head, to try to induce the Unknown to save the city. Despairingly the three ministers call on him to leave his star-gazing and listen to them. Death threatens every house in Pekin. What is it he wants? Is it love? They surround him with beautiful maidens, whose blandishments he rejects. Is it riches? Gold and gems are displayed before his eyes, and Ping, Pang and Pong sing the praises of them. Is it glory? they will help him to found empires, if only he will be content to know himself to be the only one to have vanquished Turandot, and leave Pekin for ever.

Every temptation of the body, every blandishment of the spirit having failed, the exasperated ministers resort to threats. He does not know this Turandot of theirs, they tell him: she is infinitely crafty, infinitely cruel, and China is rich in subtle, fantastic tortures unknown to the rest of the world. Turandot, frustrated, will never forget and never forgive: he himself will die a horrible lingering death if he remains in the city and does not divulge his name. The crowd, now maddened with fear, surges round him, cursing him for his obduracy and threatening him with their knives. His sole reply to appeals and threats is that he wants Turandot, and her alone.

Suddenly a commotion and cries of "Here is the name!" are heard from the direction of the garden, and some guards rush in, dragging with them Timur and Liù. The drama has reached its highest point of emotional tension. The startled Prince calls out that these two know nothing: he alone knows his name. But Ping remembers them as the two with whom the Unknown had been seen talking the day before. He hurries towards the pavilion, calling, with the crowd, "Princess! Princess!" Turandot, accompanied by her motive (No. 3) in triumphant and terrible trumpet tones, appears on the threshold of the pavilion. Bending low before her, Ping informs her that they have discovered two people who know the name, and that they have hooks with which to tear the secret from their lips if the Princess commands. Ignoring all the others, she addresses herself with cold irony to the Prince, to the accompaniment of No. 2 in the orchestra. He is pale, she says tauntingly. It is her own fear, he replies, that she sees reflected on his face in the pallid light of dawn; and he swears again that the old man and the maiden do not know him. "We shall see!" is Turandot's answer. She orders Timur to speak; but the old man, frightened and bruised and bleeding, only turns on her a look of mute misery. The ministers seize him to torture him; but before they can get to work Liù turns to Turandot and declares that she alone knows the name the Princess is seeking. The crowd utters a jubilant cry, which changes to one of baffled fury as Liù goes on to say that the name is her secret and will remain so.

The Prince breaks out into threats against the mob. He is seized and bound by the guards, and the horrible scene of the torture of Liù begins. She is forced by the guards to her knees, and as she still refuses the name, her arms are twisted at the command of the maddened Ping. The torture increases till the child can bear no more, but still she will not yield. As she falls almost dead near the steps of the pavilion, something in Turandot seems to break. She is faced by a mystery beyond her understanding: what gives her, she asks Liù, the strength to suffer like this? It is love, the child replies, a love for her lord which she has never yet confessed to anyone. She bids the guards torture and destroy her: she glories in her pain, which is the last and greatest sacrifice she can make to the being she loves.

It is only for a moment that Turandot has weakened. They are to tear the secret from the girl, she says; and the crowd cries out for Pu-Tin-Pao and more and worse torture. When the sinister figures of the executioner and his assistants loom up through the darkness, Liù's resolution fails her. The demented child—the spectator should never forget that Liù is supposed to be only a child—runs to Turandot, calls out that she, the ice-cold Princess, will yet love the Unknown as she loves him, and that her death will be his triumph:

13

Andantino mosso ♩ = 69

then snatches a dagger from the belt of one of the guards and plunges it into her heart. She dies, with a last fond look at him, at the feet of the Prince. The orchestra repeats sadly the melody of No. 13, to the strains of which Timur pours out a pitiful lament over his "little dove". The body is carried away, the old man walking beside it, holding the little hand in his.

The three masks, the crowd, and even Turandot—after a spasm of rage in which she snatches a whip from one of the executioner's assistants and slashes the face of the soldier who has allowed his dagger to be taken from him—have been moved to pity and remorse by these horrible happenings and their still more horrible ending. The superstitious mob is afraid that the dead girl's spirit will haunt them. Ping, Pang and Pong feel something human surging up within them the very memory of which had almost faded from their minds during these long years of cruelty. Turandot's attendants have covered her face with a white veil. When the last of the crowd has disappeared, following the body of Liù, and only the Prince and Turandot are left on the stage, he tears her veil aside, bidding her forget her coldness and be a woman again. She repels him with scorn: she is divine, she says, and he must not profane her even by touching her veil. But he takes her in his arms and kisses her. At this her defences break down; tremblingly she begs him to leave her—she is afraid of this new something that life has brought her. The old Turandot, she laments, is no more: "The dawn is here", she stammers, "and Turandot's sun is setting." Yes, replies the Prince; it is indeed the dawn—and the coming of a sweeter, purer day.

Now she has fully found her new self. Transfigured, exalted, she confesses that at the first sight of him she had loved him, and, with the memory gnawing her of those who had been sacrificed to her, her hate of him was only her love for him making her dread for him the fate that had overtaken the others. She hated him, too, for very pride: she had to conquer or be conquered. Now that he has triumphed, she begs him to be content with his victory and to leave her, taking his mystery with him. He replies that his mystery is his no longer, now that Turandot is his. His name he gives into her keeping, and with it his life—he is Calaf, the son of Timur. For a moment she becomes almost the old

Turandot once more, as she realises that he has placed himself utterly in her power. But he has no fear of her; and as the trumpets sound to proclaim that the appointed hour has come, he goes with the still proud beauty to the supreme trial.

After a brief orchestral interlude the curtain rises on the exterior of the palace, glowing in the red light of dawn. The Emperor is sitting among his court, awaiting, as the vast crowd in front of the palace is doing, the last fateful act of the long-drawn drama. The Prince and Turandot enter. She ascends the staircase at the top of which the Emperor is sitting, and says, "I know the stranger's name: it is—Love!" Calaf rushes to her and folds her in his embrace, while the crowd gives a great cry of joy and strews flowers around them.

The musical world will never cease to regret that Puccini died before he could complete this his greatest score. He laid down his pen at the point where, after the death of Liù, Prince Calaf begins his appeal to Turandot to descend from her lonely ice-cold heaven to the warmth of earth with its human love. Alfano has done his loyal best with the material available to him; but nothing can compensate us for the loss of the Master's touch. It is evident that the librettists had considerable difficulty with the last stages of the drama, and indeed the dénouement they finally decided on is not wholly convincing; but we have the feeling that Puccini's music to the duet between the Prince and Turandot would have carried a conviction of its own.

GIANNI SCHICCHI
Puccini (1858-1924)

PRINCIPAL CHARACTERS

GIANNI SCHICCHI	*Baritone*
LAURETTA	*Soprano*
ZITA	*Contralto*
RINUCCIO	*Tenor*
LA CIESCA	*Mezzo-soprano*
NELLA	*Mezzo-soprano*

I

In 1915, while he was engaged upon what was to prove the least successful of his works—*La Rondine*, produced in Monte-Carlo on the 27th March 1917,—Puccini felt an urge to try his hand at a one-act opera. Hence arose in the course of time the so-called *Trittico*, three short works in contrasted genres—tragedy, sentiment and comedy, as Puccini described them—consisting of *Il Tabarro*, *Suor Angelica*, and *Gianni Schicchi*. The triptych received its first performance at the Metropolitan Opera, New York, on the 14th December 1918. The first Italian performance was at the Costanzi Theatre, Rome, on the 11th January 1919. Since then *Il Tabarro* and *Suor Angelica* have been unjustly neglected by the theatres; *Gianni Schicchi*, however, has become a repertory piece.

The libretto of this, by Gioachino Forzano, is based upon a historical episode in Florentine life during the Middle Ages. (The date of the action of the opera is 1299). The hopes and fears of the expectant relatives of rich, or supposedly rich, testators have long been a favourite theme for comic art: in our own day we have been given, in addition to Puccini's masterpiece, a bright comedy by Zola—*Les héritiers Rabourdin*—and Lord Berners' ironic *Funeral March for a Rich Aunt*, in which the sparkling eye of the gratified heir can be seen peeping out of the black-edged handkerchief. Perhaps the best swindle in actual history connected with a last will and testament is that recorded of a Florentine rogue,

Gianni Schicchi, who placed his gifts as a mimic at the service of certain relatives of old Buoso Donati, who had just died, and whose wealth was worth taking a bit of extra trouble to secure. Concealing for a while the fact of the death, they placed Schicchi in Buoso's bed, where the consummate comedian dictated to a lawyer, in proper form, a will of the required type, which included a bequest to himself of a valuable mare known as "the lady of the stud".

As if Schicchi's achievement of itself were not sufficient to ensure a humorous immortality for his name, Dante must needs empty the vials of his wrath on him in the 30th Canto of the *Inferno*, placing him in the Eighth Circle among a crowd of thieves, panders, swindlers, barrators and other gentry of that type. Dante describes

> *due ombre smorte e nude,*
> *che mordendo correvan di quel modo*
> *che 'l porco quando del porcil si schiude.*

(Two pallid, naked shades which ran biting like the hog let out from the sty). One of these was Myrrha, who had loved in illegitimate fashion her own father, the King of Cyprus. The other

> *giunse a Capocchio, ed in sul nodo*
> *del collo l'assannò, sì che, tirando,*
> *grattar li fece il ventre al fondo sodo,*

(came at Capocchio and buried its teeth in the nape of his neck, and then dragged him so that he made his belly scrape on the hard bottom). It is explained to Dante that

> *Quel folletto è Gianni Schicchi,*
> *e va rabbioso altrui così conciando;*

(that goblin is Gianni Schicchi, and he goes raging and dealing in this manner with the rest). It appears that just as Myrrha had counterfeited for her own ends the form of another, so Schicchi had stooped,

> *per guadagnar la donna della torma,*
> *falsificare in sè Buoso Donati,*
> *testando e dando al testamento norma.*

(to impersonate Buoso Donati, making the will in due form, that he might get for himself the lady of the stud).

It is evident that the tight-lipped Dante, who probably never saw a joke in all his life, felt particularly venomous, even for him, towards Gianni Schicchi; and were he writing a supplement to the *Inferno* today he would no doubt find a place for Puccini in it,—probably in the section of the Eighth Circle of hell reserved for the makers of discord.

2

The curtain rises on a bedroom in the house of Buoso Donati. It is nine o'clock on an autumn morning in Florence: the light in the room is part sunlight, part candle-light. On the right is the big bed in which the old man has just died. On the left are a large window giving a view of the tower of Arnolfo, and a smaller window opening on to the terrace. There are staircases right and left. A table with various silver objects on it catches the spectator's eye. Through the half-closed curtains of the bed we get a glimpse of the red coverlet under which is supposed to be the body of Buoso. Beside the bed are four candelabra with lighted candles, and in front of it another with three candles that have gone out. To these candelabra we shall owe a couple of rich comic touches later.

With hope and fear contending for mastery in their hearts, the relatives of the dead Buoso are on their knees in front of the bed. They have lost no time in coming to the house when the news has gone round that the rich old man is dead. Their ages range from seven to seventy or more, from little Gherardino, the son of Gherardo, a nephew of Buoso, and his wife Nella, to old Simone, one of Buoso's cousins. Simone's son Marco is there, with his wife La Ciesca. The very old woman present is Buoso's cousin Zita, who is accompanied by her young nephew Rinuccio. The company is completed by Betto di Signa, a brother-in-law of the deceased, a ruin of uncertain age, and obviously a very poor relation. Buoso seems to have left behind him no more direct relatives than this miscellaneous collection of interested mourners. All are behaving themselves in a conventionally proper way, moaning and mumbling prayers, except little Gherardino, who is obviously bored by the proceedings: with his back to the others he is amusing himself with some wooden balls. Soon he upsets a chair, and the mourners suspend their lamentations for a moment to "Sh!" him. A little later he plucks his father by the sleeve and whispers something to him; whereupon the exasperated Gherardo runs him out of the room.

There is no formal prelude to the opera—merely a preamble of some twenty-five bars during which we hear a phrase that runs through most of the opening scene and recurs frequently later:

It begins at a great pace, but by the time the curtain rises it has slowed down to a *largo*, and it suffers a further change by passing from major to minor now and then. It is a curious phrase, in that it keeps us perpetually suspended between the comic and the tragic: the merest trifle of exaggeration in this direction or that during the playing of it would suffice to make it either. It is accompanied in the preamble by a little figure:

which is also much used later. No. 1 we may perhaps call the death motive. It begins, as has been said, at a great speed—the composer's marking is *tumultuoso*—suggestive of the frantic haste with which the expectant relatives have made their way to old Buoso's house, while the slower tempo later and the switch over to the minor show them composing their features to the proper degree of affectionate concern as they enter the death chamber. Example No. 2, which keeps on insinuating itself into the texture every now and then, suggests, apparently, the shadow of Gianni Schicchi already playing impishly over their hopes and fears.

Even while they are assuring the shade of the departed Buoso that they will not cease weeping for so good a man for the rest of their lives it is evident that their minds are not on his past but on their own future. While the others cease their wailings for a moment to gabble a prayer or two Betto and Nella begin whispering to each other about "what they are saying at Signa", where the deceased had some property. Gradually we learn what it is that the gossips have been saying lately at Signa—that if Buoso dies the monks will do well, while others know for certain that everything has been left to a convent. The mourners begin to be a trifle worried. They ask Simone's advice, he not only being the oldest among them but having been at one time mayor of Fucecchio. After profound deliberation Simone gives his verdict —if the will is in the custody of a notary, that may be good for the monks but bad for them, but if by any chance it has been left in this room, that may turn out bad for the monks but promising for them.

New hope springs up in their hearts, and especially in that of young Rinuccio, who breathes a prayer that the document will turn out to be just what they would all like it to be, so that he may marry his adored Lauretta, the daughter of Gianni Schicchi. The tempo of No. 1 changes to *allegro vivo* again as the relatives, now in a state of high fever, begin to turn the place upside down in the search for the will. Old Betto does not take part in this search, but furtively tries to pocket some of the valuable silver articles on the table. The others pull out drawers, open lockers, look under the bed. Soon the room is littered with papers. One false alarm succeeds another. At last Rinuccio opens a parchment which he thinks may be the will, and we hear in the orchestra a suggestion of a melody:

that will later be associated with him and his Lauretta: if all goes as well as he hopes it will, they can marry next May-day. He gives the document to old Zita, and all gather round to see what it contains. Zita looks about for the scissors that were on the table a few moments ago, but cannot find them, for the excellent reason that they are in Betto's pocket. In the end she tears off the ribbon with her hand. Inside the parchment is yet another parchment, and inside this the will—at last.

Zita reads the inscription on it—"To my cousins Zita and Simone". The sap of hope rises high in them both: Simone, overcome by his pleasurable emotions, lights again the three candles that had gone out; nothing could be too good for this excellent Buoso. The others begin to speculate as to what the old man may have left each of them—the house, perhaps, or the mills and the mule at Signa, or, who knows, all these and more. Zita now stands in the centre of an excited group, all of them with their eyes turned eagerly on the fateful parchment; and the solemnity of the occasion is marked by a theme of almost legal deliberation in the orchestra—the "will" motive, we may perhaps call it:

It shows to what excellent use the notes and the simplest harmonies of the scale of C major can still be put, all modern developments notwithstanding. No. 2 is heard fluttering ironically round it.

The lips of the relatives move as they read the will. Their faces register first of all anxiety, then incredulity, and finally rage as they realise what has happened to them. They throw themselves, exhausted, wild-eyed, despairing, into any seat that presents itself. Simone alone has a bit of action left in him: he puts out not only the three candles he had lit a few minutes ago but all the others— a richly humorous touch in performance. Now they know! they say bitterly: the monks are going to get rich and fat at their expense; out there at Signa heaven knows what *they* will be drinking while the monks are doing themselves well with the products of the vineyards; Rinuccio's happiness will have vanished for the benefit of the scheme for reconstructing Santa Reparata. They all shake their fists and heap curses on the heads of the friars, whom they call by every opprobrious name they can think of, the orchestra all the while pouring out a flood of rage exceeding even their own in volume.

Gradually fury gives way to depression once more. Some of them begin to shed tears of self-pity: who would ever have believed this of Buoso? And the worst of it is that there's no altering it now. Once more they appeal to old Simone as the doyen of the family and the former mayor of Fucecchio: surely he can think of something? But the old man merely shakes his head sadly and hopelessly. Rinuccio comes forward. There is only one man, he says, who can advise and, perhaps, help them—Gianni Schicchi. They are all about to swear that, as members of a respectable family, they will have nothing to do with that rascal or his daughter when Gherardino rushes in, shouting "Here he comes!" At the commencement of the scene of the search for the will, Rinuccio, without saying anything to the others, had sent the boy with a message to Gianni to come to the house at once. The relatives continue to abuse Gianni, and to cry out at the idea of a Donati marrying the daughter of a man like that; but Rinuccio reasons with them. Gianni is artful, he says; there isn't a nook or cranny of the law that he doesn't know. He is a jester of the first order; why, they have only to look at those shrewd eyes of his, at his great nose like an old ruined tower, to see that he is capable of carrying any trick through to the end, and only a trick of the cleverest kind is going to be of much use to them now. Enough of this silly talk about his being a rustic! Florence itself, that lofty, lovely tree, with its branches reaching almost to heaven itself, Florence, with its palaces and towers, does it not renew its roots in the valleys? Rinuccio's song in praise of Florence, its arts, its sciences, its great men:

5
Andante mosso ♩ = 92

Fi - ren - ze è co - me un al - be - ro fio - ri - to

has something of the flavour of a popular melody. It ends with a
cry of "Enough of these miserable animosities and recrimina-
tions: good health to the new breed and Gianni Schicchi!" A broad
orchestral phrase that occurs in the middle of Rinuccio's song:

becomes of importance later.

3

As the strains of the aria die away, Gianni himself enters,
followed by Lauretta. The arch-rogue pauses on the threshold,
amazed at the woe-begone looks of the relatives, which the man
of the world in him can account for only on the theory that
Buoso has had the bad taste to recover. While Rinuccio and
Lauretta are greeting each other affectionately to the strains of
No. 6, Gianni, who has observed the candles round the bed, and
now guesses what has happened, hypocritically assures the relatives, to the accompaniment of No. 1, that he knows why they
are grieving. Still, death is an everyday matter, and there is always
the deceased's estate. They break it to him that this has gone to
the monks, every bit of it; and Zita swears that now there is no
money in the family she will not allow her nephew to marry a
penniless girl like Lauretta. A lively ensemble is built up, Lauretta
and Rinuccio vowing eternal fidelity to each other, Gianni
Schicchi calling Zita, among other things, a sordid, miserly old
curmudgeon, Zita returning his insults in kind, and the others
interjecting every now and then a remark to the effect that what
they ought to be thinking about is the will. As the dispute mostly
concerns the lovers, it is naturally accompanied by a broad
version of No. 3:

Ad-di-o,   speranza bel-la,   speranza bel-la

The indignant Gianni is for leaving the scene, and it takes all the persuasive powers of Rinuccio and Lauretta—the latter in a charming little appeal to her father which she sings on her knees to the tune of No. 6—to get him to change his mind: Lauretta's trump card is the assurance that unless she can go to Porta Rossa and buy the ring she will throw herself into the Arno.

"Give me the will", Schicchi says at length. He strides up and down studying it, with the relatives following him mechanically, while the lovers, forgetful of all the rest, bid a sad farewell, to the melody of No. 3, to their dream of a wedding on May-day. At first Gianni has no hope that the will can be got round. Then we see from his face, as the agonised relatives do, that an idea has struck him. He gets rid of his little Lauretta by telling her to go out on the terrace and give the bird some crumbs. Then he asks the company if anyone except themselves knows that Buoso is dead. Their reply is "No". Then no one must hear of it just yet, he says. But what about the servants? Zita tells him that no one except themselves has entered the room since the end came. And now Gianni becomes the man of action. He orders them to carry the body and the candelabra into an adjacent room and to re-make the bed; which they do.

A knock at the door makes everyone's heart jump into his mouth. "It's Maestro Spinelloccio, the doctor!" says Zita in a scared whisper. While the others crowd round the barely open door and hold the doctor in conversation, and Betto darkens the room by closing the window shutters, Gianni conceals himself behind the bed-hangings. Spinelloccio, speaking in a nasal tone with a Bolognese accent, asks after his patient, and is assured that he is going on nicely. He tries to approach the bed, but the others block his way, and from behind the curtains comes a thin, weak, tremulous voice begging the physician not to insist. Perhaps Spinelloccio can call again in the evening. Buoso is much better, but he needs rest, and he is feeling very drowsy. At the sound of what for the moment they take to be the voice of Buoso himself, so good is the imitation of it, the relatives almost jump out of their skins: but as soon as they realise that it is only Gianni speaking they manage to steady themselves—all except old Betto, who, in his fright, lets fall a silver dish he had been hiding in his sleeve; Zita

picks it up and replaces it on the table, giving Betto a nasty look
and threatening him with her finger, but saying nothing. The
doctor lets himself be edged out of the room, attributing, as he
goes, this marvellous recovery to the well-known skill of the
Bologna school of medicine. (In the old commedia dell'arte the
doctor was generally a Bolognese).

As soon as he has gone, Betto reopens the shutters, once more
letting in the light of day, and Gianni comes into sight again.
"Was the voice anything like correct?" he asks them. They assure
him that it was absolutely right. "Victory! Victory!" he cries,
but still they do not understand. He tells them to send to the
notary and bid him come without a moment's delay to old Buoso
Donati, who has got much worse and wants to make his will.
When he arrives, he, Gianni Schicchi, lying in the bed, concealed
behind the curtains in a darkened room, will impersonate the
dying Buoso: the orchestra gives humorous point to what he says
by harping on the death motive (No. 1) of the genuine Buoso. In
a passage of the utmost slyness he describes how all the notary
will see will be a head with a nightcap on it and a face covered with
a kerchief, except for a nose that will look like Buoso's but will be
his, Gianni Schicchi's; and in that guise he will dictate a will, a
proper will! His head is bursting with the brightest, maddest joke
that ever was, a joke that is a challenge to heaven itself. The
others think it is a magnificent idea, which could only occur to a
genius like him. While Rinuccio rushes off for the notary the
others crowd round Schicchi, kissing his hands and his clothes,
and blessing the day when he thought of this scheme for circum-
venting the monks. They even go to the extent of embracing each
other and singing the praises of love among relations.

Then they give Gianni instructions as to the dictating of the
will. Simone wants the Fucecchio farms; others claim those of
Figline, or Prato, or the property at Empoli, and so on. But the
most valuable of all are the mills and the mule at Signa, and everyone wants these. Simone thinks they ought to come to him
because he is the oldest and because he has been the mayor of
Fucecchio; the others stake out their own claims. They are all
shouting each other down when the tolling of a funeral bell is
heard. It strikes dismay into them: the whole town knows, then,

that Buoso is dead! Even Gianni Schicchi's nerve fails him for
a moment. "All's lost!" he says. It is precisely at this critical
moment that simple little Lauretta chooses to come back from the
terrace with the information that the bird won't eat any more.
"Then give him something to drink", says her father tersely: at
all costs she must be out of the way while he is putting his fraud
through.

As Lauretta goes out, Gherardo, who has gone to see what is
happening in the street, rushes in panting for breath, only just
able to gasp out that it is a false alarm; it is only the Moor baptised
by the captain who has come to grief. "Requiescat in pace!" sing
the relieved relatives cheerfully; and immediately the mills and the
mule and the house at Signa come uppermost in their thoughts
again. This time, instead of wrangling about the matter, they
agree to leave it to the decision of Gianni Schicchi. He consents
to act as arbiter. Zita, Nella and La Ciesca dig out for him one
of Buoso's nightgowns, a kerchief and a nightcap. While he is
putting these on, the relatives in turn edge up to him and whisper
into his ear promises of bribes if he assigns the house, the mule and
the mills to them. His reply to each of them is "All right!", but
the typical motive of his slyness (No. 2), peeping out in the
orchestra through it all, bodes ill for the relatives. Each of them,
however, retires well satisfied, rubbing his or her hands.

While Simone goes to the window to look out for the notary
and Gherardo clears the table for the latter, the others sing the
praises of Gianni's lifelike impersonation of Buoso—nose, voice,
everything is perfect. The ensemble reaches its climax of ecstasy
in a great cry of "O Gianni Schicchi, our saviour!":

They push him towards the bed, but he halts them with a solemn gesture. He has a warning for them. They know the law, he hopes: "If anyone substitutes himself for another in a matter in which a legacy is concerned, both he and his accomplices shall lose one hand and then be exiled"; and in that case, farewell for every one of them to beautiful Florence! The relatives, thoroughly sobered, repeat his final words: none of them can bear the thought of dragging out existence under another sky than that of Florence, and with only one hand at that.

4

A knock at the door sends Gianni scurrying to the bed, while the others darken the room, place a lighted candle on the table, and make other preparations for the notary, who, with Rinuccio and a couple of friends of Buoso, Pinellino the shoemaker and Guccio the dyer, enters to the motive of No. 4 in the orchestra. This makes way for the death motive (No. 1) as the pseudo-Buoso greets the newcomers and thanks them for coming to witness his will. The notary seats himself at the table and spreads out his parchments and seals, the two witnesses standing by him. Schicchi, in a feeble voice, explains that it had been his intention to write out his will with his own hand, but his paralysis having made that impossible for him he has sent for this worthy notary. To demonstrate his paralysis, Gianni raises a trembling hand to the accompaniment of the mocking No. 2, the relatives registering compassion and murmuring "Poor Buoso!" At the sick man's special request the relatives are allowed to remain in the room during the making of the will, which is carried out to a development of the motive quoted as No. 4. The notary gabbles the long Latin preamble as he gets it down on the parchment—he, Amantio di Nicolao, a notary of Florence, on this first day of September 1299, inscribes at the request of Buoso Donati this last will and testament, which revokes and annuls all preceding ones —a clause which meets with the warm approval of the relatives.

First of all the notary asks about the funeral. Does Buoso wish it to be an ostentatious one? No, no, says Gianni; it is not to cost more than a couple of florins. Once more the relatives thoroughly approve. Then Gianni begins his dictation of the will. At his

opening words—"To the Frati Minori and the fund for Santa
Reparata I bequeath"—the relatives start up in terror; but they
sit down again, with a sigh of relief, when he continues, "five lire".
They commend his charity and his piety alike; good works should
always be remembered in one's will. The few florins in ready
money left by the deceased are next bequeathed to the relatives in
equal shares. Other legacies follow in quick succession—to Simone
the property at Fucecchio, to Zita the farms at Figline, to Betto
the Prato fields, to Nella and Gherardo the property at Empoli,
to La Ciesca and Marco that at Quintole. Each beneficiary in turn
murmurs his grateful thanks. And now, they say under their
breath, for the things that really matter, the Signa mule, house and
mills! The mule, the testator continues, the best mule in Tuscany,
which cost three hundred florins, he leaves to—his devoted friend
Gianni Schicchi. While the notary is getting that down in his
Latin the relatives jump up in affright. Simone, forgetting himself, asks what on earth Gianni Schicchi can want with the mule;
but the testator cows him with the rejoinder that Gianni Schicchi
knows perfectly well what Gianni Schicchi wants; and poor old
Simone subsides, muttering "Ah! the rascal!"

The house in Florence is next bequeathed by Buoso to his dear,
devoted, affectionate friend Gianni Schicchi. This is too much for
the relatives, who cry out in a wild chorus against such injustice;
but he brings them to reason by singing a line or two of the farewell to Florence and its divine sky, with its reminder about the
loss of one hand. The sentiment seems to the notary beautifully
appropriate to the dying Florentine, but the relatives understand
its darker significance. Anyhow all is not yet lost; there are still
the mills to be disposed of. The rogue leaves these also to his
dear, affectionate friend Gianni Schicchi; but between each
phrase of his dictation he inserts another subtle reminder to the
relatives of the penalties attaching to complicity in the making of
a false testament. Caught in their own net, they can do nothing
but groan.

Rinuccio now slips out to join Lauretta on the terrace. Adding
insult to injury, the testator directs Zita to give twenty florins out
of her own purse to the two witnesses, and a hundred to the
notary. The three go out expressing their gratitude to this excel-

lent Buoso and regretting that soon they will see him no more. When they have gone, the relatives rush in force towards Gianni Schicchi, calling him a rascal, thief and traitor. They tear off his nightgown. He leaps from the bed and assails them with Buoso's staff, ordering them out of his house. They begin to pillage the place, each going off with as much as he can carry, while he pursues them with the stick. When they have all gone, Rinuccio opens the great window from outside, revealing Florence in all its beauty in the full sunlight; and the lovers pour out their hearts to each other and to the city they love to the broad melody of No. 3.

Gianni Schicchi returns from the fray loaded with things he has retrieved from the marauders. As he throws them down in triumph he catches sight of Rinuccio and Lauretta. His heart melts: he smiles understandingly, removes his cap, and turning to the audience asks them, in a speaking voice, if Buoso's money could have come to a better end than this. For this little pleasantry of his he has been consigned to the Inferno; but, by permission of the great Dante, if they have been amused he will ask them for a verdict of extenuating circumstances. He starts the applause with his own hands, and bows to the audience as the curtain descends. And of course he carries us with him; for whatever Dante may have to say on the subject, and however regrettable it may be from the point of view of the moralist, the world has generally found its rogues more companionable than its saints.

THE BARBER OF BAGDAD
Peter Cornelius (1824-1874)

PRINCIPAL CHARACTERS

MARGIANA	*Soprano*
NUREDDIN	*Tenor*
ABUL HASSAN ALI EBN BEKAR (THE BARBER)	*Bass*
THE CALIPH	*Baritone*
BABA MUSTAPHA (THE CADI)	*Tenor*
BOSTANA	*Mezzo-soprano*

I

It is generally unsafe to regard an artist's work as the counterpart of himself; but there are cases in which the resemblance is too close to be fortuitous, and that of Peter Cornelius and his *Barber of Bagdad* is one of them. The opera is typically Cornelius both in its shrewd but kindly humour and its modest independence of manner. Of all the people who came into Wagner's orbit, either as man or as artist, Cornelius was the one who surrendered least of his real self to the tyranny of the giant's personality. As a man, indeed, he often annoyed Wagner seriously by his refusal to be blind to his faults. He had an immense admiration and affection for both Wagner and Liszt; but he clung tenaciously to his right to judge each of them objectively, and he stoutly refused, from first to last, to be, as he put it, merely the nought behind Wagner's one. He had no illusions about either the extent or the depth of his own musical capacity. He knew just how much he could and what he could not do; but he held that what he had to say was worth saying, and his healthy nature preserved him from the dangers of too close a dependence either on Wagner or on Wagner's art. Almost from the beginning he seems to have realised that the field in which his talent could most fully realise itself was that of comic opera—a genre, it must be borne in mind, in which Germany was not particularly rich in the mid-nineteenth century.

He analysed himself quite objectively when he was no more than twenty-five, in a letter to his friend Hestermann on Christmas Day, 1849. "If I were to pass judgment on myself, it would be in these terms. I have a fair talent for composition, in spite of the fact that nature has not endowed me with the inexhaustible invention of a Mozart or a Rossini. . . . I can quietly lay claim to one good thing—what little I have is my own property. I do not dig in other people's fields, or adorn myself with others' feathers; so I may hope that when I come to my years of discretion I shall have, God willing, a certain individuality to display. There is still one path open to us composers: music has had its three great tragedians, but . . . the Aristophanes has not yet appeared. I do not know of one purely comic opera among modern German works: since Dittersdorf we have not possessed a single composer who was strictly speaking a comic writer; the Italian opera buffa has still to come to flower in Germany. . . . Years ago I sketched out several comic opera subjects, but my feeling that I was not yet ripe enough has kept me from setting to work at them, so I went back to my purely theoretical studies. Now, however, I have done the text of a little one-act opera,[1] which I hope to finish by the spring, as the music naturally will not aim at anything learned or exceptional, but must flow easily and unaffectedly." He composed, of course, in several genres, writing, in addition to *The Barber of Bagdad*, a number of delicately conceived songs and other vocal works, a fair quantity of religious music, and two serious operas, *Der Cid* and *Gunlöd*, the latter of which was unfinished at his death. But the best Cornelius is in *The Barber*.

It was in 1852 that he drifted, as so many others of the more ardent young German musicians of that period did, to Weimar, to become the friend, the helpmate, and to some extent the pupil of Liszt. (It was not until some time later that he became at all familiar with Wagner's music). Weimar remained, off and on, his headquarters for about seven years. During that period the strongest musical influence on him was that of Berlioz, a number of whose larger works were brought to a hearing in Weimar by Liszt, some of them under the baton of the composer himself. Cornelius, who was not only an accomplished linguist but a poet,

---

[1] This appears to be lost.

translated the texts of some of Berlioz's works into German, among them that of the opera *Benvenuto Cellini*. This work seems to have made a deep impression on him; traces of its example are to be found in more than one place in *The Barber*.

Cornelius confided to Liszt his aspirations in the direction of comic opera, but Liszt—who, excellent creature though he was in some respects, had no more sense of humour than could balance itself comfortably on a pin-head—tried to convince him that his true line was church music. It was not until 1855, when Cornelius had settled down in Weimar as Liszt's secretary and literary man-of-all-work, that he began to put into shape his ideas for a comic opera based on the story of the famous Barber of Bagdad. He read his text to Liszt, who seems to have expressed himself rather coolly about it. The music was begun in November 1856. Cornelius kept making various small alterations in his design, and it was not until February 1858 that his composition was complete. By the following April the full score was ready; and it was the study of this that reconciled Liszt somewhat to the subject, which had formerly been antipathetic to him. No opera, he now assured Cornelius, had interested him so much since *Benvenuto Cellini*.

He put it into rehearsal in the Weimar theatre at the earliest possible moment; and there it was produced on the 15th December 1858, Liszt himself conducting. This first performance was also the last in the composer's lifetime. A cabal set itself from the commencement to ruin the chances of the work; the evening ended, says Cornelius, in a ten minutes' contest between the many well-wishers of the work and the gang that was bent on killing it. Towards Cornelius himself, whom no one could ever help liking, or towards his opera in and by itself, there could be no question of any real enmity on any one's part. The traditional explanation of the affair is that the opposition had been worked up by the director of the dramatic side of the Weimar theatre, Dingelstedt, who objected to so large a proportion of the financial resources and the energies of the institution being expended on music. So, in part, it may have been; but from all we know of Liszt in Weimar it seems probable that he aroused the antagonism he undoubtedly did not because as an artist he was too lofty in his idealism for the little town, but purely and simply because his own defects of character and the ways of his unofficial wife, the Princess Wittgenstein, had made the pair of them cordially disliked by many of the inhabitants. Liszt was deeply wounded by this exhibition of personal ill-will towards him: from that evening he severed his connection with the Weimar Opera, for which he had done such splendid work since 1848.

Cornelius had originally cast his opera in one-act form—"in seven scenes", as he said, "with an extended final scene occupying something like a third of the whole work." Later he decided on "two acts of equal length . . . twelve scenes, each with its outstanding lyrical moment."[1] The overture was in B minor: Cornelius describes it as "an objectively-handled comedy overture" —that is to say, an introduction of the type of Mozart's *Figaro* overture, which establishes a general mood of gaiety and humour without making any specific reference to the themes of the opera itself. This at first found favour in Liszt's eyes, perhaps precisely because it was "objective". He approved, says Cornelius, of the form, and "found the melodies and harmonies, for the most part, very interesting and piquant", though "his antipathy towards the subject, even if unexpressed, remains the same as before: which is quite natural, for the comic is not in his line." Liszt was wrong about many things in connection with *The Barber*. But he was right in urging Cornelius later to write a new and more descriptive overture, in which the Barber should announce himself straight away with his characteristic motive. Cornelius completed this second overture, which is in D major, in 1873, but died before he could orchestrate it. That pious task was performed for him by Liszt.

Three years after the composer's death the opera was given in Hanover (on the 24th May 1877), in an abbreviated form. It then disappeared from the boards for a further seven years: on the 1st February 1884 it was revived at Karlsruhe by Felix Mottl, but drastically curtailed, and with the orchestration touched up at

[1] In the final libretto there are ten "scenes" to each act. This division, however, is purely formal: there is only one setting for each act, and music and action are continuous from the beginning of each act until the end of it.

innumerable points to suit a Wagnerian conductor's notions of what was right and proper. Hermann Levi followed with a Munich production on the 15th October 1885, restoring a good many pages which Mottl had omitted, but making still further changes of his own in the scoring. He was of the naïve opinion that "in its original form the opera is impossible on the stage": he assured the publisher Kahnt, indeed, that an imprint of the original score would be "at best merely a literary document, which could never be utilised in connection with a performance." Kahnt accordingly published the Mottl-Levi version of the score, without the name of either of these worthies, however, appearing on the title-page.

It was largely owing to the vigorous polemic of Max Hasse against the "improvements" of this score that *The Barber* was at last given in Weimar in its original form on the 10th June 1904; and the success of it proved that in this, as in so many similar cases in the history of the opera house and the concert room, the composer knew his own business better than any of the prime donne of the baton who had taken it on themselves to teach him.[1] As the composer's son, Dr. Carl Maria Cornelius, put it in a letter to these gentry, "No one would deny that you can orchestrate better, more cleverly, more effectively than Peter Cornelius could. It is not a question of that, however, but simply this— Which of the two orchestral scores is more in keeping with the style of the work? . . . The new instrumentation may be as brilliant and effective as you please, but it is alien to the style of the *Barber*." Today *The Barber of Bagdad*, if not everyone's opera—its flavour and aroma are perhaps a trifle too delicate for

---

[1] It is true that in 1860 Cornelius himself thought of rearranging *The Barber* as a one-act opera. But it was no doubt in the pathetic belief that in this form the work might stand more chance of acceptance by the theatres and the publishers; and we can now congratulate ourselves that he never carried out his intention. Today we agree with Bülow, who wrote to Cornelius's widow in 1886, *à propos* of a successful revival of the work in Hamburg, "In heaven's name do not suggest or permit a condensation of the opera into one act. According to my own 'slight' knowledge of the theatre, that would be murder pure and simple." The "splendid work", he said, "has more wit and more music in a single page of it than there is in the whole of the stuff sweated out by the imitators of Wagner."

that—is the joy of everyone with a palate that can appreciate the refinements of humour in music. Cornelius was right when he described his own humour as *liebevoll*, at the furthest remove from the broad *Kladderadatsch* grin that makes the greater appeal to the greater number.

The plot of *The Barber of Bagdad* is derived from the group of stories, one enclosed within the other like a set of oriental boxes, that commences with the twenty-fourth night of *The Thousand and One Nights*. The Tailor tells a story of an entertainment given to certain tradesmen of his acquaintance, at which a rich-looking young man of the handsomest appearance and the comeliest form —except that he was lame in one leg—refused to sit down with the rest of the company when he perceived among them a barber who hailed, like himself, from Bagdad. He is induced to tell his story. In his native town, it appears, he had fallen in love with the beautiful daughter of a Cadi, who at last consented to receive him one day when her father was at prayers in the mosque. The young man called for a barber to make him more presentable after the long illness caused by the cruel indifference of the maiden. The barber who was sent to him brought him to the verge of madness by his loquacity. At last he escaped from him and went to the Cadi's house. But the barber followed him, believing it to be his mission to protect the youth, whom, he declared, he loved as a son, against the wiles of women and the hand of the law. As luck would have it, the Cadi arrived at his house almost immediately after the lover. He had occasion to punish a slave, whose cries were heard in the street below by the barber, who, jumping to the conclusion that the young man was being murdered, roused the populace and entered the house. The lover had concealed himself in a large chest: guessing where he was, the barber walked out with the chest on his head:[1] the lover leaped out, broke his leg, sold his property, and left Bagdad in the hope of escaping for ever from the accursed barber who had been the cause of all his misfortunes.

[1] A truly remarkable feat, even for a man so remarkable as the barber by his own admission was; for we learn later that he is at least ninety years old when the Tailor's story is told, and even at the time of the adventure he was already old enough to have numbered the young man's father among his customers.

Cornelius, of course, dispenses with the detail of breaking the lover's leg: so unhappy an ending would never do for a comic opera. But for the rest he keeps closely to the piquant details and rich characterisation of the original; and he has condensed the Tailor's story, and those told later by the barber of himself and his six elder brothers, into a libretto that is a little masterpiece of dramatic design and gentle humour.

2

As already mentioned, the original overture to the opera, in B minor, was a comedy overture in the older sense of the term, establishing a general mood of gaiety without direct reference to the thematic material of the work itself. How great was the influence of Berlioz on Cornelius at this time can be seen from a comparison of the main theme of the overture:

with the opening phrase of the *Benvenuto Cellini* overture:

the notes are not at all the same, yet the filiation of the one theme with the other is unmistakable.

The score of the D major overture to *The Barber of Bagdad* now in general circulation is an orchestration by Mottl of Cornelius's second overture, written at the suggestion of Liszt. (A later scoring by Waldemar von Baussnern is not so well known). The overture begins with a bold statement of the Barber theme (No. 7 below) in the brass, followed in turn by the theme of the Barber's song "Bin Akademiker" (No. 9), the melody of Nured-

din's appeal to Margiana (No. 3), the "assignation" duet between
Nureddin and Bostana (No. 6), a suggestion of the chorus of
Nureddin's servants at the end of the first act (the scene of the
plaguing of the Barber) with angry interjections of No. 7, and an
expressive melody, fluctuating between 4/4 and 5/4 time, that is
not to be found in the opera. All these themes are worked up in
the liveliest fashion, and the overture ends with the brass voci-
ferating the simple little phrase to which, in the opera, Nureddin
says to the departing Bostana, "Don't forget the barber!" Cornelius no doubt intended the reminder of this at the end of the
overture as a gentle admonition to the public not to forget his
own *Barber*.

Nureddin is lying on a couch in a room in his house, sick with
hopeless love for Margiana. His servants are bending over him
anxiously: on a table near by stand medicine bottles and other sick
room appurtenances. It is early dawn. The servants sing, with
hushed voices, a sympathetic little chorus over the sufferer, whom
they evidently regard as being on the point of death: from time to
time he sighs out the name of Margiana, whom he implores to deign
to look down on him once more from her window—for the last
time, perhaps, for his suffering soul is bound for Paradise:

Komm Deine Blu-men zu be-gie - ssen, o Mar-gia - na!

The servants are no less convinced of that than he is; and to
console him they paint the delights of the next world with its
dates, its pomegranates, its flowers, its purling streams, and, not
least, the houris with their honeyed kisses:

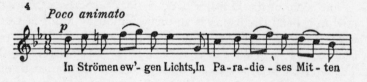

In Strömen ew'- gen Lichts, In Pa-ra-die - ses Mit - ten

All in all he will be exchanging, in their opinion, a bad proposition for a good one. But Nureddin can think only of Margiana; and for a while his appeal to her (No. 3) accompanies contrapuntally the mortuary consolations (No. 4) of the chorus.

The servants creep out silently, and Nureddin summons up strength enough to rise from his couch and pour out his passion and despair in an agitated *allegro*. In his mind's eye he once more sees Margiana at her window, watering the flowers, as when he beheld her first; but on the fire that is consuming him, alas, never a cooling drop falls:

His only hope is the old go-between Bostana, who enters at the conclusion of his song, when, exhausted by his paroxysm, he has flung himself into a chair with his head in his hands. This Bagdad ancestress of Mrs. Quickly is old, and grotesquely costumed: her manner varies between the unctuous, the cunning and the playful. She has good tidings for him, she says, tidings that surely deserve a handsome present, she hints. His imagination at once takes fire: "You are the dove", he cries, in the true oriental vein of imagery, "that after the flood alights on the ark of my heart, in which the serpent of sorrow hisses, where despair whines like a jackal and wild jealousy howls like a tiger, and ah! the nightingale of longing warbles!" And each reference to animal and bird and reptile is given its special humorous point in the orchestra.

Bostana goes on to say that at last she has persuaded Margiana to take pity on him; he shall see her that very day if he will follow the old woman's instructions implicitly. Her father the Cadi, like the pious mussulman he is, will be going to the mosque at mid-day as usual: what can be easier, then, with the father out, the door open, and the maiden willing? All this is told at some length, along with Nureddin's eager reactions, in a charming canonic duet (*molto presto*):

the lively give-and-take of which is obviously modelled on the racy trio, "Demain soir, mardi gras", in Berlioz' *Benvenuto Cellini*. The resemblance extends even to the repetition of it. Berlioz, unwilling to let so good a thing as this trio pass away before the audience has had a real chance to appreciate it, manufactures an excuse for its repetition by making Cellini ask Teresa whether she is quite sure that she has the details of the plot correct. Cornelius does likewise. Nureddin is all impatience to get to Margiana's house at once; and Bostana has to remind him that it is some hours yet to mid-day. Nor can he hope to make a good impression on a lady in his unshorn and generally untended condition. She prescribes a barber and a bath. For the former she can recommend an old friend of hers, "a hero of the sciences and the arts, and withal a virtuoso at barbering", none other, indeed, than the great

Nureddin bids her send the man to him at once. But Bostana, equally anxious to make sure that there is no mistake about the assignation with Margiana and to give the composer a pretext for savouring his own charming music once more, asks him to go over it all again with her. The duet is accordingly repeated.

Nureddin, having hurried Bostana out with a parting admonition not to forget the barber, indulges himself, in an agitated monologue, in a vision of the more than paradisiacal joys that are in store for him. At the height of his ecstasy the Barber enters. He carries with him, in oriental fashion, the apparatus of his craft—a particoloured napkin, a small brass basin, a hand mirror hanging from his girdle, and under his arm a box containing other implements. He is very old, with a long white beard; his skin is almost yellow. What distinguishes him from the mere ordinary barber is the astrolabe he carries.

It is some time before the self-absorbed Nureddin becomes aware of the strange figure that keeps bowing and h'ming beside him; it takes a touch on the shoulder from Abul to tear the young man out of his trance. He tells the Barber to begin shaving him at once. But that is not Abul Hassan Ali Ebn Bekar's way of doing things. In a vocabulary of his own—an admirable idea of Cornelius's carried out with inexhaustible inventiveness and unflagging zest—he expresses his delight at Nureddin's recovery and the young man's wisdom in calling on *his* services:

He is never at a loss for a compound rhyme:

> *Heil dir! Du Krankgewesener,*
> *Du glücklich Neugenesener,*
> *Du Übelüberwindender,*
> *Dich wieder Wohlbefindender,*
> *Dem Tode froh Entschlüpfender,*
> *Durch's Leben rüstig Hüpfender,*
> *Du jüngst noch Heiltrank Schlürfender,*
> *Nur meiner Kunst Bedürfender,*

C*

> *Schwer unter Haarlast Ächzender,*
> *Nach meinem Messer Lechzender,*

and so on. Every one of his lines is couched in the same rhythmic mould, with the same type of cadence (as shown at A and B in our quotation No. 8); yet Cornelius manages to achieve constant variety throughout all this uniformity.

Nureddin cuts him short, urging him to make haste with the shaving, as he has urgent business on hand. But no one could ever hustle Abul Hassan. Showing the young man his astrolabe, he tells him that, having lately cast his horoscope, he can assure him that he has had the good luck to choose the best of all possible times for being shaved: Mars and Mercury, it seems, are favourable, though a suspicious eye will have to be kept on Venus. Nothing that Nureddin can say or do can either stop the old man's chatter or induce him to set to work. He launches into one of the finest episodes of the score, the long aria in which, hardly pausing to take breath, he sets forth all his claims to respect as doctor, chemist, mathematician, aesthetician, and everything else under the sun:

Once more we admire Cornelius's verbal dexterity as well as his musical inventiveness:

> *Bin Akademiker,*
> *Doktor und Chemiker,*
> *Bin Mathematiker*
> *Und Arithmetiker,*
> *Bin auch Grammatiker,*
> *So wie Ästhetiker,*
>
> .   .   .   .   .

Astrolog, Philolog,
Physiker, Geolog,

.   .   .   .   .

Linguist und Jurist
Und Tourist und Purist.

.   .   .   .   .

Dabei ein Sokrates
Und Aristoteles;
Bin Dialektiker,
Sophist, Eklektiker,
Zyniker, Ethiker,
Peripathetiker,

.   .   .   .   .

In fact, as he modestly assures Nureddin, a universal genius.

Nureddin, whose temper is getting out of control, makes the mistake of calling him a chatterer. That starts Abul Hassan off again on a long disclaimer. His brothers Bacbouc the lame, Heddah the bastinadoed one, Bacbac the blind, Alcouz the one-eyed, Alnaschar of the cropped ears, Schacabac, whose lips were cut off,[1] these were indeed babblers whom there was no stopping; while he, the youngest of the family, was always the virtuous one, the silent one. But Nureddin can stand no more. He shouts to his servants to come and throw this intolerable windbag out. The stage instructions are that the last of the servants to enter—one Motavakel—shall catch the spectator's eye by reason of either his unusual height and bulk or his comical smallness. In a chorus which, in the profusion of its manufactured epithets and the ingenuity of its rhymes, goes beyond even what Abul Hassan was able to achieve in these genres, the servants manage to edge the Barber as far as the door; but there he turns on them with his razor, and Nureddin has to call off the baying pack. The Barber, still flourishing his razor, accelerates their exit, paying special attention to Motavakel.

His consciousness of triumph soon makes him amiable and

[1] These, of course, are the names and descriptions of the brothers given in *The Thousand and One Nights*. Cornelius varies them somewhat.

paternal again, especially as Nureddin, realising that diplomacy is likely to get him further than fury will do with a man of this sort, now overwhelms him with flatteries and courtesies, begging him only to shave him without further delay. Nureddin seats himself in a chair in the centre of the stage, and the Barber, having arranged his utensils on a table, makes a lather in his basin and fastens the particoloured napkin round the young man's neck. Nureddin, finding himself, as he imagines, in sight of port at last, begins to sing of his Margiana—a fatal error, for it reminds Abul Hassan of the days of his youth when he too was in love with a Margiana. He favours Nureddin with the song he used to sing to the maiden; words and music, he says, are both his own invention:

The ditty and the lathering go on simultaneously.[1] So long as Abul is making any progress at all with the shaving, Nureddin can join ecstatically in his absurd invocations of Margiana. But it is not long before the artist in Abul succumbs to the fatal fascination of his own virtuosity. He loses himself in a seemingly interminable coloratura cadenza, in the best old-Italian opera style, on the words "O Margiana!", meanwhile, of course, forgetting his shaving entirely. Nureddin at last, with a pluck at his sleeve, brings the artist back to reality, and implores him, as a one-time lover himself, to have pity on him, for *his* Margiana is at that very moment awaiting him: "if ever one breath of love was in you, here on my knees I entreat you to do just one thing—shave me!"

Abul Hassan is beside himself with joy to hear that Nureddin is

[1] In present-day performances the Barber lathers, and then half-shaves, Nureddin's chin. Cornelius, however, true to oriental practice, makes him shave the head, as in the story in *The Thousand and One Nights*.

in love. He clasps him enthusiastically to his bosom. "I too!" he says: "Learn from this heart how I, who am now ninety years old, once loved!" On the topic of Margiana the pair are of one heart and soul; they accordingly sing a rapturous duet on the subject to the melody of No. 10. Then Nureddin takes his seat in the chair once more and the shaving is resumed.

Fresh trouble is not long in coming. Abul Hassan learns that Nureddin's Margiana is the daughter of the Cadi Baba Mustapha. "A villain!", he cries, "a man whom I hate like nothing on earth! May Allah make an end of him; may the plague seize the barbarian; the rascal shaves himself!" He undertakes to accompany Nureddin to the assignation and keep watch and ward over him. But Nureddin only laughs at him, and, the shaving being at last finished, goes into the next room to be dressed, advising the Barber to get back with all speed to his no doubt numerous other customers.

Instead of going, Abul Hassan broods sadly; a woman has only to beckon, he says, and these young fellows go out gaily to danger and even death. His brothers, now—what brought them to their ruin, all six of them? Love! What turned Bacbac's heart to dust? Love! And got Bacbarac his drubbing?[1] Love! And made Alnaschar take ratsbane? And got Alcouz hanged with the other thieves? Love! And gave Schacabac the cold that carried him off? Love! And what is it that torments even him, the youngest of the seven? Love! And Cornelius, employing a favourite and most ingenious technique of his, maintains yet varies each time the same low-lying cadence of the voice on "Lieben":

11

Allegro assai

Was hat Euch Brü - der in den Tod ge -

trie - ben? Lie - ben!

[1] We follow Cornelius's text here.

He is still sighing at the recollection of all these family catastrophes when Nureddin returns, splendidly dressed and in the highest spirits. He is surprised to find the Barber still there, and not only surprised but annoyed to learn that the old man really means to accompany him to Margiana's house. As a duet, angry on the one side, paternally affectionate on the other, fails to settle the question, Nureddin calls his servants in once more: Motavakel, as usual, brings up the rear. Nureddin tells them that the poor old Barber is very ill with a fever. They are to put him to bed, pile cushions on him, and dose him with pills and potions: if he refuses to swallow them he is to be beaten till he does. They are to get a surgeon to bleed him, and to do everything else they can think of to effect a cure. Nureddin goes out. The servants, delighted to have a chance to get their own back, overpower the Barber and drag him to the couch, promising him the most comprehensive treatment in the whole annals of medicine. They hold him down on the couch and heap cushions on him till only his cap and beard are to be seen. The fun grows faster and more furious. In spite of his appeals and struggles, some flourish razors and lancets at him; one brushes his feet with a big broom; another fans him with a large cloth; some make as if to pour Nureddin's medicine down his throat; others clap a big black plaster on his forehead and nose. Our last view of him, as the curtain falls, is with Motavakel bending over him with the end of the Barber's long beard in one hand and a handsaw in the other, while the whole pack of them deafen the old man with his own "Abul Hassan Ali Ebn Bekar" in five-part harmony.

2

According to Mottl, it was on Liszt's advice (in 1880), that he condensed the *Barber* into a single act. "The final scene of the first act must go", said Liszt; "after Abul Hassan's exit with the words 'Lieben! O!' the curtain must fall, and the music run on to the Intermezzo in F sharp minor." Mottl acted on this suggestion; but today we can see that both he and Liszt were wrong and the composer right.

The Intermezzo is a tone-picture of extraordinary beauty. It is a moving meditation on the Muezzin's call to prayer, which is heard in the first bar, over a quiet open fifth:

Cornelius repeats the phrase again and again, always with a fresh melodic turn, a fresh colour, a fresh depth of romantic suggestion, and with the most enchanting imitations between the parts, as in the following example:

The curtain rises on the women's apartment in the house of the Cadi Baba Mustapha. There is a large door at the back, in one wall a tapestried opening, and on the other side a curtained-off recess. Towards the left of the stage stands a table covered with gorgeous flowers; before it there is an ottoman and a kneeling-cushion. On the left, near the footlights, is a window, and on the opposite side of the room a small door.

Margiana enters in a flutter of excitement: "He comes! he comes!" she carols, this ideal lover of hers whom she has never met before but of whom she has often dreamed:

14

Er kommt! Er kommt! o Wonne meiner Brust! Wie

werd' ich ju-beln ihn zu se - - hen

Then enter successively Bostana and the Cadi, each in a similarly happy mood, and each to the same words—"He comes! he comes!" —sung to the same long melody as Margiana's. Cornelius was very fond of this device of making the canon form subserve at the same time his musical and his dramatic purpose; and this is one of his happiest and most skilful efforts in this field. Bostana's "He comes!" relates, of course, to Nureddin, about whose coming she is almost as pleased as Margiana herself. The Cadi, who enters through the great door at the back with a letter and a key in his hand, is pleased for another reason. His rich friend Selim is on his way from Damascus to ask for Margiana's hand; meanwhile he has sent her a chest full of presents of the most expensive kind. Four servants bring in the chest as the Cadi is speaking: he opens it, lifts the costly stuffs out of it, and drapes them admiringly over the side of the chest. Margiana, like a dutiful daughter, is pleased not only with the presents but because her father is pleased; but every now and then she asks Bostana, in an aside, when the eagerly expected lover will arrive. This longish trio is based on a charming phrase:

15

Bass: A _____ G♯ __ F♯ _____ E ___

which passes from mouth to mouth and from one instrument of
the orchestra to another with perfect dramatic appropriateness: as
usual with Cornelius, the musical and dramatic elements of the
scene play expertly into each other's hands.

Suddenly there strikes into the delicate texture the voice of a
Muezzin (bass) from a distant mosque, with the melody of No.
12. He is answered by another (tenor), and in turn by a third,
also a tenor. "Allah is great!" they cry, "and Mahomet is his
prophet! Come, ye faithful, to prayer." Margiana, Bostana and
the Cadi, forgetting for a moment their personal affairs, repeat the call, blending their voices with that of the third
Muezzin; and the solemn strain swells and ebbs away again
in the orchestra as the pious Cadi goes out, still casting cove-
tous glances at the chest. This episode of the Muezzins is one
of the most enchanting in all opera; and the curious thing is
that for all its heart-piercing solemnity it never for a moment
strikes one as an alien patch upon the comic-opera tissue of the
rest of the work.

As soon as the Cadi's back is turned, Bostana slips out through
the tapestried doorway, returns with Nureddin, and then discreetly retires. Nureddin at once launches into a respectful declaration of his love, in a quiet melody that fluctuates between
triple and quadruple time:

Margiana answers him in the same style. A frenzied outpouring
of passion would of course be out of keeping with the general
character of the work, but there is a note of idyllic ecstasy in the
ensuing duet, sung in unison throughout:

17

Allegro moderato

So mag kein and - res Wort er - klin - gen,

Als das die blühn - de Ro - se sprach,

While the orchestra is softly repeating the melody there is heard through the window the voice of the Barber, bidding Nureddin have no fear, as his devoted Abul Hassan Ali Ebn Bekar (No. 7) is keeping guard without. Bostana rushes in with the news that the crazy fellow is outside, shouting Nureddin's name loudly enough for the whole neighbourhood to hear. She goes out again to see if there are any signs of the Cadi. After an anxious moment or two Nureddin draws Margiana to the ottoman and kneels before her on the cushion; and they try to resume their dialogue. It is broken in upon all the time, however, by the voice of the Barber singing his own song to *his* Margiana (No. 10). And as if this were not disturbance enough, the air is made hideous by the howls of a slave somewhere inside the house. Bostana explains that the Cadi, having found, on his return from the mosque, that the slave had broken a fine vase, is now administering the bastinado with his own hand.

The Barber calls on the whole street for help against the Cadi, who, he tells the people, is murdering his friend. A crowd quickly gathers and joins in the outcry, and escape is impossible for Nureddin. Bostana and Margiana hastily empty the chest of its contents, which they stow away in the recess: then Nureddin gets into the chest. Bostana locks it, puts the key in her pocket, and pushes Margiana into the room on the left: she herself remains for a while to face Abul Hassan, who bursts in with four of Nureddin's servants, armed with sticks. Abul demands the body of his poor murdered friend. Bidding him shut his mouth and not be such a fool, Bostana tells him that the young man is in the chest, which she advises him to get away before the Cadi comes.

He misunderstands her, taking her to mean that it contains the corpse: he throws himself weeping on the chest, lamenting Nureddin's sudden end, and cursing Mars and Mercury for their evil influence.

The servants are on the point of going out with the chest when the Cadi enters and bids them leave it alone; he takes them, of course, for thieves of the treasure. He and Abul begin abusing each other; and in their interchange of alliterative epithets there may be a sly dig on Cornelius's part at Wagner and the peculiar diction of his *Ring*: the poem of this had been privately printed in 1853, and Liszt possessed a copy which Cornelius must certainly have seen:

> *Du glaubst mich närrisch, Narr, und willst mich narren,*
> *Brandschatzen um den unschätzbaren Schatz,*

says the Cadi; to which the Barber replies:

> *Ruchloser Richter, der sich ungerecht rächt,*
> *Doch höh're Richter richten, Richter, dich!*

The more each tries to explain, the more they misunderstand each other, for while the Cadi means it in one sense of the word when he says that the chest contains his daughter's "treasure", the Barber says he knows that full well, but takes "treasure" in the other sense.

By now the stage is full of people—the Cadi's friends, women in long white robes, with black veils, mourning for the dead Nureddin, and miscellaneous inhabitants of Bagdad. Charges and counter-charges of theft and murder are bandied about in a big ensemble, soaring above the hullaballoo of which we hear the voices of the women wailing and reproaching the Cadi. In a general struggle between the Cadi and his friends and the servants of Nureddin for the chest it is turned upside down, and in that position it remains until the end of the next scene.

The young Caliph now enters, preceded by four of his armed officers and followed by his suite: he has heard the uproar from the street, and has come to demand an explanation. The Cadi states his case against the Barber, who, ordered by the Caliph to speak, launches into a description of his six brothers—from whom he himself, it appears, is distinguished by his exceptional taciturnity—and a rhapsody on his own unique accomplishments. At last he is induced to explain that he is no thief, as the Cadi has said, but the friend of the young man whom the latter has murdered, and whose body is in the chest. The Caliph orders the chest to be opened: it is placed right way up, and at a sign from Margiana, who has now returned with Bostana, the old woman produces the key. "Come, my child", says the Cadi; "show us your treasure as proof that I speak the truth"; and, still playing neatly on the double meaning of treasure, Cornelius lets us hear in the orchestra the melody of Nureddin's confession of love (No. 16). The "treasure" turns out to be insensible when Abul Hassan has lifted him up and propped him on the edge of the chest in everyone's view.

The Cadi cannot believe his eyes. He looks round him as if in a dream. "Ah, Mustapha!" he apostrophises himself in a dazed kind of way:

and first the Caliph, then Abul Hassan, take up the droll phrase after him. An admirable ensemble follows, in which Margiana and Bostana call upon the still insensible Nureddin to awake:

while the Barber laments that the young man will never awake—"shaved this morning, and this afternoon a corpse", as he pathetically puts it—and the others express themselves according to their several characters. In the end the storm concentrates upon the head of the poor, puzzled Cadi Mustapha, for whom, it appears, the sword of justice is waiting: he, good man, still in a state of dream, keeps reiterating "O Mustapha, O Baba Mustapha, awake!"

At last the Barber, who has been weeping over the body, turns to the Caliph with the joyous news that Nureddin is still alive, though only just. The Caliph suggests that here is an excellent opportunity for him to give them a demonstration of the art he has been boasting of. The spectators opine that recalling one from the dead is a task beyond any barber's skill. But there is no beating Abul Hassan. He motions them all away from the chest, bends over Nureddin, and first of all sings into his ear his old song about Margiana (No. 10). There is no response. Pulling Nureddin's nose and ears and holding a smelling bottle under his nose are equally ineffective. Then the Barber sees that the young man is still clutching a rose given him by Margiana during their duet in the earlier part of the act. He holds this to his nose, and Nureddin slowly recovers consciousness and staggers to his feet. Abul leads him to Margiana, and the two men join in the melody of No. 10: this eulogy of Margiana, even if not the same Margiana, is the one and only thing on which the pair have been able to agree since they made each other's acquaintance.

The still dazed Cadi joins the lovers' hands at the Caliph's suggestion; and then the latter bids his officers arrest the Barber and hold him in safe keeping, in order, as he explains to the terrified old man, that he may hear the full story of his life and profit by his arts. The rest of the company are to go their several ways until the Caliph himself invites them to the wedding of Nureddin and Margiana. And so we reach the finale, which fitly crowns the delightful work. Abul Hassan starts a song in praise of the Caliph:

The rest of them repeat the "Salamaleikum", bowing to the Caliph as they do so. This procedure is repeated a further seven times: it is yet another illustration of Cornelius's gift for extracting the utmost imaginable variety out of a series of phrases and refrains that are basically the same. We feel that we would be content to have the process go on for ever, so exquisite is the music. But an end has to be made at some time or other, and it comes with a last enthusiastic cry from them all:

THAÏS

Massenet (1842-1912)

PRINCIPAL CHARACTERS

ATHANAËL	*Baritone*
NICIAS	*Tenor*
PALEMON	*Bass*
THAÏS	*Soprano*
CROBYLE	*Soprano*
MYRTALE	*Mezzo-soprano*
ALBINE	*Mezzo-soprano*

I

Anatole France's famous story *Thaïs* appeared in 1890. He had already treated the same subject, however, in a poem of 1867, when he was about twenty-three years old; and his attitude towards his characters, especially towards Paphnuce,[1] the monk who "saves" Thaïs, changed considerably in the interval. He never seems, indeed, to have been quite able to make up his mind whether he sympathised with or disliked Paphnuce. At times he fills us with the pity which he himself evidently feels at the moment for this not very intelligent cœnobite, who so sincerely longs to bring the courtesan to Christ and is at the same time the victim of carnal desires of which he himself is mainly unconscious until near the end of his career. Desire played a leading part in France's own spiritual as well as physical make-up. "Desire", he wrote in 1913, when he was in his seventieth year, "has governed the entire course of my life. I can truly say that my existence has been nothing but one long desire. I love desiring: I love the joys and the sufferings of desire."

With a temperament and a philosophy of this kind it was inevitable that, for all his pity for Paphnuce, he should feel a certain repugnance towards him, a certain contempt for his bovine incapacity to realise the supreme beauty of desire. More than once

[1] In the opera this name is altered to Athanaël.

77

we see a faintly ironic smile playing about the corners of France's mouth as he limns his Paphnuce. Subconsciously, it is evident, he disliked and despised the type. These hermits of the Thebaïd were pious and continent, he gravely assures us. Then comes the ironic side-glance of the man of the world at their extravagances of contrition for peccadilloes which, in all probability, they had never had vitality or courage enough to commit. "As an atonement for original sin, they refused their bodies not only all pleasures and satisfactions, but even the attention which our own age regards as indispensable. They believed that our souls are purified by the diseases of our members, and that the flesh could have no more glorious adornment than ulcers and wounds: thus was fulfilled the word of the prophet who had said, 'The desert shall blossom as the rose'. . . . The odour of their sanctity rose to heaven."

The quiet, mocking smile becomes something like a laugh as France tells us how the monk, who had been born of noble parents in Alexandria, used to reproach himself with having "led a life of dissipation, after the manner of the Gentiles. He recalled the memory of those days with shame and only for his own confusion. 'At that time', he used to say to the brethren, 'I seethed in the cauldron of false delights'. By this he meant that he had eaten meats properly cooked and had frequented the public baths." France cannot even show us Paphnuce escaping the snare of the fascinating Thaïs in his hot and callow boyhood without making him look a trifle ridiculous. The adolescent Paphnuce, it appears, had once been tempted to visit the courtesan. "But he had been restrained on the threshold of her house by the timidity natural to extreme youth—he was only fifteen at the time—and by the fear of being repulsed for lack of money, for his parents took care that he should run into no great expense. God, in his mercy, had used these two means to prevent him from committing a great sin."

The author's secret contempt for his maladroit puppet seems to increase as the story nears its close; it certainly becomes more plainly evident to the reader. As Paphnuce thinks of Thaïs dying —Thaïs, whose grace and loveliness and sweetness had made so many happy—the sensualist manqué which he really is at heart curses the God who created him only to dupe and frustrate him. "Thou God whom I hate, hear me. Overwhelm me with damnation. To compel Thee, I spit in Thy face. I must find an eternal hell, to exhaust the eternity of rage that is in me." He folds his arms about the dying Thaïs, and cries, "I love thee! Do not die! . . . I have deceived thee. I was but a wretched fool. God, heaven, all that is nothing! There is nothing true but the life of earth and the love of its creatures." But by this time whatever pity there originally was in the author for Paphnuce has hardened into not only scorn but something like loathing. The end of the book is terrible in its unexpected cruelty. Thaïs dies. The virgins of the house of the saintly Albine chant the song of Zacharias: "Blessed be the Lord, the God of Israel." But the song dies in their throats at the sight of the monk's face. They fly in terror, crying "A vampire! A vampire!" "He had become so hideous that, passing his hand over his face, he could feel his own deformity."

From all this it will be seen that Paphnuce as Anatole France portrays him is a character much too complex for opera. It is he, indeed, not Thaïs, who is the central personage of the book, and should be the central personage of the opera, just as Don José, not Carmen, is the true psychological and dramatic centre of Merimée's story, and Des Grieux, not Manon Lescaut, that of Prévost's. It is a quaint paradox that each of the works containing these master-studies of male mentality should be known by the name of a female character who in neither of the three instances is anything more than the medium through which a light is thrown for us on the more complex and more tragic male. Opera audiences being largely made up of women, they naturally feel much more professional interest in a Carmen, a Manon or a Thaïs than in a Don José, a Des Grieux or an Athanaël: And if the stage happens to have provided us with so many better Carmens, Manons and Thaïses than Josés, Des Grieux and Athanaëls, that is partly because the women are all broadly typical, while each of the men concerned is an individual; and it is far easier for the average actor or actress to reproduce a type than to create an individual.

But Anatole France's Thaïs also, no less than his Paphnuce, is a character rather too subtle for opera, or at all events too complex for all the gradations and nuances of her mentality to be made clear to us in the limited time that the music of an opera has to spare, as a rule, for psychological refinements. More than one member of the audience on a *Thaïs* night has wondered, with a smile, at the suddenness of the courtesan's conversion in the second act: an uncouth, ragged, faintly unpleasant monk, blackened by the desert sun, and, in spite of all that Nicias' dainty slaves have lately been able to do for him in the way of ablutions and adornments, perhaps not too convincingly clean, has only to walk into the house of the beautiful pampered courtesan and talk a trifle of rudimentary theology to her for her to turn her back without a qualm on everything which until then had made life so enjoyable for her. The indulgent spectator, noting all this, merely remarks to himself that emotion in opera is generally as swift as it is overwhelming. Des Grieux is madly in love with Manon within ten seconds of catching a glimpse of her in a hotel courtyard for the first time in his young life; and after Thaïs, in the second act, true to type, has been passionately invoking Venus —"Vénus, descends et règne! Vénus, éclat du ciel et blancheur de la neige! Splendeur, Volupté, Douceur!"—the monk has only to exhort her to curse, with him, the flesh and become the bride of Christ, and she is already nine-tenths on the way to complete conversion.

This is the way things have to be done in opera. In Anatole France's story, however, the change that comes over Thaïs is subtly led up to by the moving pages in which he shows her, as a little child, visiting the secret conventicles of the Christians with the gentle old black slave Ahmes,—who is later martyred and becomes St. Theodore—and drinking in, almost unknown to herself, something of the beauty of a life devoted to purity and loving-kindness. These early experiences of hers had left her with an ever-present vague sad sense of the impermanence of worldly things. "She feared death, and she saw it everywhere. When she was yielding to pleasure, it would suddenly seem to her that an icy finger was touching her on the bare shoulder, and she would turn pale, and cry out in affright in the arms that embraced her." She has her own simple religion, that of her own warm youth and bodily loveliness. These she would fain make eternal: the thought of losing them is anguish to her. It is for this reason that, in the novel, Paphnuce finds the conquest of her not very difficult. She thinks, indeed, that this crude, wild creature with the burning eyes is perhaps "a mage who knows secret charms against old age and death", the two things she most dreads. "Do not use your science against me", she cries. "Do not pronounce magic words which would destroy my beauty, or change me into a statue of salt. Do not terrify me! I am already too frightened. Do not kill me! I am so afraid of death." She is infinitely weary of an existence that to others seems so enviable. Yet she does not want to die. "Monk, if you love me", she says to Paphnuce, "can you prevent me from dying?" "If I abjure my pleasures and do penance", she asks him, "is it true that I shall be born again in heaven, my body intact in all its beauty?"

The "conversion" of Thaïs means then, in the novel, a good deal more than the opera is able to make clear to us—a point we do well to bear in mind when we are listening to Massenet's work in the theatre. Strictly speaking, of course, we ought not to be thinking of one work of art while we are listening to another. It is not quite playing the aesthetic game, we admit, to supplement what is lacking in the text or the music of an opera by our know-ledge of what was said and thought at this point or that in the novel or the play from which the opera has been taken; but the procedure, though aesthetically improper, is sometimes tempt-ingly convenient. After all, the composers themselves are always urging us, or at least expecting us, to do something of the kind. Without the programme of *Till Eulenspiegel* we should often be at a loss to understand just what Strauss is driving at; while the listener who knows his Cervantes sees and hears a hundred subtleties in the score of *Don Quixote* that pass unperceived by the unlettered hearer.

Liszt is perpetually nudging our elbow and bidding us listen for something which music itself cannot possibly make manifest but a knowledge of which is necessary if we are to hear in the work all the composer tried to put into it. As early as the second bar of his *Hamlet*, for instance, he marks a couple of chords in the horns and a note or two in the kettledrums "schwankend". Obviously what he has in mind is the irresolution of Hamlet's character: but it is equally obvious that by themselves the notes, without the marking, would suggest nothing whatever of that sort. A little later, a single soft trumpet note is marked "sehr düster"; but how the trumpeter, who must have played that particular note many times in the course of his life, is on this one occasion to make it clear beyond question to the audience that it depicts the gloom of Hamlet's soul, Liszt does not pause to tell us. Later still, Hamlet, one gathers, is supposed to be a trifle cynical at Ophelia's expense. Anyhow, Liszt marks a jerky little figure that appears first in the violins, then the bassoons, then the violas and 'cellos, "ironisch", blandly oblivious of the fact that for the players there is no possible way, short of winking at the audience, by which they can possibly convey to it that the figure is intended to suggest irony. In all these cases, and in a thousand others, the indulgent listener is asked to supplement the mere evidence of his ears by a draft on his memory or his imagination. And so if, while the famous "Meditation" of Thaïs is being played in the opera house, he chooses to close his eyes and imagine he sees Thaïs, in the seclusion of her chamber, musing upon her past and her future life in the way suggested in the novel, he may be committing a sin against strict aesthetic, but at all events he is sinning in excellent company. And anyhow, he is only doing what Massenet manifestly wanted him to do, though the atmosphere of the opera house does not always assist him.

2

The libretto of *Thaïs* is by Louis Gallet, who prefaces his "book" with an interesting little essay on what he calls "poésie mélique". In the 1890's, we are told, "the question of prose in music" was occupying the serious consideration of French musicians and others. The Press had even asked a number of eminent or notorious French composers, among them Massenet, Gounod, Saint-Saëns, Reyer, Ambroise Thomas and Benjamin Godard, for their opinions on the matter. These opinions differed considerably, though some of the composers—Gounod in particular —were quite in favour of prose texts for operas. As Gallet points out in his preface, composers invariably upset the rhythms and ignore the rhymes of verse for their own purposes: why then, he asks, go on with the ancient farce of casting words intended for music in the stereotyped moulds of verse form? Why not give the composer a simple prose text and be done with it—for inevitably he will turn whatever lines are given to him into prose: as Gallet ironically puts it, "a 'lyrical poem' [i.e., a poem written for the "lyric stage"] is a work in verse that is handed over to a musician so that he may convert it into prose." The footfalls of poetry and of music rarely coincide: "what rhymes poetically does not always rhyme musically."

Yet oddly enough, when Massenet asked for a prose text for *Thaïs*, Gallet pleaded for a compromise that would allow him, as a man of letters, some scope for the classical niceties of French verse. For this compromise he adopted a name that had been suggested some time earlier by the Belgian composer and savant Gevaërt—"poème mélique", signifying a form in which music and poetry would each assert its own inalienable rights while at the same time being politely accommodating towards the rights of the other. Gallet's text, while almost entirely avoiding rhyme, affects a kind of free rhythm that differentiates it from out-and-out prose, a rhythm designed to help rather than impede the composer.

In large part, Massenet has been obliging enough to cut his melodic periods to the size and shape of those of his librettist. In the second act, for instance, Gallet writes: "Je suis Athanaël—moine d'Antinoé!—Je viens du saint désert—et je maudis la chair —et je maudis la mort qui te possède!—et me voici devant toi, femme—comme devant un tombeau;—et je te dis: Thaïs, lève-toi, lève-toi!" The dashes represent the natural sense-endings of the irregular phrases, which suffer no constraint of formal rhythm or number of syllables. Massenet makes his musical phrase-divisions, in the main, at the same points. There is, however, one notable departure on the composer's part from the pattern set him by the poet. Finding the word "femme" superfluous, for his particular purpose, in the long declamatory line he has projected for the sentence "Et me voici devant toi, femme, comme devant un tombeau", he calmly omits it, although it is *the* vital word for Gallet! His procedure here is typical: after having asked for a prose—or near-prose—libretto in order that he might not be perpetually succumbing to the temptation to maltreat a verse-text for the purposes of music, he does not hesitate to behave just as tyrannically as any other composer towards his "melic" librettist whenever it suits his convenience to do so.

Thaïs was produced for the first time at the Paris Opéra on the 16th March 1894, with Sybil Sanderson as Thaïs, Delmas as Athanaël, and Alvarez as Nicias.

3

The opening scene is set among the huts of the cœnobites on the banks of the Nile. Seated at a long table are the venerable Palemon and twelve other monks: the empty place at the table is that of Athanaël. The frugal evening meal is in progress. The brief orchestral prelude breathes the tranquillity of evening; the main motive of it:

which runs like a thread through a great part of the scene, will have for many ears a suggestion of the early Christian church, an effect no doubt due to the first four or five notes, which constitute an opening gambit met with in many plainsong melodies. The bread and salt and water are passed from hand to hand, and simple old Palemon returns thanks to God for the blessing of his quiet garden. All pray for their long-absent brother Athanaël, "the elect of God", the hour of whose return should now be nigh. They have hardly spoken when the monk himself appears, accompanied by his characteristic dragging motive, expressive of his weariness and his disillusionment:

He declines the food the others offer him. His heart is full of
sorrow and bitterness: his visit to Alexandria has shown him, he
says, that the town is wholly given over to sin under the corrupt-
ing influence of the beautiful courtesan Thaïs, "a priestess of evil,
vowed to the worship of Venus." He recalls, half shame-facedly,
half in agitation, how he himself had one day gone as far as the
threshold of the temptress, but the divine grace had there arrested
his steps; and, thus saved from perdition, he had fled to the peace
of the desert, imprecating the sin he had almost committed. But
the memory rankles in him: having saved himself, he yearns to
save others; he must win the soul of Thaïs for God.

The sage and gentle Palemon advises him not to meddle in the
affairs of the profane, for the world is full of snares for the
godly. To the strains of No. 1 the cœnobites intone their evening
prayer and then disappear into the shade, leaving Athanaël alone,
stretched out on a hard couch in front of his own hut. He too,
with joined hands, commits his soul to God.

Night falls, and a short orchestral *adagio* fills the air with a
grave sweetness. Sleep comes to all—at last even to Athanaël. His
mind still runs, even in his dreams, on Thaïs, and his fevered vision
becomes visible to us through a mist that now descends upon the
scene. We see the vast theatre at Alexandria, filled with an immense
crowd applauding the half-nude actress, who, with veiled face, is
miming the loves of Aphrodite. The orchestra paints her seductiveness and the delight of the spectators in a pair of motives:

that are developed at some length. Within the theatre the delirium
grows: shouts of "Thaïs" reach our ears.

The vision fades: day dawns, and Athanaël leaps in a frenzy from his couch. He can endure this infamy no longer. In a long and expressive monologue:

he declares his double mission of saving Alexandria from this siren and saving the siren from herself. He calls the brethren together. The wise old Palemon repeats his gentle warning, but in vain; Athanaël, accompanied by the chanted prayers of the monks, disappears slowly into the desert of the Thebaïd. Thus ends an admirably handled scene which, in spite of its many fluctuations of mood, is cast in the one musical mould from beginning to end.

With the second scene comes a complete change of atmosphere. The brief orchestral prelude, with its rippling figures of this kind:

interspersed with a more flowing melody:

paints the lightness and brightness of rich and gay Alexandria. When the curtain rises we see the terrace, overlooking town and sea, of the house of Nicias, a rich young devotee of pleasure.

Athanaël appears at the foot of the terrace—a fearsome figure in surroundings so elegant as these. A servant tries to drive him away with hard words and threats, but the monk at last manages to persuade him to take in a message to his master. Left to himself for a few minutes, Athanaël harangues in passionate terms the beautiful corrupt city that gave him birth, which he once loved but now hates—hates it, as only a monkish fanatic could, for its wealth, its learning, its loveliness, its careless gaiety. His cry to heaven for help in his crusade is broken in upon by the merry, artless carolling of a pair of charming young female slaves, Crobyle and Myrtale, upon whose bare shoulders rest the arms of the approaching Nicias. The elegant, rather languid young patrician at once recognises in the unkempt, sun-blackened creature before him—looking, as he says, more like a beast than a man—the companion of his boyhood's days. Athanaël informs him that he has come to make the acquaintance of Thaïs. Does Nicias know her? Nicias, as it happens, knows her so well that he has not only ruined himself for her sake but has written three books of elegies in her honour. She is to be his for just one day more. He smiles indulgently at Athanaël's idea of converting her, and warns him of the danger of offending omnipotent Venus, whose vengeance can be terrible. He will gladly, however, bring Thaïs and his pious friend together: as a matter of fact the actress, who is at the moment delighting the theatre, will soon be with him.

At an order from Nicias, slaves bring in all that is necessary for making Athanaël more presentable; and Crobyle and Myrtale, for ever rippling with childish laughter at this monkish gawk and at the world in general, take him in hand to the accompaniment of chattering figures in the orchestra:

"He is young, he is handsome", they sing; but his beard is rough,

D

though his eyes are full of fire. He suffers himself to be given a rich robe and to be adorned with rings and bracelets; to be perfumed and gold-sandalled; but when they try to deprive him of his coarse monkish cilice he repulses them so violently that for a moment even they are disconcerted. In the end they effect a compromise: the hair-cloth remains, but it is hidden under a gorgeous robe belonging to Nicias. The whole scene is carried on in a tone of good-humoured banter on the part of Nicias and the slave girls, with an occasional burst of petulance from Athanaël.

Nicias, with a smile, warns the transformed monk that his "terrible enemy" is now approaching. A crowd of actors, actresses and philosophers—we are in ancient Alexandria, be it remembered, where even philosophers went to the theatre and rhapsodised over actresses—appears on the terrace, to the accompaniment of a gay little theme:

that suggests how lightly they are accustomed to take life; and at last the resplendent Thaïs herself appears. Nicias detains her for a moment while the others go in to the banquet that is prepared in an inner room.

There is a brief dialogue between the two, conducted in one of those gracefully-flowing 12/8 rhythms that Massenet always handles so well, and that give such an air of ease and naturalness to an operatic conversation. It is their last day together, and there is an under-current of sadness in the farewells of this man and woman of the world.

A few philosophers pass slowly across the scene, gravely discussing problems of the kind that philosophers are supposed to discuss. Among them is Athanaël, whose wild look attracts the attention of Thaïs. Nicias informs her ironically that the stranger is a monk from the desert, come to convert her to his own severe way of thinking—"scorn of the flesh", as Athanaël himself puts it, "love of suffering, austerity and repentance." Indifferent and a trifle bored, Thaïs assures him that she believes only in love, and bids him go his way. She reads him a little lecture, charming and sinister at the same time, in that graceful feminine style of which Massenet had the secret: through it all runs an orchestral phrase:

that seems to play at once seductively and ironically about the awkward, joyless fanatic. Why is he so hard and obstinate, she asks him, he who knows nothing of the world, has never drunk from the cup of life? Truth? Wisdom? There is neither truth nor wisdom except in love: let him therefore crown his head with roses like the rest, and join them in their merriment. Athanaël's only reply is a threat to bring salvation to her in her own house. She dares him to do so, and, by way of adding to the force of the defiance, begins to mime the loves of Aphrodite as she had done in the monk's vision in the first scene. Athanaël flies in horror, pursued by the laughter of them all.

4

The second act opens in a room in the house of Thaïs, who, to the strains of No. 9, is bidding goodbye to her departing guests. She is weary and depressed, disillusioned alike with regard to men and to women, and above all fearful that some day her youth and beauty will leave her. In another of those typical Massenet monologues in which the words fall so naturally, so trippingly from the singer's mouth, she implores her glass to reassure her that she will be for ever lovely, for ever Thaïs: then she calls on Venus herself to give her the same assurance.

Athanaël enters silently, and, with a prayer that his resolution may not fail him in the face of so much charm, begins his siege of Thaïs' soul. He loves her, he says, but not as she conceives love. She assures him that as she already knows love through and through he can have nothing new to offer her. But gradually, by his sincerity and intensity, he wears down her defences. She is about to let fall her mask of irony and scepticism, when, burning a little incense to Venus, she decides to make a last appeal to her protectress. The sight of the heathen rite goads Athanaël to fury. Tearing off his rich robe and showing the coarse monkish cilice beneath it, he cries, "I am Athanaël, the monk of Antinoë. I come from the holy desert; I anathematise the flesh and the death that claims you for its own; and I cry, 'Thaïs, arise!'" His vehemence frightens her. "Have pity on me!" she says: "do me no ill! I am so afraid of death!" Rising to his greatest exaltation of passion, Athanaël promises her not death but eternal life as the bride of Christ. A sweetness and freshness unknown to her descend upon the weary, anxious soul of Thaïs. Just then the voice of Nicias is heard outside: he has come to see his adored one for the last time. The hateful thought of this sybarite and all he represents in the world goes far to complete the conversion of Thaïs, though she makes a last desperate stand against the doctrine of the monk, swearing that she is and will remain Thaïs the courtesan, believing in nothing and wanting nothing, neither him nor his God. She breaks down in an hysterical mixture of laughter and sobs after Athanaël has gone: his last implacable words to her have been, "I will await you on your threshold until the dawn".

A conversion such as that wrought on Thaïs by Athanaël is pretty fast going, even for opera. Massenet does what he can to make it seem less abrupt by the famous "Meditation" which is heard in the orchestra during the change to the next scene. The prelude to this episode shows us, by means of motive No. 4, Thaïs, alone with her thoughts, looking back with a kind of nostalgic regret on her former life. Gradually the music softens into the "Meditation" proper, beginning with the long violin solo that is familiar not only to our operatic but our concert audiences:

Its suavity goes against it with some musical purists; but we do well to remind ourselves that it is precisely in some such silken, caressing terms as these that a Thaïs would embrace a new faith —she would see the new life opening out before her as promising, for all its renunciations, something of the sensuous happiness that had been the very breath of her being in the old life. Unfortunately the violin solo is almost invariably made far more sickly than it need be or should be, purely and simply because it *is* a violin solo. It is the great chance of the evening for the leader of the orchestra. What concern of his is dramatic psychology? What's this Thaïs to him or he to Thaïs? The one thought in his mind is that here and now is the chance to show the audience what a good violinist he is; and so he sugars the solo with so much "expression" of the type traditional among violinists that it becomes, on occasion, not merely saccharine but maudlin. Nothing of that sort was in Massenet's intention. The essence of the "Meditation" has already been heard in the orchestra in the scene of Athanaël's vision of the theatre in the first act, where it suggests the immensity of Thaïs' seductive power. The violinist and the orchestra should bear this in mind while playing the interlude: they should try to convey something at least of the contest that goes on within her, in those long night hours of lonely musing, between old passions and present regrets and aspirations.

It would have been well if Gallet and Massenet could have gone straight on here to the psychological climax of the scene. That, however, was impossible. The audience must be allowed to suppose the lapse of a reasonable interval between the parting of Thaïs and Athanaël and their meeting in the early hours of the next morning; besides, a climax so soon as this would have made the act inconveniently short. So librettist and composer were compelled to resort to an episode that plays a rather different part in Anatole France's story. When the curtain rises for the second scene of this act we see the outside of Thaïs' house. Under the portico is a little statue of Eros, before which a lamp is burning. It is not yet day: the light in the street is that of the moon. At the foot of the steps in front of the house Athanaël lies stretched on the ground. Further back, on the right of the stage, we see the lighted windows of a house in which Nicias is feasting with a company of his own kidney.

An orchestra behind the scenes maintains, during much of what follows, a soft accompaniment supposed to be coming from the house of the feast; the music has a faintly oriental flavour:

Thaïs descends the steps of her house, lighting her way down by the lamp that is before the statuette. She sees Athanaël, restores the lamp to its place, and, another and very different Thaïs now —addressing him humbly as "Père",—tells him that his words have been a balm to her heart: she has prayed and wept, and a great light has come to her: she has seen the nothingness of the senses, and has come to obey his commands. He tells her that she shall go with him to a house in the desert in which there are women living a life of poverty and complete seclusion from the world, chaste but happy, the brides of Christ: there he will immure her in a narrow cell until the day when Jesus himself shall come to deliver her and wipe away her tears.

Before they go, however, she must destroy every vestige of her former life of impurity. She humbly submits, but pleads pathetically to be allowed to spare from the general destruction the little statue of Eros. For love, she says, is god of all; and she herself has sinned not through him but against him. She would like Athanaël to give it to some monastery, where its artistic charm and its warm human symbolism may perchance turn some souls towards God. But she is indiscreet enough to mention that it was the gift of Nicias. At that name Athanaël breaks out into a fury in which, it is clear, jealousy plays as large a part as piety: he dashes the fragile thing of beauty down and tramples on the pieces: everything that was once hers, he tells her, must similarly be ground to dust.

At this point the action takes one of two lines, according to whether the theatre gives the ballet or not. In the former case, no

sooner have Athanaël and Thaïs re-entered the house—to set
about the work of destruction—than Nicias and his friends pour
out tumultuously from the house on the right. Nicias is a trifle
flown with wine. He has won back at play all he had squandered
on Thaïs, and more, and he intends not only his friends but the
whole town to celebrate his good fortune with him. The taverns
and the streets all about are scoured for revellers, and for the
jugglers and buffoons who are to amuse them. There follows a
series of ballet divertissements, in which not only Crobyle and
Myrtale take part but a certain La Charmeuse, who, not content
with dancing, displays her skill in vocal coloratura.

When the excitement is at its height, Athanaël appears on the
steps of Thaïs' house with a lighted torch in his hand. Nicias and
his friends recognise the monk and make merry over his coming
at that hour from such a house. He bids them be silent. Thaïs, he
tells them, is now the bride of God: the old Thaïs is dead; the new
Thaïs—behold her! And the Thaïs who now descends the steps
is in truth changed: her hair is disordered, her cloak is of mere
wool.[1] She is followed by her slaves, who glance back mournfully
at the house, which is now seen to be on fire. Nicias and his
friends would bar the passage of Thaïs and the monk. So would
the crowd, though for another reason—many of them are tradesmen and other beneficiaries of the courtesan, who see their profits
going up, like the house, in smoke. They cry out for Athanaël's
blood: one of them hurls a stone at him which wounds him in the
forehead. A dangerous situation is saved by Nicias, who throws
handfuls of gold among the canaille. While they are scrambling
to secure this, Athanaël and Thaïs make their escape, Nicias, a
gentleman and a poet, even if only a minor one, to the last, assuring Thaïs that the memory of her will remain for ever like a perfume in his soul.

5

The third act opens with a mournful orchestral prelude mainly
descriptive of the sufferings of Thaïs and Athanaël as they stumble

[1] Singers of the part might be respectfully asked to take note of this.
More than one Thaïs has been known to start her long tramp across the
desert in the next act looking as if she had been turned out by Paquin.

across the inhospitable desert. There are two chief themes:

By the time the curtain rises the pair have reached an oasis. Near by is a well beneath the palm trees: in the far distance, on the confines of the sand, the white walls of a nunnery gleam in the midday sun. Silent women approach the well, go down to draw water, return, and disappear.

Thaïs enters, broken by fatigue, but urged on relentlessly by Athanaël: No. 13 is now seen to be more particularly associated with the fanatical severity of the monk, and No. 14 with the stumbling, suffering Thaïs. Athanaël takes a sadistic delight in seeing her beautiful body racked by pain, "that exquisite body", he says, "which you gave to the heathen, to the unbelievers, to Nicias", thereby letting us into the secret of at least one half of his zeal for her conversion—his jealousy of Nicias and his own subconscious hunger of the flesh. But as she faints under her pain a wave of pity and tenderness passes over him; he draws her into the shade of the trees, prostrates himself before her, covers her bleeding feet with kisses, and brings her fruits and water from the well. She thanks this "messenger of God" who, for all his harsh-ness, has yet opened heaven to her: her flesh, she says, may bleed, but her soul is filled with joy. Their voices blend in a quiet duet, first of all outlined in the orchestra:

In the distance are heard voices chanting the Paternoster: it is the venerable Albine, daughter of the Caesars, and her nuns, who now approach, bearing the black bread for the convent. A great peace descends upon the music as Athanaël delivers into the keeping of Albine this soul he has saved from the burning to consecrate it to God. He bids Thaïs a last farewell, through the calm of which, for a moment, we feel the surge of his own secret suffering. As she passes out of his sight with the others, and the sensuous melody of No. 11 eats its way into the depths of him, he breaks down at the thought that he will never see her again. Leaning on his staff he follows in his mind's eye the now invisible procession of women, the while the orchestra soars aloft with a last reminder of No. 11.[1]

The scene changes to the Thebaïd, where we see once more the huts of the cœnobites, who, to the strains of No. 1, are finishing their simple evening meal. A storm is brewing; from afar the howling of the jackals is heard, and the monks are filled with a vague terror. They talk anxiously of Athanaël, who has scarcely tasted food or water during the twenty days that have elapsed since his return to them. His typical motive (No. 2) is heard as he himself appears, a broken man, with the air of one possessed; he passes through their ranks as if he did not see them. The monks retire, leaving him alone with the venerable Palemon, to whom he pours out his pitiful story—how the sense of holy triumph that followed his conversion of Thaïs has forsaken him, and he himself is now a prey to the sensuality from which he had gone to Alexandria to save the courtesan. In vain he has scourged himself: the beauty of the woman has

[1] This scene in the oasis, one of the finest features of the opera as we now know it, was not in the original version of the work. The ballet in the second act was also an afterthought.

D*

entered like a demon into his soul, haunting him even in his sleep:

En vain j'ai fla-gel-lé ma chair

Sleeping or waking he sees "only Thaïs, who is not merely Thaïs but Helen, and Phryne, and Venus Astarte herself, all voluptuousness in a single body." Palemon tries to comfort the wretched man with his customary formula of wisdom—"Let us not meddle, my son, in the affairs of the profane, for the world is full of snares for the soul of man. Ah! why did you ever leave us? Why? God be with you! Farewell!"

Palemon goes slowly out, leaving Athanaël in prayer. He falls asleep, and peace seems to descend upon him as the orchestra gives out slowly and softly the music (No. 5) to which, in the first scene of the opera, he had thanked God for all His goodness to him. But in his dream he sees the desert once more. Thaïs is there; she stretches out her arms to him, and, accompanied by the motive of her seductiveness (No. 10), upbraids him ironically for his folly in flying in the face of his destiny—he, a man made for love. As the vision fades he hears her laughing crazily, obscenely, at this fool who, disregarding her own and others' warnings, has dared to affront Venus. Athanaël is near madness when he fancies he hears, in the distance, a sweet and solemn chorus of the nuns: "A saint is leaving the world; Thaïs of Alexandria is nigh to death!"

He awakes and pours out a flood of reproaches and regrets and longings. Why was the universe created, if Thaïs is to die? He must see her again, and make her his, he cries; and he rushes out into the darkness and the storm that is now lashing the desert. A wild orchestral figure:

depicts his agitation now and during much of what follows.
During the orchestral interlude that accompanies the changing
of the scene the "Meditation" (No. 11) is heard once more in the
softest of tones and colours.

When the curtain rises we see the garden of the nunnery: Thaïs
lies dying under a great fig-tree, surrounded by Albine and the
nuns, singing and praying. Athanaël rushes in, haggard and distracted. The nuns group themselves round him so as to hide
Thaïs from him. Albine gives him a pious greeting. He has come,
she assumes, to bless the soul of the dying saint whom he had
placed in her care: Thaïs, she says, had submitted uncomplainingly
to every discipline imposed on her at his command. At last he
catches sight of her, and sinks on his knees beside her with a
mournful cry of "Thaïs!" She opens her eyes, and for the last
time we hear the melody of the "Meditation" as, in an ecstasy,
she recalls to his memory the stages of their journey together
across the desert, their tranquil hour in the oasis, his pious exhortations. Through him she has learned the meaning of the only
veritable love; and now she sees the heavens opening, angels,
prophets and saints greeting her with a smile, their hands full of
flowers. In her illumination she does not hear the wild cries with
which he now and then interrupts her musing, his ardent protestations that he remembers only the unappeased and un-
appeasable desire she has kindled in him. When he had spoken to
her of holy love, he says, he was lying. Heaven is only a word;
nothing exists, nothing is true, but life and the love of earth's
creatures—such love as his for Thaïs. But she remains deaf and
blind to everything but her vision and the sound of the celestial
harps:

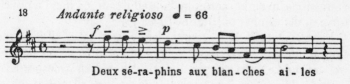

She dies unconscious of his torture; and Athanaël can only give
one last cry of "Pity!" that summarises the futility of all his
strivings, all his sufferings.

EUGEN ONEGIN
Tchaikovski (1840-1893)

PRINCIPAL CHARACTERS

TATIANA	*Soprano*
OLGA	*Contralto*
MME LARIN	*Mezzo-soprano*
EUGEN ONEGIN	*Baritone*
LENSKY	*Tenor*
PRINCE GREMIN	*Bass*
TRIQUET	*Tenor*

I

Tchaikovski conceived the idea of an opera based on Pushkin's *Eugen Onegin* in May 1877. Apparently the first section he set to music was the Letter Scene in the first act. The work was complete in every respect by February 1878, though two years and a half later Tchaikovski added an *écossaise* to the opening scene of the second act for a Petersburg performance, and made a few changes in the finale. The first performance was given in the theatre of the Moscow Conservatoire, by students of that institution, on the 17th (29th) 1879. The composer, by the way, gave his work the title not of "opera" but of "lyrical scenes in three acts".

Pushkin, Russia's greatest poet (1799–1837), took from 1823 to 1831 to write his *Eugen Onegin*, a narrative poem, with many digressions, in eight cantos: he himself described it as "a novel in verse in the manner of [Byron's] *Don Juan*".

Eugen Onegin is a young dandy and rake, disillusioned, cynical, blasé in the Byronic manner of the 1820's: "his malady", we are told, "was simply the British spleen transported to Russia". His father having died, and he himself possessing nothing but debts, he leaves Petersburg to visit an uncle in the country; but before he can arrive the uncle dies, bequeathing his estate to Onegin. There the young man, tired of the large towns, their follies and deceptions, settles down and tries to find some new interest in life. He lives almost entirely alone, for those of his neighbours whose acquaintance he has not been able to avoid making bore him.

An estate near his belongs to a young man named Vladimir Lensky, who has been studying at Göttingen, where he had imbibed all sorts of romantic notions, become infected with all sorts of enthusiasms, and developed the habit of poetising about platonic love: he is handsome and rich, but hardly fonder of society than Onegin is. Neither of them is yet twenty. The two young men become fast friends, in spite of, or perhaps because of, their fundamental dissimilarity of mind and temperament. Each acts as a foil to the other, Onegin, from the heights of his superior experience as a man of the world, condescending amusedly to the more ardent, idealistic Lensky. He is especially entertained by the latter's naïve views on love, a subject with which Onegin has long ago finished.

Lensky is engaged to Olga Larin, the younger daughter of a widowed lady who has a small property near by. Olga is a healthy, modest, cheerful girl, with an older sister, Tatiana, who is in most respects her antithesis. She is not beautiful, not brilliant. She is not unsocial, but the fripperies of social life have no attractions for her: she loves solitude and contemplation. She reads Rousseau and Richardson, from whom she has imbibed in full measure the "sensibility" of the epoch.

Lensky persuades his friend to visit the Larins with him. Onegin is not greatly taken by either of the girls, but of the two he finds Tatiana more interesting than her superficial sister. Seeing them together, friends of the Larins believe they scent the possibility of a "match". Certainly Tatiana herself, at long last, is in love: she reads more novels of "sensibility" than ever, and in her imagination dramatises herself and Onegin. Sleep deserts her. One night, excited and restless, she dismisses her old nurse after having made her bring her pen and paper, and writes Onegin a long letter in which she lays her whole soul bare to him. She sends the letter to him the next day by the nurse's little grandson.

Two days go by without a reply from Onegin. Then he rides over to the Larin house, where he finds Tatiana in the garden.

The blasé young man of the world has indeed been "touched with sympathy", as he expresses it, by Tatiana's letter, but for all that he cannot take it or her seriously. His heart has grown too cold in the larger world for that. He compliments her on her charming sincerity, and says he will meet frankness with frankness: he would not wish to beguile such candid naïveté. If he were a marrying man he would marry her. But he is not: the most he can feel for her is a brother's affection. She will fall in love again, he assures her. But if she does, perhaps he may give her a piece of advice that will be useful to her: she should cultivate more self-control, for the next man to whom she so imprudently pours out her inmost self may not be one like himself. She returns to the house on his arm, his cold words burning into her like a fire. She becomes silent, falls ill, and is intensely unhappy. Onegin, for his part, also retires within himself, striving to make the growing burden of life more endurable by means of exercise, games and good living.

In the following winter Lensky persuades his friend to visit the Larins again on the occasion of Tatiana's fête-day. Onegin becomes more and more bored with these worthy provincials, and determines to revenge himself on Lensky for having brought him there. For no reason that anyone can discover he pays such attention to Olga that Lensky leaves the party in a fury of jealousy, gallops home, and sends a challenge to his friend by the hand of one Zaretzki, a worthless gambler, bully and one-time duellist. The bored Onegin accepts the challenge without anger and without compunction: the silly affair is a nuisance, but as it is he must see it through. Lensky, paying what may be a last visit to Olga, finds that she is really as simple and innocent and as much in love with him as ever. He spends the night before the duel in sleepless torment, writing a poem on the vanishing of his golden youth and his forebodings for the future. (Pushkin's reflections at this point on the unfulfilled promise of Lensky as a poet have a melancholy interest for us in view of the fact that he himself was killed in a duel a few years later, in his thirty-eighth year).

Lensky is killed by Onegin. The amiable, superficial Olga soon consoles herself: she marries a lancer and leaves the village

23750

in which she had spent all her life till then. Onegin also goes away for some years. When we meet him again he is twenty-six, a wanderer on the face of the earth, unhappy, unquiet, trying vainly to forget the tragedy of Lensky. As for Tatiana, left more than ever alone by the departure of Olga, her thoughts gradually begin to turn again in the direction of the strange, unapproachable, yet attractive Onegin. She goes to his deserted house and turns over some of his books; and as she reads the comments in them the baffling workings of his mind become a little more comprehensible to her. By way of distraction for the suffering girl her mother takes her to Moscow one winter. She is not a success in society: the frivolity of it wearies her, and the gallants pronounce her provincial. But an honourable gentleman of middle age, Prince Gremin, who has sensed the exceptional quality of her nature, falls in love with her and marries her.

One night Onegin is persuaded by some one or other to accept an invitation to a ball. There he sees Tatiana, who, matured now and happy, has shed all her provincialism and developed into a calm, dignified woman of the finest breeding. He learns from the Prince's own lips that she is his wife, and that they have been married some two years. When Onegin is introduced to Tatiana there is nothing of the embarrassed provincial girl of their former acquaintance about her: she greets him with perfect poise, and leaves him after a formal word or two. There begins for him now a period of agitation such as had fallen to Tatiana's lot in the days gone by. He finds himself madly in love with her. He haunts her house and anywhere else where he is likely to meet her—a gloomy, distraught figure; while she is invariably tranquil, courteous, the self-possessed mistress of the situation. He writes letter after letter to her, recalling their past, pleading his unhappiness and begging for her love. She does not reply. But one day he calls on her and finds her reading one of his letters and weeping: for the moment she has reverted to the Tatiana of long ago. They talk of the past. She was young and foolish then, she says: now she can see everything more clearly. He had wounded her cruelly by his frankness; but today she can only thank him for it. She would prefer even his old cynical coldness and sarcasm to the lawless love he now demands of her. In herself she would gladly give up her present riches and enviable position for the old house and little garden of her girlhood, and for the golden days when happiness seemed for a moment to be approaching her, then turned aside and passed her by. Now her lot is fixed and her determination immovable: she still loves him, but he must give up all thought of ever making her his. With that she turns on her heel and leaves him—as does the author of this "novel" in verse, after another three stanzas of semi-humorous reflection. Pushkin thought more than once in later years of continuing his seemingly incomplete tale, but wisely decided that after all the best possible ending was the "half-close"—to employ a musical term—in which he had left Onegin suspended in his eighth canto.

2

The action of the opera follows so closely that of the original poem that detailed analysis of Tchaikovski's work is almost superfluous, except to indicate at this point or that how the composer has dealt with the subject in terms of his own special medium.

The short orchestral prelude is entirely devoted to the presentation, in one form and another, of a motive always associated later with Tatiana:

It is typically Tchaikovskian in its drooping lines.

The opening scene shows us the Larin garden, with the house on the left. It is evening. In the background is a hedge, beyond which the village, with its church, is visible. Mme Larin is sitting under a tree, engaged in preserving fruit: the elderly nurse,

Filipievna, is helping her. Tatiana and Olga are singing a duet, which becomes a quartet as the two older women take part in it. The girls' song takes Mme Larin back to her own young days, when she used to read Richardson and behave, like all well-brought up Russian girls of that epoch, with appropriate "sensibility". The nurse agrees with her that those were the good old times, when Mme Larin was young and impressionable and society was distinguished by its elegance. We gather that Mme Larin's sensibility had brought her rather near danger at one time, but that she had escaped it by throwing herself heart and soul into her duties as wife and mistress of a household.

Behind the scenes is heard a chorus of peasants, singing, as they approach the house, of the joy of abandoning work at the harvest for a while. They have come to present the family with the last sheaf. At Mme Larin's request they sing and dance in true Russian style, to a melody which will be familiar to many concert-goers in other connections:

Meanwhile Tatiana and Olga have ascended to the terrace of the house, whence they survey the pleasant, friendly scene.

Tatiana, who, as usual, has a book in her hand, tells her sister, to the expressive strain of No. 1, how these songs of the people transport her in fancy far away. Olga smiles at her passion for day-dreaming; as for her, the only effect these country melodies have on her is to make her want to sing and dance herself. Dreaming has no charms for her, she assures her mother and Tatiana; why spend the night in tears when each day is so bright? Her little song is charming enough, but there is just a little too much of Tchaikovski in it for it to be quite as care-free as Olga intends it to be.

Mme Larin having dismissed the harvesters with thanks, she turns with some concern to Tatiana, who, as is generally the case with her, is absorbed in her book; this particular one, according

to her, describes the sorrows of two lovers in such affecting
fashion as to move her to tears. Her mother is trying to impress
it on her that life is not like novels when a coach is heard approaching. Olga's fiancé Lensky is coming, and with him his neighbour
Eugen Onegin. At the mention of the latter, Tatiana, greatly
agitated, would leave the company, but the others persuade her
to remain. The two friends enter. Lensky introduces Onegin, and
the mother leaves the two young couples together.

A brief quartet follows: Onegin asks Lensky which of the two
girls is Tatiana. His frankly critical opinion of the blonde Olga is
that she is a trifle colourless both physically and mentally—she
reminds him, he says, of a Vandyck Madonna. He finds "the other
one, the dark silent one", rather more interesting, though he admits he is speaking more as a poet than an ordinary individual.
Tatiana is at the same time ill at ease and happy, for in this
Onegin, with his distinguished manners and his strong self-
containment, she finds the incarnation of her romantic dreams.
Lensky's quiet comment on it all is that he could imagine ice and
flame matching each other better than these two who have just
met.

Lensky goes apart with Olga, with whom he indulges in a
warm-hearted little duet, the poetic theme of which is that to
lovers the separation of a day is like eternity:

Meanwhile Onegin casually engages the embarrassed Tatiana in
conversation: his manner throughout is polite but cold. Does she
not feel bored in this out-of-the-way spot? he asks her. She

assures him that her whole pleasure is in reading and dreaming in
the garden, to which he replies, with a touch of superior irony,
that she seems too much inclined to indulge her imagination: he
himself, he says, was at one time very much like her in that
respect. They are still on this somewhat awkward footing when
Mme Larin reappears to summon them all in to supper.

The second scene of this act shows us Tatiana in her simply-
furnished bedroom, lost in meditation before her glass. Feeling
sure that she will not sleep, she asks Filipievna to tell her one of
the stories that used to soothe her when she was a child. The nurse
begins instead the story of her own wooing and marriage, long,
long ago. The music here, of course, is in the Russian national
vein:

which contrasts markedly with the motive of Tatiana (No. 1),
which plays a large part in this and the following scene.

Flinging her arms around her, Tatiana pours out her soul to the
old nurse: she loves, she says, and suffers:

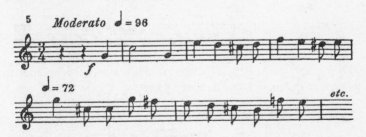

She bids Filipievna bring her pen, ink and paper and then leave
her; for in her innocence and inexperience of the world she is
resolved to write to Onegin, to say to him what she had not
strength to say when he was present. Thus begins the famous
"Letter Scene", which is one of the masterpieces of musical-
dramatic psychology. The main motives of it are (a) the agitated

No. 5, (*b*) the theme that accompanies her decision to write the letter:

(*c*) the feverish orchestral figure that accompanies the hurried putting of the glowing words on paper:

(*d*) the melody of her assurance to Onegin that she had never loved anyone before, that her destiny had been to wait for her total fulfilment in him:

(*e*) the grave strain to which she asks him whether he comes to her now as guardian angel or as tempter:

and (*f*) the melody accompanying her decision to give her life to him, whatever may befall, for she is alone, helpless, misunderstood, and will go under if he does not see how she suffers and rescue her:

The music models itself faithfully on every nuance of the fine poetry: this suffering, this self-doubt, this self-torment, was something that Tchaikovski well understood.

She seals the letter with a passionate cry to Onegin not to misuse the trust she places in him. The nurse finds her dreaming by the window as the day dawns, and, at Tatiana's urgent request, sends her little boy with the letter to Onegin. As the curtain falls, Tatiana buries her head in her hands, sunk in thought.

The next scene—a short one—shows us a different part of the Larin garden from the one we saw at the commencement of the opera. In the background a chorus of girls is singing a pleasant little song of the Russian folk-type. Tatiana enters in great agitation: she has seen Onegin coming. She wonders what his answer to her letter will be, and half regrets having sent it. She hangs her head in confusion and apprehension as he approaches. As usual, he is completely self-possessed, formally polite, but ice-cold. "You wrote to me", he says to her without preamble, "and opened out your soul to me. I honour you for your candour, which rekindled in me, for a moment, a spark that had long died out in my breast. But I cannot flatter. I will be as open as you have been." Then, in that conversational tone which Tchaikovski always had at such easy command in his songs and operas:

he assures her that had fate destined him to be a husband and a father he would have recognised his ideal mate in Tatiana. But he was not born for happiness of that or any other kind. He is not in harmony even with himself; harmony with another is quite impossible. He can love her as a brother, but no more. The future will justify him in what he is now saying: love, in a maiden's life, is nothing but illusion, deception. His advice to her is to learn to know herself and to hold her romantic feelings in check; for inexperience such as hers generally leads only to disaster. He holds out his hand. She gives him a long, imploring look, then takes his arm as if in a dream and allows him to lead her away to the others.

3

The first scene of the second act takes place in a room in the Larin's house, where a ball is in progress in honour of Tatiana's birthday.

The short orchestral prelude is mostly based on the motive (No. 9) of Tatiana's passionate appeal to Onegin in her letter. As the curtain rises this merges into a waltz:

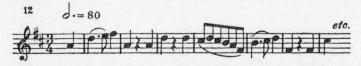

to which the guests sing a chorus in praise of a life of pleasure in house and field. Onegin dances with Tatiana, to the admiration of the older ladies, who scent a wedding in the offing, though they do not by any means approve of Onegin, who, we learn from their chatter, has the reputation of being unmannerly, a Freemason, and too fond of wine. The young man, happening to overhear them, resolves to punish Lensky for having brought him to so boring a place by dancing with Olga and so making him jealous. The waltz music runs through the whole of this episode.

At the first opportunity that presents itself Lensky seeks an explanation with Olga. She does not take his indignation seriously, and to show him that he is upsetting himself and her about nothing at all she goes off again to dance with Onegin. A momentary mild diversion is brought about by an elderly Frenchman, Monsieur Triquet, who, somewhat to Tatiana's annoyance, persists in singing some couplets in her honour, couched in the formal terms, poetic and musical, of a French genre that was beginning to be old-fashioned even in Russia at that time. M. Triquet having retired, overwhelmed with the compliments of the company on his charming couplets, the master of the ceremonies leads off a mazurka with Tatiana. Onegin appropriates Olga, and Lensky watches the pair in increasing trouble of soul.

The dance over, Onegin rallies his friend on being "as gloomy as Childe Harold". At first Lensky answers him quietly; but his anger mounts in face of Onegin's cold cynicism. Not content with the conquest of Tatiana, he says, his friend must needs take from him now his own bride, turning her head only to laugh at her later. Onegin's loftily ironic attitude infuriates Lensky still further. The quarrel at length attracts the attention of the other guests. Realising how seriously his friend has taken this trifling matter, Onegin tries to convince him that he is exaggerating the importance of it all; but finally, seeing that it is hopeless to reason with him, he shrugs his shoulders and says no more. Lensky, now beside himself with rage, challenges Onegin before them all. The scene ends with a big finale, in which Lensky laments this sorry ending to his golden dream of love. Onegin, serious and noble at last, regrets that he has tried too far this good friend whom he sincerely loves, and the rest of the company comment on the affair in their several ways. Though Onegin admits to himself that he is in the wrong, he cannot refuse the challenge; and his temper rising dangerously as the maddened Lensky calls him a seducer without honour, he hurls himself on him. The guests separate the two men. Lensky rushes out, followed by Onegin; while Olga, the innocent cause of all the trouble, falls in a faint.

The next scene takes place in a lonely spot by the river. It is early morning, and the countryside is deep in snow. Lensky and Zaretzki arrive for the duel; and while the latter paces impatiently up and down awaiting Onegin, Lensky sits in moody meditation under a tree. At length his second goes off to talk with the miller whose mill stands by the river bank, and Lensky launches into a melancholy aria, bemoaning his vanished youth and his lost happiness, and looking forward with foreboding to the result of the coming duel. The situation is of a type that always called out what was most characteristic in Tchaikovski's genius; and the aria, which ends with a cry of passionate love to Olga, is one of the finest things he ever wrote:

It is an almost constant succession of those falling phrases of which Tchaikovski was so fond, corresponding as they did to his own wilting spirits on most occasions of life.

Onegin arrives with his servant Gillot, who carries the pistols. While the two seconds are discussing the ritual of the duel, Onegin and Lensky, in a short duet in canon form, lament the sad turn their friendship has taken; honour requires that one of them shall now kill the other. The two men take up their positions, and a last thought of Olga (No. 3) flits through Lensky's tortured mind. Zaretzki gives the signal, and Onegin, firing before his opponent, kills him. He runs to the dead man and makes a gesture of horror and despair, while the orchestra gives out a last mournful reminiscence of No. 13.

4

The third act opens in a fashionable house in Petersburg, where the guests are dancing to a polonaise:

In the gay company, but not part of it, is Onegin, sunk in gloom, regretting his twenty-six wasted years, and still haunted by the memory of Lensky. Travel has failed to still the voice of conscience; and now, in sheer desperation, he is seeking forgetfulness in society again. Tatiana enters and seats herself on a sofa, where, to a gracefully-flowing accompaniment in the orchestra:

various guests come and pay their compliments to her. Onegin can hardly believe his eyes, so lovely, so dignified now is the one-time provincial maiden. From Prince Gremin he learns that she is now the latter's wife; and the good Prince breaks into a song in praise of love:

the sober musical terms of which are psychologically quite in keeping with his age. In Tatiana, he assures Onegin, he has been fortunate enough to find the one good and true thing in a world of hypocrisy, treachery and lies. As he presents the young man to his wife there wells up from the orchestra the melody of No. 5. The pair exchange only a few conventional words, Onegin being deeply moved, Tatiana calm: then, to the accompaniment of No. 15, she moves away on her husband's arm, pleading fatigue. Onegin follows her with his eyes, lost in wonder at the transformation that has taken place in her. Can this be the Tatiana, he asks himself, to whom he had once given a schoolmasterish lesson in conduct, down there in the country? And what is this strange emotion he now feels at seeing her again, and so changed—dejection? repentance? wounded vanity? And then he realises that it is none of these, but love, such love as he has never known or understood before; and Tchaikovski gives a curious musical point to this realisation by making him announce it to the same melody (No. 6) as that to which Tatiana, when writing her letter, had made the same discovery within herself. As Onegin goes out, perplexed and troubled, the dance music is resumed and the curtain falls.

The final scene takes place in Tatiana's boudoir. An orchestral introduction, based on what seems to be intended as a partial translation into the minor:

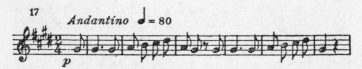

of the song (No. 16) in which Prince Gremin had spoken of his quiet happiness in Tatiana's love, no doubt aims at showing us the reverse of that picture: Tatiana's happiness, perhaps we are to understand, is less complete than his, for at the core of it lie memories of a dead self which she can never cease to mourn in secret.

She enters with a letter in her hand—a letter from Onegin, announcing that he will call on her. She looks forward with some apprehension to the interview, for she feels that it will disturb the peace of soul which she has won for herself by so many hard fights against fate. While she is musing thus, he appears at the door. Seeing that she is weeping he rushes to her and throws himself at her feet. Mastering her emotion, she bids him rise, for she has an explanation to make to him. Gently she recalls to him, to the melody of No. 17, the day when, an inexperienced country girl, she had poured out to him the naïve confession of her love and he had crushed her with his cold cynicism: yet through it all he had behaved like a man of honour. She was despised then because the world did not understand her. But why does he pursue her now? Is it because, thanks to her husband, a man of worth and distinction, she has wealth, power, social position? Or is it in the hope of boasting of a conquest of a kind on which the vulgar world will felicitate him? If he really knew her he would pity her, for cold reason is her only shield in the fight that is now going on within her heart. "Alas!" they both sing, "how near to us was happiness once!" But honour, she tells the wretched man, now binds her irrevocably, and he must leave her. He pleads to be allowed to be where she is, if only to die in happiness and peace. The confession is at last wrung from her that she loves him, and he clasps her in his arms. But she frees herself instantly, and, in spite of his anguished appeals not to cast him off, she repeats that honour holds her fast to Gremin, and she will not be false to it. With a last mighty effort she summons up strength enough to bid him adieu for ever, and leaves him crushed and hopeless. With a final cry against the hardness of his fate he too rushes out as the curtain falls.

Tchaikovski had no great range of dramatic characterisation: he could not transport himself easily into more than a few psychological types of more or less his own fundamental cast. Hence a certain monotony in his operas as a whole, in spite of fine moments in each of them. But in *Eugen Onegin* we get the best of him as a musical dramatist, because each of the main characters is to a great extent himself. They are all, in this way or that, defeatists; and for defeatism and frustration Tchaikovski could always find convincing musical expression.

PRINCE IGOR
Borodin (1834-1887)

PRINCIPAL CHARACTERS

PRINCE IGOR	*Baritone*
JAROSLAVNA	*Soprano*
VLADIMIR	*Tenor*
PRINCE GALITSKY	*Bass*
KONTCHAK	*Bass*
KONTCHAKOVNA	*Contralto*
OVLOUR	*Tenor*
SKULA	*Bass*
EROSHKA	*Tenor*

I

"The funny thing about these Russian operas", a man in the
audience at Drury Lane was heard to remark during the great
Russian season of 1914, "is that they're all written by someone
else." That is particularly true of *Prince Igor*. Ostensibly the
composer of it was Borodin. But, faithful to the Russian habit, he
left a good deal to be done to it by other people after his death,
which occurred with tragic suddenness at a musical party he was
giving in his own house. Rimsky-Korsakov scored the Prologue
(i.e., the opening stage scene), the first, second and fourth acts and
the Polovtsian March in the third. Glazounov orchestrated the
remainder of the third act as Borodin had left it, and completed
the composition of this act from the composer's sketches.
The choral accompaniment and the introductory recitative to
Kontchakovna's cavatina in the second act were Rimsky-
Korsakov's work. The overture and the short chorus of Russian
prisoners in this act were given their present form by Glazounov
from his recollections of Borodin's playing of them on the
piano: the scoring of the overture is Glazounov's. (The feat
of putting the overture into shape is not so remarkable a one
as would appear at first sight, for there is practically nothing in it

that is not in the opera itself). In addition to all this, Borodin, after using some of his projected *Prince Igor* music for a co-operative ballet-opera, *Mlada*, which came to nothing—Borodin was to have written the fourth act of this, while the others were to be contributed by Cesar Cui, Moussorgsky and Rimsky-Korsakov—put it back again into *Prince Igor*, along with some music that had been specifically written for *Mlada*. Finally, we cannot be sure whether some of the melodies in *Prince Igor* that seem to be folk-tunes are really such, or Borodin's own, though influenced by his eager study of Russian and Central Asiatic folk-music.

It was the critic Stassov, who co-operated so closely with the Russian composers in so many of their schemes, who, in the spring of 1869, suggested the story of Prince Igor to Borodin as a likely subject for an opera. Stassov's scenario appealed to him so greatly that he started work on it almost immediately; yet, as we have seen, when he died some eighteen years later his score was still in a sadly unfinished state. Whether this was due to his having been halted from time to time by some difficult problems in connection with it, or whether it was simply that his routine duties as a professor of chemistry took up more and more of his time as he grew older, it is impossible to say.

The Song of the Army of Igor is the title given to a Russian poem a manuscript of which, apparently dating from the fourteenth century, was discovered in a monastery in 1795 and published five years later. This manuscript perished in the Moscow conflagration of 1812, but another came to light in 1864. The subject of the poem is the expedition made in the year 1185 by Prince Igor of Novgorod against the Tartar tribe of the Polovtsy. The epic rather than dramatic nature of the poem necessarily commits both librettist and composer to a certain looseness of construction; but this is generally atoned for by the beauty of Borodin's music and the copiousness of his invention.

2

As the overture consists of a concatenation of some of the principal themes of the opera, consideration of it had better be postponed till the reader has become acquainted with these in their proper places in the body of the work.

The scene of the Prologue is a public place in the town of Poutivle, whence Prince Igor is about to set out with his army against the Polovtsy. As the curtain rises, Igor is seen leaving the cathedral, accompanied by princes and boyars (noblemen), while the populace sing a chorus in praise of his exploits and those of his house. A prominent feature of the chorus is the frequent reiteration of the word "Slava" (glory) to musical phrases of this type:

(Apparently Borodin's intention had been to *end* his work with this "Slava" chorus).

While Igor and his adherents are breathing fire and slaughter against their enemies, however, the stage is suddenly darkened by an eclipse of the sun. Igor's brother-in-law, Prince Galitsky, and several of the others are dismayed by what they take to be a portent of evil. They urge Igor to abandon the expedition, or at least postpone it. But the self-reliant Prince refuses to be discouraged, and as the sky lightens again he despatches his troops to the seat of war. Two curious characters, Skula and Eroshka, remain behind, their intention being to desert Igor and enter the easier and more congenial service of Galitsky. They are by profession gudok-players. (The gudok was an ancient Russian stringed instrument). They are rogues and clowns who are brought on at fairly frequent intervals to afford light relief. Apparently they owe their introduction into the opera to Borodin, who is known to have been highly pleased with them; but we meet with essentially the same type of buffoon, generally running in couples, in more than one Russian opera. Perhaps the best-known specimens of the genre are the two monkish topers in *Boris Godounov* and the buffoons Duda and Sopiel in Rimsky-Korsakov's *Sadko*.

Igor's wife Jaroslavna anxiously tries to persuade her husband against the expedition, but he is not to be moved. Commending her to God, he confides her to the care of her brother Galitsky,

who accepts the charge, hypocritically professing deep gratitude
to Igor for his help and protection in difficult days gone by. An
old priest having given the army his blessing, it sets out with Igor
and his son Vladimir and the princes at its head, to the strains once
more of the "Slava" chorus.

3

The first scene of the first act is set in the court of Galitsky's
house. Galitsky has been appointed not only guardian of Jaroslavna but governor of Poutivle, and he is secretly plotting Igor's
downfall. At the rising of the curtain we see the mob, whom
apparently he has bribed with the contemporary Russian equivalent of bread and circuses, lauding him for his joviality and
open-handedness: life in Poutivle, we gather, is for the many-
headed well worth living under Galitsky and his gang. Eroshka
and Skula are among the crowd, encouraging them in that view
with their songs. Galitsky confesses that he is quite content to
leave the hazards and fatigues of war to Igor. For his own part he
prefers peace and plenty, feasting and love-making: let them only
elect him Prince of Poutivle and wine will flow like water, and
every hour be one of enjoyment. There is something very
suggestive of the bibulous-irresponsible in the melody as well as
the words of his song:

His sister Jaroslavna, he declares, can enter a nunnery if she likes,
so long as she does not interfere with his drinking and other
sports by night and day.

A number of young girls rush in, appealing agitatedly to
Galitsky for his protection against some of his men, who, it
appears, have carried off one of them. Galitsky declines to
take a trifle of that kind seriously: the maiden, he assures them,

will be better off with him than with them. The girls run away in terror.

Galitsky also having left the stage, Skula and Eroshka again work up the feelings of the malcontent mob against Igor and Jaroslavna. A barrel of wine is rolled in by servants of Galitsky and broached; and the two buffoons praise the liberality of the Prince in a song of clumsy gaiety in a three-bars rhythm:

The delighted crowd ask each other why, now that the army is away, the benevolent, pleasure-loving Galitsky should not be put on the throne in the strenuous Igor's place, and after one of those choruses, of which Russian composers seem to have the secret, that somehow or other hit off the populace to the life, they go off well primed and exceedingly pleased with themselves, leaving behind them Skula and Eroshka, who are hardly sober enough to follow them.

The second scene of this act takes place in a room in the women's quarters of the palace, where Jaroslavna, alone, is sadly counting the days since the departure of Igor and his son, from whom no word has yet come. The melody of her long aria:

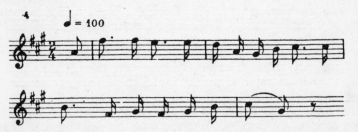

brings a new and warmer atmosphere into the work. At the end of it, lost in premonitions of evil, she buries her head in her hands and abandons herself to the luxury of her grief. She is roused by the entrance of her old nurse, bringing with her the frightened girls who had been so rudely treated by Galitsky and the crowd

in the preceding scene. They appeal for Jaroslavna's intervention
on behalf of the one of their number who had been carried off. In
fear and trembling they give the name of the ravisher—none
other than the powerful Prince Galitsky, who, with his undiscip-
lined partisans, has been spreading terror through the town since
Igor left.

Just then Galitsky himself enters. In reply to Jaroslavna's up-
braidings he coolly claims the right, as regent, to do as he pleases
with everyone and everything in the town. In the bluff musical
style characteristic of him he laughs at Jaroslavna's threats to have
him punished when Igor returns. He has the multitude with him,
he says; and he goes so far as to advise his sister to look out for a
successor to Igor in her affections. She has no difficulty in putting
this debauched brother of hers in his place. Bowing before the
storm he has raised, he promises to return the maiden to her home
—though he will compensate himself, he says, by taking another
and more amiable one in her stead.

The story of Prince Igor, as has already been pointed out, is
more epic than dramatic, a leisurely point-to-point chronicle
rather than a compression and shaping of the material to a single
definite end. Nothing could better illustrate this haphazard
construction than the fact that after this scene with Jaroslavna
Prince Galitsky disappears completely from the opera. Yet the
prominence given to him in this act cannot be said to be a total
misdirection of dramatic effort: the tragedy of Igor's expedition is
thrown into higher relief by this vivid picture of the difficulties
that beset his kingdom during his absence.

Left alone for a moment, Jaroslavna soon has to undergo a new
trial. The council of boyars enters with the news that fresh misfortunes have befallen the country—the terrible Khan Gzak has
descended on the town, and word has come that not only has Igor
been wounded and totally defeated, but he, his brother and his son
have been made prisoners. The boyars swear to defend Poutivle
to the last. But the alarm bells peal out while they are speaking,
and the windows reflect the flames in the burning city. Jaroslavna
and a number of women in the streets below break into loud
lamentations and appeals to heaven: the boyars draw their swords
and rush to attack the enemy.

4

With the second act the scene changes to the camp of the Polovtsian Khan Kontchak, the vanquisher of Igor. All the music associated with the Tartar tribe of the Polovtsy has a quasi-oriental tinge, which is noticeable at once in the langourous, highly-decorative melody of the song of the maidens with which the scene opens:

The exotic interval of the augmented second, of course, plays a considerable part in creating this atmosphere:

which is admirably maintained also in the choral accompaniment to the solo phrases:

The song is followed by a dance, and this by the cavatina of the Khan's daughter Kontchakovna, a voluptuous nocturne, as it were, addressed to the soft night that is descending on the camp, and to the beloved for whose coming her heart is hungering. The song is rich in chromatics and melodic arabesque:

At the conclusion of the song the Russian prisoners, returning from their labours, pass across the background, escorted by Tartar guards; Kontchakovna and the maidens greet them kindly and offer them food and drink as they go by. The women also gradually leave the stage, which is now occupied only by a Polovtsy night patrol, which, being an operatic patrol, indulges, as a matter of course, in a chorus having as its thesis the noble resolve to perform its duties faithfully during the night that is now so obviously descending on the camp. Ultimately it goes off on its rounds, leaving behind only the potential renegade Ovlour, of whom we shall hear more shortly.

The young Prince Vladimir, Igor's son, now enters and pours out his soul in an ecstasy of love for the beautiful Kontchakovna:

The cavatina is one of the most exquisite things of its kind in all Russian music. There may be no particularly valid dramatic reason for the introduction of this tangled "love interest" into the epic story of the expedition of the Army of Igor against the Polovtsy; but there can be no question that, having seen fit to introduce it, Borodin makes us eternally grateful to him for having done so.

Vladimir is joined by Kontchakovna, and the expected love duet follows. We learn from it that while the broad-minded Khan, her father, would not oppose their union, Vladimir has no hope of obtaining his own father's consent to it. Hearing footsteps they separate.

The newcomer is Igor, whose gloomy mood is pre-announced by the orchestral phrase that accompanies his entrance:

In a fine aria he recalls his happiness in the past:

and bewails his present misery. Everything is lost: his army has been exterminated, and he himself, beaten, wounded, is a prisoner. But his spirit is unbroken; if only he can regain his freedom he will still drive the foe out of his land. Then he thinks tenderly and sadly of the Jaroslavna who is weeping for him in Poutivle:

the thought of whom inspires him to hope for liberty again. But as the sombre No. 10 recurs in the orchestra he abandons himself once more to despair.

He is furtively approached by Ovlour. Pointing to the first rays of dawn, which are now beginning to strike across the scene, Ovlour sees in them, he tells Igor, a symbol of the latter's escape and Russia's re-birth. He has waiting for him, he says, a fast horse, ready and saddled. But the Prince rejects with scorn the idea of flight, and Ovlour departs crestfallen.

The Khan Kontchak enters. He is one of the finest creations of Russian opera, a Tartar marauder but a magnanimous conqueror and a great gentleman. He offers to do all he can to soften Igor's captivity: the Prince has only to command him, for he looks upon him as his guest rather than his prisoner. The fortune of war, it is true, has gone against Igor; but for the rest, he can now, if he chooses, live among them as a Khan in his own right: his chains shall not weigh intolerably on him. Kontchak protests in soothing phrases his high regard and warm friendship for Igor:

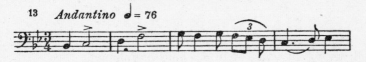

What can he give him to make him happy? Horses? Tents? Treasure? Female slaves? The sword of his ancestors? All he has is his for the asking, for he admires Igor's courage in war and would gladly form an alliance with him. Igor thanks him and pays tribute to his nobility of soul, but declares that he can never be happy in captivity. Thereupon Kontchak offers him his liberty, on condition that he pledges his word not to resume the war after he has reached his own land again. But this Igor refuses to do: once he is free, he swears, he will assail Kontchak in greater force than before. The urbane Khan commends his frankness, accepts his decision with real regret, and places Igor by his side during the rich entertainment he has ordered to be prepared in his guest's honour.

The stage fills with slaves, male and female, singers, dancers, and players of instruments. The maidens begin a dance to a languorous choral song:

This is the prelude to the famous sequence of Polovtsian dances with which every concert-goer and every balletomane is now familiar—a riot of colour and passion. If anything, surely, could have persuaded Igor to take kindly to the idea of making his permanent home with Kontchak it would be the prospect of being able to enjoy this kind of thing whenever he liked! The man, we feel, must have been made of stern stuff to turn all this down at the prompting of patriotism and duty.

5

Before the curtain rises on the third act we hear a Polovtsian March, which works up from a quiet beginning:

to a high pitch of excitement as the trumpets peal out behind the scenes and we get a view of the Polovtsian camp, where the Tartars are eagerly awaiting the return of the victorious army of Khan Gzak. The warriors march in to the strains of No. 15, bringing with them many Russian prisoners and much booty: they are greeted with cries of barbaric joy by the crowd, and a chorus praising their valour. The brilliant pageant reaches its climax with the entry on horseback of Gzak himself and his body-guard. Kontchak advances to give them a ceremonious greeting, while Igor and the other Russian captives hold themselves aloof, surveying it all in sombre silence.

Kontchak welcomes the returning warriors in a vigorous aria, in which, showing the reverse side of his nature to the one he had exhibited in his colloquy with Igor, he exults in Tartar fashion over the devastation that Gzak and his hordes have left in their wake. The chorus breaks in from time to time with cries of "Glory to Gzak! Glory to Kontchak!" At last Kontchak bids the trumpets sound:

orders the division of the spoils, and commands a council of war for the morrow. The Khans, in a savage chorus, joyfully discuss the prospect of a new expedition, this time against Kiev or Poltava, and then depart, leaving only the Russians on the stage.

Igor and Vladimir and the other prisoners agitatedly debate the

report of the capture and sack of Poutivle by Khan Gzak.
Vladimir urges on his father the necessity of escape to save what
is left of their native land, and Igor now begins to believe that
Ovlour was right. The anger of the Russians rises as the waggons
loaded with booty traverse the back of the stage, accompanied by
crowds of ravenous Polovtsy, and followed by a number of new
prisoners.

The depressed Russians go into their tents, before which a few
of the Polovtsy take up positions as sentries. They sing a rough
chorus in praise of the two invincible warriors Kontchak and
Gzak, and then call for koumiss to drink. This is brought to them
in leathern bags by Ovlour. They drink and dance until one by
one they are overcome and fall to the ground, where they are soon
all asleep.

This gives Ovlour his chance. Approaching Igor's tent with
the utmost circumspection, he whispers that the guards are all
dead-drunk, the night is dark, his horses are ready by the river,
and everything favours the escape of the Prince and his son. Igor
gives him authority to make the final arrangements for flight, and
Ovlour creeps off in the darkness. Just then Kontchakovna enters
in great agitation. She has learned of the plan for escape, and is
distressed at the thought of losing Vladimir. He pleads that he
must obey the call of duty, whereupon she begs to be taken with
him. Igor, who has overheard the conversation, emerges from his
tent and sternly bids his son follow the course dictated by honour.
Vladimir bids Kontchakovna a sad farewell. She pours out her
soul's distress in a fine melody:

declaring herself willing to leave everything for his sake, and
passionately imploring him to let her be with him wherever he
may go. While Vladimir is obviously hesitating between love for
Kontchakovna and the stern admonitions of his father, Ovlour's
signal whistle is heard in the distance. Igor becomes still more
urgent; and at last the desperate Kontchakovna, seeing no other

way of keeping the man she loves, pounds madly on a sheet of iron suspended near the tents. Igor rushes out as the Polovtsy pour on to the stage. Kontchakovna reveals Ovlour's treachery to them; and while some of them pursue the flying Igor, others threaten the life of Vladimir.

Aroused by the clamour, Kontchak and the other Khans enter, and are told of the machinations of Ovlour and the flight of Igor. Kontchak takes a characteristically calm and broad-minded view of the affair. It is what he himself would have done had he been in Igor's position, is his philosophical comment on the escape. It is precisely this indomitable spirit that he has always admired in his enemy. Why had not the Prince accepted his offer of an alliance? In combination they could have conquered the world! Then, with a quick transition from the philosophical to the practical, he orders the peccant guards to be hanged. His resolve to spare Vladimir does not meet with the approval of the Khans, who point out to him that now the old hawk has taken flight the young one will not be long in following him. They are in favour of killing out of hand not only Vladimir but all the other prisoners. But Kontchak is wiser than they. The fact that the old hawk has returned to his nest is one reason more for retaining the young one as a hostage and a lure. Vladimir shall marry his daughter; and meanwhile the war against the Russians shall begin again. The curtain falls with the trumpets ringing out again with a call to arms.

6

The setting of the fourth act is a square in Poutivle, adjoining the city walls; on a terrace surmounting these, Jaroslavna is alone, lamenting in a long aria her misfortunes and those of Igor, to the same melody (No. 12) which, in the second act, had voiced the captive Prince's tender thoughts of his wife. Will the Dnieper, that flows into the land of the dread Polovtsy, ever bring back her loved ones to her? she asks. While she is sunk in melancholy reflections of this kind a number of peasants pass across the scene, singing in chorus of the devastation that Gzak has wrought in the land. But as Jaroslavna gazes hopelessly across the burned and pillaged fields she sees two horsemen in the distance, riding towards the town. One of them is clearly a Russian warrior of noble rank, the other as clearly a Polovtsian. Does their coming portend new misfortune, or is the noble Russian a rescuer of the land?

At last, with a cry of joy, she recognises Igor, who rides in with Ovlour. The latter leads the horses away, and the re-united pair express their happiness in a rapturous duet:

They go slowly towards the citadel, leaving the stage free for Skula and Eroshka, to whom Borodin was too attached for him to be able to endure separation from them for very long. It goes without saying that they are slightly drunk. To the accompaniment of their gudoks they comment ironically on the misfortunes which Igor has brought not only on himself and his army but on the whole land, which has now, according to them, nothing for him but curses and hatred. But even as they reach the end of their song they catch sight of Igor, just then going into the citadel with Jaroslavna, and they begin to regret having expressed their sentiments about him so frankly and audibly a moment ago. Eroshka is dolefully certain they will both be hanged, but Skula hopes there may still be a way out for them. The prospect of flight with all its privations not appealing to them, they decide to remain where they are and trust to their wits. Skula soon manages to solve their problem: why not sound the alarm bells that lie so conveniently handy, rouse the town, and be the first to announce the happy miracle of the Prince's return? This they do, and though at first the townspeople believe that it is merely a drunken freak on the part of the two notorious rascals, they have to believe them when Igor himself comes into view once more.

Soon the square fills with an excited crowd, to which Ovlour tells the story of the Prince's escape. Skula and Eroshka are quick to take the credit for having been the first bringers of the good news, and they hasten to assure everyone that if there is anyone in Russia whom they dislike and with whom they have never had anything to do it is Galitsky. It ends in the rogues being hand-

somely rewarded by the boyars for their patriotic services; and
the pleasing prospect of being able to buy more drink sets them
singing and gudok-playing once more. The boyars and others
sing a chorus of thanks to God for the safe return of the Prince:

While they go towards the citadel to greet him, the townspeople
continue to flock into the square, some of them bearing offerings
of bread and salt. At length Igor and Jaroslavna emerge from the
Kremlin and greet their cheering subjects, who hail them jubilantly with a cry of "Long live our good and brave Prince Igor!"

With the story of the opera and the leading themes of it in his
mind the reader will find the overture the plainest of plain sailing.
It begins with the sombre phrase (No. 10) which prefaced Igor's
aria in the second act. Then comes, in a faster tempo, the stirring
figure (No. 16) associated with Kontchak's triumph, which is
soon succeeded by the melody (No. 17) of Kontchakovna's
appeal to Vladimir before his attempted flight. This, after due
development, merges into the passionate theme of Igor's lament
for his lost liberty (No. 11), and that of the mutual love of Igor
and Jaroslavna (No. 12). The remainder of the overture consists
for the most part of fresh presentations of this clear-cut thematic
material, with a somewhat conventional peroration. Kontchak is
hinted at now and then by means of a vigorous descending bass:

taken from his colloquy in the second act.

The length of *Prince Igor* makes a certain amount of cutting
inevitable in the theatre, while of course the looseness of its
dramatic construction makes it an easy prey for the modern producer, who sometimes makes no bones about omitting certain

scenes altogether and re-distributing others to suit his own notions of what is right and proper. But if the construction is technically loose it is not incoherent; and the chief result of the producer's monkeying about with it is generally to confuse the spectator who is doing his best to follow the story by depriving him of some main connecting thread or other. Reduction to the time-limit of an ordinary performance is easily obtainable by declining to follow Borodin slavishly to the end in some of his needless musical repetitions: the score benefits, indeed, by a fairly lavish use of the blue pencil in this respect. But the one thing that should not be interfered with is the ground plan of the work.

THE GOLDEN COCKEREL
Rimsky-Korsakov (1844-1908)

PRINCIPAL CHARACTERS

KING DODON	*Bass*
PRINCE GUIDON	*Tenor*
PRINCE APHRON	*Baritone*
GENERAL POLKAN	*Bass*
AMELFA	*Contralto*
THE ASTROLOGER	*High Tenor*
THE QUEEN OF SHEMAKHA	*Soprano*
THE GOLDEN COCKEREL	*Soprano*

I

The Golden Cockerel, Rimsky-Korsakov's last opera, seems to have been written between the late summer of 1906 and the early summer of 1907. The conclusion of his autobiography is dated the 22nd August (O.S.) 1906: in the closing pages he makes no mention whatever of *The Golden Cockerel*, though he speaks of certain other plans for new works in conjunction with Bielsky (the librettist of a couple of his earlier operas). It was intended to produce *The Golden Cockerel* in Zimin's Theatre, Moscow, shortly after its completion, but the censor raised objections to some features of it. The librettist and the composer having made a few alterations, the ban was removed in the spring of 1909—that is to say, some nine months after Rimsky-Korsakov's death. The first performance was given in Zimin's Theatre on the 24th September 1909.

The plot of the work was derived by Bielsky from a fantastic folk-tale told to Pushkin by his nurse, and given literary form by him about 1831–2. Bielsky claimed that it was what Wagner was fond of describing as "purely human": dealing as it does with passions and weaknesses of poor humanity which are themselves ubiquitous and eternal, the story, he contended, is above and beyond all limitations of time or space. The censor, however, must have felt that it touched certain failings of the Russian régime on the raw. Perhaps it did, either by accident or design. But one of the things that constitute the charm of *The Golden Cockerel* for us today is the fact that not only are we not sure what it all means but we are not quite sure that it means anything at all, or that it meant anything in particular for either Bielsky or Rimsky-Korsakov beyond opportunity after opportunity for humour, beauty, burlesque, and, occasionally, sincere feeling. And all the ingredients of the pot are so good in themselves that it does not worry us in the least that we cannot find the right name for the strange dish that is the totality of them.

The first thing we hear, before the curtain rises, is a muted trumpet giving out the characteristic motive of the Cockerel:

At the seventh bar there steals in the sinuous chromatic melodic line that will be associated later with the Queen of Shemakha:

which runs on into another figure from her aria in the second act:

Then a thin tinkle:

prepares us for the entry of the Astrologer, who steps in front of the curtain with a key in his hand, and, to the melody of No. 4, informs the audience that by virtue of his magic arts he is going to re-create for it a fantastic tale which, though it is only a fable, has a moral well worth taking to heart. We shall meet with the Astrologer again on much the same footing at the end of the opera, when he will have something further to tell us about the story and the characters.

Having said his little piece, the picturesque old gentleman disappears down a trap, and the curtain rises on the first scene. The setting is the richly and fancifully decorated council chamber in the palace of King Dodon, with a view of the town in the distance. On one side of the hall is a colonnade, with stairs running down from it. We can see people moving about below; we see also that the heavily-armed soldiers who are supposed to be guarding the entrance are fast asleep. On the other side of the chamber the great lords of the kingdom are ranged on benches;

they look very important and very solemn. Among them is
General Polkan, a sturdy, assertive, not very intelligent old
soldier. In the centre is the absurd old King on a magnificently
adorned throne; he wears his crown and is gorgeously robed.
Close by him are his sons Guidon and Aphron.

A march-like strain in the orchestra gives us a hint that military
matters are occupying the attention of the King and his councillors. Looking extremely worried, Dodon explains why he has
summoned them. He is very sorry for himself: he finds the burden
of the crown increasing as he gets older, and does not quite know
how to deal with the new order of things. When he was younger
it was his habit to carry war into his enemies' territories; now that
he is old, they all descend on his without the smallest regard for
him. They do not play the game. Does he expect them from the
North? They make a special point of advancing from the South;
and so on. He could weep for pure vexation. And what he wants
to know is, what is to be done about it. Can his elder son make a
suggestion?

Guidon leaps from his seat, ready and anxious to oblige. The
naïve self-satisfaction and self-confidence that never desert him
speak through his typical motive:

The problem his father has raised is one which, he assures the
meeting, has been occupying his own attention for some time.
What they have to do is to be cleverer than their enemies. The
strategy he suggests is this. The immediate trouble is that the
enemy is too close to them. Very well; let them recall their own
troops to the capital, accumulate food and drink and stores of
every kind in the town, then sit down inside their ramparts, and
while the enemy is laying waste the surrounding country they
can consider what to do next. Dodon, radiant with paternal pride,
congratulates his first-born on this brilliant idea, and the lords
also overwhelm the Prince with compliments; truly this young

man, this saviour of his country, is worthy of his remarkable father! The only jarring note is struck by old General Polkan, who jumps up in a very bad temper, and, without mincing his words, makes it clear that he thinks Guidon's fine plan of campaign pure balderdash. Polkan's motive is thoroughly suggestive of the obstinacy and irritability that seem to be the two main features of his character:

King Dodon, who evidently does not like his too plain-spoken Chief-of-Staff, gives him a nasty look, whereupon the courtiers dutifully call Polkan an old donkey. All the same, Dodon has his secret doubts about Guidon's plan, in which he scents possible danger to himself. Can his second son suggest anything? he asks. Thereupon Aphron takes the floor. He has nothing but contempt for the crude strategy of Guidon. He himself, as his motive would seem to indicate:

is intellectually of sounder stuff than his brother. His plan is simplicity itself. The army is to be disbanded and the soldiers sent to their homes; then they are suddenly to re-assemble and fall lustily on the enemy, and, having mopped them up, return in triumph.

Once more the council admires and approves, and once more the King felicitates himself on having brought so brilliant a son into the world. Almost weeping with pleasure, he folds Aphron in his arms. But again the general harmony is marred by a dissenting voice—that of the irascible, self-opinionated Polkan, who, to the strain of No. 6, declares the Prince's scheme to be no good at all. It might work admirably if they could leave the enemy out of consideration. But they cannot; while they are carrying out the subtle strategy suggested by Aphron the enemy, refusing, as usual, to play the game, would fall on them without a moment's warning and annihilate them.

This scepticism is really more than Dodon can stand. He hurls at Polkan's head every object he can lay his hands on. The Princes call the old General a traitor; the nobles use physical violence towards him. All in all the War Lord has had rather a bad press.

Still, when tempers have cooled down, everyone recognises that the problem of strategy is still unsolved. Various forms of augury and magic are tentatively suggested: and the presence of superstition in the air is subtly hinted at by a return of No. 4 in a modified form. The lords have begun to quarrel among themselves as to the best brand of soothsaying, and the old King is sitting unheeded, lost in thought, when suddenly—to No. 4 in its original form and colour—the Astrologer appears on the stairs. He is a striking figure with his white astrakhan cap and his star-embroidered cloak. Under his arm are an astrolabe and a bag of many colours. Silence falls on the assembly. He walks slowly towards the King, falls on his knees before him, and, addressing him in his peculiar musical idiom, tells him that he is an ancient counsellor of Dodon's father, returning to advise and help the present King. In the bag, he says, he has a marvellous Golden Cockerel. All Dodon will need to do is to put the bird high up somewhere where it can get an all-round view of things: when there is nothing to worry about it will remain silent and immobile, but at the first distant sign of an approaching enemy it will raise its head, extend its wings, and cry "Cocorico! Have a care!"

The King being a trifle incredulous, the Astrologer releases the bird from the bag. At once it cries, to the melody of No. 1, "Cocorico! Cocorico! Sleep in your bed!" Everyone is delighted, especially the King, who is now sure that no harm can come to him or the kingdom. He orders the Cockerel to be placed on the point of a lance, so that he may have a good view all about him. He does not quite know, he tells the Astrologer, how to recompense so great a service, but he promises to perform whatever may be asked of him. The Astrologer assures him that he desires neither treasure nor honours. He thanks the King for his verbal oath, but hints that he would like it in writing, in due legal form. The astonished Dodon refuses this, but again assures him that he can have full confidence in his gratitude; and with that the Astrologer leaves him.

The King dismisses the council; and now, as the Cockerel repeats his assurance that he can sleep in peace, he looks forward to a very pleasant time, ruling the kingdom from his bed, from the comfortable depth of which he will be able to enjoy an endless succession of pleasures, dances, tales, and so on, and forget that there are such things in the world as cares of state. He stretches himself out luxuriously in the sun-rays that strike across the chamber: everything invites him to a nap, he says. Just then his housekeeper Amelfa enters. She fully agrees with him. At a sign from her the servants carry in a great ivory bed, covered with furs. She persuades Dodon to lie down, and offers him a large dish of dainties of all kinds. He amuses himself also for a while with his parrot. Then, as the Cockerel once more assures him that all is well, he surrenders himself to the delightful drowsiness that is stealing upon him. Soon he is fast asleep, with Amelfa keeping affectionate watch over him: all the guards, by the way, are by this time sunk in slumber. The 'cellos sing a lulling melody, over which the wood wind repeat a variant, equally lulling, of the bird's assurance that all is well:

Finally Amelfa herself is overcome and falls asleep by the side of the bed. A beatific smile illumines the face of Dodon, and No. 2 in the orchestra tells us why: he is dreaming of fair women.

But from this ecstasy of *dolce far niente* everyone is roused by a sudden cry from the Cockerel: "Cocorico! Cocorico! Open your eyes and beware!" Behind the scenes the "Cocorico!" (first two bars of No. 1) rings out in the trumpets, against clashing harmonies. The fanfares are repeated from all quarters, with greater and greater urgency. The town awakes in alarm; frightened crowds rush to the palace, crying out that the land is threatened. Polkan runs in, wakens the King, and manages bit by bit— Dodon's first thought is that the palace must be on fire—to knock it into him that the Cockerel is in a state of wild excitement, and that the people are scared out of their wits. Realising at last that it is up to him to do something, Dodon bids his servitors hasten to their camps—first, however, levying six months' taxes on the community. Aphron and Guidon and the nobles come in, all armed to the teeth, though none of them, one gathers, is particularly keen on setting out. The King delivers a solemn official address, pointing out to them their duty: then he embraces his sons, wishes everyone the best of luck, and packs them off to the seat of war with the injunction to return without unnecessary delay. Outside in the streets the army is heard assembling, to the accompaniment of a lively march in the orchestra.

As this dies away, the Cockerel is heard giving the King the good news that he can safely go to sleep once more. He orders Amelfa to prepare the bed again, settles down in it, closes his eyes, and prepares to resume the interrupted dream. He cannot, unfortunately, remember precisely what it was about, though he knows it was something delightful. Amelfa makes one or two suggestions about it that are very pleasant and flattering to him. Finally Amelfa guesses right; and she enlarges on the subject in such voluptuous tones that before long the King, the guards and she herself are once again fast asleep, the orchestra pouring out all the while the soporific No. 8. As the suggestions of No. 2 gradually become more and more definite we seem to see the King's dream taking more precise shape.

But once more the alarm cry of the Cockerel shrills out; once more the trumpets sound; once more the terrified people stampede through the streets about the palace. No one cares, however, to disturb Dodon, until Polkan rushes in, rouses his master, and tells him of the peril threatening him. Very reluctantly the King gets up and allows himself to be dressed for battle by his servants. It is a comic spectacle. His armour is dusty and rusty: his cuirass has grown a bit tight for him: his sword is too heavy: nothing fits, nothing looks serviceable. With great difficulty they get him down the stairs, where, with even greater difficulty, he mounts a white horse—the kind of horse, of course, one sees only in panto-mimes—makes sure there is unlikely to be any shortage of food, and rides off to the respectful acclamations of his subjects.

2

With the second act a complete change comes over the char-acter of the music. So far it has been to perfection just what one would expect in so delightful and nonsensical a fairy tale; and something of the same exquisite unreality—or beyond-reality—will return to it in the third act. But in the second there steals into the music now and then an indefinable something which is as near the tragic as makes no matter.

This new quality is already to be sensed in the opening bars of the orchestral introduction. The curtain rises on a narrow pass in a rocky country; it is the scene of the recent defeat of Dodon's army. In the livid light of the moon we see the bodies of the slain: among them are those of Guidon and Aphron, over which their horses stand motionless, with lowered heads, as if turned into stone. A cold white mist fills the air. Birds of prey are bending over the corpses; they fly away every now and then as a strong wind beats down from the mountains. After a few solemn pre-ludial bars there comes a grisly sound from the wood wind, like the squawking of evil birds:

Then we hear, but now in subdued tones, the march to which the army had set out so gaily at the end of the first act. What is left of

Dodon's force advances across the scene, in couples, looking round it apprehensively at every step. The sinister No. 9 is heard again as they shiver under the cold wind and shudder at the sight of the vultures at work among the bodies.

Dodon and Polkan enter, sunk in melancholy. They stumble over the corpses of the two Princes, and the King bemoans their fate and the ruin of all his hopes for them:

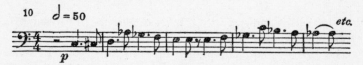

His threnody ends with a wailing phrase of the type often used in Russian opera for the expression of grief:

This is certainly not the grotesque King Dodon of the first act. Yet somehow or other even No. 11 acquires a faintly comic tinge when the army sobs to it; and we seem to be approaching the realm of farce again when Polkan and the soldiers talk of a fresh advance against the enemy as soon as they can find out where he is.

Just then the mist begins to disperse, and the morning sun beats full upon a gorgeous particoloured tent which has been invisible until now. All are astonished; but Polkan has the bright idea that it houses the enemy's generalissimo. He orders his troops to capture him; but they show so little inclination to advance that we cannot help wondering how so many of them managed to get near enough to the battle to get killed the day before. They suggest that a better plan would be to bombard the tent from a safe distance. Accordingly a farcical cannon is dragged in and put into position, farcically fired, and then as farcically abandoned by the scared warriors as a beautiful young woman is seen stepping out of the tent. She is richly robed, and wears a white headdress with a long feather in it. She is accompanied by four slaves, each carrying a musical instrument. She advances with apparently unseeing eyes, and, with hardly the pretence of a preamble, launches into the famous hymn to the sun:

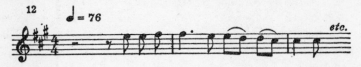

that sun which endows with a myriad delights and lovelinesses her own far-off natal land.

The lovely song, abounding in exotic intervals, rich harmonies and glowing colours, having run its long course, she looks fixedly at the old King, who, with Polkan, at length ventures to approach her and ask who she is and where she comes from. In the same voluptuous, caressing strain she tells him that she is the Queen of Shemakha, that she is alone, and that she has come from afar to subdue him and his kingdom by the sole force of her beauty. She claps her hands, and from the tent come two slaves with cups of silver, into which they pour wine. She asks Dodon to drink with her, but he draws back rather suspiciously, only to feel once more a strange trouble in his soul as she raises her eyes to his and smiles. The slaves spread a carpet in the centre of the stage, placing on it three cushions. The corpses, now become a trifle incongruous, are removed by a few of the soldiers, who, at a sign from Polkan, take up positions by the carpet.

The Queen, the King and Polkan seat themselves on the cushions. The two men are ill at ease. Polkan, by way of making conversation, asks the Queen if she had slept well the night before. Not too badly, she replies, though at morn she had wakened suddenly; the warm air and the perfume of the flowers had filled her with thoughts of love, and she had imagined she heard a voice sighing, "Come, my beloved!": but there was no one there. "Did you look under the bed?" asks the fatuous Polkan. "It was dark", she replies: "Oh thou whom I love, come to me!" He will come one of these days, Polkan assures her. By now she has had enough of his drivelling facetiousness. This crude fellow, she tells the King, annoys her. At her bidding Dodon sends Polkan away with a rebuke for his bad manners:

the old general retires to the side of the tent, where we catch sight
of his nose and long beard sticking out every now and then as
something particularly interesting in the conversation reaches his
ears.

The Queen now sets herself to the conquest of poor Dodon.
It is little wonder that he does not quite know what to make of
her, for we ourselves, who have had more opportunities than he
of studying her, do not. She is neither wholly real nor wholly
fantastic, neither entirely woman nor entirely puppet, but something between the two, though precisely where the one aspect
of her ends and the other begins we find it impossible to say.
When we ask ourselves why she should be spreading her feminine
net in this way round old Dodon, of all persons in the universe,
or just why the Queen of Shemakha happens to be where she is
at this particular moment of the opera, we are compelled to admit
that we haven't the faintest idea. All we know is that she sings
some captivating music, much of which is very subtly poised
between comedy and gravity, and that her seduction of the
doddering old King is at once laughter-making and slightly
repellent.

As she proceeds, her song becomes by turns more luxuriant
in its oriental arabesque and more heartfelt in its expression—or
as near the genuinely heartfelt as one can imagine this curious
creature ever getting. In another situation, with another vis-à-vis,
much of her music might ring as true as anything of its particular
kind in Russian opera. At length, tired of listening to herself, she
persuades the old King to take the goussli in his hands and sing
to its accompaniment. Trying to recall the sentimental hours of
his youth, the pathetic old fool croaks his way through a little
song that sounds all the more preposterously naïve after the
luxury of line and colour to which the Queen has been treating us:

She applauds his effort ironically. Then she goes off into a sort of
dream-state in which she sees the gay and brave young lovers

who worship her in the earthly paradise from which she has come; and then again, with another of her sudden changes of mood, she confesses that she is weary of it all, and dissolves in tears of self-pity. Where, she asks, will she find someone to make life bearable for her by contradicting her, opposing her, dominating her? This gives Dodon his cue. He himself, he fatuously declares, will be the despot she is looking for. She thanks him gaily, and then maliciously insists on his dancing for her as she is sure he used to dance in his young days. In vain he pleads his years, his bulk, and the weight of his armour. She takes off his helmet and cuirass, ties a kerchief round his head, puts her fan in his hand, flatters him, and forces him to dance to a slow melody played by the slaves:

The Queen, a tambourine in her hand, also dances, approaching him, evading him, cajoling and insulting him, and mocking with her own gracefulness the clumsy antics of the dotard. When her poison has done its full work within him she sits on the edge of the carpet and laughs at his absurd pirouettes. At last he falls down exhausted, and, as soon as he has recovered his breath, offers the Queen his hand, his heart and his kingdom: they will spend their days, he tells her, in feasting, sleeping and story-telling. Her first stipulation is that Polkan shall be whipped. Better than that, Dodon promises her; he shall be executed.

The Queen is anxious to set out at once for this new country of hers. Slaves pour out of the tent, gather up the carpet and the rest of the apparatus, and prepare their mistress for the journey. Dodon's army reappears. The King's chariot is brought in, and he and the Queen seat themselves in it; as they drive off, the slaves comment ironically on this latest conquest of the beautiful Queen of Shemakha. But Dodon, in the seventh heaven of fatuous happiness, bids Polkan sound the fanfares for the triumphant lover, and the grotesque procession moves off to the cheers of the soldiers and the malicious laughter of the slaves.

3

The third act takes us back to Dodon's capital. We see a street crowded with excited people; others are visible at the windows and on the roofs of the houses. One of the first objects to catch our eyes is the Golden Cockerel, perched on the top of a pole. The street is bathed in sunlight, but clouds are gathering in the east, and a storm seems to be on its way. Every now and then messengers run in, out of breath, bringing the latest news of the approaching King.

Some members of the crowd are vaguely ill at ease; others try to reassure them, pointing out that all must be well, since the Cockerel is quiescent. When Amelfa appears at the top of the flight of stairs that runs up to the palace the people eagerly ask her if she has any authentic tidings of the army. They learn from her that it has been victorious, that King Dodon has gallantly saved a young Queen from a dragon, and that he is bringing the beauty back with him. The Princes, unfortunately, will not return, their father having made an end of them—a statement which the crowd, scratching their heads, accept without understanding what it means.

As Amelfa retires into the palace the trumpets are heard heralding the coming of the King. A fantastic cortège comes into sight —soldiers preening themselves under the admiring public gaze, attendants on the Queen of Shemakha, queer-looking creatures with animal heads or only one eye, dwarfs, giants, negroes, and many other oddities, the sight of whom sends the populace into an ecstasy of childish wonder. The procession files across the stage to the accompaniment of music almost as strange as itself. At last the gilded car containing the King and the Queen comes into sight. Dodon looks much older, evidently as the result of new worries; the Queen, for her part, seems a trifle bored, although the crowd greets her and the King with the most lavish assurances of undying fidelity.

The innocent enthusiasm is at its height when the Astrologer, dressed as in the first act, suddenly appears on the steps of one of the houses. He attracts the attention of the Queen, who stops the King as he is about to descend from the car and asks him who this

wise-looking person may be. Dodon, joyfully recognising his
former acquaintance, enquires what he can do for him on this so
happy day. The Astrologer comes forward slowly, his eyes fixed
all the while on the Queen. The King, he said, had promised him
at their first meeting whatever he might ask in return for the
invaluable Golden Cockerel. He now demands in payment—the
Queen! Dodon is disconcerted; the Queen is highly amused, the
crowd a trifle scared. The King admits his promise, but, he
pleads, there are limits to everything. The Astrologer explains
that, old as he is, he is contemplating marriage: the Queen pleases
him, and he wants her. Dodon tries to get him to see reason: he
can have anything else he likes, even to the half of his kingdom
—but not the Queen. As the Astrologer still insists, Dodon,
losing his temper, orders him to leave the land at once. The
guards seize the old magician and drag him away: but as he seems
inclined to go on arguing the point the King kills him with a blow
on the head with his sceptre. Not only do the spectators shudder
but nature itself seems to be appalled at the crime, for thunder
growls angrily in the distance and dark clouds obscure the sun.
Dodon himself is a little disturbed at the turn events have taken:
this, he reflects ruefully, is a pretty omen for his wedding day!
The only person to find amusement in it all is the Queen, who, as
usual when anything serious happens, bursts into a peal of
laughter; the man, she declares, richly deserved what he got.
Reassured by her attitude, Dodon tries to embrace her, but she
repulses him with insults and curses, and prophesies the speedy
punishment of his crimes.

Just then the Cockerel flies down from its perch with a cry of
"Cocorico!" and a threat to the King himself. Flying over the
heads of the frightened crowd it drives its beak into the head of
Dodon, who falls dead. There comes another and louder peal of
thunder, and through the complete darkness that descends upon
the scene the heartless laughter of the Queen is heard. When at
last the clouds roll away, both she and the Cockerel have disappeared. The people pour out wave after wave of lamentation
for the King, in wailing phrases of the type of those shown in
No. 11. Now that he is dead they remember only the virtues of
the deceased monarch: who can replace this father whom they

have lost? And the curtain falls with them prostrating themselves, beating their breasts and sobbing their hearts out.

But this is not the end of the curious story. The Astrologer comes in front of the curtain, and, to the music of No. 4, exhorts the spectators not to be upset by this tragic *dénouement*, for the figures that have been set before them are mere illusions of the imagination—all of them, that is to say, except the Queen and himself. With that somewhat enigmatic announcement he disappears. And so ends an opera of which no one on earth has been able yet to discover the precise meaning, or even establish that it has a meaning; which trifling drawbacks, however, do not prevent the work being one of the most charming in the whole field of Russian opera. Bielsky's foreword to his libretto, for all its air of explaining matters, does nothing whatever to lighten our darkness. Nor does it matter in the least. It is probably the utter inconsequence of the story that makes it so suitable to the ballet form which Fokine has recently given it.

It is not wholly clear what the censor objected to in the text of *The Golden Cockerel*; but presumably the grotesque plans for conducting war in the first act were regarded as having too pointed a Russian application, while there is something very characteristic of the old régime in Amelfa's instructions to the populace in the last scene—"Demonstrate your loyalty, dance and grimace, but don't expect anything in return!"

ELEKTRA
Richard Strauss (1864)

PRINCIPAL CHARACTERS

ELEKTRA	*Soprano*
CLYTEMNESTRA	*Mezzo-soprano*
CHRYSOTHEMIS	*Soprano*
AEGISTHUS	*Tenor*
ORESTES	*Baritone*

Elektra was produced at Dresden on the 25th January 1909. It was the first opera in which Hugo von Hofmannsthal co-operated with Strauss as librettist.

The subject had already been treated, in different styles, by Sophocles and Euripides in their *Elektra* dramas, and by Aeschylus in his *Choephoroi* (*The Libation-Bearers*, the second play of his Agamemnon trilogy). For the roots of the story we have to go back to certain events preceding the Trojan War. Atreus, King of Mycenae, had two sons, Agamemnon and Menelaus. The former had for wife Clytemnestra, and the latter her sister Helena, who was carried off by Paris, the son of Priamus, King of Troy. Out of this there sprang the war between Greece and Troy, which lasted ten years. On the way to Troy the Greek fleet was becalmed at Aulis, for Artemis was wroth with Agamemnon for having killed one of her sacred hinds. To placate the goddess, Agamemnon sent for his daughter Iphigenia and sacrificed her.

After the destruction of Troy and the recovery of Helena, Menelaus, on his journey home, was driven by contrary winds to Egypt and elsewhere, his wanderings lasting several years. Agamemnon returned to Mycenae, where, during his long absence, he had been supplanted in his Queen's affections by Aegisthus. Clytemnestra's hatred of Agamemnon was justified by her as having sprung from a mother's resentment at his sacrifice of her daughter Iphigenia. The Queen and her paramour murdered

Agamemnon while in his bath, and Aegisthus reigned in his stead. The great King left behind him a young daughter, Elektra, and a son, Orestes, of whose possible vengeance the guilty pair now live in constant dread. Elektra is degraded to the state of a slave in the palace: the little Orestes had been rescued from death by a faithful slave who placed him in safe keeping at a distance from Mycenae.[1] In due course he returns to Mycenae, where, giving himself out to be a messenger bringing Clytemnestra the welcome news of the death of Orestes, he obtains admission to the palace and slays both her and Aegisthus, as filial duty to the outraged dead required.

It is fundamentally a story of violence, for all the profound moral implications with which the Greek conscience endowed it; and the tremendous expressive apparatus of modern music has enabled Strauss and Hofmannsthal to intensify the violence to an extent that would have astonished and perhaps horrified a Greek. This same apparatus, however, makes possible to librettist and composer a beauty at the very heart of horror that was beyond the scope even of the finest minds of the ancient world.

The opera is in one long act, but analysis of its structure shows that Hofmannsthal's plan has seven main psychological stages, to each of which Strauss gives a different musical cast. It may assist not only the listener in the opera house or on the radio but the home student to have these stages enumerated and summarised here:

1. Elektra. (Pp. 5 to 34 of the German vocal score).
2. Chrysothemis. (Pp. 35 to 59).
3. Clytemnestra. (Pp. 59 to 114).
4. Elektra and Chrysothemis. (Pp. 114 to 161).
5. Orestes. (Pp. 162 to 182).
6. The Recognition. (Pp. 182 to 202).
7. The Vengeance. (Pp. 203 to end).

The emotional climax comes, after a slow ascent from the opening scene, with the despair of Elektra when she hears that Orestes is

---

[1] In some versions of the story it is Elektra who sends her brother away, looking to him to avenge some day their murdered father. The complex myth, indeed, comes down to us with many variations in detail. The reader will understand that the version here given is the one adopted by Hofmannsthal.

dead. Then the tension relaxes in a long solo in which the avenging fury softens into the tender sister welcoming the loved brother home again; after which the action gradually slips back again into its former atmosphere of hate and strain and lust for vengeance, until, the double deed accomplished, the moral law vindicated, Elektra's *Verklärung* is expressed in a sacred dance.

1. There is no overture, the orchestra launching at once into the arresting motive of Agamemnon:

The setting is the inner courtyard of the palace at Mycenae, which is overlooked by the back of the palace and the servants' quarters. On the left is a draw-well, from which some female slaves, watched by the overseers, are drawing water. Night is falling. Elektra runs out of the house—a ragged, unkempt, hardly human creature, recoiling on herself at the sight of the others, instinctively holding one arm before her face as if to protect herself against them, so used is she to brutal usage:

The orchestra gives out the motive of her undying hate of her mother and Aegisthus:

The maids discuss in fear and horror this almost dehumanised

woman who seems hardly more than a wild beast, always
sobbing:

and cursing and spitting at any one who tries to approach her.
With some of them, fear has long ago hardened into hatred;
while one or two are touched with something approaching pity
at the thought of the misery and degradation Elektra suffers in
the house that was once her father's, lodging with the dogs and
eating from the same platter with them. The Fifth Maid, a gentler
creature than any of the others, makes no secret of her sympathy
with this child of kings who suffers such shame: none of them, she
says, is fit to breathe the same air as she. The others turn on her
angrily. "Were she my daughter", says one of them, "I would
keep her under lock and key"; and we hear in the orchestra the
motive of Orestes, who, like Elektra, is the victim of his mother's
hatred and fear:

It is when one of the maidservants shows a faint gleam of pity for
Elektra that we hear the motive that symbolises her degradation:

which, as the Fifth Maid speaks of her as a King's child, is linked with the motive of her brother (No. 5). The maids go into the house, from which we hear a cry of "Help, they are beating me!" from the one who alone had ventured to speak a word of love for Elektra and understanding of her.

When the stage is empty, Elektra comes forward and launches into a fine monologue (commencing with the motives No. 2 and No. 1), in which, in an ecstasy of love and pain, she addresses the shade of the great King who had been so foully murdered. Her imagination darts forward to the day when those who wrought that deed will in their turn be victims raining their life-blood on her father's tomb, along with that of the chargers from his stables and the dogs that once licked his sandals, while she, with her brother and her sister, will dance the royal dance of victory about the tomb. It is a magnificent outburst—most magnificent of all, perhaps, in the figure, symbolising the shade of Agamemnon as avenger of his own wrongs, that rises threateningly from the depths to the heights of the orchestra like a great fist clenched above the house that was once his:

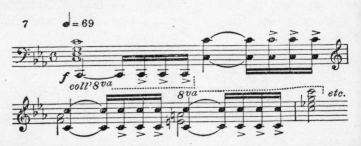

Another theme, which becomes of great importance later, represents the Children of Agamemnon:

It is used here to the words, "Father, leave me not this day alone!
Show thyself to thy child as thou didst yesterday, like a shadow
in the recess of the wall!" The final stages of the monologue
foreshadow the mystical dance to which Elektra looks forward in
imagination:

2. As Elektra's last cry of "Agamemnon!" dies away, Chrysothemis enters. This younger sister was designed by Hofmannsthal,
as his letters show, to contrast with Elektra as the human with
the demoniac. Chrysothemis is as weak through love as her sister
is strong through hate. She bids Elektra beware, for Clytemnestra
and Aegisthus intend to immure her in a tower into which
neither the light of the sun nor that of the moon ever penetrates.
Elektra tries to infect Chrysothemis with her own religion of
hatred and her lust for revenge. But Chrysothemis shrinks from
all this violence. She herself is almost demented with fear; her one
desire is to escape from this hag-ridden house, to become the
wife of some good man, were it only a peasant, and bear him
children:

It is because of Elektra that she too is a prisoner in the house,
because of the fear that Elektra inspires in her mother and
Aegisthus; and it will come to nothing with all Elektra's hopes, for
no news ever reaches them of their brother, and meanwhile these
years of suffering are breaking down the bodies of the sisters
and ageing their faces with care. It is unfortunate that nowhere
in the opera does the music of Chrysothemis rise to the height

of that of Elektra. Strauss has not Wagner's gift for endowing his second-line figures with the inner vitality, the dramatic veracity, of those of the first line. Gudrune, for instance, says and does very little in the *Götterdämmerung*; but minor character as she is, she is given a characteristic phrase or two that limn her to the life. Strauss's Chrysothemis music is certainly what he intended it to be—a contrast to that of Elektra; but it nowhere carries the same conviction.

From within the palace is heard the sound of hurrying feet drawing nearer and nearer; and torches are seen in the passage to the left of the door. The Queen, says Chrysothemis, has been dreaming again—this time her dream was that she was being pursued by Orestes, and she awoke shrieking with fright. She is now on her way to propitiate the gods, driving before her the slaves with torches, and the beasts she means to slaughter, and the priests with their sacrificial knives. "Sister, when she trembles she is most terrible. Cross not her path today." Elektra's only answer is that today, as never before, she desires to have speech with her mother. Chrysothemis flies from her in horror.

3. Past the crudely lighted windows figures are seen rushing wildly, driving forward, with resounding whip-blows, a procession of struggling and stumbling cattle. At the broad window Clytemnestra herself at length appears. She is so horrible a spectacle that the Greek imagination, surely, would have shrunk from it. Sleepless nights, remorse, haunting fears have undermined her. Her sallow, bloated face shows up in the lurid light of the torches against her scarlet robe. Her eyelids are unnaturally large, and she seems to hold them open with difficulty. She is covered with jewels, rings, armlets, all of them talismans against evil. She leans heavily on her Confidante, whose dark violet robe contrasts sombrely with hers, and on an ivory staff set with gems. Clytemnestra's train is carried by an Egyptian-looking woman, whose jet-black hair is combed straight back from a smooth yellow face like that of a snake rearing its head to strike.

The music takes on a sombre tinge once more: that allotted to Clytemnestra is full of dragging harmonic clusters of this kind:

which suggest her constant effort to bear up against the load of physical corruption and mental torture that weigh on her by day and by night.

She begins by reproaching the gods for having given her this Elektra for child, this nettle which she cannot endure to touch yet cannot bring herself to exterminate. Gradually, as Elektra draws her into conversation, Clytemnestra leaves the window and comes down with her attendants to the doorway. She turns a deaf ear to their warnings about Elektra. She has come to the end, she says, of what body and spirit can endure, her body rank with disease, her spirit sapped by her dreams and visions. Victims she sacrifices in endless succession, yet no peace comes to her soul. Perhaps this hated and hating daughter of hers may know of a medicine against torture such as hers.

She orders the Confidante and the Trainbearer to leave her, and they go, though reluctantly, into the palace, and with them the torchbearers, so that only a dim light from the windows is left to define the figures of the two women now facing each other in the courtyard. There are simples, could one but know them, for all ills, Clytemnestra tells Elektra wearily. She describes her nights of choking anguish, the evil eyes that seem to watch her as she lies sleepless in the haunted darkness, the sleep that is even more terrible than wakefulness, for in her sleep she dreams. And yet each demon can be appeased if only the right blood be made to flow! There follows a dialogue which, with its swift verbal give-and-take and its wealth of double meanings, harks back to the technique of the Greek tragedy in moments when the action has reached its supreme tension. In each of Elektra's answers to the Queen's eager questions there is a sinister meaning that is hidden from Clytemnestra but perfectly plain to the audience.

There are many respects in which the structure of the ancient Greek drama resembles, in essentials, that of the Wagnerian music drama, though the latter has this great advantage, that it can always call on music not only to recall to our memory what has happened in the past but to suggest to our imagination what the future holds in store. To some extent the Greek audience itself supplied this element of backward-glancing and fore-knowing: as every detail of the myth on which a play was founded was known to the spectators, their imagination could always supply what was sometimes designedly left unsaid by this character or that. But opera, with its leading motives that look before and after and its capacity for supplementing, or even contradicting, in the orchestra what is being said on the stage, is incomparably more potent than any mere verbal drama can be in this regard.

She will slay anything that creeps on the earth or flies in the air to rid herself of her spectres, says Clytemnestra; and Elektra assures her that once the appointed victim has bled under the axe she will dream no more. (Clytemnestra does not know that Elektra has hidden away, for the great day of vengeance, the axe with which Aegisthus had slain Agamemnon). The destined sacrifice, it seems, is not yet consecrated, nor even bound: it still runs free. Clytemnestra demands the name of this beast that must die. It is a woman, replies Elektra. Question after question comes swiftly from Clytemnestra's tongue. One of her servants? A child? A maiden unwed? A wife? Yes, answers Elektra tranquilly, a wife. And what the hour and the manner and the place of killing? At any place, at any hour of day or night. Shall Clytemnestra herself take part in the slaying? No; this time she will not take part in the hunt with net and axe. (According to the legend, Clytemnestra herself had entangled Agamemnon in a net in his bath for Aegisthus to smite him with the axe). Who is to deal the blow? A man. Aegisthus? Elektra laughs contemptuously at the application of the word "man" to one so effeminate and degenerate as her mother's paramour. Will the victim be slain by a member of her household or by a stranger from afar? By a stranger, in sooth, yet one akin to her and to Elektra.

The orchestral texture during this dialogue is an elaborate

network of thematic references, with the motive of Elektra's dance of triumph (No. 9) especially prominent.

The two women begin to speak of Orestes, who, Clytemnestra has been told, has lost his reason, and stammers in his speech, and has his abode with the dogs, being no longer capable of distinguishing man from beast. She hypocritically claims to have sent much gold to those into whose keeping he had been given, so that they may treat him as beseems a royal child. Elektra retorts that the gold was sent as a bribe to them to slay the boy, for his mother lives in perpetual dread of his return. As to that, Clytemnestra professes confidence in those whose duty it is to guard her, and turns again to what is uppermost in her mind— the discovery of the one sacrifice that will rid her of the sick terror that haunts her. She reminds Elektra of her power over her and threatens her with chains and hunger if she will not tell her what she so desires to know—what blood it is that must flow that she may sleep once more.

Thereupon Elektra throws off the mask. She leaps out of the shadow and comes nearer and nearer to Clytemnestra, crouching and threatening. She takes up her mother's last words. Yes, blood must flow, but from Clytemnestra's own throat when the huntsman shall have seized her. She sees the slayer creeping through the chambers of the palace till he comes where Clytemnestra lies. He draws back the curtain from the bed. She wakens, and flies screaming: he pursues her through halls and down the great staircase, and she, Elektra, she who has set him on, follows her windings like a hound, heading her off to the huntsman. And at last they come to a shadow in the depths of the darkness cast by a wall: it is Agamemnon, and at his feet the two avengers strike the wretched woman down, but not until she has had time to live in imagination through an eternity of terror and suffering. The axe falls, and Clytemnestra's anguished dreaming is for ever at an end, nor is there need any more for Elektra to dream, for all living things, this load of horror and infamy lifted from them, can now rejoice and be glad.

Clytemnestra stands trembling under the vehemence of Elektra's speech and before the madness in her eyes. But just then lights appear in the palace, and the Confidante runs out and whispers something in Clytemnestra's ear the significance of which she seems not to grasp at once. When she does, her expression changes from one of fear to one of evil joy in triumph. She raises her hands towards Elektra with a menacing gesture. Meanwhile the serving-maids have poured into the courtyard, flooding it with the reddish-yellow light of their torches. Leaning on her Confidante and her staff, Clytemnestra makes her way hurriedly into the palace. During the whole of this episode no word is spoken on the stage, the orchestra alone, with its interlacing motives, carrying on the action and supplying what comment is necessary.

4. Elektra is left alone for a moment, wondering what this sudden gladness on the part of her mother can portend. She is soon enlightened. Chrysothemis comes running in through the courtyard gate, howling, as the direction in the score puts it, like a wounded beast. "Orestes is dead!" she shrieks; and we hear in the orchestra the motive of the Children of Agamemnon (No. 8), but now in the minor. Chrysothemis tells her sister the whole story in her customary three-four rhythm. (See No. 10). Two strangers, an old man and a younger, have brought the news to the palace: Orestes has been dragged to death by his own horses in a chariot race. A young slave hurries through the courtyard, calling imperiously for a horse, the swiftest that can be had; he must fly with the long-desired news to Aegisthus, who is in the country.

For a while Elektra is stunned: she cannot bring herself to believe what she has heard. Then, recovering herself, she turns to Chrysothemis. They twain, she says, must do it, and here and now. Realising what this means, Chrysothemis shrinks from her sister in horror. She learns for the first time that Elektra has hidden the axe with which their father had been slain, hidden it for the day when Orestes should return and wield it. Now it is for the sisters to kill the Queen and her paramour with it—that very night, in their sleep. Elektra cannot do the double deed alone. Her long sufferings have weakened her: she will need the youthful strength of Chrysothemis to help her. Feverishly she implores that help; let Chrysothemis only give it, and Elektra will henceforth be her slave, living only for her happiness and that of her

children. But the weaker spirit of Chrysothemis cannot rise to
these heights of fury. With a final cry of "I cannot!" she runs
into the house, followed by a curse from her sister.

   5. Elektra's resolution is taken: since the others have failed her,
she must and will do the deed alone. She goes to a place by the
wall of the house, where she begins to dig, noiselessly, untiringly,
like an animal, for the axe. After a while she seems to sense that
she is not alone. She turns round and sees a figure by the gate,
standing out in black relief against the expiring light: a wailing
theme in the orchestra (see No. 12), announces him as the herald
of woe. He tells Elektra, whom he takes to be one of the serving-
maids, that he and another are the bearers of a message which
they must deliver in person to the Queen. He tells the whole sad
story to Elektra, to the accompaniment of the wailing figure just
referred to:

He was the companion of Orestes, he says; they were of the same
age. Orestes had perished before his eyes, trampled to death by
his own horses. Elektra pours out her unendurable sorrow in one
of the most moving passages of the opera. Why has this herald
of misfortune come to her? Could he not trumpet the tidings to
others, who would rejoice at it? "Thine eye stares at me, and the
light of his is quenched. Thy mouth moves to and fro, and his is
stopped with earth. Thou livest, and he, who was better and
nobler a thousand times than thou, he is dead!"

   Gravely the herald tells her that it was meet that Orestes
should die, for the gods look with unfriendly eyes on one who
rejoices in life as he had done. But Elektra laments once more that
the child will never return to the house of his fathers, while those
within it live out their foul life in safety and joy, and she herself
is hideous and alone, like some miserable beast of the forest.
The passion of her grief surprises the herald. Who can she be, he
asks, that mourns like this over the death of Orestes and Aga-

memnon? Is she, perchance, of kindred blood with them? She
tells him that she is the fatherless and brotherless Elektra, the
oppressed of her mother and Aegisthus. The herald's heart melts
within him as he looks on her wild eyes and wasted form. "Give
ear to me", he says softly: "Orestes lives!" She bids him, in that
case, rescue him before those who hate him can murder him.
"By my father's corpse", he replies, "it is for that I have come
hither!"

6. "Who then art thou?" she asks in wonderment; but before
he can answer, an old servant, followed by three others, comes in
from the courtyard, prostrates himself, and kisses the herald's
feet, while the other three kiss his hands and the hem of his garment. "The very hounds in the courtyard know me", says the
stranger softly, "but my sister not!" She gives a great cry of
"Orestes!" and all her savagery falls from her in a moment. The
music of the Recognition scene, which now follows, brings us the
first grateful relaxation of the terrific tension of the last hour or
more. Elektra forgets everything in the bliss of reunion, though
Orestes, she fears, is only a vision that may fade away. The music
of this great scene is based mainly on the theme of the Children
of Agamemnon (No. 8) and a new motive, which may be called
that of Elektra's ecstasy:

As in Sophocles and Euripides, she tells her brother the story of
her sufferings at the hands of Clytemnestra and her dedication of
herself to the one task of avenging her father. Orestes promises
her that he will take the expiatory deed on himself, and she
blesses him for the relief he has brought her. She becomes the
possessed Maenad again as she sings a paean in honour of the man
who can do what he has set his hand and his will to do, and on all
who help him, who dig the axe and hold the torch and open the
door for him. But the figure of an old man with fiery eyes suddenly appears in the doorway. It is the Tutor of Orestes, who bids

him be silent, lest they betray themselves to those within before their work be done.

7. A servant with a torch appears in the doorway: behind her is the Confidante, who makes a sign to the two strangers to follow her within. Orestes and the Tutor do so, Orestes, with closed eyes, mastering his horror by a mighty effort. When the door has closed behind them, Elektra, who, on the appearance of the Confidante, had hidden herself in the shadows, runs to and fro like an excited animal again, crying out apprehensively, "They have gone, and I could not give him the axe! There are no gods in heaven!" But from within there comes a shriek from Clytemnestra. "Strike again!" cries Elektra; and there is a second shriek as the shade of the great King (No. 7) seems to rise in all its majesty in the orchestra.

The death-cries of Clytemnestra have aroused everyone. From another quarter Chrysothemis and a number of attendants come running towards the palace; but Elektra, standing with her back to the door, bars their way. They scatter distractedly as Aegisthus appears at the door on the right of the courtyard, shouting to the slaves to bring torches. A strange-looking figure, so wild that it affrights him, takes a torch from its socket, approaches him in the gloom, bows low before him, and offers to light him. He recognises Elektra, and eagerly asks where are the strangers who have come with the news of Orestes' death. They are inside, replies Elektra; they have found a friendly hostess, with whom they now make merry: they are, indeed, not merely expressing their joy in words but proving it by deeds. She accompanies him to the door with a great display of ironical deference; there is even a hint in her movements of the dance that will later celebrate his destruction.

He enters the house. A few moments of silence follow; then Aegisthus appears at a window, tearing back the curtain, and crying "Help! They are murdering your master!" He is dragged away, but reappears at the window, gives another anguished cry, and is torn away again.[1] To his shriek of "Does no one hear

---

[1] The Strauss-Hofmannsthal correspondence shows that the poet and the composer had some difficulty in deciding on the details of this episode. Strauss wanted Aegisthus to be killed in sight of the audience. The procedure finally agreed upon seems to have been a compromise.

me?" Elektra answers jubilantly, "Agamemnon hears thee!" She
stands in front of the house, almost insane with excitement.
Chrysothemis and the women rush out, and the cry goes up that
it is Orestes who has slain Aegisthus and the Queen, and that all
within who loved the line of Agamemnon, drunk with joy, are
fighting to the death with the slaves of Aegisthus. The women
run off, leaving Chrysothemis alone with Elektra, to whom the
sounds of slaughter within are heavenly music.

To the motive of her joy at the return of Orestes (No. 13) she
sings that her great hour has come, the time for her to lead the
dance. But her limbs are heavy, she laments, as she crouches on
the threshold, while Chrysothemis, in growing excitement, tells
how Mycenae seems transfigured, how men are weeping for joy,
and the high gods have endowed them all with a new life. At last
strength returns to Elektra. She sees herself as the instrument
through which the gods have wrought their tardy justice, and
she exults: the gods, she says, to a theme which has already been
hinted at in an earlier scene between herself and Chrysothemis:

the gods go their own way through mortals like a sword-blade.
She herself had sown the seeds of darkness and reaped a joy above
all joys; and now whoso looks on her face must either die or
dissolve in bliss. While the happy Chrysothemis runs into the
house to embrace her brother,[1] Elektra, in whom reason has
snapped through excess of happiness, flings back her head like a
Maenad and breaks into a wild dance, to the strains of No. 13,
No. 14 and other leading motives. Chrysothemis reappears at the
door, in the midst of a crowd of men and women, and calls to her
sister by name. But Elektra bids them all be silent and join her in
the dance; and once more motive is interwoven with motive in
the complex tissue of the orchestra, till at length the theme of
Elektra's hatred (No. 3), that of the shade of Agamemnon (No. 7),

---

[1] Orestes does not appear on the stage again after going into the palace.

and that of Orestes (No. 5) come to the forefront together or in quick succession. As Chrysothemis runs to the door and beats on it with a wild cry of "Orestes!", and the orchestra thunders out for the last time the name of Agamemnon (No. 1), Elektra falls lifeless.

The natural sequel to an Elektra drama in antiquity was one in which Orestes, in his turn, was shown paying the penalty for his offence against the moral law in the murder of his mother. It is interesting to learn that in 1912 Hofmannsthal expressed the hope that Strauss would now write a symphonic poem on the subject of Orestes and the Furies. Apparently the music was to accompany a ballet, the scenario of which Hofmannsthal enclosed with his letter. "Think of Orestes as represented by Nijinsky, the greatest genius among mimes today!" Strauss's reply has not been published; but no doubt he was too full just then of his *Ariadne auf Naxos* to feel much interest in the world of Orestes and the Furies. When, a year or two later, he began to coquet with ballet, it was in connection with the less exacting subject of Joseph and Potiphar's wife.

ORFEO ED EURIDICE
Gluck (1714-1787)

PRINCIPAL CHARACTERS

ORFEO	*Contralto*
EURIDICE	*Soprano*
AMOR	*Soprano*

I

Gluck had already more than thirty works to his credit when, in 1762, he produced his *Orfeo*. This is the work with which he began his famous "reform of the opera"; and it is the oldest opera now in the repertory.

The poem is by Ranieri Calzabigi, an Italian who managed to combine culture with business in a way peculiar to his century. Born at Livorno in 1714, he settled in Paris, where he attracted attention not only by his writings on music and poetry and the arts in general but by a scheme for a lottery that was intended to restore health to the ailing French finances. Nine years later he was in Vienna, in the capacity of "Chamber Councillor to the Exchequer of the Low Countries". There he came into close contact with the Austrian Chancellor, Prince Kaunitz, through whom he met Count Durazzo, the director of the Vienna theatres. As Calzabigi was known to hold advanced views on the subject of opera libretti, Durazzo seems to have invited him to give them practical shape; whereupon Calzabigi wrote the poem of *Orfeo*. He must have met Gluck shortly after his arrival in Vienna, as the pair collaborated in the ballet *Don Juan*, which was produced in October 1761. According to Calzabigi's own account, written some years later, at a time when his relations with Gluck were a little clouded over, it was he who suggested Gluck as the composer of *Orfeo*. The question who began the rapprochement is, however, of no more than academic interest today. The two men had for some time been approaching the same problem along different but converging lines; and it was inevitable that as soon as they found themselves side by side at Durazzo's dinner table they should plan to co-operate in a solution of that problem, which was none other than to substitute a "return to nature" for the formalities and frigidities that had been weighing on opera seria for so long.

Calzabigi alleged that he "consented" to the production of his drama on the sole condition that the music to it should meet with his approval; whereupon Durazzo "sent" Gluck to him. This is no doubt an exaggeration: Gluck's reputation and official position in Vienna just then were not of the kind that would make it likely that Durazzo would "send" him to Calzabigi; nor would a man of his tough fibre allow himself to be "sent". According to Calzabigi, he read his poem to the musician, repeated several sections of it for him in order to show him how he wished his lines to be "declaimed", and generally indicated the procedure the composer was to follow. No doubt he did something of that kind; but the respect in which *Orfeo* is held today, and consequently the very survival of Calzabigi's poem, are due not to the composer having "declaimed" the text as the poet would have had him do—on his copying, as Calzabigi says, "the nuances I put into my declamation, the suspensions, the slackening of the pace, the rapidity, the greater or less intensity and emphasis of the voice, which I desired him to employ in his composition"—but to the quality of the *music* written by Gluck. The most correct declamation in the world would not have saved the score from oblivion, and with it would have vanished the poem had the music not been what it is. Calzabigi certainly owes as much to Gluck as Gluck did to him. Even without Calzabigi, indeed, Gluck would still have been a great figure in the history of opera, whereas but for his association with Gluck, Calzabigi would today be almost forgotten. Who, apart from students who specialise in the subject, is aware even of the existence of the libretti the Italian wrote for certain other composers?

Gluck, for his part, frankly acknowledged his indebtedness to his collaborator in the famous preface to a later opera of his, *Alceste*, in 1769, in which he says that Calzabigi had "conceived a new type of lyric drama, in which flowery descriptions, futile similes, and cold, sententious moralising were to be replaced by strong passions, interesting situations, the language of the heart, and a constantly varied spectacle." Four years later, in a letter to the Paris *Mercure*, he paid still more generous tribute to his former colleague.

Ever since the middle of the seventeenth century the feeling against certain deficiences or absurdities in the dramatic basis of opera had been growing in more than one European country. But the immense literature on the subject would have been impotent to effect any substantial reform without the musical genius of Gluck: the poets and the aestheticians might have talked till they were black in the face had the *musician* not arrived just at the right time to achieve in practice what they could no more than aspire to do in theory. The situation was exactly paralleled half a century later in the case of Wagner. In the very year of Wagner's birth one Ignaz Franz Mosel published a book in which he suggested most of the later Wagnerian reforms; but had Wagner died in his childhood we should still, in all probability, be theorising very much as Mosel did, and still awaiting the coming of the great practician.

Orfeo was first given in Vienna on the 5th October 1762, under Gluck himself; Calzabigi "produced" it on the stage. The text used, of course, was the original Italian one. The Orfeo was the male contralto Gaetano Guadagni, the Euridice Marianna Bianchi, the Amor Lucia Gelbero-Claverau. Twelve years later Gluck recast the work for Paris, the French version being made by Moline. As the French stage did not use male soprani or contralti, Gluck rearranged the part of Orfeo for the tenor voice, besides making a few further alterations in, and additions to, his score.

It is an endless subject for debate whether the part of Orfeo should be sung today by a female contralto or a tenor. The advocates of the latter course insist that the drama becomes more human when the Orfeo is a man, and that the ear, as well as the eye, finds an opera with the three principal characters in it women a little monotonous. Besides, they say, did not Gluck's willingness to recast the part for a tenor show that he was not inseparably wedded to the idea of a contralto Orfeo? To this it is rejoined that if Gluck had preferred a tenor to a contralto in the Vienna production he had only to cast the part for a tenor when writing his original score: the fact that he wrote it for a contralto suggests that he saw the character in terms of contralto colour, and consequently to substitute the tenor colour for this is to alter the whole scheme of psychological as well as musical values. To this argument, in turn, it is replied that the timbre of the female contralto voice is a different thing altogether from that of the male contralto, in which the eighteenth century took such keen delight. No final solution of the problem is, or will ever be, possible.

In its new form the work was given in Paris on the 2nd August 1774, with Legros as Orfeo,[1] the brilliant, witty Sophie Arnould as Euridice, and Rosalie Levasseur as Amor. In the ballets there figured not only the two famous Vestris, père et fils, but the Mlle Guimard who was the victim of some of Sophie Arnould's brightest *mots*. Sophie seems to have regarded Mlle Guimard as more a statuesque *poseuse* than a dancer. The lady once had the misfortune to break her arm. "What a pity it wasn't her leg", said Sophie: "then it wouldn't have prevented her from dancing." It is interesting also to note that among the dancers mentioned in the French playbill of the 2nd August 1774 were the brothers Gardel. Mlle Guimard, it seems, was rather long and lanky; and Sophie Arnould said that whenever she saw her dancing a pas de trois with Gardel and another male dancer, Dauberval, it reminded her of two dogs disputing with each other the possession of a bone. We can only hope that the lady cut a better figure in Gluck's Elysian Fields than she does in the biographies of Sophie Arnould.

2

The multiform legend of Orpheus has been dealt with by Calzabigi in a way of his own; and though, while in conscious revolt against the conventions of his day, he has not been able

---

[1] As Legros insisted on something "effective" for his exit at the end of the first act he was given a bravura aria, "L'espoir renaît dans mon cœur", that was at one time believed to be the work of one Bertoni, but is now known to have been written by Gluck himself for a performance of *Orfeo* in Frankfort-on-the-Main in 1764.

entirely to free himself of them subconsciously, his poem is on the whole admirably planned for both musical and dramatic effectiveness. As the opera is always given today with a contralto Orfeo it is the original Italian version of it that we shall analyse here, with an occasional reference to the changes made in the French score.

The short overture is not one of Gluck's most distinguished efforts in this line: it merely plays the opera in, in the most general terms, without any specific reference to the drama, and without having very much to commend it musically. The real *Orfeo* begins when, after an expressive orchestral preamble of fourteen bars:

the curtain rises showing the tomb of Euridice in a vale in Thessaly: nymphs and shepherds are adorning it with flowers, while at the foot of an adjacent tree Orfeo abandons himself to his grief. From time to time he ejaculates a mournful "Euridice!":

which does not interrupt the chorus but blends with it, taking on itself the harmonic aspect of the particular moment; for example:

The orchestral colouring is at once sweet and sombre. Here, at the very commencement of the work, we can see how much greater Calzabigi's debt is to Gluck than Gluck's to him. We can visualise the poet reading this opening chorus of his to the composer and indicating, as he says, the proper scansion of the words. Gluck does indeed follow the prosodic values in the melody he puts into the mouths of the nymphs and shepherds:

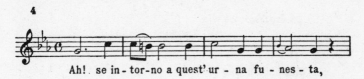

This is the soprano part: in the other three parts the composer's fidelity to the poet's prosodic pattern is still more manifest:

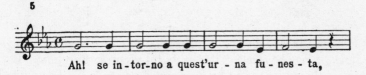

But throughout virtually the whole movement Gluck maintains in the *orchestra* the syncopated rhythmic scheme:

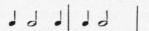

shown in example No. 1; and it is these cross-beats—a purely musical effect, beyond the powers of poetry—that before everything else give the episode its accent of grief.

Orfeo, in a short recitative, bids his companions be silent, continue their work of bedecking the tomb with flowers, and leave him undisturbed in his sorrow. They circle in solemn antique fashion about the tomb in what was called in the eighteenth century a "pantomime":

Before leaving they repeat their first strain (No. 1, etc.) in a curtailed form, and Calzabigi and Gluck show their fine sense of style by omitting this time the distracted cries of Orfeo to the beloved dead; for he is now about to make a longer, more stylised, and still more moving lament over the lost Euridice. "I call on my loved one at dawn of day and at fall of even", he sings:

(The melody is said to be an adaptation of a Czech popular song: Gluck, it may be recalled, had spent his youth in Bohemia). "But vain is all my grief: my love responds not to me." The tender cadences of his phrases are echoed softly by a few instruments behind the scenes. Orfeo continues his complaint in an expressive recitative, which also has its echo effects—it is as if all nature were listening sympathetically to him. The aria (No. 7) is repeated to other words; then there follows a third recitative, in which once more the woods and streams repeat his dolorous cries of "wretched Orfeo" and "loved Euridice", and after this comes another repetition of the aria. The whole lay-out of this opening scene of the opera is admirable in the way it preserves the one fundamental note of overwhelming grief and pain through the many variations of technical device.

A more agitated recitative follows, in which Orfeo bitterly reproaches the gods for their cruelty: he will pursue Euridice to where she now is, he says, and tear her from their keeping. Whereupon Amor (Eros) appears, to tell him that the gods, in their pity for him, will allow him to descend to Lethe; and if there he can overcome the Furies with his song, Euridice shall return to the light of day with him. But the gods impose a hard condition: until the pair have left the shores of the Styx behind them he is not to turn his eyes on her, on pain of losing her for ever. In the French version this scene is more spun out than in the Italian. In the former, Amor has two arias, in the latter only one, in which, in the "galant" musical style of the period, he exhorts Orfeo to be of good cheer:

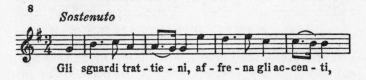

Gli sguardi trat - tie - ni, af - fre - na gli ac-cen - ti,

and the act ends with a vigorous and varied recitative, in which Orfeo affirms his resolve to dare the great adventure, and a brief orchestral postlude (*presto*) that underlines his resolution.

3

The second act takes place at the entrance to Tartarus, with the river Styx in the distance. A majestic orchestral prelude depicts at once Orfeo's resolution:

and his grief:

There follow three bars of harp arpeggios that announce the singer's coming; then the chorus of the Furies—the four voices in a hard unison—asks who is the mortal that thus dares to brave the terrors of their abode:

11
Andante

Chi mai dell' E - re - bo fral - le ca-

li - gi - ni sull' or - me d'Er - co - le

A short dance of the Furies follows this: then the chorus is repeated, with a new phrase hinting at the horrible fate of the
intruder if he be not a god:

12

D'orror l'in-gom - bri-no   le fie - re Eu-me - ni-di,

Against these harsh harmonies and colours the pleading of
Orfeo and its harp accompaniment stand out in complete contrast:

13   *Più lento*
p

Deh pla - ca - te - vi   con   me!

Fu-rie,   lar-ve,   om - bre sde - gno-se,

Between the broken phrases of his appeal to them to have pity on
his misery the Furies thunder an uncompromising "No!"—for
example, at the points represented by minim rests in the foregoing
quotation. In the orchestral basses we hear also the growling and
barking of Cerberus. The next ensemble of the Furies, however,

suggests that some spark of pity is already beginning to show itself in them. He appeals to them in still more urgent accents:

Mil - le pe - ne, om - bre sde - gno - se,

And so it continues, with further solos of Orfeo:

Men ti - ran - ne, ah! voi sa -

res - te al mio pian -to, al mio la -men -to,

and a further softening of the Furies, until at last they confess themselves vanquished by his song: their ranks divide, and the victor passes through. (In the French score Gluck inserts at this point a "pantomime" of the Furies, the music of which is drawn from his *Don Juan* ballet of 1761).

The scene changes to the Elysian Fields, which are bathed in the purest of light; some of the happy shades are dancing to a tranquil melody:

Andante

To the Paris score Gluck added for this scene a long melody for a single flute, with string accompaniment, that is without parallel for its romantic beauty in all Gluck's music; and may fairly claim to be still the loveliest of all solos for the flute. Berlioz quoted the movement in full in his treatise on the orchestra. He shows with what consummate art Gluck has exploited the peculiar timbres of the instrument. No other instrument, as Berlioz says, would be adequate to express "this very sublime lament of a suffering and despairing departed spirit." "It is at first", he continues, "a voice scarcely audible, which seems to fear to be overheard; then it laments softly, rising into the accent of reproach, then into that of profound woe, the cry of a heart torn by intolerable wounds, then falling little by little into complaint, regret, and the sorrowing murmur of a resigned soul. What a poet!"

An aria by Euridice depicts in soft lines and colours the felicity of these blest spirits:

the chorus joining in from time to time.

Orfeo enters. He is dazzled by the clearness of the light, intoxicated by the sweetness of the air, ravished by the song of the birds, in this place where all is pure contentment. Shall he find his Euridice here? he asks. His long scena, which commences with a melody in the oboe:

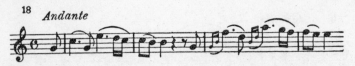

flows along suavely, unhurriedly, the orchestra supplying, in the eighteenth century manner, all kinds of pictorial touches suggested by the images aroused by the words. (This music was taken over by Gluck from a couple of his earlier works and adapted to the present situation. In the French version it underwent further modifications).

The happy spirits, in a tender chorus, lead Euridice to the impatient Orfeo: and the general joy finds expression in a dignified ballet. The act ends with a repetition of the previous chorus.

4

At the commencement of the third act we see the re-united pair in a wild region of dubious light, somewhere between the Elysian Fields and the world of men. Orfeo holds Euridice by the hand, but, true to his compact with the gods, keeps his eyes averted from her. Gluck sets the emotional tone of the long dialogue between them (in recitative) in a few preliminary bars in the orchestra that convey clearly to us that the time for the happiness of the pair is not yet. Euridice can hardly believe that she is with her lover again, and asks how this good fortune has come about: Orfeo, anxious and fearful, begs her to think of nothing but pressing on until the end of the journey is reached. After a while she begins to wonder why he is so scant of speech, why he does not embrace her, why he keeps his eyes turned away from her. Has she changed? she asks him. Is she less beautiful than of old? She implores at least one glance from him: he tells her that it would bring evil on them. She reproaches him for his coldness: it is for this, then, that the deceiver has torn her from the bliss of Elysium!

The psychological cross-currents continue in the duet that follows, in which Orfeo in vain begs Euridice to have faith in him and to hasten with him to their goal:

·19

Andante

Vie-ni,   ap - pa - ga il tuo con - sor-te

Death, she tells him, would be preferable to life with one so heartless.

The misunderstanding grows until Euridice can bear no longer the thought of having exchanged death and its serene oblivion for this living misery. She so works upon him that his resolution at last breaks down: in sheer desperation he turns his eyes on her, and at once the gods exact the penalty—she sinks dead in his arms. Orfeo pours out his grief and despair in one of the most famous of operatic arias, "Che farò senza Euridice?":

It is the tendency nowadays to regard this aria as having been over-rated by its contemporaries. The truth probably is that our singers no longer possess the style for music of this kind; and we may take it as certain that the way they sing it was not the way of Guadagni.

His aria concluded, Orfeo is on the point of slaying himself in order to follow Euridice when Amor enters, to tell him that his constancy is to have its reward. Euridice is forthwith restored to him, and while the lovers are expressing their satisfaction at this happy conclusion in brief exchanges of recitative we cannot help feeling that Calzabigi has managed the *dénouement* of his opera none too well, and that Gluck, with nothing vital to work upon here, has failed to give us the musical climax we had a right to expect. All that he and his poet can do now is to stage a brilliant ballet in a temple dedicated to Eros,—in which the happy ending of the adventure is celebrated by all the participants in the drama —and dismiss us with a final chorus in praise of Eros himself.

LAKMÉ
Delibes (1836-1891)

PRINCIPAL CHARACTERS

LAKMÉ	Soprano
MALLIKA	Mezzo-soprano
ELLEN	Soprano
ROSE	Soprano
MISTRESS BENTSON	Mezzo-soprano
GERALD	Tenor
FREDERIC	Baritone
NILAKANTHA	Bass-baritone
HADJI	Tenor

I

The life of Léo Delibes affords little scope for the biographer: he was a modest, indeed rather self-depreciating man, in whose inner existence there was nothing dramatic, and whose public life amounted to not much more than the success of two or three works, with *Lakmé* as the climax. He was a poor provincial with a liking for music who came up to Paris in his twelfth year and enrolled himself at the Conservatoire, where he seems to have troubled to learn little more than was necessary for the simplest practical purposes. When, some thirty-five years later, Ambroise Thomas, the then head of the Conservatoire, asked him to join the staff of the institution as teacher of composition, Delibes was reluctant to do so. He knew nothing, he said, of counterpoint or fugue; to which Thomas replied, "Never mind; you'll learn." Presumably he did so; for he taught "advanced composition" at the Conservatoire until his death.

He picked up some sort of a living, for a few years after his arrival in Paris, as organist, opera chorister, chorus master, theatre accompanist, and so on. Various small commissions for bits of light operas and ballets came his way, till in time he was entrusted with more important things. He established himself in the ballet world in 1870 with his charming *Coppélia*, scoring another success in the same genre six years later with *Sylvia*. Between these two works he had produced an opera, *Le Roi l'a dit*, in 1873: the political circumstances of the time rather hindered the success of this, but it sufficed to show that in this sphere also Delibes had a note of his own. In *Jean de Nivelle* (1880) he attempted something larger in scope than the normal light opera of the period, but with only partial success. He found his real vein again three years later in *Lakmé*. This was the last of his completed works: another opera, *Kassya*, was finished by Massenet, produced in 1893, and quickly forgotten. Delibes died suddenly on the 16th January 1891.

Lakmé was produced for the first time at the Opéra-Comique on the 14th April 1883. No expense was spared in the production. The decorations were sumptuous: the costumes, in particular those of the bayaderes, were as authentic as possible: and the instruments shown on the stage in one section of the ballet were copied from a genuine set presented to the Conservatoire by an Indian rajah. The first player of the part of Lakmé was Marie van Zandt, a young soprano who had already been very successful in such rôles as Mignon, Rosina, Zerlina and Cherubino, less, one gathers, in virtue of her voice than of her youthful figure, her grace and the charm of her personality. There was something exotic in her appearance that marked her out from the beginning for Lakmé; and it seems to have taken some time to convince the public that Delibes' opera was possible without her. Today the rôle seems to be regarded as the perquisite of any coloratura soprano, mainly because of the famous "Bell Song" in the second act. A genuine Lakmé, however, needs rather more than laryngeal agility and the intellectual innocence which many people look upon as the main ingredients in the make-up of the ideal coloratura soprano: a good deal of the part calls for intelligent acting and for expressive singing of music of the non-coloratura type.

Lakmé, in its original form, is an opéra-comique—that is to say, the action is carried on at times by means of spoken dialogue. Although one or two themes are employed to a small extent as "leading motives", Delibes studiously keeps clear of what were at that time regarded as dangerous modernities. He casts his music into the accepted forms of solo, duet, and so on. The style, of course, is to some extent inconsistent, with its exoticisms of tonality and harmony at this point and its conventional diatonicism at that: one seeks in vain for a convincing reason why Lakmé, for instance, should be all occidental penny-plain at one moment and all oriental twopence-coloured at another. But 'twas ever thus in operas set in a non-European milieu.

The idea of *Lakmé* seems to have originated with Edmond Gondinet, under the literary influence of Pierre Loti, then in the first flood of his enormous vogue. Delibes did not take warmly to the plan at first, but became converted to it after a reading of Loti's recent novel *Le Mariage de Loti*. The text-book of the opera was the work of Gondinet and Philippe Gille. The plot has no definite connection with any work of Loti's in particular, but flowered out of a certain type of novel which he popularised, in which a European hero—Loti himself for preference—is loved too well by a beautiful maiden of one of the inferior races. (This motive, of course, had frequently done duty in opera and elsewhere already; it is found, for instance, in Meyerbeer's *L'Africaine*. The vogue of it in the last twenty years or so of the nineteenth century was, however, almost entirely Loti's work). Their brief idyll always had an ending that dissolved the impressionable reader in tears. The maiden, as a rule, did the correct thing and died of a broken heart after the inevitable parting. The young naval lieutenant also sailed away with his heart broken, but not so badly broken as to prevent him from letting the public into the secret of his romance in a novel that could count on reaching at least its fifty-third French edition in the first year or so.

The librettists and the composer of *Lakmé* found themselves faced with a grave problem in the third act. Delibes' idea was that Lakmé should die through eating a leaf of the *datura stramonium*. Gondinet, no less proud of his botanical knowledge, insisted that the plant was non-poisonous, so that some other method of disposing of Lakmé would have to be found. Gondinet was right in his facts: the stramonium variety of the datura is grown by many an amateur gardener, who knows it, perhaps, under the homelier name of thorn apple, and is unaware that the modest little thing has ever been promoted to operatic rank. In the end Gondinet and Delibes agreed on a compromise: it was settled that while the leaves of the *datura stramonium* are quite harmless in Europe they shall be a deadly poison in India; and to forestall any scandalised toxicologist in the audience who might feel inclined to rise to his feet in the third act and protest that Lakmé would find herself in her usual sound health after her dose of datura, the remarkable distinction between the effects of it in Europe and in Asia was made clear in the first scene, as we shall see in a moment.

2

The prelude—Delibes refrains from calling it an overture—is a simple piece of work, consisting of a few themes from the opera strung together without any attempt at summarising the drama. The first is taken from the chorus of Brahmins in the second act:

The second accompanies the sacred dance in the second act:

Next there is a brief reference in the flute to Lakmé's address to the goddess Dourga:

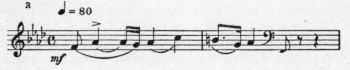

followed by the strings singing the melody of Gerald's impassioned declaration of love in Act II:

With another hint of No. 3 the prelude runs straight on into the opera.

The setting of *Lakmé* is English India, and the opera contains some pleasing pictures of the English as seen through French eyes.

An old Brahmin, Nilakantha by name, denied by the brutal English the profession of his religion, has hidden himself with his daughter Lakmé and a few of the faithful in a secluded spot where he indulges himself in dreams of vengeance on his oppressors. The opening scene shows us a shady garden, rich in flowers of every colour and surrounded by a palisade of bamboos. At the back of the stage is a small house with the lotus sign over its entrance: we see also a statue of Ganesa, the elephant-headed god of wisdom. It is dawn. Nilakantha's two faithful servants, Mallika and Hadji, open the gate to a number of Hindoos, men and women, who, after a brief orchestral preamble:

address a prayer of propitiation to Brahma. They are joined before long by Nilakantha, who is looking forward to the day when the gods will bring him deliverance and revenge. He trusts in the intercession of his daughter, whose voice is now heard within the house, invoking Dourga, Siva and Ganesa. Her melody:

which is accompanied by the twanging of harps off-stage, acquires an exotic tinge through the augmented second and the harmonies that go along with this. The prostrate Hindoos supply a choral background to her song, which is cast in the coloratura mould from first to last.

Nilakantha dismisses the worshippers, who repeat their chorus (No. 5) as they leave. The old Brahmin, to the accompaniment of a broadly-flowing melody in the clarinet:

pours out his love to the one thing dear to him in the world—his daughter, to whose favour with the gods he owes his own protection by them. He must leave her for a little while, he tells her: he must go in secret to the festival to be held next day in the near-by town, in a pagoda that is still open for their cult. Lakmé he leaves in the care of Hadji and Mallika. After he has gone, Hadji re-enters the house, while Mallika and Lakmé prepare, in a charming duet in barcarolle form:

to bathe in the sacred stream that flows by the house. Lakmé, who is troubled by a foreboding which she cannot understand, divests herself of her jewels before she goes, placing them on a stone table in the garden. She and Mallika enter a small boat that had been moored among the rushes, and the pair disappear down the stream, repeating their duet (No. 8) as they go.

From outside the garden we hear ripples of laughter, and soon the English characters of the opera appear. There are five of these. Gerald and Frederic are officers in Her Majesty's Indian Army. Ellen is the daughter of the governor of the province, and the fiancée of Gerald. Rose is Ellen's cousin and inseparable companion; while Mistress [*sic*] Bentson is Rose's governess. All are true to the British type as conceived by the average Frenchman. The governess is more or less the traditional duenna of southern comedy; she is always slightly ridiculous, always bothered about something or other, but always likable even when we are laughing at her. She speaks, in a fashion more French than English, of the day when M. le gouverneur deigned to confide to her the charge of his daughter and his niece. The others invariably address her, or speak of her, as "Mistress Bentson"; and Gerald improves even on this when he calls her, to her face, "vénérable Mistress Bentson".

The conversation between the newcomers is carried on in spoken prose. They have stumbled upon this delightful spot by accident. Frederic, who knows something of these matters, sees by the lotus leaf on the door of the house that it is the abode of a Brahmin; and he warns the others that these are dangerous people to trifle with. The girls, of course, will not listen to him: the thrill of exploring a real Brahmin's garden is more than they can resist. In spite of the protests of Mistress Bentson and the warnings of Frederic, who tells them that he has heard of the dangerous fanatic whose abode this is, Ellen and Rose, aided and abetted by Gerald, break through the bamboos into the garden. The girls admire everything they see, especially the plants and flowers. Frederic warns them not to touch certain of them. "They are daturas, Miss Ellen", he says, "*daturas stramonium*: they are quite harmless in England, but under this Indian sky you would have only to put a single leaf between your teeth and you would be poisoned." "An abominable country!" as Mistress Bentson justly remarks.

Frederic gives them the story of Nilakantha and his beautiful daughter Lakmé. The girls would very much like to see her, but Frederic explains that according to Indian notions she is divine: she shows herself to no one, and is indifferent to all that goes on outside her home. In a charming quintet the English people philosophise about the different ways of women in India and in Europe: Ellen thinks it is a sin for any woman to hide herself if she is pretty:

while Frederic explains that everything in India is peculiar:

Frederic is in the end outvoted, the sage verdict of the other four being that women are women everywhere.

Soon the girls catch sight of the jewels that Lakmé has left behind her. Frederic advises them not to touch them. They have committed profanation enough in entering the sanctuary: a Brahmin never forgets and never forgives an insult to his religion. They are in a conquered country, he reminds them. "Oui! Oui!" says the venerable Mistress Bentson, who takes the characteristic

British view of all "foreigners": "when I think how comfortable
we might be now in London, in Hyde Park, inhaling that delightful fog that gives us our clear complexions!" Gerald suggests a
compromise. He happens to be, in addition to a soldier, a romantic
and a bit of an artist; and Ellen has said she would like him to
copy the design of the jewels. "Do you, therefore, respectable
Mistress Bentson", he says, "return to the town with the others,
while I stay and copy the jewels for Miss Ellen."

As soon as Gerald is left alone in the garden he feels vaguely
troubled by its solitude and its profound quiet. He takes in his
hands one ring and clasp and armlet after another, musing the
while upon the fair owner of them, trying to recall to himself the
sober realities of his situation:

but becoming more and more the victim of the milieu and of his
romantic imagination as he proceeds:

He has just decided not to profane the objects by sketching them
when the voice of Lakmé is heard from the boat. He conceals himself. Soon Lakmé enters with Mallika; and once more their voices
unite in a prayer for the protection of Ganesa.

Mallika leaves Lakmé, who, when alone, asks herself pensively
why today all nature seems lovelier, more intoxicating than
before. She is troubled but happy:

G

Pour - quoi dans les grands bois   ai -
mé-je à m'é - ga - rer   Pour y pleu - rer?—

(This is one of the episodes that demand of the singer of the part
a capacity for expression and a command of vocal colour that are
not generally in the equipment of the coloratura soprano pure and
simple).

As she finishes her meditation she catches sight of Gerald and
gives a frightened cry that brings Hadji and Mallika rushing to her
aid. Recovering her poise, she dismisses them with a reassuring
word or two and then turns to Gerald, whose infatuation she can
read in his eyes. She warns him of his danger: a word from her a
moment ago and he would have been killed in front of her. She
bids him go: the place where he is is sacred, and she herself is
a daughter of the gods. He refuses to leave her. Ignorant of the
world as she is, she wonders what it can be that gives him the
superhuman courage to brave a terrible death in this way: what
god is it that sustains him? "The god of love, the god of spring!",
is his reply:

C'est   le   Dieu   de   la   jeu -
nes - se, C'est   le   Dieu   du   prin - temps,

Lakmé is vanquished. But while their voices are blending to the
strain of No. 14 she hears her father approaching with Hadji and

others. Nilakantha sees the breach in the palisade and catches a glimpse of the fleeing Gerald; and the act ends with a cry of vengeance from the Hindoos.

3

The scene of the second act is a square in the city, with a pagoda in the background. On the right is an awning in front of a refreshment house, with bamboo chairs and little tables all about. The stage is filled with a motley crowd of promenaders, sailors, and traders of all kinds crying their wares. A brief orchestral interlude, with its drums and fifes (two piccolos):

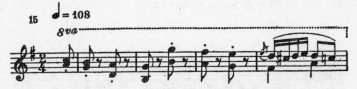

is a reminder that there is a British regiment marching past.

The scene opens with a lively chorus in which the vendors or every variety of goods recommend them to possible customers:

Everybody is very gay except the venerable and respectable Mistress Bentson, who has got separated from her party, is jostled by all sorts of shady characters, and has her watch purloined by a sepoy:

A fortune-teller offers to read her venerable and respectable hand. An optimistic merchant tries to sell her an elixir of youth and beauty. At last she is rescued by Gerald and the others, and the charming scene ends with a repetition of the chorus of vendors.

The market is closing and the fête commencing: the crowd is now about to enjoy itself, as is hinted at in the careless little No. 17 in the orchestra, which accompanies the talk of the English group. Frederic informs Mistress Bentson that the bayaderes are going to dance, discreetly explaining, in answer to her enquiry, that they are vestals, of a sort, attached to the pagoda. All is now ready for the ballet, which consists of four divertissements in varied musical styles, including a slow exotic terana:

a vivacious rektah:

and a Persian dance with appropriate melodic arabesques and unusual harmonies.

As the dancers leave the stage, Nilakantha enters disguised, accompanied by Lakmé: Frederic explains to his friends that it is a mendicant monk, attracted to the fête by the hope of gain, the function of the girl being to regale the crowd with one of the dramatic narrations in which the Hindoos delight. They hark back to the adventure of the garden. Gerald is quiet and thoughtful. He admits that he had seen the Brahmin's daughter; but to Ellen's eager enquiry whether she was beautiful he replies only that she was "strange". Frederic tells him, out of hearing of the ladies, that their regiment is to march at three o'clock next morning against the rebels. Gerald leaves with Ellen and the governess, followed in a little while by Frederic and Rose.

Nilakantha, to the accompaniment of the Dourga motive (No. 3), keeps up, with the crowd, the pose of a poor mendicant monk, but all the time his eyes are searching for the barbarian who had desecrated his sanctuary. Sadly and tenderly he tells Lakmé all that she is to him:

The intruder, he knows, would not have risked death had he not loved Lakmé. She is therefore to sing, and when the barbarian hears her his eyes will betray him. Beginning with a series of improvisatory roulades designed to attract the attention of the crowd, she sings, at her father's command, the legend of the pariah's daughter. This is the famous Bell Song.[1] It tells of an Indian maiden, a pariah:

[1] As *Lakmé* is sometimes put on today merely in order that a star soprano may show herself off in the Bell Song, it is interesting to recall that in the 1880's the number was almost universally condemned by the critics as being merely a display of vocal virtuosity for its own sake.

who is shunned and repulsed by all. In the depths of the dark forest she sees one day a lost traveller surrounded by wild beasts waiting for their prey:

22

Allegro moderato

Là-bas dans la fo-rêt plus som-bre,

Quel est ce voy-a-geur per - du?

"He is fairer than any rajah! Alas, he would be shamed did he know that he owed his life to a pariah woman!" She will save him by charming the savage beasts with the little bells she carries with her. But the stranger is not a mortal but the god Vishnu, the son of Brahma, who casts his enchantment on her and transports her with him to the skies; and ever since that day the traveller in the forest hears the tinkle of the charm-bells. The aria is rich in quasi-oriental orchestral and coloratura effects, among them an imitation of the bells by the voice, to the syllable "Ah!":

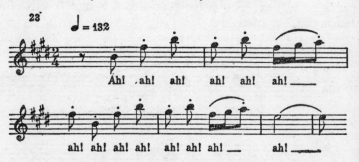

23

$\downarrow = 132$

Ah! ah! ah! ah! ah! ah! ____

ah! ah! ah! ah! ah! ah! ah! __ ah! ____

Nilakantha, scanning the spectators, can see no one making the emotional response he expects; and at his bidding Lakmé resumes her song just as a number of British officers, Gerald and Frederic among them, appear on the scene. Lakmé perceives Gerald, and in her emotion has difficulty in continuing, in spite of

the constant urging of her father. Her song breaks off in a wild
cry, and it seems as if she would faint. Gerald, rushing to the
singer's aid, discovers that it is Lakmé. She recovers in a moment
and makes a desperate effort to continue her song. But Nilakantha has seen it all: the barbarian has betrayed himself, and the
rest will be easy. In the distance are heard the drums and fifes of
the English troops (No. 15), who are soon seen marching across
the background. Gerald allows himself to be dragged away by
Frederic. The crowd runs after the soldiers, and the stage is left to
Nilakantha and his followers, who elaborate their scheme for
revenge. Later in the evening, when the crowd is intent on the
procession of the goddess, a number of them are to isolate the
victim from his companions: the rest can be left to Nilakantha.
Lakmé begs to be allowed to accompany her father, but he refuses, as she might cause him to weaken when the moment for the
avenging blow has arrived. He leaves her with the faithful old
Hadji, who, realising her distress, out of his love for her offers to
serve her in whatever she may command, be it an enemy to be
injured or a friend to be saved.

As he leaves at her bidding, Gerald enters. There is a long and
passionate duet between the pair:

24   ♩ = 132

Dans le va-gue d'un rê-ve Je t'ai vue en pas-sant.

in which Gerald draws from her a confession of her love for him,
though her god, she reminds him, is not his; the music reaches its
climax with the theme already quoted as No. 4 of the prelude. Near
her house, she tells him, there is hidden a little hut in the forest,
under the shelter of a great tree, known to no one but herself:

25   ♩ = 63

Dans la forêt près de nous, Se cache toute pe-ti-te,

Thither he is to follow her, and there she will come in secret each day to see him. He pleads that honour and duty call him to his regiment: she rejoins that she would not have him die. Their duet is cut short by the arrival of the spectators who have come to see the procession of the Dourga image. Lakmé, catching sight of her father, leaves Gerald, who rejoins his English companions when, to the sacred dance motive (No. 2) in the orchestra, the procession comes into sight, headed by the priests and accompanied by the temple dancers. The Brahmins sing an impressive invocation to the goddess:

as, with the bayaderes, they pass into the pagoda.

While Ellen and Rose are expressing their naïve delight in the spectacle, and Mistress Bentson is wondering how anyone can be so foolish as to lose his head over a goddess with ten arms, Frederic amicably rallies Gerald on his infatuation for the Brahmin's daughter: he might, he says, be really anxious about him were the regiment not leaving for duty the next day. By this time night is falling. The procession pours out of the pagoda again, the Brahmins now bearing the statue of Dourga in a palanquin. Torches light up the scene. The sacred dances are resumed, together with another massive chorus to the goddess (No. 26). Gerald's enemies meanwhile have marked down their prey. He is irresistibly drawn to Lakmé again, conscious once more of nothing but her beauty. Nilakantha stealthily follows him, strikes him down, and escapes among the crowd. Lakmé runs to Gerald and bends over him. Her face becomes transfigured as she realises that his wound is not dangerous: now he will be hers for ever. She summons Hadji, who helps her to remove the fainting man.

4

The orchestral entr'acte that precedes the rising of the curtain for the third act is mainly based on the gentle, lulling theme:

that accompanied Lakmé's short monologue at the end of the preceding act. The final scene takes place by the hut in the forest of which Lakmé had told Gerald: it is almost lost in a profusion of acacias, tulip trees and daturas. Gerald is lying on a couch of leaves, with Lakmé singing a lullaby over him:

He wakes, but can only dimly recall what has happened. She helps out his feeble memory: Hadji had carried him here, and she herself

brought him back to life by her knowledge of the healing properties of plants. He will live there for ever with her, he promises,
in the profound peace of the forest, both of them forgetting the
world without:

She, for her part, will teach him the legends of her gods, the gods
who have united them. In the distance they hear a chorus of happy
lovers visiting the sacred spring near by: Lakmé explains that
when two people have drunk of it from the same cup they belong
to each other for ever, and the gods bless their love:

As she leaves him to go to the spring herself, Frederic enters:
he has succeeded in following the track of his friend through the
tall ferns by his blood. He warns Gerald of the danger of an
attachment of this impossible kind, but the young man is now the
slave of Lakmé's enchantment. It is only when Frederic appeals to
his honour as a soldier that Gerald becomes sobered: he will be
with the regiment, he promises, at dawn the next day. Satisfied
with this assurance, Frederic leaves him as Lakmé is seen returning.

She has brought with her a cup of the sacred water. She is
describing ecstatically the happiness of the pledged couples at
the spring when she becomes aware of a change in Gerald. He
responds in indulgent European fashion to her grave question

whether he wishes his destiny to be for ever blended with hers: he is ready to do anything, he assures her, to gratify a caprice of hers and to see her smile. Reminding him of the solemn nature of the pledging in the sacred water she holds out the cup to him, bidding him swear to love her always. But at that moment the regimental march (No. 15) is heard in the distance. Gerald hesitates, and Lakmé sees that all is over: he will not even allow his downcast eyes to meet hers. Sadly she lays down the cup, and then, in an access of despair, tears off a datura leaf and chews it unperceived by him, the orchestra meanwhile giving out the motive of Lakmé as priestess of Dourga (No. 3). She thanks him for the divine dream he has given her, brief as it has been:

Something in her eyes frightens him, and he swears that come what may he will remain hers. She raises the cup to her lips, drinks from it, and hands it to him: it is the festival of their love, she tells him. He drains it in exaltation:

and their voices blend for the last time. Then she discloses to him that she has taken poison, and nought remains but to die in his arms.

Nilakantha rushes in, and the desperate Gerald bids him strike home; but Lakmé checks the old fanatic with the confession that she and the stranger have drunk together from the ivory cup. Gerald therefore is now sacred; if the gods still desire vengeance, they have an expiatory victim in her. She dies with a smile on her lips, singing No. 31 once more; while Nilakantha becomes transfigured as, in a final solemn phrase, he announces her reception in the skies.

LES HUGUENOTS
Meyerbeer (1791-1864)

PRINCIPAL CHARACTERS

VALENTINE	*Soprano*
MARGUERITE DE VALOIS	*Soprano*
URBAIN	*Soprano*
RAOUL DE NANGIS	*Tenor*
MARCEL	*Bass*
COMTE DE SAINT-BRIS	*Bass*
COMTE DE NEVERS	*Baritone*
BOIS-ROSÉ	*Tenor*

I

Meyerbeer, in the opinion of some people, was not so much a composer as a composite. The successive metamorphoses of his name are symbolical of his whole career, with its cool material calculations, its prudent trimming of sails, and its occasional ironic futilities. He began life, in 1791, as a Prussian Jew of the name of Jakob Liebmann Beer. His maternal grandfather, the rich Berlin banker Liebmann Meyer Wulf, guaranteed the promising boy, in his will, an income of some 300,000 francs for life in order that he might devote himself entirely to music—on the sole condition that he should add Meyer to his name. For a while, then, Jakob Beer went about the world as Meyer-Beer. When his youthful hopes became centred in the Italian stage he converted Jakob into Giacomo, and abolished the hyphen between his two surnames. Then, having half-Italianised himself in this fashion, he left Italy, made Paris his spiritual home, and became the leading light of French "grand opera"; while the King of Prussia made this international composite the musical head of the German national opera in Berlin, though his duties there were for a large part of the time merely nominal.

A similar eclecticism characterised everything he did. He began as one of the rising hopes of German music, studying under

Clementi for the piano, and for composition first under Bernhard Anselm Weber, the Berlin Kapellmeister, and then with the famous Abbé Vogler in Darmstadt, where one of his fellow-students was Carl Maria von Weber, later to achieve immortality as the composer of *Der Freischütz*. Some early attempts at opera-writing having failed in Munich, Stuttgart and Vienna, Meyerbeer decided to try his fortune in Italy, where, between 1818 and 1823, he had considerable success in the theatre. In the latter year he returned to Berlin, where he found, to his chagrin, that his cautious compatriots placed little value on his triumphs in the south; and some of his friends, notably Weber, urged him to try to fulfil the hopes they had built on him as a *German* composer. But Meyerbeer's eyes were already turned longingly on Paris, which was at that time the centre of the European operatic world. Paris alone could offer everything he desired in the way of "effect", which was always the first consideration with Meyerbeer. Paris, with its long dramatic tradition, insisted on a certain degree of literary substance even in such a thing as an opera libretto. Paris was rich enough to command the services of the best singers, orchestral players, designers and decorators. Finally, the last thing Paris would ask of Meyerbeer would be to follow in the footsteps of Beethoven and write what the French of that epoch called "learned" music. Paris loved effect; and effect, Meyerbeer already felt in his bones, was his leading suit.

His opening move in Paris—in September 1825—was with *Il Crociato in Egitto*, which had already been given in Italy. It was only moderately successful, but, oddly enough, this half-success made the Berlin authorities think that after all this young townsman of theirs might be worth cultivating. Meyerbeer's fate, however, was to be decided not in Berlin but in Paris, and that comparatively soon. The French public was in the mood just then for something different from its usual fare, without quite knowing what, except that it would have to be something "actual", "contemporary". The "classical" spirit in French opera, of which Gluck had been the leading representative for so many years, had virtually spent itself by the eighteen-thirties. The public taste was veering round towards a mixture of the remotely romantic and the immediately topical: in favour of the latter was the growing political and social unrest of the epoch that followed the collapse of Napoleon's empire. A significant sign of the times was the excitement caused by Auber's *Masaniello* (1828)—the story of a popular rising against a tyrant in Naples in 1647: it was after a performance of this work in Brussels in 1830 that the riots began which ended in the expulsion of the Dutch. In 1829 came another historical—or near-historical—opera, Rossini's *William Tell*, the central motive of which is again the rights of man against his oppressors. Into this atmosphere of nervous excitement Meyerbeer plunged with his *Robert the Devil* in 1831. The romanticism of this was so pungent as to have the very tang of contemporaneous actuality; and the success of the work was surpassed only by that of *Les Huguenots* five years later. With this latter, Meyerbeer became unquestionably the leading figure of the operatic world.

2

We ask ourselves today, in some astonishment, how it ever came about that a man with so many and such obvious defects as an artist managed to capture the interest and bulldoze the critical faculty of his own generation as he did. The explanation, however, is simple: for his own generation, what we now regard as his failings constituted his supreme virtues. We of today reproach him for his "eclecticism": but it was precisely because he was "un génie *composé*", as an adoring critic of the 1860's called him, that he seemed to his contemporaries to symbolise the very soul of the epoch. For that age prided itself on being "intelligent" beyond any of its predecessors. It demanded of its composers that they should be capable of something more than merely writing music. They had to be thinkers as well; and the great thinker among musicians was held to be Meyerbeer. From his stage interpreters also the age demanded gifts of much the same order. It was not enough that they should charm men's ears with the sensuous beauty of their voices; they must further be able to drive home the "ideas" of the particular Meyerbeer opera in which they happened to be singing. Meyerbeer, in fact, was the acknowledged epitome of his epoch—nay, more than its epitome, its leader, for he was regarded as not merely "marching with the times" but striding far ahead of them.

This estimate of Meyerbeer was not that of the easily gulled theatre mob alone but of many of the most intelligent people of the second and third quarters of the nineteenth century. Meyerbeer, they maintained, had not merely, like some of his predecessors, created individual characters in opera; he had depicted masses, tendencies, historical forces, general ideas. Heine, in 1837, wrote that Meyerbeer "is the man of his epoch, and the epoch, that always knows how to choose its man, has tumultuously raised him on its shield, has proclaimed his overlordship, and celebrates in him its own joyous entry into possession." In the hero of *Robert the Devil* the generation of 1830 recognised itself— the then "modern" individual who, as Heine put it, "does not know precisely what it is he wants, who is in perpetual conflict with himself" . . . "the very symbol of an epoch that was vacillating restlessly and painfully between virtue and vice, fretting itself in endeavours and galling itself against obstacles, and, like Robert, sometimes lacking the strength to withstand the assaults of the devil."

That generation, in fact, failed, as so many other generations have done, to grasp the seeming paradox that in art the surest way to go out of date fairly soon after your death is to be terrifically up to date during your lifetime. Bach is the classical proof of this: regarded by the younger generation in his own day, for the most part, as an old fogey addicted to obsolete literary ways and discredited musical means, he continues to be the contemporary of each successive age, while many of his colleagues who were the palpitating moderns of their own day are now not much more than interesting museum pieces. Wagner himself, even as late as the 1860's and 1870's, was regarded in some German quarters as having damaged his prospects of survival by not being sufficiently abreast of his time, harking back for his subjects to the legends of the Middle Ages instead of deriving them from contemporary life or from authentic history. Adolf Bernhard Marx, in 1855, gravely doubted whether operas like *Tannhäuser* and *Lohengrin* would be able to survive such deplorably outmoded legends. "Impossible!" he cried. "These sagas and fables of the wicked enchantress Venus and the Holy Grail, with their clash of weapons, their worthy heroes, their ordeals by combat, come to us now only as the echo of long-dead times that are quite foreign to our spirit."

3

It is popularly supposed that Meyerbeer acquired his successes by purchase, and particularly by bribery of the Press. It is true that he used his large fortune not only to buy the best of everything for his works inside the theatre but also to secure for them in advance the goodwill of the critics. His *diners de la veille*—the forethoughtful entertainment of the Press a day or two before the curtain was to rise on a new work of his—were notorious everywhere; and many a worthy journalist's wife was able to boast of a piece of jewellery that might never have fallen to her lot had not Meyerbeer been both a composer of operas and a wealthy man. Heine, who himself had benefited handsomely by his compatriot's generosity, and who, like the brilliant blackguard he was, did not hesitate to denigrate his benefactor when he found him resisting further blackmail, put it that "Meyerbeer will be immortal during his lifetime and perhaps for a little while after, for he always pays in advance." Popularity such as that of Meyerbeer, however, could never have been wholly acquired by mere purchase. The public adored him not because the critics praised him but because he gave it what it wanted—subjects that appealed to its passion for "actuality" in the theatre, plus a wealth and variety of effect, and a skill in the manipulation of it, that left his competitors far behind.

That many of the effects were there for their own and Meyerbeer's sake rather than for the sake of the opera as a work of art—that they were, as Wagner said, "effects without causes"—was not always so evident to that generation as it is to a later day. There was little in a Meyerbeer opera that was not coolly, even coldly, calculated. He was under no illusion as to his own limitations: he had had too good a schooling under Vogler not to be aware what was beyond him in composition, and would always be beyond him. He knew that the extended logical evolution of a musical idea was not his strong point: therefore he took good care never to land himself in a situation where it would be demanded of him. Like a character in one of Bernard Shaw's plays, he believed that if one has a fault one should make a virtue of it. And so, as his talent was mostly for small detached pungencies of expression, he saw to it that his scores were full of these, and that his librettists presented him with endless opportunities for them. He believed in providing from the shelves of his universal stores a little of everything for each one of his possible customers,[1] in allowing them just time enough to be smitten by an effect and then diverting their attention to another before they had time to become too critical of the first. The too frequent trouble was that he either lacked or drugged the faculty of self-criticism that might have warned him that too many of his effects were of so cheap an order that they were bound to be found out before long.

He was not, as his admiring contemporaries imagined, a great dramatist but only a cunning craftsman of the theatre—the theatre, that is to say, as it was in his day. He pondered long over several of his works, holding them back year after year from completion and then from production, not because of any passion for the supreme perfection of inner logic, but merely because he was uncertain about this contemplated effect or that and wanted to make sure, or because he was hopeful that he or his librettist would one of these days light upon a more striking new effect to replace an old one. He hoarded in his memory and carefully docketed for future use every novel effort of orchestration he chanced to hear, and incessantly exercised his restless brain upon some new combination or other of colours; till at last, being sure of it and of the means by which to realise it, he would make a place for it willy-nilly in his score, the colour thus being, in many instances, not an emanation from the psychological situation but the cause and origin of it. He himself confessed that he was never fully sure of anything in a work of his until he heard it. At rehearsal he would sit in his stage box with his score in front of him and his pencil in his hand, trying to place himself at the mental point of view of the average man in the average audience, ear-marking this or that phrase, this or that episode, for alteration

---

[1] "A monstrous motley, historico-romantic, diabolico-religious, fanatico-libidinous, sacro-frivolous, mysterious-brazen, sentimental-humbugging dramatic hotch-potch" is Wagner's description of the type of "drama" with which Meyerbeer insisted on his librettists supplying him.

because it seemed to his coldly calculating eye and ear to fall short of the desired "effect". And even when his work was really finished he would hold it back from the theatres until he was sure he had found the interpreters who seemed to him to have been created by nature expressly for it.

4

On the whole, *Les Huguenots* is his best work. The fourth act is generally admitted to be not only the finest of the five but the best thing Meyerbeer ever achieved. Even Wagner could find in his heart to praise certain features of it, notably the duet between the lovers Raoul and Valentine; and it is ironically characteristic of Meyerbeer that this scene was an afterthought, suggested to him by the tenor Nourrit after the rehearsals had commenced. The "poet" of *Les Huguenots* was Eugène Scribe, the most indefatigable libretto manufacturer of that epoch. Scribe, as an opera "poet", lived in a strange world of his own, in which any situation, any motive, any psychology was valid so long as it avoided too close contact with common sense. He knew all the rules of the game as the composers and audiences of that day had agreed to play it, and he could turn out the appropriate doggerel in any quantity with the utmost facility at the shortest notice. Meyerbeer, of course, co-operated with him in the texts to which he was to supply the music, suggesting an addition here, an omission there, a modification in some other place, all for the sake of greater "effect"; and though the amour-propre of the great Scribe was occasionally wounded, he always found it politic to fall in with the wishes of the recognised dictator of grand opera. Wagner was right, in the main, when he said that Scribe's Meyerbeer libretti are his worst—"the silliest bombast, the lamest galimathias: actions without happenings, situations of the most insane confusion, characters of the most absurd caricature"—all because Meyerbeer had in mind, at this point or that, some effect or other of surprise, of contrast, of rhythm or of colour, for the exploitation of which he demanded the necessary words.

Both Scribe and Meyerbeer were perhaps born a century too soon: in these days they would have found the ideal sphere for the exhibition of their peculiar talents in Hollywood. The films would have been the perfect instrument for the realisation of their sound commercial policy of a bit of everything for everybody, and the more sensational the better. In *Robert the Devil*, Meyerbeer had sent a thrill through his audience by a scene in the third act in which certain nuns who, when they were alive, had forgotten the lessons learned at their mothers' knees, rise from the dead and indulge in a voluptuous ballet. In *Le Prophète* (1849) there is a ballet of skaters. The connection of these people with the world of the Dutch Anabaptists of the mid-sixteenth century is not very obvious, and indeed they did not appear in Meyerbeer's original score, which had been finished about 1843. But not long before the production of the opera the inventor of the roller skate had been delighting the Parisians night after night with a demonstration of the giddy delights to be had from his invention, and Meyerbeer thought the effect too good to be neglected: so in his new opera there had to be inserted a skating ballet.[1] In *Les Huguenots* he had what in itself was an excellent subject in the conflict of the Catholic and Protestant faiths, a subject, moreover, palpitatingly up to date, for religious controversy had sprung up once more in France in the 1830's. But Meyerbeer seems to have reflected that while not every Frenchman was interested in sects, every Frenchman worthy of the name was sure to be interested in sex; and so he graced the second act of this religious drama of his with a display of bathing belles. The Universal Provider was never at a loss for something that would be sure to pack the house.

5

The first performance of *Les Huguenots* took place in the Paris Opéra on the 29th February 1836. No money had been spared

[1] In *L'Étoile du Nord* (1854) Peter the Great of Russia plays the flute—not for any historical reason but because this opera in its first form, as *Ein Feldlager in Schlesien* (1844), had contained a couple of solos "off" for Frederick the Great of Prussia, who, as everyone knows, prided himself on his flute-playing. When the scene of the opera was transferred from Prussia to Finland and Russia, and the German Frederick became metamorphosed into the Tsar Peter, Meyerbeer thought the flute effects too good to be sacrificed, so he blandly had opportunities made for them in his new score.

to make the *mise en scène* as brilliant as any that Paris had yet seen. The Raoul was Adolphe Nourrit, the leading French tenor of the day. Maria Falcon was the Valentine, Mme Dorus-Gras the Marguerite, and Nicolas Prosper Levasseur, of whom more will be said later, the Marcel.

The action of the opera takes place in August 1572. Of the eight civil wars of religion that racked France in the second half of the sixteenth century, the third, which had begun in 1568, had been terminated in 1570 by the Peace of Saint-Germain, under which the French Protestants were assured toleration. In 1572 Marguerite, the sister of King Charles IX of France, married in Paris Henri of Bourbon, son of the Huguenot Queen of Navarre. A number of Protestant notables attended the wedding, among them the Admiral Coligny. A week or so after the ceremony, on the night of St. Bartholomew, the Catholics rose and massacred some thousands of their rival religionists, Coligny among them. It is in this atmosphere of religious fanaticism that the main action of *Les Huguenots* is set.

For his overture—or rather prelude—Meyerbeer relies entirely on the chorale "Ein' feste Burg", which he uses throughout the opera as the symbol of militant Protestantism:

1

The melody is familiar enough to everyone today, Protestant or Catholic, but it seems to have been a novelty to the Parisians of 1836: a note in the score, indeed, informed the French reader that "the melody of this chorale is by Luther, and dates from 1530." Meyerbeer does not do much more with the chorale in the overture than dish it up several times in harmonies of his own which by no means show it to the best advantage, either musical or religious, and with alternations of *pianissimo* and *fortissimo* that may add to its theatrical effect but certainly not to its dignity. He further annoyed his German contemporaries by quickening the pace of it towards the finish:

and in other ways "hotting it up" so as to make it run more or less smoothly into the music of his opening scene.

The first act takes place in Touraine, in the early days of August 1572. The curtain rises on a room in the château of the Comte de Nevers, a gay young Catholic nobleman; at the back, great open windows give us a view of the gardens, and of a lawn in which a number of gentlemen are playing a ball game. (That, at least was the original intention of Scribe and Meyerbeer. But this piece of realism had to be dropped, because it was found at rehearsal that the players could not hit the ball in time with the corresponding effects in the orchestra). In the front of the stage are Nevers and a choice collection of young bloods of his own type—Cossé, Thoré, Tavannes, de Retz, Méru and others—busy with dice and other games. Nevers leads the others in a song in praise of youth and the pleasures appropriate to it:

"Let us consecrate our lives to gaming and folly, forgetting everything but pleasure", is their simple philosophy of existence:

The chorus finished, Tavannes asks their host why dinner is so long delayed. Nevers' reply is that he is awaiting yet another guest, a young gentleman who has just obtained an appointment in the lansquenets by the influence of Admiral Coligny. That name of itself raises in the company the suspicion that the new-comer is a Huguenot:

Nevers agrees, but begs them not to be prejudiced against the young man on that account: is not the King himself doing his best to reconcile the two faiths, and have not the Protestant Coligny and the Catholic Catharine de Médicis, mother of the King, solemnly sworn eternal peace? The nobles, being men of the world, are much amused at this "eternal peace": eternal as it may be, they comment ironically, it will not last long:

The two little episodes illustrated by our quotations 5 and 6 are excellent examples of Meyerbeer's technical skill in securing points of contrast at the same time that he keeps the action and the music in constant movement.

While the cynical noblemen are promising themselves the pleasure of taking in hand the education of this disciple of Calvin and converting him to the cult of "the only true gods, love and pleasure", the gentleman himself, Raoul de Nangis, makes his appearance. He introduces himself to Nevers with a modest allusion to the honour which he, a simple soldier, feels in being admitted to such brilliant company: Meyerbeer places in his mouth a sober strain that is in marked contrast to the light-hearted, cynical music of Nevers and his associates:

The latter are favourably impressed by Raoul's appearance and demeanour; they think him, to be sure, a trifle provincial, but under their skilled tuition and with the benefit of their example he will soon improve.

Servants bring in a table laden with delicacies, at which Nevers and his friends seat themselves, singing, as they do so, a chorus in praise of wine:

which becomes more and more orgiastic as it proceeds:

10 *Presto*

De la Tou-rai - ne Ver-sez les vins,

Nevers gives them a toast, "Our mistresses!", inviting Raoul
to join in it. For his own part, Nevers explains, he is on the point
of bidding farewell to love, for he is now committed to matrimony
—a fact which, ever since it became known among the ladies of
the court, has increased embarrassingly his popularity with them:
never, he complacently assures his friends, has he been so pursued.
He suggests that each of them shall tell the story of his amours,
commencing with the latest addition to their circle. Raoul
smilingly consents, though, it appears, he knows neither the name
nor the station of the lady he loves. He describes to the company
how one day in Amboise he saw a rich litter approaching. It was
surrounded by a band of students who began to embarrass the
occupant: Raoul drove them off, approached the litter, and was
dazzled by the beauty of the lady within. He sings her praises in
the romance "Plus blanche que la blanche hermine":

11 *Andante* ♪ = 126

Plus blan - che - que la blanche hermi   ne

which Meyerbeer accompanies with an obbligato for the viola
d'amore that won the admiration of Berlioz, who, in his treatise
on orchestration, quotes in its entirety the instrumental prelude
to the romance as an illustration of the effects that can be drawn
from this expressive instrument under the hand of a master of
colour.

The burden of Raoul's song is that he there and then vowed to
himself eternal homage to the "angel or mortal" he beheld that
day, who is still as completely unknown to him as she was then.
Nevers and his friends, of course, make merry over so naïve a
story: the idealism of it is something outside not only their
practice but their comprehension.

Just then there appears in the background a strange-looking
creature whom Raoul introduces to the company as an ancient
servant of his house. It is Marcel, a tough old warrior and bigot
whom Meyerbeer puts before us as the incarnation of uncompromising Protestantism. Marcel will have no truck with Catholics, or indeed with anyone, Catholic or Protestant, who prefers
a merry life to a religious one: his first words to his master are to
reproach him for sitting at the table of the ungodly, his second, to
describe the gay company as "the camp of the Philistines":

Raoul apologises for this rough old retainer of his; he was brought
up by Raoul's grandfather, it seems, "between a sword and the
Bible, taught to swear only by Luther, and to hold in equal horror
love, the Pope, and hell—faithful but inflexible, a rough diamond
set in iron." Throughout the score Marcel's part has an orchestral
colouring of its own, bold, biting, sometimes aggressively
harsh.

At the command of his master, Marcel moves some distance
away from the revellers, but a remark of Nevers' about "nos
maîtresses" and "leurs vives tendresses" goads him to make one
more effort to save Raoul from perdition. With this object in view

he breaks into "Ein' feste Burg", the first words and notes of
which are sufficient to make Raoul lower his eyes in confusion and
put down his glass:

Meyerbeer was not content with the simple stark effect of this
solemn melody, contrasting as it so markedly does with everything that has preceded it in the opera. He must needs load it with
one theatrical effect after another of his own. One of these effects
consists in making Marcel deliver the lines of the chorale alternately *fortissimo* and *pianissimo*, as had been done in the overture.
For the end of the hymn Meyerbeer has a further effect up his
sleeve: Marcel descends note by note *pianissimo* from the middle
C to the low E, from which point he makes a quick ascent to the
higher E, *via* a trill and a big *crescendo* followed by a *diminuendo*:

The explanation of this somewhat odd procedure is to be sought not in the psychology of Marcel but in the voice of the first player of the part. Levasseur had a particularly powerful bass voice, of exceptional range, and capable of sudden changes of colour; and Meyerbeer knew perfectly well when to play so sure a winning card as this with the Parisian public of 1836. If he ever reflected that for the most part he was making Marcel so purely theatrical a figure that he almost ceases to be dramatic—or rarely rises to the dramatic,—that thought, we may be sure, did not greatly worry him. The effect of the moment was all that interested him.

The German chorale might have been enough to characterise Marcel and the Protestant faith. But it was not sufficient to display Levasseur; so a pretext has now to be found for letting the singer exploit his powers in another way. Cossé recognises Marcel as the tough old warrior who, during the fight at La Rochelle, had dealt him a wound of which he still bears the scar. Cossé, who feels no ill will, good-naturedly invites Marcel to drink with him. Marcel, of course, refuses with pious horror. Thereupon Nevers intervenes: "If he will not drink, let him sing", he says. Marcel snatches joyously at this "cue for song": he will give them, he says, a ditty the Protestants used to sing at La Rochelle, to the accompaniment of the drums, the cymbals, and the "piff, paff, pouf" of bullets. This "chanson huguenote" as it is called in the score, was one of the most admired of Meyerbeerian *tours de force* in its own day. Marcel begins by miming the action of firing, accompanying each pull of the trigger with a "piff, paff, piff, paff" now in the lower, now in the higher octave, for all the world as if he were not Marcel but Levasseur. The song itself is an outpouring of implacable hatred of the Catholics, and a refusal to grant quarter to any of them, monks, nuns, or "the Delilahs who imperil men's souls":

15   *Allegretto*   ♪ = 176

Pour les   cou-vents c'est fi-ni! Les moines à   ter-re,

Each stanza terminates with a pungent fantasia on "piff, paff":

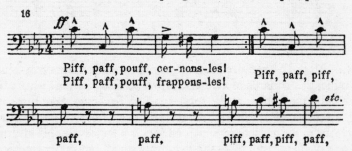

Piff, paff, pouff, cer-nons-les!
Piff, paff, pouff, frappons-les!   Piff, paff, piff,

paff,   paff,   piff, paff, piff, paff,

The reactions of the Catholic noblemen to the "chanson huguenote" are not disclosed; for no sooner has Marcel finished his second couplet than a servant of the Comte de Nevers appears in the background, conducting a veiled lady, who disappears into the garden. The servant informs Nevers that some one desires to speak with him. Nevers, who is by this time pleasantly warmed with wine, swears that not for the King, not even for the ruler of the universe himself, would he put himself out when at table with his friends.

But when the servant tells him that it is "a young beauty" who wishes to see him, his tone changes: it is unbelievable, he complacently remarks to his friends, how the women persecute him with their attentions. Is it the Marquise d'Entrague this time, he asks, or "the young Countess", or possibly Madame de Raincy? He becomes really keen about the visitor only when the valet tells him that he has not seen the lady before: a "new conquest" is worth following up, if only out of "curiosity". Begging his friends to continue their "joyous orgy", which "love" has only temporarily interrupted, he goes out with the servant.

The gentlemen comment lightheartedly but a trifle enviously on Nevers' good fortune:

L'a - ven - ture est sin - gu - liè - re,

Tout   lui   cède, et   sûr   de   plai - re,

while Marcel once more laments his master's lapse from true-blue Huguenot standards of virtue. Curious to discover the identity of the lady, the nobles, at the suggestion of Tavannes, take turns in looking out of a window on the left that affords a view of an oratory in the garden, in which Nevers is interviewing his visitor. None of them recognises the lady, though all praise her face and figure. The only member of the party not the least interested in all this is Raoul. At last, merely to satisfy Tavannes, who has rallied him on his Protestant indifference to female charms, he lets himself be persuaded to go to the window. He recoils angrily. The lady is the one he had rescued at Amboise, and to whom he had sworn eternal allegiance; now he finds her *tête à tête* with a libertine like Nevers. His love instantly turns to fury: he swears he will be revenged for this perfidy, the while the others, men of the world, mock at his innocent ardours.

Nevers and the lady come into sight again in the garden: he salutes her respectfully, bids her adieu, and re-enters the room to inform his friends that his marriage project is at an end. The visitor, it appears, was his betrothed, the favourite lady-in-waiting of Queen Marguerite; in obedience to the Queen's wish she had come to beg him to release her from the contract. He is naturally a trifle annoyed at this blow to his prestige as a lady-killer, and his friends do not let the opportunity go by to laugh at him, in a chorus of mock praise of the all-conquering hero:

18   *Allegro* ♩ = 144

Bonheur au conquérant   Dont le pouvoir galant,

A new character now appears: it is the young Urbain, the favourite page of the Queen. He bears, he says, a message to one

of them from a noble lady of whom even kings might be jealous.
His cavatina, "Une dame noble et sage", was one of the Meyerbeerian pieces most admired by our grandfathers:

19. *Andantino* ♪= 126

U - ne da - me no - ble et sa - ge,

Dont les rois se - raient ja - loux,

Nevers, of course, complacently assumes that *he* is the favoured
gallant: a man cannot escape his fate, he sighs, inconvenient as it
sometimes is to possess so much "merit"; and he holds out his
hand for the letter carried by the page. Urbain asks him if he is Sir
Raoul de Nangis, for it is to him that the letter is addressed.
Raoul is a little incredulous, as he knows no one in these parts
who could be interested in him. He reads the missive aloud: "At
close of day some one will wait for you at the old tower: you are
to submit to have your eyes bandaged, and, asking no questions,
to accompany your guide." Concluding that some one is amusing
himself at his expense he promises to see the adventure through,
but only in order to punish whoever is taking this liberty with
him. He carelessly passes the letter to Nevers, who, after an
ejaculation of surprise, passes it round among the others. "It is
her seal!" says one, *sotto voce*. "Her device!" says another. "Her
own hand!" whispers a third. There can be no doubt about
it: the message is from the King's own sister, Marguerite de
Valois.

At once their tone towards Raoul changes: he is no longer the
young greenhorn from the country, to be patronised and serve as
a butt for their humour, but a royal protégé whom it will be well
to court. Meyerbeer paints admirably their rather suspect protestations of eternal friendship when, after a whispered colloquy
among themselves, they crowd round the young man and take

him affectionately yet respectfully by the hand. Nevers begins with an assurance that Raoul has no more devoted friend than himself:

20 *Allegretto moderato* ♩ = 96

Vous sa - vez si je suis un ami, un ami sûr et tendre

the others taking up the theme in a sprightly ensemble. Everything, they assure the astonished Raoul, is now within his capacity; the fruit is ripe and he has only to pluck it; and they hope he will "remember them later". The act ends with an ensemble expressive of the general joy. Even the dour Marcel cannot help rejoicing at his master's good fortune: "Te Deum laudamus!" he booms, in one of those commanding *fortissimi* in which Levasseur excelled; "Samson has overthrown the Philistines!"[1] At the height of the "orgy", in which we hear once more the melody of No. 8, though now to different words, some masked men appear in the background. Advancing to Raoul, one of them shows him the scarf he holds in his hand; and the somewhat bewildered Raoul suffers himself to be led off by Urbain, though Marcel—rather inconsistently, one cannot help thinking—tries to restrain him.

6

The first act having been devoted entirely to men, Meyerbeer, true to his principle of keeping the audience's attention perpetually on the alert by variety, makes Act II almost entirely an affair of women. The place of the action is still Touraine.

The scene is laid in the garden of the château of Chenonceaux, a few miles from Amboise. A stream winds sinuously across the

[1] Here, as elsewhere, the text in the score differs from that in the collected edition of Scribe's works. For example, in Scribe the mysterious assignation is for mid-day, and in or near Nevers' house, whereas in the opera it is "près de la vieille tour" "vers le déclin du jour." All these afterthoughts were no doubt Meyerbeer's. When, as sometimes happened, Scribe "struck", Emile Deschamps supplied the necessary new words.

further half of the stage, disappearing every now and then behind clumps of trees and re-emerging from them. To the right of the scene is a broad stairway leading down from the château to the garden. As the curtain rises we see Queen Marguerite surrounded by the ladies of her court. She has just completed her toilette: Urbain is on his knees before her, a mirror still in his hand.

The lines and colours of the music in this opening scene are a complete contrast, in their elegance and suavity, to the bolder ones of the preceding act. The introductory instrumental figure:

runs its graceful course all through the Queen's opening aria, which is a song in praise of the beauty of Touraine:

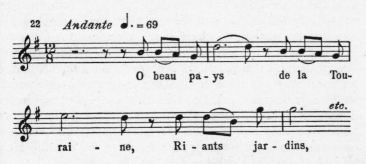

Let a Luther or a Calvin, with his religious animosities, set the rest of the world by the ears as he likes: here in Touraine, and at her court, "austere reason" and "serious moods" must yield place to the smiles of the god of love. The ladies repeat these assurances, which are further repeated by an intelligent echo from the adjacent woods. The pastoral charm of the scene, with its light wood-wind touches in the orchestra, cannot be denied.

Urbain bears a certain resemblance to Siebel in Gounod's *Faust*: he is still little more than a child, a creature just emerging into puberty, troubled with vague amorous desires, and cherishing a hopeless passion for the Queen, who treats him indulgently throughout as the precocious but harmless thing he is. After he has sighed his sentimental heart out over the spectacle of Marguerite's beauty, the Queen turns to one of her maids of honour. Valentine, and asks the result of her visit to Nevers. Valentine informs her that the Comte has agreed, on his honour, to decline her hand. The Queen promises her another marriage more to her liking, but the blushing maiden doubts whether she will have the courage to raise her eyes to the Raoul whom the Queen has in mind. The scene is managed better in Scribe's original text than in the version adopted by Meyerbeer. Scribe makes it fairly clear to the spectator—which the opera cannot be said to do—that neither Valentine nor Marguerite is aware that the Raoul whom the Queen designs her favourite to marry is the stranger who had come to Valentine's rescue at Amboise. The marriage projected by the Queen is a purely political one, between Raoul de Nangis as the scion of a leading Huguenot family and Valentine as the daughter of the Catholic Comte de Saint-Bris. As a further step towards the reconciliation of the rival sects, the Queen herself, it now appears, intends to marry at the same time the Protestant Henri of Navarre—a piece of news that calls forth fresh lamentations from the suffering Urbain. Valentine has her doubts about it all, but these are swept aside by Marguerite, who assures her that she already has the consent of Saint-Bris to the plan, and has no doubt that Raoul will respond to the very unconventional invitation sent to him in the first act. All this is of vital importance to our understanding of this stage of the action; and it is difficult to see why Meyerbeer decided to dispense with much of it.

Perhaps it was because he was impatient to get on to the next of the big surprises he had in store for the audience—the scene of the bathers. The cue for this scene is given by a maid of honour who opportunely points out to the Queen that the sun is strong and the water and the shade of the trees promise coolness. (Meyerbeer seems already to have forgotten that whereas the visit of Raoul to the court had been arranged by Scribe for mid-day, he himself had altered this to "the decline of the day"). Some of the younger girls now begin, as the libretto puts it, to occupy themselves with their "toilette de bain". Others, who are already appropriately half-concealed, half-revealed in robes of gauze, dance and play games before plunging into the stream; they are watched admiringly and indulgently by the Queen, who reclines carelessly on a bank. The girls who have been disrobing behind the trees are soon seen disporting themselves in the Cher, and it now becomes evident why forethoughtful nature had bestowed on that river the "sinuosities" of which the stage directions speak—it was manifestly to allow Meyerbeer's stage manager to exhibit the largest possible number of female bathers in the smallest possible stage space. A touch of comic relief is given to the proceedings now and then by Urbain, who keeps concealing himself behind a tree and playing Peeping Tom as long and as often as the Queen and the ladies permit him. The chorus sung by the bathers runs on the same smooth lines as the music of the earlier part of the act.

At last Urbain is able to announce the coming of "un beau chevalier", whereupon the ladies, Valentine included, modestly run for safety to the neighbourhood of the Queen. The "chevalier" is of course Raoul, who, with bandaged eyes, is led slowly down the staircase on the right, to the accompaniment of an admiring chorus of the ladies.[1] Marguerite dismisses them all, no one remaining on the stage but herself and Raoul. The scarf is removed from the young man's eyes, and he is duly dazzled by

[1] At this point Meyerbeer added, at a much later date, a roguish rondeau for Urbain, " Non, vous n'avez jamais, je gage", which was not in Scribe, and which, in some editions of the opera, is relegated to a supplement. It was written for Madame Alboni, and its prime object was undoubtedly to give that lady plenty of chances to show off her high and low notes:

23 Allegro grazioso ♩ = 100

Non,   non,non,non,non, non,   vous n'a-

vez   ja - mais,   je   ga - ge,

the beauty of the lady, as yet unknown to him, who stands before him. He makes no secret of his passionate admiration:

Beau - té di - vine, en-chante - res - se,

while the Queen handles the situation throughout in a tone of friendly badinage, shaking a roguish finger at the young man, and saying to herself how easy it would be to make a conquest of him if she did not destine him for Valentine:

Si j'é-tais co-quet - te, Dieu!

Pa - reil - le con-quê - te, oui __

At this point Meyerbeer once more alters Scribe's scheme for his own purposes, and by no means for the better. In both versions, however, it is clear enough that Raoul is indulging himself in the pleasant prospect of "vengeance" upon the fair lady of Amboise for the perfidy of which he imagines her to have been guilty.

The Queen has just extracted from Raoul a promise that he will obey her in everything when the ubiquitous Urbain enters once more. This time his mistress is seriously annoyed with him. He bears, however, an important message: "The gentlemen of the region, whom you have summoned hither, have come to pay homage to your Majesty." Raoul is abashed by this revelation of the unknown lady's rank, but Marguerite reminds him of his oath, and tells him of her plan to marry him to a young and charming heiress, the daughter of an ancient enemy of his house, the Comte de Saint-Bris.

The gentlemen of the court now enter, with Saint-Bris and Nevers at their head, the Catholics ranging themselves on one side of the stage, the Protestants on the other. Raoul is presented to Nevers and Saint-Bris. They are polite enough to him, though it is evident that there is not much love lost between the rival sects. Marcel, who has come in with the others, naturally warns his master against having anything to do with "the daughter of a Midianite."

A courier enters with letters for the Queen. Having read them, she announces that her brother, Charles IX, requires the presence of the chief Catholic nobles in Paris immediately, to carry out some "vast project" not disclosed to her. Before they leave, however, they and the Protestants are to swear eternal peace with each other. This they do in a very effective ensemble:

note the telling effect of the quiet opening, the *crescendo*, the strongly accented notes in the third bar, and the *fortissimo* on "Nous jurons!" Once more we see, by comparing the score with the original libretto, how keen an eye Meyerbeer had for theatrical effect. Scribe puts into the mouths of the singers four lines of verse—"By our honour, by the name borne by our ancestors, by the King, by our swords, by the God who detects and punishes traitors, we swear eternal amity". But Meyerbeer knows a trick worth two of that: at the end of each line—delivered *pianissimo*—he inserts a *fortissimo* "We swear!" of his own. Marcel, needless to say, does not join in the oath: he sings with the other three, but his words are a threat of eternal war against Rome and all that Rome stands for. The lines allotted to him are not in the original text: presumably they were an afterthought suggested at the rehearsals. It is surprising that so skilled a craftsman as Scribe should not have seen that since Marcel was on the stage he, of the whole male company, could not alone be silent, while if he had to sing at all he would have to utter sentiments consistent with his character. In the score, again, though not in Scribe, is a supplementary quartet:

27 Andante ♩. = 42

Pro - vi - den - ce, mè - re ten - dre, Sur la ter - re fais des-cen - dre

in which the four principals pray for brotherhood and peace. This quartet seems to have been omitted in Paris at an early stage in the opera's career.

Valentine is now brought in by her father. The Queen presents her to Raoul, who, recognising her as the lady of Amboise and of the supposed assignation with Nevers, recoils angrily with a cry of "Betrayal! Perfidy! I her bridegroom? Never! Never!" There is a long, fateful silence: then Meyerbeer launches the big ensemble that ends the act. The Queen and Valentine are shocked and hurt at Raoul's refusal: Saint-Bris and Nevers, furious at the insult to their houses, cry out for the Huguenot's blood: Raoul, beside himself with rage, hurls defiance at them all: the chorus add in their several ways to the clamour, and Marcel exults *fortissimo* to the familiar strain of "Ein' feste Burg". The ensemble is worked up musically in exciting fashion. Murder is in the air: it is averted only by the Queen's command to Raoul to give up his sword. At last Saint-Bris and Nevers drag the fainting Valentine away, both of them reviling Raoul, who tries to follow them but is held back by the Queen's bodyguard.

7

The remainder of the action takes place in Paris.

The third act opens in the Pré-aux-Clercs, the great meadow, running down to the banks of the Seine, that is now the site of the Faubourg St. Germain. It is six o'clock on an afternoon in the same month of August. In the centre of the stage stands a great tree. On the left, a little way back, the portal of a chapel is visible. On either side of the stage is a cabaret: in front of one of these sit a number of Catholic students and girls, while outside the other are Huguenot soldiers drinking and playing dice. Elsewhere we see lawyers' clerks sitting at little tables with grisettes, and a perambulating, chattering crowd of workers, merchants, monks, and bourgeois of all kinds.

After a lively orchestral preamble the promenaders break into a chorus on the theme of Sunday and the rest and recreation it brings. The Huguenot soldiers, with one Bois-Rosé at their head, indulge themselves in the luxury of a song in praise of war in general and of Coligny in particular. This is the famous "Rataplan" chorus that made such a sensation in its own day. The soldiers begin with hand-claps intended to represent drum-rolls:

and these rhythmical effects persist throughout the song. This is succeeded, in accordance with the immutable Meyerbeer formula of incessant contrast, by a chorus for Catholic women's voices alone, accompanying the nuptial procession of Nevers and Valentine as it wends its way into the chapel. Marcel appears, making enquiries after the Comte de Saint-Bris. The rough old soldier, whose manners, it must be admitted, are never of the best, goes out of his way to annoy the Catholics in the first place by jostling the procession, and in the second place by not removing his hat during a religious ceremony. His truculence, however, wins him the approval of the Huguenot soldiers, who break out into their defiant "Rataplan" chorus once more, as a counterpoise to the chant of the Catholic women. Tempers begin to rise; and the crowd is about to lay violent hands on the Huguenots when there occurs one of those opportune diversions that are less frequent in real life, perhaps, than in grand opera, where they serve the double purpose of preventing the action from reaching its climax too quickly and of providing the management with an excuse for a ballet.

Just as a free fight seems inevitable, a troupe of gipsies of both sexes invades the scene, bringing with them their musical instruments: they invite the other occupants of the stage to dance with them or to have their fortunes told. After a lively opening chorus comes an elaborate ballet, comprising, in the score, five numbers, though these are generally cut down in performance.

After this light relief the serious business of the opera is resumed. Saint-Bris, Nevers, and another Catholic gentleman, Maurevert, come out of the chapel, Nevers explaining to his father-in-law that Valentine, in fulfilment of a vow she had made, wishes to remain in the chapel, in prayer, until the evening. He has acceded to her wish, and will return later "to conduct her in pomp to my abode", as he puts it in the libretto-language of that epoch. Valentine, of course, may have made such a vow, and may really wish to remain in the chapel for no other purpose than to pray. One suspects, however, that somewhere at the back of her mind is another motive—to help Scribe and Meyerbeer out of a little difficulty that now confronts them in the working-out of their plot. For it is essential to that working-out that Valentine shall overhear a little scheme for the murder of Raoul.

After Nevers has left the stage, and while Saint-Bris, who is still smarting under the affront put on him by Raoul, is breathing fire and slaughter against him if they should ever meet again, Marcel appears with a letter for him from his master, who, it seems, has just arrived in Paris with the Queen and her Court.

Saint-Bris, to his joy, finds that the letter is a challenge to meet him, for a settlement of their differences, in the Pré-aux-Clercs that same evening at an hour when the meadow will be deserted. The Catholics agree that the Lord has delivered their enemy into their hands. Saint-Bris suggests that the challenge shall be kept from the ears of his son-in-law, who must not be exposed to the danger of a duel on his wedding day. Maurevert goes further. There is no need for anyone to expose himself to risk of that sort. He knows of a better plan; and he takes Saint-Bris into the chapel to communicate the details to him.

Evening is now falling. A constable enters, announces that it is curfew time, and clears the stage of the promenaders: the Huguenot soldiers go into one of the cabarets. Saint-Bris and Maurevert come out of the chapel. The plot is complete: Raoul is to be set upon in this very place, within an hour.

Valentine now emerges from the chapel, in great agitation; from her brief recitative we learn that, hidden behind a pillar, she has overheard the conversation of the two men. She must save Raoul—not so much for his own sake as to redeem the honour of her father. But how to warn him of the danger that threatens him? The problem is solved for her by the entry of Marcel, who, uneasy at the turn events have taken, has returned to protect his master or to die with him. As he soliloquises aloud, Valentine soon knows him by his voice: her veil, however, prevents him from recognising her, and she tells him no more than that his master is in great danger if he comes to the duel alone. Their brief duet, through which the following figure runs in the orchestra:

29

Allegro con spirito ♩ = 88

is admirably written.

Marcel rushes out to warn Raoul, leaving Valentine free for a lyrical expression of her love for the man who had so cruelly offended her:

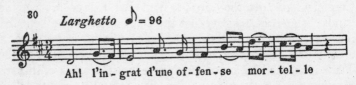

But Marcel is back again instantly—in his agitation he had forgotten that Raoul will already have left his house—and the pair unite in another duet, in which Valentine continues on the broad lines of No. 29, while Marcel, whose agitation and whose feeling of helplessness increase every moment, sobs out his fears and his love for the Raoul whom he would die to save. Marcel is no Kurvenal—Meyerbeer's characterisation of him is as a rule too consciously theatrical for that; but in this scene the old man does become dramatically alive, and for perhaps the first time in the opera we really believe in him. He tries to make Valentine disclose her identity, but she will say no more than that, like him, she loves Raoul and desires to save him. Over a surging orchestral accompaniment that well expresses her agitation she describes the torment of her soul, divided as it is between love and duty:

Marcel, deeply moved, gives her an old man's blessing.

She takes refuge in the chapel just as Raoul enters, accompanied by Saint-Bris and the four seconds—Tavannes and Cossé for Saint-Bris, de Retz and Méru for Raoul. Marcel warns Raoul that treachery is afoot, but the young man merely turns to the seconds and orders them to arrange the details of the duel. There follows a spirited ensemble in which all parties express their confidence in the justice of their cause:

while Marcel invokes the protection of heaven for Raoul. The climax comes with a sweeping phrase of which the text is "Each for himself and God for all!"

The fight between Saint-Bris and Raoul begins.

Just then a confused noise is heard "off". Marcel, sword in hand, turns to meet the newcomers—Maurevert and two other armed men, who take up positions near Saint-Bris. Raising the cry that several Huguenots are attacking a single Catholic, Maurevert summons the "defenders of the true faith" whom he had brought with him in accordance with the plan revealed in an earlier scene.

A dozen armed men come out from behind the large tree in the centre of the stage and surround Raoul, his two seconds and Marcel.[1] The Huguenots are hard-pressed when there is heard from one of the cabarets the truculent "Rataplan" refrain of the Huguenot soldiers. Marcel breaks through the cordon, pounds on the door of the cabaret, and calls the Protestants out in the name of Coligny to defend the faith against its enemies. At the sound of the familiar chorale they rush into the open. Saint-Bris,[2] crying "Treason!", summons the Catholic students from the hostelry opposite. The two groups, in an animated chorus, hurl insults and threats at each other; so do the women of the rival sects, who now, in their turn, pour out of the cabarets.

The two parties soon come to blows, with half the women trying to stop the bloodshed, the other half throwing themselves on their knees and praying. Marcel has snatched an axe from some one's hands, and with it stands guard over Raoul. At the height of the turmoil the Queen enters on horseback, with her train: she is on her way to the palace. Each section of the combatants accuses the other of violence and treachery, and Marguerite does not know whom to believe. It is left to Marcel to clear up the situation

[1] Meyerbeer seems to be in some confusion over his characters in this scene. Scribe, in his original text, gives no names to any of the seconds. Obviously he intends two of them to be Catholic and two Protestant; for he speaks of "the four Huguenots standing back to back to confront their enemies, who press on them from all sides". It is only in Meyerbeer's score that the four witnesses are named specifically as "Tavannes and Cossé for Saint-Bris, de Retz and Méru for Raoul". But in the list of dramatis personae the two last-named figure among the "gentilshommes catholiques", in which capacity, indeed, they have taken part in the festivities in Nevers' house in the first act. The only "gentilhomme protestant" in the cast is Raoul. How de Retz and Méru can now be Protestants, fighting with Raoul and Marcel, is not explained.

The confusion becomes worse confounded a little later. When, in the ensemble, Marcel thunders out his Lutheran chorale—an episode not in Scribe's text, by the way—he is joined by Raoul, Tavannes and Cossé. But as the two latter are Saint-Bris' *Catholic* seconds, it is quite inconceivable that they should help Marcel in his singing of "Ein' feste Burg". It looks as if Meyerbeer was not very particular what nonsense he perpetrated if the spectators were not likely to notice it.

[2] Maurevert in Scribe.

by appealing to a masked woman who just then comes from the church. Saint-Bris having torn away her mask, Valentine stands revealed. Raoul is astonished at the proof which, he now learns, she has given of her regard for him, but still cannot understand the "perfidy" of which she had been guilty in Touraine. It is all explained to him by the Queen, who further informs him that Valentine is now the wife of another. (Thus in the opera. Scribe had handled the situation much more tellingly: he had made Saint-Bris deliver this knock-out blow to Raoul, having first drawn from the young man a confession that he loved Valentine. The implacable old Catholic is thus able to gloat over a revenge that has surpassed all his hopes or expectations).

As if to give further point to the dagger thus plunged into Raoul's heart, just then the joyous strains of the wedding cortège (No. 34) are heard "off". On the river appears a large gondola, gaily decorated, brightly lit, and filled with musicians, pages and ladies of the court. From it Nevers disembarks. He salutes Valentine in the most courtly tones, inviting her to "le banquet d'hymenée", where she will find him "a captive proud of his chains". To the choral melody of the cortège:

he conducts her to the boat, surrounded and followed by the gipsies, who strew flowers, dance, and wave lighted torches—altogether a very effective piece of theatrical spectacle: Meyerbeer, with his usual eye for effect, throws everything he has, from the Queen to the gipsies, into his final assault on the audience. Even here the rival religious sects cannot refrain from threatening each other, in spite of the Queen's appeal to them to forget their animosities; but the dominant note to the fall of the curtain is one of gaiety on the part of everyone but Valentine, Raoul and Marcel.

8

From this point the action of the opera runs on swiftly to the end. The fourth act is particularly well-handled by both the poet and the musician. Not only does Meyerbeer score his points here without the sometimes excessive expansiveness, the desire to win over his listeners with incessant contrast, that have stretched the canvasses of the first three acts to such unusual lengths: he seems, in spite of a characteristic lapse or two, to be more truly and simply sincere in this fourth act than anywhere else, to be sunk in his characters to the point of as complete forgetfulness of himself and of his audience as was ever possible with him.

The setting is a room in Nevers' house. At the back of the stage are a door and a window: on the left, a door leading to Valentine's room: on the right, a great fireplace, and near to it the door, covered with a tapestry, of a smaller room. Further back, on the same side, is a window overlooking the street. It is the night of St. Bartholomew's day, the 24th August 1572.

As the curtain rises we see Valentine sitting on a couch, alone, as she says, with herself and her grief: her state of mind is painted in some agitated phrases in the orchestra. She reproaches herself, her father, who gave her to Nevers, and Raoul, who might have frustrated the marriage. Scribe gives her a romance to sing before she has been on the stage three minutes—"De mon amour faut-il, triste victime". Meyerbeer, however, uses other words—"Parmi les pleurs mon rêve se ranime"—for *his* romance. The whole episode, however, seems to have been omitted in Paris, and to have been relegated to a supplement in the published scores. Perhaps it was realised from the first that any aria here would merely hold up the action; and as the melody that Meyerbeer puts into Valentine's mouth:

Parmi les pleurs mon rê - ve se ra - ni - me,

is far from being one of his best efforts, from every point of view it was wise to sacrifice it.

In the acting version, then, Valentine's short soliloquy is interrupted by the entry of Raoul, in sombre mood, through the door at the back of the stage. He has come to bid her farewell before dying, as he expects to do and is resigned to doing, in that same room under the swords of her father and her husband. The steps of these two are, in fact, already audible in the room on the left. Distractedly Valentine begs Raoul to avoid them to save her honour; and he allows her to conceal him behind the tapestry on the right. The colloquy is very much more extended in Scribe than in the opera. Whether Meyerbeer ever composed the music for Scribe's long dialogue we do not know; but no doubt every-one connected with the production of the work saw from the beginning that the less time that was wasted on non-essentials the better it would be for the act as a whole.

Saint-Bris enters with Nevers, Tavannes and other Catholic noblemen, whom he has brought there to confide to them the Queen Mother's plan for the destruction of the Protestants. Saint-Bris orders Valentine to leave them; but Nevers obtains permission for her to remain, her Catholic zeal, he says, being above suspicion. The noblemen now learn that the details of the plot are complete: that very day will see the Huguenots exter-minated. The only one who shows any horror at this is Nevers, whose sense of honour revolts at a scheme for murder of this treacherous kind: his ancestors, he says, pointing to the portraits of them that cover the walls of the room, have numbered among them many a soldier, but never an assassin; and he breaks his sword across his knee to save it from dishonour. As his co-opera-tion evidently cannot be had, nor his discretion be counted upon, Saint-Bris hands him over to some of the town authorities who enter, armed, just at that moment, bidding them take him away and keep him under guard until the following day. As for Saint-Bris himself, he neither knows doubt nor feels compunction in a matter of this kind, in which it is for God and the King to com-mand and for him only to obey:

36

Pour cette cause sain-te   J'o - bé-i-rai sans crainte,

which pious sentiments are echoed by the other noblemen present. The melody of No. 36, by the way, is taken from a trio in an earlier opera of Meyerbeer's, *Margherita d'Anjou* (1820).

Valentine, at a sign from her father, has gone to her own room at the time of Nevers' arrest. The coast being clear, Saint-Bris now gives the conspirators and the city authorities their orders. All strategic posts are to be silently occupied by the faithful:

37
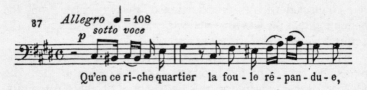

Qu'en ce ri-che quartier   la fou - le ré - pan - du - e,

One of them is to see to the slaying of Coligny, another to attacking the house in which the leading Protestants are that evening attending the fête of Marguerite and the King of Navarre. At the first sound of the bell of St. Germain's the Catholic soldiers are to be ready in hiding everywhere: at the second stroke they are to rush out to the slaughter. Meyerbeer's music all through this scene is full of nervous fire.

Through the great door at the back there now enter three monks, carrying baskets containing white scarves. They advance slowly down the stage, and the celebrated chorus of the Benediction of the Poniards begins. Swords and daggers are drawn and held out to be blessed by the monks, which they do to a series of effective alternations of *fortissimo* and *pianissimo* chords in the orchestra:

38

at the same time bidding the men spare no one in their vengeance; the white scarves are for them to know each other by. The musical ensemble is worked up furiously, the conspirators advancing *en masse* to the front of the scene and brandishing their weapons: then, with a final exhortation of each other to secrecy, they leave the stage in silence, to meet again at midnight.[1]

As soon as they have gone, Raoul, who of course has seen and heard everything, raises the tapestry and makes for the door at the back, but pauses as he hears it being bolted from without. He runs next to the door on the left, through which Valentine comes from her room to meet him. And now begins the famous duet to which so much of the success of the opera has always been due. To appropriately agitated figures in the orchestra Raoul declares his intention of flying to the aid of his brothers, to warn them of the plot and bid them arm. He will listen to none of Valentine's pleadings for her father, her husband and her co-religionists: arrayed against him and his he sees none but assassins who must be punished. Time presses, the danger grows, and he must be gone:

In vain does she try to hold him back from what she feels to be certain death. It is only when she confesses that she loves him that

---

[1] The reader who may be following this analysis with a piano score will be puzzled by the "sopranos and contraltos" who figure in this chorus, for nowhere, either in the text itself or in the stage directions, is there the smallest hint from first to last of any women having entered to take part in these operations. The explanation is that Meyerbeer, unable to reconcile himself to the lack of female voices in this scene, introduced at the last moment a bevy of nuns, who join with the male conspirators in invoking Heaven's blessing on the coming slaughter!

his mood changes. "Your lips have said it!" he cries in the famous *andante amoroso* in G flat major: "Yes, you love me! What star is this that has come to lighten my night? I am born again: I breathe the pure air of heaven itself";

Orchestral echoes of the vocal phrases intensify the sensuous appeal of these; and at the end of the duet the music soars to a height of passion that is rare in Meyerbeer.

Raoul would have Valentine fly with him, but she still entreats him to remain. Suddenly the church bell strikes in with its solemn, sinister clang. It recalls Raoul to his senses and dissolves his brief dream; his duty to his brothers must come before even the joys of love:

In vain does she appeal to that love:

and while she is struggling to hold him back, the bell booms out again. This finally decides the now maddened Raoul. He rushes to the window on the right, and shows Valentine the carnage going on in the street below. The dreadful clamour of the bell increases, and above it is heard the clash of arms. Commending the fainting Valentine to God, Raoul throws himself from the balcony and disappears along the street.

9

The reader need never hope to hear an integral performance of *Les Huguenots*. Almost from the commencement of its career it has been cut according to the exigencies of each theatre and the fancy of the producer, partly because it is excessively long, partly because it is not of uniform quality throughout. One easy way of dealing with the problem is to delete the fifth act altogether—a practice that probably began, even during the composer's life-time, through many people leaving the theatre after the stirring fourth act. On the principle, indeed, that the best is the enemy of the good, the fourth act of *Les Huguenots* has always been the enemy of the fifth. Heine summed the situation up in one of his characteristically malicious but amusing *jeux d'esprit*. Almost as well known in Paris as Meyerbeer himself was a certain amiable Gouin, a minor postal official, who managed the composer's affairs with a competence and a devotion beyond praise. Some joker or other having put into circulation the story that Gouin not only looked after Meyerbeer's business matters but composed his music for him, Heine was asked whether he thought it possible that Gouin might have written *Les Huguenots*. "Not all of it", said Heine; "I don't believe Gouin wrote any of it but the fourth act."

There are two reasons why the fifth act should be retained in modern performances. In the first place, without it the story of the opera is shorn of the major portion of its dramatic interest: why, indeed, invite the public to see an opera called, by its librettist and composer, *Les Huguenots*, unless the really important thing in it is not the love of Raoul and Valentine but the clash of the Hugue-not and the Catholic faiths? In the second place, the fifth act, if it has faults of its own, has also qualities of its own, both dramati-cally and musically.

At the very moment when the personal drama of Raoul and Valentine has been rising to its climax in Nevers' house, the larger drama of the Huguenots and the Catholics is being played out elsewhere. The scene is laid in the hôtel de Nesle, where a ball is in progress in celebration of the recent wedding of Marguerite and Henri of Navarre. Even during the brief orchestral introduction the warning sound of the bell is faintly heard: it increases in power until the dancers are perturbed by the sinister quality of it. They continue dancing, however, until Raoul rushes in, frenzied, haggard, his clothes covered with blood. He tells his co-religionists what he has just seen—Coligny dead, the streets running with the blood of murdered Huguenots. Wildly he calls on them all to answer force with force. The women fly in terror; the men draw their swords and rush pell-mell through every door of the great room.

The scene changes to a cemetery. (In Scribe, a cloister). In the background is a Protestant church, its windows shattered by bullets. On the left is a small door opening into the church, on the right an iron gate leading into a street. The stage is filled with Huguenots, the men hastily constructing a barricade, the women, with their children, running to take refuge in the church: Marcel, sorely wounded, is directing them. Raoul enters, to learn from Marcel that the place is surrounded, and that nothing remains for them all but to die bravely. Raoul is quickly followed by Valentine; she has come, as she thinks, to save him. She holds out to him a white scarf; wearing this he can pass through the ranks of the enemy to the Louvre, where his life will be spared if he will embrace the Catholic faith: they can then reap the reward of their love, for Nevers has most opportunely fallen a victim to the assassins.

For a moment Raoul hesitates, but Marcel's mournful reproaches turn the scale with him. He will stay with the brave old man, he says, and perish honourably; whereupon Valentine, in increasing excitement, declares that now she will show him how a woman can love—she will imperil her immortal soul by turning Protestant: all that matters is that they shall be for ever united, be it in Paradise or in hell. Raoul asks Marcel to act as their priest and join their hands; and, by a telling stroke at just the right

moment on the part of both Scribe and Meyerbeer, the purely
personal drama being worked out before our eyes suddenly rises
into the higher religious atmosphere; from inside the church come
the strains of the Lutheran chorale, sung by the women alone.

The lovers sink on their knees before Marcel, and there follows
the trio of the "bénédiction nuptiale":

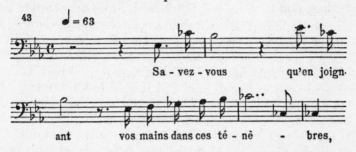

The sombre colour given to the episode by an obbligato bass
clarinet was one of the many features of the *Huguenots* score that
won the commendation of Berlioz.

The chorale heard from within the church comes to an abrupt
end: the Catholics have broken in, and we hear nothing for a while
but the noise of arms and the shouts of the soldiers, adjuring the
Protestants to recant or die, alternating with the last dismembered
fragments of the chorale. Within the church, it soon becomes
evident, the bloody work is over. Raoul, Valentine and Marcel
kneel in prayer. Suddenly Marcel rises to his feet, in an ecstasy of
religious exaltation, to sing of the vision of Paradise that hovers
before his eyes:

Valentine and Raoul echo his phrases, and the harps give the trio
a super-terrestrial colour of its own.

Soldiers break through the iron gate on the right. They offer
white scarves to the three Huguenots, giving them a last chance

to recant. The three refuse: they advance slowly, intoning the chorale and defying their enemies, who at last bear them down and drag them off through the street to the right.

The final scene shows us one of the Paris quays the same night. (One of the technical weaknesses of this fifth act is the shortness of each of the three scenes). Raoul, mortally wounded, staggers in, supported by Valentine and Marcel. From the opposite side of the stage Saint-Bris enters with a company of arquebusiers. In spite of Valentine's attempt to close Raoul's mouth, he cries out defiantly that he is a Huguenot, whereupon, at Saint-Bris' command, the soldiers fire on the little group. As Valentine falls on the dead body of Raoul, Saint-Bris recognises his daughter. She dies praying for her father. There is a cry of "Make way for the Queen!" Marguerite enters in her litter, on her way to the Louvre. At the sight of Valentine's body she gives a cry of horror, and tries with a gesture to impose quiet upon the soldiers, who, however, are still cursing the heretics and vowing their extermination when the curtain falls.

COSÌ FAN TUTTE
Mozart (1756-1791)

CHARACTERS

FIORDILIGI	*Soprano*
DORABELLA	*Soprano*
FERRANDO	*Tenor*
GUGLIELMO	*Baritone*
DON ALFONSO	*Basso buffo*
DESPINA	*Soprano*

I

Così fan tutte,[1] which was first produced in Vienna on the 26th January 1790, was the last but two of the operas of Mozart's maturity: it had been preceded by *Idomeneo* (1781), *The Seraglio* (1782), *Der Schauspieldirektor* (1786), *Figaro* (1786) and *Don Giovanni* (1787), and was followed by *La Clemenza di Tito* and *The Magic Flute* (both 1791). Its fate has been somewhat peculiar. It has been revived again and again in the theatre in one form or another during the last century-and-a-half, and invariably with the same result. People go away remarking how charming most of it is, and wondering why it is not given oftener; but after a few performances it again disappears from the bill for another longish interval. Various theories have been put forward to account for the work never having become a real repertory piece. Some have blamed the subject itself, some the treatment of it by the librettist, Da Ponte: a few, like Wagner, have been frank enough to admit that the music is not always Mozart at his best, and have excused him on the ground that even his consummate genius could not always grace a poor text with fine music. This, of course, is really to lay the blame once more on Da Ponte at a further remove. No one explanation, however, will cover all the facts of the case. The fault certainly is not wholly Da Ponte's. Many a composer, in-

[1] The original title in full was *Così fan tutte, o sia La Scuola degli Amant* (*They All Do It, or The School for Lovers*).

cluding Mozart himself, has written enduring music to an opera "book" no better in essentials than that of *Così fan tutte*. When due allowance has been made for Da Ponte's lapses, there still remains a certain amount of blame to be debited to the account of Mozart. It is just as well for us to recognise frankly that there were limits even to his genius—limits in part personal, rooted in his mentality and his temperament, in part due to the fact that music in general in the eighteenth century lacked the vocabulary and the apparatus for the expression of several things which it was reserved for a later epoch to encompass in opera.

Mozart seems to have received the commission for a new opera in the autumn of 1789 at the instance of the Emperor Joseph II himself, who, it is said, further suggested, as the subject, a story from real life that was amusing all Vienna at that time—the story of two gentlemen who, concealing their identity, had made love to their respective fiancées in other semblances, and had found the fair ones regrettably frail. It may have been so; but scholars hint vaguely at previous stage plays on much the same theme, and industrious research would probably establish the fact that the alleged incident in Vienna, if it ever happened, was merely one more instance of life imitating, or pretending to imitate, art.

In Da Ponte's libretto everything goes in pairs: equilibrating the two sisters and their lovers we have the old cynic who sets the action going and the maidservant who aids and abets him in all his devices. Though the librettist makes an occasional attempt to differentiate psychologically between Dorabella and Fiordiligi, and again between Ferrando and Guglielmo, he often handles each pair as a unity in itself; Mozart has necessarily to follow his lead in this, with the result that on several occasions he has to give up the attempt at individual characterisation and fall back on a generalised kind of musical utterance for each couple—a procedure in which he does not always manage to command our full interest.

No opera of Mozart's has been so persistently and so absurdly overwritten as *Così fan tutte*; and the overwriting has generally sprung from the curious passion of many biographers and critics for crediting Mozart with all kinds of psychological profundities and subtleties of the possession of which he himself was blissfully ignorant. The plot of the opera has been gravely censured for its "improbability and frivolity"—as if the Muse of Comedy were bound to go everywhere with John Stuart Mill's *System of Logic* under one arm and Law's *Serious Call to a Devout and Holy Life* under the other. If we are not to laugh at the improbable, what becomes of *Alice in Wonderland?* If the moralist in us is to frown on the frivolous, which of us can ever again book his seat for *L'Heure Espagnole* or *Die Fledermaus* without a sense of shame?

One odd feature of the *Così fan tutte* matter is that people who raise disapproving eyebrows at the "improbability" of the action are the same people who docilely accept the legend that it was derived from an actual contemporary occurrence, known to everyone in the theatre, in the very city in which the work was first produced! Some of the German commentators assure us, of course, that Mozart, as was his wont, raised this "sordid" comedy into the higher sphere of "universal humanity" by means of his music. The libretto, we are asked to believe, must have been distasteful to him in many respects, because it expected him to find amusement in an exposure of feminine frailty; Mozart's ideal being the Eternal Womanly, it must have gone terribly against the grain with him to associate himself with an irreverent jester of the type of Da Ponte, to whom, for the purposes of comedy, one woman was very like another, and women in general no better than they ought to be. Accordingly, we are given to understand, the divine element in Mozart rose in protest against the immorality of the plot, and this protest took the practical form of his writing serious music for more than one situation in which Da Ponte had seen only humour. Upon all which the only fitting comment is that if Mozart accepted with his eyes open a libretto designed by its author as a comedy, and intended to be listened to as a comedy, and then, because he disapproved of its ethics, deliberately "raised it into a higher sphere" by being serious where his job was to be funny, then Mozart was an ass. But Mozart was very far from being an ass; and if he sometimes fails, as we must frankly recognise, to strike the sure note of comedy in the music of his *Così fan tutte*, that is purely and simply for the reasons given above—that even a genius like his was unable to transcend either its personal limitations or those of the music of his epoch.

We may be sure that when, as sometimes happens in *Così fan tutte*, we find his sense of comedy in music not at its finest, or are unable to see much difference between an idiom which he apparently means to be comic and the idiom he employs elsewhere in connection with perfectly serious characters or situations, he was doing his musical best according to his lights and those of his epoch; and he would have been amazed, and probably annoyed, at the suggestion that he had allowed, even unconsciously, his dramatic sense of what was due to his subject to be over-ridden by "loftier" considerations. To regard his handling of Dorabella and Fiordiligi, Ferrando and Guglielmo as his special "contribution to the problem of sex" is to go beyond the limit of solemn absurdity permissible even to a German critic philosophising about Mozart. And even when one of these critics sensibly protests that it is unreasonable of us to play "the schoolmaster and moralist" towards Mozart, "the most sensuous of all German composers", he cannot refrain from adding that in forgetting sometimes the "idea of the whole" and losing himself in "the situation of the moment"—which is perfectly true—Mozart "forgot that he was making music for the impure souls of two seducers, who transform their loves into wenches (Dirnen)."

2

It is not to be wondered at that in a country predisposed to take this hyper-serious, not to say solemn, view of the nature of comedy, the most frantic attempts should have been made to rid the libretto of *Così fan tutte* of its "improbabilities" and purge it of its "frivolities". Da Ponte's story is of two army officers who, stung by the remark of their cynical friend Don Alfonso that all women are alike, consent to put their fiancées to the acid test. They depart, ostensibly, to join their regiment, but return disguised. Each of them now makes love to the fiancée of the other, with complete ultimate success, the ladies' servant, Despina, a minx who is obviously not a paragon of propriety herself, co-operating with Don Alfonso to throw the two couples together and break down the women's resistance; finally, disguised as a notary, she celebrates a double mock-marriage between the re-shuffled pairs. Mozart had not been in his grave many years before the German theatre began to rationalise and moralise the action of the opera in its own virtuous way. In one version, some sort of exculpation was devised for the two erring ladies by making Don Alfonso a magician; not even the most eternally-feminine of women, of course, could be blamed for straying from the strait path of virtue when the ordinary wiles of male seduction are reinforced by necromancy. In this version Despina became Celerio, the ministering spirit of the magician doctor. In another version the ladies' fidelity is assailed not by the original pair of lovers in disguise but by two other characters created by the librettist solely for that purpose. Another arranger, also desperately anxious to prove that the sisters are not as black as Da Ponte has painted them, makes the servant betray the plot to them, so that in the final scene they are able to disconcert their peccant lovers by maintaining that their surrender was merely feigned. Another way of making the intrigue less offensive to "morality" was to have each of the ladies courted by her own lover in disguise, instead of by the lover of her sister; apparently the racy humour of the original version in this respect was far too frivolous for an ethically-minded German audience.

In most of these well-intentioned versions and perversions, Mozart's music, of course, was curtailed and mutilated in shocking fashion. In 1909 Karl Scheidemantel, a baritone famous in his own day, reverted to a plan that had been adopted in Paris a generation or so earlier. He scrapped Da Ponte entirely, concocting a new text of his own out of a play by Calderon, and adapting this as best he could to Mozart's score. The construction of the Spanish comedy enabled him to preserve, in the new milieu, the formal dualism that is so characteristic a feature of Da Ponte's text—once more we have two male and two female lovers, while Despina has her parallel in Dona Angela's maid Isabella, and Cosme, Don Manuel's servant, takes over the music of Mozart's Don Alfonso. The action, of course, is transferred to Spain, and the period is the mid-sixteenth century. Scheidemantel's version, which, under the title of *Die Dame Kobold*, was produced for the first time in Dresden on the 6th June 1909, had a certain success; but his libretto is of a naïveté that makes Da Ponte's text, flimsy as it is, seem in comparison almost oppressively intellectual. The final result of all these attempts to revive *Così fan tutte* by murdering it has been to convince the modern world that, with all its little faults, the opera is best given today as Da Ponte wrote it, or as near thereto as may be possible.

The parts of the sisters Dorabella and Fiordiligi, who are described in the opera as "two ladies from Ferrara", derived an additional mild piquancy for the Vienna audience of 1790 from the fact that Luisa Villeneuve, who played Dorabella, was the sister of Adriana Gabrielli del Bene, who played Fiordiligi, the latter lady being professionally known as Ferrarese Del Bene, or Ferrarese for short. She was notorious for her gallantries, and at the time when *Così fan tutte* was produced she was the mistress of Da Ponte. It was more or less for this reason, one surmises, that she was entrusted with the part of Fiordiligi, for she was not popular, either in the opera house or in Vienna society; she received, indeed, a Court order to leave the town in 1791. Da Ponte, who devised for her the soprano parts in three or four other operas, could not, in his Memoirs, find her beautiful, even in distant retrospect: but he speaks of the charm of her voice and of her exceptional talent. Mozart, however, does not seem to have had an equally high opinion of her; writing to his wife in April 1789 he says that a new singer of the name of Allegrante is much better than the Ferrarese, "though that isn't saying much." It was for the latter that he had added to the score of *Figaro* the coloratura aria "Al desio di chi t'adora" when the opera was revived in Vienna in 1789 with the Ferrarese as Susanna.[1] The music of Fiordiligi indicates that the Ferrarese's voice, besides boasting considerable flexibility, was of unusual range: in one of her arias in *Così fan tutte* Mozart takes her from the A below the stave to the B flat above it; and it is evident that the high C was also in her voice. How Mozart made use in *Così fan tutte* of the lady's vocal range for the purposes of rough-and-ready comedy will appear later.

[1] The brilliant coloratura and the general character of the aria, which are inconsistent, of course, with the mentality of Susanna, are explained by the fact that in the scene for which this aria was planned the Countess and her maid are each impersonating the other. For the Ferrarese as Susanna Mozart wrote also the arietta "Un moto di gioja mi sento in petto". These two pieces are printed as supplements in some scores of *Figaro*.

3

The overture employs only one theme from the opera itself. This is the actual "Così fan tutte" as sung by Don Alfonso and the two lovers towards the end of the second act:

In the overture it comes at the end of the brief *andante* introduction, which runs to no more than fourteen bars. This is followed by one of those gay quick movements that bubbled so spontaneously from Mozart: noticeable in it are passages of lively orchestral give-and-take of this type:

and this, which is always sandwiched between crashing orchestral tuttis:

Near the end the "Così fan tutte" motive returns.

The opera opens with a lively argument about the constancy of women between Don Alfonso, Ferrando and Guglielmo in a café in Naples. When the curtain rises the dispute has evidently been going on for some time, for the first thing we hear is Ferrando denying vehemently everything that the man-of-the-world Alfonso has been saying. His Dorabella is as good as she is beautiful, he maintains; and Guglielmo at once swears that that goes, so to speak, for his Fiordiligi also. Alfonso, for his part, is not going to be browbeaten by a couple of young greenhorns out of an opinion that is the product of a lifetime of experience. Woman's fidelity, he says, resembles the phoenix—everyone says it exists, but no one knows where to look for it. Swords come near being drawn; but in the end they agree to have a bet of a hundred sequins on the matter. The terms are agreed upon: for the next twenty-four hours the young officers are to do everything Alfonso tells them, but they are not to breathe a word about it all to "their Penelopes", as he cynically calls them. Already the lovers have decided how they will spend the money when they have won it: Ferrando will lay it out on a serenade for Dorabella, while Guglielmo will give "a dinner in honour of Cytherea" to which the discomfited Alfonso will be generously invited. They all raise their glasses on it. The music to the scene centres round a sequence of three trios, each of them striking a different vein of pure musical comedy.

The scene changes to the garden of the house, overlooking the Bay of Naples, of the two sisters who have been the unwitting cause of the dispute. Each has in her hand a medallion of her lover, which she is contemplating in sentimental rapture. They draw each other's attention to the many charms of the portraits: is there anything on earth to compare, for example, with Guglielmo's beautiful mouth or Ferrando's flame-throwing eyes? The comedy is mainly in the words and the miming, for the exquisite music would for the most part go with any of Mozart's serious operatic situations: from the opening bars of the orchestral prelude, with its clarinets in thirds softly cooing over string harmonies that rise and fall as gently as the Mediterranean itself in its most placid moments:

we are in the very land of romance. When the sisters sing together it is more often than not in thirds and sixths. Here and there is a touch of broad comedy, as when the women sigh their sentimental souls out in a cadenza in thirds on the word "amore".

They are behaving in a very kittenish kind of way, looking forward to speedy matrimony and wondering why their lovers are so late, when Don Alfonso enters in a great hurry. To an orchestral accompaniment that imitates his pantings for breath he pours out his agitated story. The ladies must steel themselves to receive bad news. The worst that could have happened to Ferrando and Guglielmo has happened—they have been ordered to join their regiment for active service. The officers follow almost on his heels. They are hardly able to speak for emotion, and the ladies are duly sympathetic, even going so far as to express a wish that their lovers will plunge their swords into their faithful, sorrowing hearts. The young men delightedly call Alfonso's attention to this striking proof of feminine fidelity; but he merely ejaculates "Finem lauda!" The voices then unite in a quintet on the subject of the shocking trials that destiny imposes on the hopes of poor humanity—a quintet of finely varied expression, sometimes obviously comic, sometimes coming as near entire seriousness as makes no matter. The little duet between Ferrando and Guglielmo that follows, in which they express the hope that soon they will be restored to their ladies, is hardly worthy of Da Ponte and not at all worthy of Mozart. It is therefore generally omitted in performance.

At the conclusion of the quintet, then, we hear a stirring drumroll "off". It is the summons to depart for the wars. A ship has arrived at the foot of the garden: a regiment marches across the stage to embark, and the townspeople run to cheer the soldiers, singing a charming little chorus in praise of the military life, which is all pipes and trumpets and guns and glory. The music here is of a type that only Mozart has ever been able to achieve: it is completely unlike anything that could have been anticipated from the situation and the text, yet in some unexplainable way infallibly right.

Dorabella and Fiordiligi are in tears, and their lovers seemingly not in much better condition, now that the time has come to say farewell. One of the many difficulties in connection with the score of Così fan tutte is that of deciding whether Mozart is serious or not at this moment or that. His humour in its broader aspects, of course, admits of no misunderstanding; but in these aspects neither his humour nor the musical means by which he expresses it are invariably above criticism. At times both his humour and his wit are of the finest kind. There are times also when we can only say to him frankly, "Master, if you are asking us to believe that these are the accents of comedy, please tell us in what lines and colours you would paint a serious situation." The quintet that follows the first chorus of the townspeople is a case in point. On the stage the situation can always be counted on to extract a laugh from the audience; but the lovely music, in and by itself, breathes, surely, the very pathos of parting. These, we feel compelled to say as we listen, are not the wire-worked puppets of the preceding comic scenes, jerked this way and that by librettist and composer to wring an easy laugh out of us: if we listen to the music alone they are human beings touched to the heart by the pain of farewell. But Mozart's perfect tact enables him to work even Don Alfonso into this expression of truly romantic feeling without the smallest suspicion of incongruity: the cynic's dry laughter never strikes a jarring note.

After the boat has gone we get a trio in which the two ladies and Don Alfonso pray for gentle winds and a calm sea for the voyagers: and once again we feel that, so far as the music is concerned, we have left far behind us the atmosphere of broad comedy in which some of the preceding episodes have been set.

The ladies having left, Don Alfonso has a recitative and aria in which he expounds to his own satisfaction his philosophy of women—the man who puts his trust in them is ploughing the sea and sowing in the sand.

The scene changes to a room in the sisters' house. Their maid Despina enters: she is one of the stock figures of the older comedy, clever, self-assured, impudent and likable, the female counterpart of the valet who has more brains than his master and knows how to express his contempt for him without overstepping the bounds of prudence and decorum. She introduces herself with a tirade against domestic service, and samples the mid-day chocolate she has prepared for her mistresses. When Fiordiligi and Dorabella come in we are once more in the field of frank farce. Da Ponte lays on the colours with the heaviest brush he can find, and there is nothing for the composer to do but to follow him. The ladies indulge in the most exaggerated protestations of grief at the departure of their lovers. They rave about the Eumenides; they demand dagger and poison; they order Despina to close the windows, for light and air are hateful to them now.

Mozart gives Dorabella a recitative and aria in the grand style: much of the music we should take quite seriously did we not know that we are meant to be amused at the contradiction between these grand-opera heroics and the absurd figure that is enacting a farce in full view of us. It has often been remarked that

I

not a single aria from *Così fan tutte* has established itself really firmly in the concert room, as arias from so many other Mozart operas have done. It is safe to say that were this fine aria of Dorabella's—"Smanie implacabili", with its recitative, "Ah, scostati!" sung at a concert today by a competent dramatic soprano who had no idea whence the thing came, and so had no suspicion that in its original environment it was sung by a comic character, an audience also ignorant of the Italian language, and therefore of the occasional rant in the text, would listen to it all with complete gravity.

Despina evidently does not take this outburst seriously. Her advice to the languishing ladies is that instead of dedicating themselves to a life of misery until their lovers return they should take advantage of their absence to have a good time—as the men are doing, no doubt, in camp. Her philosophy, which she sets forth in an aria "In uomini, in soldati", is the feminine equivalent of that of Don Alfonso—men were deceivers ever, and should be paid back in their own coin. She is still preaching this doctrine when the indignant Fiordiligi and Dorabella flounce out of the room in a state which a Victorian lady in a similar situation would have described as high dudgeon.

Don Alfonso now enters, and, having bribed Despina to help him in his plans, introduces Ferrando and Guglielmo disguised as gentlemen from Albania, sporting the national costume and their false beards with grotesque exaggeration. Despina is most disrespectfully amused by the sight of them; but the men console themselves with the reflection that if *she* does not recognise them her mistresses are not likely to do so. As the ladies are heard approaching, Despina pushes Don Alfonso into a place of hiding. Fiordiligi and Dorabella are of course very angry with their maid for allowing these two strangers into the house, and still angrier when the strangers begin to make love to them. In due course Don Alfonso makes a formal entry and asks what all the fuss is about. "Just look!" says Dorabella; "men in our house!" Alfonso is surprised, when his attention is thus drawn to the Albanians, to find that they are old and valued friends of his whom he is delighted to see again. Ferrando and Guglielmo play up as they are told to do, making love to the ladies in terms of the wildest hyperbole.

Dorabella having had her big aria a little while before, it is now Fiordiligi's turn. She rounds on the two men in a recitative of the approved high-dramatic type, bidding them depart and not profane this chaste abode with their infamous words: no power on earth can make them unfaithful to the men they love. The recitative is followed by the famous aria "Come scoglio" ("Like a rock stands my heart, unmoved by wind or sea"). The aria is burlesque of the broadest kind, and at the same time a coloratura piece for the glory of the singer. In the theatre we laugh at the great leaps the voice has to take now and then—in the opening bars, for instance:

and again later:

The wit of this is not precisely of the finest, and one sometimes wonders to what extent Mozart was deliberately guying not only Fiordiligi but the first singer of the part. Everybody who has heard one of these female voices with an exceptional range knows how difficult it is, even when the voice and the art behind it are both first-rate, to repress a smile at some of the sudden changes from soprano to contralto and back again. As we have seen, Mozart was not particularly fond of the Ferrarese; and it is fairly probable that while flattering her vanity by providing her with the kind of vocal line that would enable her to display the particular virtuosity on which she prided herself, he slyly raised a horse-laugh in the theatre at her expense. Be that as it may, the aria is the broadest of musical farce.

Guglielmo ripostes with one of the most charming numbers of the score, the little aria "Non siate ritrosi":

which is as fine-fingered, in both the vocal and the orchestral part, as "Come scoglio" is thick-thumbed. But Guglielmo's appeal to the ladies to be kind to two such fine young fellows as these new lovers of theirs has no effect on Fiordiligi and Dorabella, who go out with their heads in the air even before Guglielmo has finished his song. He and Ferrando throw themselves into chairs and have a hearty laugh at the expense of Don Alfonso, whom they imagine to have as good as lost his bet already. They offer to let him off with twenty-five sequins. He laughs at them in turn for their juvenile simplicity, and reminds them that they are still under his orders. With that he leaves them.

One of the defects of the construction of the libretto of *Così fan tutte* is its very symmetry. Everything goes in pairs, and whatever is entered at one moment on one side of the account must be balanced by an entry a little later on the other side. The baritone having had *his* aria, operatic justice insists that the tenor shall have his. Accordingly we now have Ferrando immobilising the action in order that he may sing a long aria—"Un' aura amorosa"—setting forth the regulation operatic thesis that a breath of affection from the one we love restores the heart of the lover, an admirable sentiment, no doubt, but perhaps one that does not bear repetition quite so many times as Ferrando and Mozart seem to think. Following Otto Jahn, it is the custom to regard this rather sickly-sentimental aria as a particularly delicate piece of witty characterisation on Mozart's part. We might perhaps be inclined to grant that contention, even against our critical judgment, if the aria were not so excessively long, and, if the truth must be told, sometimes not merely conventional but commonplace. There were occasions when even Mozart's almost infinitely adaptable genius could not find anything vital to put into the mouth of a character in whom he himself, seemingly, found it a little difficult to believe.

The exit of Ferrando and Guglielmo is succeeded by a dialogue between Alfonso and Despina, in which the plan for the under-mining of the constancy of the latter's mistresses is further elabo-rated. Then the scene changes to the garden of the house, where, in the loveliest surroundings of land, sea and sky, the ladies are indulging themselves in romantic reflections upon life with its fleeting joys. Here we say good-bye to burlesque once more: the music is Mozart at his most enchanting. The sisters have barely finished their duet when Ferrando and Guglielmo rush in, followed by Alfonso. Each of the lovers has in his hand a bottle containing, we are soon given to understand, arsenic. They swallow the poison, and the place is soon in an uproar. It is supposed to be a particularly humorous touch on Mozart's part to make the sisters say "Heavens! it was poison?" in the most casual way imaginable. But perhaps this is just another instance of our reading into Mozart's scores significances and subtleties of which he himself was quite unconscious. This little ejaculation of Fiordiligi and Dorabella amounts to no more than five words in the flood of words that is being poured out. Mozart is fully set for his grand ensemble; and it is impossible for him to interrupt the continuity of the orchestral line merely to make Fiordiligi and Dorabella say their five words in a more emphatic or more pseudo-tragic way. He just lets the words flow with the stream and leaves it at that. It was not, indeed, the first occasion on which he had acted in that very way in his operas, putting a musical sentence of the most matter-of-fact kind into the mouth of some character or other in the course of an ensemble the totality of which was of far more importance to him, and to his audience, than this or that part. It may be praiseworthy piety, but it is hardly sound criticism, to try to persuade ourselves that even Mozart's occasional little lapses are not really lapses at all but subtleties beyond the range of any other composer—making him an accredited wit who, as Sydney Smith said of himself, has only to ask someone to pass the salt to set the table in a roar.

Mozart is always happy when he can get the action moving and let the players toss the ball from one to another in quick succession; and he is at the top of his form in this long ensemble. The fun is fast and furious, notwithstanding the fact that every now and then the comic posturings and sentimentalisings are expressed in what would be in any other Mozartian situation a musical language of undoubted seriousness. Despina and Alfonso go off to fetch a doctor. While they are away the ladies, in spite of themselves, begin to find the unhappy suicides rather interesting. The music takes on a new character when Alfonso returns with Despina, the latter amusingly transformed into a doctor of what was in 1790, no doubt, the most advanced kind, one who put into practice the latest scientific discovery—the "mesmerism" that took its name from that same Dr. Mesmer whom Mozart himself had known as a child. After a lot of delightful nonsense in the best vein of medical pomposity the physician applies the infallible cure—a big magnet which makes the suicides heave and writhe to the accompaniment of similarly descriptive writhings in the orchestra, but which eventually restores them to life.

They raise their heads, and, naturally a bit weak at first, after all they have been through in the way of poison and antidote, try to take their bearings. Their first thought, it appears, is that they have died and wakened up in some paradise or other. Is this Pallas they see before them, they ask, or perhaps Cytherea? No, on closer inspection they turn out to be the beauteous ladies for whom they had wanted to die. They beg for a kiss; but though the doctor recommends the treatment on medical grounds, and is backed by Don Alfonso, the sisters mount their high horse again at this bold suggestion, and the curtain comes down on another big ensemble into which Mozart puts all he knows in the way of opera buffa excitement. While the ladies are protesting volubly that, poison or no poison, the strangers have no right to be so "forward", Mozart seems to remember that it is some time since he gave the Ferrarese an opportunity to make a bit of a donkey of herself with her stunt of a shift from soprano to contralto and back again. He accordingly lets her play fast and loose with the general texture of the sextet with a couple of passages of this sort:

We cannot help laughing, nor does it matter very much whether it is at Fiordiligi or the singer of the part.

4

Da Ponte's invention was always better in the first half of an opera than in the second, and in *Così fan tutte* he runs true to form in this respect. The mechanical symmetry of the characters, for one thing—two women and two lovers who have at one and the same time to run in pairs and be to some extent individualised, plus two intriguers of whom much the same is true—begins, in the second act, to hinder not only his own freedom of movement but Mozart's.

At the commencement of the second act, which opens in a room in the sisters' house, we have Despina once more telling her mistresses how silly they are to refuse a good thing when it comes their way; even a girl of fifteen, she assures them in a long aria of the sprightly buffa type, ought to know by instinct how to flirt and not be caught. Left to themselves, the sisters begin to wonder whether, after all, Despina may not be right. They decide that there can be no harm in amusing themselves with these two attractive strangers, so long as they are careful. Dorabella chooses the dark one (Guglielmo), because he is so merry; Fiordiligi's preference is for the blond. They settle this important question of the division of the spoils in a charming duet:

Don Alfonso enters hurriedly, bidding them come down at once to the garden, where they will see and hear something worth their while.[1] They do so, and find the two new lovers there in a boat, with a number of singers and players of instruments. Ferrando and Guglielmo sing in duet a short serenade to the ladies. The orchestral colouring of this (flutes, clarinets, bassoons and horns) has a strongly rustic tang:

10 *Andante*

it suggests the divertimenti which eighteenth century composers were so fond of writing for some local occasion or other. Perhaps what was in Mozart's mind at this point of the opera was to suggest something which, if not authentically "Albanian", would stand out from the rest of the score as "foreign".

As there is at first a certain shyness on both sides, Alfonso and Despina give the two couples a lesson in the art of wooing and coyly accepting. Then they leave them together, remarking *sotto voce*, as they go, that if the ladies don't succumb now they must be superhuman. The lovers begin the great assault. After a little while Ferrando and Fiordiligi disappear, and Guglielmo takes up the attack on Dorabella in earnest. In spite of her putting up a fairly good resistance he has little trouble in hanging round her neck a heart that is meant to be symbolical of his respectful but ardent affection, while her own necklace, with the miniature of Ferrando attached to it, he removes from her neck to his,

[1] In one of the silliest of the many silly attempts to improve on Da Ponte —that of Eduard Devrient, made for the Karlsruhe theatre in 1860, and the text-book of which is still sold in Germany—a scene is interpolated here in which Despina, suddenly succumbing to an attack of virtue, discloses to Fiordiligi and Dorabella that the "Albanians" are their own actual lovers, and that the whole thing has been from the beginning a scheme on Don Alfonso's part to test their fidelity. From this point to the end of the opera, therefore, the ladies are only pretending to be duped! Thus was virtue triumphant, vice vanquished in the German operatic world of the latter half of the nineteenth century.

murmuring as he does so, "Poor Ferrando! I wouldn't have believed it!" The little duet strikes the happy medium between comedy and sentimental seriousness:

especially delightful are the realistic touches when a reference comes in the text to the pit-a-pat of their hearts.

The pair then pass down an avenue, their place on the stage being taken by Ferrando and Fiordiligi. Fiordiligi has been putting up a better fight than her sister. At once we are in the domain of farce again: she rants about his having behaved like "a snake, a hydra, a basilisk". She begs to be left alone: Ferrando at once obliges—or almost at once, for of course he has to stay long enough to sing an elaborate aria in which he fluctuates between confidence as to his ultimate victory and doubts about it:

When at last Fiordiligi really is alone she launches out into a detailed exposition of her state of mind. She is on "fire", it seems, but no longer with the fire of "virtuous love": "frenzy, grief, remorse, repentance, levity, perfidy, betrayal" are contending for mastery within her breast. All this in a highly dramatic recitative, with appropriate effects in the orchestra. The aria that follows is one with which even the Ferrarese must have been satisfied, so many opportunities does it give Fiordiligi to play the high-stepping opera heroine and at the same time display her vocal range and her coloratura technique. The aria is a rondo with a good deal of obbligato work for the horns: it commences with a pseudo-pathetic *adagio*:

I*

Pér pie - tà, ben mio, per - do - na

which is succeeded by an imposing *allegro*:

A chi mai man-cò di
fe-de que - sto va - no ingra - to cor!

When she has trilled her way off the stage, Ferrando and Guglielmo meet to report progress. Ferrando is sincerely delighted to be able to give his friend so comforting an account of Fiordiligi's resistance. Guglielmo, on the other hand, finds it far from easy to tell Ferrando all that has happened between himself and Dorabella, but cannot refrain from showing him the miniature. Thereupon Ferrando comes as near seeing red as is possible to a light tenor in an opera buffa. At first he talks about tearing the faithless one's heart out; but very soon he is asking his friend's advice as to what he ought to do. Perhaps Guglielmo's success has slightly turned his head; anyhow we find him now apostrophising women in a genuine opera buffa aria the thesis of which is the favourite one of Don Alfonso—that the sex is frail and cannot be trusted. But Ferrando is not to be consoled in that way; and as he is entitled to an aria of his own after that of Guglielmo, he lets us know at proper length that in spite of Dorabella's treatment of him she still possesses his too fond heart. He is not at all consoled by Don Alfonso's admission later that he has lost half his bet, for one of the ladies at least has been faithful to her lover. And the old philosopher proposes yet another experiment, which will prove even to the cock-a-whoop

Guglielmo that it is foolish to count your chickens before they
are hatched.

The next scene is set in a room in the ladies' house. Despina
congratulates Dorabella on having at last behaved like a sensible
woman; while Dorabella's excuses for her recent conduct run on
much the same lines as those of Polly Peachum in the *Beggar's
Opera*:

> *But he so teaz'd me,*
> *And he so pleas'd me,*
> *What I did, you must have done.*

When Fiordiligi enters she is obviously not in the best of tempers; apparently while disapproving of her sister's capacity for
fickleness she cannot help envying it. Dorabella, in yet another
aria, which is so uninteresting that it is generally omitted, argues
with her very much as Despina herself might do.

Fiordiligi, when she is alone, thinks the matter over. A brilliant
idea strikes her: she rings for Despina and orders her to bring
from the wardrobe two uniforms of Ferrando and Guglielmo
respectively. (It is a sign of the helplessness that Da Ponte was
by now beginning to feel with regard to the untying of his knots
that he should not make the slightest attempt to explain to us how
these uniforms come to be where they are. At this stage of a long
libretto almost anything was good enough for Da Ponte, who,
as a dramatist, was first-rate at the hundred-and-twenty yards, so
to speak, but lacked the wind for the mile). Fiordiligi, we are
given to understand, has arrived at the desperate conclusion that
the only way for the sisters to preserve their innocence is to don
these uniforms and go to the seat of war themselves, she in Ferrando's, Dorabella in Guglielmo's, there to rejoin their legitimate
lovers as soldiers and die by their sides if necessary. She is regaling
herself with the thought of a reunion with her lover under these
romantic conditions when Ferrando himself, who has been
watching the proceedings through the open door, comes in, still
in the guise of an Albanian, and entreats her not to make him die
of despair: if he really must perish, let it be by the sword she has
in her hand. The struggle within Fiordiligi does not last long this
time. "Yield, dearest!", cries Ferrando; and Fiordiligi sinks into

a chair with no more than a feeble "Dei, consiglio!" Ferrando swears eternal fidelity to her, as lover, then as spouse; she falls on his breast, completely vanquished, and they go out of the room in an embrace that is not at all to the liking of Guglielmo, who, with Alfonso, has been watching it all from outside the door.

Alfonso has hard work to restrain Guglielmo, who, forgetting his own complacency when, a little while before, he had won over Dorabella, goes into something like the male equivalent of hysterics at the perfidy of his Fiordiligi. When Ferrando returns, looking most objectionably pleased with himself at having turned the tables on his friend, there is a moment or two of slight unpleasantness: then they both listen to the sage counsel of Don Alfonso. What are they making such a fuss about? he asks them. True, they could easily find any number of women to take the place of a Dorabella and a Fiordiligi. But will the others behave any better than these have done? If not, what's the use of changing? They still love the frail ones, don't they? Very well, let them take them as they are, for they cannot be otherwise; and meanwhile let the young men listen to a little song he will sing them. The burden of it is: "Everyone speaks ill of women, and I'm not surprised. If they change their lovers a thousand times a day, well, some people may call it a vice, others a habit, but in my view it is a necessity for them. If a lover is tricked he should blame not the lady but himself; for young or old, pretty or plain—come now, repeat it with me—they all do it!" And the young men dutifully repeat it with him, to the strain of No. 1.

But the joke is not yet played out, the imbroglio not yet cleared up. The ladies having consented to marry the fascinating strangers and to migrate to Albania with them, we next find ourselves watching the servants preparing the table for the wedding feast, under the supervision of Don Alfonso and Despina. Soon the betrothed couples come in, followed by a numerous company who sing a chorus of congratulations and good wishes. The two pairs of lovers unite in a quartet in which they thank the good Despina as the first cause of all their happiness; and the chorus having departed, the happy couples drink to themselves and to each other. Fiordiligi starts a melody which Ferrando and Dorabella take up in turn in a charming canon: Guglielmo, however, who has still not recovered from the shock of Fiordiligi's infidelity, only mutters in his beard a wish that what the others are drinking may poison them.

Don Alfonso had left with the chorus. He now returns with the notary, who, needless to say, is Despina in yet another of her disguises. The notary reads out in a professional nasal voice the contract of marriage between Sempronio and Fiordiligi and between Tizio and Dorabella—between, in fact, as he puts it, "these noble Albanians and these Ferrarese ladies"; the latter point was one which the Vienna audience of 1790 would not be likely to miss. He is just launching into the subject of dowries and settlements when the four of them declare that they will leave it all to him, and clamour for the contract and a pen. But the two ladies have no sooner signed than a distant drum roll is heard, followed by the "military" chorus from the first act. The sisters are terrified. Don Alfonso runs to the window, looks out, and confirms their worst fears—the regiment has indeed returned, and Ferrando and Guglielmo with it.

The agitated brides push their Albanian spouses into an adjoining room, wondering what is going to happen to themselves now, and putting up a prayer to heaven for help. Heaven does not answer them, but Don Alfonso does: they have only to leave it to him and all will be well. The lovers, meanwhile, who have slipped out of the room into which they were bundled, re-enter by the main door, not as the Albanians, of course, but as Ferrando and Guglielmo. The King, it seems, has countermanded the order to the regiment, so here they are again, safe and sound, and happy to be once more with their loving and faithful fiancées. But why are the ladies so pale, so speechless? they ask. Because, says the gallant and resourceful Don Alfonso, they are paralysed with pleasure at seeing their dear ones again.

The remaining threads of the intrigue are soon untied. Guglielmo, under the excuse of depositing his knapsack in the next room, opens the door and discovers a man hiding there—a notary! What is the meaning of this? Despina explains that it is no notary, but she herself, changing her costume after having been to a fancy dress ball. The ladies are a bit puzzled by this, but at the same time relieved. But they are dumbfounded when Ferrando picks up and reads the marriage contract, which Don Alfonso has rather ostentatiously dropped in front of him. The lovers bitterly upbraid Fiordiligi and Dorabella, who are now thoroughly beaten: they can only confess their fault and beg to be slain there and then. Their last faint hope is that Don Alfonso will do something for them. But apparently the traitor is against them, for he suggests to the lovers that they shall take a look in the next room, where they will find the proof they want of their fiancées' infidelity. They do so, and return once more in Albanian guise. Guglielmo hands over to Dorabella the miniature she had given him; and he and Ferrando praise "the magnetic doctor" who had been so clever.

The game is entirely up so far as Fiordiligi and Dorabella are concerned. They throw the blame for their lapse, of course, on Don Alfonso, who takes it in quite good part. It is true he has fooled them, he says, but it was for the education of their lovers, who will be wiser in future. He advises them to make it up and forget it all: he has had his laugh, let them now have theirs. "You are betrothed", he tells them: "now embrace and say no more about it." This they do. But do the couples now pair off as they were at the beginning of the opera, or as we found them at the signing of the marriage contract? We are not told: perhaps Da Ponte and Mozart themselves did not know and did not care. The lively finale ends with an ensemble to the text of "Happy is the man who takes everything as it comes, and in all the vicissitudes of life lets himself be guided by reason; who laughs when others weep, and remains unmoved when the whirlwind blows."

THE SERAGLIO
Mozart (1756-1791)

PRINCIPAL CHARACTERS

CONSTANZE	*Soprano*
BLONDE	*Soprano*
BELMONTE	*Tenor*
PEDRILLO	*Tenor*
OSMIN	*Bass*
THE PASHA SELIM	*Speaking Part*

I

It is of course impossible for that rather terrible by-product of the contemporary theatre, the producer, to keep his meddling hands off *The Seraglio*; and so we seldom see the charming work given precisely as it is, in spite of the fact that it is virtually the one opera of Mozart's that does not require any re-arrangement for the modern stage. There are dull numbers in *Figaro* and *Don Giovanni* to which no amount of piety can induce us to listen with any pretence of rapture, and the conductor or producer who omits these today is doing us in the audience a service. But in *The Seraglio* there is not a single really dull number from start to finish. In his later operas and instrumental works Mozart develops admirable qualities that were not present, at any rate to the same degree, in his earlier ones; but in some of his creations of the period between about 1775 and 1782 there is a peculiar romantic glow that somehow or other faded out of him as he matured.

In 1818 Weber introduced *The Seraglio* to Dresden under his own baton, and in a preliminary article he commended the work to his fellow-townsmen in words that bear quotation today. Weber hit the nail on the head when he said that *The Seraglio* presents us with a picture of "what every man's joyous youthful years are to him, years the bloom of which he will never recapture. . . . I venture to say that in *The Seraglio* Mozart had attained the peak of his artistic experience, to which only experience of the world had to be added later. Mankind was entitled to expect from him several more operas like *Figaro* and *Don Giovanni*; but with the best will in the world he could never have written another *Seraglio*."

In 1781 Mozart was living in Vienna. He had cut the ties that had so long bound him to his father and his father's employer, the Prince Archbishop of Salzburg, and he had fallen in love with Konstanze Weber, the daughter of a former ticket-seller in the Vienna National Theatre. It was while he was waiting for his father's consent to his marriage that he received a commission for a German Singspiel—the order being given in accordance with the desire of the Emperor Joseph II that his Court Theatre should aim at being more German in its future policy and less Italian. For the text of the new opera recourse was first of all had to the actor Friedrich Schröder; but as he had nothing useful to contribute the commission was turned over to Gottlieb Stephanie (actually Stephan), who figures in theatrical history as Stephanie Junior to distinguish him from his brother. Mozart's father has some nasty things to say about Stephanie in his letters to his son; but to have been disparaged by the envious, suspicious Leopold Mozart is regarded today as more of a testimonial for any man than an indictment of him.

On the 1st August 1781 Mozart wrote to his father, "The day before yesterday young Stephanie handed me a 'book' to compose. . . . It is very good. The subject is Turkish, and is called '*Bellmont* [sic] *und Konstanze, oder Die Verführung* [sic] [1] *aus dem Serail.* For the symphony [i.e. the overture], the chorus in the first act, and the final chorus I will write Turkish music. . . . I am so delighted with the book that I have already done the first aria for the Cavalieri, that for Adamberger, and the trio that concludes the first act." [2] The music to this act was complete by the 22nd August. Then it was announced that the production

[1] The ultimate title of the work was *Die Entführung aus dem Serail* (*The Abduction from the Seraglio*).

[2] Caterina Cavalieri was the Constanze, and Adamberger the Belmonte, in the first performance of the opera.

would have to be postponed owing to the inability of the Emperor to visit the theatre on the date originally intended. Mozart was consequently able to work in more leisurely fashion at his score, which was finished in June 1782. The first performance took place in Vienna on the 16th July. On the following 4th August Mozart was at last able to marry his Konstanze.

"Turkish" operas and plays and stories were highly popular in the seventeenth and eighteenth centuries, when pirates still made the Mediterranean unsafe for quiet people, and no one undertaking a voyage anywhere between Jaffa and Gibraltar could be quite sure that it would not end, if he were an able-bodied man, in a slit throat or slavery, or, if she were a young and good-looking woman, in a harem. The "Turkish" theme, in fact, communicated to the romantic mind in those days something of the thrill for which the youth of the nineteenth century used to turn to the Red Indian, and the youth of today turns—or did so as late as the day before yesterday—to the American gangster. Of the many previous incursions into the "Turkish" world only one has any interest today in connection with *The Seraglio*. In 1781 there was produced an opera entitled *Belmont und Konstanze*, the text of which was by one Christoph Friedrich Bretzner; this was laid under contribution by Stephanie with the gay nonchalance characteristic of the days when copyright protection for authors and composers was unknown. Bretzner, however, managed to immortalise himself by a communication he sent to a Leipzig journal in 1782: "A certain person of the name of Mozart, living in Vienna, has had the impudence to misuse my drama *Belmont und Konstanze* for an opera text. I hereby protest most solemnly against this encroachment on my rights, and reserve further action." The name of Herr Bretzner thus goes down to history coupled with that of one Franz Schubert, a minor composer of the early nineteenth century, who indignantly protested that *he* was not the Franz Schubert responsible for a certain setting of *The Erl-King* about which everyone was talking. In any case Bretzner had small claim to sympathy on the ground that he had been robbed, for his own work had been the result of all-round pillage: everyone and everything in his *Belmont und Konstanze* is a stock character or a stock situation of the period.

2

The main themes of the charming overture—which, with its piccolo, big drum, cymbals and triangle colouring, is in the best vein of eighteenth century "Turkish" music,—are the vigorous one given out in the opening bars:

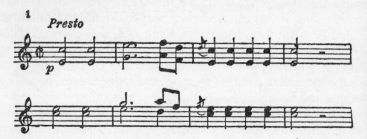

and its counterpart in the key of the dominant:

but midway in the development of his material Mozart inserts a tender reference, in the minor, to Belmonte's first song, which we shall soon hear in the major:

The overture has no formal close, but runs straight on into the song of Belmonte's just mentioned:

The scene is the terrace of the Pasha Selim's house, overlooking the sea, in which Belmonte believes his long-lost Constanze, who had been taken by pirates, to be a captive. His immediate problem is how to get access to her in the conditions that obtain in the establishment of a Turkish Pasha. While he is thinking this out the Pasha's head gardener and factotum Osmin enters, singing a little love song of his own, for the old curmudgeon, as we discover later, is over head and ears in love with Constanze's maid Blonde, who had been captured with her mistress.

Belmonte thinks that this old fellow may be able to give him the information he wants, but Osmin is too much absorbed in his own lyrical reflections to be open to general conversation. Belmonte has to ask him several times whether this is the Pasha Selim's house:

before he can get an answer. When this comes, it is in a musical form that shows how conclusive a plump drop into the tonic key can be after one has been kept poised for some time on the domi-

nant, as we have been during Belmonte's questions: the tonality
of Osmin's reply leaves nothing further to be said on the subject:

6

Das ist des Bas - sa Se - lim Haus!

It appears, moreover, that the gardener is in Selim's service. In
that case, says Belmonte, can he have a word with one Pedrillo,
who, he understands, is also engaged there? The knowledge that
the young man is a friend of Pedrillo's does not endear him to
Osmin, for Pedrillo—a veritable gallows bird, according to him
—is his rival in the affections of Blonde: he would have the
rapscallion hanged, drawn and quartered if he could. All this we
learn in an amusing duet, which ends with Osmin shooing Belmonte off the scene.

Pedrillo now enters, full of an impudence and self-assurance
that are especially exasperating to Osmin, because the gallows
bird has somehow or other managed to get on the soft side of the
Pasha. There is a lively scene between the pair, Osmin swearing
by the beard of the Prophet that he will get the better of his saucy
young rival one of these days, Pedrillo making him madder and
madder by laughing at him. As soon as Osmin has stormed out,
Belmonte returns. He and his former servant are rejoiced to see
each other again. Pedrillo gives Belmonte all the news. He and
the two girls had had the good fortune to be bought from the
pirates by the Pasha Selim, whose favourite Constanze has become—though, he hastens to assure Belmonte, there is nothing
whatever to worry about on that account. Pedrillo's own poor
little Blonde has not done quite so well, for she is daily pestered
by the attentions of an ugly old clodhopper to whom the Pasha
has seen fit to assign her—the same with whom Belmonte has just
been talking, not only the Pasha's gardener but his handy man
and spy. Still, taking one thing with another, things might be
worse. Thanks to the Pasha's liking for Pedrillo, he is allowed to
be about the garden when the ladies of the harem come out to
take the air. Belmonte informs him that he has a ship lying just

off shore; and Pedrillo, though not underrating the difficulties, thinks they may be able to get the girls away. Then, seeing Constanze and the Pasha in the distance, he hurries away to meet them and, if possible, put in a good word for Belmonte.

The latter, left alone, launches into a song of love to his Constanze:

the orchestral accompaniment to which, as we learn from one of Mozart's letters to his father, is full of touches descriptive of the lover's state of mind. "The throbbing of the loving heart is indicated by the first and second violins in octaves. . . . One sees the trembling, the faltering, the heaving of the breast (expressed by a *crescendo*), one hears the whispering and sighing (first violins, muted, and a flute in unison)." It was doubtless to his own Constanze, as much as to Stephanie's, that Mozart was pouring out his heart in this aria.

Pedrillo comes running back with the news that the Pasha is close by, whereupon Belmonte conceals himself. Selim, who is accompanied by Constanze, lands from a boat, and is greeted with a chorus of welcome from his janissaries:

"As regards the janissaries' chorus", says Mozart in the same letter, "this is all that a janissaries' chorus ought to be—short and merry, and the very thing for the Viennese."

Addressing Constanze in the most courteous fashion, although she is his property, Selim laments that he has not yet succeeded in winning her love. She recognises his nobility and forbearance, but explains that her thoughts always run on the one she loved in the days of her freedom; to him she will for ever be true. Her aria, "Ach, ich liebte" is of the coloratura order and takes her at one or two points up to the high D; but for all that the dominant expression of it is that of grief. When, in the dialogue that follows, she tells the Pasha once again that no one will ever have her heart but the lover from whom she has been torn, his anger rises for a moment. He bids her reflect once more, and for the last time: he will wait for her answer till the morrow. But when she has left him he softens again; never will he employ violence, he says, against one so loving and so lovable.

Pedrillo now approaches with Belmonte, whom he introduces as a friend from Italy who, having heard glowing accounts of Selim's magnificence, has come to offer him his services as architect. The Pasha promises to consider the matter and to see the stranger again the next day. He goes into his palace, and Belmonte and Pedrillo, congratulating themselves on the success of their scheme, are about to follow him when Osmin comes out and bars their way. Neither Belmonte's haughty assertion of his rank nor Pedrillo's gay impudence and his assurance that the stranger is now in the Pasha's service has the smallest effect on the surly Osmin. He knows, he says, how easy it is to impose on the good Pasha, for he is as soft as butter: but he, Osmin, is a tougher proposition altogether. The scene culminates in a lively trio, in the course of which the pair manage to push him aside and run into the palace.

3

The opening scene of the second act, which takes place in the Pasha's garden, introduces us to the sprightly Blonde, who, as the curtain goes up, is telling poor Osmin, not for the first time, apparently, what she thinks of him. It isn't a Turkish slave he has to deal with, she gives him to understand in her aria. It appears that she is English; and English girls don't stand any nonsense from people like him. All this bullying and threatening and sulking and snarling gets a man nowhere: the only things that impress a nice girl like herself are smiles and tender speeches and flatteries:

Durch Zärt - lich - keit und Schmei-cheln, Ge-fäl - lig-keit und Scherzen,

As none of these happen to be in Osmin's repertory, he tries the high hand with her. Are they not in Turkey? Has not the Pasha given her to him? Is he not the master, she the slave? But Blonde, as a free-born Englishwoman, does not care a rap for any Osmin, Pasha, or Turkey. Let him wait till she knows the place a bit better: then she will raise the banner of revolt among the ladies of the harem. For her part she is in love with that charming young fellow Pedrillo. At the mention of his detested rival, Osmin, as usual, sees red; but when he threatens violence Blonde reminds him that her mistress is the Pasha's favourite—one word from her, and it's fifty of the best on the soles of Osmin's feet! This cools him down; and after a lively duet, in which the most that Osmin can do is to apostrophise the English race, telling them they must be crazy to give their women so much liberty, she bundles him unceremoniously off the stage.

As she does so, Constanze enters from the opposite side, looking very sad. Blonde feels sorry for her: *she*, at least, can see her Pedrillo by stealth every day, while her mistress can only dream of her Belmonte. Constanze pours out her heart in a melancholy aria, descriptive of her sufferings since the day she was torn from her lover:

10

which is laid out on the broadest concerto lines, with four solo
instruments and an orchestral introduction of some sixty bars.
It is not easy for either of the characters to keep the action alive
while this long introduction is playing, or for the Pasha to know
what to do while the aria itself is running its lengthy course. That,
however, is the actors' and the producer's problem; and since
Mozart wanted things thus, they had better get their brains to
work at it. Towards the end, Constanze approaches the Pasha to
hurl her final defiance straight in his face: "Patiently will I bear
the worst you can do. Command, storm, rage, do what you will:
death will release me from it all."

She leaves him, and he does some thinking. What gives her the
courage to defy him like this? Is she planning to escape? No, it

Blonde tries to console her: surely, she says, a young man so rich
and so resourceful as Belmonte will find some means of rescuing
them, even from a Turkish harem. But Constanze has given up
all hope.

Blonde retires as the Pasha enters. He woos Constanze once
more, and once more is repulsed. Never can she love him, she
says; neither the threat of death, nor, what is worse, of torture
can shake her resolution. She proudly assures him of this in the
long and brilliant aria "Martern aller Arten":

11

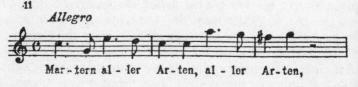

cannot be that, otherwise she would take another line with him, and try to put him off his guard by seeming complaisance. But as neither prayers nor threats avail, he must try craft.

Blonde, returning to the scene, is astonished to find neither Constanze nor the Pasha there. Have they come to an understanding at last? she asks herself. This poor mistress of hers is really too faithful to her Belmonte. As for herself, she is fortunate enough to have Pedrillo always at hand. Were it not so, there is no saying what might happen; she might be tempted, as she puts it, to become quite mussulmanised in her way of thinking. Pedrillo breaks in upon these meditations of hers with the news that great plans are on foot—Belmonte has come, he has obtained admission into the palace as an architect, he has a ship waiting in the bay, and he intends to rescue all three of them before many hours are over. At midnight he will be at Constanze's window with a ladder: Pedrillo will be at Blonde's window with another: as for Osmin, Pedrillo is going to put a sleeping-draught into his drink in the course of the evening. Blonde is to give the good news to her mistress. Left to herself, Blonde pauses only long enough to give vent to her feelings in a joyous song:

and then runs into the palace.

Pedrillo returns to await Belmonte: he has with him a basket containing two flasks of wine, one large, the other small, and a couple of drinking-cups. Now that the hour for action is approaching, the bright little fellow does not feel quite so pleased with himself as he did a little while ago. If only they were safe on the sea with their maidens, never to see this accursed land again! To give himself courage he sings a ditty in which he assures himself again and again that "only cowards are afraid".

Osmin enters, and a richly comic scene ensues between the two. Pedrillo, the soul of gaiety once more, commiserates with Osmin on being a Mahommedan, and so forbidden wine. Bit by bit he manages to overcome the old fellow's suspicions and inveigle him into drinking with him, assuring him that Mahomet, who has long been dead, has something better to do than to bother about Osmin and his drop of wine. The pair sit down back to back, become eloquent on the themes of wine and women, and drain glass after glass, until Osmin is so completely tipsy that he can even address Pedrillo as "brother". He refuses to go indoors, denying that he is sleepy; but Pedrillo scares him by dropping a hint about the Pasha. He somehow manages to prop the bulky Osmin up against a tree and then take him on his own back and drag him off the stage. Then he returns to keep the rendezvous with Belmonte, considerably happier than he was a little while ago. It is only three hours now from midnight, and Osmin can be trusted, he thinks, not to recover consciousness within that time.

Belmonte enters, followed in a moment by Constanze and Blonde. Pedrillo draws the latter on one side and, judging by his miming, gives a humorous account of the trick he has played on Osmin. Belmonte begins to pour out his soul to Constanze, though not, as one might have expected, in an impetuous aria but in an *adagio* one: his first thought is of all they have suffered since their separation. It is only towards the end, when he looks forward to their future bliss, that the tempo changes to *allegretto*. Constanze replies in much more passionate tones, and gradually communicates her ardour to Belmonte. Pedrillo and Blonde, going over the arrangements for midnight, join with the leading pair of lovers in a quartet. This is not without its clouded moments, for Belmonte cannot help expressing a timid hope that Constanze has resisted the Pasha's advances, which emboldens Pedrillo to put a question or two of a similar kind to Blonde. Constanze convinces Belmonte by the simple process of bursting into tears: the indignant Blonde's only argument is a box on the ear for Pedrillo. Each of the lovers thereupon craves pardon for ever having doubted, and is soon forgiven. The curtain falls on their complete reconciliation.

4

The setting of the third act is an open space before the palace, overlooking the sea, with the main building on one side and Osmin's quarters on the other. It is midnight. Pedrillo enters with the captain of Belmonte's ship, one Klaas, who is carrying a long ladder which he places against the wall of the palace. Then he goes back to his ship, leaving Pedrillo to give yet another exhibition of that shrinking from danger that has been one of the characteristics of the comic stage servant from the earliest days of the drama. Pedrillo is a distant descendant of Sosia, for example, the slave of Amphitryon in the comedy of Plautus. These plaguey Turks, according to Pedrillo, have no sense of humour; and though the Pasha Selim is a renegade, when it comes to chopping off heads he is just a Turk like the rest. (This is the first intimation we have had that Selim had changed his religion: it is no doubt inserted here to prepare us for his most un-Turk-like generosity later to a lady who has tried to abscond from his harem).

Klaas returns with a shorter ladder, which, being intended for Blonde, he places against the wall of Osmin's house. Then he goes off to his ship again to make the final preparations for the flight.

Belmonte enters. Pedrillo leaves him in order to take a last look round and see that there are no spies about. Meanwhile, he says, Belmonte is to burst into song, for apparently the inhabitants of the palace in general and Osmin's quarters in particular are so accustomed to hearing Pedrillo serenading Blonde every night that they will suspect there is something wrong if for once some one does not give a recital. So Belmonte launches out into a long aria, "Ich baue ganz auf deine Stärke":

13   Andante

Ich bau-e   ganz   auf dei - ne Stär - ke,

the burden of which is the power of love to accomplish whatever it sets its hand to. This finished, Pedrillo returns. He looks at his watch. It is just twelve o'clock—time for the signal to Blonde. Bidding his master keep watch on the other side of the stage, he takes up a position near Osmin's house and sings two stanzas of a delightful little romance about a pretty maiden who was taken captive by the Moors and waited and waited till the rescuer came. Strange to say, this evokes no sign of life from within; so Pedrillo confides to the night air a further couple of verses, which tell how the elopement was achieved at precisely twelve o'clock one night. At last the song awakes Constanze, who puts her head out of an upper window. Belmonte ascends the ladder, and a moment or two later makes his exit with her through the palace door. They disappear into the darkness, leaving Pedrillo, whose heart is in his boots again, to follow with Blonde when he can. He ascends the shorter ladder and disappears through the window which is now opened in Blonde's room.

But his singing has awakened a mute, who in turn has roused Osmin. Befuddled as the old man still is, he guesses there is something wrong, and comes out to investigate. Soon the mute spots the ladder in front of Osmin's house. Sending the dumb man to rouse the guard, Osmin climbs the ladder, and reaches the upper window just as Pedrillo and Blonde appear at it. They go back hurriedly into the room, slamming the window in Osmin's face. He begins to descend the ladder, but so cautiously and clumsily, as befits a man of his years, that he is only half-way down when Pedrillo and Blonde come out by the door and escape under his very nose. As soon as Osmin reaches earth again he is arrested by the watch under suspicion of having put the ladder where it is. He is still explaining who he is and what has happened when Pedrillo and Blonde return in custody, followed a minute or two later by the captured Belmonte and Constanze.

Pedrillo tries to convince Osmin that he had merely been taking Blonde for a little walk, seeing that his "little brother" Osmin is hardly in a condition to do that himself today—a gentle reminder of the episode with the bottles, designed to frighten Osmin, who, as a professing Mussulman, has laid himself open to dire penalties by indulging in wine. But Osmin is not so easily

terrified. When Belmonte and Constanze are brought in, he asks
ironically if perhaps the Herr Architekt has also been planning to
take a walk. Belmonte tries to bribe him, but Osmin prefers his
revenge: with Pedrillo in particular he has long wanted to get
even. He pours out his detestation of poor Pedrillo in a vigorous
aria in which he gloats over the prospect of seeing him and his
companion strangled:

14   *Allegro vivace*

Ha!   wie   will ich tri - um - phi - ren,
Wenn   sie   euch zum Richtplatz füh - ren,

und   die Häl-se schnüren zu, schnüren zu,

The final scene takes place in a hall in the palace, in the early
hours of that same morning. The Pasha, who has been awakened
from his sleep by the noise, has just ordered his servants to find
out the meaning of it all, when Osmin enters, still a trifle heavy
from the sleeping-draught that had been put into his wine. He
tells the Pasha of the plot of the pseudo-architect and Pedrillo to
abduct Constanze and Blonde, a plot which, thanks to Osmin's
devotion and intelligence, has been frustrated. Belmonte and
Constanze are brought in by the guards. The Pasha reproaches
Constanze for her perfidy. She pleads, in excuse, that this "architect" is the man to whom her heart has long been pledged; let the
Pasha take her life if he will, but spare her lover's. Belmonte,
though it goes against the grain with him, also begs for clemency.
He is, he explains, the son of one who will pay anything to free
him—a rich Spaniard of the name of Lostados. Selim looks up in
astonishment. Lostados? Does Belmonte know a Commandant
at Oran of that name? "My father", replies the young man.
Thereupon the Pasha rejoices that fate has thrown into his hands
the son of his deadliest enemy, the man who had robbed him of
his betrothed, ruined and degraded him, and driven him from his

fatherland. What would that Lostados do, he asks, if he were now in the Pasha's place?

He will deal with Belmonte, he says, as once Lostados did with him; and he leaves the hall with Osmin, ostensibly to give orders for the torture. Belmonte bitterly reproaches himself for having brought Constanze to this pass; but she consoles him with the assurance that she is willing to die with him. At the conclusion of their long duet Pedrillo and Blonde are brought in by the guards. They too face torture and death with composure, though their views on those subjects are necessarily not expressed at such length and in such elegant language as those of their master and mistress. The Pasha returns. Belmonte defies him to do his worst, but Selim surprises him by telling him that his contempt for Lostados is too vast for him to imitate him in anything, even in revenge. "You are free. Take your Constanze, return to your own land, and tell your father that though you were in my power I set you free, to prove to him that there can be more satisfaction in returning good for evil than in requiting one crime with another." Constanze also, who thanks him and implores his forgiveness, he dismisses with a kindly word. Then Pedrillo, who looks like being forgotten, puts in an appeal for similar magnanimity towards himself and Blonde. This he obtains, in spite of the protests of Osmin at being robbed of his female slave, the Pasha humorously assuring him that it will be better for him too, in the long run, that he shall lose her.

Belmonte begins a little song of praise of the Pasha:

the final strain of which:

kann,   den seh' man mit Ver - ach - tung an!

s repeated by the whole assembly. Then Constanze takes up the
melody, followed by Pedrillo and Blonde in turn, the refrain
being repeated each time as on the first occasion. A passing
reference of the irrepressible Blonde to Osmin goads the old man
into an angry reply, in which he hankers once more after the
vengeance that will now never be his. The janissaries sing the
praises of the Pasha in a chorus which, like that in the first act,
has a pleasant pseudo-"Turkish" touch about it here and there,
and the curtain falls with the two happy couples making their
way to the ship that is awaiting them.

5

The modern producer, as we have said, cannot keep his offi-
cious hands off *The Seraglio*; but the more he tries to re-shape the
work as he imagines it ought to be the more convinced we become that it is better as Stephanie and Mozart wrote it. That it
has one or two little awkwardnesses and weaknesses of con-
truction cannot be denied; but every attempt to remedy these
only substitutes a fresh set of flaws, and a worse set, for the old
ones. Several of the so-called "defects" of the opera are more
imaginary than real; we cease to be perturbed by them as soon as
we try to look at the work from the point of view of its own period
and milieu, instead of making it an absurd grievance against the
past that it did not shape its theatrical practice in accordance with
certain notions of today. Some critics have succeeded in per-
uading themselves that it is a blot on the opera that the Pasha has
only a speaking part—a circumstance said to have been imposed
upon Mozart and his librettist by the limited number of singers
t their disposal. But for many of us the fact that Selim uses only
he speaking voice lends a special interest to the character and
confers a peculiar distinction on it. Whatever strict aesthetics
may conceive it to be its duty to say on this matter, there can be
no doubt that telling dramatic effects can sometimes be drawn
from the co-operation of the speaking with the singing voice

in opera. In any case, *The Seraglio* is not "grand opera" but a Singspiel. It is only in the more highly-lit emotional moments that the characters break into song: the whole of the action is carried on by means of ordinary speech. It is not, then, as if the Pasha alone spoke always while everyone else always sang; it is merely a matter of his continuing to speak in one or two situations in which the modern theoretician assumes he ought to sing. One critic laments that there is "no musical answer" on the Pasha's part to Constanze's big aria (No. 11—"Martern aller Arten"). But why on earth should Selim any more reply in music to *this* expression of Constanze's sentiments than he does to so many others? "Martern aller Arten" is a very extended piece of musical design: a musical reply to it on Selim's part would constitute, if short, an anti-climax, while if long it would upset the proportions of the act as a whole. Moreover, since he has so far been able, and later will be able again, to express in speech, with perfect effectiveness, every emotion set up in him by Constanze or anyone else, is there any particular reason why the resources of language should prove insufficient for his purpose in just this one instance?

The experiment has been tried of giving Selim, somewhere or other in the course of the work, an opportunity to sing one of the finest of the many arias—"Per questa bella mano"—written by Mozart for concert room use. But the only result has been to make us feel that a two-dimensional Selim, so to speak, has been arbitrarily substituted for Mozart's one-dimensional Selim without any corresponding gain in psychological verisimilitude or dramatic effectiveness. There is another consideration to be borne in mind. The fact that Selim has not to sing makes it possible to entrust the part to an actor—not a singer—entirely qualified for it by appearance, vocal timbre, and skill in elocution; and no one who has seen the rôle played as it can and should be played can regret that Mozart did not see fit to substitute for this grave, dignified figure—whose curiously dominating intellectual position in the drama is accentuated by his never breaking, like all the others, into song—just one more bass or tenor to add to the evening's tale of technical shortcoming.

Another reproach that is brought against the libretto is that the whole scene of the abduction in the third act is carried on by means of speech alone: no singing occurs between Pedrillo's "Romanze"—"In Mohrenland gefangen war"—and the aria of Osmin—"Ha! wie will ich triumphieren"—after the frustration of the plot. But once more we have to bear in mind the genre to which *The Seraglio* belongs. It would no doubt have been an excellent thing had Mozart's librettist been able to supply him, for the abduction episode, with a text that would have enabled him to cast the whole scene, packed as it is with action, into music from start to finish, in the style that makes the second act of *Figaro* the miracle it is. But it is not easy to see just how Stephanie could have got through all he has to get through in this scene in the way of action and at the same time provide Mozart with a series of opportunities to "spread himself" as a musician. Let us once more accept the fact that *The Seraglio* is a Singspiel—a sublimated specimen of it, thanks to the genius of Mozart, but for all that just a Singspiel, a genre in which music as a matter of course surrenders some of its own claims for the convenience of the drama.

As for the changes that are sometimes made in the disposition of the arias, it can only be said uncompromisingly that they weaken rather than strengthen the action. The only possible excuse that can be put forward for transferring "Martern aller Arten" from the second act to the third is the fact that while in this last act Belmonte, Pedrillo and Osmin all have arias of one kind or another, Constanze has none: she joins the rest of them, of course, in the finale, but apart from that, Stephanie and Mozart make her sing only in the duet with Belmonte—"Welch ein Geschick!"—which follows the capture of the lovers. But to transfer "Martern aller Arten" to this point involves first of all holding up the concluding action of the opera while Constanze tells the Pasha at great length what she thinks of him, and in the second place weakens the effect of the scene between him and Constanze in the second act. "Martern aller Arten" is best left where Stephanie and Mozart chose to put it. So with the cut that is sometimes made in the second act, necessitating the removal of Belmonte's Aria No. 15—"Wenn der Freude Thränen fliessen" —to the beginning of the third act; and with the experiment occasionally made of leaving No. 15 in its proper place but transferring Belmonte's aria—"Ich baue ganz auf deine Stärke" (No. 17)—from its proper place in the third act to the commencement of that act.

Some sort of case might be argued for modifying the construction of *The Seraglio* were its little peculiarities the result of incompetence on the part of either the librettist or the musician. But they were not: they were merely the result of indifference on their part to considerations that seem more important to us of a later day than they did to them. Mozart, like the other opera composers of his epoch—apart from Gluck—was blissfully free of aesthetic or historical prepossessions: nor did he ever pause to consider whether theatrical humanity a century or two later would approve or disapprove of what he was doing at this moment or that. What he had to do, and all he thought of doing, was a job of work: he had been commissioned to produce an opera, and given a certain local personnel to produce it with; and he would have thought anyone crazy who suggested to him that he had a duty to posterity as well as to himself, and that he must not so much as embark on his share of the work until he was satisfied that psychologically and dramatically Stephanie's "book" would stand the strictest scrutiny by critics and aestheticians to the end of time. The eighteenth century opera audience was completely lacking in our own highly developed historical sense. It knew next to nothing of the remote past of the art, and cared absolutely nothing about its distant future; and Mozart, the least theoretical of musicians, would have been the last to imagine it to be his duty to try to impose a new water-tight, objection-proof ideal of opera on his collaborators and his listeners. He sensibly applied himself not to aesthetic speculation but to throwing himself heart and soul into whatever dramatic character or situation appealed greatly to him, and where the appeal was less strong he availed himself of his unique faculty for turning out, at a moment's notice, and in response to any stimulus or even to no stimulus at all, a piece of music which, if it does not particularly elevate the critical modern listener, at any rate never lets him badly down—music that manipulates the most serviceable clichés of the period with consummate skill and the most perfect taste.

It is true that he generally did some thinking of his own about the subjects and texts submitted to him. But, as the references to *The Seraglio* in his letters to his father are alone sufficient to show, his thinking was that not of an arm-chair theoretician but of a practical man of the theatre. If he thought there was a better way of making a particular episode effective than the one provided by his librettist, he would tell him so. But he would, and could, suggest improvements only within the framework dictated by plain common sense and the theatrical practice of his day; the vast field of speculation lying outside that framework had the minimum of interest for him. Moreover, like other composers of the period, he had perforce to see every work of his in terms of the human material at his disposal for the first production of it; and since a radical change of cast for the benefit of an opera was out of the question, the only thing to do was to shape the work with an eye constantly on the cast allotted to him. The main reason why his Osmin is given so much to sing is that he was a first-rate singer. The original player of the part, Ludwig Fischer, had a bass voice of exceptional tonal range and remarkable flexibility. Considering himself fortunate to have such an asset in his opera, Mozart decided to make the utmost possible use of him; and Osmin becomes a more important character in Stephanie's libretto than he was in Bretzner's merely because Fischer was exceptionally competent in his particular line.

The reader will recall that *The Seraglio* begins with an aria by Belmonte, after which Osmin sings his little ditty, "Wer ein Liebchen hat gefunden"; then comes a longish duet between him and Belmonte. Stephanie had evidently cast this scene, apart from Osmin's song, in the form of spoken dialogue; and it was Mozart who insisted on its being sung throughout. On the 26th September 1781 he writes thus to his father: "The opera [as originally submitted to him] began with a monologue. This I asked Herr Stephanie to make into a little arietta—and further, that instead of making [Belmonte and Osmin] chit-chat together after the latter's little song, they should have a duet. Since the rôle of Osmin is intended for Herr Fischer, who has a really capital bass voice . . . we must make good use of him, especially as he has the great public with him. In the original libretto Osmin had nothing whatever to sing except this *Liedchen* and a share in the trio [1] and the finale. So now he gets an aria [No. 3, "Solche hergelaufne Laffen"] in the first act, and he will be given another in the second." [2] Mozart goes on to say that in the aria in the first act he has taken care to make good use of Fischer's effective deep notes: moreover, he has been so intent on Fischer, rather than on Osmin, that not only did the suggestion for the aria come from himself but he actually wrote the bulk of the music without any text, leaving it to Stephanie to fit words to the melody as best he could later.

Mozart, it will be seen, knew perfectly well what he was doing in *The Seraglio*; and if we have to choose between him and the modern producer there ought to be no hesitation in our choice. We go to see and hear the opera for Mozart's, not the producer's, sake; and it is really much easier for us to make the slight mental effort necessary to listen to the work in its proper historical perspective than to accommodate ourselves to changes in it that have their origin, for the most part, merely in the conviction of the producer that in order to justify his position in the theatre he must at all costs "produce". [3]

[1] I.e., with Belmonte and Pedrillo at the end of the first act.

[2] As a matter of fact Osmin did *not* get an aria in the second act, though he takes part in a duet with Pedrillo.

[3] It is true that while in the middle of his labours Mozart desired a drastic change in the lay-out of the end of the second act and the beginning of the third; but for one reason or another this was not done. What would have been the final effect on the opera of this re-modelling it is useless to conjecture. The only *Entführung* we have is the actual one bequeathed to us by the librettist and the composer; and the broad fact remains that this is better in the form in which Stephanie and Mozart left it than in any new form imposed on it by the modern producer.

LES TROYENS
Hector Berlioz (1803-1869)

PRINCIPAL CHARACTERS

CASSANDRA	*Mezzo-soprano*
DIDO	*Mezzo-soprano*
ANNA	*Contralto*
AENEAS	*Tenor*
CORŒBUS	*Baritone*
IOPAS	*Tenor*
NARBAL	*Bass*
HYLAS	*Tenor*

I

In the somewhat unmusical France of the first half of the nineteenth century a composer's quickest way to fame and his only way to fortune was *via* the opera house. At opera, accordingly, Berlioz tried his hand as soon as he had obtained some sort of standing in Paris. His *Benvenuto Cellini* was produced on the 10th September 1838. It was given again on the 12th, and for the third time on the 14th; the fourth performance did not take place until the 11th January 1839, after which the work disappeared for ever from the local repertory. Seeing little chance now to establish himself at the Opéra for some time to come, Berlioz was driven back into the concert room, where he experimented for a while with a genre that was essentially dramatic in intention but did not require a stage setting. To this mixed genre belong his *Romeo and Juliet*, first given in November 1839, and *The Damnation of Faust*, produced in December 1846. Each was a failure so far as the larger French public was concerned.

In his heart of hearts, Berlioz must have recognised that there was a certain amount of justice in the public refusal to become wildly enthusiastic over a nondescript form that was too operatic for the concert room yet not dramatic enough for the theatre; but he remained to the end of his days not only hurt but puzzled at the failure of *Benvenuto Cellini*, in which, indeed, there is much excellent stuff. No amount of re-arranging and re-writing on his part ever sufficed to rehabilitate the work, either in Weimar (under Liszt) in 1852, or in London in 1853. Thanks to Liszt, Weimar, in the 1850's, was given one opportunity after another of hearing Berlioz's major works, whenever possible under the composer himself. In February 1856 the little town had a Berlioz Festival: Liszt conducted a revised version of *Benvenuto Cellini* on the 16th of the month, and Berlioz the *Corsair* Overture on the 17th and *The Damnation of Faust* on the 28th.

It was during this visit of his to Weimar that Liszt's friend the Princess Wittgenstein urged Berlioz to forget his many discouragements and take seriously in hand a project for a grand opera on the subject of the Trojans that had apparently been occupying his thoughts for a long time. He seems to have had a good grounding in Latin as a child, and from his earliest years Vergil had been a passion with him. It is therefore not surprising that when, during the 1850's, his thoughts turned once more in the direction of opera, the great figures of the early books of the *Aeneid*, which, like himself, are at once classical and romantic, should have sprung to life in his imagination; and presumably the Princess did no more than add, by her sympathy and encouragement, fuel to a fire that had long been smouldering within him. At any rate he began to cast his ideas on the subject into literary form as soon as he returned to Paris. It soon possessed him as no other subject had ever done: he felt that the greatest task of his life was now before him.

The theme called, of course, for an exceptionally large canvas. For the bulk of his material Berlioz, who was his own librettist, relied on the stories of the fall of Troy and the tragic love of Dido and Aeneas as told by Vergil in his first, second and fourth books. For the love duet between the Carthaginian Queen and the Trojan hero, however, he laid Shakespeare under contribution, adapting to his own purposes the dialogue between Lorenzo and Jessica in the fifth act of *The Merchant of Venice*, commencing

The moon shines bright; in such a night as this . . .

These Shakespearean images had no doubt always had definite

Vergilian associations for Berlioz, for besides a reference to Troilus and Troy the English poet describes how

> *in such a night*
> *Stood Dido with a willow in her hand*
> *Upon the wild sea banks, and waft her love*
> *To come again to Carthage.*

2

The modelling of the text of his work cost Berlioz infinite trouble; to the last he kept adding here, deleting there, re-arranging, re-touching, sometimes restoring a passage that had been cut out, again removing and again restoring it. When at last, imagining his poetic agonies to be at an end, he settled down to the composition of the music, he found that this in its turn was perpetually suggesting fresh alterations to him. He had begun by assuring the Princess that he had steeled himself to resist the temptation to embark on the music until his poem was quite complete. In the very next breath, however, he confesses that the temptation had proved too strong for him in the case of what he calls "the Shakespeare duet" in the fourth act, the music of which he had already drafted. (It is not improbable, indeed, that he had tried his hand at setting these lines long before he became engaged on *Les Troyens*). In March 1857, taught by many a harassing experience, he was assuring the Princess that the libretto would never be really finished until he had written the last bar of his score. The music was completed in April 1858.

It was not long before he realised that his enthusiasm for his subject was causing him to over-write it. "My score is too long", he told his correspondent in Weimar: "I must allow at least twenty-five minutes for the ballet." But the crucial problem of length he never succeeded in solving. His own final timing of the work was as follows: Act I, 52 minutes; Act II, 22 minutes; Act III, 40 minutes; Act IV, 47 minutes; Act V, 45 minutes; making a total of 206 minutes. "With four intervals of a quarter of an hour each", he noted in his score, with an optimism so desperate as to be indistinguishable from self-delusion, "the performance will take four hours twenty-six minutes; commencing at 7.30, it should finish shortly before midnight." He might have foreseen that no theatre could be counted on to achieve each change of scene in an average of fifteen minutes, so that under the most favourable conditions conceivable the evening would be a long one for the most heroically-enduring audience. It was a foregone conclusion that the moment any opera house took the work in hand it would be subjected, whether with the composer's consent or without, to the cruellest curtailments.

Long before his score was finished, Berlioz had to plunge shoulder-deep into the morass of diplomacy and intrigue that blocked all the approaches to the Paris Opéra. The usual strings were pulled to secure the interest of Napoleon III or of the Empress; but, as might have been expected, poor Berlioz got no more than the conventional assurances of regard and good will. He was invited to a reception at the Tuileries at which he hoped to be able to put in a word for his *Troyens*; but the crowd was so great that it was impossible for him to get a moment's speech with the Emperor. By the Opéra direction he was duped month after month by means of the regulation promises, flatteries and evasions. "The Opéra", he told Princess Wittgenstein bitterly in February 1858, quoting a recent remark of Prince Napoleon's (a son of the former King Jerome of Westphalia), "is a shop carried on not for art but for money: it has no desire to produce anything new so long as the ancient repertory continues to bring in good receipts." And just then the Opéra had no time to spare for a mere Berlioz. It was busy with a new work by a notorious society amateur of the period, Prince Poniatowski; and it was committed, after that was launched, to one by the Grand Duke Ernest of Gotha, a dilettante German princeling whose grand-ducal boots Liszt, when in charge of the Weimar theatre, was always painfully willing to lick. It was not until the June of 1861 that the Paris Opéra came to a vague provisional arrangement with Berlioz. But he was given to understand that it would be at least two years before a production could even be contemplated; for already-existing contracts with Gounod and Gevaert would first have to be carried out, and neither composer's score was as yet ready.

His constant disappointments in connection with his darling work were largely answerable for Berlioz's wretched health during all these years, and they account, in some measure, for his behaving so meanly to Wagner in 1860 and 1861; for it soured and exasperated him to see the German intruder given *carte blanche* in the matter of expense for his *Tannhäuser* at the Opéra by the Emperor's direct command, while he, the most notable French composer of the epoch, seemed condemned to knock for ever at doors that refused to open, and to pluck humbly at the sleeve of a crowd of functionaries the insincerity of whose promises he could read in their eyes as they made them.

3

When at last the hour of *Les Troyens* did arrive, it was not in the national Opera House but in the new Théâtre-Lyrique of an impresario named Carvalho, who had received a state subvention of 100,000 francs in July 1863. The sorely ailing Berlioz was now made to realise the full enormity of his crime in doing his best to provide the French stage with a work worthy of it. As *Les Troyens* in its proper form was too long for an ordinary evening, the work had to be divided into two. The first two of the original five acts now became *La Prise de Troie*, an "opera in three acts (five tableaux)". The remaining three acts became *Les Troyens à Carthage*, "poème lyrique en quatre actes et cinq tableaux".[1]

It was *Les Troyens à Carthage* that was produced for the first time at the Théâtre-Lyrique on the 4th November 1863. To acquaint the audience with the course of events covered by the missing two acts of the original, Berlioz now began with an instrumental prelude which he describes, in a letter of the 19th November to Princess Wittgenstein, as a "prologue explicatif", "a combination of music and recited lines". It is "novel and grandiose", he adds; "this instrumental *Lamento*, this invisible chorus, this recalling to memory the Trojan catastrophe, make a striking effect." The poor man was deluding himself; the *Lamento* created more astonishment and hilarity than anything else. The spectators found the curtain depicting Troy in flames neither informative nor impressive; while the words of the chorus explaining it all behind the scenes must have been even

---

[1] In the modern text-books this section of the work is described as being "in five acts, with a prologue".

K*

less intelligible to the audience than the words of a choir on a concert platform normally are. Some of the principal singers were none too well acquainted with their parts, while the unfamiliar idiom of Berlioz created many difficulties for even the most willing of them. The stage machinery ran awkwardly; one interval alone extended to nearly an hour. The superb "Chasse royale" fell flat; the French public was not used to "symphonic music" of this sort in the theatre, and the stage action accompanying the piece seems to have been most imperfectly realised. One or two of these classical characters, again, to say nothing of the music they were given to sing, were hard to fit into the conventional French operatic frame of that period. The septet, however, was encored, and the duet between Dido and Aeneas inspired respect.

On the whole, the reception of the work on that first night could not be considered unfavourable. A second performance followed on the 6th November; and between then and the last performance of all—the twenty-second—on the 20th December, life for poor Berlioz was one long *via dolorosa*. The director, the singers, the machinists, all clamoured for cuts and still more cuts. At the second performance the "Chasse royale" was omitted; what that meant for Berlioz we can dimly imagine. The song of Hylas in the third act was the next thing to go: it disappeared while Berlioz was absent from the theatre with an attack of bronchitis. "Cabel", he says in his *Memoirs*, "was required for the piece played the day after [the first performance of] *Les Troyens*, and as his engagement only bound him to sing fifteen times in the month, they would have had to pay him two hundred francs for each extra night. Carvalho therefore suppressed the song for the sake of economy, without giving me notice."

In all, ten cuts were made from time to time. Berlioz tabulates them thus:

1. The entry of the builders.
2. That of the sailors.
3. That of the labourers.
4. The instrumental interlude (Hunting scene and tempest). (Mention has already been made of this).
5. Scene and duet between Anna and Narbal.

6. Second air de ballet.
7. The strophes of Iopas.
8. The sentinels' duet.
9. The song of Hylas. (Referred to above).
10. The grand duet of Aeneas and Dido: "Errante sur tes pas".

Finally the Dido, Madame Charton-Demeur, who seems to have done her best for Berlioz in difficult circumstances, had to leave the cast in order to resume her Verdi rôles at the Théâtre-Italien. In his *Memoirs* Berlioz cannot say much more for her than that she "did admirably at times", though he admits that she was "the only woman who could sing Dido's part". Of the Aeneas, the tenor Monjauze, the best he could say in retrospect was that he was "occasionally spirited and animated".

For some of the difficulties attending not only the original but any future production of *Les Troyens*, Berlioz would have had to confess that he himself was to blame. It was somewhat un-practical of him, for instance, to create, in Cassandra, a character calling not only for a great singer but a consummate tragic actress, and to demand, for Corœbus,[1] a baritone possessed of hardly lesser gifts, and then make no further use of either of them after the second of his five acts. Theatre directors could be for-given for jibbing at an expense of this kind. What Berlioz was not prepared for was the mean hostility of some of those who should have co-operated with him, and the bestial delight a certain section of the Paris public took in fouling the noble work with its moron wit. Berlioz gives us, in his *Memoirs*, a faint notion of what he had to go through in this way. They laughed at the four-stringed lyre of the rhapsode in Greek costume who appeared in the prelude: "Ha! ha! ha! a tetrachord! An antique lyre, striking only four notes! Ha! ha! ha!"

"Aeneas must not appear on the stage in a helmet", they told him.

"Why not?"

"Because Mangin, who sells pencils in the street, also wears a helmet; a helmet of the Middle Ages, certainly, but still a helmet;

---

[1] Berlioz, after the French fashion with classical names, calls him "Chorèbe".

and the gods in the top gallery will begin to laugh and call out 'Hello! here's Mangin'!"

"Oh, of course, a Trojan hero must not wear a helmet, because people will laugh. Ha! ha! ha! a helmet! ha! ha! Mangin!"

"Suppress Mercury; the wings to his heels and head will make people laugh. No one has ever seen wings except on the shoulders."

"Oh! human beings have been seen with wings on their shoulders? I did not know that. However, I can understand that wings on the heels, and still more on the head, will make people laugh; ha! ha! ha! And so, as we don't often meet Mercury in the streets of Paris, let him be suppressed."

Berlioz never heard *La Prise de Troie*. The bitter thought that after all he had done for France, France had no use for him in its national opera house, rankled in him to the wretched end of his days. "Ah, my noble Cassandra, my heroic virgin", he cried; "I must then resign myself to never hearing thee!" "I am in my sixty-first year", he wrote in his *Memoirs* shortly after the disappearance of *Les Troyens à Carthage* from the stage. "I have neither hopes, nor illusions, nor great thoughts left. My son is nearly always absent; I am solitary. My contempt for the folly and meanness of men, my hatred of their detestable ferocity, are at their height, and I say hourly to Death: 'When you will!' Why does he delay?" He died in 1869. It was not until 1879 that his great work began to raise its head again after its defeat of sixteen years earlier. At first, however, it had to be content with concert performances: it was not until 1890 that the complete opera was given in the theatre. The honour of this achievement belongs to Felix Mottl, who produced, in Karlsruhe, *La Prise de Troie* on the 6th December 1890, and *Les Troyens à Carthage* on the following evening. The Paris Opéra-Comique revived the latter work in June 1892, and some notable performances of a condensed single-evening version of the original *Les Troyens* were given at the Paris Opéra in 1921. The first—and so far the only—production of the entire work (apart from a few cuts) in Britain was that of a gallant band of Glasgow amateurs, under Dr. Erik Chisholm, in March 1935, in an English version made by Professor Edward J. Dent.

Perhaps the main cause for the general neglect of the work has been the virtual impossibility of getting an adequate idea of it from the piano score. Berlioz's music as he conceived it for the orchestra and Berlioz's music as translated into terms of the piano are always two very different things; and even the best piano set-out is more likely than not to misrepresent him, as thousands have at last come to realise in the case of the *Nuits d'Été*. When the piano arrangement is about the worst conceivable it is hopeless to expect true understanding of Berlioz's music; and the original piano version of *Les Troyens*, which was made by Berlioz himself, is about as misrepresentative of the work as anything our fancy could picture. A later transcription, made by someone whose name is not given on the scores, is much better; but even here the rule holds good that Berlioz simply cannot be translated idiomatically into the language of the piano.

4

The action of *Les Troyens* begins in the tenth year of that war between Greece and Troy the cause of which had been the abduction of the beautiful Helen, wife of King Menelaus of Sparta, by Paris, the son of King Priam of Troy. On the Trojan side the great Hector has been slain, on the Greek side Achilles and Patroclus. At last the Trojans are induced to believe that their enemies, weary of the conflict, have set sail for their homeland again. But they have only retired to the neighbouring island of Tenedos, leaving behind them on the beach near Troy a huge Wooden Horse packed with warriors.

Berlioz's opera opens on the day when the Trojans discover that the enemy, as they think, has fled. The scene is the abandoned Grecian camp on the plain in front of Troy. On opposite sides of the stage stand a throne and an altar, symbols respectively of the regal and the sacerdotal power. Towards the back of the scene is a funeral mound—the tomb of Achilles—on which are seated three shepherds ostensibly playing antique double flutes, though the sound is that of modern oboes. The people of Troy, soldiers, citizens, men, women and children, pour into the plain, rejoiced at being once more free to savour the delights of the country after ten years of confinement within the city walls.

The work opens with thirty bars of joyous orchestral prelude, into the tissue of which, as well as into that of the chorus which follows, the iterative melody of the shepherds strikes from time to time with curious effect:

The burden of the splendid choral song is the load that has been lifted from the heart of Troy by the flight of the Greeks. While some of the younger people are dancing:

others exhibit gleefully the Grecian trophies they have picked up —here a helmet, there a javelin, elsewhere a huge shield. Whose was the tent that stood on this spot? some ask. "Achilles'", replies a soldier; and at that dread name the crowd shrinks back with a cry of terror. The soldier reassures them. They have nothing to fear from Achilles now. He is dead, and over there is his tomb; and he points to the funeral mound, from which the flute-players fly in fear of even the shade of the redoubtable Greek. But the people quickly forget their terror when they hear of the colossal Horse which the Greeks have left behind them as an offering to Pallas. They rush off to the beach to see this curiosity, leaving the scene free for the great figure of Cassandra, that sister of Hector whom Apollo had endowed with the gift of prophesying truly but condemned to the curse of never having her prophecies believed.

She comes forward to the accompaniment of an impressive unison orchestral figure that suggests at once her majesty and her agitation:

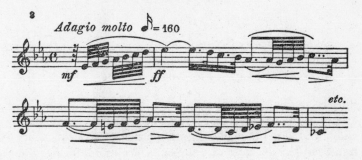

In a grave recitative and aria she gives voice to her disquietude. What lies behind the inexplicable sudden departure of the Greeks? She has seen the shade of Hector on the ramparts at night, gazing fixedly and sombrely across the water. But the unthinking crowd sees in the departure only an occasion for joy; and Priam himself leads them in their rejoicings! "Unhappy King!" she cries, "it is decreed that you shall descend into the eternal night: but neither you nor your doomed people will believe my words":

Corœbus himself, she laments, believes her mind to be deranged. She sinks into a tender reverie at the thought of her lover, who now enters to ask her why she alone takes no part in the rejoicings of this day of days for Troy. In a short *larghetto*, that shows how deeply rooted was one side of Berlioz's musical mind in the classicism of Gluck, he exhorts her to raise her sad eyes to the skies and let hope enter her troubled heart:

Re - viens à toi. Vierge a - do - ré - e!

But Cassandra is not to be consoled. In the book of destiny, she tells him, she has read that Troy's fate is sealed: soon its streets will be red with blood, its virgins ravished, and Corœbus himself transfixed by the spear of a Greek. Once more, to the strain of No. 5, he tries to dispel these gloomy thoughts, but once more in vain. She implores him to fly that very day to save his life:

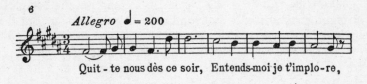

Quit - te nous dès ce soir, Entends-moi je t'implo-re,

but he rejects with scorn so base a course. This melody is then made the subject of a passionate duet. Finally Cassandra, unable to shake the heroic resolution of Corœbus, gives him her hand and solemnly pledges herself to him as his bride: already, she says, jealous death is preparing their bridal couch for the morrow.

The setting of the next scene is an open space in front of the citadel, with a throne on one side and an altar on the other as in the preceding scene. In the distance the summit of Mount Ida is visible. A long procession enters—Priam, his wife Hecuba, their son Helenus and daughter Polyxena, the hero Aeneas and his little son Ascanius, Corœbus, the priests of Jupiter and Neptune, among them Panthus, and a multitude of soldiers and magistrates and other Trojan dignitaries. A splendid chorus is built up, on a melody which, in its curious alternations of tonality:

Dieux pro-tec - teurs de la ville é - ter - nel - le,

and its combination of rigidity and athleticism, reminds us, as
Adolphe Boschot has happily expressed it, of the warriors who
march in angular profile across some ancient sculptured frieze.
The chorus is a hymn of thanksgiving to the gods of Troy for the
deliverance of the town from the Greeks; and it rises in power
with each stage of the procession, the main features of which are
the entries successively of (1) the ordinary people, (2) Ascanius
and a band of children, (3) Hecuba and the princesses, (4) Aeneas
and the warriors, (5) Priam and the priests.

Priam and Hecuba having seated themselves on the throne,
there follows a mimic combat of young men, to music couched
in one of those irregular rhythms in which Berlioz delighted.
Then comes one of the most impressive episodes of the whole
work. Andromache, the widow of Hector, enters, leading her
little son Astyanax by the hand. They are both clothed in white—
the colour of mourning among the ancients. A hush falls upon the
excited crowd at the sight of them, and the chorus greets them
with respectful sympathy:

While Astyanax places a basket of flowers at the foot of the altar,
Andromache kneels and prays for a few moments: then she rises,
conducts the boy to the throne, presents him to Priam and
Hecuba, and presses him to her bosom in a convulsion of tenderness, while orchestra and chorus comment tenderly on the situation. The King and Queen bless the child, who clings timidly to
his mother. Cassandra, traversing the back of the scene, prophesies to herself, to the accompaniment of a wailing theme in the
orchestra:

an even greater sorrow that is soon to overwhelm Hector's widow. To a development of the solemn strain of No. 9, which resembles a funeral march, Andromache, holding Astyanax by the hand, slowly passes from the scene, the people greeting her, as she goes by them, with further signs of sympathy and respect.

Hardly has this extraordinarily moving episode come to an end, with the funeral march dying away in a sigh in chorus and orchestra, than there is a great clamour outside, and Aeneas rushes in, to tell Priam and the people, in agitated accents, of the horror just enacted on the shore: the priest Laocoon, suspecting that the Wooden Horse concealed some menacing perfidy of the Greeks, had hurled a javelin into its flank, whereupon two huge serpents had come from the sea, thrown themselves furiously on Laocoon, and devoured him before the eyes of the terrified Trojans. The general horror at this news is expressed in a magnificent ensemble movement in which eight solo voices—Aeneas, Helenus, Corœbus, Ascanius, Cassandra, Hecuba, Panthus and Priam—unite with the chorus. An ascending chromatic line:

is followed by a slow chromatic descent, to the words, "O dire chastisement! Mysterious horror! My blood freezes in my veins!" The phrase, which began on F sharp, terminates a tone lower, on E. It is then taken up by a new set of voices on this lower note, ending this time, therefore, on D. The same procedure is repeated a third time, thus achieving a sort of round. There is something curiously suggestive of the ebbing spirits of the Trojans in this continuous fall of pitch. Further developments culminate in a broad melody first launched by Cassandra:

over broken ejaculations of "O dire chastisement!", etc., by the
chorus, and worked up dramatically in the most masterly fashion.
The impressive movement ends with awe-struck mutterings of
"Laocoon, a priest, a victim of the anger of the gods!", and
a final despairing cry of "Horror!" There are few ensembles
in all opera to compare with this for expressiveness and craftsmanship.

Aeneas tries to restore the fainting spirits of the Trojans. He
suggests that the fate of Laocoon was a sign of the displeasure of
the goddess Pallas at the outrage committed on the Horse, which
had been dedicated to her; and he orders them to conduct it in
solemn procession to the Palladium (an image, preserved in the
citadel, on which depended the weal of Troy). This it is decided
to do, in another fine ensemble worked out technically in close
imitation between the parts. No one listens to the warning voice
of Cassandra, who, when all the others have left the stage, gives
voice to her despair over their blindness in a long scena posed
mainly upon an agitated accompaniment figure:

that is repeated again and again in the orchestra. The nearer she sees the infatuated procession advancing the more profound is her anguish:

In the far distance is now heard the only theme which recurs in the later stages of the opera, a "Trojan March in the Triumphal Mode"[1] which has a strange tint and tang that only the imagination of a Berlioz could have hit upon:

One development of it:

[1] It is true that the theme of the duet between Cassandra and Corœbus recurs in the prelude to *Les Troyens à Carthage*; but this prelude has no real

might serve once for all to illustrate the immense psychological difference between a Berlioz phrase in the colour-medium in which it was conceived and the same phrase in the black-and-white of the piano. Later we shall hear the March in the minor, for the mood of it changes with the changing fortunes of the Trojans. But on the present occasion it is in the major, corresponding to the joyous, confident spirit with which they go about the fateful business of taking the Horse into the city. We first become aware of the procession while it is still some distance away, through the medium of an orchestra behind the scenes giving out No. 14, accompanied by a chorus, also far away, praying for the protection of Pallas. The successive stages of the cortège we can follow with the eyes of the distressed Cassandra, who stands in magnificent isolation at the front of the stage.

Night is falling by now, and the background is lit up by the torches of the soldiers who constitute the advance guard of the procession. "The enemy nears, and the town lies open!" cries Cassandra. There follows, again to the melody of No. 14, a second chorus, followed by a third as the head of the marching column comes into sight. But this time the song breaks off abruptly; one senses that a feeling of disquietude is spreading among the people who have not yet come upon the scene, and communicating itself to those who have. Some among them enquire the cause of the alarm; and a few of the women who have run off to investigate come back with the strange story that from within the body of the monstrous Horse the clatter of weapons has been heard. The others, in their blindness, take this as a happy omen, and the chorus greet the monster with the wildest joy as it now passes across the back of the scene, drawn by a number of the Trojan warriors. By this time, too, the various hidden smaller orchestras which Berlioz has been using for his gradually cumulative effect are fused into one in a shattering immensity of sound. The despair of Cassandra mounts with the joy of the populace. As the Horse disappears she cries to them, "Stay! Stay! Bring axe and fire and find out what the monster holds within it! Laocoon! The

place in the work. It was an afterthought on Berlioz's part. On this point see below, p. 304.

Greeks! It conceals a deadly trap for Troy!" But the deluded crowd pushes her aside to follow the cortège, the last triumphal strains of which die away gradually in the distance. Cassandra sees the Horse enter the citadel, and knows that the fate of Troy is sealed. "It is finished!" she cries. "Destiny has seized its prey! Sister of Hector, go thou too to perish beneath the ruins of Troy!"

5

The first scene of the second act takes place in the palace of Aeneas. It is night; by the dim light of a single lamp we see the hero stretched out on his couch, semi-armed. A sombre orchestral prelude is broken in upon from time to time by suggestions of military fanfares:

and other sinister noises far away in the town. The music takes on a lighter character for a moment as little Ascanius enters, listens and looks round him in terror, approaches the bed as if to rouse his father, hesitates timorously to do so, and finally returns to his own apartment. This is the prelude to a short scene that is without its like in opera. The superb episode in Vergil's second book in which the shade of Hector appears to the sleeping Aeneas, warns him of the fate which is in store for Troy, and bids him save the household gods and fly with them to the great new city which it is decreed he shall found somewhere across the seas, must have been well known to Berlioz since his boyhood; and it would have been impossible for him to omit it from an opera on the subject of Troy. His treatment of it is worthy of its Vergilian source. The shade of the hero strides majestically across the room:

17
Andante maestoso ♩ = 138

It pauses, gazes for a while in silence at the sleeping Aeneas, and gives a profound sigh—"largosque effundere fletus". Aeneas awakens with a start; he asks the spectre whence it comes and why its features are so seamed and its eyes so heavy with suffering. The shade solemnly adjures him to fly before it is too late—"Seek out Italy, where your people, after many wanderings by sea, shall know a new birth and accomplish a new mission, the founding of an empire that shall rule the whole world." [1] Each line of Hector's monologue is declaimed on a single note; this falls a semitone line by line, the music thus traversing, in its total course, a whole chromatic octave. Then the shade majestically recedes, to the accompaniment of the impressive No. 17, and gradually fades away into the darkness. No one who has seen and heard this tremendous episode adequately realised on the stage will ever forget it.

As the vision of Hector fades away Panthus runs in, bleeding from wounds, and carrying in his arms the gods of Troy. He tells

[1] The Romans of the Augustan age flattered themselves that Aeneas was the ancestor of their race. Hence the necessity for Vergil to put this prophecy into the mouth of Hector.

Aeneas how, the Horse once within the citadel, a horde of Greek soldiers had sprung from its inside and massacred the guards: Priam is dead and the town given over to blood and flame. Ascanius enters with the further news that the palace of Ucalegon has been destroyed: he is followed by Corœbus and a band of armed warriors, come to summon Aeneas to make a last stand in defence of the citadel. They all rush out, under Aeneas' leadership, to the accompaniment of far-off cries and noises that tell of the ruin that has suddenly fallen on Troy.

The scene changes to the temple of Vesta. In the background is a colonnaded gallery, enclosed by a low parapet over which a view is obtainable of the burning town. Between the columns, in the far distance, Mount Ida can be seen. Lights are flickering on the altar of Vesta-Cybele, round which lie or crouch a number of terrified women, among them Polyxena, daughter of Priam and one-time bride of Achilles. They address a wailing, curiously-phrased prayer to Cybele, invoking her protection:

As the tumult without increases, Cassandra enters, with hair dishevelled, to announce that at least Aeneas and his heroic band have escaped with the royal treasure and are on their way to Ida: some day they will raise in Italy a new and greater Troy. But Corœbus is dead, and nothing remains for Cassandra but to put an end to her own life. Too late the others see now that had they listened to her prophetic warning these misfortunes would not have fallen on the doomed city. Cassandra points out to them their only way of escaping from worse things—to throw themselves from the gallery. A few only of the younger and more craven of the women shrink back from so awful a sacrifice: most of them, in a frenzy of despair, seize their lyres and in a fiery chorus swear they will never fall into the hands of the Greeks. Under Cassandra's urging they drive out with contumely the weaker souls among them. "Go then," they cry, "and live out your lives as Thessalians! Shame on you! Go! You are not women of Troy!"

The delirium of those who remain with Cassandra increases. While they are still chanting to their lyres a Greek chieftain enters. He advances sword in hand, but is halted by the involuntary feeling of respect with which the women inspire him. An expression of ironic admiration is wrung from him by the sight of Cassandra raging like a Bacchante. A number of Greek soldiers rush in, bent only on finding out where the Trojan treasure is. They threaten the women with their swords. Cassandra defies them; plunging a dagger into her breast she offers the weapon to Polyxena, bidding her follow her example. Still more Greeks pour in, furious at the escape of Aeneas and the loss of the treasure. By this time the women—all except Polyxena, who is dead—have assembled on the gallery. Waving their scarves in the direction of Mount Ida and crying "Aeneas! Save our sons! Italy! Italy!" they go to their death each in her own way, some stabbing themselves, others leaping over the parapet. Cassandra, mortally wounded, tries to follow them, but her strength fails her. She sinks to her knees, raises herself by a supreme effort, stretches out her hands towards the mountain, cries in her turn "Italy!" and falls dead at the foot of the altar. The whole scene in the temple is handled by Berlioz in unforgettable fashion.

6

This brings us to the end of the Troy section of the opera, the two original acts of which Berlioz divided into three in order to form *La Prise de Troie*. The remaining three acts of *Les Troyens* were divided into four acts to make *Les Troyens à Carthage*. There is in general a marked change of musical style, corresponding to the complete change in milieu, in incident and in psychology, between the two sections of the work. So far Berlioz the classicist has mostly been to the fore; now the romantic has his say. Henceforth Shakespeare, as well as Vergil, leads him by the hand.

The wanderings and sufferings of the Trojan band have at last brought them to Carthage, the city in north Africa alleged to have been founded by Dido, an Asiatic princess who had fled from her native Tyre after the murder of her husband Sychaeus by her brother Pygmalion.

Les Troyens à Carthage opens with an orchestral prelude—a "Lamento instrumental: Légende et marche troyennes"—which was not in the original *Les Troyens*.[1] Berlioz had to acquaint the 1863 spectator of the second section of the opera, as well as could be done in the circumstances, with some of the events antecedent to the episodes at Carthage. The means he employed for this purpose were (a) the aforesaid orchestral prelude—a "lament" over Troy in general and Cassandra in particular—(b) a "prologue" on the following curious lines. After the prelude the front curtain was raised, disclosing a second curtain depicting Troy in flames. A rhapsode in Greek costume came to the footlights, faced the audience, and told (in a speaking voice) the story of the ten years of the Trojan war, the pretended retirement of the Greeks, their stratagem of the Horse, the vain warnings of Cassandra, and the entry of the Horse into the town. The Trojan March (Nos. 14 and 15), "dans le mode triomphal", was then played, and a group of rhapsodes behind the second curtain sang the chorus which, in the final scene of the first act of *Les Troyens*, had accompanied the cortège of the Horse. The rhapsode next described the irruption of the Greeks from the belly of the Horse, the destruction of the town and the death of Cassandra, and made his exit. Then, after a "fragment symphonique", followed by a short silence, the curtain rose on the opening scene of *Les Troyens à Carthage*.

The scheme was a desperate *pis aller*, and, as we have seen, it did little more than perplex one half of the first audience and

---

[1] This is sometimes erroneously referred to as "the overture to *Les Troyens*". It is not that, of course. There was no "overture" in Berlioz's original conception of the opera, consequently this prelude does not figure in his own piano score, though it has been added, from the manuscript full score now in the Library of the Paris Conservatoire, to the later edition of *Les Troyens à Carthage*.

amuse the other half. Today, if *Les Troyens* is being performed in
its original form there is no need for any introduction at all to the
third act, even if the work is given on two evenings. Berlioz, in
1863, wanted the listeners to *Les Troyens à Carthage* to become
acquainted with the Trojan March from the suppressed first
section of the opera because it plays a vital part in the second
section; but the modern hearer who has heard *La Prise de Troie* on
the first evening has no need to have the March brought to his
notice in this fashion. From every point of view the "lamento" is
best omitted from present-day performances, for Berlioz, in one
of those curious lapses from good taste that were not uncommon
with him, has here presented the melody of the duet between
Cassandra and Corœbus (No. 6) in so slow a tempo, and with
such crudity of cornet and trombone colour that for those who
know it in its original form it becomes intolerably vulgarised.[1]
Dramatically the reminiscence has no meaning whatever, for the
last thing in *La Prise de Troie* that can be conceived as having
any bearing on Aeneas and the Queen of Carthage is the duet
between Cassandra and her lover. As for "playing the audience
into its seats", this is no more necessary in the case of *Les
Troyens à Carthage* than it had been in the case of *La Prise de
Troie*.

At the time when the second section of the opera is supposed
to open, the building of Carthage has been proceeding for seven
years, and the people have now been called together to celebrate
the progress that has been made. The scene shows us an open
space in the gardens of Dido's palace. On one side is a throne,
surrounded by symbols of agriculture, commerce and the arts.
On the other side is an amphitheatre, the terraced seats of which
are occupied by an immense assembly.

The act opens with a chorus expressing the Carthaginian
people's joy in the beauty of the festive day, which, apparently,
has succeeded a great storm. As Dido enters, the whole crowd in
the amphitheatre rises to its feet, and a second chorus, much more
numerous than the first, greets her enthusiastically:

[1] The original melody is in 3/4 time, with a metronome marking of
crotchet 200: in the "lamento" it is phrased in common time, crotchet
66!

She seats herself on the throne, with her sister Anna on one side and her minister Narbal on the other. She speaks to her faithful subjects of the seven years that have elapsed since she and they fled from Tyre—seven years in which, thanks to them, Carthage has risen in all its glory. She exhorts them to fresh efforts, for the kingdom is now threatened by Iarbas, the savage chief of the Numidian hordes that surround it. This aria of Dido's has something of Gluckian majesty about it, touched, however, by the more romantic spirit which in the main distinguishes the music of the Carthage episodes from that of the events in Troy.

The people swear to defend her against Iarbas, who has had the insolence to demand her hand in marriage. She thanks them, and proceeds to distribute appropriate rewards for their industry and devotion to representatives of the various groups as they file before her in a long cortège—to the builders an axe and a square rule, to the sailors two ivory oars,[1] to the husbandmen—who are led by an old man of vigorous aspect, on whose head the Queen places a garland of flowers and ears of corn,—a golden sickle. The arts and sciences having thus been duly honoured, to the accompaniment of suitable processional music in the orchestra, the people break out again into praises of Dido (No. 19), and with Narbal at their head file out in front of her throne, demonstrating their loyalty by their gestures as they pass her. Dido and Anna are left alone on the stage.[2]

[1] Thus in the text book: in the score it is an oar and a helm. There are many trifling discrepancies of this sort between the two versions.

[2] According to the modern text book, the scene that now follows takes place in a room in the palace. There is no hint of this in the score, nor does

It is at this point that the music of the work takes a definitely
romantic turn. The scene begins with a short orchestral preamble.
Then Dido addresses her sister. She is no longer the Queen, but
simply a woman; the pomp and circumstance of the celebrations
done with, she finds the calm around her very grateful to her
heart. Anna, in a suave melody phrased above a gently-flowing
accompaniment of this type:

tries to console her: what fears, what anxieties can she feel, she
the Queen of a vigorous young kingdom, she whom all admire
and adore? The gracious strands of No. 20 run through the whole
tissue of the dialogue that follows. Dido, we learn, is consumed
by a sadness for which she cannot account and against which she
cannot contend: sometimes the tears start unbidden to her eyes.
Anna tells her, with an affectionate smile, that love will one day
come and banish her grief, for she is still young and beautiful, and
Carthage needs a King. But Dido is shocked at the suggestion
that she could ever love again: may the gods and her people overwhelm her with curses if ever she is untrue to the memory of
Sychaeus, whose ring on her finger she shows to Anna. The
latter again assures her that Venus will not sanction such a vow,
and the gods will refuse to record it. The charming scene ends
with a duet between the sisters, in which Dido's resolution can
already be seen to be yielding—"Sychaeus, o my spouse", she
murmurs, "forgive me for even harbouring such a thought"—
while Anna tenderly contemplates her work, knowing well
that the day will come when the inconsolable Dido will find
consolation:

any break occur in the musical sequence. But it is more credible that Dido
and her sister would be exchanging tender confidences in the seclusion of
their room than in the vast open space of the first scene. On the other hand,
the amphitheatre setting is essential for the closing stage of the present
scene.

Dido: Si-chée! ô mon é-poux, par-don-ne, Di-don! ma tendre sœur, par-don-ne,   Anna:

At the conclusion of the duet the poet Iopas—the "crinitus Iopas" of Vergil—enters with the news that a strange fleet, having survived the recent storm, has drawn up by the shore and the leaders crave audience with the Queen. Dido despatches Iopas to them with the message that the doors of her palace are always open to suppliants; then, in a short aria, she recalls her own unhappy flight across the sea from Tyre.

In the distance is heard the Trojan March (No. 14), but now in the minor—"dans le mode triste", as the score expresses it. Dido, at the sound of it, feels a strong curiosity about the newcomers, and at the same time an unaccountable fear. Soon Aeneas, Panthus, Ascanius and the other leading Trojans enter, to the strains of the March: Aeneas, however, is disguised as an ordinary mariner. Ascanius speaks for his companions. A band of men pursued by misfortune, he tells the Queen, asks refuge for a few days. They have come from far away; they are Trojans, as is proved by the gifts he now lays at Dido's feet—the sceptre of Ilione, daughter of Priam, Queen Hecuba's crown, and the gold-embroidered veil of the fair Helen herself. Yes, they are Trojans, and their chief is Aeneas, father of the youth who is now addressing the Queen. Panthus next steps forward and further explains that in obedience to the will of the gods Aeneas is seeking Italy, where a new country and a new home await him and his.

"Who has not heard the name of that prince, the friend of the great Hector?" asks Dido. "Carthage resounds with his fame. Take him word that my port is open to his vessels. Let him land, and at my court may he forget the sufferings he has endured." Just then Narbal enters in great agitation: Iarbas is advancing

with his savage hordes upon Carthage, and is even now slaughter-
ing the cattle and laying waste the fields; the town itself is
threatened, for many of the brave Carthaginians are unarmed, and
the fight will be an unequal one. Thereupon Aeneas steps forward. Discarding his disguise, he now reveals himself in splendid
armour, though without either helmet or buckler. In ringing
accents he declares that he is Aeneas, and that he places himself,
his men and his fleet at the service of the Queen. Dido gratefully
accepts, with a murmured aside to Anna, "O my sister, how
proud the mien of this son of the goddess! [1] What grace, what
nobility, his face and form bespeak!"

Aeneas, in vigorous terms, summons the Carthaginians to
rally and march with him to victory over the African invader; and
in a big ensemble, in which Dido and Anna join, they accept
enthusiastically the leadership of this son of Venus. By this time
his helmet, shield and javelin have been brought him. He sends
Panthus to call the remainder of the Trojan band to arms; then he
confides his young son Ascanius to the care of Dido, a maternal
charge which she accepts in tender words. [2] The people of Carthage
pour in from all sides, some of them armed, others carrying only
scythes, slings or axes; and singing a vigorous chorus of defiance:

they all march out to battle against Iarbas.

[1] According to the legend, Aeneas was the son of Anchises and Venus. In
the Vergilian version of the story it was the hatred of Juno for Venus that
brought so many woes upon the latter's protégé, the Trojan race.

[2] Berlioz seems to assume as a matter of course that the audience knows
that in the *Aeneid* Venus, unknown to Dido, substitutes her own son Cupid
for Ascanius, to sow the seeds of love in the young Queen's bosom.

In the original version of the opera the next scene commences with a "symphonic intermezzo", the now famous "Royal Hunt and Storm". The scene represents a virgin African forest, with a high rock in the background, to the left of which is an opening into a grotto: a small stream flows from the rock into a natural basin bordered by reeds and rushes. We catch a glimpse for a moment of two naiads as they plunge into the basin; but at the sound of a hunting fanfare somewhere in the forest they take fright and hide themselves among the rushes. The royal hunt is in progress; Ascanius and a number of Trojan huntsmen pass by. A terrific storm breaks out, through the thunders and lightnings of which the hunting horns blare now and then. Dido and Aeneas enter and take shelter from the tempest in the grotto: the Queen is costumed like Diana the huntress, with a bow in her hand and a quiver on her shoulder; the Trojan hero is in almost military equipment. As soon as the pair have entered the grotto, woodland nymphs rush about in wild excitement: from time to time their cries are broken in upon by the word "Italy!" The storm increases. The rock stream becomes a cascade. Satyrs, fauns and other wild creatures of the forest execute grotesque dances in the dim light. The lightning strikes a great tree, which crashes to the ground in flames: the satyrs and fauns pick up the burning branches, dance for a while with them in their hands, then disappear with the nymphs into the depths of the forest. Gradually the tumult of the tempest dies down, the clouds drift away, and profound peace descends on the scene.

In Berlioz's original scheme, this episode marks the end of the third act. In the modern scores the intermezzo is transferred to the end of the following act. Perhaps it does not matter greatly where it is placed, for the episode, which in Vergil marks the culminating point of Dido's passion for Aeneas:

> *Speluncam Dido dux et Troianus eandem*
> *Deveniunt.*
>
> . . . .
>
> *Ille dies primus leti primusque malorum*
> *Causa fuit. Neque enim specie famave movetur,*

Nec jam furtivum Dido meditatur amorem:
Conjugium vocat; hoc praetexit nomine culpam: [1]

may come as appropriately in the opera in the one place as in the other. It is anything but an easy scene to stage, for the slightest exaggeration of its realism may make it ludicrous. One listens to the music best in the concert room, with the scenario at the back of one's mind, but without any crudities of stagecraft to fetter the wings of the imagination. But whether it is staged well or ill, or not staged at all but played purely and simply as an intermezzo, it should never be omitted from a theatrical performance, for it is the most perfect in idea and execution of all Berlioz's orchestral pieces. It is the finest and most sustained piece of nature painting in all music; it is like some noble landscape of Claude come to life in sound. The reader who has never heard it on the orchestra, however, should be warned that no idea whatever of its magic can be had from the piano score.

The main thematic elements of it are the placid theme in violins and flutes with which it opens:

the flute melody that accompanies the episode of the bathing nymphs:

[1] In Conington's translation:
> That day she first began to die:
> That day first taught her to defy
> The public tongue, the public eye.
> No secret love is Dido's aim:
> She calls it marriage now; such name
> She chooses to conceal her shame.

the horn fanfare, heard from behind the scenes, which heralds the approach of the royal hunt and puts the nymphs to
flight:

the climax of the development of the hunting calls:

and the theme, given to the trombones behind the scenes,
which suggests the passing of the hunt into the depths of the
forest:

It is at this point that the storm breaks out; through it is still
heard the blaring of the horn fanfare (No. 25) with a new hunting
call:

It is over this last theme that the woodland nymphs utter their wild cries, while the shouts of "Italy!" by the fauns and satyrs are accompanied by No. 27.[1] The passing of the storm is announced by the reappearance of the tranquil No. 24, in the cool tones of the flutes as before. There follows a last faint echo of No. 25 in the horns, and the splendid picture fades away like a white cloud melting into the serene blue of the sky. The reader who knows his Vergil will not make the mistake, however, of seeing in "The Royal Hunt and Storm" only a piece of nature painting in music, dragged in for its own pictorial sake. He will listen imaginatively to it as Berlioz certainly intended him to do, as the passionate climax to the realisation by Dido and Aeneas of their love for each other. The storm itself, the blasting of the tree by lightning, and the cries of the wild things of the woodland were part of Juno's magnificent stage management of the episode as described by Vergil:

> ... *prima et Tellus et pronuba Juno*
> *Dant signum: fulsere ignes, et conscius aether*
> *Conubiis, summoque ulularunt vertice Nymphae.*[2]

7

The fourth act of the original version of *Les Troyens* shows us Dido's gardens by the sea. It is evening; Carthage has come out to celebrate its deliverance at the hands of Aeneas.

[1] All these striking vocal effects, which are so vital to Berlioz's scheme, are necessarily omitted in concert performances.

[2] Then Earth, the venerable dame,
         And Juno gave the sign;
    Heaven lightens with attesting flame,
         And bids its torches shine,
    And from the summit of the peak
         The nymphs shrill out the nuptial shriek.
                              (Conington).

While the other Tyrians promenade in the gardens, Anna and Narbal discuss the new situation created by the coming of the Trojans and the prowess of Aeneas. Dido, according to Narbal, now devotes her days and nights to hunting and feasting, to the neglect of the affairs of Carthage. Anna tries to reassure him: the Queen and Aeneas, she says smilingly, are in love, and where could Carthage find a nobler King? The only trouble which she dimly foresees comes from the conflict in the hero's breast between his love for Dido and the destiny appointed him by the gods: while one voice calls to him "Stay!", another cries "Italy!" Narbal, unconvinced, expresses his forebodings in an aria; he is not to be calmed by Anna's assurance that all will be well.[1]

A suggestion in the orchestra of the choral hymn "Gloire à Didon" (No. 19) announces the coming of the Queen, who enters with Aeneas, Panthus and Ascanius. At once the festivities in celebration of the victory over Iarbas begin, for the time has arrived, of course, for the inevitable opera ballet. The ballet music —dances of Nubian slaves, etc.,—is varied and expressive. In due course Anna, at a hint from her sister, makes a sign to the dancers to retire: Dido's mind is on something other than "cette fête importune", as she calls it. She leaves the platform from which she has been watching the proceedings and reclines on a couch towards the front of the stage. Berlioz gives detailed instructions as to the tableau she and the others are to form, to which he evidently attaches some importance. Dido, on the couch, presents her left profile to the spectator. Aeneas stands near her for a while. Anna bends over Dido with her elbow on the back of the couch. The graceful young Ascanius, "standing on the Queen's left and leaning on his bow, resembles a statue of Eros."

Dido bids Iopas sing them his "song of the fields",—apparently a repertory piece of this poet-musician—"sur un mode simple et doux". The minstrel does so: his lay is a charming little one in praise of Ceres, and it is accompanied by a Theban harpist in a religious Egyptian costume:

[1] The whole of this scene can be omitted from a modern performance without much loss. The words of it are not printed in the most recent textbook.

O blon - de Cé - rès,_____

Quand à nos gué-rets   Tu rends leur pa - ru - re

But after his third stanza he is interrupted by the love-sick Queen, who today has no more appetite for the lyric than for the ballet. Aeneas seats himself by her side, and she begs him to finish the story he had begun elsewhere of the misfortunes of Troy, the long wanderings of the Trojans, and the fate of the beautiful Andromache, in which she is particularly interested. Alas! Aeneas replies; taken by Pyrrhus as his slave, the widow of Hector had at first prayed for death; but the love of her captor prevailing, in the end she became Pyrrhus' wife and ascended the throne of Epirus.

There follows upon this one of the loveliest numbers of the opera, one that reveals an aspect of Berlioz that will be new to the casual listener to him in the concert room: rarely has he shown himself so fine-fingered a psychologist as here. The occasion is a quintet. Dido leads off softly, meditatively:

O pu - deur!   tout con - spi - re,   tout con-

spire   à   vain - cre mes re - mords____

Everything, she says, conspires to shake her resolution to preserve her widowhood: Andromache, for all-powerful love's sake, had given herself to the slayer of her father, the son of the warrior who had dealt Hector his death-blow! The spaces between the vocal

portions of her soliloquy and Aeneas' reply are filled by a unison
line in the orchestra:

31

that is like a secret thought threading its way silently through the
Queen's mind. Aeneas takes up the strain, continuing the exquisite melody begun by Dido. Anna, with an understanding and
affectionate smile, bids Iopas and Narbal, in a quiet aside, observe
the charming tableau that is forming itself in front of them—
Dido's left arm has been resting on the shoulder of Ascanius, with
her hand hanging down on his breast; smilingly he draws from
it Sychaeus' nuptial ring; she redeems it, but in her distraction
places it on the couch and leaves it there, forgotten:

32

Vo - yez, Nar - bal,___ la main lé -

gè - re   De cet enfant sembla - ble à Cupi - don,

The lovely, unforgettable quintet having run its gentle,
thoughtful course, Aeneas and the Queen rise to their feet, and,
to banish the latter's melancholy, turn to contemplate the beauty
of the night that is now descending on the garden and the sea. It
is the signal for the celebrated septet of Dido, Aeneas, Anna,
Ascanius, Iopas, Narbal and Panthus:

33   *Andantino* ♪ = 120

Tout __ n'est que paix   et __ charme au-tour de

nous.   La nuit é - tend son voi - le,

in which the chorus also takes a discreet part. The fullness of
Dido's heart speaks in a murmurous, caressing melodic line
entrusted to her alone among the voices:

La nuit é-tend son voi - le,

et   la mer en-dor - mi-e murmu - - re

The enchantment of night by the sea truly lies on this exquisite
movement.

By now Berlioz's imagination is in full romantic flood. Everyone but Dido and Aeneas having left the stage, the lovers, in the
garden that is now lit only by the moon, pour out their rapture in
a long duet, "Nuit d'ivresse et d'extase infinie". As has been
pointed out in the introduction to this analysis, the general poetic
idea of the duet is derived from the dialogue between Jessica and
Lorenzo in the last act of *The Merchant of Venice*: "The moon
shines bright: in such a night as this", etc. Over a gently-swaying
accompaniment-figure in the orchestra:

the voices begin the first of their interlocked phrases:

Berlioz makes skilful use of the French equivalent of Shakespeare's reiterated "In such a night", his own "Par une telle nuit"
serving, each time it recurs, to launch a new musical idea:

with a more intensive expression than any of its predecessors. The
melodic line attains its maximum of freedom and flow in a passage
just before the final *reprise* of No. 36, where Aeneas answers
Dido's

> Par une telle nuit le fils de Cytherée
> Accueillit froidement la tendresse enivrée
> De la Reine Didon,

which runs along in a single musical sentence, with another long melodic sentence that clinches the idea both poetically and musically:

As the murmuring voices and orchestra die away into the night, and after the pair have slowly left the stage with Dido's head resting on the shoulder of Aeneas, Mercury suddenly becomes visible in the rays of the moon, close by a broken column on which are suspended the Trojan hero's arms. With his caduceus he strikes two blows on the buckler, which gives forth a long lugubrious note; then with a cry of "Italy! Italy! Italy!" he disappears. The reader of Vergil will remember that Mercury was sent by Jupiter to recall the infatuated Aeneas to a sense of the mission entrusted to him by the gods. In the *Aeneid*, of course, the warning message is delivered to "pius Aeneas" in person.

8

When the curtain rises on the fifth act we see a beach covered with the Trojan tents, and the Trojan ships lying in the harbour. It is night. Hylas, a young Phrygian sailor, stationed on the mast of one of the ships, sings a simple little nostalgic song about his far-away home, while two sentinels guarding the tents listen sympathetically to the home-sick boy.

The tired Hylas having sung himself to sleep, Panthus and other Trojan chiefs enter hurriedly and give orders for everything to be made ready for the departure from Carthage: Aeneas, we learn, has bowed to the will of the angry gods, and will somehow find strength to tear himself away from Dido. Too long, the Trojans agree, have they dallied here; and as if to add to their resolution and exacerbate their fears, a mysterious cry of "Italy! Italy!" comes from a chorus of invisible shades.

The chiefs having gone into their tents, the two sentinels march backwards and forwards in contrary directions, stopping now and then, when they meet, to exchange views about the situation so far as it affects them personally. The order to weigh anchor, and indeed all this romantic-prophetic talk about Italy, makes no appeal to their prosaic minds. They like Carthage, where the food is good and the wine plentiful and the women are kind to them: and now they are expected to exchange these amenities for yet another perilous voyage into the unknown, for hunger and thirst and wounds and sufferings of all kinds, merely to find this problematic Italy about which they know nothing and care less! However, they are soldiers, and when the word of command is given they must obey. The racy popular humour of the duet, with its pungent orchestral colouring, makes an effective break in the tragic action of the story, and serves to throw into the highest possible relief the aria of Aeneas which follows—one of the finest things in the opera.[1]

The hero enters in great agitation. In a preliminary arioso recitative he tells how he had broken the news to Dido that he

---

[1] From the fact that Purcell has a comic chorus of sailors at the corresponding point in his *Dido and Aeneas* it has been conjectured that Berlioz may possibly have been acquainted with the English composer's work. Evidence of such acquaintance, however, is completely lacking. There is a scene in Monteverdi's *L'Incoronazione di Poppea* (1642) in which a couple of soldiers grumble, very much as those in Berlioz's opera do, at being kept so busy by the wars that they cannot get a single lazy hour to themselves. But it would be unwise to infer from this superficial similarity that Berlioz had even so much as heard of the Monteverdi work.

must leave Carthage, and how stupefied and sad she had been, how indifferent to the purposes of the gods and the high destiny laid on the Trojans. Then follows the great aria. He looks forward with dread to the hour when he must bid Dido farewell:

For he cannot depart without seeing her again, though the grief of the parting will consume him. The aria is difficult not only because of its high tessitura (it touches C *in alt.* at one point) but because of the demands it makes on both the musical style and the dramatic intelligence of the singer.

As he reiterates that he cannot go without holding her hands in his again and bathing her feet in his tears a warning cry of "Aeneas!" is heard coming from somewhere in the darkness. Four shades appear in succession, one from each side of the stage, the other two from the back. As they speak and unveil their features in turn we discover who they are—the shades of Priam, of Corœbus, of Cassandra and of Hector. One by one they adjure Aeneas to remember the duty that lies before him, and to fly from Carthage at once. The solemnity of the apparitions is increased by the ghostly scoring of the music. "I yield to your pitiless command", cries the distracted Aeneas; "if I show myself cruel, ungrateful, it is your work: I avert my eyes from the destruction I bring on Dido!"

A feverish new version of the Trojan March accompanies him as he strides up and down among the tents, rousing the men within. One of the chiefs he despatches to Ascanius with the order to embark at once and with the whole fleet weigh anchor before dawn: "To sea! Italy!" The Trojans hurry away, and soon we see the ships preparing to sail. Aeneas turns in the direction of the palace and addresses a passionate and remorseful farewell to Dido.

Thunder growls in the distance and flashes of lightning rend the sky as Dido enters. In a dialogue of agitated give-and-take between herself and Aeneas she learns her fate. Her tears, her reproaches, her appeals are alike in vain. He pleads that he is only obeying the command of the gods; and when, for a moment, it looks as if his resolution were about to break, the Trojan March, sounding faintly in the distance, recalls him to his duty and steels his heart. Then, finding his will unbreakable, the distracted Queen curses him and his gods and leaves him.[1] Shouts of "Italy!" come from the ships, towards which the soldiers and the chiefs, accompanied by Ascanius, are now hastening. The word reanimates Aeneas. He himself cries out "Italy!" at the top of his voice and goes into one of the ships: the curtain falls with the Trojan March "dans le mode triomphal" ringing out in all its glory.

The scene changes to an apartment in the palace. In wavering accents the wretched Dido, her pride having left her, asks Anna and Narbal to go to Aeneas and implore him not to abandon her. Anna blames herself for having ever put thoughts of love into her sister's mind; but there is no fighting against the gods, she says. It is decreed that Aeneas shall go; yet who can doubt that he loves Dido? The Queen once more urges them to seek out the hero with a message from her: but she does not presume to command him, she humbly implores that he will delay his going for at least a few days. Can he be utterly unmindful of all she has been to him? But even while she is speaking there come excited cries from outside: "Look! On the sea! Six vessels! Seven! Nine! Ten!" and Iopas rushes in with the news that the Trojan fleet, which had left port at dawn, is now almost out of sight.

Hearing this, Dido becomes a ravening fury. She gives orders that the Carthaginian galleys are to go out in pursuit of the escaping ships and destroy them by fire. So this was the supposed fidelity, she cries, of this "pius Aeneas" to whom she had given her love and offered a throne! She should have sensed the perfidy

[1] This fine scene does not appear in the most recent text-book of *Les Troyens à Carthage*. Under no circumstances should it be omitted in performance.

of these Trojans from the first, burned their boats, exterminated the vile race and thrown their bodies into the sea; on Aeneas she should have avenged herself by serving him with the flesh of his own son at a horrid banquet of death. She calls on all the gods of Olympus to come to her aid, to fan the flame of hatred that now burns in her for this man she had once been weak enough to love. She gives orders that the priest of Pluto is to be summoned at once, for she will offer a sacrifice to the dark divinities of the underworld, committing to the flames everything that can remind her of her betrayer.

Narbal and Anna, appalled at her frenzy, leave her. Left alone, Dido, tearing her hair in true Vergilian fashion, brings the terrible scene to a fitting end with a great monologue. She will die on the pyre, hoping that Aeneas, across the sea, may catch sight of the flames of it. For a moment she softens as she sadly recalls their hours of love. Then she resigns herself to the inevitable end. She bids a sorrowful farewell to the city she had founded, to her tender sister, to her people, to the shore that had given her refuge in days of old, to nights of rapture with Aeneas under the stars of the glorious African sky. Never will she see or know any of these again: her end has come! At the words "Adieu, beau ciel d'Afrique, astres que j'admirai aux nuits d'ivresse et d'extase infinie" there is a touching reminiscence of the love duet (No. 36). She goes slowly out, sunk in melancholy memories and visions.

The scene changes to a terrace overlooking the sea. A lofty funeral pyre has been erected, access to which is by lateral steps. On the top of the pyre is a couch, a toga, a helmet, a sword with its belt—all of them once associated with Aeneas—and a bust of the hero. Lights are burning on two altars, round which are grouped the priests of Pluto in funeral robes. Anna and Narbal enter, followed by Dido, who is veiled, with a fillet on her brow. The priests sing a solemn invocation to Pluto, and Anna and Narbal, stretching out their arms towards the sea, call on the gods to curse the false Trojan. Dido, speaking as if in a dream, calls on the priests to perform the last rites preparatory to the sacrifice. This having been done, Dido mounts the steps, throws on the pyre her gold-embroidered veil and the toga that had once belonged to Aeneas, looks sadly for a while at his sword and casque, throws herself sobbing on the couch, and, embracing it convulsively, draws the sword from its scabbard and plunges it into her breast. But before she does so she sees, as the ancients believed the dying could do, into the distant future. "My memory will endure through the ages", she says, still to herself, as if in a dream; "a heroic destiny awaits my people. Some day there will spring from the soil of Africa a glorious avenger of my wrongs. Already I hear his mighty name. Hannibal! Hannibal! My soul is filled with pride. Away from me, bitter memories! Thus does it befit me to go down to death!"

A great cry of "Help! The Queen is wounded!" goes up, and the people come running in anxiously from all quarters. Anna raises her sister and tries to stanch the wound. Dido raises herself on one elbow, looks up to heaven, summons up her last strength to deny her own vision of a moment before—"Implacable fate!" she stammers; "Carthage ... will perish! Rome ... Rome ... eternal!"—and dies in Anna's arms. And at the moment when Dido cries "Rome!" there appears, high above the pyre, yet invisible to all but herself, the Capitol, with "ROMA" inscribed on its pediment; in front of the noble building stands the Roman Emperor, surrounded by poets and artists, and before him file his conquering legions. The Carthaginians, who see and sense nothing of all this, burst out into imprecations against the Trojans, swearing eternal hatred to the brood of Aeneas, which one day they will blot from the earth:

But their vows and their curses are accompanied by the Trojan March, thundering out defiantly in the orchestra as the symbol of Rome's ultimate victory over Carthage.

DON PASQUALE
Donizetti (1797-1848)

PRINCIPAL CHARACTERS

DON PASQUALE	*Buffo Bass*
DOCTOR MALATESTA	*Baritone*
ERNESTO	*Tenor*
NORINA	*Soprano*
A NOTARY	*Bass*

I

Historians speak respectfully, as in duty bound, of Paisiello's *The Barber of Seville* (1780); but the fact remains that of the enormous repertory of Italian comic opera in the last quarter of the eighteenth century and the first half of the nineteenth only three works still keep the boards intact, not merely respected as museum pieces but admired as masterpieces that seem, for all the changes that have taken place in music since their day, to be perennially young. These three works are Rossini's *The Barber of Seville* (1816), Donizetti's *L'Elisir d'Amore* (1832), and his *Don Pasquale* (1843), which was nearly the last of its composer's sixty-odd operas. Already in 1843 he showed signs of exhaustion and a tendency to morbid melancholy: he was, in fact, suffering from a cerebro-spinal disease.[1] In 1845 he became paralysed. Almost the whole of 1846 and the first six months of 1847 he spent in an asylum at Ivry. In October of the latter year he was removed to his native town, Bergamo, where he died on the 8th April 1848.

The libretto of *Don Pasquale* is from Donizetti's own pen. He seems, indeed, to have had a decided gift for this kind of thing: the book of more than one of his early operas is his own work,

---

[1] The cause of his malady does not seem to have been determined beyond question. That the seeds of it had been in him since his youth seems to be suggested by the fact that of his three children (born respectively in 1829, 1836 and 1837) the first lived less than a fortnight and the other two were stillborn.

and one at least of these, *Il Campanello di Notte,* is a little gem of humorous inventiveness, even if, as is probable, he derived the fundamental idea of it from a farce he had seen in Paris. For the general idea of *Don Pasquale* he was indebted to a comic opera produced in Milan in 1810, *Ser Marcantonio,* the composer of which was one Stefano Pavesi and the librettist Angelo Anelli. The plot of this hinges upon two eternally popular themes of the Italian comic theatre, that of the anxiety of the relatives of a rich man as to the dispositions he may have made in his will, and that of an elderly bachelor who suddenly decides to plunge into matrimony, and is given reason to regret it later.[1] Old Marcantonio perturbs his expectant relations by informing them that he intends to marry and hopes to become a father. The news is particularly unwelcome to his nephew Medoro and his niece Dorina: the former is engaged to a milliner named Bettina, the sister of one Tobia, a stockbroker, who, as the laws of theatrical symmetry demand, is in love with Dorina. Together they hatch out a plot by which Bettina is passed off on Marcantonio as the very wife for a man like him, she being an exceptionally inexperienced and modest girl: the mock marriage ceremony is performed by Tobia made up as a notary. Bettina, however, quickly reveals a shrewish temper and a passion for domestic extravagance that frighten the old gentleman out of his wits; so that he is easily persuaded to let Medoro take her off his hands in consideration of a handsome annuity, while Tobia, of course, marries Dorina.

In construction, as will be seen, the play ran true to a well-established type: there were two hopeful young relatives, two other lovers, and two servants, one attached to Medoro, the other to Dorina. Donizetti wisely rid this traditional pattern of its superfluities. He made shift with only one relative—old Pasquale's nephew Ernesto,—and consequently a single love interest. This left him room to treat more extensively the character who hatches the ingenious plot against the old bachelor; Tobia now becomes Dr. Malatesta, the trusted friend of Don Pasquale. This drastic simplification and condensation of the too crowded

---

[1] The latter of these two themes is probably of great antiquity. A variant of it is found in Ben Jonson's comedy *Epicœne, or The Silent Woman.* Richard Strauss's opera *Die schweigsame Frau* (1935) is based on this.

canvas of *Ser Marcantonio* gave Donizetti, of course, more opportunity to expand his simple musical forms and to extract the last ounce of humorous expression out of each situation. The chorus is equally skilfully and economically handled: it appears only twice in the three acts, and on each occasion with perfect appropriateness, consisting as it does of Don Pasquale's house servants.

2

The wit and humour of the music, the composition of which is said to have occupied Donizetti no more than eleven days, ensured popularity for the work from the beginning. It was first performed in Paris on the 4th January 1843, with a cast that sends our thoughts back wistfully to the great days when singing *was* singing: Lablache was the Pasquale, Tamburini the Malatesta, Mario the Ernesto, and Grisi the Norina. Mario must have made a handsome and sympathetic Ernesto; he not only looked but was a gentleman, by birth as well as training—something of a rarity on the Italian operatic stage of that period. The charming Grisi was his wife. Tamburini was a baritone of unique quality, both as a singer and as an actor. As for Lablache, opera has perhaps never seen or heard his like before or since. He was equally great in serious and in comic rôles. Henry Chorley, who knew something about opera singing, and had heard again and again all the finest artists of the first half of the nineteenth century, described him as "taking him all for all the most remarkable man whom I have ever seen in opera. . . . An organ more richly toned or suave than his voice was never given to mortal." He was "gifted with personal beauty to a rare degree. A grander head was never more grandly set on human shoulders." He was of gigantic stature, "yet one never felt on the stage how huge he was. His shoe was as big as a child's boat. One could have clad the child in one of his gloves; and the child could almost have walked on his belt. But every article of his dress was so excellently fitted to its wearer, was worn so unconsciously, and was so thoroughly in agreement with all that it accompanied, that there was neither time nor temptation for comparison. . . . This handsome young French-Neapolitan had got an amount of general and genial and solid musical culture . . . which, for a singer, has been something with too little precedent

. . . Lablache's perfect acquaintance with the great Roman style, his marvellous voice and, little less marvellous, his power of sustaining and animating his comrades without bearing them down, afforded a distinct idea of how such music might be sung, and how, when well sung, it might move, impress and exalt those who heard it as a portion of a rite."

The reader might do worse than to try to picture to himself, the next time he hears some ill-trained, weary, wobbly victim of the modern mania for pushing people on to the stage before they have acquired much more than the rudiments of a technique, how the recitatives and melodies of Don Pasquale used to be *sung* by Lablache. And when, as is more than likely, he sees some lubberly lout of a bass, who has never been taught anything better, laying on the humour in the grossest fashion, the reader should try to visualise Pasquale as Donizetti conceived him and as Lablache represented him—"the farce of fatness", as Chorley says, "trying to make itself seductive", "the dear silly hero of the farce-opera" wearing a coat "which stuck to him with as terrible a closeness as the outside garment of a sausage does to its contents within", yet, for all that, never for a moment angling for the horse-laugh of the mob. "Throughout the entire farce of Lablache's performances nothing was more admirable than his entire avoidance of grossness or coarse imitation. There was, with him, that security which belongs only to persons of rare and admirable tact; and, with that security, the highest power of expressing comedy, tragedy or grotesque—because it belongs to one who will risk nothing hazardous, but who is not afraid of daring anything extraordinary. When I hear of this person's style, and that person's high note, and when I think of Lablache, I am tempted to feel as if I had parted company with real comic genius on the musical stage for ever."

The part of Don Pasquale should never be clowned. The work was at first performed in what was then contemporary costume, an innovation in opera which, however, did not appeal to every spectator. But the very fact that Pasquale, as did Norina, Ernesto and Malatesta also, looked precisely like someone in real life is of itself a proof that the part was never intended by Donizetti as a vehicle for conventional clowning. Pasquale, for all his amorous foolishness, was a gentleman in an epoch when good breeding still counted for something.

3

The gay overture passes in review two or three of the many delightful melodies with which the work is strewn, without any attempt at arranging them in such a sequence or developing them in such a way as to summarise the story of the opera. After a few bars of quick preamble we hear in the clarinet the melody of Ernesto's serenade in the third act (See No. 21 below); the theme is then continued in turn by horn and flute. It is succeeded by the gay melody of the second part of Norina's cavatina in the first act (No. 6), which, with some lively connective tissue between its several returns, dominates the remainder of the overture.

The setting of the first act is the frequent stage one of a room with a door at the back and one at each side. Don Pasquale is seen walking impatiently up and down with his watch in his hand. A brief orchestral introduction of no more than a dozen bars indicates as conclusively that he is plunged in thought as the prelude to *Siegfried* suggests the profound cogitation of Mime. Then a pleasant melody steals out in the orchestra:

as Don Pasquale complains that it is nine o'clock and Dr. Malatesta is still not here to keep his appointment. Pasquale is preparing, he lets us know, a nice little pill for his nephew. While the orchestra continues with the strain of No. 1, Malatesta enters; as always, he is the soul of self-assurance and hearty humour. He is able to assure the impatient old bachelor that the bride he has commissioned him to procure for him has been found. Malatesta sings her praises in an aria every word of which Pasquale drinks in as the thirsty soil drinks in a shower of rain: it appears that the maiden is beautiful as an angel, fresh as a lily opening its petals to the morning sun; she has eyes that slay at sight, hair blacker than ebony, and a smile that is pure enchantment. So much for the person of this paragon; as for her moral qualities, she is blessed with a soul so innocent, so ingenuous, that it is ignorant even of itself; she is of a modesty without its parallel on earth; she is beloved by all for her goodness, her gentleness, her sympathy; heaven, in fact, created her purely and simply to make some super-fortunate man or other uniquely happy:

Pasquale swallows it all, licks his lips, and asks for more. Her family, he next learns, is well off, and her name is Malatesta—she is none other, in short, than the sister of the Doctor, who has to implore his old friend to control his ardour just a trifle longer, for he will bring the maiden to him this same evening. With that he leaves him. Don Pasquale, in a lively 3/8 rhythm, gives vent to his enthusiasm over this news:

The burden of his more than sixty years, he says, has fallen from him; he feels a mere twenty again; already he hears the patter of baby feet about the house. And now he will put that obstinate nephew of his in his place.

Ernesto enters at that very moment, and Don Pasquale at once

becomes the man of affairs again. He looks severely at the young
man. Is it true or isn't it, he asks him, that two or three months
ago he gave him the chance to marry a certain rich, noble and
beautiful maiden, promising him a handsome allowance if he
obeyed, and threatening to disinherit him if he refused. Quite
true, replies Ernesto; but he loves his Norina, he is pledged to her,
and he cannot give her up: she may be poor, but she is virtuous.
Thereupon Pasquale tells him that he will have to keep himself in
the future, for as for him, he is going to get married. Ernesto is
at first incredulous and inclined to be satirical; his uncle must
surely be joking. Pasquale assures him that he is not; and to a
tripping melody in the orchestra:

he tells his nephew that "I, Pasquale da Corneto, here in the flesh
before you, being of sound mind and body, have the honour to
inform you that I am going to marry, and that immediately."

Ernesto's amusement evaporates when he realises that the old
gentleman really means what he says; and in a melancholy little
aria, punctuated by the unfeeling comments of his uncle, he bids
eternal farewell to his own dream of love:

Too poor now to marry his Norina, he nobly renounces her for
ever. He warns Pasquale, however, not to take so rash a step
without consulting Dr. Malatesta, a man of proved judgment and
probity. His uncle triumphantly assures him that he has already
done so, and that so far from trying to dissuade him the Doctor
himself has found him a bride in the person of his own sister. At
the revelation of this perfidy on the part of Malatesta, whom he
had always looked upon as a friend, poor Ernesto breaks down
utterly: he has lost faith in everyone and everything. He gets no
sympathy from Pasquale, whose only comment is that he has
brought it all on himself through his pigheadedness. The curtain
descends with Ernesto still bewailing his martyrdom and his uncle
still chuckling over his discomfiture.

The scene changes to a room in Norina's house, where the
pretty young widow is reading aloud, from a book she has in her
hand, an episode in which a cavalier transfixed by a glance from
his lady falls on his knees before her and vows eternal and un-
divided homage. Norina laughs merrily: she too, she says, knows
all the arts and crafts—smiles, tears, and all the rest of it—by
which men are enslaved:

So anch'io la virtù ma-gica d'un guardo a tempo e lo-co,

She is capricious, fond of a jest, she admits, a trifle hasty, and
inclined to fly into a temper, but for all that the best-hearted
creature in the world; when it comes to managing men no one can
teach her anything; and as she is not only a young woman of the
world but a heroine of Italian comedy opera she says all this with
an abundance of sparkling coloratura.

She is impatient for the coming of Malatesta with news of how
his little scheme for some good joke or other at Don Pasquale's
expense is going. Just as Malatesta enters and begins the gay story
of how beautifully the fish rose to the bait, a servant enters with a
letter for Norina. After a glance at this she tells Malatesta that she
washes her hands of the business: she has more serious things to

think of now. She hands him the letter, which he reads aloud: "My Norina, I write to you with death in my heart. Don Pasquale, worked upon by that two-faced Doctor, is going to marry the scoundrel's sister; he has turned me out of his house and has cut me out of his will. Out of love for you I must renounce you: I shall leave Rome this very day, and Europe itself as soon as I can. Farewell. That you may be happy is the ardent prayer of your Ernesto". Malatesta tells Norina not to take the young donkey too seriously: he will disclose the plot to him, and then there will be no fear of his leaving. But what precisely is the plot? she asks. She knows already that Don Pasquale has talked about getting married to punish his nephew for his disobedience; but what else is there? She now learns that Malatesta, having been consulted by the old bachelor, has concocted a plan for doing her and Ernesto a good turn. If *he* doesn't plant a bride on Don Pasquale, some one else will—someone with an axe of his own to grind. Pasquale knows that Malatesta has a sister in a convent; the Doctor accordingly proposes that Norina shall impersonate her. His cousin Carlotto will pose as the notary and draw up the marriage contract: once they have that they can do what they like with the old man. Norina is willing to do anything that will not involve infidelity to her lover. Her lively and humorous imagination at once begins to run riot, to the accompaniment of an impish figure in the orchestra:

at the thought of the tricks she will play on Don Pasquale. Dr. Malatesta takes up the congenial theme: now, he hopes, she can see that he is a real friend of Ernesto, and that the sole purposes of his stratagem are to help the lovers and to have a bit of fun at Don Pasquale's expense.

Norina at once begins to practise her part, under the tuition of Malatesta. Is she to act the haughty dame? she asks him. No! Melancholy? No! Tearful? Shrewish? No, no! that isn't the idea at all. She must be the timid simpleton, the shrinking female, looking as if butter wouldn't melt in her mouth. Easy! she says; and she gives Malatesta a few specimens of her art of playing the simpering ingénue. Each is now eager to get to work on the victim:

They will fool Don Pasquale to the top of his bent: already they taste the sweets of vengeance. The duet, from start to finish, is of an irresistible vivacity, of a type and in a tempo only possible with a language so liquid as Italian and a music so purely melodic as that of Italian comedy. Incidentally we realise, from some of the passages that Donizetti gives Malatesta to sing, that in that epoch even a baritone or a bass was occasionally expected to be something of an expert in coloratura.

4

The second act also is played in Don Pasquale's house. Ernesto is alone, indulging himself in the luxury of a little Donizettian self-pity before he carries his broken heart with him to a foreign land. The main melody of his aria (No. 9 below) is first of all given out in full in an orchestral prelude. It is one of those melodies for which Donizetti had a curious aptitude—melodies that bring gravity enough into a comedy to make us take the character immediately concerned quite seriously for the time being, but still not too seriously: never do we feel that we have been snatched out of the comedy atmosphere of the work as a whole. Sorry as Ernesto is for himself, we know all along, though as yet he does not, that all will come right with him in the end. Meanwhile we listen sympathetically to his sad assurance that he is going into banishment, there to mourn to the end of his days his lost Norina, whose sweet image will never fade from his heart:

Cer-che-rò lon-ta-na ter-ra do-ve
ge-mer sco-no-sciu-to;

Even should Norina, in his absence, find consolation elsewhere, he will not reproach her, but be glad that she is happy:

E se fia che ad al-tro og-
get-to tu ri-volga un gior-no il co-re,

to which handsome sentiment he makes his exit.

Don Pasquale now enters with a servant, to whom he gives instructions that he is not at home except to Dr. Malatesta and whoever may accompany him. When he is alone he struts up and down, pluming himself on being in such good condition for a man of his years; but all the same, when he hears his visitors approaching he nervously commends himself to the protection of the god of matrimony.

Malatesta enters, leading a veiled, very shy, and almost fainting "sister" by the hand and exhorting the poor little thing to keep up her courage. Don Pasquale makes to approach her, but at a sign from the Doctor he retires to a corner. "For pity's sake do not leave me, dear brother", begs Norina. Malatesta goes to Don Pasquale and apologises for his sister; fresh from the convent as she is she is naturally a little scared on such an occasion, and Pasquale must be very gentle with her. While the men are colloguing in this fashion Norina completes the trio with a malicious aside:

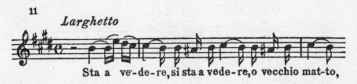

Sta a ve-de-re, si sta a vede-re, o vecchio mat-to,

that bodes no good to Don Pasquale. Then, the clinging female of the species once more, she turns to her brother with a new appeal for protection. To reassure her he points out that she is not alone: *he* is with her, as well as Don Pasquale. Norina, horrified at this discovery that there is another man in the room, wants to run away. The trio is repeated, with Norina reiterating her sotto voce warning to the old bachelor, Pasquale lost in admiration of her simplicity and modesty, and Malatesta chuckling over the perfection of the little slut's acting.

Don Pasquale, he informs his sister, is the last man in the world of whom she need be afraid; he is a friend of his, and the best of men. She makes him a curtsey, but does not dare raise her eyes to him. The three of them sit down, Malatesta in the middle. At his suggestion Pasquale asks his bride a few questions bearing on their future married life. No doubt she will want company in the evenings? "Not at all", she replies: "in the convent I was always alone." "A theatre occasionally?" The modest creature does not know what a theatre is, and does not want to know. "An admirable sentiment!" says Don Pasquale, "but all the same one must pass one's time in some way or other." But the prospective bride asks for no better way of passing the time than sewing, knitting, cooking and embroidering. Just what he would have ordered in the way of a bride! thinks Pasquale. But when Norina, after much pressing, is persuaded so far to overcome her modesty as to raise her veil in the presence of a man, the conquest of the old bachelor is complete. Words fail him; he can only stammer out a request for Malatesta to speak for him. Very timidly Norina accepts Pasquale's hand. Malatesta goes into the next room and returns with the pseudo-notary—"This Doctor thinks of everything!" says Don Pasquale to himself—and the masterly scene of the final fooling of Pasquale begins.

The four having seated themselves at a table, the notary—a familiar Italian comedy figure—takes down from the dictation of Dr. Malatesta, repeating, in his thin, high, nasal voice, the last word or syllable as he gets it on paper. The melodies mostly sing out in the orchestra, the voices speaking through them in the way so favoured by the composers of the old comic opera: Donizetti in particular has an inexhaustible supply of these charming tunes on tap. We begin with an insinuating orchestral melody:

12 *Moderato*

to the accompaniment of which the Doctor dictates the terms of the marriage contract between "Sofronia Malatesta, etc., etc., of the one part, and Pasquale da Corneto, etc., etc., of the other part, both here present and willing." Don Pasquale continues the dictation: the bridegroom settles on the bride half his property, movable and immovable; she is further to be absolute mistress of the household. When Don Pasquale has signed, and as Norina is about to do so, the notary points out that another witness besides Malatesta is necessary. Just then the voice of Ernesto is heard without, expostulating with the servants who are trying to bar his entrance. Norina lays down the pen, a trifle scared. Malatesta also is for the moment worried, for it seems that he has not yet had time to communicate the plot to Ernesto, and, as he says under his breath, "It looks as if the whole thing is going to be ruined." Here, then, are all the materials for a fresh comic imbroglio.

Ignoring the others, Ernesto goes straight to Don Pasquale to bid him goodbye. His uncle tells him he has arrived in the nick of time to witness the marriage contract; and Ernesto nearly collapses when he sees that the bride is Norina. This is more than he can be expected to stand! Dr. Malatesta takes him aside, and in agitated tones that are a test of the coloratura technique of the best baritone:

Ah!   fi - gliuol, non   mi   far
sce - ne, fi - gliuol, non mi far sce - ne,

implores him not to make a scene, as all that is happening is purely
for his benefit. Although he feels he is going mad under the
intellectual and emotional strain he is induced to sign after Norina;
and the notary, joining the hands of Don Pasquale and Norina,
solemnly declares them to be man and wife. Instantly Norina's
manner changes from timidity to audacity: "Now", she says sotto
voce, "the battle begins." The notary leaves.

Pasquale tries to embrace his Sofronia, but she tells him to wait
for her permission to do that. Ernesto laughs loudly. His uncle
orders him out, but Norina asks him what he means by manners
so countryfied and clownish as these. The orchestra plays lightly
and humorously round the characters all the time, especially when
Pasquale, hardly able to believe his ears, says to Malatesta,
"Doctor, she's not the same!" He has good reason to think this,
for Norina tells him that an old gentleman like him, fat, heavy,
decrepit, must not treat a young man in this fashion: Ernesto shall
be her cavalier. Pasquale protests in vain: Norina reminds him that
she has been given absolute command of the household, and gives
him to understand that she will tolerate no nonsense from him.

Malatesta takes the lead:

È   ri - ma - sto   là im-pie -
tra - to. Ve - gli,o so-gni non ___ sa be - ne.

in a slow emphatic quartet in which each of the characters comments on the situation after his own fashion, Malatesta, like the good friend he is, urging the abashed Pasquale not to be discouraged by this unexpected turn of events, and some notion of what it all means beginning to soak at last even into Ernesto's brain.

Norina snatches up a bell from one of the tables, rings it violently and orders the whole of the domestic staff to be brought in. A major-domo and two servants appear. She laughs this meagre ménage to scorn. Promptly she doubles the astonished major-domo's wages, and, to a merry little theme in the orchestra:

orders him to engage a new staff of bright young people, to buy a couple of new carriages at once, together with the necessary horses, to clear out the rubbishy old furniture, which is fit only for a museum, and replace it by something smarter and more modern, and to engage such necessaries for her as a hairdresser, a tailor and a jeweller. When Don Pasquale begins to protest against the cost of all this she rounds on him in good earnest, calling him by every unpleasant name she can think of. He is now pretty well sure that she is out of her mind. Ernesto is delighted by the storm she has raised, while the artful Malatesta begs his dear sister not to try his old friend too far.

All is now set for the grand finale. Don Pasquale realises at last that Norina has fooled him:

and swears he will not tolerate any more. Ernesto sees how mistaken he has been about Norina; and Dr. Malatesta advises his over-heated old friend to go to bed, leaving him to deal with this spitfire sister of his, whose conduct is as much a surprise to him as it is to her husband. The curtain comes down with them still arguing it out among themselves.

5

The setting of the third act is once more a room in Don Pasquale's house. Tables, chairs and floor are strewn with every species of female finery—costumes, hats, furs, scarves, lace, and so on. The unhappy Don Pasquale is sitting at a table that is hardly visible for tradesmen's bills. New servants stand all around. From a neighbouring room—that of Norina—comes a hairdresser carrying all the apparatus of his profession: he crosses the stage and goes out by another door.

The servants sing the liveliest of choruses as they try to cope with the mass of goods in the room, while poor Don Pasquale sits examining one account after another and lamenting over the madhouse that his once quiet home has suddenly become. When the servants have left, Norina enters hurriedly, magnificently dressed, with a fan in her hand: she takes no notice of her husband, but makes to go out by another door. He detains her, and asks with studied politeness where she is going. To the theatre, she says, and without him. His temper rising, he orders her to go at once to her room; but she only laughs at him and advises him to go to bed and have a nice sleep. They get to calling each other "coquette" and "impertinent fellow" respectively; and the climax comes when she slaps his face. "It's finished, it's finished; Don Pasquale, you have got yourself into a pretty mess!" he says sadly, the orchestra pointing his words with a melancholy motive of its own:

There is nothing to be done now but to go and drown himself.

Norina, in a quiet aside, agrees that the old man is being rather severely tried, but it had to be done, and the scheme must be carried through to victory. The little duet, with its clear differentiation of the two characters, is one of the best things in the opera: there is a tenderness in Norina's phrases:

that shows she is not bad at heart, and that she is really sorry for the old simpleton.

At the end of the duet he tells her she can leave the house if she likes, but she need never return. She assures him amiably that she will be back again next day; to which he replies that if she does she will find the door bolted. In the most dulcet of tones:

like a mother talking to a naughty and somewhat backward child, she advises the old man once more to be good and go to bed and sleep well; his wife will come and wake him in good time. "Divorce!" he cries. "Bed? Wife? A worse union there never was in this world! Wretched fool that I have been!"

When she has finished teasing and exasperating him she goes out; as she does so she lets fall a piece of paper, which Pasquale picks up, imagining it at first to be a bill. He reads: "Adored Sofronia, Between nine and ten this evening I shall be in the garden, in the part looking north. For extra security try, if you can, to admit me by the secret gate. We shall be in the shade of the grove. I forgot to tell you that you will know when I am there by my serenade. Your faithful one." This is the last straw: almost out of his mind he rings for a servant and sends him to Dr. Malatesta with orders to come to him at once.

When he has left the room the servants comment in a charming chorus on the strange goings-on in the house. None of them can get a moment's peace for the incessant ringing of bells; all the same it's a fine place, where money is poured out like water. Those who had heard the altercation between the master and the mistress give a full report of it to those who had not; others hint darkly at there being a nephew somewhere in the offing. After they have filed off the stage the Doctor appears on the threshold of the room, making the last arrangements with Ernesto, who goes down into the garden to play his own part in the coming comedy. Malatesta, hearing Don Pasquale approaching, composes his features in the best professional style.

Don Pasquale pours into his ears his long tale of woe, with the letter of assignation as the climax. Malatesta finds it hard to believe that his sister could have done any of the things of which Don Pasquale accuses her. Don Pasquale unfolds his plan for catching the faithless one. He and Malatesta will go into the garden; the servants will surround the grove:

the couple will be caught and taken before the magistrate. But Malatesta, also to the strain of No. 20, counsels quieter and subtler methods: he and Pasquale alone will surprise the pair, and get all they want without a scandal, by the mere threat of exposure; after all, Sofronia is his sister. After some argument he gets Don Pasquale to agree to *his* plan—they two will conceal themselves in the grove, and if what they overhear proves Sofronia's guilt, Pasquale will get rid of her there and then. Gloating over his coming revenge, Pasquale pours out his words in such profusion and at such a pace that one wonders how he can articulate them at all: the effect is irresistibly comic, and again one that is possible only in Italian. Malatesta follows his example in this respect as he remarks, sotto voce, that Pasquale is going to be caught in his own net.

The scene changes to the grove adjoining the house: on the left is a flight of steps leading from the house to the garden: on the right is a terrace: in the distance a gate. Ernesto is heard singing his serenade:

21 Andante mosso

Com'è gen-til____ la notte a mezzo A-pril!

to an accompaniment of chords on the guitar, and with a small chorus behind the scenes joining in occasionally. Norina enters from the right, and goes cautiously towards the gate to admit Ernesto, who now lets fall the cloak that has enveloped him. The lovers sing a tender duet, mostly, as Italian opera tradition dictated, in intertwining sixths and thirds. Seeing Pasquale and Malatesta creeping along with dark lanterns from the direction of the gate they conceal themselves behind some trees. Pasquale flashes the light in Sofronia's face and demands to know where her lover is. She denies that anyone is with her; she has been taking the air alone, she swears. While the two men are groping about in the wood, Ernesto slips into the house.

Don Pasquale orders Sofronia to leave him, but she refuses to go, as the house is hers. The Doctor now takes charge of the imbroglio, Pasquale having given him carte blanche. Malatesta tells his sister that tomorrow another woman will be settling in the house—Norina, the bride of Ernesto. "This is your cue for flying into a temper", he whispers to her. The sister passionately refuses to live a single day under the same roof as this Norina, a coquette whom she despises. ("Splendid, Doctor!" says Pasquale:

M

nothing will please him better than for Sofronia to go). Turning
next to Pasquale, the Doctor advises him to consent to his
nephew marrying Norina. Ernesto having been sent for, Malatesta informs him that Don Pasquale is not only willing that he
shall marry his Norina but will settle on him an annuity of four
thousand scudi. Ernesto joyously assents, but Malatesta's "sister"
opposes the idea, which fact, of course, is of itself sufficient to
recommend it to Don Pasquale. The latter tells Ernesto to send
for his Norina and he himself will marry them there and then.
"No need to go far for that", says Malatesta; "this lady is Norina.
Sofronia is still in the convent, and your 'marriage' was only a
scheme of mine to stop you from getting really and truly married."
Delighted at his escape and profiting by his lesson, Don Pasquale
forgives the conspirators; and led by Malatesta they join in
singing the moral of it all, which is that matrimony is an adventure which it is better for a man of Don Pasquale's age not to
embark upon:

22   *Allegretto moderato*   *etc.*

Bra-vo,   bra-vo ___   Don Pa - squa-le! ___

LA JUIVE
Halévy (1799-1862)

PRINCIPAL CHARACTERS

RACHEL	*Soprano*
ELEAZAR	*Tenor*
LEOPOLD	*Tenor*
CARDINAL DE BROGNI	*Bass*
EUDOXIE	*Soprano*
RUGGIERO	*Bass*
ALBERT	*Bass*

I

More than one of the Jewish Jacques François Fromental Elias Halévy's relations, by blood or by marriage, achieved distinction in the nineteenth century world of music, art or letters. First of all there was his brother Léon, archæologist and dramatist. Heine, who disliked both the Halévys, polished them off together in a single epigram: asked what he thought of Léon he replied: "He's as dull as if his brother had composed him." Léon's son, Ludovic, produced, in collaboration with Henry Meilhac, some of the best light-opera and opéra-comique libretti of his own or any other period, notably those of Offenbach's *La Grande Duchesse de Gérolstein*, *La Vie Parisienne* and *La Belle Hélène*; while the pair turned Prosper Mérimée's *Carmen* into a "book" for Bizet. The Meilhac-Halévy comedy *Le Réveillon* was the immediate source of the libretto of *Die Fledermaus*. Halévy's daughter married Bizet, who completed two works left unfinished by his father-in-law at his death.

Heine's epigram must not be taken too seriously: Halévy was anything but a dull composer, though it is true that of his many operas only *La Juive* keeps the stage today. This, as it happened, was a comparatively early work, produced in Paris on the 23rd February 1835—that is to say, between *Robert the Devil* and *The Huguenots*. After the huge success of the latter (1836) Halévy

seems to have succumbed to the temptation to follow to some
extent in Meyerbeer's footsteps; apparently he had not force
of character enough to concentrate doggedly on the development
of his own unquestionable individuality. Wagner, who never
showed much appreciation of the French genius in general, and
was never greatly drawn to the Jews, thought really well of
Halévy. During his distressful Paris period of 1839–1842 Wagner
did a good deal of "arranging" for the publisher Schlesinger; and
one of the newest successes he had to dish up in this way was
Halévy's *La Reine de Chypre* (1841). Close acquaintance with the
score of this gave him a higher opinion of contemporary French
opera than certain other works had done; and this favourable
opinion was confirmed, in spite of some absurdities in the work,
when he saw *La Reine de Chypre* on the stage. "I sincerely rejoiced", he says in his autobiography, "to see once more the
better side of Halévy, to whom I had taken a great fancy from the
time of his *La Juive*, and of whose vigorous talent I had formed
a very favourable opinion." Wagner made Halévy's personal
acquaintance about that time: he found him a modest, amiable
man, devoid of vanity where his own work was concerned, but
at the same time comprehensibly sceptical as to the worth of
contemporary opera in general.

It is never good for an artist to doubt the validity of the genre
in which it is his lot to work; and perhaps it was this spirit of critical
scepticism, combined with a constitutional tendency to indolence,[1]
that accounted for Halévy's never quite fulfilling in later life the
high promise of *La Juive*. Wagner saw him again fairly frequently in Paris in 1860-1: he found, to his regret, that Halévy had
given up in discouragement the struggle against the tendencies
of the epoch. "From my final visit to him", he says, "I came
away grieved at the enervation, moral and aesthetic, of one of the
last of the significant French musicians", and with a clearer
perception of "the universal hypocrisy or the frankly impudent
exploitation of the prevailing degeneracy on the part of all who
could be regarded as Halévy's successors." There are plentiful
grounds, indeed, for surmising that Halévy had more in him than
ever came to full fruition.

[1] He died of consumption.

The libretto of *La Juive* is one of Scribe's best efforts: this was certainly one of the operas Wagner had in mind when he said [1] that the famous text-manufacturer of that epoch could turn out a really good piece of dramatic carpentry when uncorrupted by Meyerbeer. It is true that both the construction and the diction of *La Juive* are grand-operatic in the manner of the Paris of the first half of the nineteenth century: each of the characters sometimes says and does things which no human being could ever be imagined saying or doing anywhere but in opera. But for all that, the plot bears critical examination, the action is admirably planned for progressive theatrical effect, and the characters in general, and especially the Jew Eleazar and his adopted daughter Rachel, are entirely credible. There is abundant scope not only for fine singing but for intelligent acting in both these rôles.

The scene of the drama was originally laid in the Spain of the Inquisition period, and the part of Eleazar was designed for a high bass. Later it was re-cast for the leading French tenor of the period, Adolphe Nourrit, to whom we owe the present ending of the fourth act. Apparently Scribe had terminated the act with a short chorus following on the scene between Eleazar and Brogni. Nourrit suggested that a monologue was called for here in which the Jew could express to the full the conflict of emotions in his breast,—the struggle between his desire to save Rachel and his thirst for revenge on the persecutors of his race; and Halévy agreed with him. Although the words of this long scene—commencing with the recitative "Va prononcer ma mort" and continuing with the aria "Rachel! quand du Seigneur la grâce tutélaire"—are printed as Scribe's in the complete edition of the latter's plays, they are said to be from Nourrit's pen. They are interesting for the light they throw on the points which an intelligent singer of that epoch regarded as likely to prove especially effective.

2

The scene of the drama is the Swiss town of Constance in the year 1414, and the main theme of it the eternal antagonism of Christian and Jew. Cardinal de Brogni, by the way, was a

[1] See p. 201.

historical character: in August 1414 he presided in Constance over a council of princes and ecclesiastics that had been convened to try to establish peace between the various sects within the Church.

The Overture presents us with some of the leading themes of the opera, strung together in the fashion of that epoch. The theme with which it opens:

is that which later will introduce the opera itself. Also taken from the introduction are:

and

this last being presumably intended to characterise the Jewish element in the story, while Nos. 1 and 2 as obviously represent the Christian element.

To this preludial *andantino* there succeeds an *allegro agitato ed appassionato*, in which the composer gets to grips with the more tragic elements in the action. Syncopated chords:

serve to suggest the perturbed atmosphere of the work, while
thunderous octave passages of varying outline, but of much the
same type:

are associated with the power of the Church as represented by
Cardinal de Brogni. When the fury of this section has died down,
we hear the broad cantabile melody of the passage at the end of
the fourth act in which the condemned Jew looks forward
rapturously to eternal reunion with his daughter:

Developments of this, and of the element of agitation represented
by Nos. 4, 5 and 6, culminate in a fresh melody of a tranquil
character:

which plays no part in the opera itself. The further course of the overture is dominated by the psychologically important No. 7.

The first act of the opera takes place on the day of the opening of the council. The scene is a crossways in the town of Constance: on one side of the stage we see the porch of a church, and on the other side, at the corner of the street, the house and workshop of the rich Jewish goldsmith and jeweller Eleazar. On the steps of the church a number of people are kneeling for whom there has been no room inside: others are promenading in the open space in front of the church. Before the curtain rises there is an expressive orchestral introduction which runs, to some extent, on the same lines as the first section of the overture, though the key is now E flat instead of E natural: we hear in succession Nos. 1, 2 and 3 (in the latter the melody is now given to the oboe), and various phrases of the same general kind as No. 4. Solemn organ strains are heard from inside the church, terminating in a "Te Deum laudamus" sung by the congregation.

At the rise of the curtain several of the people are resenting the fact that while the rest of the town is holding festival in honour of the ecclesiastical assembly, work is going on in the shop on the left of the stage. The word is passed round that this is the shop of the wealthy Israelite Eleazar, who just then comes into sight, accompanied by his daughter Rachel. The girl, terrified at the hostile attitude of the crowd, draws her father into the shop: he throws the Christians a defiant look as he goes within. The crowd makes its way towards the church, from which there now comes a song of praise in voices and organ.

Leopold, Prince of the Empire, enters, enveloped in a cloak. He is recognised, however, by Albert, a sergeant-at-arms in the service of the Emperor, who respectfully expresses his surprise at seeing the Prince thus disguised. Leopold imposes silence on him: the Emperor, he says, must not hear of his presence in Constance before nightfall at the earliest. He inquires the cause of the excitement in the town. Albert tells him that the Hussites, thanks to the Prince himself, having been suppressed, the Emperor Sigismond is opening in person a grand council of princes and prelates, whose function it will be to blot out heresy and unite all Christendom in the one true faith. As the pair go out together, Leopold casting a glance at the house of Eleazar as he leaves, a great choral cry of "Hosanna" comes from the church; trumpet fanfares ring out, and the congregation pours into the streets. They are ordered by Ruggiero, the provost of the town, to listen to the reading, by the public crier, of a proclamation just issued by the Emperor: "Prince Leopold having chastised, with God's aid, the insolent Hussites, the Emperor, the Cardinal Brogni and the council now assembled in Constance have ordained that the people shall enjoy largesse at their hands: in the morning thanks will be given to God in all the churches, and in the afternoon the public fountains will flow with wine." The crowd greet the edict with acclamations.

From the shop on the left of the scene comes the insistent sound of the tapping of workmen's hammers. Once more the crowd rages against the profane Jews, and Ruggiero sends his soldiers into the shop with orders to bring the heretics before him. Eleazar and Rachel are dragged out, the old man, as always, truculent and defiant, and the girl concerned, as always, not for her own sufferings but for those of her father. Eleazar sees no reason, he tells the crowd, to consider their wishes or angle for their good will. Their faith is not his: and if he detests and insults theirs, is he not justified in doing so? Has he not seen his own sons burnt at the stake by Christians, reaching out impotent hands to him in their agony? Ruggiero threatens him and his daughter with death for their insolence; and the soldiers and the crowd, delighted at the prospect of wreaking their malice on the Jews, are dragging the couple away when the venerable Cardinal, emerging from the church, halts them and asks the meaning of it all. It is explained to him that these Israelites have wilfully profaned the festival. He orders them to be brought before him. When Eleazar gives him his name, Brogni seems to remember having heard it before, and to have seen the bearer of it somewhere, though he cannot recall when or where.

Eleazar refreshes his memory for him: it was in Rome, he says, where, in days long ago, Brogni, not yet a minister of the Church, had had a wife and a daughter whom he loved. The Cardinal checks him with a gesture: he has lost all who were once dear to him, and he would fain forget. Now he is only a servant of the Church, working for the salvation of men's souls, including

those of Jews if they will let themselves be saved. Has he forgotten, rejoins Eleazar, that when he was head magistrate of Rome
he had driven into exile the very Jew who now stands before
him? (Scribe's original text, but not the opera libretto, makes it
clear why Eleazar had thus been banished from Rome. He had
been convicted of usury; the people had demanded his execution,
and Brogni had saved his life by exiling him). The Cardinal now
orders the soldiers to release the Jew, whom he asks to forget the
past and be his friend and brother. The crowd murmurs at this
clemency, and Eleazar himself rejects it. He refuses the friendly
hand offered him by Brogni, declaring that nothing will ever
abate his hatred of Christians or induce him to forget what they
have done to him. The Cardinal expresses his desire that Eleazar
may some day be brought to a better way of thinking, in a little
cavatina:

which is developed into a short ensemble, in which the people
express a pious hope for a change of heart in the Jews, Rachel
thanks the Cardinal for his kindness, and Eleazar vows implacable
enmity towards the persecutors of his race and of himself.

All leave the stage except Leopold, who, taking up a position
under the window of Eleazar's house, sings softly a serenade to
Rachel, the piquant opening rhythm of which:

contrasts with the more conventional one of the second section:

11

Mais voi-ci le jour, ô maî-tres-se ché-ri - e,

in which Leopold speaks of the joy of reunion with the beloved after a long absence.

After the second stanza of the song Rachel appears on the balcony of her house, and, addressing her lover as Samuel, inquires if the journey abroad that had separated them has been as successful as he could have desired. (The spectator soon discovers that Leopold has wooed Rachel in the guise of a Jewish artist named Samuel). He evades her questions as best he can, and asks when they can meet again. "This very night", she replies. They will be celebrating the Passover according to the ancient rites of their faith; and Samuel, as one of their own race, will be welcome at their board. Leopold, greatly embarrassed, seems on the point of giving her some kind of explanation when the noise of an approaching crowd is heard, and Rachel exhorts him to leave her now: they will see each other again that same evening, she says.

Flinging his cloak around him, Leopold disappears in the crowd that now fills the stage, to the sound of joy-bells from all parts of the town. The populace have come out to take advantage of the edict that the city fountains—there happen to be several of these within sight—shall spout wine; and they express their satisfaction, and their intention of having a merry time till morning, in a lively chorus:

12 *Allegro*

Hâ-tons-nous, car l'heure s'a - van - ce, et bien-

tôt la fê - te com - men - ce,

which runs on into another in praise of the Emperor:

Ah! quel heur-eux des - tin, oui, bé - niss- ons, bé -niss-ons no - tre bon sou - ve - rain!

(Halévy is generally at his best when he can get his choral masses moving).

By now all the fountains are yielding wine, and the crowd are filling cups and passing them on to each other with great gusto, toasting gratefully not only the Emperor but all the members of the council: they would be glad, the jovial fellows say, to drink the separate health of every one of these benefactors, did they number even a thousand. One or two of them begin to quarrel as to whose cup is whose, but these little difficulties are soon smoothed out. This chain of choruses—which, as is generally the case with Halévy, develops fresh vigour as it proceeds—leads to a vigorous dance in waltz rhythm, and this into another fine chorus as the now half-tipsy crowd see the procession of the notables approaching.

Just then Eleazar and Rachel leave their house and try to cross the square, but are so jostled by the excited crowd that in the end they have to mount the steps of the church and stand close to the wall for safety. There they are recognised by Ruggiero as the Jews of the episode of a little while before. He incites the mob against the heretics who are thus polluting a Christian sanctuary. Some of the faithful drag the furious Eleazar off in one direction, intending to throw him into the lake: others are about to carry off Rachel in the opposite direction when Leopold intervenes. Rachel, believing "Samuel" to be of her own race, implores him to save himself by flight; but he draws his sword and sets on the mob. He is once more recognised by Albert, at whose command the people relinquish their prey, to the great astonishment of

Rachel; neither she nor the mob can account for the influence "Samuel" has over the soldiers of the Emperor.

The attention of the people is now opportunely diverted to the procession which is at last coming into sight: the whole town seems to have come out to see the superb spectacle. Soldiers and councillors and their retinues lead the way, followed by the Cardinal with his esquires and pages, halberdiers carrying the banners of the empire, and finally the Emperor himself, on horse-back, accompanied by the princes. When the Emperor appears, Leopold, covering his face with his cloak, disappears in the crowd. Rachel observes him with increasing wonderment and anxiety, while Eleazar surveys the Christians in general with proud contempt. The curtain descends to cries of "Honour and glory to the Emperor!"

3

The scene of the second act is a room in Eleazar's house. In the centre is a large table covered with a white cloth, at which a num-ber of Jews and Jewesses are celebrating the Passover: Eleazar is at the centre of the table, Leopold at one end of it, Rachel at the other. On the left side of the room is an easel, and beside it a small table containing the usual apparatus of the painter's craft.

The prayer in which Eleazar and his guests are taking part has a peculiar rhythmical structure of its own, of which Eleazar's opening phrase is typical:

14

Andante moderato

O Dieu, Dieu de nos pè - res, par-mi nous descends!

Having invoked the wrath of heaven on any unbeliever who should dare to profane their devotions with his presence, they proceed to the distribution of unleavened bread. The last to be served is Leopold. He hesitates for a moment, and then, after a nervous glance round to make sure that he is not observed, throws the bread away. His action has been seen, however, by Rachel, who is puzzled and disturbed by it.

After a somewhat undistinguished cavatina by Eleazar there

comes a loud knocking at the door. The lights on the table are hastily extinguished, and then the table itself removed. From outside a voice commands them to open the door in the Emperor's name. Soon the room is empty save for Eleazar, his daughter, and Leopold. Rachel asks "Samuel" to follow her into an adjoining room, for she wishes to have a word with him about his strange conduct at the table. Eleazar, however, detains him: the young man, he says, will be able to defend him should danger threaten. Rachel thereupon goes out with the others, after she and Leopold have exchanged glances of mutual understanding.

By the time the door has been opened, Leopold has stationed himself by the easel, with his back to the centre of the room: there he pretends to be painting when Eudoxia (Eudora), the Emperor's niece, enters with two of her own liveried servants, carrying torches. Who is the man at the easel? she enquires. Eleazar replies that he is a painter, a famous artist who is of great service to him in his craft: should she desire it, he will ask him to leave them. Eudoxia assures him with a smile that there is no need for that, as there is nothing mysterious about her visit. She has heard that Eleazar has for sale a magnificent specimen of the jeweller's craft. He sings its praises—a gold chain, richly set with jewels, that once had hung round the neck of the Emperor Constantine himself. Eudoxia asks to see it: she wishes, she says, to present it to her betrothed—Prince Leopold, the suppressor of the Hussites, whose return she expects that very day. A short trio is built up out of the musical phrase:

15

Ah! dans mon â-me son image chérie est gravée à jamais,

to which she speaks of her love for Leopold. It is taken up in an aside by the Prince, who is filled with remorse for his unfaithfulness to her and his deceit of Rachel, and carried on by Eleazar, whose hatred of the Christians is for the moment mitigated somewhat by the thought of the handsome profit he is going to make on the deal. Eudoxia is fascinated by the chain, which she buys without demur at Eleazar's price of thirty thousand florins. She tells the Jew to engrave her own and Leopold's monogram on it and have it delivered at the palace the next day, when she intends to present the gift to her betrothed in the presence of the Emperor and his court. The trio based on No. 15 is resumed, this time on larger lines; and after it Eudoxia leaves, escorted to the door of the house by the deferential Eleazar.

Rachel enters, anxious to know the meaning of the mystery she feels to be surrounding her "Samuel". He begs for a more secret meeting later, at which he will explain everything. When Eleazar returns he notices his daughter's agitation, and vague suspicions spring up in him. Concealing his thoughts, however, he dismisses Leopold and turns to Rachel with an affectionate word or two. But when he takes her hand in his he is struck by the coldness of it, and he chances also to intercept a significant look between her and the young man. He still keeps his thoughts to himself, however; and having bidden Leopold farewell he goes off with Rachel to say the evening prayer.

Soon Rachel returns, in great perturbation of spirit, to keep the assignation she has made with Leopold. She seats herself at a window on the right of the stage: she is torn between love and a dim foreboding of evil. Her heart leaps as Leopold appears at the window; but she is terrified at the unhappiness she reads in his face. He confesses that he has deceived her, that her God is not his. This deadly blow, she tells him, she had not expected: when she had pledged him her love in secret she had known she was being untrue to honour and to her father, but not to her God:

16   Allegro

Lorsqu'à toi je me suis don-
né - e j'ou-tra-geai mon père et l'honneur,

Distractedly she reminds him that for a Christian to love a Jewess means death for them both. There is only one thing that can save them, he tells her—flight together from Constance: let her only have trust in him and all will still be well:

She recoils at the thought of abandoning her father, but he assures her that he himself will have to make a sacrifice no less great. The long colloquy, which becomes ever more despairing on Rachel's side, ever more urgent on Leopold's, ends with her promising to forsake everything, even her God, for love of him.

But as their excitement reaches its climax Eleazar enters. He has overheard the latter part of their conversation. Whither, he asks them, can they fly and escape a father's curse? An ominous phrase in the orchestra:

introduces a trio in which Leopold and Rachel express their fear and remorse, while Eleazar reproaches them both for their treachery. Then he turns angrily to Leopold. He upbraids him for his deception and ingratitude, and swears he would slay him there and then were he not, like them, an Israelite. Leopold bids him strike without mercy, for he is a Christian. The maddened Eleazar draws a dagger and hurls himself at him, but is restrained by Rachel, who implores him to pardon her lover, pleading that she is equally guilty with him, equally worthy of death. The old man's infinite love for her softens his heart, and in the end he consents that Leopold, Christian though he is, shall become her husband. But Leopold distractedly declares that that is impossible, though he cannot reveal to them why. Eleazar's anger flames out afresh at what he regards as this further proof of Leopold's baseness, and his part in the agitated trio that concludes the act consists of a furious denunciation of the sacrilegious Christian and the calling of the vengeance of Israel's God on his head. As the curtain falls he sinks into a chair with his head in his hands. Leopold rushes away; and a moment later Rachel flings round her the cloak he had left behind him and follows him.

4

In the third act we see a magnificent garden in which the Emperor is feasting with the princes, dukes, Electors and other notables. His own table stands high above the others, under a gorgeous canopy. The seat of honour on his right hand is occupied by the Cardinal de Brogni; close by at the same table are Eudoxia and Leopold. Servants are busy bringing dishes and pouring out wine. Sundry gentlemen and ladies who have not been invited to the banquet are enjoying the spectacle from rows of elevated seats. The townspeople also would very much like to see what there is to be seen, but the guards prevent them from getting too close.

The act opens [1] with a hearty chorus in commendation of the Emperor and of the feast; and the words of Scribe's original text

[1] In some scores of *La Juive* the act begins with a scene inside the palace. After Eudoxia has sung of her joy at Leopold's return Rachel enters: seemingly she has followed him to the palace from her father's house. She asks Eudoxia to take her as her slave for at least a day; and the Princess, though she sees at a glance that Rachel is not of the slave class, agrees. Rachel, we gather, is already planning revenge on her false lover. Rachel having been dismissed, Leopold enters, and there follows a short scene between him and the amorous Eudoxia, which is terminated by a trumpet

are a charming specimen of that vein of facile doggerel on which
he could draw so inexhaustibly:

> *Jour mémorable!*
> *Jour de splendeur!*
> *Vois-tu la table*
> *De l'Empereur?*

The chorus is followed by a pantomime and a ballet. The Emperor—his is not a singing part, by the way—either does not
think much of this branch of art or has affairs of state to attend to:
anyhow he leaves the moment it begins, though he kindly signifies by a gesture to the Cardinal and Ruggiero, who are following
him, that they can stay for it if they choose to do so. (In the
original scenario and score the pantomime represents the defeat of
the Moors by Christian knights and the rescue of damsels from
an enchanted castle). After the ballet there comes another chorus,
in which Leopold and Eudoxia take part, the latter making the
most of the opportunities given her to display her high notes and
the agility of her voice. Her song is in praise of the conquering
hero Leopold, the saviour of the Christian faith; he, however, is
ill at ease, brooding darkly over his own unworthiness and fearing
what the future may have in store for him.

A major-domo enters, conducting Eleazar—carrying the golden
casket that contains the chain—and Rachel. They are not only
astounded but shocked to see "Samuel" sitting in a place of high
honour among the ungodly. Eudoxia bids Leopold kneel before
her to receive the chain from his betrothed. At this last word
Rachel throws herself between them, tears the chain out of
Leopold's hands, and returns it to Eudoxia: the man is not

fanfare summoning them to the festivities. After that the action takes the
course indicated in the present analysis, i.e., from the chorus "Jour mémor-
able" onwards.

None of this supplementary matter is in the official Scribe text: presumably
it was an afterthought on the part of some one or other.

On the other hand, there is a passage in Scribe's text later—in the scene of
the recognition of Leopold by Rachel—which is not in Halévy's score. It is
evident that the insertion of new matter at the commencement of the act
necessitated a change in the management of the recognition scene as originally planned.

worthy, she tells the Princess, of such a mark of honour. Eudoxia resents this aspersion on her betrothed. "Call him not that!" answers Rachel; "he is a traitor, a dastard, whom I denounce before you all." Eleazar tries to silence her, but she advances to where de Brogni and the members of the council are sitting, and proclaims in a frenzy of hatred and despair that for having loved a Jewess Leopold deserves death, and that the Jewess, who by the law has incurred the same penalty, is herself. All rise from their seats in horror.

Over an arresting figure in the orchestra:

Leopold confesses, more to himself than to the others, his shame and self-contempt. Eudoxia, Rachel, Eleazar, the remaining principals and the chorus take up the strain and build up a fine ensemble, in which the several characters and their respective reactions to the disclosure are admirably differentiated.

Eleazar then steps forward, holding Rachel in his arms, and boldly demands the punishment of Leopold—or is it only for the Jews, he asks them with bitter irony, that they reserve their Christian laws, their chains, their executioners? As Leopold makes no attempt to deny Rachel's accusations, Brogni advances and proclaims the anathema of the Church on him and the two Jews. They are to be shunned by all, and their bodies, accursed on earth and in heaven, are to be left unburied and unprayed for. The act ends with a big ensemble, in which Leopold admits the justice of his punishment, Rachel begs that at least her father, who has had no part in her crime, be spared, and Eleazar truculently answers Brogni with curse for curse. At a sign from the Cardinal, Ruggiero and the guards approach the trio. Leopold draws his sword and throws it at Brogni's feet. He, Eleazar and Rachel are taken away, while Eudoxia, the princes and the Cardinal raise despairing hands to heaven.

5

One of the best features of *The Jewess* is the way the dramatic interest mounts with each of the five acts: the fourth is an intensification of the crucial third, yet even after that the librettist and the composer have still their strongest card of all to play.

The setting of the fourth act is a Gothic apartment adjoining the council chamber. Eudoxia enters and hands the officer on duty a written order from the president to allow her a short interview with Rachel. The Jewess is brought in—to meet, as she thinks, the death for which she longs. She is surprised to see Eudoxia— her enemy, as she calls her. The Princess, however, has come only to humble herself to her rival, to beg her to save Leopold's life by declaring that he is innocent. Rachel passionately refuses: it is because she loves Leopold as she does, quite as much as because of her jealousy of Eudoxia, that she desires his death and her own. All the Princess's tears, all her frenzied entreaties, are in vain until, at the ominous sound of bells and drums behind the scenes, love wins the victory over every other emotion in Rachel's breast: she will show this woman, she says in an aside, that a Jewess can surpass a Christian in greatness of soul.

Eudoxia leaves as Brogni and the guards enter to take Rachel before the tribunal, there to make her confession and receive her sentence. She will do her duty to her God, she declares, and save not herself but the one most dear to her. When she has been taken away, Brogni, who is filled with pity for her, orders Eleazar to be brought in: he sees that his only chance to save the girl's life is to persuade the Jew to renounce his faith.

In grave but kindly terms he tells Eleazar that the fate of Rachel, who is at that moment before the tribunal, lies in her father's hands: she can be saved from the flames only by his abjuring his religion. Eleazar rejects the suggestion with scorn: he would rather die than be false to the faith of his fathers: the God of Israel will some day liberate His persecuted people. He himself is prepared for death; but before he dies, he says, to the accompaniment of a figure that is always symbolical of his inappeasable hate and passion for revenge:

he will be avenged on at least one Christian—the Cardinal himself. He, Eleazar, is not the only one, he reminds the prelate, who will have been robbed by the flames of the one he held most dear. When, years before, the Neapolitans had taken and sacked Rome and the Brogni palace had been burnt to the ground, Brogni had lost his wife and his infant daughter. The Cardinal, greatly distressed, begs Eleazar not to recall to him those tragic days in which everything had been lost that he had most treasured. No, not everything, Eleazar replies: for the Jews—those very Jews whom Brogni had treated so harshly—had been the first to defy the flames and save what could be saved in the devastated city: and one of them had found Brogni's child still alive, rescued her from the ruins of the palace and taken her away with him. But he refuses to give the distracted father the name of the Jew who had done this, though Brogni goes on his knees to him:

Ah! j'implore en tremblant ta ⸺ clé - men - ce,

Eleazar answers him to the same melody. What right has he, he demands, to ask a favour now of one whom he had injured in the past? The Jew glories in his sense of mastery. Brogni's daughter lives, he says, and he alone knows where; and he will take the secret to the grave with him. Let the Cardinal, then, do his worst on him. Thereupon Brogni reluctantly abandons the fanatic to his fate, and returns to take his place at the council.

Left alone, Eleazar gloats fiendishly for a moment over his triumph: he has planted in his old enemy's heart a barb which the victim will never he able to pluck out. Then his heart softens as he thinks of his beloved Rachel, whom he is sacrificing to enjoy the sweets of revenge. In the finest aria of the opera, to which the warm dark tones of basset-horns give a peculiar colouring, he reminds himself how Rachel's happiness had been his one care throughout her life:

Rachel! quand du Seigneur la grâce tu - té - lai - re

and now it is he who is delivering her over to the executioner! In imagination he hears the beloved voice calling to him, begging for pity; and for a moment his fierce heart melts. Then, as a savage cry of "To the flames with the Jews!" is heard outside, he resolves that as she is Israel's child she shall die with him for the glory of the God of Israel. They shall enter Paradise together, he declares ecstatically to the melody of No. 7. Then Ruggiero and the guards enter and sign to him to follow them to the council chamber.

6

The final scene shows us a great tent from which a view is obtainable over the whole town of Constance. A prominent feature of the prospect is the great square, on the far side of which stands a huge brass cauldron in the centre of a fire. The square is built up in tiers, on which are seated the populace, drunk with pleasurable anticipation of the spectacle about to be set before them. Some of the crowd force their way also into the tent prepared for the council, from which they can get a still better view of the square.

The mob expresses its naïve delight, in the opening chorus, at not only having a day off from work but being able to spend it in so charming a fashion as seeing Jews plunged into boiling water.

As usual, Halévy finds within him resources for the expression of mass-feelings which are not always at his command for the portrayal of his individual characters.

The bells ring out, and, to the strains of a march, an imposing procession—monks, prelates, the Cardinal, guards, penitents and many others—makes its way from the imperial garden to the square. Eleazar and Rachel are led in by soldiers from opposite sides of the stage: Rachel is in a white robe, and her feet are bare. At the sight of the grim apparatus in the square she throws herself, with a frightened cry, into the arms of Eleazar. He exhorts her to have courage: soon, he promises her, they will be together again, never to be parted. Ruggiero, accompanied by the secretaries of the council, steps forward and reads the decree condemning the two Jews to death: Leopold, it appears, has been spared by the Emperor but banished from Constance. Eleazar cries out furiously against the Christians' one-sided notions of justice. He is told that a witness has sworn to Leopold's innocence; and to his profound grief Rachel, at Ruggiero's summoning, proclaims to them all that the charge she had laid at Leopold's door was false, and had been prompted only by jealousy. The infuriated crowd clamours for her death. Ruggiero pronounces the sentence of the council upon Rachel and Eleazar: for having traduced a prince of the empire they must both of them die. Brogni breathes a short prayer for them, and then implores Eleazar, for the last time, before they part for all eternity, to end his anguish by telling him what had become of his daughter.

Rachel is being taken away to the scaffold when Eleazar, his mind at last made up, orders the soldiers to stop. With the Cardinal's eyes fixed anxiously on him he asks Rachel if she desires to live after he himself is dead. She scorns the suggestion that she can save her own life by being baptised: rather the flames than that, she cries. Joyously Eleazar bids the procession form again. Just as Rachel is mounting the steps that lead to the cauldron, Eleazar finds himself close to Brogni. The Cardinal clutches him by the arm, and in a low voice implores him once more to tell him if his daughter still lives. Turning his head in the direction of Rachel, Eleazar answers "Yes!" His face lit up with joy, Brogni asks where she is. "Behold her!" cries the Jew, pointing to Rachel, who at that moment is being thrown by the executioners into the cauldron. Eleazar passes on to his own death with a smile of cruel triumph on his lips. Brogni covers his face with his hands and falls on his knees, while the crowd, their blood-lust sated, shout their thanks to God for having destroyed the enemies of their religion.

MANON

Massenet (1842-1912)

PRINCIPAL CHARACTERS

MANON LESCAUT	*Soprano*
CHEVALIER DES GRIEUX	*Tenor*
LESCAUT	*Baritone*
GUILLOT DE MORFONTAINE	*Bass*
DE BRÉTIGNY	*Baritone*
POUSSETTE	*Soprano*
JAVOTTE	*Mezzo-soprano*
ROSETTE	*Mezzo-soprano*

I

As has been pointed out elsewhere in this volume, the psychological centre of the Abbé Prévost's famous story (1733) is not really Manon but des Grieux: Prévost's own title for the work, indeed, is *Les Aventures du Chevalier des Grieux et de Manon Lescaut*. It is said to have been founded on experiences of the author's own; and whoever the original Manon may have been, it is certain that, as Michelet put it, "the author and the hero are one". The story is told to the supposed narrator of it by des Grieux, and it is through the latter's eyes alone that we see Manon throughout. And the tragedy, when all is said, is far less Manon's than his, because his is the more complex nature of the two.

Massenet's *Manon* was produced at the Opéra-Comique, Paris, on the 19th January 1884, with Talazac as des Grieux and Marie Heilbronn as Manon. Puccini's *Manon Lescaut* followed nine years later. Long before either Massenet or Puccini, however, the subject had been treated twice by Scribe—in a ballet pantomime in 1830, with music by the future composer of *La-Juive*, and in an opéra-comique, with music by Auber, in 1856. This latter work is one of those curiosities of operatic literature which perhaps only Scribe could have achieved. The third act, which takes place in Louisiana, opens with a chorus of negro slaves

367

expressing such sentiments as perhaps no slaves have ever cherished with regard to their master except in opera: "when a slave has a good master he loves to serve him: to defend him and work for him is a real pleasure." Then a young male slave of the name of Zaby obliges the company with what he calls "une chanson du pays". It commences thus:

> *Mam'zelle Zizi,*
> *Mam'zelle Zizi,*
>
> *Un peu d'espoir*
> *Au pauvre noir,*
> *Pitié pour lui!*
> *Le teint n'y fait rien,*
> *Quoique noir, on aime bien.*

But even Zaby and Mam'zelle Zizi are no remoter from Prévost than some of the other characters and incidents of this amazing specimen of the French opera libretto of the 1850's.

2

The libretto of Massenet's work is by Henry Meilhac and Philippe Gille, who have made a very fair job of converting into an opera a story the essence of which defies operatic treatment. In the first place, Prévost presents the librettists with only three full-length portraits—the Chevalier, Manon, and her brother Lescaut. Prévost's Tiberge, the sober friend of des Grieux in his school days and his moral support and prompter of conscience later, is useless for operatic purposes. Neither des Grieux's father nor the men with whom Manon betrays her young lover are anything like full-size studies in the novel, but Meilhac and Gille get out of this difficulty quite well: des Grieux *père* is easily converted into the traditional heavy father of opera (he is first cousin, indeed, to the elder Germont in *La Traviata*), and Guillot de Morfontaine and Brétigny are near enough as makes no matter to some of the older and richer lovers of Manon as sketched by Prévost.

In the second place, the final American adventure of the Chevalier and Manon, which has been included in Puccini's work but omitted from Massenet's, is not good operatic material, in spite of the easy opportunities for pathos which it affords. Librettist and composer lack space in which to set forth in any detail what happened to the young lovers in the New World, as narrated in the thirteenth chapter of the novel. If all they are to be shown doing in America is for one of them to die and the other to be broken-hearted over it, Manon may just as well quit this life at Havre, as Meilhac and Gille make her do, as go to Louisiana for that purpose, as in Puccini: for there is not a word anywhere in Puccini's work [1] to explain just how and why their idyll has come to so sad an end in the neighbourhood of New Orleans, and why they happen to be painfully toiling through the desert on the particular day of Manon's death.

In the third place, many of the effects that are the very essence of Prévost's art are from their nature impossible of reproduction in opera. Take, as an example, the episode that immediately follows the death of Manon, as told by des Grieux:

"For four-and-twenty hours I remained without taking my lips from the face and the hands of my dear Manon. It was my intention to die like that: but at the beginning of the second day I reflected that after my death her body would become the prey of wild beasts. So I resolved to bury her and await my own end on her grave. The weakness due to my fasting and grief had brought me so near my end that it was only by the greatest effort that I could keep on my feet. . . . The soil was sandy, so it was not difficult for me to open it. I broke my sword to dig with, but found my hands of more use. I made a deep grave, and in it I laid the idol of my heart, after having wrapped her in my own clothes so that the sand should not touch her; but not before I had kissed her ten thousand times, with all the ardour of the most perfect love. Once more I seated myself near her and contemplated her for a long time, for I could not bring myself to close the grave. At last, feeling my strength leave me and fearing it

---

[1] The only words in the Italian text that have the smallest bearing on the question are Manon's "Ahi! mia beltà funesta ire novelle accende. Strappar da lui mi si volea" (Alas! My fatal beauty has caused new misfortunes. They wanted to tear me away from him [des Grieux]). But not a word of explanation is vouchsafed as to who "they" may be, and what are the "new misfortunes" that have followed in the wake of Manon's charms in New Orleans.

would fail me wholly before my task was done, I committed to the earth for ever the sweetest, the most perfect thing that had ever trodden it. Then I laid myself on the grave with my face turned towards the sand, and, closing my eyes in the hope of never opening them again, I invoked the protection of heaven and awaited death impatiently."

It is touches of this kind, incomparable in their simplicity and their pathos, that make Prévost's book what it is: and the things they describe all take place in the soul of des Grieux. It is only through him, indeed, that we know Manon at all. In and by herself, if the truth be told, she is sometimes hardly likable. Certainly the real Manon, complex, in a paradoxical sense, only through her very lack of complication, is not translatable into terms of an art so forthright as music. She is not even immoral: she is simply amoral, not a creature who has forgotten virtue but one who has never learned it and whose constitution makes her incapable of ever learning it. Des Grieux describes her as "a being of a most curious kind. Never had any woman less craving for money; but the fear of lacking it left her without a tranquil moment. It was only pleasure and amusement that she wanted: she would never have desired to possess a sou if pleasure could be purchased without cost. . . . She would have preferred me, even with a moderate fortune, to the whole world; but I could never doubt for a moment that she would abandon me for some new B . . . when I had nothing more to offer her than constancy and fidelity." From first to last she is utterly and honestly unable to see either that she does des Grieux any wrong in betraying him whenever his purse is low, or in robbing and deserting, and then callously deriding some rich lover or other when he has served his financial purpose. So it was that des Grieux could say of her paradoxically after many a betrayal, "Elle pèche sans malice; elle est légère et imprudente, mais elle est droite et sincère." But he at once adds that "L'amour seul suffisoit pour me fermer les yeux sur toutes ses fautes." It is always through des Grieux's eyes that we see her; and we feel more for him than for her. But in an opera next to nothing of all this psychological involution can be suggested. The only thing to be done with Manon is to make her what Massenet and his librettists have done—a charming piece of

feminine frailty, lovable and pitiable both for the Chevalier's sake
and for her own. Massenet in particular, with his unique gift for
expressing certain elements of female sensibility in music, has
produced what is undeniably a masterpiece in its own genre.
And his opera is so purely Massenet and so purely French that
we learn without surprise that certain sapient Paris critics accused
him, in 1884, of merely "following in Wagner's footsteps" and
of having "imposed German music on a French subject."

3

The brief prelude (Massenet does not call it an overture)
passes in quick review two or three of the characteristic melodies
of the opera, but without any attempt either to summarise the
story by the sequence of the themes or to construct a miniature
symphonic poem out of them. We get first of all:

the lively music of the fête in the Cours-la-Reine in the third act,
to which is tacked on a suggestion of the graceful minuet—
though now in a much faster tempo—with which that act opens.
No. 1 is repeated; then comes a quiet suggestion of the song of the
archers in the fifth act:

which modulates into des Grieux's passionate invocation of
Manon in act 4:

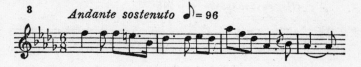

This is allowed due scope to spread its lyrical wings; but at its climax it breaks off suddenly, and we get No. 2 once more, this time rounded off by a curious harmonic progression taken from the scene on the road to Havre in the fifth act:

It will be gathered from this that no theme positively representative of Manon herself appears in the prelude; we see her, in truth, as we do in Prévost's story, only through the eyes of des Grieux, by the instrumentality of No. 3.

The opening scene shows the courtyard of an inn in Amiens, with a gateway at the back opening on to the street, some steps on the right, leading up to a pavilion, and on the left an arbour with a well and a stone bench in front of it. A little further back is the entrance to the inn. It is the hour when the coach from Arras is due. Standing by the pavilion are two rich Parisians, the elderly Guillot de Morfontaine and his friend Brétigny, about to dine, they hope, with the three mistresses of Guillot, Poussette, Javotte and Rosette, who are inside, looking out of the window. At the moment when the curtain rises all five are appealing mock-pathetically to the apparently deaf or dead inn-keeper to do something to save them from dying of hunger and thirst. They have almost abandoned hope when he comes out of the inn followed by scullions bearing a number of dishes in solemn procession towards the pavilion, to a melody as ceremonious as themselves, but made comical by its sudden changes of volume and colour:

This theme, in one form or another, runs through the whole of the gay ensemble that ensues. The menu proving to be everything they could have desired, the Parisians joyously follow the procession of hors d'œuvre and buisson d'écrevisses and poulet and pâté de canard ("un objet d'art", as the host proudly describes it) and the vieux vins into the pavilion, the door and windows of which are then closed.

Left to himself, the innkeeper indulges in a sage reflection or two upon the crowd of idlers and sightseers who now begin to filter into the courtyard to see the coach arrive: he himself hurries away to book a place in the coach for the young Chevalier des Grieux, as he had promised to do. Among the townspeople are three gardes-françaises in uniform, one of whom is Lescaut. He tells his two companions to go to the neighbouring tavern and await him there; he himself must stay behind to meet his little cousin Manon, who will arrive by the coach now due. (In Prévost she is his sister). The gaping bourgeois are aptly characterised in a ponderous phrase which accompanies all their chatter:

while Lescaut's motive:

suggests the self-satisfied swagger that never deserts him. Lescaut is the one character in the opera who can become, in performance, just what the actor can make, or chooses to make, of him, stressing chiefly his broad humour, or his rough geniality, or his incurable rascality as the case may be, and according to how much or how little the singer knows of Prévost's Lescaut, or, knowing him, how much or how little he tries to model himself on the original. Generally speaking, however, the players of the part merely reproduce a familiar stage military type.

The place fills with intending travellers and porters carrying their luggage, and soon the coach arrives. There is an amusing scene, which may be paralleled any day (in peace time) at any continental port, everyone having lost his luggage or his porter or both, everyone speaking at once, and everyone wanting to be attended to first. The whole character of the music, which so far has been of the sprightliest kind, suddenly changes as a young girl, who has just descended from the coach, looks at the jabbering, gesticulating crowd in astonishment. It is Manon, on her way to the convent to which her people have consigned her; and her perturbation at this first experience of humanity in the mass is indicated by the hesitating syncopated phrase that accompanies her as she comes into our view:

Lescaut soon finds her, and comments, sotto voce, that her looks do credit to the family. In the prettiest fashion she apologises for her girlish gaucherie: this is the first time she has ever been away from home, and everything she has seen en route has been a wonder to her, she tells her cousin, in one of those chattering bird-like phrases that fall so naturally from the mouths of Massenet's female characters:

Sometimes, it appears, she could have wept from sheer distress, and we hear once more the timid No. 8; then she makes a sudden transition to young-girlish laughter.

The coach at length sets out again, to the accompaniment of another animated and humorous chorus, leaving no one on the stage but Manon and her cousin. The latter goes out in search of her luggage. Just at that moment Guillot, stepping out on to the balcony of the pavilion to order more wine, catches sight of Manon, and at once loses what the years have left of his heart to her. He goes straight to the point, as is the way in opera: he tells her his name, and assures her that he is rolling in money and would give most of it for a single word of love from her. She laughs at the decayed old amorist, and her laugh is repeated by Brétigny and the others, who have come out on to the balcony to see what is going on. They gaily advise Guillot to come back before he burns his fingers; but he manages to tell Manon, unheard by his friends, that he will have a carriage and postilion ready immediately in which to carry her away. There follows a little trouble with Lescaut, who, returning just then, demands to know what the stranger has been saying to his cousin. Guillot goes back into the pavilion in some confusion, which is increased by the ironic comments of his friends; and Lescaut is about to speak seriously to Manon when one of the guards enters to remind him that the cards and the dice are awaiting him at the tavern. He does not go, however, until he has given Manon a quasi-paternal warning to mind her step, as it were—"Ne bronchez pas"—and to bear in mind that he is the guardian of the honour of the family.

Manon, when she is alone, has a moment of sober reflection: she must put all frivolity out of her thoughts, she muses. Then she remembers wistfully and enviously how well-dressed and opulent-looking Poussette, Javotte and Rosette had been. Still, she says, in another of those typical Massenet phrases that have the natural accent of a spoken sentence:

she must leave fancies of this kind behind her at the door of the convent. And yet how seductive is the glimpse she has just had of that other life! While the child is turning all this over in her mind she perceives a stranger, and hastens to seat herself demurely on the stone bench. It is the young des Grieux, not much more than a seminarist yet, whose serious nature is indicated by his characteristic motive:

We learn that he has missed the coach, but that anyhow on the following evening he will be with the good father whom he so loves. But in the middle of his musings he catches sight of Manon, and he feels at once that a crisis in his life has been reached. All through this scene—and indeed throughout the opera—Massenet characterises him admirably. In his most ardent or furious moments the Chevalier never loses his dignity; he is always a young aristocrat of the finest breeding. The spectator will be lucky if he finds the portrait even approximately realised once in a lifetime of opera-going: the tenor with the right combination of appearance, vocal timbre, youth, grace and polish for the part can hardly be said to exist.

Des Grieux approaches Manon respectfully, accompanied by a motive symbolical of the future love of the pair, a motive:

which will reappear in the last moments of the opera, when Manon is dying in des Grieux's arms. Timidly and simply she gives him her name; she is a poor girl, not bad at heart, she says, whom her family are placing in a convent because they suspect her of being too fond of pleasure. "Et c'est là l'histoire de Manon Lescaut", she concludes simply, to the wistful little melody of

No. 10. Des Grieux cries out against the barbarity of immuring so much charm and loveliness in a convent, and he has little difficulty in winning her round to his way of thinking.

Just then the postilion who has been told by the infatuated Guillot to await the young lady's orders becomes visible at the back of the stage. A smile passes over Manon's face: here is an opportunity to profit at the expense of the old gallant who had forced his attentions on her. She tells des Grieux of that episode and suggests that they shall use the carriage to fly to Paris together. Des Grieux agrees, and the lovers sing a simple little duet on the subject of the happiness that awaits them in some romantic love-nest or other in Paris:

Any lingering doubts that Manon may have as to the prudence or the morality of their flight are dissipated by another burst of merry laughter from the care-free cocottes inside the pavilion. "Ah! how pleasant it must be to amuse oneself one's whole life long!" she sighs; and she rushes away with des Grieux just as Lescaut returns from the tavern, drunk and bankrupt. When Guillot comes out, looking for Manon, he is seized by Lescaut, who takes him for the abductor of his cousin. They get at cross-purposes, to the amusement of the crowd that filters into the courtyard, attracted by the noise; and the amusement becomes universal when the innkeeper tells them that the pretty girl who was here a little while ago has gone off with a young man in a carriage belonging to old Guillot. Brétigny and the three girls try to console Guillot, whose thoughts, however, are now concentrated on vengeance for this perfidy.

4

The second act takes place in a little apartment in the rue Vivienne, Paris, in which the Chevalier and Manon have installed themselves. Des Grieux is writing a letter to his father, telling him how he has met a paragon of beauty and charm, a girl named Manon, sixteen yesterday, whom he proposes to marry. Manon and des Grieux read the letter aloud together: the two main motives of the exquisite scene are the grave one of the young Chevalier, quoted above as No. 11, and a more light-hearted one, symbolical of Manon, that hovers about it caressingly:

and at the same time a little ominously, for Manon is no longer the timid ingénue of the scene at Amiens. The coquette latent in her has come to the surface, and the rippling laughter of No. 14 seems at times almost a mockery of the naïve sincerity of her lover. Already there is in the room a bouquet of flowers the sight of which troubles him somewhat; but she assures him that it was thrown in through the window by an unknown hand, and he believes her.

Lescaut enters, accompanied by Brétigny, also in the uniform of a garde-française. Apparently Brétigny has already managed to cultivate the acquaintance of the pretty girl he had seen at Amiens: he and Lescaut have traced her to her apartment, and his plans for separating her from des Grieux are laid. Lescaut begins by taking a high tone with the Chevalier, but the swashbuckler is soon put in his place. He then explains that, Manon being his cousin, he has merely come to ask whether or not the Chevalier intends to marry her. To satisfy him on that point des Grieux takes him towards the window to read the letter he has just written to his father. Brétigny seizes this opportunity to tell Manon that he has been in communication with des Grieux *père*, who intends to have his son taken away from Paris by force that same evening. At first Manon refuses to countenance the scheme, declaring that she loves the Chevalier, and him alone. But Brétigny cunningly works upon her weakest point: does she prefer perpetual poverty with this young man to a brilliant life with one as rich as himself? By the time that Lescaut, professing himself quite satisfied with the letter, has returned to the other two, des Grieux's fate is sealed. The musical texture of this scene is admirably varied and at the same time unified. Lescaut preserves his own physiognomy throughout, more especially by means of a motive:

that is thoroughly characteristic of his pose of the bluff but honest broker. The ensemble writing is rich in ironic touches. The Chevalier and Manon are musically their now familiar selves; while Brétigny's passion breaks out every now and then in a phrase:

which, whenever it recurs, stands out markedly from the rest of the tissue.

Lescaut and Brétigny having gone away, entirely satisfied with the state of affairs, Manon and des Grieux are about to sit down to their modest supper when he remembers that he has not yet posted his letter. He begs for an assurance that Manon loves him: he gets it, but the frivolous No. 14 in the orchestra—now somewhat subdued, it is true—hints at the cross-currents in her soul. When he has gone out with the letter Manon sincerely laments her own fragility: then, in a touchingly sad and simple little monologue ("Adieu, notre petite table") she bids farewell to the happiness that has been hers with des Grieux in spite of their poverty, when one glass sufficed for them both to drink from, for then each drank from the other's lips.

Des Grieux returns, heralded by the motive of his love for Manon (No. 12). He tells her of a dream he has had—of a tiny house in the woods, which ring with the song of birds: it will become a paradise when Manon joins him there. But there comes a knock at the door, and an agitated variant of No. 16 (the Brétigny motive) in the orchestra makes clear the significance of it. A mournful "Adieu!" slips out of Manon's mouth almost without her volition. Then, recovering herself, she tells the Chevalier not to open the door, for she does not wish to leave him. Unable to understand her emotion, des Grieux goes out to order the inopportune caller away: he will return to her in a moment, he says, and they will laugh together at her foolishness. But outside is heard the sound of a scuffle, followed by that of carriage wheels. Manon goes to the window and gives a dolorous cry of "Mon pauvre Chevalier!" and the triumph of Brétigny is emphasised by a *fortissimo* statement of No. 16 in the orchestra.

5

The first scene of the third act, which opens with a dainty orchestral minuet that brings with it fragrant memories of the elegant eighteenth century, is set at Cours-la-Reine, where all Paris is enjoying itself. Vendors of all sorts of wares who have established their stalls under the great trees importune the gay crowd that passes up and down to buy. On the right of the stage is a ballroom.

The opening chorus, which makes liberal use of No. 1, is devoted to the cajoleries of the shopkeepers and the replies of the passers-by. A reminiscence of the opening minuet is heard as Poussette, Javotte and Rosette emerge from the ballroom: they are still under the protection of Guillot, but have for the moment evaded him to flirt with younger game. In time they all three pass off the stage, and the chorus is resumed. Lescaut comes into sight with some of the tradesmen pursuing him and pestering him to buy their wares. He is in a good humour, for, thanks to his skill at cards and dice, his finances are flourishing just then. Why economise, he enquires blandly of the universe, when one has a dice-set in one's pocket and knows the route to the hôtel de Transylvanie (a famous Paris gambling resort)[1]:

[1] Prévost refers to the place as "l'hôtel de Transylvanie", "where there was a faro table in one of the rooms, while various card games and dice were played in the gallery. This academy was carried on for the profit of the Prince de R.... who at that time lived at Clagny...." Modern research has

Then, growing sentimental, he sings a "madrigal", in the pseudo-classical style of the period, to one Rosalinde; after which he disappears in the crowd, pursued by all who have benefited, or hope to benefit, by his liberality.

The three cocottes come out of the ball-room again, but happening to run into their elderly protector they scurry away as fast as they can. Guillot is furious, for, as he says, he maintains three of the species in the hope that one at any rate will be faithful to him. While he is in this unpleasant mood he is accosted by Brétigny, who, indulging in his usual irony at his old friend's expense, implores him, in mock terror, not to take Manon from him. This gives Guillot an idea. Brétigny, it appears, has refused to gratify a too fantastically expensive whim of Manon's—to engage the personnel of the Opéra to perform for her at Cours-la-Reine. He, Guillot, will profit by this mistake of Brétigny's to rob him of Manon. He goes off rubbing his hands at the pleasant thought.

To a new theme:

the crowd of bourgeois now celebrate the arrival of a number of elegant Parisian beauties, the queen of whom is Manon, now in the heyday of her prosperity. Brétigny having assisted her to alight from her sedan chair she pours out her little soul in an aria that expresses to the life her frivolity and caprice: naturally No. 14

established that the house was that of Franz Rakoczi II, Prince of Transylvania, who, driven from his own territory by the Germans, had to live more or less by his wits in Paris. The house stood at what is now the corner of the Quai Malaquais and the Rue Bonaparte.

plays a large part in it. She has everything a woman can desire, she informs the company—beauty, power, horses, adorers: in short, she is the happiest creature on earth. She winds up with a gavotte, in which Brétigny and the other men join her, in praise of youth and spring-time:[1]

Manon and her companions retire to the background as Brétigny encounters an old friend. It is des Grieux *père*, who, we soon learn, has come up from the country to Paris to see and hear his son, now no longer the Chevalier but the Abbé des Grieux, preach his first sermon that very evening. The elder des Grieux, discovering that the former object of his son's affections is the pretty girl pointed out to him by Brétigny, understands now, as he says ironically, how it came about that the latter took so much interest in the moral welfare of the Chevalier. But Manon happens to have overheard the name "Comte des Grieux". She approaches the two men, gets rid of Brétigny by a simple pretext, and asks the Count for news of the Abbé des Grieux, who, she tells him, was at one time in love with one of her friends. (Their dialogue is accompanied by the strains of the minuet in the distance). She would like to know how the young man had borne the blow of separation. Has he been able to forget the one who had dealt it him? Has he suffered greatly? Does he ever repeat her name? Does he upbraid her? The Comte assures her gravely that his son has borne all his sufferings in silence; the wound had healed, and now he has done what men should always do in matters of this kind—he has forgotten. "Forgotten!" repeats Manon dolorously as the Comte takes leave of her.

The crowd fills the scene again, among them Brétigny, Guillot and Lescaut. Guillot plays what he regards as his trump card against Brétigny—he has brought the ballet of the Opéra to

[1] For one of his Manons, Mme Bréjeau-Silver, Massenet wrote a tricky "fabliau" to take the place of the gavotte in the original score.

Cours-la-Reine at terrific expense, simply to please Manon.
Everyone runs to see the show; but when the ballet is over and
Guillot turns to Manon for the expected thanks, he learns, to his
vast mortification, that she has "seen nothing". Her mind, in
truth, has been all the time on des Grieux: and as the gay crowd
breaks once more into the melody of No. 1 she calls for her chair
and sets out for Saint-Sulpice.

The second scene of this act opens with the strains of a distant
organ. When the curtain rises we see a parlour in the seminary of
Saint-Sulpice. It is filled with devout women, grandes dames and
bourgeoises, praising the eloquence and piety of the young man
who has just delivered his first sermon: how admirably he had
spoken of St. Augustine and of Santa Teresa! They leave the
stage as the young saint himself enters, accompanied by his
father, who compliments him on his fine performance in a tone of
affectionate irony: the family should be proud to possess a
Bossuet of its own! He tries to persuade his son against the
adoption of the priestly calling. Des Grieux replies that he has
experienced in life nothing but bitterness and loathing; and the
orchestra comments mournfully on his words with a tender
reminiscence of the love music (No. 12). The Comte, reminding
him that he is still too young to know much of life, hopes that he
will marry some girl worthy of him and of his ancient family, and
find uneventful but solid happiness with her and his children. But
the young man's resolution is not to be shaken. As the Comte
takes his farewell of him, he tells him that he shall receive at once
the 30,000 livres due to him from the estate of his mother.

When des Grieux is alone he feels old memories surging up
within him and troubling the peace of soul he had set himself to
win in the bosom of the Church. He would forget Manon, but
cannot, he cries in a passionate aria ("Ah! fuyez, douce image"):

20 *Andante* ♩ = 60

pp

Ah! fuyez, douce image, à mon â-me trop chère,

He is summoned by a functionary to the service about to commence in the church; and Manon, who enters the parlour shortly after, obtains permission, by bribing the man, to remain there until the Abbé returns. She muses sadly, the while a Magnificat is being chanted behind the scenes, on the pass to which she has brought both des Grieux and herself, and prays heaven for pardon and a reunion with him. When he returns, and she has uncovered her face and he recognises her, he at first bids her begone. She confesses her fault, but he reproaches her with her perfidy and swears that she has no longer a place in his heart or in his memory. She implores him, to the strain of No. 12, to love her again if he would have her live; then, as is the way with her, she suddenly abandons the note of passion for that of cajolery. In her—and Massenet's—most caressing accents she appeals to him to say whether it is not still the Chevalier's hand that she holds between hers, still the voice, still the eyes of her whom he had once so loved; is it not still his Manon who supplicates:

His resolution begins to weaken. As a distant bell tolls, summoning him to prayer, he makes a last effort to break from her, but she will not let him go. At last, with a great cry of "Ah! Manon! Je ne veux plus lutter contre moi-même!" he confesses his undying love for her and folds her in his arms. The passionate No.12 peals out in the full orchestra as the curtain falls.[1]

[1] The seminary scene was not in the original text. It was suggested to the librettists by Massenet, whose artistic instinct no doubt told him that the high-light of the work should be the emotional conflict in des Grieux's soul between his native seriousness and his passion for Manon, that this conflict would be most fittingly expressed in an aria, and that the only time and place for such an aria would be when des Grieux was alone. The original plan of the opera did not provide any opportunity of that kind.

6

The setting of the fourth act is the hôtel de Transylvanie.[1] To the accompaniment of a feverish theme in the orchestra:

the gamblers stake and lose and win and wrangle, and the croupiers summon the faithful to their devotions. Among the crowd that circulates about the tables are Poussette, Javotte and Rosette, ready and willing, as always, to make the acquaintance of any man who has been favoured by fortune; as they sagely remark, while ordinary people win only occasionally, people of their sort invariably do. Sharpers are everywhere, looking out for possible victims; and Lescaut, who is in his element in a dubious place like this, has a passing difference of opinion with another punter as to which of them had won a certain coup. Fortune continuing to smile on him, he obliges the company with a piquant song, which is accompanied by the clinking of gold at the various tables—a song in praise of the only goddess he worships, "la dame de pique" (the queen of spades).

Guillot joins the group, and fatuously assures Lescaut and the three cocottes that he also, when occasion calls, can "bestride Pegasus". He has actually, it appears, composed some verses against the Regent: but as they are too dangerous for the ears of all and sundry, he contents himself with conveying the substance of them to his friends with many eloquent omissions and much gesture. The vain old noodle is mightily pleased with himself, and the others laugh at him under the pretence of laughing with him.

All eyes now turn towards one of the doors, at which the beautiful Manon and her Chevalier are seen entering, to the accompaniment of the melody of No. 18. Guillot cannot conceal his annoyance at the sight of des Grieux, whom he hates for being more successful with Manon than he had been. Lescaut, seeing an opportunity to profit pecuniarily by Guillot's ill-will, draws

[1] This scene also seems to have been Massenet's own idea.

him aside for a confidential talk. Meanwhile, everyone else being absorbed in play, des Grieux and Manon are left alone in the forefront of the scene. Des Grieux is sad: Manon has quickly run through the 30,000 livres given him by his father, and something within him warns him that he has taken the first step on the road to ruin by accompanying her to the hôtel de Transylvanie. To the passionate melody of No. 3 he opens out his heart to this baffling, perturbing Manon of his, Manon, the siren, the incomprehensible sphinx, with nothing in her heart and her mind but the thought of pleasure and gold, this Manon whom he hates but also loves. She too would love him, she replies, if he would but consent to try to retrieve his fortunes at the faro table. Lescaut, joining them at that moment, adds his counsel to hers—a few lucky coups, and all will be well with the three of them again. The Chevalier turns from the suggestion with horror; but Lescaut whispers in his ear a warning that "Manon does not like poverty": and the fitful No. 22, playing continually round the conversation, gives added point to Lescaut's words. Lescaut confidently promises des Grieux the traditional "beginner's luck": Manon assures him of her eternal love and devotion. The conflict is fought out in des Grieux's soul to the melody of No. 3, which is now built up into a trio.

Guillot approaches them and challenges the Chevalier to a game: he would like, he says, to see whether he is fated invariably to lose to des Grieux. The latter consents and the game is played with ever rising stakes, to the accompaniment of delighted comments, according to their several characters, from Manon, Poussette, Javotte and Rosette. Manon in particular sees in imagination a life opening out to her that will be a continuous shower of gold. Lescaut, for his part, goes to try his own luck at another table, where he soon loses every pistole he had. Des Grieux keeps winning from Guillot, much to Manon's delight, and to Guillot's increasing chagrin. At last Guillot gives up the game, accuses the Chevalier loudly of having cheated him, and leaves the room breathing threats against both des Grieux and Manon.

This scene is dominated musically by the "gambling" motive (No. 22), which continues, in subdued tones, throughout what follows. A loud knocking is heard at the door, followed by a

voice outside ordering them to "open in the name of the King".
A police officer and several soldiers appear, whereupon Lescaut
slips out of the room. Guillot orders the officer to arrest des
Grieux and "his accomplice" Manon, both of whom he maliciously begs to observe the completeness of his revenge. Des
Grieux, beside himself with rage, threatens to throw Guillot out
of the window, but is checked by a word from his father—whose
presence in the gambling den, by the way, is not accounted for.
The Comte repudiates his unworthy son, remaining unmoved
even by the passionate appeal of the whole company to pardon
him in consideration of his youth. The scene ends with des
Grieux being carried off to prison, at his father's own request;
while Manon is taken to the penal institution reserved for women
of notoriously scandalous life.

7

The short fifth act takes place at a melancholy spot on the
road to Havre. Manon had been condemned, along with a
number of other women of bad reputation, to the American plan-
tations: and des Grieux, released from prison, has followed the
convoy, which is being escorted by soldiers to Havre, in the
hope of rescuing her. A brief orchestral prelude hints at the song
of the soldiers (No. 2), which will be heard in full later. Its
curious cadence, quoted in our analysis as No. 4, resembles a
well-known phrase in Beethoven's "Les Adieux" sonata; hence
it has been suggested that Massenet has consciously applied the
associations of the Beethoven phrase to the situation in which
Manon and des Grieux now find themselves. It may be so,
though proof is impossible. The melodic sequence shown in
No. 4 happens to be that also of the final bar of the song itself,
from which it may conceivably have been derived in the ordinary
way. At the same time Massenet plainly attached considerable
importance to No. 4, for in the course of this scene he repeats it
again and again in every variety of colour.

When the curtain rises, des Grieux is sitting by the roadside,
thinking sadly of Manon. He is approached by Lescaut, who has
held out hopes to him that somewhere about the spot where they
now are an attack might be successfully made on the escort. But,

he now informs the Chevalier, at the first sight of the soldiers' muskets gleaming in the sunlight the men whom he had hired for the rescue have proved cowards and deserted them. He tries to excuse himself and his confederates to des Grieux, who dismisses him angrily. But just then there is heard a little way off the song of the approaching soldiers. Des Grieux, in his frenzy, is for attacking them; but Lescaut, who never seems to have much stomach for fighting, counsels another method. He drags des Grieux away as the soldiers enter, still chanting their regimental ditty with its curious instrumental refrain (No. 4). They are thirsty; and while they halt for a while in order to drink, they fall to discussing the odd collection of women whom they have in charge: one of them, it seems, who is already half-dead, does nothing but weep and cover her face when anyone speaks to her. Des Grieux, who, hidden in a bush with Lescaut, has overheard the conversation, gives a mournful cry. Lescaut silences him, and having obtained his purse from him he approaches the sergeant of the troop, of whom, as a fellow-soldier, he asks a favour—to be allowed to speak for a moment with the poor girl whom the soldiers have just been discussing, who happens to be a relation of his. He bribes the sergeant to leave Manon with him for a while, on condition that he brings her back to him in the near-by village before nightfall.

The soldiers, still singing, resume their march and soon disappear—all except one of them, who has been left by the sergeant to keep an eye on Manon and her relation. Lescaut has no difficulty in persuading him to take himself off after the others. Lescaut discreetly follows him; and soon Manon comes slowly into sight, bowed down with fatigue, to the strain of No. 4. She gives a wild cry of "Des Grieux!" as she sees her lover: the Chevalier can answer only with a broken murmur of "Manon! Manon! Manon!" as he takes her in his arms. Their parting duet commences with a new and dark-coloured motive in the orchestra:

He tries to comfort her with the assurance that they can escape. But her strength has gone, and she can only weep and humbly and affectionately implore his pardon for having brought so much misery on him. He tells her there is nothing to pardon, that his heart will be hers for ever. As if transfigured, she too promises herself and him a new and happier life, but with a meaning in her words which at first he does not perceive. Her mind reverts wistfully to cherished incidents in their past—their first meeting at the inn, the coach, the ride to Paris, the letter to his father, their little table in the Rue Vivienne, his black robe at Saint-Sulpice— the orchestra giving out meanwhile the softest of reminiscences of No. 12.

He exhorts her to come with him, but her strength is at a final end. "I love you, and this kiss is my last farewell!" she murmurs in a voice that is hardly audible, the orchestra again playing mournfully round her words with No. 12. He tries to re-animate her with the words of her own appeal to him in the scene in the parlour, and to the same music (No. 21)—"Is it not my hand you hold in yours?"; and they take up the melody in unison in a last ecstatic cry of love. But the final words, "Soon our happiness of old will come again", are hardly out of her mouth before we hear in the orchestra a fateful roll in the kettledrums, a soft clang in the tamtam, and some faint, irregular pulsations in the plucked strings, as if Manon's heart had already almost ceased to beat. She suddenly collapses with a murmured "I am dying: it had to be! it had to be!" There passes through her failing mind a last reminiscence of the days before she knew anything of the world and its wickedness (a faint suggestion of No. 10 in the orchestra); and half-unconsciously she repeats the very words she had used when, in the courtyard of the inn at Amiens, she had told her simple story to des Grieux—"Et c'est là l'histoire de Manon Lescaut." As the Chevalier falls with a despairing cry on her dead body, the orchestra comments on the tragedy with a final recall to our memories of No. 21.

FALSTAFF

Verdi (1813-1901)

PRINCIPAL CHARACTERS

FALSTAFF	*Baritone*
FENTON	*Tenor*
FORD	*Baritone*
DR. CAIUS	*Tenor*
BARDOLPH	*Tenor*
PISTOL	*Bass*
MISTRESS FORD	*Soprano*
ANNE FORD	*Soprano*
MISTRESS PAGE	*Mezzo-soprano*
MISTRESS QUICKLY	*Mezzo-soprano*

I

Never what one would call the sunniest of men, Verdi became decidedly gloomy in his last years. As he looked back on his life, he said in 1895, he could see little more than an immense number of notes, and unfortunately he had his doubts whether the notes were worth very much. This was merely the exaggerated self-criticism of a sincere and modest artist. *Otello*, produced in 1887, when Verdi was in his seventy-fourth year, would have been an honourable enough ending to the career of any composer. But the old warrior was not finished even yet. Six years after *Otello* came *Falstaff*; and one of the most serious and seemingly least humorous of men bade farewell to the world of art with a comedy of a light-fingeredness unique in that or any other epoch. And after *Falstaff* the grand old man had still eight years to live.

Held in universal admiration as it is among musicians, *Falstaff* does not appear in the general operatic repertory as often as one could desire. The exact reason for this is not easy to discover. It may be that its very lightness of touch and its delicacy of texture go against it in our large opera houses, with their too-long intervals between the acts: the sparkle, the aroma of each of the first two acts is lost by the time the audience reassembles for the next. It has to be admitted, too, that the final scene as a whole is neither musically nor dramatically on the same level as the other two. For here Falstaff, who has so far been the life and soul of the work, passes, at times, almost unobserved; and a *Falstaff* scene without Falstaff is as lame as *Hamlet* without the prince. A lover of the delightful work may perhaps be allowed to suggest that as Verdi's librettist Boïto has dealt so freely in the first two acts with the Shakespearean—or pseudo-Shakespearean— material presented to him by tradition, he might have exercised his rights in this respect still more fully, and invented an ending of his own for the opera. "Reverence for Shakespeare" is all very well in its way; but what if we are asked to fall down on our knees to something that is not Shakespeare at all?

Neither Boïto nor Verdi could be expected to be *au fait* with even the Shakespeare scholarship of their own and an earlier day; still less could they have anticipated that of a generation or two after their time. Perhaps they did not even know that *The Merry Wives of Windsor* has always been a stumbling-block to Shakespeare scholars. The older perplexity with regard to the work, and the vague older doubts about it, were frankly expressed by Professor A. C. Bradley in 1909: "Falstaff", he said, "was degraded by Shakespeare himself":

"The original character is to be found alive in the two parts of *Henry IV*, dead in *Henry V*, and nowhere else. But not very long after these plays were composed, Shakespeare wrote, and he afterwards revised, the very entertaining piece called *The Merry Wives of Windsor*. Perhaps his company wanted a new play on a sudden; or perhaps, as one would rather believe, the tradition may be true that Queen Elizabeth, delighted with the Falstaff scenes of *Henry IV*, expressed a wish to see the hero of them again, and to see him in love. Now it was no more possible for Shakespeare to show his own Falstaff in love than to turn twice two into five. But he could write in haste . . . a comedy or a farce differing from all his other plays in this, that its scene is laid in English middle-class life, and that it is prosaic almost to the end. And among the characters he could introduce a disreputable fat old Knight with attendants, and could call them Falstaff, Bardolph, Pistol and Nym. And he could represent this Knight assailing, for financial purposes, the virtue of two matrons, and in the event baffled, duped, treated like dirty linen, beaten, burnt, pricked, mocked, insulted, and, worst of all, repentant and didactic. It is horrible. It is almost enough to convince one that Shakespeare himself could sanction the parody of Ophelia in *The Two Noble Kinsmen*."

All which means, in somewhat franker language, that Professor Bradley, like a great many other people before and after him, thought, although he did not like to say so outright, that *The Merry Wives of Windsor* is for the most part so poor a piece of work that it is difficult to believe that Shakespeare in his prime could have been responsible for very much of it. Nor is this the only difficulty in connection with the play. No one has ever yet succeeded, for example, in bringing sense into the chronology of it, particularly where the ages of Falstaff and Mrs. Quickly are concerned. Other incongruities abound.

The truth of the matter is in all probability that set forth by the late Mr. John M. Robertson in a paper on *The Problem of 'The Merry Wives of Windsor'*, read before the Shakespeare Association in 1917. Although the legend that the Queen, having been delighted with the robust humours of *Henry IV*, said that she would now like to "see Falstaff in love" is not met with earlier than the eighteenth century, it need not be summarily rejected. The Queen may quite possibly have been referring to an *already existing* play in which the fat Knight *was* shown in love—an earlier form, in fact, of the play which now figures among the works of Shakespeare as *The Merry Wives of Windsor*. This play, in which, as Mr. Robertson shows by means of verbal fingerprints, Chapman in all probability had a hand, was apparently touched up here and there by Shakespeare about 1593: it is as certain that some strokes of humour and certain felicities of style in it are from his hand as it is that he was never capable of turning out such poor stuff as much of it unquestionably is, and more especially of grinding out such wretched blank verse as that of the final act.[1]

[1] For further light on these and other points the reader who is interested in the subject must be referred to Mr. Robertson's paper.

Now Boïto never hesitates to play fast and loose with the tissue of *The Merry Wives of Windsor* when it suits his purpose to do so. He resorts, whenever it suits him, to the character-drawing and the actual words of *Henry IV*. He transfers to Dr. Caius, in the opening scene, the episode of the robbery which in the play is associated with Justice Shallow. He abolishes Page. He dispenses altogether with Slender, making Fenton the only lover of Anne, apart from Caius. He makes Anne herself (Nanetta) not Page's daughter but Ford's. He reduces the number of duperies of which Falstaff is the victim at the hands of the wives and Mrs. Quickly; and so on. Another liberty or two on the top of all these would have made no difference, and there are two in particular which one could wish Boïto had taken. The first would have been to devise a better ending to the opera than is afforded by the fifth act of the play. The other would have been to reduce the age of Falstaff.

In the play, as Bradley mournfully pointed out, Falstaff is not only treated most despitefully but hatefully: particular malice is imported into some of the references to the advanced age of this would-be seducer—"Old, cold, withered, and of intolerable entrails" is one of Page's descriptions of him, while Mrs. Page wonders that "one that is well-nigh worn to pieces with age" should try "to show himself a young gallant". But, as Mr. Robertson was the first to show, of the six references to Falstaff's age in the first Folio, from which our present text is derived, five are "entirely absent" from the earlier Quarto, which represents, apparently, the play in something like its original form. (In the Folio it is nearly double the length of the version in the Quarto). In the latter, Falstaff himself asks "Ah, Jack, will thy old body yet hold out?"; but "old" is no more necessarily to be taken in its literal sense here than in a thousand other uses of the word in colloquial speech; and whereas the Folio makes him say "I'll make more of thy *old* body than I have done", in the Quarto the corresponding passage runs "*Good* body, I thank thee, and I'll make more of thee than I ha' done." No stage performance of the play ever takes the text quite literally in this matter of Falstaff's age; that is to say, it stops short of making the man "old, cold, withered" and "well-nigh worn to pieces", so as not to alienate the sympathies of the audience. There seems no good reason why producers should not go a step further and reduce the Knight's age still more: he can be made as fat and as fatuous as you please, of course. From every point of view it is a pity that Boïto did not adopt a still freer attitude towards "Shakespeare" than he has actually done.

Verdi's correspondence shows that he embarked with a certain reluctance on this final opera of his, fearing that the labour of it would put too great a strain on the health of a man of his advanced age. He seems, however, to have allowed himself to be persuaded by Boïto somewhere about 1889; and by the summer of 1892 the score was finished.

The first performance was given at the Scala, Milan, on the 9th February 1893, under the conductorship of Mascheroni. Maurel was the Falstaff. With this gentleman Verdi had had a little trouble. True to the traditions of his type, the famous singer had tried to secure for himself in advance the sole right to play Falstaff for a certain number of performances. Verdi refused: his view was that in an opera of his no one part, and therefore no one singer, was more important than another. Couldn't the man see, he wrote to his publisher, Giulio Ricordi, that all he had to do was to play the part in superior style and it would be his by artistic right, without their needing to offend other people? He resented the intrusion of Madame Maurel into the matter: "I simply ask to be allowed to be owner of my own belongings, without ruining anyone. Let me add that if I were confronted with the alternatives—'Either accept these conditions or burn your score'—I would at once get the fire ready and myself throw on it Falstaff and his paunch." Fortunately it never came to that!

2

The curtain rises on a room in the "Garter" Inn at Windsor. That it is occupied by Falstaff is indicated by the number of bottles on the table; and apparently he has not long finished breakfast. At the moment when he comes into view he has Bardolph and Pistol for company. He himself is sealing a couple of letters: that done, he stretches his limbs luxuriously and

drinks deeply, to the accompaniment of a bustling orchestral
phrase:

which runs through a good deal of the present scene.

Falstaff orders the landlord to bring him another bottle of
sherry, taking no notice for a little while of Dr. Caius, who comes
in in a great hurry and angrily accuses the Knight of having
broken into his house, beaten his servants, and ridden his bay
mare. Falstaff calmly admits it all, but advises Caius not to make a
public fuss about it unless he wants to become a public joke. Caius
then turns on the other two. He had drunk copiously, it appears,
with Bardolph and Pistol the night before, and when he was
fuddled they had picked his pocket. Each of the rascals solemnly
denies that he ever did anything of the kind: Bardolph opines that
Dr. Caius must have dreamt it while he was drunk, and Pistol
threatens personal violence. "You see", says Falstaff judicially,
"the charge has been denied; depart in peace." Poor Caius
swears, in the words of Slender in *The Merry Wives*, "I'll ne'er
be drunk whilst I live again, but in honest, civil, godly company
... if I be drunk, I'll be drunk with those that have the fear
of God, and not with drunken knaves"—which looks, by the
way, like a real Shakespearean touch. Even Verdi has found it
impossible to convey the rich tang of the English words in
music.

Bardolph and Pistol sing "Amen" to the pious sentiment,
making quite a little canon of it in the approved ecclesiastical
style; as they do so they ceremoniously escort Caius to the door,
Pistol beating time,—a delicious burlesque effect that would be
impossible, of course, in any other art but music. Falstaff,
seemingly, does not think much either of their melody or their
performance of it—one gathers that he imagines them to be

unable to keep time, whereas what Bardolph is really doing is
to take up and imitate Pistol's phrase at a half-bar's distance.[1]
Falstaff bids the precious pair cease their antiphon, as he calls it,
and gives them the sage advice, equally good in music and in
their particular profession, if they must steal [2] to steal gracefully
and *a tempo*: as it is, they are mere crude artisans, not artists, he
tells them contemptuously.

Having run his eye over the host's bill, he is shocked to
discover how little there is in his purse to meet outgoings such
as his. It is true that Bardolph saves him something, for that
m onstrous red nose of his serves the three of them as a lantern
when they make their way from tavern to tavern at night:

So che se andiam, la not-te, di ta-ver - na in ta-ver-na

But what Falstaff economises in this way on lamp oil he spends
and more, on wine to light up this human beacon. And this has
been going on now for thirty years! The pair of them are ruining
him. The thought is so grievous that he has to call to the host for
another bottle; for as to himself, were Falstaff to lose anything
of that generous bulk of his he would no longer be Falstaff.
"This is my kingdom", he says, stroking his paunch, "and I
mean to extend it." But for that and other things money is
necessary, and for the raising of money he has worked out a nice
little scheme. In Windsor, it appears, there is a rich burgher of the
name of Ford, rich in gold and fortunate in a handsome wife—

[1] The idea and the text here are an ingenious embroidery on the original
on Boïto's part. In *The Merry Wives*, Falstaff merely says of the stupid
Bardolph, "I am glad I am so acquit of this tinder-box: his thefts were too
open; his filching was like an unskilful singer; he kept not time"; to which
Nym adds, "The good humour is to steal at a minute's rest." Boïto, being
himself a musician, saw the opportunity this gave him and Verdi to make
Bardolph and Pistol sing canonically "at [metaphorically] a minute's rest",
and to make Falstaff imagine that they do so because they "cannot keep
time".

[2] A neat allusion to *tempo rubato*.

what eyes! what a neck! what lips! he rhapsodises, to a suave, caressing phrase in the orchestra:

And this pearl among women, this Alice, had set his heart on fire by smiling at him as he passed her window—yes, at him, with his fine figure, his ample chest, his well-turned leg; and her heart had so melted within her at the sight of him that she seemed to be sighing "I am Sir John Falstaff's". (He imitates the female voice in falsetto). But this is not all. There is another lady of Windsor, he tells his dazzled entourage—one Margaret Page (known to her intimates as Meg, Pistol interjects), who also has succumbed to his charm. Each of these desirable beauties has the key of her husband's money-box; and together they shall be his Golconda, his Gold Coast!

He gives Bardolph and Pistol the glowing letters he had just finished writing when the curtain rose, and bids them deliver them to Mistress Alice and Mistress Meg, whose virtue he means to put to the test forthwith. The myrmidons refuse, Bardolph pleading his honour, and Pistol swearing that he is a soldier, not a Pandarus. Falstaff thereupon sends the notes by little Robin, the page-boy of the hostelry, turns contemptuously on Bardolph and Pistol, and gives them an eloquent lecture on the subject of honour. Has not he himself to pawn his own occasionally? And yet these evil-looking, evil-smelling bundles of dirty rags, these pole-cats dare to prate about *their* honour! and he launches into an impressive catalogue of the things that honour cannot do, on the lines of the famous "catechism" in *I Henry IV*, Act V,— "Can honour set to a leg? no: or an arm? no:" and so on—which Boïto has paraphrased admirably and Verdi set incomparably. As for Bardolph and Pistol, the honest Knight has had enough of such rascals. He takes a broom and chases them round the stage and finally out of the room.

3

The second scene of this act shows us the exterior of Ford's house. The short and lively orchestral preamble:

introduces us to the two merry wives, Mistress Ford's daughter Anne, and Mrs. Quickly. Each of the wives has a letter which she is dying to show the other. Both missives prove to be from the same gallant wooer, the noble Knight Sir John Falstaff; and when the ladies come to compare them they find, to their vast amusement, that they are couched in identical terms; the burden of them is that Alice (or Meg as the case may be) is a gay gossip and Falstaff a merry fellow, and together they would make an ideal pair. The letters culminate in a grandiose lyrical outburst on the part of the amorous knight—"Let your face shed its refulgent rays on me like a star in the immensity of the night":

E il vi-so tu - o su me ri-splen-de - rà

The four women make merry over the fat old fool in a lively, light-fingered quartet.

As they leave the stage—though they are still visible occasionally among the trees—Ford, Caius, Bardolph, Pistol and Fenton enter. Falstaff's quondam henchmen have been hinting to Ford that his domestic security is in danger; and being of a jealous nature he takes the suggestion seriously. Fenton does not like Sir John, Dr. Caius has grievances of his own against him, and Bardolph and Pistol are out for revenge for the indignity recently inflicted on them; so trouble seems to be blowing up for Falstaff from every quarter. They all express their feelings about him simultaneously in a quintet which every now and then becomes a nonet through the addition of the chatter of the women. The ensemble is most skilfully managed by Boïto, and Verdi's tripping music is a joy even if we do not understand a word of what is being said. But we enjoy the whole thing still more when we do understand, and the only way to do that is to get thoroughly familiar with the words apart from the music; for as the characters are all saying different things at the same time it is rarely possible for the listener to get the sense of a single sentence. Poor Ford seems to be in the same difficulty himself, for he complains that while the men talking to him are four, he is only one; and he wishes he could make up his mind which of the four to listen to— "If you would only speak one at a time", he remarks plaintively, "I might be able to hear you."

At last Pistol, speaking solo, makes it clear to him that Falstaff, meditating an attack on the virtue of Mistress Ford, has already written her a letter, of which he, Pistol, has nobly refused to be the bearer. Ford resolves to keep an eye on his wife. The women return for a moment, still cackling about the plan for Falstaff's discomfiture which they have evolved among themselves; then all leave the stage except Fenton and Anne, who seize the opportunity to sing a tender little love duet:

Lab-bra di fo - co! Lab-bra di fio - re!

Their love-making, charming as it is in its way, is perhaps more Boïtian and Verdian than Shakespearean; but that, of course, is equally true of many other things in the opera.

As the older women are seen approaching, Fenton hides among the trees. The two wives and Mrs. Quickly enter, and, to appropriately fussy music, begin to elaborate their scheme for dealing with Falstaff. It is decided that Mrs. Quickly shall take him a letter from Alice, making an assignation with him at her house. The three women are then shuffled off the stage on the rather clumsy pretext that they catch sight of someone spying on them among the trees, the truth being that the librettist and the composer want the stage free once more for a continuation of the duet between Fenton and Anne. The pair of love-birds bill and coo as prettily as before; then they too run off as they see someone approaching.

It is Ford, who is followed by Caius, Bardolph and Pistol; Fenton also insinuates himself among them. It is arranged that Falstaff's two former companions shall introduce Ford to him under another name; and as this is an opera, and we are now nearing the end of the act, the women are brought in to combine with the men in a delightful ensemble on the subject of Falstaff and what is coming to him before long. Here, as elsewhere, the women and the men preserve their own group-individualities within the frame of the choral texture as a whole, while Fenton, who can never think of anyone but Anne—and besides is a tenor —takes his own melodic course independently of the others. The men having left the stage, the women have a last chuckle among themselves over the fun in prospect, rolling over their tongues delightedly the quotation from Falstaff's amorous letter quoted as our No. 5.

4

The setting of the second act is once more the interior of the "Garter". Falstaff's porcine bulk is stretched out in an armchair: he has finished breakfast and is now drinking sack. Bardolph and Pistol stand before him, professing penitence, begging forgiveness, and beating their breasts in unison every now and then. The Knight regards them both with lofty indifference until Bardolph announces that a lady desires to see him. It is Mrs. Quickly. She approaches Falstaff with a phrase of mock humility that is one of the gems of the opera: it is a veritable genuflection in music:

After the exchange of many courtesies between them, she tells the
"great seducer", as she calls him, that she comes from Mistress
Alice Ford, who is crazy with love for him. Alice thanks him for
his letter, and wishes him to know that her husband is always
away from home between two o'clock and three:

e - sce sem - pre   dal - le due al - le tre.

He smacks his thick lips over this "dalle due alle tre" as he
fatuously repeats it. But he has no sooner assured her that he will
be there at the right time than Mrs. Quickly tells him that she has
another message for him: the beautiful Mistress Page, an angel if
ever there was one, has also succumbed to his charms, though
unfortunately *her* husband is seldom away from home. The
Knight, preening himself monstrously, dismisses the messenger
with a reward, and breaks out into a song of triumph to an Italian
version of the monologue in *The Merry Wives*—"Say'st thou so,
old Jack? go thy ways; I'll make more of thy old body than I
have done.... Good body, I thank thee." The scoring of the
soliloquy admirably underlines the grossness of the fat fellow's
self-satisfaction.

Bardolph now introduces Ford, under the name of Brook (in
the Italian, Fontana). He commends himself to Falstaff straight
away by his generosity in the matter of wine. He is rich, he says,
and fond of pleasure, and he has come to solicit Sir John's help in
a certain matter. Bardolph and Pistol, who are enjoying the joke,
having been sent out, Brook offers Falstaff a bag of gold to help
him win one Mistress Ford, of Windsor. He has squandered large
sums on her, it seems, but alas, her virtue seems impregnable. He
places his last hope in the diplomacy of a gentleman so distinguished, so gallant, so courtly, as Sir John Falstaff. The Knight
promises him complete success, for he himself happens to stand
high in the favour of this Mistress Ford, who only that morning
had sent him word that her lout of a husband is always out
between two and three. Master Brook has come to the right

quarter for assistance; he, Falstaff, will see to it that this poor Brook is treated as he deserves.

In high exultation he goes out to dress himself, taking care not to leave the bag of gold behind him. In his absence Ford indulges in a long and passionate monologue, the subject of which is the faithlessness of women. He has just finished swearing that he will have revenge on Falstaff also when the latter returns, dressed in his best, to take a walk with Brook. The short scene that follows is perhaps the opera's high water mark of musical grace and wit. The pair ceremoniously yield each other the precedence for some time, but finally solve their problem by going through the door arm in arm, the orchestra giving out the while the theme of Falstaff's self-satisfaction ("Say'st thou so, old Jack? . . . I'll make more of thy old body than I have done. . . ."). A neater "curtain" has never been devised in comedy. Humpty-Dumpty is on the top of the wall; but the great fall is coming.

5

The next scene is played in Ford's house: we see a large room with three doors, two staircases, a large cupboard, a screen, etc. Alice and Meg are in conversation, the subject, of course, being Falstaff. Mrs. Quickly and Anne enter: the latter, whose thoughts run on her hopeless love for Fenton, stands sadly apart from the others. Mrs. Quickly tells delightedly the story of her successful mission to Falstaff, mimicking her own hypocritical humility and the pomposity and condescending courtesy of the over-blown amorist. The scheme has succeeded to perfection; Falstaff will soon be there. At Alice's order, two serving-men bring in a huge buck basket full of dirty linen. The room in general is arranged for the reception of the chief actor in the coming comedy, the women keeping up a gay running commentary all the time:

Ga-je co-ma-ri di Vind-sor! è l'o - - ra!

Then, as Falstaff is seen from the window to be approaching, Mrs. Quickly, Meg and Anne hurry out.

When the Knight enters it is to find the love-lorn Alice pensively striking chords on her lute. He makes love to her in the most grotesque fashion, wishing that Ford were in the next world so that he might lay at her feet his ancient name and title. She responds simperingly that she has no taste for riches or splendours, to which he replies with the famous description of himself as he once was, the slender page of the Duke of Norfolk:

The precise bearing of this little monologue on the action is not quite clear; but as it gives Verdi a pretext for writing a couple of pages of his most delicate music we need not be too critical as to the way in which the episode is spatchcocked into the general tissue of the scene. But the last thing, surely, that a grossly corpulent and vain lover would do would be to add to the handicap of his fatness by describing to the lady he is trying to seduce how slender he was in the days *before* she knew him.

The dialogue is broken in upon by Mrs. Quickly, who announces that Mistress Page, who has arrived in great agitation, wants to speak with Mistress Ford. Falstaff hides behind the screen, where he hears, when Meg enters, just what he is intended to hear—that the jealous Ford is hot on the track of Alice's lover, whom he believes to be now in his house. Soon Ford comes in with Caius, Fenton, Bardolph and Pistol. The hunt is up. Some of the men search the room, others run into the corridors to cut off his retreat. Ford, who is beside himself with rage, after hurling an insult or two at his wife begins to throw the linen out of the basket. But Falstaff is not there, nor, apparently, anywhere else in the house; for no one thinks of looking behind the screen which Mrs. Ford has folded round him. He emerges when the coast seems to be clear, and the three older women stow him into the basket; while they are doing so, Anne and Fenton steal behind the screen for a bit of love-making.

The men return, and the search for Falstaff is resumed more frantically than before, and with an even greater abundance of comic touches. At last a suspicious sound from behind the screen is heard. It is only Anne and Fenton kissing; but the hunters think they have run their quarry to earth at last. While they are gathering stealthily round the screen, the women pile the clothes on to the protesting Falstaff, who looks like being stifled. Behind the screen the sound of billing and cooing increases: obviously it comes from Falstaff and Alice! The hunters are in no great hurry to pounce on their prey, for first of all they have to build up an animated musical ensemble. At long last, after a "one, two, three" from Ford, the screen is thrown down, only to disclose the embarrassed young couple. Ford rails at them both, swearing that they shall never marry; and at a fresh view-hallo from Bardolph, the men, with the exception of Fenton, who has already left the stage with Anne, run up one of the staircases. While they are following up this false alarm, Anne returns with four menservants, who, at an order from Alice, hoist the basket on their shoulders and heave it out of the window into the shallow river, just as Ford and the others return. Shaking with laughter, Alice takes her husband to the window and shows him a spectacle that ought to rejoice his heart.

6

At the opening of the third act we see a very disillusioned Falstaff sitting meditating outside the "Garter". It is now evening. He intones his immortal comment on the wickedness of a world that can treat a good man as he has just been treated—pushed into a basket stuffed with foul linen and flung into the river like an unwanted kitten or puppy. Fortunately his roundness and cork-like substance had made it impossible for him to sink; otherwise the world would now be lamenting the passing of one of the best of men. He takes a deep draught of sack to dilute the Thames water he has swallowed. Wine is good, he muses; and as his spirits begin to revive we are treated to one of the most brilliant effects in the whole score—an orchestral trill that commences with the utmost quietness and gradually extends to a *fortissimo* in the whole orchestra; we seem positively to see the new life within the man rising from a faint trickle to a mighty flood.

Mrs. Quickly enters, greeting Falstaff once more with the hypocritical No. 7. At first he sends her and her beautiful Mistress Alice to the devil: he has suffered enough on her account, he says. While he is fuming in this fashion, Alice, Meg, Ford, Anne, Caius and Fenton emerge from behind a house on the left, and, alternately peering out and hiding themselves, listen to the conversation that follows. Mrs. Quickly begs Falstaff to believe that Alice was not to blame for the regrettable little incident with the basket. She is, in fact, most unhappy about it: and the old go-between gives Falstaff a letter from her, making an assignation with him by Herne's Oak in Windsor Park at midnight. He is to disguise himself as the Black Huntsman. (There seems to have been a tradition in Shakespeare's day that a certain Herne, one of the keepers of the royal Park, had hanged himself on an oak, which was consequently haunted by his ghost). Falstaff takes Mrs. Quickly into the inn, to talk the matter over in quiet; and the group outside naturally pounce on this opportunity to come into the open and settle, in the audience's hearing, the details of the new plot against Falstaff. Anne, dressed in white, is to be the Queen of the Fairies; Meg, in green, will be a woodland nymph, and Mrs. Quickly a goblin; while Alice will be in charge of a number of children made up as sprites and imps, who will gather round Falstaff and plague him:

11   ♩ = 138

leggiero stacc.

A-vro con me dei put-ti Che fingeran fol-let-ti

until, in due time, all the conspirators reveal themselves to him and leave him to profit by his lesson. As Mrs. Quickly comes out of the "Garter" again she overhears Ford assure Caius, sotto voce, that he shall marry Anne, who, he impresses on him, will be robed in white: at the proper moment Caius and she are to come secretly to him, and he will give them a matrimonial blessing. Darkness has by now set in. The stage gradually empties, and the last thing we hear as the curtain falls is the piquant No. 11 in the orchestra.

7

The setting of the final scene is Windsor Park, with Herne's Oak in the centre, showing up in the moonlight. Distant horns are heard, as of some spectral hunt. Fenton enters and sings a sensitive little aria in praise of love:

Dal labbro il canto esta-si-a - to vo-la,

which ends with a refrain we have already met with in the duets between Fenton and Anne: it is completed by Anne herself in the distance.

Mrs. Ford enters, not masked, but carrying on her arm a black cloak and a mask, which she orders Fenton to put on. (She is bent on countering the trick of her husband to marry Anne to Caius with a trick of her own).

All of them make a hurried exit as some mysterious chords in the orchestra announce the approaching Falstaff, who, according to plan, is enveloped in a heavy cloak and carries antlers on his head. A distant clock strikes twelve. Falstaff, more than a little scared at the eeriness of the hour and the place, commends himself to the protection of the gods. Alice enters, and Falstaff makes love to her in his usual twopence-coloured fashion. He is pleased rather than otherwise when she tells him that Meg also is somewhere about: they can carve him up between them, he says, like a buck at table! Meg's voice is now heard, calling for help, and Alice runs away in pretended terror. The demons, it appears, are coming. Falstaff throws himself on the ground face downwards when he hears a voice (that of Anne) summoning the elves, goblins and what not, for, as everyone knows, it is death for a

mortal to look on the fairies. Anne now enters, dressed as the
Fairy Queen, with nine other fairies in white and nine in blue.
Soon the whole force of those engaged in the masquerade are
present—Fenton, Bardolph, Alice, Meg and Mrs. Quickly in one
mask or another, Ford undisguised and not masked, and another
crowd of fairies. Anne calls on the fays to come out and sing and
dance in the moonlight:

This they do, afterwards advancing en masse to Herne's Oak.
Bardolph halts them: he has stumbled over the prostrate body of
Falstaff. As a man has no business there among their revels, they
order him to get up; but he pathetically explains that this will be
impossible for him without the assistance of a crane. Thereupon,
at the instigation of Bardolph, goblins, demons and imps of all
sorts descend on the Knight and pinch and flog and plague him.

Meanwhile, seeing Caius looking about for Anne, Alice removes her and Fenton to a little distance off, and soon the lovers
and Mrs. Quickly slip away among the trees. Falstaff is assaulted
and tormented by almost everyone until he begs for mercy. Ford
crows over him; Alice shows herself to him unmasked; Mrs.
Quickly curtsies ironically to him as she had done in the tavern
(No. 7); his humiliation is complete.

Ford now thinks it time to spring his great surprise on the
company—the betrothal of the Queen of the Fairies. Caius, still
masked, comes forward, leading, as he imagines, Anne by the
hand; but in reality it is the red-nosed Bardolph, heavily veiled.
Alice brings forward at the same time Fenton, cloaked and
masked, and Anne, draped in blue; Alice asks for Ford's permission, which is readily given, to include "this other ardent

young couple" in the ceremony. The two couples join hands, and, after being solemnly blessed by Ford, Fenton and Caius unmask, while Anne removes her veil. Mrs. Quickly snatches the veil from Bardolph, and all laugh at the discomfiture of Caius. Ford, when he has recovered from his astonishment, takes his defeat in good part, and he and Falstaff invite them all to join him in a chorus as the preliminary to a carouse. The whole company comes down to the footlights for the chorus, the text of which is to the effect that the world is just one huge joke, and man the greatest of jesters: everyone has his laugh at the expense of everyone else, and he laughs best who laughs last. This lively finale is an elaborate fugue on the following subject:

which, we note, is given out by Falstaff.

LOUISE

Charpentier (1860)

PRINCIPAL CHARACTERS

LOUISE	*Soprano*
JULIEN	*Tenor*
THE MOTHER	*Mezzo-soprano*
THE FATHER	*Bass*

I

Gustave Charpentier was born in Lorraine; but after the war of 1870 his father, a baker, migrated to France and settled in Tourcoing. In 1879 the municipality of that town granted the promising boy an allowance of 1,200 francs per annum to enable him to continue his musical studies in Paris, the idea at that time being that he was destined to become a violinist. It was not until 1885 that he entered Massenet's class for composition at the Conservatoire. Two years later he won the Prix de Rome with a cantata, *Didon*. He lived in Rome, barring an interruption or two, from February 1888 to 1890, leaving behind him at the Villa Médicis the reputation of a dangerous anarchist, not so much in music as in politics and ethics. About his "anarchism" there was a good deal of blague as well as much honest conviction. He felt sincerely for the working classes, the hardness of whose lot he knew from personal experience; but when it came to putting his opinions into practice the joker in him tended at times to get the upper hand of the social reformer. Thus during a holiday from Rome he offered himself to the electors of Tourcoing as a candidate for a vacant deputyship in the Boulangist interest: he went so far as to have the usual flamboyant placards printed. Then he seems suddenly to have changed his mind. He went straight back to Rome. But the placards were too good to waste; so a perplexed Rome woke up one fine morning to find its walls plastered with an appeal from one Gustave Charpentier for the suffrages of the intelligent electors of a town in France the very name of which, in all probability, the Romans had never heard.

There was never anything of the "absolute" musician in Charpentier. He could never see any sense in such "abstract" forms of music as the fugue or the quartet: music, for him, meant the direct expression of something he had seen or experienced. His orchestral *Impressions d'Italie*, a Suite in five movements, recording his sensations and emotions in Naples and other places, made him talked about in Paris in the early 1890's as an exceptionally promising young composer. He followed this work up in 1892 with *La Vie du Poète*, a "symphony-drama", as he called it, for orchestra, chorus and solo voices. The words of this were his own; they dealt with the aspirations and disappointments of a poet who, unable in the end to square his accounts with life, abandons himself to vice and perishes in misery and degradation. The subject of the drama no less than the character of the music attracted a good deal of attention in Paris; the younger artists in particular, in revolt, as young artists always and everywhere are, even if they are not invariably quite clear what it is they are in revolt against, adopted him as their leader. In Paris he was the typical Bohemian of Montmartre, with his long hair and flowing beard, his enormous hat, his expansive cravat, and other unmistakable labels of a local type that has perhaps seen its best days. He knew nothing and cared little about the life of any class but that from which he had sprung and to which his poverty seemed at that time to condemn him irrevocably; and his head was full of plans for expressing the sufferings and longings of that class in music.

Already while in Rome he had drafted the text of an opera, *Louise*, and completed the music for the first act. The story is to some extent a dramatisation of certain youthful experiences of his own, upon which it was easy for him to graft his ardent social philosophy: there was an actual Louise, though her name has not been made public. The music was mostly completed in Paris between 1893 and 1896. In 1897 a number of Montmartre artists and men of letters organised a grand "Couronnement de la Muse", the music for which was contributed by Charpentier—a young woman, chosen by popular vote to represent the "Muse of

Labour", was to be solemnly crowned at the open-air festival in the spring. Unfortunately, owing to the bad behaviour of the weather on the appointed day, this part of the programme could not be carried out. Two years later the scheme was revived in connection with the Michelet celebrations, and the Muse was duly crowned in the Place de l'Hôtel-de-Ville, to the accompaniment of music and dancing. The picturesque ceremony was afterwards repeated, with great success, in several other French towns; and Charpentier finally worked the episode into the third act of his opera.

2

Louise was given for the first time at the Opéra-Comique on the 2nd February 1900, under the conductorship of André Messager, with Marthe Rioton as Louise, Maréchal as Julien, Mme Deschamps-Jehin as the Mother, and Fugère as the Father. At first the average respectable French bourgeois was a little doubtful about it all; the characters were too much like those he came across every day to satisfy his hunger for romance in opera, the modernity of the costumes offended him, and there was much in Charpentier's text that jarred on him. It was the students, the working people—the opposite numbers of the characters shown on the stage—who steered the opera through its first difficult days; once these had been survived the work was set for a long run of popularity.

It was the new Director of the Opéra-Comique, Albert Carré, who launched *Louise*. His predecessor, Carvalho, though he had accepted it, jibbed at certain things in it, more especially the realism of the every-day costumes. He tried hard on this account to induce Charpentier to transplant his story to the eighteenth century, but the composer was not to be moved. From his point of view and that of his day in general he was right: the whole force of *Louise* lay in its up-to-date actuality. But it has had to pay for its contemporaneity in the way that all works of art have to do, sooner or later, that pride themselves on having caught the very mood, reflected the very colour, of the day that saw their birth. The terrifically up-to-date comes, in a generation or so, to look sadly out-of-date; this is a rule from which works of art are no more exempt than the fashions of ladies' clothes. Even those of us who, deep down within us, have an affection for *Louise* which nothing can overcome, cannot pretend to ourselves that it does not "date" a little now. But the paradox of every case of this kind is that sooner or later the day arrives when the one-time liability becomes an asset. We have to distinguish carefully between a dilapidation and a ruin. A mere dilapidation is an eyesore in the landscape; it lacks the charm, the softening atmosphere, of the historical perspective, whereas that perspective lends a peculiar glamour to the ruin. The dangerous period for an idea or a belief is, so far as art is concerned, when it has got as far as the dilapidation stage but no further; and in that stage it can do nothing but wait resignedly and hopefully until time does its kindly work of sentimental restoration.

A celebrated operatic impresario, asked recently why he did not produce *Susanna's Secret*, replied smilingly that although he liked the delicious little work very much it was impossible to stage it today, for a modern audience could not be expected to take seriously an action that turned upon a woman's having to conceal from her husband the fact that she smoked. But surely the time has now arrived when a dramatic motive of that kind no longer offends our notion of actuality, for the simple reason that it has parted company entirely with our conception of the actual. It is no longer an absurdity, any more than a fairy tale is absurd. On the contrary, it has a demure antique charm of its own. Few of us today believe in ghosts; but we do not refuse to take *Hamlet* seriously on that account. As Coleridge has put it, it is not that we believe in ghosts, but that in the theatre, for the time being, we consent to suspend our disbelief in them. Literature is packed with ideas of this kind that are none the less dramatically possible because they are ruins. At the present moment the doctrine of the injustice done to women because they are not "free", which lies at the root of *Louise*, is in the dilapidation stage: it is difficult, to take one instance out of many, for an audience of today to believe that in any working-class family a grown-up girl still allows herself to be bullied and browbeaten and even chastised as Louise was by her mother. But perhaps the day will come when that picture will be so remote from not only the experience but the memory of the average man that he can look at it in an opera of 1900 as he does at the ghost in *Hamlet*, as something in which people no longer believe, though for purely artistic purposes on a given evening they are willing to pretend they do. So again with some of the Montmartre episodes of the third act, especially the crowning of Louise as the Muse. A world which, far from taking Montmartre as seriously as Charpentier did, cannot even take it today amusedly, is inclined to smile at this sort of thing in *Louise*. But that is only because, while we have parted company with dear, foolish, posturing Montmartre, it is still too close to us: it is a dilapidation that has not yet acquired the time-perspective, the dignity and the romance of a ruin. Some day it will seem as remote from men's actual lives as Troy or Carthage now does; but long before then it will have stolen back to art and literature not as an actuality, which is what Charpentier intended it to be, but as a delightful escape from actuality into the enchanting world of the unreal.

As has been pointed out in the Overture to the present volume, operatic producers cannot pick and choose their actors as they would like to do, and it is frequently bound to happen that we are given a Louise who has every qualification for the part except the appearance. Among the things, indeed, that gives the average spectator today the feeling that the opera is somewhat out of date are the episode in which the Father rocks Louise on his knees, and that in the first scene in which the girl's mother loses her temper with her and smacks her. These two episodes, particularly the second, are all the more likely to create a laugh when, as is often the case, Louise is a strapping wench who looks as if, in a contest under Marquis of Queensberry rules, she could put her mother down and out in the first minute of the first round. This, of course, is not what Charpentier intended, and not what the first spectators of the opera saw. Marthe Rioton seemed born for the part. She had only just finished her studies at the Conservatoire: Louise was her first rôle. She was slightly built, with an adolescent timbre in her voice, and with intelligence enough to double by art the suggestion of the pathetic ingénue that her appearance lent her. According to a French writer who, one gathers, based his story on information supplied to him by the composer himself, there was never anything improbable about this first Louise. When she told Julien how her mother had ill-treated her, no one in the audience doubted that with such a Louise and such a mother the thing was physically possible. When her father petted her like a child, that again was thoroughly in keeping with her appearance and her manner of the moment. And when this half-awakened fledgeling answered Julien's ardour with a passion warmer than his own, once more it all seemed absolutely true to life.[1]

On the 4th June 1913 the Opéra-Comique produced *Julien*, a sequel to *Louise*. This ran to some twenty performances in Paris, and the work was given later in New York and one or two other towns. Since then it seems to have disappeared completely from the boards, and it is hardly likely to be revived. Musically it is not often Charpentier at his best, while dramatically it is vague and sprawling. Louise herself, for instance, reappears not only *in propria persona* but as La Beauté, La Jeune Fille, La Fille, and L'Aïeule; and what with a Hiérophante, a Mage, Filles du Rêve, Fées, Chimères and other symbols or abstractions flitting about among starkly realistic characters such as a Bohemian, a Stone-breaker, a Workman, a Student, a Bourgeoise and Garçons de café, to say nothing of a crowd of supernumeraries specified in the score as Levites, Augures, Sages, Servants et Servantes de la Beauté, Muses, Amants, Amantes, Poètes Elus, Poètes Déchus, Bûcherons, Terrassiers, Paysannes, Paysans, Bohémiennes, Bretonnes, Foule de Fête et de Carnaval, Danseuses Sacrées and Danseuses de Fête, it is evident that Charpentier had set himself an impossible task. The settings range from the Holy Mountain and the Accursed Valley to the Temple of Beauty, a landscape in Slovakia, a wild spot in Brittany, the boulevard extérieur and the Place Blanche in Paris. What anyone could ever have made of it all in the theatre it is difficult to say; but one student at least, on more than one occasion, has risen from a reading of the score with only the vaguest notion of what it is all about.[2] Charpentier's social and artistic philosophy seems not merely to have gone to

[1] Her theatrical career was very short. She married young, and quitted the stage at the desire of her husband.

[2] A good deal of the earlier *Vie du Poète* has been incorporated in *Julien*.

his head but to have descended to his feet, and to be always tripping him up. We are given to understand that the scores of other, still unperformed, operas are in existence; but Charpentier seems destined to be remembered as essentially the composer of a single opera.

His sympathy with the working classes has taken practical as well as artistic forms. For one of the early performances of *Louise* the Director of the Opéra-Comique placed four hundred free tickets at the disposal of the seamstresses of Paris. Charpentier tried to induce the theatre directors in general to make a practice of admitting working people free on certain nights of the year. Not succeeding in this, he beat up sufficient subscriptions from various quarters to enable him to found a Mimi Pinson Association having this object in view among others; and not content with this, he brought into being a "Conservatoire Populaire" for the musical education of working girls.

3

Charpentier uses a number of leading motives in his opera, but sometimes in such a way that they are to be associated less with a particular character than with some dramatic or psychological force incarnated in that character. Thus the figure marked A in the following quotation:

should be associated throughout a good deal of the work less with Julien himself than with the call, to Louise, of something in her blood which Julien stands for. Julien is, in a sense, only a minor character in the opera. The centre of it all is Louise, in whose young soul is fought out a contest between many forces—affection for her home and more particularly her father, the desire to be free of domestic restraint, the youthful longing for love, and the general feminine craving for excitement, clothes, bright lights and so on. The other leading characters in the work—with the exception of the Father, who is both himself and a symbol—are vital to the story only as operating on Louise, pulling her in this direction or frustrating her in that. Sometimes, indeed, the force acting on her is frankly a symbol rather than a character. It is Paris, for instance, rather than anything or anybody in particular in Paris, that constitutes an irresistible attraction to Louise; Paris is as truly one of the "characters" of the opera as Julien or anyone else. It should be borne in mind, then, that our No. 1 A often represents not so much Julien the individual as the call to love and freedom which, for Louise, happens to have found voice in Julien.

It is with No. 1 that the short prelude of some twenty-five bars opens. It is followed by the motive typical of the Father:

The setting of the first act is a mansard room in a working-class quarter of Paris. On the right is a door leading into the kitchen. On the left, towards the back of the stage, is a window opening on to a balcony, and giving a view of the roofs of other houses. Opposite the balcony, and quite close to it, is the terrace of another building, with an artist's studio in the background. It is six o'clock on an April evening.

Louise enters, and, hearing the voice of Julien, cautiously draws the curtains and opens the window. Julien, on the terrace opposite, is pouring out his heart in song to his fair neighbour. We gather from the ensuing dialogue between the pair that Louise has urged him to write once more to her father requesting permission for them to marry, and has promised him that if this permission is again refused she will fly with him. Louise still hopes that a less drastic solution of their problem may be found, for she is attached to her parents, and to part from them on ill terms would break her heart. She asks him to tell her in detail just how and when his love for her sprang up within him—not, perhaps, that she does not already know all there is to be known about that matter, but that the information is necessary for the enlightenment of the audience. Julien accordingly tells her how one day he had discovered that he had Louise for a neighbour, a child with great wondering eyes, ignorant of the world, whom her parents kept in a sort of prison. He, for his part, a poet, always dreaming of an ideal love and turning his dreams into verse, had suddenly realised that he had found his ideal when he stumbled one evening, in the dim light of the staircase, on Louise. His fate was sealed.

Just as his song reaches its climax of ardour, and is answered in the orchestra by the motive of Louise's own passion:

the Mother enters the room unobserved by either of them. She listens with an unpleasant curl of the lip to the romantic reminiscences of the lovers, into which there slips now and then a disparaging reference to herself on Julien's part. She learns, among other things, that he and Louise are now betrothed. She takes her daughter by the arm, drags her into the kitchen, closes the door on her, and returns to face Julien, who, from where he stands, has seen nothing of all this. She tells him frankly what she thinks of him, and threatens to come and pull his ears for him if he does not go away. She goes fuming into an adjoining room, whereupon Louise emerges for a moment from the kitchen. Julien shows her the letter he intends to send to her parents, and then disappears, singing his gay No. 1. Louise, who is obviously in a very nervous state, goes back to the kitchen. The mother returns; Julien goes off laughing at her, and she shuts the window angrily.

Louise comes into the living room again, and, in a desperate attempt to appear at her ease, begins to arrange on the sideboard the provisions destined for the evening meal. Her mother nags and jeers at her, giving a malicious burlesque of the recent exchange of lovers' confidences which she had overheard, and tells her to congratulate herself that it was not her Father who had caught her. Poor Louise asks why she cannot be allowed to marry

Julien. What have they against him? Is it that he is a poet, with the
gay manners of the artist? The Mother laughs at this description
of Julien: she prefers to call him a good-for-nothing, a debauchee,
a haunter of cabarets, a pursuer of women. Louise's defence of
her lover exasperates the Mother still further; and, losing her
temper, she is making to ill-treat her when the Father's steps are
heard outside.

He enters to the accompaniment of a figure derived from his
typical motive (No. 2)—a figure, by the way, which in a modified
form does duty at times for the Mother also. He is a very sympathetic figure—the old-style honest workman, respectable, industrious, uncomplaining, unembittered. He has in his hand a
letter that has been handed to him as he entered the building; and
he seats himself by the stove to read it, while Louise and the
Mother silently prepare the table for supper. He looks up for a
moment from his reading, and holds out his arms. Louise falls
into them and kisses him. Evidently there is more affection and
understanding between these two than between daughter and
mother; and his feelings towards Louise and her problems are
expressed in a tender phrase in the orchestra:

which recurs frequently later. During the simple meal that
follows, the Father speaks of his fatigue; the working days are
long, he says, and he is not growing younger. His wife indulges
herself, as much to hurt Louise as to express her own feelings, in
an ill-tempered outburst against the young ne'er-do-wells who
spend their days in idleness and selfish enjoyment. To this the
Father replies philosophically that people of that sort have had
the good luck to be born the sons of their parents. That is how
things are in the world; equality is only a word, for if everyone
were free to pick and choose his job, how would the more unpleasant ones get done? If one isn't born with an income, one must
work. And after all, are the rich any happier than he and his? Can

any happiness surpass that of the home in which love sits by the hearth? The good fellow seizes his wife round the waist and makes her dance with him; and for a moment even this acid creature cannot help being gratified and amused.

Supper over, he sits by the fire and lights his pipe. Louise takes him Julien's letter, which the old man had left by his plate. He reads it again, to the accompaniment of the tender No. 4. As against the Mother, he is inclined to listen patiently to what the young poet has to say for himself; they can make enquiries about him, he says, and, if these prove satisfactory, send for him and talk it all over with him. This is too much for his wife, who launches into a bitter tirade against Julien, and, when Louise protests, strikes her. The girl falls weeping into a chair, where her father speaks lovingly and comfortingly to her, in a moving monologue in which No. 2 and some transformations of No. 4 play a large part. The child believes that in the choice of a husband a girl need listen only to her own heart. He tries to show her that this is not enough, for the heart sometimes deceives. With the cross-grained Mother spitting her poison at them every now and then, the two find a way to temporary peace through their love for each other. He asks for an assurance from Louise that if what he learns about Julien is not to his credit she will forget him; for his own heart, he tells her, would be broken if ever she should fly in the face of his affection for her.

The Mother, having finished her work in connection with the remains of the meal, returns with her mending, and the three seat themselves by the table, on which a lamp has now been lit. The Father asks his daughter to read the evening paper to him. At the first sentence that catches her eye she dissolves in tears. "The spring season", she reads in a dull voice, "promises to be most brilliant. Paris, in festive mood . . ." She can go no further. "Paris!" she murmurs brokenly, her tears choking her. Her father looks pityingly at her as the curtain slowly falls. It is not simply Julien, it is Paris that is tugging at the girl's heart.

4

The second act opens with an orchestral prelude that bears the title "Paris awakes". It is a skilfully-woven tissue of three motives held together by a deep D natural which we feel to be never far away even when we are not actually hearing it. This bass symbolises the sleeping giant that is Paris: the melodic fragments superimposed on it are street cries—that of the chickweed vendor, that of the carrot seller, and that of the vendor of "plaisir".

The curtain rises on a crossways at the foot of Montmartre. On the left is a shed; on the right the establishment in which Louise works as a seamstress; and further back on the same side a flight of steps. It is five o'clock in the morning. The city is still shrouded in a mist through which we catch glimpses of several of those unfortunates whose function it is to start the wheels of a great city each day. Under the shed a Milk-woman is fixing up her booth. Near her is a girl folding the morning papers on a small table. A young female Rag-picker is busy with an overturned rag basket. A Coal-gatherer and a Junkman are also hunting for something worth taking away. These derelicts discuss their own lot and that of the happier beings who are still in bed.

The Noctambulist enters, to a modified form of the motive we have already heard in the prelude to this scene in association with the vendor of "plaisir". He is considerably more a symbol than a character. By a kind of curious play upon words and notes, he and his motive soon become identified with that "Plaisir de Paris" that exercises so irresistible an attraction upon Louise and others of her type. For the moment he is just a nocturnal reveller on his devious way home, pausing en route to flatter and make love to the pretty folder of newspapers, who will have nothing to do with him. To the Milk-woman's enquiry, "Who are you?" he replies, "I am the Plaisir de Paris"; and he throws back his cloak, disclosing a costume, supposed to represent Spring, to which some Folly bells are attached. We shall see more of him later. He requires, perhaps, a little explanation beyond that afforded by the score. The "plaisir" whose vendor's call has been heard in the prelude is a kind of crackly wafer. Charpentier chooses to make this light and flimsy "plaisir" punningly symbolical of the "plaisir" that Paris offers so generously to its devotees; and as he is so bent on it we do not mind humouring him, even against our stricter judgment. Later, of course, it is wholly as the Plaisir de Paris incarnate that we have to view the Noctambulist. One gathers that in the first production of the opera he made a dazzling apparition when he threw back his cloak, his carnival costume being lit up from inside by means of electric light bulbs—which explains the directions in the score: "The women make a gesture of surprise and admiration." The later practice of the theatres was to show him simply in evening dress underneath his cloak. Charpentier does not seem quite to have solved the problem he had set himself in this scene, that of blending the symbolic-fantastic with the real: when, for example, the Noctambulist goes on to explain at some length to his auditors—the Junkman, the Rag-picker and the rest of them—that he seeks out the girls in love who are tormented by desire, the men who have forgotten what happiness is, and other similar unfortunates, preaching to all of them their "right to folly", he himself being the "Purveyor-in-Chief to the great city", we feel tempted to reply to him that if he is speaking as a Noctambulist on his way home from a party his claims are a trifle exaggerated, while if he is speaking purely as a symbol it is not very clear what he is doing in this otherwise very realistic scene at all.

He goes off laughing, knocking down the old Ragman as he does so. The Ragman picks himself up and launches into a pathetic story of the seduction and abduction of his daughter by this very scoundrel—but whether the human actuality or the symbol we cannot be sure. The others sympathise with him but at the same time exhibit a certain philosophy about it all. In every home it is the same, says the Junkman. He himself has lost three daughters in that way; and indeed who can blame the girls of his class if they prefer the "paradise over there"—he points to Paris—to the hell in which they are brought up? At the mention of Paris we hear in the orchestra again the ground-note (D) that symbolised the great city in the prelude.

The first rays of the sun are now striking down from the top of the hill, and the scene becomes more animated. Policemen, a female Street-sweeper, a Street Arab and others come in; and the battered old Street-sweeper proudly tells her friends how twenty years ago she was the "Queen of Paris", with her carriage and pair. She has come down in the world since then; but she has no regrets, for the former life was good while it lasted. Paris is always Paris, she says, an unforgettable paradise for those who have once known it.

When the poor people have drifted off the stage one by one, Julien enters with a number of his Bohemian friends. He explains to them that Louise works in the building on the right. She is accompanied to the very door each day by her dragon of a mother; and this morning, if the parents still refuse their consent to the marriage, he intends to run off with Louise. The Bohemians —sculptors, painters, poets and so on—decide that a corner like this is just the place for serenading a "Muse" if they can find one. Servant girls and others put their heads out of various windows when a Song-Writer, pretending that his cane is a guitar, starts a little ditty in praise of "les enfants de la bohême". He and his co-artists are humorously rewarded with a shower of coppers from the windows. We gather from the talk of these wiseacres that the one desire of the working classes is to be bourgeois, the desire of the bourgeoisie is to be lords and ladies, the desire of the lords and ladies is to be artists, and the dream of artists is to be—gods! And at the word "gods" Charpentier permits himself an ironic quotation in the orchestra of a couple of motives associated in the *Ring* with Wotan and Valhalla.

As the Bohemians depart, the orchestra gives out, in combination, two themes already associated with Julien and Louise, as the lover impatiently awaits her coming and wonders what the answer will be. His meditations are broken in upon by various street cries, a Chair Mender, a Ragman, an Artichoke Vendor, a Carrot Vendor, a Bird-food Girl, sellers of potatoes, barrels, brooms and green peas all contributing to build up the picturesque tissue, with the motive of Paris underlying and reverberating through it all. The cries are music in the ears of one so wholly Parisian as Julien.

He conceals himself behind the shed on the left as the workwomen begin to invade the scene, greeting each other gaily as they go into the house on the right, for it is now eight o'clock. They are followed by Louise and her Mother, the latter telling her daughter roughly that she will see to it that in future she shall work at home, for they intend her to be an honest woman. Cold kisses are exchanged between them. The Mother goes away,

looking round suspiciously in all directions as she leaves. When
the coast is clear Julien runs out, drags the agitated Louise to the
shed, and passionately implores her not to allow herself to be kept
a prisoner in her own home. To the accompaniment once more
of some of the street cries he reminds her of her promise; but the
agitated girl replies that it would kill her father if she were to
leave him. It ends with her running into the house; and as Julien
stands gazing sadly after her we hear again some of the familiar
cries of the Paris that is now fully awake, the Paris that has been
subtly present in everything that has been said and taken place
since the curtain rose.

After an orchestral interlude in which the motive of Julien's
passion (No. 1A) plays a prominent part, the curtain rises on the
dressmaker's workroom. A number of workgirls are busy with
their various tasks, one of which is gossip. Louise sits a little apart
from the chattering mass. The others begin to comment on her
moody silence and the evident traces of tears on her face. A new
motive:

is heard as the girls launch into the subject of love; and soon they
are all lost in sentimental or sensual dreams—the seductive call of
Paris is once more in the air. They try to induce Louise to speak
of her own adventures, but she remains unresponsive.

In the street below, musicians are heard performing a crude
polka, which is followed by an aubade sung by Julien to his
Louise. Some of the girls look out of the window, approve of the
voice and still more of the appearance of the singer, and for a
little while encourage him by throwing him kisses. But the song
goes on too long and is too serious for them. Becoming unmistakably bored, they end by guying the passion of the singer and
throwing the workshop cuttings at him. What they want is something cheerful to dance to—an opportunity provided for them by
a resumption of the polka. Louise's distress has by now become

more than she can bear. Complaining of feeling unwell, she leaves the workroom, to the great astonishment of the others. The mystery is solved when they see Louise making off down the street with the singer of the song; and the curtain comes down to peals of cackling laughter.

5

Julien's song had been of "the distant city, the blue land of hope", where he knew of a "sanctuary" he would fain dedicate to his love. The prelude to the third act is entitled "Toward the distant city": it is woven out of several motives, new and old, among them one which symbolises Louise's desire for freedom:

The lovers have found their "sanctuary" in a tiny house on the heights of Montmartre, with an outlook over the vast panorama of Paris. We see them in their little garden at twilight: Julien is sitting with a book in his hand, not reading, however, but lost in tranquil contemplation, while Louise, leaning on the balustrade of the porch, smiles affectionately at him as she recalls the memories of their first kiss—"Depuis le jour où je me suis donnée":

The segment marked A is frequently used in the sequel to express Louise's new-found happiness. Her dream of freedom and love has come true, and all nature seems to rejoice with her. She tells Julien of her former misery in the workroom, where no one understood or cared for her, and at home, where her father, for all his affection for her, persisted in treating her almost as a child, while her mother was often brutal with her. And neither of her parents could believe there could possibly be any good in a poet, so that between *la mère Routine et le père Préjugé*, as she puts it, Louise has had a bitter time. She and Julien fully agree that older people, however wise and experienced they may be, however good their intentions, have no right to bar the younger ones' way to the happiness they have set their hearts on. What these older people call their greater experience is only convention, tradition, envy, hatred of the ideal; they would hold God himself in bondage if they could, says Julien, working himself into a passion of revolt as he proceeds. Everyone, he insists, has the right to freedom, everyone's duty is to love; and woe to those who would strangle the young soul that is struggling to find its place in the sun! Louise cannot quite accept his theory that parents in general, and her own in particular, are the worst of egoists; but her love for him swamps her regrets as he draws her to him and points to the city beneath them, from which there surges up a waltz-melody typifying the joy of life down there; and the pair blend their voices in an ecstatic cry to "Paris, city of strength and light, of joy and love." And as if in answer to their appeal to the great city to protect them, its lights begin to appear in the growing darkness, and its million voices seem to call to them with a promise of freedom to live their lives as they will. Locked in each other's arms, they see themselves no longer as Louise and Julien but as all the ardent souls, the faithful lovers, the earth has ever known. This long and passionate duet is the emotional climax of the opera; and once again we are conscious through it all that Paris is as much an actor in the piece as Julien or Louise.

Their duet ended, the lovers go into the house. Fireworks are seen in the distance, and drum rolls and fanfares are heard. A couple of Bohemians leap over the hedge in the background and then open the garden gate to three others, carrying large parcels from which they hurriedly unpack flags, paper lanterns, streamers, and things of that sort, with which they drape the front of the house. Beggars, grisettes, idlers and street urchins troop on to the stage, singing a chorus in praise of pleasure and of the Bohemians; some of them climb a scaffolding that stands in front of the houses on the right. They are joined by a number of the bourgeois of Montmartre, who do not altogether approve of what goes on. Presently the main body of the Bohemians arrives, carrying lanterns, streamers and banners, and followed by the Procession of Pleasure, the centrepiece of which is the Noctambulist, now attired as the King of Fools, sitting solemnly in a chair borne by the Daughters of Joy. Two of the Bohemians, one of them got up as a monkey, the other as an ass, post themselves on either side of the house; and as Louise appears on the porch—Julien having gone down to join the Bohemians—the crowd breaks into a chorus in praise of her as the Muse of Montmartre. The King of Fools comes forward, and with mock gravity brings into view a Dancer, who, he explains in language none too lucid, is his own soul, and the soul of all of them in the form of a flower. To the strains of a seductive waltz the Dancer mounts the steps of the porch and presents a bouquet of roses to Louise, while round the latter's shoulders the grisettes drape a shawl embroidered with silver, as the emblem of her sovereignty as the Queen of Bohemia and the Muse of Montmartre. Overcome with emotion, Louise offers a rose to Julien, who kneels in homage before her. A big choral ensemble is built up, in which the principals, the Bohemians, the idlers and the sober bourgeois all take part in accordance with their own characters and the nature of their reaction to the fête.

As the noise is working up to its climax a sudden hush falls on them all as a humble, miserable figure is perceived standing motionless at the back of the scene. It is Louise's Mother. At the sight of her the King of Fools laughs cynically and disappears with the Daughters of Joy and many other participants in the revels. The grisettes gather round Louise, who has swooned. The Mother, a very different creature now from what she was in the first act, comes forward slowly and timorously. What is left of the crowd comments on the situation, some of them sympathetically, some with heartless irony. At length Julien dismisses them all. Louise has crouched in terror in the vestibule. Julien places himself defiantly in the path of the approaching Mother, who, in a quiet voice, tells him that she comes now not as an enemy, but to let them know what had happened in their home since Louise had left it. They had resigned themselves, after a while, to the blows of Fate; regarding their child as dead to them, they had hung a cross on the door of her bedroom. But now the Father is ill and nigh to death, and only Louise can save him. Julien stands aloof, resentful and distrustful; but Louise listens with ever-increasing pain to the story told by her mother of how her father had longed for her, rising in the night and walking about in the darkness, vainly expecting her, or kneeling at the door of her room and crying her name; how for a while he had seemed, on the surface, reconciled to the loss of her; and how body and spirit had at last broken down. The Mother implores Julien to consent to Louise returning to them for a little while, after which, she promises them, the girl shall have her freedom again.

The pathos of her appeal is unexpectedly enforced by the old Ragman, who is seen just then passing slowly down the path at the back of the stage, singing mournfully of that lost daughter of his, to look for whom in Paris is like looking for a needle in a field of corn: Paris, he laments, never gives up those it seizes upon, for Paris has need of them! As the old man disappears into the distance, Julien, moved now in spite of himself, makes the Mother repeat her assurance that Louise shall return. Louise divests herself of her shawl and takes a pitiful farewell of Julien, who stands, as the curtain falls, with his arms held out in longing to the little figure that goes out hesitatingly through the garden gate with the Mother.

6

The setting of the fourth act is the same as that of the first. The Father, no longer the brave, cheerful fighter of the first act but a broken, embittered man, is sitting by the table. Louise is by the window sewing. A mournful orchestral prelude warns us that all is not well with the humble household; while hints of No. 1A and the first bar of No. 7 tell us plainly where Louise's thoughts are. Her parents, in fact, have not kept their promise to let her return to Julien, and she makes no secret of her discontent.

The Mother comes out from the kitchen with a bowl of herb tea, which she sets on the table by the Father. Then she urges him

to come and sit by the window, where he can get more air and
sunlight and watch the pageant of life in the city. We gather from
his reply that he has just recommenced work after an illness of
twenty days. He has worked all his life, he says, and now he
cannot reconcile himself to idleness. He is not happy—can the
poor ever be happy?—but at all events he knows how to face his
hard lot as a beast of burden with resignation: in a world where all
is injustice, enmity, cruelty, where even one's children disappoint,
going their own selfish way regardless of their parents' claims on
their love, why complain, why repine? Touched to the heart by
his misery, Louise opens the window and looks out sadly into the
night. He follows her with the eyes of a suffering animal. You
bring a child into the world, he continues; you cherish it, and
work for it, and live in it and for it, and when it has grown up it
leaves you for some passing stranger who callously blots the
memory of you out of your child's heart. Curses on these robbers
who destroy the happiness of one's home!

Taking Louise on one side and speaking to her in a low voice,
but overheard, for all that, by the wretched old man at the table,
the Mother tells her plainly that they have no intention of letting
her return to Montmartre and to Julien, whom she insults in the
old way: the girl's duty is to give up everything for her father.
Louise goes to him to say good-night. She offers him her forehead
to kiss: he takes her fondly in his arms, but she is quite unresponsive. Aching with love for her he seats her on his knee, rocks her
like a child, singing her his memories of the old happy days when
they two were all in all to each other. A sort of berceuse runs
through his monologue:

which is perhaps the most affecting piece of music in the whole
work.

Louise tries to make him see how unhappy she herself is, but
he has no eyes or ears now for any sorrow but his own. Do he and
her Mother, he asks her, think of anything but her happiness? Her
answer is that if they truly desire her to be happy they should let
her return to where joy awaits her, not keep her like a bird in a
cage, petted, indeed, but captive. She reproaches her parents with
not having kept their word to Julien. Her Father makes a last
desperate appeal to her affections; and when this looks like failing
he asserts his claim to obedience from her. "Each soul has the
right to be free, each heart the duty to love", she replies, to the
melody of No. 6, "and to suppress the soul that is aspiring to
freedom and love is to be a murderer." The Father cannot recognise his little Louise of old in the girl who talks like this, the
rebellious girl who, knowing that she is all he has in life, would
abandon him in this heartless fashion. Perhaps his passion and his
misery might in the end have softened her; but just then there
float up from the city below the strains of a waltz which has
already been heard in the workroom scene in the second act,
where it was associated with the seductive appeal of Paris. Other
motives with much the same significance follow it. "It is Paris!"
Louise cries rapturously, "Paris is calling me! The great city is
coming to my rescue with its magic! Paris, eternal festival of joy!
Break down the walls of my prison! Let my heart beat against his
once more, if only for a day! Let the poet whose love made the
humble workgirl a Muse come for me and take me away with
him again!" Her parents can no longer recognise their child
in this possessed creature, whose frenzy mounts with the mere
expression of it. The Father, in a paroxysm of rage, runs towards
her as if to strike her down; but mastering himself he flings open
the door and ragingly bids her begone to the Paris she so loves,
to the lights and the dancing and the wantons of her own sort.
Sobered and somewhat terrified by his fury, Louise for a moment
hesitates; but the demented old man pursues her round the room
till at last she has to seek safety in flight.

The lights of the town suddenly die down. Louise has gone:
the room looks dark and empty. The Father's rage has burned

itself out. He runs to the stairs and calls "Louise! Louise!". But there is no answer. He stumbles back slowly and brokenly, clutching at the furniture for support. Thinking he hears Louise returning he looks eagerly towards the door again. But she has gone, this time for ever: and all he can do is to shake an impotent fist at the Paris that has robbed him of everything he had.

PELLEAS AND MELISANDE
Debussy (1862-1918)

PRINCIPAL CHARACTERS

PELLÉAS	*Tenor*
MÉLISANDE	*Soprano*
GENEVIÈVE	*Contralto*
GOLAUD	*Baritone*
ARKËL	*Bass*
YNIOLD	*Soprano*
A DOCTOR	*Bass*

I

Pelléas and Mélisande was the product of a coincidence unique in musical history. Between 1890 and 1892 the young Belgian Maurice Maeterlinck had been feeling his way towards a new type of expression in drama. In the latter year he found himself in the five-act play *Pelléas and Mélisande*. This seemed to many readers to cry out for musical treatment; yet the current idiom of neither French, German nor Italian music was quite appropriate to the shadowy theme or the peculiar diction of the play. During precisely the same period the young Debussy had been reaching out towards a new musical language to the mastery of which he could at last feel that he had attained at the very time when the Belgian dramatist's play was published. The composer's dilemma was that of the playwright reversed: he felt that with his new musical idiom he could create a new type of opera, yet he did not know where to look for a libretto that would match the fluidity and the finesses of that idiom.

Goethe used to maintain that each man's mental life would have been something fundamentally different from what it was had he been born ten years sooner or later. He would have rejoiced at the confirmation of this theory of his supplied by the case of Maeterlinck and Debussy. The two men were born within a week of each other in August 1862. The appearance of one of them in the world

431

ten years before or ten years after that date would have meant that by 1892 he was either too far ahead of the other or too far behind him. What happened in that year was that a new form of dramatic expression, aiming at suggestion rather than statement, at showing not so much character in action as characters in the grip of a fate against which action was futile, found ready for it a new language of music that in its turn shrank in horror from the obviously assertive in melody, in harmony, in colour and in design. Debussy was bent on breaking up the old four-square type of melody, in which a phrase of two, four or eight bars is balanced symmetrically by correspondent phrases of the same length. Instead of promptly resolving dissonances in the traditional manner he prolonged and enchained them, thus giving an impression of endless harmonic fluidity. The language thus created was the only one appropriate to the expression of personages so shadowy, moods so vague, as those of Maeterlinck's play. The gods had brought it about that living within a few miles of each other there were two artists speaking the same tongue, nourished by the same culture, aiming at the same refinements of expression; each of them preferring, as it were, the soft pedal to the loud. It may have been a miracle that these two should have instantaneously found each other, but it was one of those miracles that are occasionally bound to happen. And that the coincidence of the orbits of the two men at the particular time and place of 1892 was one of those things that can happen only once in a century is shown by the subsequent history of both of them. Maeterlinck never again found a musician who understood him as Debussy had done, while Debussy, though he longed to write another opera, never again found a dramatic subject to suit him as *Pelléas and Mélisande* had done.

Maeterlinck's drama was published in Brussels in May 1892. Debussy came across it in Paris a few weeks later, and at once conceived the notion of setting it to music. It must have seemed to him as if it had fallen from heaven into his lap. Some three years before that date he had described to his friends the sort of play he had more or less dimly in mind for the only kind of opera he could imagine himself writing. There were to be no long acts, condemning him to write more music than was necessary, merely to fill up a prescribed mould. Stereotyped symmetries of "poetic" construction were to be avoided, so that his vocal music could model itself more or less on prose speech. People *sang* too much in opera, he thought: singing, in the fullest sense of the term, should be reserved only for the most highly-lit moments of the drama, and in general the vocal line should fluctuate between a melodic recitative and full lyricism, according to the emotional intensity of the situation: operatic characters should no more *sing* sober statements of fact than they should merely *say* things that rose from the very bottom of their heart. The conventional forms of music should not be allowed to determine the structure of a drama even to the extent they do in Wagner; on the contrary, it is the drama that should lead and music that must follow. When he added that in the ideal opera poem as he conceived it the personages would not "discuss" but "submit to life and destiny" he anticipated in the strangest fashion the contribution that Maeterlinck was to make to the solution of his own problem of opera; for if ever there was a world in which men and women do not "discuss" but are helpless corks on the sea of fate it is that of *Pelléas and Mélisande*.

Debussy began by making sketches for a few of the more salient features of the play. He saw a stage performance of the latter in Paris in May 1893, and it was presumably this that determined him to set to work systematically at his opera. He went to Ghent and saw Maeterlinck. He found him completely ignorant of music, but perfectly willing to turn his play over to the composer for his own purposes: he not only authorised him to make whatever cuts he liked but even suggested a few on his own account. The composition progressed slowly, Debussy ruminating over almost every bar and often rejecting later what he himself had imagined to be the definitive form of an episode. He perhaps laboured too long and too hard at this passage or that because he was almost morbidly anxious that every bar should unmistakably bear the Debussy sign manual. He was not getting on as fast with the music as he could have wished, he told a correspondent in 1893. Here and there it reminded him too much of some other composer; more especially did "the phantom of old Klingsor, alias R. Wagner", keep popping out at all sorts of in-

convenient moments, necessitating, he thought, tearing up what
he had just written and setting out afresh in search of something
more "personal".

However, by 1902 the orchestral score was complete. Long
before that, André Messager had become interested in the work.
He in his turn secured the interest of Albert Carré, the director
general of the Paris Opéra-Comique, and it was in that house that
the first performance was given, on the 30th April 1902, with Jean
Périer as Pelléas, Mary Garden (whose English accent was not
precisely an asset) as Mélisande, Dufrane as Golaud, Vieuille as
Arkël, and Mlle Gerville-Réache as Geneviève. Messager conducted. In the first performances the part of Yniold was taken by
a little boy, one Blondin. Just before the production an unfortunate impression was created in Paris by a letter from Maeterlinck
to the director of the *Figaro* which was unworthy of the author of
Wisdom and Destiny and *The Life of the Bee*, and for which the
only possible excuse was the ancient one of the woman in the
case. Maeterlinck seems to have taken it for granted that the part
of Mélisande would be played by his recently acquired wife,
Georgette Leblanc. When he realised that it was not to be so he
suddenly discovered that he totally disagreed with the modifications of his text for which he had given Debussy carte blanche ten
years earlier. The listener, he said, would be able to hear for himself "the extent to which the text of the Opéra-Comique production differs from the authentic one." The performance of the
opera would be given "in spite of him". "In short", he went on
to say, "the *Pelléas* in question is a work that has become foreign,
almost inimical to me; and, deprived as I am of any control over
my own work, I am reduced to hoping that its failure [i.e., that of
the opera] will be immediate and resounding." Far from being a
failure, however, the opera was a success from the start.

2

Debussy did not take over Maeterlinck's text just as it stood.
His most notable omissions were the opening scene of the servants
(which it would have been impossible to realise properly on the
stage), the first scene of the fifth act, in which the servants discuss
the tragedy that has just happened, the first scene of the third act

(Yniold with Pelléas and Mélisande), and the fourth scene of
Act II, in which Arkël dissuades Pelléas from leaving the castle.
Here and there the composer has dovetailed a couple of settings
or has omitted some of Maeterlinck's words: in the fourth act, for
instance, he cuts out everything between Mélisande's "Si, si, je
suis heureuse, mais je suis triste" and Pelléas's "Quel est ce bruit?
On ferme les portes!" There are several occasions when the text
of the opera differs in some small detail from that of the play; but
whether these alterations were made by the composer or the poet
we do not know.

Though certain of the themes in the opera can safely be identified with certain characters, Debussy's use of the leit-motif device
is hardly in the least like Wagner's. The modifications which the
themes undergo in this situation or that are so many and so subtle
that endless quotation would be necessary to show the intimacy
of the connection between the action and the music of the opera.
The following analysis, therefore, will mostly confine itself to a
description of the action, with an occasional citation of a motive
only in its first form, or some form near the first.

The place and time of the drama are legendary. In an ancient
castle by the sea sits an old half-blind King, Arkël by name, wise
with age, mellow with pity for the sorrows of men. With him
is his daughter Geneviève, the mother of an elder son, Golaud,
and of a much younger one, Pelléas, by a different marriage.
Golaud's father is dead; the father of Pelléas, though he does not
appear in the play, we know to be sick somewhere in the castle.

The opera opens with a brief orchestral prelude which sets
before us clearly three of the principal motives. It is difficult, if
not impossible, to attach a definite label to some of the themes of
the work. The solemn opening theme:

is heard again, some twenty-four bars later, at the entry of
Golaud; but it appears in such different circumstances and carries

so many implications in the course of the work that only for convenience' sake can we venture to call it a Golaud motive. There is more warrant for applying that term to the wavering theme which succeeds No. 1 at the fifth bar:

Repetitions of Nos. 1 and 2 bring us, at the fourteenth bar, to a third theme, given out by the oboe over a tremulous shimmer in the strings:

This is undoubtedly to be associated with Mélisande. Nos. 2 and 3 are instantly presented in combination, a symbol, as it were, of the strange blending of the destinies of Golaud and Mélisande.

The curtain rises, revealing the frail, elfin figure of Mélisande by a stream in a forest. Golaud enters to No. 1: he has lost his way in pursuit of a beast he has wounded. He is on the point of retracing his steps when he hears sobbing. Turning round, he sees what looks hardly more than a child sitting by the water's edge. He draws nearer, and at last touches her on the shoulder. She starts up and shrinks from him with a cry of "Do not touch me!", threatening to throw herself into the water if he does so. To all his questions he can get nothing but the vaguest answers. She has been hurt, but she does not know by whom. She has run from somewhere long ago, but does not know where she wants to go. She is lost and frightened. Gleaming at the bottom of the water is a golden crown that has fallen from her head while she was weeping. It was given to her by "him", but who "he" is Golaud does not learn. She will not let Golaud recover it: she will throw herself into the water if he tries. He tells her who he is

—Golaud, grandson of Arkël, the old King of Allemonde; of her he learns no more than that her name is Mélisande. She looks at him with child-like curiosity and comments on him with a child's frankness: he seems to her a giant, and his hair and beard are beginning to grey. It is characteristic of Debussy's entirely non-Wagnerian way of handling his motives that he should use the motive of Mélisande (No. 3) to accompany both her own words descriptive of Golaud, "Oh, your hair is so grey", and Golaud's remark about herself, "I am looking at your eyes. Do you never close your eyes?" Wagner would have shuddered at the thought of employing the Mélisande motive when it was a case of describing Golaud!

No. 3 accompanies also Golaud's reply, "Yes, a few, here, at the temples", but his own motive (No. 2) is heard in counterpoint with it in the orchestra. This counterpoint, however, is not disclosed in the piano score.

Golaud is fascinated and troubled by Mélisande's eyes, which never seem to close. At last he persuades her to go away with him for safety, but whither he himself cannot tell her just then. "I do not know", he says in answer to her question: "I too am lost." The words are a symbol.

The scene changes to a hall in the castle. As usual while the many simple changes of scenery are being effected, the composer carries on with a few bars of orchestral interlude. These interludes, many of which are of extraordinary suggestiveness, seem to have been suggested to Debussy by Albert Carré after his first tentative hearing of the work with the composer at the piano. The present one begins with the wavering Golaud motive (No. 2), and merges into another in the brass:

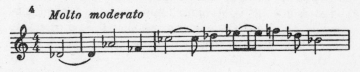

4 *Molto moderato*

The later uses of this authorise us, perhaps, to regard it as the motive of Destiny.

In the castle hall, Geneviève is reading to Arkël a long letter to Pelléas from his brother Golaud, describing how he has found

a terrified girl in the forest, and married her. That was six months
ago, and he still knows no more who the baffling, mysterious
creature is and whence she came than on the day when he saw
her first. Golaud desires Pelléas to prepare Arkël for his home-
coming with Mélisande. (It is made clearer in Maeterlinck than
in Debussy that by this inexplicable marriage Golaud has
brought to naught Arkël's schemes for his kingdom; though we
do discover in the opera, as well as in the play, that at the time
of his meeting with Mélisande in the forest Golaud was on a
mission to ask, at his grandfather's bidding, the hand of a certain
Princess Ursula in marriage). If all is well, the letter continues,
Pelléas is to light a lamp at the top of the tower that overlooks the
sea. If Golaud does not see it there on the third night after the
receipt of his letter he will sail away again and never return.
Geneviève finishes her reading, and the orchestra comments upon
the situation in three bars of lacerating sadness:

Arkël gravely consents. Age has taught him wisdom and
tolerance: what Golaud has done may seem strange, but which of
us has the right to judge the deeds of others and determine their
destiny for them? Geneviève is more troubled, though she sees
that since the death of his first wife Golaud has withdrawn more
and more inwards upon himself and gradually become almost a
stranger to them. While she is speaking Pelléas enters, to the
accompaniment of his characteristic theme:

He has been weeping. He has received, he says, at the same time
as the letter from Golaud, another one informing him that his
friend Marcellus is very ill and longs to see him before he dies.
Arkël, reminding him that his own father is also ill, here in the
castle, persuades him to delay his journey; and as the old King
and Geneviève go out, the latter utters the decisive word: Pelléas
is to light the lamp in the tower that same evening. Arkël has
unwittingly pronounced the doom of Pelléas and Mélisande.

After a few bars of interlude, based on No. 3, a new scene opens
before us. We see Geneviève and Mélisande in front of the castle;
and it is characteristic of Debussy's indifference to ordinary
realistic probability that this scene follows upon its predecessor
after less than ten bars of interlude. We are in a world where the
writ of everyday reality does not run.

Geneviève and Mélisande are discussing the sombreness of the
old castle and its surroundings when Pelléas enters. The three
watch, in the waning light of evening, a great ship leaving the
harbour down below. Mélisande realises that it is the ship that
brought her there. "Why is it leaving tonight?" she asks: she
fears it will be wrecked in the storm that seems to be brewing.
Geneviève having gone into the castle, Pelléas leads Mélisande
by the arm down the rough steep path, which is now almost
completely dark. "I am perhaps going away tomorrow", he says.
"Oh! why are you going?" asks Mélisande; and the orchestra
brings the scene to an end with a most moving reminiscence of
No. 3:

It is like an unanswered question, a question to which there *can*
be no answer. Already we sense Debussy's power to achieve the
maximum of poignancy by the very simplest means, without any
of that "insistence" that made him turn his back on so much even
of the greatest German music. Thus ends a first act in which all
the main threads of the drama have been dexterously introduced

by the dramatist, and dyed by the composer in tints no less tragic because of their extreme delicacy.

3

The setting of the first scene of the second act is a shady spot in the castle park. Pelléas and Mélisande are sitting by a spring, the waters of which, he tells her, are credited by ancient legend with the power to open the eyes of the blind; but no one seems to resort to them now that the King himself is almost blind. (Pelléas's description of this "blindman's well", and Mélisande's question, "Does it open the eyes of the blind no more?" obviously have a symbolical significance that appears to have escaped the notice of the commentators. It is by the waters of this well that the blind eyes of the fated boy and girl are partially opened to the destiny towards which they are being inexorably driven).

The profound emotion of the scene expresses itself against an orchestral background of the most exquisite pastoral beauty. The pair seat themselves on the edge of a marble basin, in the shade of a great lime tree. Mélisande tells Pelléas of her first meeting with Golaud in the forest, of which she remembers little now except that he wanted to kiss her and she would not, though she does not know why. Childlike she is fascinated by the clear water of the spring. She plays thoughtlessly with the ring that Golaud had given her, throwing it high above the water and catching it as it falls, till at last another symbol casts its shadow over the play: the ring slips through her fingers and falls into the water. "We shall never find it again, nor shall we ever find another", she says. "I thought I had it in my hands. . . . I had already closed my hands, and it fell in spite of all. . . . I threw it too high, towards the sun." And what are they to say to Golaud? she asks. "The truth", replies Pelléas, "the truth!"

After the usual orchestral interlude the scene changes to a room in the castle. Golaud, whose horse, he does not know why, had taken fright, bolted madly, thrown him and fallen on him while he was hunting—at the stroke of midday, which was the very time when the ring had been lost in the water—is lying on his bed, tended by Mélisande. She bursts into tears, unhappy for no reason that she can give. He questions her affectionately. Is it the King? Is it Geneviève? Is it Pelléas, who has always been strange, and now is sad that he cannot go to his dying friend Marcellus? Is it the gloomy castle, the sunless forest around it— for the place is very cold and gloomy, and those who live in it are well on in years. The sombreness of which Golaud speaks is painted in a few chords in the orchestra:

Mélisande does not know; she knows only that she is wretched. The sun never shines here; this morning she saw it for the first time—and we hear the briefest and softest of reminiscences, in a flute, of a melody which, in the scene before this, had described the soft plashing and rippling of the water of the stream.

As Golaud takes her little hand in his to comfort her he notices the absence of the ring. She stammers confusedly that it had slipped from her finger that morning in the cave by the sea, where she had gone to gather shells for little Yniold. In great agitation Golaud tells her she must find it immediately, before the sea rises and carries it away. He would rather lose everything he possesses than this ring. If she is afraid of the cave, she must ask Pelléas to accompany her. But she must go at once: he will not sleep until he has his ring again. She goes out weeping.

The scene changes to the entrance to a gloomy cave: Mélisande, accompanied by Pelléas, has gone there at the bidding of Golaud, though she knows well enough it was not there that the ring was lost. She is terrified at the darkness of the cave, which Pelléas describes to her. It is so vast and dangerous that no one has ever explored it to the end: ships have entered and been wrecked there. But the roof is beautiful with its incrustations of salt and crystal, which gleam fitfully when the light of the sky happens to strike on them. When at last the moon pierces the

clouds and floods the entrance, three white-haired old beggars
are seen, sitting side by side against a ledge of rock. There is a
famine in the land, Pelléas explains, and the old men have crept
inside the cave to sleep. As the beggars become visible the harmonies go strangely hollow, taking a form for which Debussy
was certainly indebted to his studies of Moussorgsky:

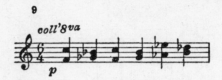

Mélisande flies from the sinister scene in terror, followed by
Pelléas, saying "We will return another day."

Debussy ends his second act here; but in Maeterlinck there
comes now a short scene between Arkël and Pelléas—in a room
in the castle—which we are surprised that the composer did not
set to music. Pelléas again wishes to leave the castle, and once
more the old King dissuades him from doing so. It is true, he
says, that Marcellus is dead, but there are other duties for Pelléas,
as for all men, than the visiting of graves. Pelléas's father is so
gravely ill that almost certainly he will not recover. The land is
threatened by enemies; the people are dying of hunger; is this the
time for Prince Pelléas to go far away? Still, says Arkël, he will
leave the decision to the young man himself—"for you must
know better than I what events you ought to offer to your being
or your destiny. I ask you only to wait until we know what is
to happen." "How long shall I have to wait?" asks Pelléas.
Thus for the second time, and in a scene in which every word
seems heavy with fate, Arkël pens the boy within the narrow plot
of earth where danger and death lurk for him: Arkël, who claims
to have learned from life at least one lesson of wisdom, that none
of us has the right to put himself in the way of the destiny of
another, becomes unconsciously the main instrument for with-
holding Pelléas from finding another destiny than the one
awaiting him in the castle. Had the profound significance of the
scene escaped Debussy, one wonders? Did he think a second
scene of this kind superfluous? Or had he, in fact, missed the

deep symbolism of the "letter" scene also, and taken this into his own plan only because, with its explanation of certain material things, it seemed to him essential to the elucidation of the action? It is impossible to say.

4

In the cruder theatrical sense very little "happens" in *Pelléas and Mélisande*, yet the drama mounts to its tragic dénouement with consummate art. All that has taken place so far has been a preparation for the warmly lyrical third act, in which the hapless lovers at last, and unexpectedly, find each other. In the fourth act, tragedy comes swift on the heels of ecstasy; and in the fifth the waves of destiny close over the heads of these pitiful creatures, in the soul of none of whom was any evil.

Maeterlinck's first scene—that of Mélisande, Pelléas and Yniold (Golaud's little son by his first marriage) in a room in the castle—is omitted from the opera, which begins with the second scene of the play. The setting is one of the castle towers, where Mélisande is combing her hair at a window. The introductory orchestral music is calm and sweet. Mélisande sings a snatch or two of a simple song, "Saint Daniel et Saint Michel, Saint Michel[1] et Saint Raphaël, Je suis née un dimanche, Un diman che à midi."

Pelléas appears on a sentry path that runs below the tower window. The enchantment of the night soon works upon them both. At Pelléas's request Mélisande leans out of the window, and he strains upward to her. He begs her to give him her hand to kiss, for he intends to leave on the morrow. She implores him to delay his departure, and as she bends lower and lower to him to reach his hand with hers, her long hair suddenly descends upon him, inundating him with its glory.

This marks the commencement of the great scene that is the lyrical high-light of the opera. It is characteristic of Debussy's

---

[1] The song that appears in all the editions of the play since about 1895—five stanzas commencing,

> Les trois sœurs aveugles,
> (Espérons encore),
> Les trois sœurs aveugles
> Ont leur lampes d'or,

—is a later addition by Maeterlinck to his original text.

horror of the insistent that after one swift surge of tone in the orchestra,—at the moment when Mélisande's hair descends— lasting no more than a couple of bars, both voices and orchestra are immediately hushed. It is now that the pair pour out their overloaded hearts to each other, and what they have to say is at once so profound and so intimate in its emotion that, paradoxical as this may seem in opera, it cannot be said in any but the quietest tones. Only rarely in the course of the long duet does the tone rise much above *piano*, but within the narrow scale of dynamics which Debussy permits himself there is plane after plane of passion. There comes a *fortissimo* gush of sound when Pelléas, intoxicated with the beauty of Mélisande's hair, which is in his hands, about his arms, around his neck and in his mouth, cries out that her tresses are like living birds in his hands, "and they love me, they love me more than you!" Then once more his emotion, precisely because of its intensity, expresses itself in a new lowering of the voice.

At the height of their rapture they are startled by a sudden fluttering of doves about them, flying from the tower; and while Mélisande, sensing the approach of evil, tries in vain to raise her head, for her hair is entangled in the branches of a tree, footsteps are heard approaching. "It is Golaud!" says Mélisande, ... "I believe it is Golaud! He has heard us!" ... and a whisper and an expressive chord or two are all that Debussy needs to make us hold our breath with apprehension, as Pelléas and Mélisande do:

10

C'est Go - laud!

Almost invariably Debussy's quietude of manner increases in proportion to the gravity of what he has to say.

"What are you doing here?" Golaud asks. Pelléas is too confused to answer. "You are children", continues Golaud. "Mélisande, do not lean so far out of the window: you will fall. . . . Do you not know that it is late? It is close on midnight. Do not play thus in the dark." And then, with a nervous laugh, "You are children. . . . What children! . . . What children!", and he goes away with Pelléas.

The orchestral interlude that follows is one of the most moving episodes in the opera: Debussy distils the last drop of poignancy out of the succession and apposition of the motives of Golaud, Mélisande and Pelléas (Nos. 2, 3 and 6).

The colouring of the interlude gradually darkens as we make our way, in imagination, to the castle vaults, where Golaud and Pelléas are discovered when the curtain rises. Perhaps Golaud does not quite know himself why he has brought his brother to this gloomy, infected place, where a stench of death comes up from the stagnant water. Pelléas walks circumspectly in front of Golaud, who carries a lantern. The older man holds the younger by the arm, ostensibly to keep him from slipping over the abyss. But the light that the lantern casts on their path is a flickering one, for Golaud's hand is trembling, like his voice. A strange episode, the force of which resides in the fact that, while not a word is said on either side about what happened outside the tower, we feel it to be the one matter really occupying the mind of each of them. At length they leave this sinister place, with its stifling odour of death, for the clean upper air.

The transition to the sunlit terrace, where the fresh morning breeze blows in from the sea, and the scent of newly watered flowers rises from the beds, and the bells are ringing as the children go down to the beach to bathe, is skilfully managed in the usual orchestral interlude. It is only now that Golaud can speak of what is uppermost in his mind. He knows, he says, that what happened yesterday evening between his brother and Mélisande was only child's play, but it must not be repeated. Mélisande is very young, very impressionable, and about to become a mother: she must be handled very delicately, lest misfortune befall her. Pelléas must avoid her as much as possible, though not markedly. Pelléas does not reply. In the play, Golaud at this point sees something in the distance that turns out to be a flock of sheep being led to the town. "They are crying like lost children", he says; "one would say they already smelt the butcher." It is curious that Debussy should have neglected to set these few lines, with their obvious tragic symbolism.[1] Maeterlinck knew well what he was doing when he ended the scene with them.

Golaud and Pelléas go out in silence, and the scene changes to a space in front of the castle. Golaud takes his little Yniold on his knee and gets him to talk about his Uncle Pelléas and his little mother Mélisande. Are they often together? the tortured man asks. What do they say to each other? Do they ever speak of him, Golaud? Do they kiss? He raises the child on his shoulders to the height of the window that looks into Mélisande's room; and in an amazingly dramatic scene—it is characteristic, by the way, both of Maeterlinck and Debussy that it is through the medium of the child's innocent prattling that the tragic tension is brought to its breaking point—Yniold describes how Pelléas is there with little mother, and they are saying nothing, only looking with fixed eyes at the light, as if they were expecting something to happen. At last terror seizes on the child, and he calls to his father to let him down. Golaud has learned nothing of what he so desires and so fears to know; and as he and Yniold go out together, No. 2 in the orchestra paints the anguish of which he cannot speak to anyone.

5

In the fourth act events move more swiftly.

Pelléas and Mélisande meet in a passage in the castle. Pelléas has come from the sick room of his father, who seems now to be out of danger. But the young man has a foreboding of catastrophe. His father had taken him kindly by the hand and said, looking at him strangely, "Is that you, Pelléas? Why, I never noticed it before, but you have the grave, friendly face of those

[1] Perhaps he did not do so because he wanted to set in full the later episode (act IV, scene 3) of the sheep being driven to the butcher. But three or four bars would have sufficed for the handling of the half-dozen suggestive lines which Maeterlinck puts into the mouth of Golaud.

who have not long to live.... You must travel; you must travel."
Pelléas has resolved to obey him; this is his last evening in the
castle, and he and Mélisande will never meet again. But he must
see Mélisande alone before he goes; and they agree to meet by
blindman's well in the park.

Pelléas having left, Arkël enters. Now that Pélleas's father is
out of danger, he tells Mélisande, he hopes that sunlight and joy
will visit the ancient place again. He has pitied Mélisande ever
since she entered the castle, pitied that bewildered look of hers
as of one who is expecting some great misfortune. He believes
that young and beautiful beings have the gift of shaping about
themselves events that are warm with youth, beauty and happiness. But Mélisande remains silent, her eyes turned to the ground;
and the old man's heart goes out to her in a fresh surge of pity.

Golaud enters, visibly distracted, and with blood on his forehead: "I have been through a hedge of thorns", he explains, in
one of the many sentences in the play that carry a sinister double
meaning. Mélisande would wipe his brow; but he repulses her
roughly and orders her to bring him his sword. His pain of soul
drives him on to a crescendo of fury and brutality. Why does she
look at him as she is doing? he asks her; and he calls Arkël's
attention to those fixed, wide-open eyes of hers. "I can see nothing in them but a great innocence", says the old King. "Great
innocence": Golaud repeats: "they are greater than innocence!
They are purer than the eyes of a lamb.... They could give
lessons in innocence to God!" Yet he will know the secrets of the
other world before he can read the secret of those eyes. "Close
them! close them!" he stammers, "or I will close them for long."
He takes her hands, then lets them go in an agony of physical
repulsion. He seizes her by the hair and forces her to her knees,
now to the right, now to the left, raging, laughing hysterically,
then suddenly growing calm again and affecting indifference.
"You shall do as you please", he tells Mélisande. "I attach no
importance to it. I am too old, and then, I am not a spy. I shall
wait to see what chance brings, and then..." Arkël stands
amazed at the half-insane outburst. Mélisande bursts into tears
after Golaud has gone: "He does not love me any more", she
moans. "I am not happy!... I am not happy!" "If I were God

P*

I should pity the heart of men", says the old King quietly; and after that it is left to the orchestra to probe the pathos of the situation to its depths.

The scene changes to the park, where Yniold is vainly trying with his little hands to raise a big stone under which his ball has run. In the distance he hears the bleating of sheep. He runs to the edge of the terrace and watches them advancing in the dying light of the sun—so many of them that he cannot count them, all huddled together as if they were afraid of the dark. They run fast till they reach the big cross-road, and from there they do not know where to go. They seem to want to go to the right, but the shepherd throws earth at them and makes them turn aside. But why are they now so suddenly silent? And the invisible shepherd gives him the answer—"Because it is no longer the way to the fold." Something seems to constrict the heart of the child, who runs out to look for someone who may comfort him. It is a great pity that this moving episode should be omitted as it is in many performances.

Pelléas enters. Soon, he muses, he will have left the castle, leaving behind him everything that binds him to life. But he must see Mélisande first, to look into the depths of her heart and say what he has not yet said. When she comes he draws her out of the edge of the moonlight into the shade of a great lime-tree, where they cannot be seen from the tower window. He bids her farewell and kisses her. "I love you", he says; and she replies, in the lowest of voices, "And I love you too." That is all! The drama has at last reached its climax, and this is all the pair have to say to each other—and they indeed say it rather than sing it, without even a supporting note from the orchestra:

11

Je t'ai - me.   Je t'aime aus - si

It is a violation of all the centuries-old rules of opera, which lay it down that when lovers find each other there shall be no limit to their rapture. But it is one of Debussy's supreme strokes of

genius: there are few things in the whole range of opera that catch
at the heart as these half-dozen simple unsung words do. This
is the veritable triumph of reticence: at what any other dramatist
and composer would have seen to it was the peak-point of impassioned statement Maeterlinck and Debussy lead us to the very
verge of silence, but what a silence! A silence which, so far from
being empty, seems to hold all the immensities within it.

The young pair lose themselves in tender poetic memories and
images:

Pelléas, in his great happiness, would draw Mélisande into the
light, but it is now she whom a dim instinct bids remain in the
shadow of the tree, though there they cannot see each other's
eyes. "I am happy", she says, "but I am sad." From the castle
comes a dull sound of doors being closed and chains being fixed
and bolts being shot. It is too late now for them to re-enter. All
is lost, says Pelléas, yet all is saved! For now there can be no
going back in any sense. As they embrace madly, Mélisande
hears a stealthy footstep and the crackle of dead leaves. Pelléas
will not listen to her warning; he hears nothing but the beating
of her heart and his own. But Mélisande's eyes, piercing the
gloom, see Golaud crouching behind a tree, no further from
them than the tip of their shadows: his sword is drawn, and
Pelléas is without his. "Do not move", Pelléas whispers, "do not
turn your head. He will rush out upon us!" They embrace distractedly for the last time as Golaud rushes on them sword in
hand. He strikes Pelléas, who falls dead beside the spring.
Mélisande flies in terror, pursued by Golaud in silence.

6

With the deletion of Maeterlinck's scene of the servants at the
commencement of Act V, only one scene remains to bring
Debussy's opera to a close.

The setting is a room in the castle. Mélisande is lying on her bed, while in a corner of the room Golaud, Arkël and a Doctor are seen in conversation. (From the talk of the servants we have gathered that Golaud and Mélisande had been found lying in front of the castle door, he with his own sword still sticking in his side, she wounded nearly to death. But Golaud is strong and is now all but cured, while Mélisande, on her deathbed, has been delivered of a puny child). It is not of so small a wound—one not big enough to kill a bird,—that Mélisande can be dying, says the Doctor, therefore Golaud need not distress himself, for it is not he who has killed her. She was born for no reason but to die, and now she is dying for no reason. But Golaud breaks out into bitter reproaches against himself. "They had simply kissed each other like little children, as if they had been brother and sister. And I . . . I did it in spite of myself."

Mélisande awakes and asks Arkël to have the big window opened, that she may see the sun going down on the sea. Never has she felt better, she tells him, but it seems to her as if she knew something. What that something is we learn from a sad little phrase in the oboe which will afterwards be associated with the new-born child:

13

She is told that Golaud is in the room, and she wonders why he does not come to her. He drags himself to the bed, and at his request the other two leave him alone with her for a while. He begs Mélisande to forgive him, but she asks him what there is to forgive. He has done her great wrong, he moans. He sees it clearly now. All that has happened has been his fault, but he loved her so! And now they are both about to die, she first, then himself; and to a dying man one must speak the truth. Did she love Pelléas? "Yes", she murmurs: "I loved him. Where is he?" But that is not what he wants to know. Did she love him with a forbidden love? Were they guilty? "No, no"; she replies; "we were not guilty. Why do you ask that?" But only one answer, the one he desires and yet fears, and desires all the more because he fears it, will satisfy the self-tortured man. He implores her, for the love of God, to tell him the truth. Then, baffled once more, he recalls Arkël and the Doctor. He bewails the ignorance in which he is to be left: "I shall never know!" he cries; "I shall die here like one blind!"

Is it true that winter is coming? Mélisande asks the King, for she is so afraid of the cold. They place by her the child, of which till now she knew nothing; but she is too weak to take it in her arms. The servants enter one by one and range themselves along the walls of the room in silence—a sign that death is near at hand. Golaud breaks out in impotent rage against them, but they answer nothing. He turns again to Mélisande in a last passionate desire to speak alone with her once more. But Arkël bids him leave her in peace, for the human soul, he says, is timid and silent and loves to steal away alone. Suddenly the servants fall on their knees at the further end of the room. The Doctor approaches the bed and touches Mélisande. "They are right!" he says. Golaud breaks into sobs. Arkël leads him away, trying to comfort him: "She needs silence now. It is terrible, but the fault is not yours. She was a gentle little soul, so timid, so silent, a poor little mysterious creature, like all the world. She lies there as if she were her child's big sister. . . . The child must not stay here. . . . It must live now in her stead: it is the poor little one's turn." The theme of the child (No. 13) threads its way delicately through the texture, and the curtain falls to a last murmured suggestion of the Mélisande motive (No. 3).

THE BARTERED BRIDE
Bedřich Smetana (1824-1884)

PRINCIPAL CHARACTERS[1]

KRUSCHINA	*Baritone*
KATHINKA	*Soprano*
MARIE	*Soprano*
MICHA	*Bass*
AGNES	*Mezzo-Soprano*
WENZEL	*Tenor*
HANS	*Tenor*
KEZAL	*Bass*
SPRINGER	*Tenor*
ESMERALDA	*Soprano*
MUFF	*Tenor*

I

When the centenary of Smetana's birth was celebrated in 1924, all Czechoslovakia, we are told, made a point of doing him honour. During his lifetime, however, his services to the cause of Czech music were not so fully recognised.

Born in south-east Bohemia in 1824, it was not until his twentieth year that he succeeded in persuading his father to let him go to Prague in order to devote his life to music. Lack of opportunities in the capital drove him, in 1856, to Gothenburg, in Sweden, where he remained until 1861. During this Swedish period no one could have sensed in him the future Czech musical nationalist: he paddled in the backwash of the "New German" school, writing symphonic poems after the manner of Liszt. But

[1] The names are given as they appear in the German version of the opera because (1) it is in the German version that the ordinary opera-goer is most likely to hear the work, and (2) the German score is the one he is most likely to possess. To employ, therefore, in the following analysis such names as Marenka, Jenik, Kecal and Vasek (instead of Marie, Hans, Kezal and Wenzel) would only confuse the non-Czech reader.

by the time he returned to his native land the current of national revival had set in fairly strongly in Bohemia; and Smetana became as ardently national as the best of his compatriots. Till then the country had been thoroughly Germanised where art was concerned: Hanslick, who had lived in Prague in his youth, assures us that in the first half of the century people of quality might send their servants to theatrical performances in Czech, but they would never have dreamed of going to anything of that kind themselves. Smetana's own education had been mainly along German lines: as late as 1860 we find him apologising to a correspondent for possible errors of grammar and orthography in a letter he had written in Czech. German, in fact, was the ordinary language of the upper and the educated classes and of those engaged in trade: the Czech aristocracy employed their native tongue only for conversation with their native servants.

In 1862 the rising national spirit of the Czechs found expression in the establishment of a Provisional National Theatre; and it was here that Smetana's first opera, *The Brandenburgers in Bohemia*, received its first performance in January 1866, the composer conducting. The librettist of this work, Karel Sabina, provided Smetana also with the text of his second opera, the now famous *Bartered Bride*. The music to this was written between May 1863 and March 1866; the opera was produced, under Smetana himself, on the 30th May of the latter year. Originally it was in two acts. It was given in a revised and expanded version on the 29th January 1869, still nominally in two acts, though the first was now divided into two tableaux. A third version, this time in three acts, saw the light on the 1st June of the same year; for this production Smetana added the Furiant and the Polka. To give the opera its definitive form the composer had now only to replace the spoken portions by recitative. In this form *The Bartered Bride* was first given in the Prague Provisional Theatre on the 25th September 1870.

Smetana completed six other operas during the next dozen years or so; but the chances of most of them were prejudiced for a long time by the increasing popularity of *The Bartered Bride*, which became more and more a symbol, for the Czechs, of their national spirit. This work received its hundredth performance in

1882; and on that occasion Smetana publicly declared that he himself had never taken *The Bartered Bride* as seriously as the public had done: he had written it, he said, without particularly believing in it, just to show that he could be as national as anyone when he chose to be so, he having been annoyed in 1866 by the verdict of the critics and some of the public that *The Branden-burgers in Bohemia* was too heavy and too Wagnerian. No one, however, has taken this declaration literally: it is generally held that Smetana was merely trying to pay back the Czech public for its relative coolness towards his later operas. It took that public, in fact, a fairly long time to perceive how fundamentally Bohemian he was even when not writing so specifically in the national vein as he had done in *The Bartered Bride*. For the Germans he was mostly a Czech; while for many Czechs he was either too Czech, or not Czech enough, or Czech in the wrong way. He had to pay the penalty usually exacted by the world of the artist who achieves a striking success in a particular vein—henceforth he departs from that vein at his peril, while if he continues in it he is perpetually reproached for not rising in his new works to the level of the model he himself had created.

So in the last few years of his life Smetana was an embittered man; even his popularity had a sourish taste about it for him. From the mid-1870's he had been afflicted with deafness; a distressing feature of the malady was the persistent ringing of one high note in his brain, an experience which, he himself assures us, he has drawn upon in the finale of his E minor string quartet—one of the two works of his in this genre that bear the general title of "From My Life". (In the quartet the note in question is E; but as a matter of fact the note that haunted Smetana was the high A flat). By the early 1880's his health had deteriorated beyond repair; and not the least tragic feature of his case was that he realised all along, from his doctor's reports, that there was a possibility of his losing his reason. That disaster fell on him while he was engaged on his last opera, *Viola*. He was not in a condition to attend the concert given in Prague on the 2nd March 1884 in honour of his sixtieth birthday. A few weeks later, on the 20th April, he voluntarily entered an asylum, where he died on the 12th May.

2

The lively overture, which has become so popular in the concert room, makes use of some four or five themes from the opera itself. It begins with the lusty melody of the folk-rejoicings at the end of the second act (No. 15), which, at the eighth bar, shifts over from F major to D minor, in which latter key the true first main theme of the overture (No. 16) is launched and developed quasi-fugally till it reaches No. 17—a melody sung by the villagers in the finale to the second act. No. 17 passes through various metamorphoses before it reaches its climax in No. 18, which in the opera also is the logical continuation of No. 17. The next theme (No. 19) is taken from the same finale. This constitutes the whole of the thematic material of the overture, the remainder of it being devoted to developments and repetitions. It will thus be seen that the overture is from first to last a picture of Czech rustic life.

The setting of the opening scene is a village in Bohemia; on one side of the stage is an inn. It is the spring of the year, and the fête-day of the consecration of the church: the whole village, including the priest, is enjoying itself to music of the popular type, such as:

The people break into a chorus in praise of spring:

through which, however, runs a rather significant warning to the young not to plunge into matrimony without taking due care. Two people who do not seem as hilarious as the rest are Hans and Marie. They love each other, but there are difficulties in their path, for the beautiful Marie Kruschina is much sought after in the locality, while Hans, though undeniably good-looking, is as poor as a church mouse; nor does anyone know much more about him than that he had come to the village a longish while ago from afar. By a simple transposition of No. 2 into the minor, Smetana gives the lovers all the musical material they need for the exchange of their sad confidences. It appears that Marie's mother has told her that this very day the husband chosen for her—of whom she as yet knows nothing at all—will be coming to claim her. Hans exhorts her to stand firm. The crowd also are quite sympathetic, but they have other things to think about than Marie and her troubles: they soon resume their merry chorus (No. 2), and then, to the enticing strain of No. 1, go off to dance, leaving Hans and Marie alone.

In simple accents she tells Hans how much she loves him:

(The rhythm here, the change in the third bar, and the echo in the fourth, are all very characteristic of Smetana). Marie reminds Hans that she still knows little about himself and nothing about his origins, for he never speaks to anyone of his early days: she has given herself to him trustfully, and it would break her heart if he were to prove untrue to her now. He tells her that if he speaks so little of his youth it is because the subject is a painful one: he comes of a rich family, but his mother died, his father had married again, and the second wife had turned her husband's heart against his son, who had been driven from home and forced to seek a living far away from his native place. Marie comforts him, and they pour out their simple love for each other, and their hopes of a happy union, in a succession of those snuggling, cuddling sixths:

which are almost immemorially associated with lovers in opera.

Hans goes away and Marie conceals herself as three people are seen approaching. They are her father, Kruschina, her mother, Kathinka, and a personage peculiarly Czech, the professional marriage broker Kezal. The latter is a figure that hits the eye, his calling, apparently, requiring a good deal of strong accent in the colour and cut of his clothes. He has come to tell the parents that, thanks to his well-known skill in these matters, everything is as good as arranged: he has found a husband for Marie, and all that remains to be done now is to bring the young couple together and for the parents to confirm the deal. What he has to say he invariably says with a great deal of breathless repetition, both of words and notes:

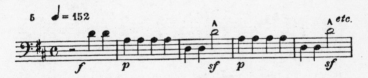

and especially with a flood of fussy, gabbling quavers:

The music flows on in broader lines when the less excitable

Kruschina and Kathinka discuss the affair. The father is inclined to leave the whole business to Kezal, but the mother thinks that Marie ought to have some say in the matter. Kezal, for his part, thinks this unnecessary; the parents' consent being all that is required, the rest of the arrangements can safely be left in his competent hands. The destined bridegroom is the younger son of the rich peasant Tobias Micha. Kruschina replies that he knows Micha well enough, but he hardly so much as remembers the names of his two sons. Kezal reminds him that years ago he had promised his daughter, in quite binding form, to Micha's son. But which son? asks Kruschina. He has only one, Kezal answers —the younger one, Wenzel by name, for the other one, by the first marriage, disappeared years ago and is regarded as dead.

But why has Wenzel himself not put in an appearance? asks Kruschina. Kezal explains that the young man would certainly have accompanied him but for the too exquisite delicacy of his sensibilities; few people, it seems, can compare with him for either soundness of morals or refinement of manners. Kezal unrolls the long catalogue of Wenzel's virtues in a solo based on a series of purling imitations between the outer and the inner parts:

The solo becomes a trio as Kruschina and Kathinka add comments of their own to Kezal's seemingly interminable laudation of the young man: they could wish that the bridegroom had presented himself in person, but all the same they are conscious of the honour that is being done them by marriage into so rich a family.

Just then Marie re-enters. She is told that they have a husband in prospect for her, but her mother whispers in her ear that if she does not approve of him she has only to refuse to marry him.

Kezal suggests a wedding within a month. Marie rejoins that there is one insuperable objection to that; and a reminiscence in the orchestra of the honeyed sixths of No. 4 makes it clear enough to us what that objection is. But for a while she will not give them the name of the man she loves, let Kezal, who is not accustomed to obstacles of this kind in his business, protest and rail at her as he will. At last she confesses that she has become betrothed to Hans that very day. The father is annoyed at this, the mother thinks she has been rather imprudent, and Kezal flourishes before Kruschina's eyes, as his trump card, the written contract with Micha. But Marie knocks the paper out of his hand and flounces out with her nose in the air. Even Kezal is for the moment thrown a bit out of his stride by this opposition. Kruschina repeats that it is a pity he has not brought the wooer with him; and the broker can only assure him once more that the reason why Wenzel did not come was that he is excessively modest and shy, and not at his best in female society. The broker suggests that the parents had better go and talk the matter over themselves with Tobias Micha, who is alone in the inn, everyone else in the village having gone off to the dance.

When the three have left the stage the villagers pour in from all sides. The elders seat themselves at the tables in front of the inn, the younger ones prepare to dance. The act ends with a charming polka:

that is completed by a snatch of choral song that includes a delightful little piece of melodic and harmonic naïveté:

The curtain falls with them still dancing and singing, and Kezal sorely puzzled at the unexpected bit of grit that has got into his machinery.

3

The second act, the scene of which is the interior of the inn, opens with a chorus, in true Czech rhythm, in praise of beer. Kezal has come there to get in touch with Hans, who, though drinking with the others, is sunk in moody reflection upon his and Marie's troubles. When, however, Kezal toasts money as the only thing worth having, he rouses himself sufficiently to say that love appeals to him more.

Girls come in, and the peasants dance to a fine furiant:

the middle section of which is composed of the contrapuntal combination of two expressive melodies. After the dance the room empties, and Wenzel comes in very shyly and hesitatingly. He achieves the feat—easier perhaps, on the stage than in real life—of looking as silly as he is. He cannot speak without stammering, a defect which Smetana plays upon graphically not only in Wenzel's vocal line but in the orchestral accompaniment:

The burden of his song is that his mother has told him that it is time he plucked up courage enough to face the problems of wooing and marriage. He obviously does not like the job, but he is afraid of being laughed at if he returns without having tackled it. Marie enters, and, sensing at once that he is the prospective bridegroom, begins to take advantage of his all too evident simplicity. She enquires if he is the young man intended for Marie Kruschina. He replies that he is. In that case she is sorry for him, she says, as indeed, are all the other girls of the village; for he is so handsome, and this Marie whom the elders are trying to foist on him is no better than she should be: she is, in fact, in love with another man, and will only make a fool of Wenzel. He is horrified: he *must* get married, he tells her, because his mother said so when she sent him here. Marie assures him coquettishly that she knows a maiden who will suit him very much better:

and who has long admired him at a distance. But his mother will cry blue murder, says poor Wenzel; moreover, what about the effect on this Marie Kruschina of a transfer of his attentions to another? Marie assures him that he need not trouble about all that; Kruschina's daughter will soon console herself, and the other maiden of whom she is speaking is just as young, just as beautiful and just as good a match as she is. It gradually dawns on Wenzel's intelligence that the proposed substitute may be the very attractive girl now talking to him; and in the end, though not without some difficulty, she manages to make him swear that he will refuse Marie. He tries to embrace her, but she evades him; and as he runs after her on one side of the stage, Hans and Kezal enter on the other.

The broker has particularly set his heart on carrying through the marriage of Kruschina's daughter and the rich son of Tobias Micha, because his commission on the transaction will be an unusually large one. In view of that he feels he can afford a little expenditure to get Hans out of the way. He learns that the young man is unknown in the locality, friendless and very poor. He points out to him that there is any number of nice girls to be had for the asking, argues that nothing in this world can be done without money, and, in a charming duet with the young man:

hints that he knows a maiden, not without means, whom any man would consider himself fortunate to marry. In the end he suggests that Hans shall transfer his right to the hand of Marie Kruschina to Tobias Micha's son for the sum of three hundred gulden, cash down. Hans agrees, having first obtained from Kezal an assurance that the girl shall marry no one but Micha's son, and further that when this son and Marie are joined in matrimony the groom's father shall not demand repayment of the money. Kezal goes off exceedingly pleased with himself. Hans smiles at the beautiful thought that the broker has fallen into the trap he had set for another, and sings a tender little song to Marie:

Thanks to his strategy, he thinks, all will soon be well with both of them.

The villagers, who can never be kept for long out of this Bohemian folk-comedy, now come upon the scene for the finale to the act. Among them is Kezal, who gives them to understand that he has something of importance to tell them. The orchestra pours out a flood of lively music in the true folk-vein: as we have seen, indeed, it is upon this finale that Smetana draws for the entire material of his overture. The finale begins precisely as the overture does:

This is followed by:

which, however, is not developed here as it is in the overture. Kezal promises the villagers some exciting news if only they will keep quiet for a moment; they are to witness the signing of a certain document and then declare whether it is in order or not:

to which they joyously consent:

They crowd round Kezal and look over his shoulder as he reads out the projected agreement with Hans—"I renounce the bride" —to which Hans, also reading from the document, adds, "in favour of no other than the son of Tobias Micha." All the principals, Kezal, Kruschina and Hans seem very pleased at the way the matter has been settled:

The villagers, however, are a trifle puzzled by it all; but when they learn that Hans has agreed to renounce Marie in consideration of a cash payment of three hundred gulden they are shocked at his callousness and cupidity; even old Kruschina would never have believed this of him! Hans signs amid general execration—"Shame on him! He has bartered away his bride!" But Hans has his own private views about the affair.

4

The setting of the third act is the same as that of the first. When the curtain rises we see Wenzel sitting there alone, brooding over his new troubles to the accompaniment of No. 11 in the orchestra. He is exceedingly depressed, he assures us in an amusing stuttering monologue:

20

Love is more difficult than he could have imagined: the charming damsel who had torn from him a promise to forget Marie has left him in the lurch, and he trembles at the thought of what his mother will say to him when she hears the mess he has made of things.

His lamentations are interrupted by the arrival of a troupe of travelling comedians, accompanied, of course, by the villagers, all agog to see the show. The director of the company, Springer, promises them a rich entertainment later in the afternoon; among the wonders they will see is the beautiful Esmeralda, a genuine Spaniard, without her equal in the world on the tight-rope, and a real bear from the American backwoods, who will dance a pas de deux with Esmeralda. To prove the truth of what he says, the villagers shall have a specimen here and now of what the troupe can do. The comedians thereupon dance, to some of Smetana's most delightful Czech tunes, and afterwards go off followed by the gaping crowd.

Only Esmeralda, the director and Wenzel remain behind. A

messenger comes running in with the dreadful news that the man who plays the part of the bear has got so drunk that a performance of that part of the programme is out of the question. The director is greatly perturbed; not only is his honour as an artist at stake but he fears he will be pelted by the populace if he does not deliver the goods he has promised them. The messenger— one Muff, who plays "Indian" parts in the company—assures the distracted man that he has sought high and low for a substitute, but in vain—this villager is too fat, that one is too thin, a third does not like the idea of getting into the bear's skin, and so on.

But Esmeralda has an idea. Why not rope in the vacant-looking gawk who has been staring at her with wide-open eyes all this time, evidently fascinated by her? As the Indian remarks, this booby is just the right size and build for the part. The director plays the fish—how would he like to dance with the beautiful Spanish lady? he asks him—and Esmeralda lands him. What a chance, they point out, for him to become an artist like themselves, seeing all there is to see of the world, to say nothing of the good time he can have in private! Esmeralda encourages Wenzel at any rate to make a trial. He stammers out that he does not think his mother would like him to be a bear; but she assures him that she will not recognise her darling son. She makes him practise, in grotesque fashion, a few steps with her, and gives him an elementary lesson in ursine love-making.

The director and Esmeralda go off, signing to Wenzel to follow them. He is about to do so, but thinks better of it when he catches sight of his father and mother. He is practising a few more steps, and congratulating himself on his run of success with pretty girls, when Agnes (his mother) enters, accompanied by Tobias, Kezal, and a number of the peasants. Agnes and Micha want to take him away with them to meet the bride they have found for him and sign the marriage contract. But when he hears the name of the bride—Marie Kruschina—he recoils in horror. He has been warned against this Marie, he tells them, by a charming maiden who had confessed that she was in love with him. When he admits, however, that he does not even know the maiden's name, and runs away from them with more defiance than they would have thought him capable of, they feel it is high time they took their rebellious offspring in hand.

Before they can decide on anything a commotion is heard outside. Marie enters in great agitation, followed by Kruschina and Kathinka. She refuses to believe that Hans has sold her for three hundred gulden until Kezal proves it to her in black and white. Then she breaks down, bursts into tears, and, to the soft accompaniment of No. 4 in the orchestra, recalls how only an hour or so ago he had sworn eternal truth to her. Her mother tries to comfort her with the assurance that they have already found a better husband for her, but poor Marie is not to be consoled so easily. Kezal, seeing Wenzel a little way off, calls to him. Wenzel's sulky expression changes to one of rapture when he sees the delightful maiden who, not so long ago, had told him how much she admired and loved him. The others see their problem solved for them at last. "Why, this is the very bride we had chosen for you!" they tell Wenzel. Though he does not quite grasp the new situation he goes off rather pleased with himself. The others, after having exhorted Marie to think it over and be sensible, also go away.

Marie, now alone, pours out her grief in an expressive aria. How changed the world is since yesterday! she sighs: how beautiful everything was then, how cold and joyless it is now!

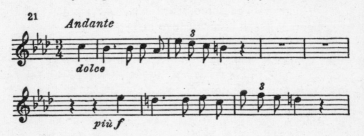

Spring seems to have fled, and autumn to have come before its time. Then a quick change comes over the spirit of her song. The world, after all, is as lovely as ever, she sings; it is only because her eyes are dim with tears that it looked so grey to her a moment ago. How lovely is the spring time, even if her own broken heart will never thrill to its warmth again!

She is still in this melancholy mood when Hans comes in, in the highest spirits. She turns on him angrily, and it takes him a little while to realise that she has taken his supposed treachery quite seriously. She, for her part, finds it difficult to understand how the faithless fellow can be so cheerful about it. He is vastly amused when she tells him that she is now betrothed to Wenzel, and he asks her just to listen to him for a moment while he tells her something that will interest her:

On this theme a delightful little duet is built up, Marie, of course, refusing to be taken in by him a second time.

They are still arguing it out when Kezal enters and spoils everything with the remark that Hans can have his money as soon as Marie has signed the wedding contract, when the business between them will be finished with. For a little while they are all three at cross-purposes. Hans wants to make it clear that Marie shall wed no one but Tobias Micha's son, Marie refuses indignantly to accept Wenzel as her husband, and Kezal is certain that the contract he has in his pocket is fool-proof. When at last Hans bets Kezal that he himself will see that the girl marries Micha's son, poor Marie can hardly believe her ears: never would she have thought her Hans capable of such baseness! He asks her to take his word for it that the course of true love will still run smooth, and that the bartered bride will be amply compensated for what she has lost:

for this Micha's son loves her truly, and her faithfulness to him will meet with its due reward. Both she and Kezal by this time look upon him as about as bad a piece of work as nature ever turned out; and Marie, though her heart is heavy, sees nothing for it now but to fall in with her parents' wishes. Kezal goes out to summon witnesses. When he has gone, Hans assures Marie again that she is going to wed Micha's son: her only reply to what she takes to be an extra insult is to tell him to get out of her sight.

As in the case of the end of each of the two preceding acts, the folk play a large part in the finale of the third. Kezal, happy in the consciousness of a business triumph and the coming of a good commission, returns with Kruschina, Kathinka, Micha, Agnes and the villagers generally. They are all delighted to hear that a marriage has been arranged and will shortly take place, though they find the bride a trifle paler and more melancholy than they would have anticipated. Marie's mind is now made up: she will go through with it if only to be revenged on Hans for his treachery and his callousness to her sufferings. The people rejoice over the prospect of a speedy wedding, and Hans, stepping forward, surpasses them all with the fervour of his assurance that such a bride and bridegroom have never been seen before. But at the sight of him Agnes and Micha give a cry of "Why, if that isn't Hans!" The young man admits it; after years of wandering, he says, he has come to make a home of his own in his native place.

Each of the characters reacts to this dramatic disclosure in his or her individual way. Hans's step-mother considers this latest trick of his quite worthy of him. Kezal has an uneasy idea that he has not been quite so clever as he had imagined. Marie is quick to grasp the meaning of it all, though in her natural anxiety to pay Hans out she will not at first admit that she is pleased. Hans, in reply to a remark of Kezal's, points out that he cannot possibly be dead, as his own parents have just recognised him; moreover, if he is driven from his native place again, this time he will take Marie with him. He reminds them of what is in the bond, and Kezal has to admit that he is right. Then he asks Marie whether she chooses him or the other son. Her answer is to fling herself into his arms with a cry of joy.

Kezal's mortification at being outwitted is so manifest that everyone, including the parents of the lovers, laughs at him and teases him till he rushes out in the vilest of tempers. As he does so a confused noise is heard "off", and a number of boys come running in, shouting "Look out! The bear is loose!" But the bear turns out to be only poor silly Wenzel, who tells them not to be afraid, for he is not really a bear. His mother rounds on him for making such a fool of himself, and drags him out. With Agnes thus out of the way, matters are easier for everyone. Marie's parents ask Micha to agree with them that not Wenzel but Hans is the right man for their daughter. The lovers kneel before Micha, who gives them his blessing; and the opera ends with a lively chorus:

in which principals and peasants all wish long life and good luck to the bartered bride.

DIE FLEDERMAUS
Johann Strauss (1825-1899)

PRINCIPAL CHARACTERS

GABRIEL EISENSTEIN	*Tenor*
ROSALINDE	*Soprano*
FRANK	*Baritone*
PRINCE ORLOFSKY	*Mezzo-soprano*
ALFRED	*Tenor*
DR FALKE	*Baritone*
DR. BLIND	*Tenor*
ADELE	*Soprano*
FROSCH	*(Speaking Part)*

I

The professional critic is sometimes heatedly told by unfriendly readers that "criticism ought to be constructive, not destructive". If this means that the musical critic, instead of merely saying that Paganini played none too well at his recital last night, ought to have taken the fiddle out of the magician's hands and shown him how the "Carnival of Venice" Variations really ought to be played, the critic can plausibly reply that doing a thing and talking about it are quite different matters, and that the housewife who refuses an egg because it does not seem to her quite fresh would not be impressed by the grocer's reproof that this was merely destructive criticism, which the lady ought to follow up with the constructive criticism of laying a better egg herself. Mephistopheles, it is true, politely offers to provide the singer of the Rat Song in *Faust* with a piece of genuinely constructive criticism: "Pray, sir", he says to him in the noble version of Gounod's opera that has delighted so many generations of English provincial opera-goers,

> *Pray, sir, conclude the canticle so well begun,*
> *And I will sing, when you have ended, a better one!*

But Mephistopheles was Mephistopheles; *he* could say that sort of thing with impunity because he knew he could do what he had promised. Mere human musical critics have to be more careful.

For all that, it has occasionally happened that an artist *has* criticised a fellow-craftsman's work constructively, by taking it to pieces and putting it together again in a rather better form—though whether the artist of the second part would ever have been able to do anything at all in the matter but for the artist of the first part may be doubted. But for Aristophanes, Maurice Donnay would perhaps never have thought of the racy Lysistrata theme as the basis of a drama; yet few people who have read both the ancient Greek play and the modern French one would deny that Donnay has improved upon his brilliant predecessor at several points. And, to turn at last to the specific subject of the present chapter, there cannot be the least doubt that each successive re-handling of the central dramatic motive of the *Fledermaus* story has been an improvement deserving to rank as constructive criticism.

The kernel of the story is the arrest of one person in mistake for another, the voluntary surrender later of the person who was really "wanted" by the police, and the humorous complications that ensue when the pair meet in the prison. As there are so few really original plots in literature it is quite on the cards that this one had been current before it was exploited by the German play-wright Roderich Benedix (1811–1873). In December 1851 there was given in Berlin a comedy of his—*Das Gefängnis* (*The Prison*) —that may serve as the starting-point for our enquiry into the origins of *Die Fledermaus*.

The German play in its totality does not concern us here; we must confine ourselves to the portion of it that bears on the later opera. A young German, Baron Wallbeck, has so impoverished himself by his gay life in town that his creditors are about to force a sale of his ancestral estate in the country. He receives a call from a Dr. Hagen, a scholar engaged in research into a period of German history in connection with which, he believes, valuable ancient documents exist at Schloss Wallbeck. The Baron, who himself has no interest whatever in matters of this kind, tells Hagen that he will be visiting his estate in a day or two, and that he will then gladly be of any service he can to him in connection with the manuscripts. He has already fallen in love, however, with Hagen's pretty young wife, and he now plans to make an attempt on her virtue before leaving town. He knows that Hagen, who, by the way, is fond enough of his wife in a scholarly sort of way but not very demonstrative in his affections, is in the habit of taking a country walk to Helldorf at six o'clock each afternoon and returning about eight. Wallbeck's scheme is for a common friend of the pair, one Ramsdorf, to come casually, as it were, upon Hagen in an inn *en route*, to inveigle him, over a glass of wine, into a game of chess, of which Hagen is inordinately fond, and to engross him into prolonging the game until well into the night. Ramsdorf having agreed, Wallbeck goes off to Hagen's house, where he is duly repulsed by the virtuous Mathilde.

Wallbeck is unaware that Hagen, having used some strong language about a professor with whom he has been engaged in a controversy, has been sentenced to fourteen days' detention, and that he intends to present himself at the prison that very evening after having had his usual walk, without returning to the house. (This prison seems to be not at all an unpleasant place: Hagen looks forward to getting on there with some literary work he has in hand). If anyone should ask Mathilde, during the fortnight, where her husband is, she is to say he has gone on a journey. And this is the story she tells Wallbeck indignantly before flouncing out of her sitting-room, having bidden the vile seducer find his own way out of the house. While he is trying to swallow the rather bitter pill she has administered, a prison official comes through the garden, and, assuming him to be the master of the house, arrests him: it appears that they have got tired of waiting for Hagen to come to them of his own accord. Afraid of compromising the wife and getting himself into trouble with the husband, there is nothing for it but for Wallbeck to go off to the prison as Dr. Hagen, and hope for the best.

Meanwhile the game of chess has lasted much longer than either of the players had anticipated; and at midnight, as it is now raining heavily, they decide to stay the night at the inn, Hagen, of course, not being in the least perturbed about this, because his wife is not expecting his return. But when he goes to the prison the next

morning to give himself up, no one will accept his assurance that
he is Hagen—for "Dr. Hagen" had been arrested the evening
before. He is allowed half-an-hour's talk with the supposed
Hagen, and they come to an arrangement that suits both of them
admirably. The inflammable Wallbeck, having fallen in love at
first sight with the prison director's daughter, is not in the least
anxious to leave; and it equally well suits Hagen to go to Schloss
Wallbeck, conduct his researches in the library there, and have
the fun of impersonating the proprietor in his dealings with
creditors and others. (Wallbeck, it should be explained, has not
been near his estate for many years, so he is not known by sight
to the people there: he sends along with Hagen his faithful old
retainer Gunter, who alone has been let into the secret). Wallbeck,
for his part, may as well stay where he is and serve the light
sentence which, in the circumstances, is rather a lucky thing for
him; for the certain result of the disclosure that he had given the
authorities a false name would be a further term of imprisonment,
plus a scandal involving Frau Hagen and likely to lead to complications with Hagen. He has already told the latter that he had
happened to be arrested in his house, though without revealing
the real reason for his being there: and, as he rightly points out,
evil tongues will begin to wag if the facts should become known
in the town. Obviously the best thing for everyone concerned,
therefore, is to leave matters as they are for the fourteen days; and,
in fact, everything finally turns out for the best in this best of all
possible worlds.

2

That is as far as we need go with *Das Gefängnis*, in which the
prison motive, as we may call it, is only one of several. The next
dramatists to take that motive in hand, however, perceived possibilities in it of which Benedix had not dreamed; and so they made
it occupy, in one way and another, their own play from first to
last. These authors were Henry Meilhac and Ludovic Halévy.
Benedix's play was some twenty years old, and perhaps forgotten by
the public, when Meilhac and Halévy laid their hands on it and produced from it *Le Réveillon*, a comedy in three acts, which was produced in the Théâtre du Palais-Royal on the 10th September 1872.

This time it is a worthy French provincial, Gabriel Gaillardin, living on his small property at Pincornet-les-Bœufs, who has got into a little trouble through calling a garde-champêtre an imbecile. The play opens on Christmas Eve with the Gaillardin's maidservant, Pernette, lamenting that she is not free to go and spend the evening with her lover. Outside the house some one is playing on the violin a fantasia on Donizetti's *La Favorita*. Madame Fanny Gaillardin, having heard this, enters the room in great perturbation: who can it possibly be but a former lover of hers, the violin virtuoso, Alfred, playing his well-known "air varié No. 3", and what can be the purpose of his doing so but to reproach her for her unkind behaviour to him some years ago? Pernette asks for the evening off to visit her "sick aunt"; but her mistress is too agitated on her own account to be in the least responsive. Pernette having gone out, Alfred enters, violin in hand: he is dressed in Hungarian costume. We discover, in due course, that four years ago he had been Fanny's music-master in Paris; the pair had fallen in love with each other, but Fanny's father having refused to let her marry a man who at that time was merely the impecunious conductor at the Tivoli-Vauxhall, Alfred had gone away to make his fortune. He has become "chef d'orchestre hongrois" to a rich Russian nobleman, Prince Yermontof, whose taste in serious music, it appears, enables him to recognise the exceptional merits of an artist like Alfred. Chance having brought the Prince to the neighbourhood of Pincornet-les-Bœufs, Alfred has decided to look up his old love and indulge himself in the luxury of upbraiding her for having married another man in his absence. He has heard of Gaillardin's little affair with the police, which, in fact, is being dealt with in court at that very moment. He promises not to do anything to compromise Fanny just now; but if, as he ardently hopes, his successful rival is sent to prison, he will return, he tells her, and make a longer stay.

Gaillardin comes home from the court in a very bad temper: he has been sentenced to eight days' imprisonment, to commence that evening. What rankles, however, is not so much his sentence, in which, indeed, he finds certain compensating features—it will see him nicely over the tiresome and expensive period of Christmas and New Year's Day, for instance—as the fact that the magistrate had refused to acquit him although he was a personal friend of his, in the habit of dining with the Gaillardins at least once a week. He tells his wife to get out his oldest and shabbiest clothes, which are good enough for prison; and he sends Pernette to the Golden Lion to order a tip-top dinner for him—the last thing of the sort he is likely to get for some days.

His wife and Pernette having left him, his bosom friend Duparquet, a notary, enters with news which, he thinks, will cheer Gaillardin up. Duparquet has been acting professionally for Prince Yermontof, who has rented a house in the vicinity for the hunting season; and the notary has brought Gaillardin an invitation to a party which the Prince is giving that very evening—a party at which there are to be some actresses from Paris, to say nothing of unlimited champagne. As Duparquet points out, Gaillardin's condemnation, looked at in the right way, is really a blessing in disguise: Fanny would never have allowed him to go to such a party alone, but as it is, he can slip away to it under the pretence that he is going to serve his sentence, can spend a few gay hours with the champagne and the Paris actresses, and deposit himself at the prison in the early hours of the morning. When Fanny returns she is astonished to find her Gabriel, whom she had left angry and dejected, now in exceptionally good spirits, and with no use at all for the old clothes she has fished out for him: he is actually going to prison in evening dress. As he is leaving, in the gayest humour, Pernette comes in with a dish on which is a *gâteau de Savoie* that has been ordered from the Golden Lion. It is adorned with a huge rose, which Gaillardin snatches up and puts in his buttonhole as he goes out.

Fanny now prepares herself for the ordeal of the visit with which Alfred had threatened her when the coast should be clear. For safety's sake she has already given Pernette the evening off to see her mythical sick aunt: she now tells her to take with her, as a present for the invalid, the *perdreau* that has come from the Golden Lion. Alfred arrives about nine o'clock; but he has not had time to do much more than go over, very much to his own sentimental satisfaction, the sad story of Fanny's infidelity to him when there are three loud knocks at the door, followed by the entry of two men—the prison director, Tourillon, and his servant Leopold. It is now ten o'clock: having got tired of waiting for Gaillardin they have come to fetch him. For appearances' sake neither he nor Fanny dares deny that he is the husband of the lady with whom he is obviously about to sup at that late hour. Before Alfred is taken away, however, he has at least the consolation of being able to fold Mme Gaillardin in his arms a few times.

Though Gaillardin does not know it, the party at Prince Yermontof's has been arranged entirely to get a good laugh out of *him*. The Prince, though only eighteen and immensely rich, is very blasé; and Duparquet has promised him, for this evening, a farce which will really divert even him. A few years before, it appears, Gaillardin had played a malicious practical joke on Duparquet, who was at that time a rising young lawyer. They had been out of town to a fancy dress ball, Duparquet wearing a costume of blue feathers, with a yellow beak. Gaillardin had made him drunk, taken him to the local railway station after the ball, deposited him in the train, and told the guard to put him out when they reached town; and the budding notary had had to stagger home in his blue bird costume in the light of the morning under the admiring eyes of his fellow-townsmen. Now, at last, Duparquet has seen his opportunity for a revenge that will cause a lot of fun and laughter and do no one any harm in the end. He is aware that Gaillardin has to go to prison for eight days, also that a new director of the prison has just arrived at Pincornet-les-Bœufs, who as yet knows hardly any of the inhabitants of the place even by sight. Duparquet's first move in the game, as we have seen, is to get Gaillardin to attend the party before going to prison. His second move is the still brighter one of bringing Tourillon, the prison director, also to the party, and introducing him to the Prince and the guests as the Count de Villebouzin. (The Prince, of course, does not get the clue to all this mystification until later, when the joke has been played out to its end: nor does Duparquet himself know anything of Alfred's visit to Fanny and his arrest as her husband). Gaillardin, not wishing his real name to be known, persuades his friend to pass him off at the party as the Marquis de Valangoujar.

There are four actresses, or alleged actresses, at the supper—

Métella, Toto, Mme de Sainte-Esplanade, and Adèle. The party
is rich in complications of all sorts. The Prince cannot understand
why his gifted chef d'orchestre hongrois is not there: the band
has to perform as best it can without him. Gaillardin soon
establishes an entente cordiale with Métella. Complaining that she
does not feel very well, she begs him to time her heart-beats with
his watch. The episode reminds her, she tells Gaillardin, of an
earlier one in her career, when, in this very neighbourhood, a
certain hunter had won his way to her heart—he was the very first
to travel the course, according to her—by promising her his
watch. This, she recalls, bore a singular resemblance to the one
she now has in her hand; and very soon the pseudo-Métella and
the pseudo-Marquis de Valangoujar recognise each other as the
Jeanne and Gabriel of that amorous incident in the past.

The servants of the Prince have orders to keep on filling the
glasses of the "Count" and the "Marquis"; and the tipsier the
pair get the more sentimentally fond they become of each other,
to the vast amusement of the ironic Duparquet. Gaillardin tells
the story of the blue bird as a huge joke against Duparquet, but
does not understand, as yet, the meaning of the latter's promise
to the company of a still better farce before the night is out. At
five in the morning Gaillardin and Tourillon, both of them very
tipsy now, tear themselves away from the party, the one to
surrender himself at the prison, the other to take up his official
duties there. They leave by opposite doors, after some confusion
as to their respective hats.

The third act opens in the director's room in the prison. Here
Leopold, the chronically tipsy warder, comes into his own with
some fruity comedy of the ancient red-nosed order. Tourillon
arrives, his head still buzzing with actresses and champagne: Toto
had made a particular impression on him at the party. Leopold
makes his report: nothing out of the common has happened over-
night, though No. 12 has made himself a bit of a nuisance by
keeping on demanding to see a lawyer. (No. 12, of course, is
Alfred). Gaillardin arrives a little later to give himself up, and the
Count and the Marquis are very much astonished to find each
other there; Gaillardin jumps to the natural conclusion that the
Count has been arrested for making a tipsy disturbance in the

street in the early hours of the morning. He thinks it just the Count's little joke when the latter assures him that he is not the Count de Villebouzin at all but Tourillon, the director of the prison; and he is only convinced when Leopold is called in and told to take him by the collar. Gaillardin's assertion that he, for his part, is not the Marquis de Valangoujar but Gabriel Gaillardin, come to serve his sentence, is not so easily proved: how *can* he be Gaillardin, when Gaillardin was arrested last night and is now in No. 12? Tourillon swears he arrested him himself, and goes into details: it was in a room decorated in red, with a clock on the mantelpiece representing the Chevalier Bayard; Gaillardin was dressed in a blue dressing-gown; he was tête-à-tête with his wife, who took a touchingly affectionate farewell of him. Gradually the wealth of authentic detail begins to impress Gaillardin, muzzy as he still is after the party: this must be looked into!

Leopold announces a lady caller, whom Tourillon goes out to greet; has Duparquet, he wonders, carrying the jest still further, given his address to Toto? While Gaillardin is trying to get the hang of this puzzling situation his own lawyer, Bidard, comes in: for it happens to be he whom Leopold has sent for in response to No. 12's request for a solicitor. Gaillardin makes the astonished and frightened Bidard give him his cap, his robe, and his brief-case; then, impersonating the lawyer, he worms the whole story out of Alfred, who is still wearing Gaillardin's dressing-gown and smoking-cap. The scene is rich in humour: Alfred gives his supposed solicitor detailed instructions how to handle the interesting case in court—he is to make the husband out to be a ruffian, but not a word is to be said against the charming wife, while he, the lover, is to be presented in the most sympathetic way possible to the jury,—and Gaillardin, his fury rising as detail succeeds detail in Alfred's story, keeps forgetting that he is not Gaillardin but Bidard, speaks of "I" and "me" when he really means "the husband", and can hardly keep his hands off the musician, whose self-complacence exasperates him beyond bearing. Alfred, who has never seen a lawyer behave like Bidard before, does not quite know what to make of it all. "I say", he remarks at one point after Gaillardin has flown at him in his temper, "there's no mistake about this, is there? You really did

come here to defend me?" He urges the lawyer to take notes of
what he is saying, as he mistrusts the memory of so obviously
excitable a man; and once more he asks, as Gaillardin takes him
by the throat and tries to strangle him, "Excuse me, but there's
no mistake, is there? It really was to defend me that you came
here?"

The scene ends, a trifle abruptly, with the irruption into the
room of the members of last night's party, all in the highest
spirits. Duparquet asks Gaillardin how he likes *his* little farce.
Gaillardin recognises in it Duparquet's revenge for the practical
joke of long ago; but, a trifle dense of understanding to the last,
he explains it all in his own way, to his own satisfaction and to the
amusement of the others: his complacent theory is that the Prince,
having been let into the secret of Duparquet's plans, had sent his
chef d'orchestre to his (Gaillardin's) house to obtain his dressing-
gown, which his dear little wife had unsuspectingly handed over,
along with his velvet cap. He understands everything perfectly,
he assures them. Leopold enters to announce that Mme Gaillardin
has called and wishes to see her husband. Gaillardin is a little perturbed by this at first, but, as the others are kind enough to point
out to him, she has come on the natural assumption that he has
been in the prison all night. He exacts from them all a promise of
secrecy as to the events at the party, and is calmly saying good-
bye when Tourillon, now quite sober and the perfect official
again, reminds him that he is not free to leave until his eight days
are up. The play ends rather weakly, the authors evidently not
quite knowing how to wind it up satisfactorily. Tourillon, as in
duty bound, turns a deaf ear to Gaillardin's suggestion that he
shall set him free, but advises him to appeal. "But to whom?" asks
Gaillardin: "I know no one in Paris." "No need to go as far as
that", replies Tourillon; and, taking the obvious cue, Gaillardin
turns to the audience, tells them that the right of pardon or condemnation rests with them, and, in his lawyer's robe, begins his
speech to the jury—it is not extenuating circumstances that
he is going to plead: no, ladies and gentlemen, he demands an
acquittal!

Q*

3

The Meilhac-Halévy play was a great improvement on that of
Benedix so far as the prison motive was concerned, in that this
motive now sufficed to animate the whole composition, everything that happens being either derived from it or flowing into it.
There was scope, however, for still further improvement, as was
shown by the next re-handling of the story. The success of the
French play led to its being bought by Steiner, the director of the
Vienna Theater an der Wien. Difficulties cropped up, however, in
the way both of translation and of adapting the purely Gallic
story to the Viennese taste; so Steiner offered his rights in the play
to Jauner, of the Carl Theatre. Jauner, not being able to come to
an arrangement with the French publisher about it, handed it
back to Steiner, who, on a hint that here was an admirable subject
for Johann Strauss, commissioned a new version of it, for musical
purposes, from two expert theatrical craftsmen of that day,
Haffner and Franz Richard Genée, the latter, who was more than
a little of a musician himself,[1] having the larger share in the
proceedings.

Some of the changes made by the Viennese librettists were
obviously dictated by the fact that they were manufacturing not
a play but an operetta, and in operettas the characters sing a good
deal, especially the leading characters. In Le Réveillon Fanny plays
almost a minor part: she appears neither in the second nor the
third act, though, as the reader knows, we hear of her having
called at the prison in the final scene to see her husband.

Such neglect of the leading lady would be impossible in opera:
she would manifestly have to appear in each act. To bring her on
in person in the prison towards the end of the opera was not a
difficult thing to manage: but to work her into the second act

---

[1] He wrote several operas of his own. Before settling in Vienna he had
been Kapellmeister in many places, including the Landestheater, Prague,
where he is said to have conducted Tannhäuser and Lohengrin from memory.
From 1868 to 1878 he was Kapellmeister at the Theater an der Wien. He is
remembered today less for his own comic operas than for the libretti
he wrote for Millöcker, Suppé and Strauss. Much of the dialogue of
his texts was supplied by F. Zell, Genée concentrating more on the musical
numbers.

was something of a problem. It was solved by a master-stroke on the part of the Vienna librettists: they make Eisenstein's (Gaillardin's) friend Dr. Falke (Duparquet) not only take *him* to the Prince's party but send an invitation to Rosalinde (Fanny). The second act of *Le Réveillon* had enjoyed much of its success in Paris owing to the robust humour of the antics of the tipsy Gaillardin and Duparquet at the supper table, and to the fact that actual dishes, steaming hot, were brought in by the servants. But if Rosalinde was to be present without being recognised by her husband she would of course have to be masked: and this fact automatically necessitated the addition of a ball to the supper. A plausible pretext for Rosalinde's coming there masked was provided by Falke's giving her out to be a Hungarian Countess: this in its turn became an excellent reason for the singer obliging the company with a Hungarian Csárdás and Frischka.

Another clever stroke was to make more, in each of the three acts, of the soubrette part represented by the maid Adele (Pernette), who appears, in *Le Réveillon*, only in the opening scenes of the comedy. Haffner and Genée work her into the second act by making Orlofsky (Yermontof)[1] invite all the ladies of the ballet of the Opera to his party. One of these happens to be Adele's sister Ida, who takes it on herself to invite Adele. By the introduction into the ball scene of these two characters (Rosalinde and

[1] Yermontof is generally supposed to have been studied from the young Prince Paul Demidof, a notorious character of the period. Immensely rich and fond of pleasure, he had descended upon Paris at the age of twenty-three and turned the town upside down with the extravagance of his fantasies. It is more probable, however, that the man whom Meilhac and Halévy had in mind was another young Russian, of the name of Narishkine, who was even richer than Demidof and quite as mad, but with certain peculiarities of his own of which we find distinct traces in the *Fledermaus*. A contemporary Parisian diarist, Comte Horace de Viel Castel, describes Demidof in 1860 as "a disgusting imbecile, worn out with debauchery." A viler creature, he said, could not be imagined: he was insolent to his inferiors, cowardly and false with those who stood up to him (*Mémoires sur le règne de Napoléon III*, I, 67). This is not at all the Yermontof of the comedy, whom we recognise, however, in Frédéric Loliée's description of Prince Narishkine—a wild young fellow, but weak and sickly and jealous of Demidof's superior vitality: he found no joy in life, for all his wealth. (See *Les Femmes du Second Empire: la fête impériale*, pp. 80-81.)

Adele) the comedy that plays around the unsuspecting Eisenstein in the second act acquires a finer irony; for whereas they both of them recognise him, he never suspects the masked Hungarian Countess with whom he is smitten to be his wife, and though he fancies he has seen Adele somewhere he cannot be quite sure. Rosalinde, for her part, not only recognises Adele but sees that the hussy is wearing one of her mistress's frocks.

Other improvements of the Viennese librettists were to make Alfred a tenor instead of a fiddler, and the Prince's singing teacher instead of his chef d'orchestre; to introduce Rosalinde, with rich comic effect, into the scene in the last act in which Alfred explains matters to the supposed lawyer; and to give a new and piquant touch to the episode of the famous repeating watch that has played so large a part in all Eisenstein's conquests. In the opera, it is not to one of the actresses but to the Hungarian Countess that he shows it: Rosalinde annexes it, foils all Gabriel's efforts to get it back, and produces it as her trump card in the prison scene of the third act. There are many more wheels within wheels in the Viennese version than in the French, and they all fit in with each other with delightful smoothness. And over and above all this there is Strauss's music, to refine away the occasional crudity of a Meilhac-Halévy incident, to give finer point to the ironies and piquancies of the situations, and to bathe the whole action in that atmosphere of refined sensuality that has always been characteristic of the Viennese operetta.

Die Fledermaus was the third of Strauss's operettas. It was not until his forty-sixth year that he embarked on this genre, the first of the series, *Indigo*, having been produced in 1871. *Der Karneval in Rom* followed two years later. *Die Fledermaus* was produced at the Theater an der Wien on the 5th April 1874.

4

Analysis of the overture had better be postponed till after the reader has become acquainted with some of the principal themes of the work.

The opening scene shows us a room in Gabriel Eisenstein's house, in a watering place near a large town. The room is at the moment empty. Outside we hear the tenor Alfred imploring the "holde Rosalinde"—a name which most conveniently rhymes with "O komm geschwinde"—whom he had known before her marriage, and whom he has met again in the little town, to take pity on him. The song is interrupted by the entry of the maid Adele with a letter in her hand, which she reads aloud to the sotto voce accompaniment of a gay little tune in the orchestra:

We learn that the letter is from her sister Ida, who is in the ballet: she tells Adele that the rich young Prince Orlofsky is giving a grand supper that evening, and if Adele can annex one of her mistress's frocks and get the evening off she can promise her a good time. Alfred had addressed Rosalinde as the "little dove" who had flown away from him. Recalling this, Adele laments that nature had not seen fit to give *her* the wings of a dove, instead of making her just a humble parlour-maid. When Alfred resumes his song she silences him angrily. Rosalinde, who now enters, has also heard the serenade; and she surmises that the singer can only be the Alfred whom she had known some years before. She is rather perturbed; she is afraid he will compromise her. Adele, bursting into tears, spins a piteous yarn about wanting to visit her poor sick aunt; but her mistress does not take the tale seriously and refuses to let her off for the evening. She will need her herself, indeed; for her husband has just been condemned to five days' imprisonment, and before he goes he must have a good supper. Adele goes out weeping.

Alfred enters. He wants to renew the warm friendship of earlier days with Rosalinde, and he sees a heaven-sent opportunity in the enforced absence of Eisenstein for a few days, of which he has somehow or other heard. His assurance that he will call again that evening, when the coast is clear, does not meet with too obstinate a resistance from Rosalinde. "O, if only he wouldn't sing!" she sighs after he has gone: "when I hear his high A my strength fails me!"

Eisenstein returns with his advocate, Dr. Blind, and there is

a lively scene of mutual recrimination, with Rosalinde interjecting a remark now and then. Each of the men blames the other
for the recent unfortunate outcome of the case in court: Eisenstein, according to Blind, had lost his temper, and Blind, according to Eisenstein, had conducted the case like a congenital idiot.
Rosalinde tries to throw oil on the troubled waters: five short
days of imprisonment, and her Gabriel will be with her again.
"Five?" shouts Eisenstein. "Eight!" Owing to the incompetence
of his advocate the court has added three days to the original
sentence. The shindy begins again. Blind suggests that as soon as
Eisenstein is free he shall appeal against the sentence and give him
a chance to show what he can do in the way of legal chicanery.
Neither of them will listen to him, and it ends with Blind being
ejected. Some of Rosalinde's music in this scene has been a
masterpiece of double meaning: did we not know that there is an
Alfred in the offing we should certainly take her lamentations
over the coming days of separation from her husband quite
seriously, so near is the music to speaking the language of
genuine grief.

When Blind has gone, Gabriel rings for Adele, who comes in
still snivelling about her poor sick aunt. Gabriel sends her to the
hotel to order a first-rate supper for him—the last of the kind that
he will get for some time,—and Rosalinde goes out to make other
preparations for his departure, and more especially to dig out
his oldest and shabbiest clothes, which he intends to wear in
prison. While she is away Dr. Falke enters, full, although Eisenstein has not the smallest suspicion of it, of a brilliant plan for
turning the tables on his friend for the practical joke he had played
on him during a recent carnival, when Falke, who had been got
up as a bat, had been shown up tipsy by Eisenstein in broad daylight. He tells him of the coming party at Orlofsky's, to which he
is authorised to invite him. Why not postpone his surrender to
the prison authorities until the next day, and meanwhile have a
last night of glorious revelry, dancing with the ladies of the ballet?
He may even be able to work off on one or two of them his
standing joke with his repeating watch, which has vanquished so
many women but is still in his possession. It is to the strain of a
polka that Falke tempts his victim—the same polka, in fact

(No. 1), that had floated through Adele's mind when reading her sister's letter. Eisenstein, sorely tempted as he is, takes a little persuading, as his conscience smites him with regard to his wife. Falke assures him that not a word will ever leak out; he will introduce him at the supper as a stranger to the neighbourhood, one Marquis Renard. Eisenstein is won over to the idea, and the pair, still to the strain of the polka, gloat in imagination over the good time they are going to have.

When Rosalinde returns, Falke having left, she is astonished to find that her husband is going to prison in evening dress and the highest spirits. He explains this strange procedure to her seeming satisfaction. (Rosalinde herself has meanwhile been doing a bit of quiet thinking; and as Alfred seems determined to carry out his threat to call as soon as her husband has gone to prison, she has decided, for safety's sake, to give Adele the evening off). Master, mistress and maid sing a trio that is one of the masterpieces of the work. Each of the characters is secretly delighted at the way things have turned out, but each has to keep a solemn face. Eisenstein is all impatience to get away to Orlofsky's party. Rosalinde's thoughts are turned, half-fearfully, half-hopefully, in the direction of Alfred. Adele has her own views about it all. Rosalinde describes in the most pathetic terms the anguish she will go through during the next week or so. Eight days without her Gabriel! Never will she cease to think of him—at breakfast, when, alas, his empty cup will stare her in the face, at the mid-day meal, when soup and boiled and roast will come and go untouched by him, and again when the shades of night fall and she realises once more the appalling blank in her life. Rosalinde's melodious lament:

moves them all to something near tears. "O Gott, wie rührt mich dies!" Gabriel ejaculates with a sob; and the others repeat the words with him:

But as they go on, cheerfulness insists on breaking in, as it did with the would-be "philosopher" in Boswell's Life of Johnson, and the strain that began so sadly ends in the most open hilarity. At last Eisenstein manages to tear himself away, after having snatched the carnation from the boar's head that had been sent in for his supper from the hotel and put it in his buttonhole.

He and Adele have no sooner left than Alfred arrives to console Rosalinde. He is delighted with the supper laid out on the table, apparently for him, and he makes himself comfortable in Gabriel's dressing-gown and smoking-cap. He gives Rosalinde instructions about his breakfast, and calls on her to drink with him, in lines embodying the typically Viennese philosophy of "Happy is the man who can forget what can't be altered":

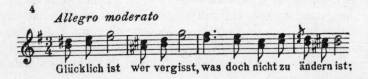

Everything, so far as Alfred is concerned, is for the best in the best of all possible worlds, until someone is heard ascending the stairs. It is Frank, the director of the prison, who has come to carry Eisenstein off to captivity. It takes the bibulous Alfred a little time to realise the mess he has landed himself in. He insists on Frank drinking with him to the tune of No. 4, and Frank is delighted that his quarry can take so humorous a view of the situation. When the prison director, however, addresses him as Herr von Eisenstein and asks him to come along with him, Alfred denies that he is the man Frank imagines him to be. But Rosalinde assures Frank that this is only Herr von Eisenstein's fun: with whom else but her capped and gowned husband would she be tête-à-tête at that time of night? Why, the man is even yawning, so ready for bed is he:

Mit mir so spät im tête à tête, ganz trau - lich und — al - lein, —

Frank, who is in a hurry to get to the Orlofsky party, tells the husband to kiss his wife good-bye, which Alfred gladly does. He sees that in order not to compromise Rosalinde he must, for the moment, impersonate Eisenstein: but he means to get the most he can by way of compensation, and so he prolongs the fond adieux until Frank becomes impatient and begs him to come without more ado and be his guest in his charming bird-house, as he calls it:

Mein schönes, grosses Vogelhaus, es ist ganz na-he hier,

At last, aided by Rosalinde, who almost sees the hand of Providence in this easy way out of her difficulties, Frank manages to persuade Alfred to go along with him. Alfred is so agitated that he forgets to take off Eisenstein's dressing-gown before leaving.

5

The second act takes place in Orlofsky's house, where a mixed company is enjoying itself hugely at his expense. This, indeed, is not merely what he would have them do but what he insists on their doing; for, as the blasé young man explains in a song that seems to be designedly gauche in its musical gait:

Ich la-de gern mir Gäste ein, man lebt bei mir recht fein,

while he himself is perpetually bored he is mortally offended if his guests are not amused; if anyone refuses to drink when he does he throws the bottle at his head. This is the tone he maintains throughout the evening; and if a guest does show any sign of being unwilling to drink when the master of the house would have him drink, he is terrorised by a big servant of Orlofsky's who says nothing, but stands over him with a menacing air. Falke promises the Prince that tonight at any rate he will have a joke he can enjoy.

Eisenstein, who has been introduced to the company by Falke as the Marquis Renard, is sure he recognises Adele in a very stylish young lady named Olga to whom he is presented; but Falke, Orlofsky and the others laugh at him for what they call his delusion, and Adele herself, in a charming little song:

Mein Herr Mar - quis,   ein Mann wie

Sie   sollt' bes - ser das ver - stehn,

asks the Marquis what parlour-maid ever had a hand or a foot like hers, to say nothing of her Greek profile, her figure and her frock (which, of course, is one of Rosalinde's). But the fun becomes really fast and furious when Rosalinde herself, to whom Orlofsky has sent an invitation through Falke, enters masked, Falke explaining that it is only in that fashion that this "Hungarian Countess" could venture into such a company. Finding her husband here enjoying himself with Adele when she had imagined him to have gone to prison, Rosalinde resolves to punish him for his deception. He, for his part, at once begins flirting with the Countess. He is certain of his conquest when she falls, apparently fainting, on a sofa, pressing her hand to her heart. It is an attack of an old malady which will soon pass, she explains; meanwhile could he take her pulse? He produces for that purpose his famous repeating watch; she gets possession of it, and foils every attempt on his part to recover it. This is a new experience for him, and he is very worried about it.

A pretext is easily found[1] for persuading the Hungarian Countess to sing for the benefit of the company a Csárdás followed by the regulation Frischka. The expressive Csárdás:

shows what depths of expression there were in Strauss had he chosen to explore them more consistently. No genuine Hungarian could sing more movingly of the pain of separation from the beloved homeland, or of the fire in the Hungarian breast that drives them to the dance:

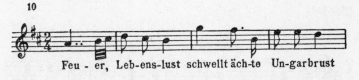

[1] Not a very brilliant one, perhaps. Adele suggests that the Unknown should unmask. Rosalinde, of course, politely declines. Adele cattishly says she is prepared to bet that the Unknown isn't a Hungarian at all; whereupon, to convince the company that she is the genuine article, Rosalinde offers to sing them a specimen of "the music of her fatherland".

Everybody's blood is by this time pleasantly warm with wine; and Frank (who has been introduced by Falke as the Chevalier Chagrin), has fallen head over ears in love with Adele and her sister Ida, but more particularly Adele. After Eisenstein has complacently told the Prince and some of the others how he had victimised Falke, as the bat, a year or two ago, and Falke has quietly remarked "Out of sight is not out of mind!", the company bursts into a chorus in praise of champagne:

the acknowledged king of wines in every land. Under its benign influence the Marquis Renard and the Chevalier Chagrin pledge each other liberally; and at Falke's suggestion:

the whole company, glass in hand, swear eternal brotherhood and sisterhood in a chorus that reaches the high-water mark of Viennese sensuousness. Coherent speech failing them, they kiss and "Du" and "duidu" and "la, la, la" each other to their hearts' content:

A ballet follows, into which it is customary nowadays to introduce the incomparable "Blue Danube" waltz. Then Orlofsky calls upon his guests themselves to dance, which they do to the tune of:

with its lilting pendant:

to which they sing of the joys of a night like this.

Frank and Eisenstein, whose glasses, by Orlofsky's orders, have been incessantly replenished, assist each other to keep upright, while Rosalinde, Falke and Orlofsky chuckle at the thought of what these two will have to say to each other when they meet in the prison. Frank asks Gabriel the time, his watch being out of order. This reminds Eisenstein that he has not yet recovered his own watch from the Hungarian Countess. He begs her to unmask, but she gives him a mysterious warning not to insist; if he were to see her face, she says, he would get a shock— a statement at which Orlofsky and some of the others, who are enjoying the joke vastly, burst into laughter. Eisenstein is not even put off by Rosalinde's assurance that she cannot unmask because she has a blemish on her nose. She escapes from him at last as the clock, striking six, recalls both Gabriel and Frank to a sense of reality. Each of them calls for his hat and coat; and after some broad humour with the wrong hats the curtain falls on the com-

pany surrounding the two tipsy figures and singing once more the
merry No. 15.

6

The first few minutes of the third act, which takes place in the
director's room of the prison, are given up to robust comedy on
the part of the warder Frosch, who has seized the opportunity
afforded him by the director's absence to get comfortably drunk.
Alfred, who is interned in cell No. 12, annoys him very much by
carolling his "Täubchen, holdes Täubchen mein" (his song to
Rosalinde in the first act). Finally Frosch threatens No. 12 that
if he doesn't stop his troubadouring he will throw him out.
Frosch staggers off to give an eye to his other prisoners, and
Frank enters, a little muzzy in the head and shaky at the knees
but still vinously happy. The orchestra announces his coming
by means of a reminiscence of his little song about his charming
bird-house in the first act (No. 6). He whistles the tune of No. 15
as he waltzes round with his own overcoat, half-on, half-off, for
partner. Then, remembering who and where he is, he takes his
coat off; but soon his thoughts are back at the party again with
Olga and Ida and that delightful Marquis with whom he had
sworn brotherhood (No. 14). It all comes back to him piece by
piece, as is shown by the quick succession, in the orchestra, of
various motives with which the reader is by now familiar. He
tries to make himself some tea with a spirit lamp, but in the end
is content with a glass of water. Then he makes an attempt to
read the morning paper, but falls asleep over it.

He is awakened by Frosch, who comes in to make his daily
report. Everything has been in order during the night, it seems,
except that Herr von Eisenstein having asked for a lawyer,
Frosch has sent for Dr. Blind. He goes out to answer a bell, and
returns with the information that two ladies would like to see
the Chevalier Chagrin. Frank is a little perturbed when they
prove to be Olga and Ida. They put him at his ease by explaining
that Olga is not really an "artiste" but would like to be one, and
no doubt the Chevalier Chagrin can be of some use to her in that
respect. To demonstrate her talent Adele sings a clever little song
in which she impersonates successively a pretendedly innocent

country girl, a queen, exuding dignity and condescension, and a Parisian Marquise flirting with a young Count.

While Frank is expressing his admiration of the performance there comes another ring at the bell. Looking out of the window, he sees the Marquis Renard. He hurriedly tells Frosch to show the ladies into another room and then to admit the new caller. As cell No. 13 is the only room vacant, Frosch takes them there. When Eisenstein enters his first thought is that Frank must be under arrest like himself; and when Frank tells him that he is not the Chevalier Chagrin at all, but the director of the prison, he laughs heartily at what he takes to be an excellent jest. When, in turn, the Marquis Renard says that he is no marquis but Herr von Eisenstein, come to serve his eight days, it is Frank's turn to be sceptical. As a matter of fact, he says, Herr von Eisenstein has been under lock and key all night: he himself had taken him into custody the night before, while the good man was sitting comfortably at supper with his wife in his dressing-gown. Eisenstein begins to be worried. The plot now works itself out much on the same lines as the Meilhac-Halévy play.

Frosch announces the arrival of a masked lady—Rosalinde, of course—and Frank goes out to see her. While he is away, Dr. Blind enters. Eisenstein demands from him his wig, glasses and papers, and they go into the anteroom to make the necessary exchange.

When the stage is empty, Alfred comes in, still wearing Gabriel's fez and dressing-gown. He is very bored: no one, he complains, seems to pay the least attention to him. He is surprised and delighted to see Rosalinde enter. She tells him that her husband may arrive at the prison any moment now, and he must on no account find Alfred there. What are they to do about it? "Perhaps", says Alfred, "the notary I sent for can suggest something. Here he is." The "notary", of course, is Eisenstein, disguised as Blind. By an effort he pulls himself together as he sees "the faithless one" with her lover. In an assumed voice he exhorts the pair to tell him the truth, the whole truth, and nothing but the truth, very much as in the corresponding scene in *Le Réveillon*. Alfred narrates the strange adventure that had befallen him the night before:

16

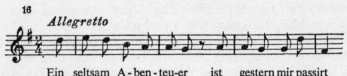

Allegretto

Ein seltsam A - ben - teu-er ist gestern mir passirt

how, while supping with the lady now present, he had had the
bad luck to be arrested. As the facts slip out, Gabriel keeps forgetting that he is not Eisenstein but Blind; and both Alfred and
Rosalinde indignantly call him to order, to the accompaniment of
an ironic little melody in the orchestra:

17

Allegretto

pp

etc.

Rosalinde assures him that her husband is a scoundrel who actually spent the preceding night supping and dancing with girls;
however, when he returns home she will first scratch his eyes out
and then leave him. This is bad enough; but when Alfred goes on
to ask the notary just how he and the lady can throw dust in the
husband's eyes, Gabriel rises in his wrath, tears off the spectacles
and wig, and announces that he is Eisenstein. "Yes, I am he who
was deceived", he cries, "but I will be avenged":

18

Allegro

Ja, ich bins, den Ihr be - tro - gen,

Rosalinde has something to say to this; but before she can say it,
Gabriel flies into a fresh temper on being asked to be reasonable
by Alfred, who, as Eisenstein points out to him, is actually sitting
there in *his* dressing-gown! At last Rosalinde manages to say
what she wanted to say; she produces as damning evidence against

her husband the watch that had been taken from him by the Hungarian Countess, and he collapses. Practically the whole company of the night before pours into the room. The only absentees are Adele and Ida. We soon hear of them, for Frosch comes in to tell the director that he is having a bit of trouble with the two ladies in No. 13, who won't let him bath them. Frank orders him to bring them in. Everyone joins in a chorus the burden of which is that the Bat should now take pity on his victim:

Eisenstein asks the meaning of this, and Falke explains it all to him, to the accompaniment of what may be regarded as the true Fledermaus motive:

Each of them confesses his or her part in the joke that has been played on Eisenstein; and Rosalinde and Alfred, quick to see their opportunity, assure him that the story of the supper in his house was only a myth, and the dressing-gown merely a means to lend similitude to Falke's joke—which Gabriel is glad to believe. The operetta ends, as it obviously should do, with a chorus in praise of champagne, which, if it causes a bit of trouble sometimes, is the bringer also of light and reconciliation. The chorus is sung, of course, to the melody of No. 11.

We can now turn our attention to the overture. This is a pot pourri of some of the main melodies of the work, strung together without any attempt to tell the story by the order in which they appear. After a few bars of preamble we hear No. 18, followed by the clock striking six (as in the supper scene in the second act), then by No. 17, No. 20, No. 14, No. 15, No. 2, and No. 3, in that order. Two or three of the themes are repeated, but there is no suggestion of any "working-out" or "recapitulation".

ROMEO AND JULIET
Gounod (1818-1893)

PRINCIPAL CHARACTERS

ROMEO	*Tenor*
JULIET	*Soprano*
GERTRUDE	*Mezzo-soprano*
FRIAR LAURENCE	*Bass*
CAPULET	*Bass*
TYBALT	*Tenor*
MERCUTIO	*Baritone*
DUKE OF VERONA	*Bass*
GREGORIO	*Baritone*
STEPHANO	*Soprano*

I

One of the incurable delusions of the musical world is that *Romeo and Juliet* is ideal material for an opera. It is not; led astray by the sympathetic figures of the young lovers, both composers and librettists have failed to perceive that apart from these two there is very little in the play that lends itself readily to the purposes of opera. Romeo and Juliet themselves have their defects in this regard. For even in opera one looks for some development of character between the opening scene and the last; and the lovers of Verona do not develop. It is events that develop, not they. Each of them is good for one aria, and together they are good for a love duet and a death duet. That, however, is about as far as the opera composer can profitably go with them. For the rest, there is hardly anyone in the play who is of sufficient importance in himself to be worth wasting much time over in an opera, or with a dramatic physiognomy definite enough to lend itself to musical characterisation. Friar Laurence is not so much a personage as a moral principle. Tybalt, Paris, Mercutio, the Nurse, the old heads of the rival families, are alive in the play, but in an opera have to be sketched in so cursorily that they necessarily become mere lay figures.

Bellini's opera on the subject (1830) is called not *Romeo and Juliet* but *The Capulets and the Montagues*. It is rich in absurdities of its own and of its epoch—for instance, Romeo's part is allotted to a female singer—but, as its title indicates, it treats the passion and the fate of the lovers as part of the age-long strife between two ancient houses. Without some such reinforcement of what we may perhaps call, without offence, the mere love interest, it is difficult to make a strong opera text out of the play. Berlioz's *Romeo and Juliet* (1839) is a cross between opera and cantata—a compromise forced on the composer by his inability to gain an entry into the Paris Opéra. Gounod's five-act work, while undoubtedly influenced here and there by that of Berlioz, is a gallant attempt on his own part and that of his librettists, Barbier and Carré, to re-cast Shakespeare's play in terms of musical drama, in the sense in which that term was understood in the 1860's.

Gounod had achieved his world-success with *Faust* in 1859. His next "grand" opera was *The Queen of Sheba* (1862); *Romeo and Juliet* did not follow until 1867. He began work on this in the spring of 1865, at Saint-Raphaël, on the French Riviera. He was deeply interested in his subject, and the music flowed from his pen with the greatest facility: if ever an artist believed from the bottom of his soul in the worth of what he was doing it was Gounod during the composition of *Romeo and Juliet*. He felt, he says in one of his letters, that he was twenty again, instead of nearly fifty; and he saw and heard his characters as if they were truly alive and in the room with him, or accompanying him on his walks.

The work was produced at the Théâtre-Lyrique, Paris, on the 27th April 1867, with great success.

2

A short orchestral prelude, consisting of (*a*) an attention-arresting *allegro maestoso*:

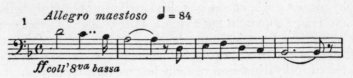

and (*b*) an agitated *fugato*, runs, by way of some solemn chords,
into a choral prologue, which is sung as the curtain rises: it tells,
as the prologue to the play does, of the ancient feud between the
two Verona houses, and the fatal love of the son of one for the
daughter of the other. At the conclusion of this the orchestra
gives out softly a strain:

which will be frequently associated later with the passion and the
tragic end of the lovers.

The setting of the first scene is a room in the Capulets' house,
where a masked ball is in progress to celebrate the birthday of
Juliet: we must overlook the trifling anachronism of making the
guests sing and dance in fourteenth-century Verona to waltz
rhythm:

After a brief conversation between Tybalt and Paris, old Capulet
advances and introduces his daughter to the company, which
greets her with a little chorus in praise of her beauty:

Ah! qu'elle est bel-le!   Ah! qu'elle est bel-le!

She expresses her girlish happiness in a naïve little monologue,
and the dance is resumed.

Mercutio, Romeo and a number of Montagues enter masked,
Romeo counselling prudence, for they are in the house of their

foe, the swashbuckler Mercutio boasting of his reliance on his sword. Romeo doubts whether they were wise to come to the ball, for he has had a dream. We are never allowed to learn what the "dream" was about, for Mercutio instantly seizes on the word as "cue for song". "So Queen Mab has been with you", he remarks—as in Shakespeare—and without further ado he launches into a ballad on that subject. A Queen Mab song, of course, was *de rigueur* in any opera after Berlioz's brilliant handling of the Shakespeare material. Gounod's descriptive setting of the words has a charm of its own.

Mab or no Mab, Romeo insists when the song is over, he has a presentiment of evil in this unfriendly house. But the words are hardly out of his mouth before he catches sight of Juliet, whose beauty at once makes him forget the Rosaline whom until then he had thought the fairest of women.

Juliet now comes forward with her nurse Gertrude, who compliments her on her betrothal to Count Paris. Little Juliet, however, has no desire for marriage; she prefers her present irresponsible condition, with its dreams and its round of pleasures suitable to her age and temperament—a philosophy which she expounds at length in a waltz song:

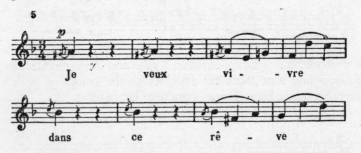

with a good deal of coloratura that is quite in keeping with the simple mentality of the singer.

Mercutio persuades Gertrude to go in to supper with him, thus making it possible for Romeo to approach Juliet. He addresses her, and receives her answer, in what is called in the score, for some reason or other, a madrigal, but is nothing more nor less than a conversational duet in Gounod's most charming vein:

Moderato ♩ = 66

Ange a - do - ra - ble, Ma main cou-pa - ble Pro - fane, en l'o-sant tou - cher,

with a great deal of refined verbal repartee on the French librettists' part: one would hardly have thought that Juliet, who has seen so little of the world, had so much wit in her.

 She has no sooner revealed to Romeo that she is the daughter of the Capulets than she is recalled to the festivities by her cousin Tybalt. He swears vengeance on the intruding Montague, whom he has recognised as Romeo by his voice. But old Capulet reappears and persuades his guests to dance again, and the act ends with a resumption of the waltz music (No. 3) with which it had begun.

3

The second act, the scene of which is the Capulet garden by night, opens with a suave orchestral prelude, descriptive partly of the milieu, partly of the unhappiness of Romeo and Juliet; it is followed by a brief chorus, in which Romeo's friends make mildly merry over his new infatuation. A light appears in Juliet's window, and at the sight of it Romeo launches into an impassioned cavatina:

Adagio ♩ = 52
p

Ah! lè-ve-toi, soleil! fais pâlir les é - toi-les,

in which, addressing Juliet as the sun, he calls on her to shine forth and put the stars to shame. The short dialogue that follows is quiet and thoughtful in tone: Juliet in particular seems to have

matured mentally to some extent since her waltz song in the first
act. They are interrupted by a chorus of Gregory and other
Capulet servants, who are annoyed to find that the intruding
Montague for whom they are looking has flown. They find some
consolation, however, in a little masculine irony at the expense of
Gertrude, who has come to look for Juliet. The lovers are soon
free to resume their talk. Juliet gravely gives her life into the
hands of Romeo, and asks him—to quote the Shakespearean
original of the scene—

> *If that thy bent of love be honourable,*
> *Thy purpose marriage, send me word tomorrow,*
> *By one that I'll procure to come to thee,*
> *Where and what time thou wilt perform the rite,*
> *And all my fortune at thy foot I lay,*
> *And follow thee my lord throughout the world.*

The adieux are fondly prolonged:

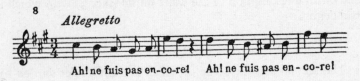

to the French equivalent of the famous

> *Good night, good night! parting is such sweet sorrow*
> *That I shall say good night till it be morrow!*

The act ends with a resumption of the quiet music of the commencement, now accompanying a paraphrase of Romeo's final
words to Juliet—

> *Sleep dwell upon thine eyes, peace in thy breast!*

The setting of the third act is Friar Laurence's cell. An orchestral prelude commences with a *fugato* which, though it soon appears to repent having assumed that scholastic form, defines sufficiently the religious atmosphere of the place. Romeo enters, and in agitated accents describes his love for Juliet, who, accompanied by her nurse, soon joins them and asks Friar Laurence to unite her with Romeo. He does so and gives them his blessing, with the hope that their union may bring about a reconciliation of the rival houses. The ceremony is carried out in a grave trio, which develops into a vigorous quartet when Gertrude joins her voice to those of the other three:

This reaches its climax in a soaring melody:

that reappears in the last scene, just before the death of the lovers.

The scene changes rapidly to the outside of the Capulet house, where Romeo's page, Stephano—a first cousin to the Siebel of *Faust*—who has not been able to trace his master since the preceding day, sings a piquant little song which, with its exhortations to the turtle-dove to fly from the vultures' nest:

R

Que fais-tu, blanche tourte-relle, Dans ce nid de vautours?

is obviously designed to exasperate the Capulet servants. This it succeeds in doing: Gregorio and his fellows come out of the house, and after an interchange of the provocative courtesies customary on these occasions they and the page draw their swords. Stephano is acquitting himself well against superior numbers when Mercutio enters from one side and Tybalt from another. These two soon come to insults and then to blows; but when Romeo appears on the scene Tybalt transfers his fury to him. Romeo tries to placate him, but the fiery Mercutio refuses to have any truce with the enemy: he attacks Tybalt again, and soon the stage is filled with the contending adherents of both houses. Mercutio is fatally wounded, whereupon Romeo in his rage kills Tybalt, whose last words are a call to Capulet to see that he is avenged. The imposing ensemble, which passes through many phases of emotion, culminates in a general lament over the tragic ending of the dispute:

Ô jour de deuil! Ô jour de lar-mes!

The Duke of Verona appears while the outcry is at its height; and in spite of Romeo's protestations that he slew Tybalt only to avenge his friend, the Montague is banished from the city, while the others are bidden to take a solemn oath to keep the peace. Romeo pours out his grief in a broad melody:

Ah! jour de deuil et d'horreur et d'a-larmes,

which is taken up by the others. The curtain falls with him vowing that in spite of his exile he will see Juliet again, and the Capulets refusing ever to make peace with their hereditary enemies.

4

Defying the ban, Romeo visits Juliet by night: and the first part of the fourth act is entirely taken up with their duet in her room. The scene opens and closes with the orchestral meditation already heard at the conclusion of the prologue to the opera, and quoted as our No. 2. The duet runs along the lines familiar to every student of Shakespeare: opening with an invocation to night, in honeyed sixths:

it passes on to the fond dispute as to whether the bird they hear is the lark, "the herald of the morning", or the nightingale, singing her song to the night:

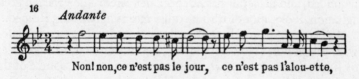

and so to the despairing parting of the lovers. The episode ends with Juliet confiding the departing Romeo to the care of the angels of heaven, to a last reminiscence of No. 2.

Her father, accompanied by Friar Laurence and the nurse, now enters to tell her that all is ready for her marriage to Paris. Juliet is in despair, but Friar Laurence whispers to her to be silent and

have no fear. After a brief quartet, Capulet leaves Juliet alone with
the Friar, who, he says, will instruct her in her duty. She turns
distractedly to him as the only one who can help her. Learning
that the thought of dissolution has no terrors for her, he hands
her a potion:

which will give her body the mere semblance of death for twenty-
four hours: her own people will cry, he assures her, "She is dead",
and the angels in heaven will reply, "She sleeps":

Romeo will be in the crypt when she awakes, and they will fly
from Verona together.[1]

The fifth act takes place in the family tomb of the Capulets.
Friar Laurence has sent a message by Stephano to Romeo in
Mantua, informing him of the device to which he and Juliet have
resorted; but the page has been attacked by the Capulets and
wounded, and his letter has not been delivered. The Friar, in great
agitation, looks about for some other means of reaching Romeo.

An orchestral interlude, based on the two themes associated
with the potion (Nos. 17 and 18), describes the death-like sleep
of Juliet. Then Romeo, who has heard from another source of the
death of Juliet—a detail for which we have to draw on our
recollections of the Shakespeare text!—enters to bid her his last
farewell. She is as beautiful in death as in life, he sings, to the

[1] When *Romeo and Juliet* arrived at the Paris Opéra in 1888 (with Patti,
Jean and Edouard de Reszke and Delmas in the principal rôles), sundry
additions were made to the original score: these included the celebration of
the wedding festivities by means of a ballet.

music of No. 2. He has no sooner taken the poison he had brought with him than Juliet awakes. A passionate duet follows, the lovers calling on each other to fly together to the confines of the world, but, unconsciously, with a contrary meaning in their words, for Juliet does not know that Romeo has taken poison. Soon he gives an agonised cry and discloses to her how, believing her to be dead, he too had made an end. In his last delirium his mind runs back to the scene in Juliet's chamber in which they had heard the song of the birds. "It is not morning", he says, "it is not the lark, but the nightingale, the confidant of love." She seizes his dagger and stabs herself, and they die in each other's arms, with their last breath imploring the forgiveness of heaven for their deed.

DER ROSENKAVALIER

Richard Strauss (1864)

PRINCIPAL CHARACTERS

PRINCESS WERDENBERG (THE FELDMARSCHALLIN)	*Soprano*
BARON OCHS AUF LERCHENAU	*Bass*
OCTAVIAN	*Mezzo-soprano*
HERR VON FANINAL	*Baritone*
SOPHIE	*Soprano*
MARIANNE	*Soprano*
VALZACCHI	*Tenor*
ANNINA	*Contralto*

I

In February 1909 Hugo von Hofmannsthal wrote to Strauss that he had just spent three tranquil afternoons drafting the complete scenario for a new opera. The situations, he said, were broadly comic, the action varied and almost as obvious as in a pantomime; there were opportunities for everything—lyricism, fun, humour, even a small ballet—and two big rôles, one for a baritone, the other for a shapely girl in man's clothes, "à la Farrar or Mary Garden". Place and period, Vienna in the time of Maria Theresa.

This was the first hint of *Der Rosenkavalier*. The musical reader will hardly require to be told that the scheme, "complete" as Hofmannsthal thought it at the time, was modified considerably afterwards: the baritone (Ochs) became a bass, and the true "big rôle" not the shapely girl-boy, not even Ochs, but the Princess. Hofmannsthal was mistaken, again, in imagining that the opera would play only "two hours and a half, i.e., half as long as *Die Meistersinger*"; *Der Rosenkavalier* is so long an opera that an uncut performance of it is virtually impossible under ordinary theatrical conditions. Strauss fell in love with the scenario at first sight of the text of Act I, though he thought this might prove "a trifle too subtle for the general public", and he foresaw that for parts like these he would need first-rate actors: "the usual opera-singers won't do at all."

He set to work at the music of the first act before the text of the other two was ready, and throughout he kept suggesting modifications of, or additions to, Hofmannsthal's text to conform to the music he already intended to write. Sometimes the poet adopted these suggestions; sometimes he rejected them or im-proved on them. Strauss wanted "a contemplative ensemble" at the end of the second act, to follow "the explosion of the dramatic bomb-shell". Hofmannsthal did indeed re-write the ending, but not along the lines proposed by Strauss. Three quiet curtains, he pointed out, would be a mistake; and as "contemplative" end-ings were indispensable in the cases of Act I and Act III, it was only Act II that could terminate in another fashion. Hofmannsthal thereupon outlined the end of the second act very much as we now have it—the intriguing Italian couple demand a fee, Ochs has them turned out, then, excellently pleased with himself, settles down to hum his waltz melody, and so on. The act as a whole, however, was still far from being what Strauss wanted it to be; and he made several admirable suggestions which Hofmannsthal had the good sense to accept. If ever a com-poser deserves to be regarded as joint author of an exception-ally good opera libretto it is the Strauss of *Der Rosenkavalier*: the reader will find it interesting to follow for himself, in the published correspondence of Strauss and Hofmannsthal, the process by which the text slowly became what it now is. The discussions went on from the early part of 1909 to the autumn of 1910.

Rehearsals began early in January 1911, and the opera received its first performance in Dresden, under Ernst von Schuch, on the 26th January: Margarete Siems was the Princess, Karl Perron the Ochs, Eva van der Osten the Octavian, and Minnie Nast the Sophie.

From the first, some of the German theatre directors jibbed at certain "risky" features of the libretto. Hofmannsthal wisely bowed to the storm he had unwittingly raised: he agreed, for instance, that, as he put it to Strauss, "the Princess shall be out of bed when the curtain rises", and he toned down some of the "coarsenesses" in the words of Ochs's part. Much more than this was required, however, before the work was deemed proper for the chaste ears of the Berlin public. The Intendant of the Berlin Opera, his Excellency Georg Hülsen-Haeseler (son of the Botho von Hülsen who, during his period of office at the same institution, showed such unfriendliness towards Wagner), simply would not produce the work in its original form; and as Hofmannsthal refused to subject the text to a drastic re-modelling, and Strauss no doubt felt that it was not for the composer to do anything of that kind, the necessary changes were made by Hülsen himself. They were many and curious.

The Princess, for Berlin purposes, was made to tell Octavian to conceal himself not "behind the bed" but "behind the screen". Beds, indeed, seem to have been a forbidden subject in the virtuous Berlin of 1911, except by way of escape from something still more shocking. In Hofmannsthal's text, Ochs tells the Princess, by way of illustration of the gracious lack of formality with which certain great ladies used to treat so distinguished a member of the Austrian nobility as himself, that when he called to pay his respects to Princess Brioche the lady made no scruple about receiving him, though she happened to be in her bath at the time, and there was nothing but a screen between them at the interview. Hülsen altered "bath" to "bed". Nor could the bold bad Baron be allowed, in Berlin, to describe himself as in matters amatory "a good hound on a good trail, keen on the scent of any sort of quarry, to right and to left." For Berlin this became "a good wind, turning the weather-vane now left, now right". Towards the end of the first act the Princess tells Octavian that she is going to church. Hülsen, for reasons best known to himself, substituted for this "going to pay a visit". Naïve little Sophie, it goes without saying, was not allowed to tell Octavian that so interested is she in the Austrian book of the peerage that she takes it to bed with her to study titles and pedigrees. In Berlin she was merely allowed to read it quietly in the evenings. After these examples of the purification the text of *Der Rosenkavalier* underwent at the hands of his Excellency Georg Hülsen-Haeseler, the reader will have little difficulty in imagining for himself the white-

washing which some of the more highly-coloured passages in
Ochs's rôle received.

2

The scene of *Der Rosenkavalier* is the Vienna of the early years
of the reign of Maria Theresa. While Feldmarschall Prince von
Werdenberg is away hunting bears and lynxes in the wilds of
Croatia, his wife, a lady who is nearing the age at which love calls
the more insistently because it feels that soon the idiom of its
call will be no longer understood, is engaged in another species
of venery. We see her, when the curtain rises, in her elegant
bedroom. The great bed stands in an alcove on the left: near it is
a threefold screen. On the other side of the large room are big
folding doors leading to an antechamber; at the back, in the very
centre of the wall, is a small door. There is a toilet table between
this door and the bed, and here and there some easy chairs,
tabourets, small sofas, etc.

It is morning: the sun streams in through the half-open window, and the song of birds is heard outside. The Princess, a
beautiful, dignified, refined and wholly sympathetic figure, is
reclining on a sofa, only one lovely hand and arm being visible to
the spectator, peeping from the sleeve of her lace gown. Kneeling
on a footstool by her side is the young Octavian—to give him his
full name and title, which we shall discover later, Count Octavian
Maria Ehrenreich Bonaventura Fernand Hyacinth Rofrano, scion
of a most distinguished Viennese family. To the Feldmarschallin
he is in particularly intimate moments Quinquin, while for him,
in such moments, she ceases to be Marie Therese and becomes
Bichette. When the opera opens, Octavian is just seventeen years
and two months old; and naturally the inexperienced boy takes
his passion for the Princess with the utmost seriousness. The brief
orchestral prelude begins with the projection, in successive bars,
of themes to be associated hereafter with Octavian:

1   *Con moto agitato* ♩ = 60

and the Feldmarschallin:

(The latter is one of those into-the-key-and-out-of-it-and-back-again melodies that are characteristic of Strauss). Nos. 1 and 2 are shown us in a close embrace, as it were; the marking is "tumultuously". At the ninth bar there comes another motive:

which is particularly suggestive of the somewhat exaggerated rapture of the boy in this his first "affair": Strauss has directed that the orchestral playing here shall be *agitato* and with a touch of excess in its exuberance. As the themes are developed, the composer notes in his score that "the working-up is to become positively parodistic".

A change of atmosphere comes with a more tranquil motive in the oboe:

which we shall learn to associate with the Princess in her graver moods; beneath it No. 2a—marked by Strauss "like a sigh"—makes its plaintive voice heard in the clarinet. No. 4 ebbs away into a phrase symbolising the resignation, a kind of *Verklärung*, that will be the only consolation of the Princess in the disillusionment which, she is already secretly conscious, threatens her where her youthful lover is concerned:

Finally, as the prelude nears its end, the love of the pair finds its simplest yet most heartfelt expression in a broad theme:

upon which Strauss dwells with particular affection.

It is just as we reach this theme that the curtain rises. Octavian launches into a flood of amorous and not always quite coherent babble: the more experienced Princess has greater control both of her emotions and of her verbal imagery. Octavian rushes from one boyish extravagance to another. He closes the window because he cannot bear that the robber daylight shall enjoy with him the sight of his beloved. When the tinkling of a bell is heard he throws himself into a heroic attitude, prepared to defend the sanctuary against all profane intruders. With some difficulty the Feldmarschallin persuades him to slip behind the screen as the small door back-centre opens,—to admit no more of a danger to their happiness than a little Black Boy in the Princess's service. He is carrying a silver salver with his mistress's morning choco-late on it. With a charming display of ceremony he places the salver on a small table, moves the latter up to the sofa, bows, and trips out again, always with his face turned in the direction of the Princess, who, while all this has been going on, has disappeared behind the curtains of the bed.

She reappears in a light dressing-gown bordered with fur; and when Octavian emerges from his hiding-place she reads him a semi-humorous little lecture on the imprudence of a cavalier leaving his sword lying about in his lady's room as he had done. He takes boyish offence at this, but she easily soothes him, and they sit down, to the accompaniment of a delightful waltz, to take chocolate together. Octavian crows lustily over the Field Marshal fooling away his time in the Croatian forests, while he, a fine young fellow, sits here, also engaged in hunting—what? A cloud passes over the Princess's brow. Let them not talk of the Field Marshal, she says: she had dreamed of him that night. This starts the jealous boy off once more. But the Princess soon hears again, this time in stark reality, the noise in the house which in her dream had accompanied the return of her husband. It *must* be the Prince, she says agitatedly, for the sound came from the back of the stage, whereas if it were some stranger who had called he would be in the antechamber. Octavian, of course, instan-taneously becomes the protective young hero again at the suggestion of danger threatening his beloved. He draws his sword and runs to the right. She recalls him: the antechamber, she points out, is by this time full of the usual morning crowd of callers and lackeys. He makes for the small centre door, but evidently there are people on the other side of that. The Feldmarschallin at last prevails on him to hide behind the bed curtains: then she turns resolutely to face whatever trouble it is that is developing outside.

Suddenly the expression on her face changes from one of apprehension to one of amusement, for the voice she has heard on the other side of the small door she recognises as that of a country cousin of hers, Baron Ochs of Lerchenau. She remembers now that some five or six days ago a letter from him had been brought to her just as she was entering her carriage with Octa-vian: she had put it aside, meaning to read it later, and then totally forgotten it from that hour to this.

Outside is heard the voice of the Major-Domo respectfully begging the newcomer to wait a moment in the gallery, and a loud domineering voice replying that a Baron Lerchenau does not kick his heels about in antechambers in that fashion. But before Ochs can enter there is a surprise in store for the Princess. Octavian reappears transformed into a serving-maid, in a skirt and short jacket, and with his hair tied up, as if in a cap, with a kerchief and a ribbon. Greatly pleased with himself for having conceived this brilliant plan of escape, he curtseys to the Feldmarschallin and explains, in working-class dialect, that he has not been long in her

Highness's service. His words are sung to the accompaniment of a waltz melody:

which will henceforth always be associated with Octavian. The Princess gives him a quick kiss as a compliment to his cleverness, and tells him to slip out of the room, go confidently through the crowd of lackeys, and return to the house in his proper clothes. She then seats herself on one of the sofas, with her back to the door, and begins to sip her chocolate.

But just as Octavian reaches the little door it is flung open, and Ochs comes blustering into the room in spite of the efforts of the footmen to restrain him. He is assuring them loftily that it goes without saying that her Highness will receive him when he catches sight of the pretty young serving-maid, who, not knowing what to do now, stands in confusion by the further wall. Ochs, who, country bumpkin as he is in many ways, has at any rate a theoretical acquaintance with the manners of society, bows three times to the Feldmarschallin in the French style, approaches her with the nonchalance of a man of the world, conducts her to her chair—she had risen at his entry—and in due course seats himself by her.[1] All through the long conversation that follows, however, his thoughts are mainly on the appetising maid, whom, by one device or another, he manages to keep in the room all the time, to the great amusement of not only the Princess but Octavian. The latter, his first embarrassment overcome, plays up to Ochs coolly and impudently, serving him with chocolate and generally acting the part of a minx to perfection. The Princess explains that the girl is Mariandel, her personal maid, fresh from the country, as yet untrained in the ways of the city; all of which makes the child still more desirable in the eyes of the Baron.

[1] There is a charming touch, of the kind possible only in music, when the Feldmarschallin apologises to Ochs for having told the servants not to admit anyone that morning, as she had a touch of migraine. The orchestra's sly comment on this is a *pianissimo* breathing of one of the love motives!

Gradually he makes it clear why he has called on the Princess at so early an hour. His explanation is really an expansion of that letter of his which she had neglected to read—an awkward little lapse which it takes all her tact to conceal from him. He has become betrothed, and is now in Vienna to complete the business arrangements precedent to the union. The bride is a certain young Fräulein Faninal. The father is unfortunately not a born aristocrat like himself, though he has recently been raised to the nobility by Her Majesty for his services as contractor for the provisioning of the Austrian army of the Netherlands. The absence of blueness in the family blood, however, is atoned for, in the Baron's eyes, by Faninal's riches; he owns a dozen houses and a palace in and about the city, and, the prospective son-in-law is glad to say, the man's health is none of the best.

It appears that Ochs, who has brought a crowd of servants from his estate in the country with him, is putting up at the moment at the White Horse. Before he can enjoy the hospitality of his future father-in-law he must, in accordance with custom, send his bride a Silver Rose; and it is especially in the matter of the selection of the bearer of this token that he has come to ask the Feldmarschallin's advice. She assures him that she is entirely at his service in this or any other matter connected with the marriage. One of the things he most needs is a good attorney to handle the question of the settlements; and the Princess is happy to inform him that her own lawyer generally waits on her about this time in the morning.

The Major-Domo having entered with the information, given with a somewhat bored air, that the antechamber is filled with the usual crowd awaiting an audience, the Baron takes advantage of the Feldmarschallin's preoccupation to ask the serving-maid whether she has ever been out to supper tête-à-tête with a gentleman. The orchestral waltz tune to which he does this:

will be put to piquant use in the third act. When the Princess comments amusedly on the frank way in which her cousin pursues his pleasure wherever he finds it, Ochs plunges into a long and extremely candid exposition of his philosophy in these matters. Compared with him, one gathers, Casanova was an amateur and Don Giovanni a mere débutant. For Ochs has elevated the conquest of women to a science, with different laws for this place or that, this season or that, one feminine physicality or mentality and another. His unapproachable ideal and the object of his professional envy, he confesses, is Jupiter, who had the truly god-like capacity to woo in a hundred male guises. As it is, though, he has a very serviceable strategy of his own for each type of campaign. As he unrolls the lengthy catalogue of his prowess in the lists of love, Mariandel, who has been listening with the greatest interest —as the Baron wished her to do—coyly tells the Marschallin that the gentleman makes her feel nervous.

He reaches the point of asking the Princess outright to give him the maid to wait upon his future Baroness, for she is a fine piece of goods: speaking as a connoisseur, he could swear that she has blue blood in her. The Princess ironically compliments him on his discernment. Such a phenomenon, he assures her, is not at all uncommon in the exalted circles in which he moves; he himself, in fact, he adds complacently, has for his body-servant a young fellow with real Lerchenau blood in him, as his features will prove when he waits on the Princess with the Silver Rose. This seems to give the Marschallin an idea. She sends Mariandel out for a certain medallion: Octavian is a little uncertain as to the wisdom of this, but she assures him sotto voce that she knows full well what she is doing. The medallion she shows to Ochs, asking him if the young man portrayed on it— her own cousin Octavian, younger brother of the Marquis Rofrano, she tells him—will suit him as Rose Bearer. Ochs is at once struck by the resemblance between this Octavian and Mariandel, but characteristically accounts for this by supposing that the serving-maid is one of the Marquis's by-blows. The Princess humours him in this notion; it was probably for that reason, she explains, that she took the girl into her personal service and now does not want to part with her. She dismisses

Mariandel, who goes out through the folding doors on the right, giving a last coquettish glance at the Baron, who has kept hard on her heels till she slams the door in his face.

The truly eighteenth century scene that follows is in the nature of an intermezzo. An old waiting-woman enters first carrying a wash-basin, a ewer and a towel. The Princess retires for a few moments behind a screen which a couple of footmen have brought forward from the alcove. Two others arrange the toilet table and a chair in the centre of the room; yet another two fling the folding doors open wide. It is the hour of the Princess's levee; and Baron Ochs, who has been visibly upset by Mariandel's saucy treatment of him, stands aside to watch the motley crowd that now pours into the room. The Head Cook enters, followed by a kitchen hand bearing a book of menus, from which the Marschallin is to choose the dishes for the day. The Princess's Attorney comes in; she presents him to the Baron, who takes him on one side to instruct him with regard to the contract to be drawn up between himself and Faninal. We see also a Hairdresser and his assistant, who, with a becoming sense of their own importance, get to work at the Marschallin's coiffure; a Milliner with the latest styles in hats; a Scholar with a folio; an Animal Dealer with some delightful little dogs and a monkey; a Noble Widow who has come down in the world, and is here, in deepest mourning, to beg the great lady's protection for the three daughters she has with her, all likewise in black; a Tenor (accompanied by a flautist) who has been recommended to her Highness and is in hopes that he will be asked to show what he can do; and finally two very dubious-looking characters, Valzacchi and Annina, intriguing Italians, living by their wits and ready to do any work so long as it is not too honest, of a type well known to the Vienna of the eighteenth century.

Hofmannsthal sets all these puppets simultaneously and successively in the most varied motion, and Strauss skilfully weaves them all into a connected musical tissue. The Marschallin has a good word or a protective gesture for all of them except the Italian couple, from whose furtive attempt to interest her in a surreptitiously printed paper containing all the latest scandal about the fashionable world she turns with disgust. (Val-

zacchi and Annina always speak in a bastard German of their own).
The Tenor, preening himself in the best tenor style, sings, in Italian,
an aria that is packed with the conventional poetic "conceits" of
the Italian aria of that period. He is getting on quite nicely—the
flautist accompanying him on his instrument—until he is approaching the effective top note of his second stanza, when he is
shouted down by the Baron. The latter has been having a lot of
trouble with the Attorney. He wants the contract for the dowry
to include a clause binding Faninal to acquire and convey to
him certain properties that used to belong to the Lerchenaus but
have latterly passed out of the family. When the Attorney ventures to point out the legal objections to this—the law providing
for a *Morgengabe* [1] from groom to bride but not from bride to
groom—the Baron flies into a temper which the man of law's
timorous explanations only make worse. Finally he gives such a
raucous howl of "Als Morgengabe!" that the poor Tenor has to
break off sharply just when he is working up to his "Ahi! che
resiste puoco cor", and go off with no more reward for his
labours than the gracious permission to kiss the great lady's hand.

While the Hairdresser has been busy with the Princess a
courier in a splendid livery of pink, black and silver has entered
with a note for her; presumably it is from Octavian. Having read
it, she lets the Hairdresser use the sheet to adjust the temperature
of his curling iron. A little later there come slouching through the
small door at the back the Baron's Body-servant—a strongly
built young lout with an expression of stupid insolence—Ochs's
Almoner—a short but sturdy figure, with a wild, gnome-like
look—and his Chasseur, who looks as if he had stepped straight
from the farmyard into his ill-fitting livery. The Body-servant
has a jewel case of red morocco under his arm. All three of them
are to the last degree boorish; after some difference of opinion
between them on the question of precedence they take up a
position near their master. After the latter's altercation with the
Attorney, the Major-Domo and the footman, on a hint from the
Princess, clear the room of almost everyone. Of the miscellaneous
crowd that had filled it a little while before there remain no one

[1] A "morning-gift" from bridegroom to bride on the day after the
wedding.

now but the Scholar, with whom the Marschallin exchanges a few
words, Valzacchi and Annina. Seeing the Princess engaged, the
two Italians steal up to Ochs and offer him their services in any
delicate situation that may occur—cause for jealousy, for example, in the case of a young bride: they could keep their eye on
such a person, they assure him, from morning till night.

Though the Baron does not anticipate needing them in that
way, it occurs to him that the shady couple may be useful to him
in another. Do they know a certain Mariandel, her Highness's
waiting-maid? he asks. They have to admit that at present they
do not, but promise that they soon will. Ignoring Valzacchi's
hand, stretched out for a reward, Ochs turns to the Princess, who
is now free again. He takes from his Body-servant the case containing the Silver Rose and hands it to the Marschallin. She promises to have it sent at once to the young Count Rofrano, who,
she is sure, will have great pleasure in presenting it to Fräulein
Faninal. And now, she says, she must beg the Baron to excuse
her, as she must go to church.

Ochs and his servants, the Attorney, the two Italians and the
Major-Domo having withdrawn, the Princess seats herself at her
toilet table and unburdens her soul of a good deal of perilous
stuff that has been weighing on it since she awoke that morning.
Her contempt for the woman-hunting, gold-digging Ochs
flashes out in a biting phrase or two. And yet, she asks, is not his
way the way of the world? Was she not herself taken, like Faninal's daughter, straight from the convent to the altar? And Time,
alas, does not stand still. Soon the "little Resi" of that distant
day will be spoken of as "the old Princess Resi, the old Marschallin". Where are the snows of yesteryear? How can the gods
look on unmoved at the sadness and bitterness of mortal things?
For in herself, she feels, she is still the woman she has always
been: and if indeed the gods will have it that onward-hurrying
life must some day pass her by, why are they so cruel as to make
her conscious of it? Would it not be greater charity to hide her
tragedy from her too clear-seeing eyes? For the tragedy is less in
undergoing this transformation than in being aware of it: and at
these words the motive of sadness and longing (No. 4) wells up
with inexpressible sweetness in the orchestra.

Her meditations are broken in upon by Octavian, who returns dressed for riding. At once he senses that the Marschallin is in one of her pensive moods; but this he puts down to the fear—for him rather than for herself—she had felt at the possibility of the sudden return of the Field Marshal. In his unthinking youthful high spirits he tries to take up the conversation where it had been broken off by the irruption of the Baron into the room. But he soon discovers, to his dismay, that the woman before him is no longer the Bichette of an hour or two before. He weeps help-lessly, pathetically, at her grey musings upon the transitoriness of all this world's joys. But when she goes on to say that some day, sooner or later, he will leave her, he breaks out into passion-ate protests. She reiterates steadily, "It will come: today or tomorrow you will leave me for one younger and prettier." For Time is ruthless: it flows ever on and on, indifferent to the happi-ness which poor mortal hearts would fain make eternal, falling silently, inexorably, like the sand in the hour-glass. And the only thing to do is to face one's fate bravely, taking one's happiness lightly when it comes, letting it lightly go when the time for that is reached.

She dismisses the now sobered and wretched boy with infinite loving-kindness, but also with a decision that brooks no answer. She is going to church now, she tells him, and after that she must visit an old bedridden relative: later she will send Octavian word when she will be taking the air, and he can join her in the Prater and ride beside her carriage. Made more thoughtful, in spite of himself, than he has ever been in his life before, he goes out with a quiet "As you wish, Bichette." Hardly is he out of the room when the Marschallin starts up with a despairing cry of "I did not even kiss him!" She rings violently. When the footmen have answered the bell she bids them hasten after the Count and recall him; but they assure her that they had seen him gallop away like the wind. She dismisses them and sends for the little Negro Boy, to whom she hands the morocco case. "Go to Count Octavian", she tells him. "Give him this and say that within is the Silver Rose. He will understand." The child trips away with the case, and the curtain falls with the Princess sitting with bowed head, lost in melancholy thoughts. So ends a scene which, from the moment of Octavian's entry to the fall of the curtain, has few equals in opera for the beauty and depth of its humanism. The closing stages of it are dominated musically by some of the motives most closely associated with the Princess, her sadness and longing in the midst of happiness, and her matured wisdom of life—No. 4, with an exquisite new pendant:

No. 5 in its full *Verklärung*, and a most moving *andante* reminiscence of the passionate No. 6 over a throbbing bass.

3

The second act is played in Faninal's house. We see a great room with a door on the left, a large window on the right, and, at the back of the stage, a centre door leading to an ante-chamber. The corners of this back wall are rounded off by a couple of fireplaces which will play a decisive part in the action later.

The household of the recently ennobled bourgeois is all excitement over the great event in the offing—the arrival of the bridegroom's messenger with the Silver Rose. Faninal's Major-Domo, who has perhaps been acquired, along with the title, to teach the army contractor the ways of high society, is reminding his master that etiquette forbids the bride's father to be there when the Rose Bearer arrives. Faninal accordingly leaves, telling his daughter Sophie that when he returns it will be with the bridegroom—"the Noble and Worshipful Herr von Lerchenau", adds Sophie's duenna Marianne, running the titles over her tongue, all feminine flutters over the honour to the family implied by this marriage.

She and Sophie watch from the window the departure of Faninal's carriage, Marianne almost hysterical with excitement, Sophie doing her best to be sincere in her maiden prayer to heaven that her head may not be turned by her elevation to the aristocracy. Her mother is dead, and she is all alone; may she be as modest and sensible in her new situation in life as in her old, not vain or haughty. But in the end her curiosity gets the better of her dutiful moralising. For she becomes more and more excited as Octavian's couriers, in the street below, are heard calling out "Rofrano! Rofrano!" ever more insistently as the gorgeous coach, the sight of which sends Marianne into an ecstasy of admiration, draws nearer to the Faninal palace. Strauss piles up the excitement in the room and in the street in skilful fashion: the "Rofrano" motive is that of Octavian (No. 7), but in a much more imposing form: the theme, in fact, now develops with a dignity which we should hardly have expected from it the first time we heard it in Act 1.

The music works up to a magnificent climax as the centre door is flung open by the footmen, and Octavian enters, a dazzling figure in white and silver: he is bareheaded, and in his right hand he holds the Silver Rose. He is accompanied by a number of his own servants in picturesque liveries of various kinds; prominent among them is a negro carrying his master's hat. One footman bears ceremoniously in both hands the case of the Silver Rose. Behind these servants of Octavian stand those of Faninal's household.

The music suddenly softens as Octavian, with inborn aristocratic grace though obviously not without a certain youthful embarrassment that has a charm of its own, advances to Sophie and hands her the Rose with a little speech couched in the formal terms usual on these occasions: "I have the honour to present to the high-and-well-born bride, in the name of my cousin, Baron von Lerchenau, the Silver Rose, the token of his love." At the mention of the Baron we hear a suggestion of a motive:

which will later be identified with Ochs in his capacity as wooer. Another new theme also heard for the first time during Octavian's little speech:

is to be associated not only with the Silver Rose but with the impression made on each other by Sophie and Octavian at this their first meeting. Its continuation:

which is more specifically connected with the Rose itself, is one of the most salient features of the score, by reason not only of its odd sequences of chords but of its curious tinkling timbre, due to the mixture of flutes, harps, solo violins and celesta. The passage remains, even after repeated hearings, strangely and rather perplexingly alien to the general texture of the work: some listeners never get quite reconciled to it.

The meeting of Octavian and Sophie brings a new something into the lives of both of them. Each of them is at once fascinated and disturbed by the beauty of the other; and from the depths of their hearts youth calls to youth. To each of them comes the same thought—"Never have I lived till today; and may this heavenly vision last to all eternity!" Their ecstasy attains its musical culmination in a phrase launched by Sophie as she savours the fragrance of the Silver Rose, upon which some drops of Persian attar have been sprinkled:

"A rose of paradise, not of earth, it is", she sings; "it is like a greeting from heaven; the perfume seems to tug at my heart." The peculiar melodic turn of No. 13—the preliminary upward leap, the momentary poise upon the highest note but one of the phrase, followed by a couple of descending triplets—is one which Strauss unconsciously employs more than once in his works for the expression of rapturous emotion: we have the counterpart of No. 13, for example, in a well-known melody in *Don Juan*:

and again in Salome's cry to Jochanaan, "Dein Mund ist wie ein Korallenzweig in der Dämmerung des Meers":

The footman carrying the jewel case hands it to Marianne, to whom Sophie gives also the Silver Rose. Case and Rose are then passed on to the Major-Domo, who goes off with them with much ceremony through the door at the right. Both Octavian's and Faninal's servants all withdraw after three chairs have been placed near the centre of the stage; two of them are for Sophie and Octavian; the other, placed a little to the back and side, is for Marianne, who remains there as duenna.

The world-forgetting emotion of the boy and girl at the first sight of each other has by now burned itself out. They are no longer disembodied spirits predestined to each other from the beginning of time, finding each other by a miracle across interstellar space. They are back in the world of commonplace reality again, and as Fräulein Sophie Faninal and the young Count Octavian Rofrano they feel a little shy and awkward. Octavian discovers that Sophie knows not only his age to a month but can reel off the long list of his baptismal names and titles better than he can himself, for, as she innocently confesses, the Book of the Nobility is her favourite reading. She even knows that among his intimates he is known as Quinquin; and as she utters that word of tender memories the orchestra gives out a soft reminiscence of a passage towards the end of the first act in which the Feldmarschallin had used it. Sophie's transparent simplicity and her ignorance of the world—as shown especially by some of her more naïve remarks about the way she intends to assert her right to precedence after her marriage, and her frank confession that Octavian pleases her more than any man she has ever met—move the young Rofrano deeply.

They are still talking along these lines when the door at the back opens and Faninal enters, ceremoniously conducting Ochs, who is accompanied by a posse of his own clumsy servants. Faninal presents the Baron to his bride. Ochs is, if anything, more completely, more fatuously at his ease than usual, for he can approach the bourgeois world only *de haut en bas*. His condescending familiarity with everyone wins the grateful admiration of Faninal and Marianne; but his coarseness, his animal possessiveness, his frankly expressed view of Sophie as a filly he has acquired and whose points and paces he admires soon bring her to the stage of open revolt. She finds him exceedingly ill-bred; what is perhaps worse, he is pock-marked. With the greatest condescension the Baron deigns to accept a glass of old Tokay from Faninal; then he turns to Sophie and compliments her on being physically the delicate type that appeals to him most. "Just what I would have ordered" would be the modern equivalent of his remarks, which end with a fatuous expression of his satisfaction with himself and his good fortune: "I have all the luck of the Lerchenaus!" And when Sophie breaks away from him with anger and disgust written in every line of her face he approves of her more than ever; these mettlesome fillies are what he likes best of all the breed! He complacently assures her that one of these days she will discover what he is to her—as the song has it, "With me, no room too small; without me, each day too dull"; and he hums for her benefit the taking little waltz-melody which, of all the tunes associated with him, characterises him best:

14   ♩. = 48

Octavian, white with rage, at last crushes his wineglass in his hand and throws the fragments on the floor. He is on the point of leaving the house without further ceremony when the Attorney enters, with whom and Faninal the Baron, after a few more compliments to Sophie on her spitfire charm, goes into the adjoining room to discuss business. His cousin Taverl, he tells Sophie, will entertain her while he is away. Octavian he assures, in his usual familiar patronising style, that he is even at liberty to cast sheep's eyes at the girl if he likes, for the less prudery a man of the world finds in his bride the better he is pleased.

As Ochs goes into the room on the left he insists on Faninal following him at not less than the regulation three paces. Faninal in turn demands the same measure of respect from the Attorney, and the latter in his turn requires it from his clerk. When the coast is clear, Octavian and Sophie quickly come to an understanding. Never, Sophie declares, will she marry such a boor as Ochs: and she begs the help of Octavian as her only friend. There comes an interruption in their talk that seems dramatically quite unnecessary. Some of Faninal's female servants are seen through the door at the back, being pursued across the anteroom by Ochs's loutish rabble. As one girl in particular seems to be in some danger, the Major-Domo invokes the assistance of Marianne, who runs off with him into the anteroom to deal with the situation. The object of all this rather clumsy manoeuvring on Hofmannsthal's part has simply been to find a pretext for getting Marianne out of the room, thus leaving the young couple alone together for the crucial scene.

Now that they are alone and unobserved, the young people freely confess their love for each other. Octavian is willing to help Sophie, but first, he says, she must help herself. She must strike a decisive blow not simply for her own freedom but for theirs; and this "Für uns zwei" seems to Sophie the sweetest thing she has ever heard. The long, rapturous colloquy ends in a passionate embrace and kiss. While they are locked in each other's arms, Valzacchi and Annina creep out from the fireplaces in the corners of the room and steal up behind the lovers. Valzacchi seizes Octavian's arms from behind; Annina takes hold of

Sophie. Then they call loudly to Baron Lerchenau to come and see the pretty picture.

Ochs comes in, folds his arms with great dignity, and asks Sophie, who meanwhile has freed herself and run to the side of Octavian, whether she has anything to say to him by way of explanation. Octavian speaks for her, though with some difficulty; at last, however, he manages to make it clear to the Baron that Sophie wants nothing more to do with him and certainly will not marry him. As Ochs, too self-satisfied and thick-skinned to take all this seriously, tries to lead Sophie through the centre door to her father, Octavian draws his sword and bars the exit. Ochs by this time does not like the way things are shaping; for if he could be accused of possessing a single virtue it is certainly not physical courage. He gives a shrill whistle, in answer to which his servants come running in. The sight of them emboldens him to draw his own sword. Thereupon Octavian, by this time beside himself with fury, rushes at him and wounds him in the upper arm.

Ochs's sawdust courage at once runs out of him. He sets up a great howl that he is murdered, calls for a doctor and bandages, and orders his yokels to set upon Octavian. But they content themselves with threats: the last thing in the world they want to do is to get within lunging distance of that circling sword. Soon the whole place is in an uproar. All Faninal's servants, male and female, among them Marianne, come pouring in and excitedly discuss the new situation, the main facts regarding which have been given them by the two Italians. The Baron's attendants want to tear up the clothes of the younger and better-looking of Faninal's maid-servants for bandages; but this drastic plan is rendered unnecessary by Marianne and a couple of maids, who run out and return with bandages, basins and sponges. They are all shouting and gesticulating round Ochs, who has been accommodated with a chair in the centre of the room, when Faninal enters with the Attorney and his clerk. The situation is explained to Faninal, who is heartbroken at this insult to so great and good a man as the Baron. He will not listen to explanations from either Octavian or Sophie; the latter, if she does not marry Ochs, will be sent to a convent for the remainder of her days.

Octavian, treating Faninal with scrupulous courtesy all the time, at last takes his leave, whispering to Sophie, as he does so, that she will soon hear from him. As he goes, Marianne marches out with the tearful Sophie; and the excited group in the centre of the stage having broken up we see Ochs comfortably extended on two or three chairs, with his arm in a sling and a doctor fussing round him. The air is rent from time to time with the lamentations of Faninal, who cannot get over the insult to the noble Baron in *his* palace.

Soon there is no one left on the stage but the Baron and his servants. By this time Ochs, having had a generous draught of wine, is feeling that matters after all are not so bad as he thought they were going to be. He can even think tolerantly of the young puppy of no more than seventeen who has defied him, and really affectionately of the little spitfire of a Sophie for the way she stood up to him. He begins to troll the melody of his favourite song (No. 14):

> *Ohne mich, ohne mich, jeder Tag dir so bang,*
> *Mit mir, mit mir, keine Nacht dir zu lang;*

which now expands joyously as he congratulates himself on having "the luck of all the Lerchenaus":

While he is in this thoroughly self-satisfied mood Annina enters with a letter for him. At his request she reads it to him, for his glasses are not handy. It is from Mariandel, confessing that his charms have enslaved her, though she had thought it prudent to conceal the fact from the Princess; she is free the following evening, and hopefully awaits an answer from the gentleman. (The identity of the writer of the letter is made clear to everyone but the Baron by the Octavian motive (No. 7) accompanying the reading of it in the orchestra). The delighted Ochs bids Annina come to his room shortly with pen, ink and paper, when he will dictate his reply. Ignoring her plain hint that a reward for the messenger would be the correct thing, he dismisses her and gaily trolls his "Ohne mich!" again, which this time the orchestra takes up and expands exuberantly. Annina goes out with a resentful backward glance at him: that stinginess of his will cost him dear before long!

4

There have been a few crudities among the incidents of the second act. There are many more of these in the third act; the librettist's handling of certain points of this, indeed, would hardly be tolerable if it were not for Strauss's music.

The third act opens with a brilliant orchestral *fugato*, played at a great pace and for the most part in a sort of whisper; it suggests that something uncanny is in the air, while suggestions of themes already met with in connection with Octavian, Ochs and the two Italians hint fairly broadly at a coming joke at the Baron's expense. Something of this sort must presumably have occurred to Octavian as soon as, or even before, he had left Faninal's house. For the working out of the practical details of it he must have been dependent on the professional technique of Valzacchi and Annina; and as only some thirty hours or so can have elapsed between the delivery of the letter to Ochs and the opening of the third act, it is evident that in matters of this kind the Italians were quick workers.

The curtain rises while the prelude is still in progress, and though a good deal of action goes on on the stage from that point onwards, it is for a considerable time only in dumb show. The scene is a private room in an inn, with a curtained recess on the left, containing, we are given to understand, a bed, a door leading to another room,[1] a door back-centre, a blind window and a sideboard on the right, and a table laid for two towards the right. There are candlesticks with many candles on this table and elsewhere, in addition to sconces on the walls. At the present moment so few of these candles are lit that the room is quite dark.

[1] The text book gives this door as "rechts", but it is "links" in the score.

We soon have a tolerably clear idea of the nature of the plot that has been hatched out against Ochs. Annina is there, got up as a lady in mourning, and putting the finishing touches to her face and costume. Mariandel looks in for a moment, to the tune of No. 7; and to prove to the spectator that she is really Octavian she lifts her skirts—to get a purse which she throws to the grateful Valzacchi—revealing a man's costume underneath, with riding boots. Five "fishy-looking men"—to quote the libretto—enter and are coached by Valzacchi in their parts; at the appropriate moments they are to pop their heads out of trap-doors and secret panels. Candles are hurriedly lit under the supervision of Valzacchi, whose watch tells him that Ochs may be here any minute now. A reminiscence of No. 8, which, it will be remembered, was first heard in Act I when Ochs asked Mariandel if she had ever been out to supper alone with a gentleman, suggests that the Baron has already arrived at the rendezvous.

At last Valzacchi opens the centre door, bowing and scraping to Ochs, who, accompanied by his Body-servant, enters with Octavian on his left arm; the right is in a sling. For a little while past we have been conscious of a pleasant little waltz being played in some other part of the inn:

When Ochs hears it he is at first for ordering it to stop, as he had not undertaken to pay for any music; but on second thoughts he decides it may as well continue. He is emphatic, however, on the point of extinguishing most of the candles and getting rid of the fishy-looking men: his own servant, he says, will wait at table.

Soon the room is clear of everyone except Ochs, Octavian and the Body-servant, who brings some bottles from the sideboard and from now on takes an impudent interest in the spectacle before him of the way of an Ochs with a maid. The Baron begins the attempted seduction to an endless flood of waltz music: it is in waltz rhythm also that Mariandel refuses wine—"Nein, nein, nein, nein! I' trink kein Wein!":

She plays up to him so magnificently that we begin to wonder where Octavian obtained his knowledge of that particular female type. She is by turns amorous, coy, startled and sentimental, this last more especially when the music weaves its soft spell around her; and as she is a good German girl her sentimentality takes, of course, the form of platitudinous philosophising. She discourses quite fluently on the standard theme of Time hurrying by them like the wind, so that soon they two, like the rest of the world, will be no more, passing away unwept, unsung. All this she says to an enchantingly insinuating waltz strain:

These flights of poetry and philosophising, of course, are beyond the prosaic Ochs. Is it the drop of wine she has had that makes her feel like that, he asks with some concern, or perhaps her stomacher pressing on her little heart?

It is as well that Strauss has been able to flood the scene with his delicious music, for the action now and for some time to come is Teutonic farce of a rather poor quality. The barrack-room baiting of the Baron is carried to wearisome lengths. Faces suddenly appear and as suddenly disappear at trapdoors and elsewhere. What seemed to be a blind window is flung open, revealing Annina in mourning, who, addressing him as Leupold, claims Ochs as the husband who had deserted her, and, in the presence of the landlord and others who run into the room to see what all the noise is about, threatens him with all the penalties of the law. She lets loose on him four young children, of ages between four and ten, who caper round him shouting "Papa! Papa!" And even when he is not being tormented in this fashion the Baron is hag-ridden by the resemblance between the face of the Mariandel whom he is pressing so closely to him and that of the vicious boy who is answerable for the pain he sometimes feels in his right arm.

It is Annina and the four children who bring matters to a climax. Feeling that he is going mad under their baiting and the warnings of the landlord that bigamy is a serious matter, Ochs flings open the window and yells for the police to come and "protect a man of quality". Soon a Commissary of Police enters with a couple of constables. Ochs starts off on a confident state-ment, all in his own favour, of what has been happening, but he soon finds that the Commissary does not take him as seriously as he takes himself. He demands proof that the bald ruffian standing before him—for Ochs, to cool his fevered brain, had some time previously taken off his wig and hung it where now he cannot find it—is really the Baron Lerchenau he claims to be. Ochs appeals for confirmation to Valzacchi, but the latter, after ex-changing glances with Octavian, declines to commit himself on that point. The Commissary next wants to know who the girl is. Ochs tries to pass her off as his fiancée, having an innocent bit of supper with him at the inn. One clumsy lie necessarily leads to another under the Commissary's close questioning. The Baron declares the girl to be Fräulein Sophie Faninal. The words are no sooner out of his mouth than Faninal himself enters: he had been summoned a little while before by Valzacchi, at Octavian's bidding, to rescue his future son-in-law, who was in great danger. When the Commissary learns that this newcomer is the Herr Faninal just mentioned, he naturally assumes that the young lady in the case is his daughter. The Baron tries to wriggle out of that by saying that this gentleman must be another Herr Faninal—not the father of his betrothed but a kinsman of some sort; but when Faninal recognises him as his prospective son-in-law he has to abandon that line of defence. The Commissary's next question to Faninal is, "Then this girl here is your daughter?" From that stranglehold there is, of course, no escape whatever for Ochs; and the situation gets still worse for him when Sophie herself arrives. Faninal broken-heartedly exposes the perfidy of her wooer—that rascal standing there with his morganatic wife and his four children; but Sophie is overjoyed at the discovery.

At this point it is necessary, for the later purposes of the action, to get Faninal out of the room for a while. This Hofmannsthal achieves by making him fall suddenly sick under all the disappointment and mortification of the last few minutes. As he appears to be on the point of fainting, Sophie and a number of others carry him into the adjoining room. By this time the Baron has recovered his wig, and with it something of his blustering self-assurance. But the Commissary still has some awkward questions to which he insists on getting an answer. Ochs tries to bribe Mariandel to support him with a whispered promise that he will marry her. She repulses him, however, and asks for a private word with the Commissary. Taking him aside, she evidently reveals the plot to him, for the officer seems vastly amused, especially when, Octavian having disappeared behind the bed curtains, Mariandel's garments are thrown out one by one, and finally Octavian's head appears through an opening.

The Baron, who has seen something of all this but as yet does not quite understand it, tries to get to the alcove, but is held back by the two constables. While he is struggling to get free of them the Princess enters.

5

At this point of the story a little digression becomes necessary.

The spectator generally wonders how in the name of dramatic probability the Marschallin turns up in such a place at such a time. On the face of it it certainly seems to be stretching the long arm of coincidence to breaking-point. But if the spectator has kept both eyes open during the scene of the baiting of the Baron he has probably noticed that shortly after the Commissary's entry Ochs's Body-servant had run out of the room: and if the spectator further happens to be a skilled thought-reader he will have surmised that the man was going to summon the Feldmarschallin. The plain truth would seem to be that Hofmannsthal had got thus far without himself having any clear idea how the great lady was to be brought to that somewhat disreputable hostelry at the critical moment. In the *score* we are told that at the point of the action just mentioned "the Body-servant, who looks very worried about the situation, suddenly seems to have been struck by an idea how to redeem it, and runs out through the centre door." But this stage direction is not in the German *text book*; apparently it was an afterthought, which probably only occurred to Hofmannsthal and Strauss when they realised, perhaps at rehearsal, that in the original text the visit of the Princess to the inn had been left quite unexplained.

The stage directions when she enters are a further proof of this. In the text book these instructions run thus: "First some men in the Marschallin's livery appear, who range themselves in a line. Then the Marschallin enters, the little Black Boy carrying her train." In the score, however, after the words "First some men in the Marschallin's livery appear", there is inserted "then the Baron's Body-servant." A little later we read, in both text book and score, that "the Body-servant goes towards the Baron, looking proud and pleased with himself; and the Baron indicates that he is satisfied with him." Which is all very well; but for one thing it is highly improbable that the spectator will be aware of this interchange of glances, for naturally all eyes turn to the Princess when she makes her imposing entry, and it is still more improbable that the spectator has noticed the exit of the Servant some time before, or, if he did observe it, grasped the intention of it. Hofmannsthal cannot be acquitted of handling most inexpertly one of the most vital episodes in the development of the action.

One wonders, indeed, to what extent his original scheme for the drama was modified as time went on. As we have seen, when he first broached it to Strauss he spoke of the situations as being "broadly comic" and almost as obvious as a pantomime, with "opportunities even for a short ballet." There is no hint of the tragedy of the great renunciation of the Princess, and, indeed, no foreshadowing of such a character as that set before us in Strauss's score. Hofmannsthal speaks of there being only two big rôles—Ochs and Octavian. The astonishing thing throughout the correspondence, indeed, is the omission, until near the completion of the work, of any reference to the Princess as an important part of the story. In May 1909 Hofmannsthal has no more to say about the plot than this: "The course of the action is simple and intelligible enough for even the least sophisticated public—a fat, elderly, arrogant suitor, favoured by the bride's father, has his nose put out of joint by a handsome young fellow: surely that is the *ne plus ultra* of simplicity!" Even at this stage he could say that the only member of the cast who need be a really gifted actor as well as singer is the Ochs! [1]

We discover from the correspondence that by autumn 1909, after Strauss has actually finished the music to the first two acts, Hofmannsthal is still not ready with the text for the third! One suspects that the published correspondence is not complete; but it is clear enough from the letters we have that Strauss did not like the third act as Hofmannsthal sent it to him in the first place, and insisted on radical alterations in it. Even now Hofmannsthal seems not to have understood his own Princess as we have come to understand her. Still obsessed with the notion that the things that really matter in his play are the "broadly comic" episodes, he actually suggested several cuts in his own text in the more serious scene that follows the Baron's exit in the third act: he could see in imagination, he said, the audience already preparing to leave, and feared boring them by detaining them too long. He "implored" Strauss to "base his composition" on his short-ened version of the original text at this point. A glance at the score is enough to show that Strauss refused to adopt the sugges-tion. It was not until the autumn of 1909 that Hofmannsthal realised, however imperfectly as yet, that in the Princess he had a front-line character from whose psychology effects of the high-est pathos could be drawn in the final stages of the opera. That the ending of the work gave him infinite difficulty is clear from a letter of the 23rd April 1910 from the composer, saying that although the score of Act II is already in the engraver's hands he is still waiting anxiously for the concluding text of Act III. [2]

Some six weeks later, Hofmannsthal realises at last that the Princess is not merely a piece of trimming in the story of the boy-and-girl love of Octavian and Sophie but a personality in

---

[1] "Strictly speaking it is only the player of the title-part who will need to be a good actor-singer." This proves that Hofmannsthal's first idea was to call the play after the Baron; for his following sentence about Leporello shows that it was a baritone whom he had in mind.

[2] Even at this stage, we discover, it was still proposed to entitle the opera "Ochs".

herself, and a personality of the profoundest human interest. After never so much as mentioning her as an integral part of his "broadly comic" play in the winter of 1909–10, he discovers by June of the latter year that now he has reached the end of the work she is the character who matters most! He has had to treat the final scene at some length, he now tells Strauss, because "the figure of the Marschallin must not be deprived of its significance. It is she whom the public, and especially the women, will regard as the leading personality, she to whom their sympathies will go out." Later he enlarges on this theme. Sophie, he says in July, is quite commonplace, just an ordinary sort of young woman; "for real charm of expression and of personality one has to turn to the Marschallin." This character, whom previously he had not thought worth referring to as in any way "principal", is now "the dominating female figure", with Ochs on one side of her, Octavian on the other, and Sophie somewhat in the background. There can seldom have been a more curious example in literature of a character gradually taking such possession of its creator that it evolves silently on lines of its own until he is surprised to find that it has turned out something quite different from what he intended it to be in the first place.

6

And now let us return to our story of the action of the opera, at the point where the Princess enters the room. We in the audience are even more glad to see her than Ochs can be, for, to tell the truth, we have grown a trifle weary of much of the clowning of the last half-hour or so, to which only Strauss's charming music has been able to reconcile us. Ochs having ful-filled his purpose in the play, he is now soon disposed of. At first he is naïf enough to think that the Marschallin will use her authority to put matters right for him; but in this he is soon un-deceived. She treats him with studied contempt. The Commis-sary, who turns out to be a former orderly of the Field Marshal, she handles easily: he soon retires, respectfully leaving the affair in her competent hands. After that, Ochs's star sets rapidly. Sophie returns from the inner room with a message from her father that he never wants to see the Baron again—a sentiment in which, she assures the astonished man, she herself heartily concurs. On the advice of the Princess he leaves the place as quickly as he can. He makes a last desperate attempt to get the situation under control again, to affect to laugh it all off as just a Viennese diversion which he would not on any account wish to spoil, and to get out with some tattered remnants of his Lerchenau dignity still clinging to him. But he is not allowed to leave without a new accumulation of farce about him. The trick of the trap doors is made manifest to him; Valzacchi makes no secret of being an accomplice in the plot against him; Annina removes her mourning cap and veil and wipes the paint off her face; the landlord presents a long bill; the boots of the inn, the waiters, the musicians, and sundry others clamour for tips for services rendered; the four children dance round him again screaming "Papa!"

When at last he escapes, most of the company follow him, the stage being left to the Princess, Octavian and Sophie. Octavian, who has long before this appeared in his proper clothes, has by now got over the shock of the Princess's finding him in such surroundings, but he is vastly mortified and embarrassed. Sophie is broken-hearted; she feels that she has lost Octavian and has been humiliated in the presence of the great lady. It is with some difficulty that the Princess, who has now taken complete command of the situation, induces the awkward, repentant boy to claim Sophie as his own, and Sophie to accept him. For her own part, the older woman bows resignedly to the will of the Fates: "today or tomorrow", as she herself had warned Octavian, the blow was bound to come, and she must bear her chastening bravely. She wins the trust of both of them by her gentleness of manner and nobility of soul. Finally, standing between them, she launches the emotional climax of the opera, the magnificent trio, the opening phrase of which is a stately variant of the almost inane little tune to which Mariandel, not so long ago, had sung her "Nein, nein, nein, nein! I' trink kein Wein!"

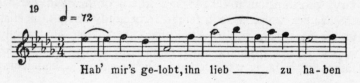

19   ♩ = 72

Hab' mir's ge-lobt, ihn lieb ——— zu ha-ben

(Why it should be this particular tune that is singled out for the honour of being made the foundation for the splendid superstructure of the trio no one has ever been able to discover). Each of the characters pursues his own reflections: Octavian is torn between love for Sophie and remorse for the heartbreak he knows to be going on within the Princess; Sophie is too simple to grasp it all, feeling that in some mysterious way the Princess is at once giving Octavian to her and keeping back something of him for herself, and she herself being sure only of one thing, that she loves Octavian; the Princess, as is shown by the insistence of the orchestra on No. 4 to the very end, even after the voices have ceased, resigning herself to her lot, yet finding a certain heart's-ease in the thought that her suffering brings happiness to the boy she has so loved.

When, to the words, "There stands the boy, and here stand I, and with this new love he has found he will be full happy—as men understand happiness! God's will be done!" she leaves the young pair to go into the adjoining room, her going is not merely a stage exit but a symbol of her passing out of the life of Octavian, a symbol poignantly driven home to us in the orchestra, where a final passionate, almost despairing meditation on No. 4a makes way for the more naïve motive of the Silver Rose (No. 11). So wrapped up are the boy and girl in each other that they do not even notice that the Princess has left them. Locked in each other's arms they pour out their love for each other in terms of the utmost simplicity: Strauss has shown fine psychological tact in refraining from putting into their mouths a language of love beyond their years.

While Sophie, the duet ended, is clinging to Octavian for support, the door on the left is opened by Faninal's footmen, who light their master and the Princess into the room. The young couple stand for a moment embarrassed, then make a deep obeisance, which is returned by the older people. Faninal, having touched his daughter on the cheek, conducts the Princess to the centre door, which is flung open by the latter's servants. "Youth is youth", remarks Faninal with paternal indulgence, to which the Marschallin merely replies "Ja, ja!", it being left to the orchestra to describe her secret heartbreak for us with a last tender re-

miniscence of the music of the closing moments of the first act
(No. 4, etc.). When the Princess and Faninal have left, the young
lovers repeat, as if in a dream, their simple little refrain of a
moment or two before; then they kiss and run off quickly hand
in hand, to the strains of the Silver Rose motive. For a few
moments the stage is empty. Then the centre door opens and the
little Black Boy trips in with a taper in his hand. He looks all
round the floor for something which he finds at last, holds it up
to our view, and trips out again. It is Sophie's handkerchief,
which she had dropped without noticing it.

CAVALLERIA RUSTICANA
Mascagni (1863)

PRINCIPAL CHARACTERS

SANTUZZA	*Soprano*
TURIDDU	*Tenor*
LUCIA	*Contralto*
ALFIO	*Baritone*
LOLA	*Mezzo-soprano*

I

Cavalleria Rusticana, which was the first of Mascagni's operas, has also been the most enduringly successful of them the whole world over. Having won the first prize in a competition launched by the Italian music publisher Sonzogno, the work was produced at the Costanzi Theatre, Rome, on the 17th May 1890. It made an extraordinary sensation; Mascagni became famous in a day.

The libretto of *Cavalleria Rusticana* was put together by G. Targioni-Fozzetti and G. Menasci from a short story with the same title by the Italian novelist Giovanni Verga, which had been published a few years earlier; Verga himself made a play out of it later. Neither the matter nor the manner of the tale differs very much from a newspaper report of the evidence in an everyday murder case.[1] Turiddu, a young buck returned from serving his term as a conscript, is given to swaggering about on Sundays in his bersagliere's uniform under the admiring gaze of the girls of the village. While making love to Santa, the daughter of a local wine-grower, he takes to visiting Lola, the wife of a well-to-

[1] This must not be taken as a denial of the effect of the story, still less as a criticism of Verga's art in general, but as a simple statement of fact. Nowhere is he so concise as in *Cavalleria Rusticana*, which runs to no more than about ten pages. As D. H. Lawrence puts it, in the Preface to his translation of this and other works of Verga, "we are here just a bit too much aware of the author and his scissors. He has clipped too much away. The transitions are too abrupt. All is over in a gasp. . . ."

do carrier, when her husband, Alfio, is away with his cart and mules. Santa having told Alfio, in a fit of jealousy, what has been going on in his absence, the two men go out one morning to settle the matter in the approved way. Turiddu magnanimously admits that he is in the wrong, but explains that as his old mother had wept copiously over him before he left the house—she had pretended she had got up so early to attend to the hens—he will be under the painful necessity of killing Alfio like a dog. The account of the fight is a charming vignette of rustic chivalry, South Italian style. Alfio scores first with a stab in the arm, for which Turiddu pays him back with one in the groin; and once more he makes it clear that since the pathetic scene in the fowl-house his mother is so constantly before his eyes that it is his plain filial duty to murder his opponent. Alfio bids him open wide the aforesaid eyes, for he is going to be repaid all he has given in full measure. Bent nearly to earth by the pain from his wound, Alfio snatches up a handful of dust and throws it into Turiddu's eyes. " 'Ah!' howled Turiddu, blinded, 'I'm done for'. He tried to save himself by desperate leaps backward; but Alfio got him again with another stab in the stomach and a third in the throat. 'That's three. . . . Now your mother can mind the hens.' Turiddu staggered and writhed a little while among the banyan trees, then fell like a log. The blood gurgled foaming from his throat, and he could not even say 'Ah! Mamma mia!' "

The subject appealed as strongly as it did to the audiences of the last decade of the nineteenth century, which had absorbed as much as they could assimilate for the time being of German sentiment in general and Wagnerian romance in particular, by reason precisely of its raw "verism"; and to this verism Mascagni had provided the perfect counterpart in his music, with its forceful if unsubtle emotionalism, its photographic appropriate-ness to each episode, its obvious melodies—drawn, as it were, with the broad of the thumb, but for all that novel and indi-vidual,—and its emphatic orchestral colouring. And that the subject and the music both answer still to something fundamental in the average man is proved by the enormous popularity of *Cavalleria Rusticana* down to the present day. Here and there in Mascagni's other operas there are pages in themselves superior to anything in this, but none of the others holds the unsophisti-cated listener in so unrelaxing a grip from start to finish as *Cavalleria Rusticana* does. Somehow or other Mascagni's very defects become virtues here. He had never, as a student, shown much liking or much capacity for labour at such refinements of craftsmanship as counterpoint, fugue, and close thematic develop-ment. But in the course of his youthful wanderings through Italy as conductor of a small touring opera company he had realised just what the average man wants, and how to serve it up to him. Verdi, who was an old man of seventy-seven when *Cavalleria Rusticana* appeared, got Boïto to play it to him from the piano score. At the third scene he stopped him. "Enough, enough", he said; "I understand." Verdi, as a practical man of the theatre, and with a *Trovatore* and a *Traviata* of his own to look back upon, could see at a glance why the new work had made so tremendous a sensation. Did he, one wonders, also sense pro-phetically that the composer of *Cavalleria Rusticana* would never rise to an *Aïda*, an *Otello*, or a *Falstaff*?

2

The prelude to *Cavalleria Rusticana* commences quietly with a melody associated later with the peace of Easter Day:

This gradually becomes faster and more insistent till it cul-minates in a *fortissimo* chord, to be instantly succeeded by a drop into a *pianissimo* statement of the melody to which Santuzza reproaches Turiddu for his cruelty towards her:

s*

This in turn is worked up with a great show of passion. Then comes an episode that made a great sensation in 1890, and is still effective today, long after the first novelty of it has worn off. Turiddu sings behind the scenes a serenade to Lola, a song that is both a eulogy of her beauty and a warning of the danger that threatens them both. Next comes a reminder of the Santuzza who is so tragically concerned in the intrigue:

the melody being derived from her passionate appeal to Turiddu not to desert her in her misery. The prelude, which has been a calculated succession of high lights and low, comes to a close with a last reminiscence of No. 2.

The rising of the curtain is accompanied by the chiming of bells from the church which stands on the right of the stage. It is Easter morning, and the townspeople, to the sound of joyous music from the orchestra:

are passing across the square and disappearing into the church. From behind the scenes we hear a chorus of field-workers singing of the joys of Easter: they come into sight still singing, pass across the stage, and disappear in the distance. The music to the whole of this scene is perfectly in keeping with the Southern milieu; it is graceful, sensuous and fragrant.

The tonality of A major has ruled through it all. This changes to F sharp minor as a brief orchestral interlude hints at the tragedy that is brooding over the place: this is foreshadowed in the sombre motive:

that winds its way in and out of the depths of the orchestra, beneath masses of uneasy syncopated chords. Santuzza meets Turiddu's mother, Lucia, of whom she anxiously begs news of her son. Old Lucia senses that there is something wrong; but before Santuzza can tell her story the cracking of a whip and the sound of waggon bells are heard behind the scenes, and soon the waggoner Alfio enters, accompanied by a number of his cronies. He sings a lively song, descriptive of the pleasures of a calling such as his, and his joy when he returns from his business trips to the home where his faithful Lola is awaiting him. The chorus, after joining in the refrain of the song, melt away in various directions, some of them drifting into the church.

Alfio asks Lucia when he can have some more of the excellent wine that Turiddu brings in from a village in the neighbourhood; and lowering his voice he gives the astonished old woman a hint that her son may not be so far away as she thinks—Alfio had caught sight of him that very morning hanging round his house. Santuzza, by a sign, checks Lucia, who is about to express her surprise at this; and Alfio, who is in no mood for church-going just then, goes his way. From within the church we hear the melody of the "Regina coeli":

which is taken up by the crowd that gradually occupies the stage, assuming attitudes of devotion in front of the sacred building. Among them is Santuzza, whose voice stands out from the rest in a broad melody:

which is afterwards taken up by them all. From inside the church the worshippers strike in occasionally with cries of "Alleluia".

When the others have left the stage, Lucia asks Santuzza why she had made that gesture of silence in the conversation with Alfio. Thereupon Santuzza tells her whole sad story—how Turiddu had been in love with Lola before he went as a soldier, and how she had married Alfio while Turiddu was away; then, on his return, he had sought Santuzza's love, and, after betraying her, had been caught once more in the net of the wicked Lola; and now, cast aside and disgraced, nothing remains for her but to weep her eyes out:

To the melody of No. 1 she sends the unhappy old mother into the church, which she herself feels she dare not profane with her presence. She will remain where she is, awaiting Turiddu.

Turiddu enters. Santuzza reproaches him with having lied to her—he has not been to Francofonte, as he had given out, for at dawn he had been seen coming from Lola's house. He tries bluff —he will not be made the victim, he says, of her foolish jealousy. But in the full flood of her entreaties and Turiddu's protestations there comes, by one of those swift and pungent dramatic effects so beloved of Mascagni and his librettists, the voice of Lola herself, singing a coquettish little song as she nears the scene. The words die on her lips as she sees Turiddu and Santuzza. She hypocritically asks Turiddu if he has seen Alfio anywhere, and then comments maliciously on the fact that Santuzza seems to be doing her praying in the street. She evidently does not share

Santuzza's scruples about entering the church, into which she goes after having infuriated Turiddu by ironically refusing to take him away from his Santuzza. The latter's tears and supplications are now in vain; after an angry scene between the pair he throws her to the ground and rushes after Lola into the church. Santuzza sends a curse after him, and the sinister No. 5 in the orchestra warns us that tragedy is coming.

At that moment Alfio enters. The demented Santuzza tells him that Lola has just gone into the church with Turiddu. She gives him the whole story of her own betrayal by Turiddu and his association with Lola. Alfio swears that if she is lying to him he will cut her heart out; but at last, convinced that she is speaking the truth, he vows vengeance on Turiddu before the close of day.

As they go out the curtain falls, and the orchestra plays the famous "Intermezzo sinfonico". The "sinfonico" seems a bit of an exaggeration, but the Intermezzo fulfils well enough the purpose for which it was obviously inserted—to give the audience an opportunity to relax for a while from the tension that has been gradually increasing since the commencement of the opera, and so prepare itself for the still greater tension that is coming. The short movement begins by suggesting the Easter atmosphere once more by means of the "Regina coeli" theme (No. 6), to which there succeeds a broad melody in octaves, which works up, in the familiar Mascagni manner, to a hammering climax and then ebbs away into silence.

When the curtain rises again it is to the joyous strain of No. 4. The congregation comes out of the church, forms into little groups, and sings a chorus expressive of the pleasure awaiting them at home, now that their religious duties have been performed. Turiddu, who has come out accompanied by Lola, goes with his friends to a nearby tavern, where, led by him, they sing a rousing song in praise of wine. Soon Alfio enters. Turiddu approaches him, glass in hand, and asks him to drink with him, but Alfio refuses: to drink with Turiddu, he says, would poison him. The women of the party, seeing that trouble is brewing, hurry away, taking Lola with them. The two men face up to each other like a couple of fighting-cocks. Turiddu "places himself at Alfio's service"; they embrace, and the traditional challenge to combat is given by Turiddu biting Alfio's right ear. Turiddu then becomes repentant and tearful. He confesses that he is in the wrong, and laments the fate of Santuzza if he should be killed: but all the same he means to plunge his knife into Alfio's heart. Alfio coldly retorts that he will await him in the orchard, then leaves him.

As he does so Lucia enters. Trying to conceal from her what is afoot, Turiddu begs her blessing, as on that morning when he left her to be a soldier, and implores her, in a voice broken by sobs, if he should not return, to be a mother to his Santuzza. The distracted old woman asks him the meaning of all this. He tries to persuade her that it is the heady wine he has just been drinking that has affected him; but his emotions overcome him. He kisses his mother frantically, bids her a distracted farewell, and runs out. Lucia calls after him in desperation; but her cry is answered only by Santuzza, who enters and falls into the old woman's arms to the melody of No. 8 in the whole orchestra, followed by a suggestion of No. 7. The *ffff* to which the latter ascends is hushed in a second to *ppp*; then, over a sinister orchestral *tremolo*, we hear shouts from the women behind the scenes, "They have killed Master Turiddu!" The chorus rush on to the stage and surround the fainting Lucia and Santuzza as the curtain falls, while the orchestra gives out with its full strength the motive that symbolises Turiddu's fault and its punishment at Alfio's hands (No. 5).

I PAGLIACCI
Leoncavallo (1858-1919)

PRINCIPAL CHARACTERS

CANIO	*Tenor*
NEDDA	*Soprano*
TONIO	*Baritone*
BEPPO	*Tenor*
SILVIO	*Baritone*

I

Leoncavallo, like Mascagni, is associated by the average opera-goer with a single work. As with Mascagni, again, the catalogue of Leoncavallo's output is a somewhat melancholy record of aspirations that came mostly to nothing, or next to nothing. The author of *I Pagliacci* seems to have taken some pains as a young man to learn the routine of composition, and up to about the age of thirty he devoted himself to opera-planning on quite a large scale. He began with an opera on the subject of Chatterton. Then he completed the first section, *I Medici*, of a trilogy—to be entitled *Crepusculum*—dealing with the Renaissance; but though this was accepted for publication by Ricordi the production of it was delayed indefinitely. All this while he was glad to earn a miserable living by teaching, and even by playing the piano at café concerts. It was probably the resounding success of *Cavalleria Rusticana* (1890) that induced him to take the score of *I Pagliacci* to the publisher Sonzogno. (It is said that the work had been technically ineligible for the competition instituted by Sonzogno in 1890 because, short as it was, it was in two acts, and one of the conditions of the competition had been that works submitted should be in one act only). *I Pagliacci* was produced at the Teatro dal Verme, Milan, on the 21st May 1892. It was an instantaneous success, and the lucky publisher—Ricordi's rival —now found himself in possession of two of the biggest box office attractions of modern times. It was not long before "Cav.

and Pag." became indissolubly linked in the repertory of opera companies all over the world.

The success of *I Pagliacci* led, as a matter of course, to a production of *I Medici* (in November 1893); but the work was such a failure that Leoncavallo never had the heart to complete the two other sections of the trilogy, which were to have dealt with Savonarola and Cesare Borgia respectively. Neither *La Bohème* (1897) nor *Zazà* (1900), in spite of some initial favour, has conquered the opera world. *La Bohème* was hampered from the start by the superior quality of Puccini's score on the same theme (1896); and even the fact that the subject of *Roland of Berlin* (1904)—celebrating the virtues of the house of Hohenzollern—had been suggested to Leoncavallo by no less august a personage than the German Kaiser did not suffice to inspire his muse: the work preceded its gifted imperial progenitor into perpetual exile by about fourteen years. As for the operas, some ten in number, that followed *Roland*, for even the titles of these we have to have recourse to the encyclopaedias.

Leoncavallo was his own librettist, and in *I Pagliacci*, at any rate, he has turned out a highly effective piece of work. The device of a play within a play is of immemorial antiquity, but it never seems to lose its attractiveness or its punch. It has been said that Leoncavallo derived *his* subject from an incident in real life; but if that be so it is merely one more illustration of life's incorrigible passion for imitating art.

2

The action of the opera takes place in Calabria, on the feast day of the Assumption of the Blessed Virgin. A troupe of strolling players (pagliacci) has just arrived in the village of Montalto, where it intends to perform the same night. The opera opens with an orchestral prelude the leading features of which are (*a*) a theme expressive of the restless life of the wandering players:

(*b*) a dolorous melody:

associated later with the grief of Canio; and (*c*) a theme associated with the lover Silvio (No. 7).

At the conclusion of the prelude the mis-shapen buffoon Tonio approaches the audience through the curtain, announces that he is "the Prologue"—in the old theatrical sense of that term—and explains that the play that will be set forth before them that night is no mere creation of fiction but a true story; he hopes that when they see the drama unfolding itself they will remember that even actors are men and women like themselves, passionate, rejoicing, suffering. "I have given you the idea", he concludes. "Now observe for yourselves how it works itself out." And turning to those behind the scenes he calls out "Ring up the curtain!"

The setting disclosed to us is the meeting of two roads on the outskirts of the village. It is three o'clock in the afternoon. Tonio is watching with considerable disfavour the antics of the villagers, who, to the accompaniment of strident and often discordant sounds in the orchestra, are awaiting with delight the coming of the troupe, which they finally welcome in a rousing chorus, with cries of "Viva Pagliaccio!" The loutish Tonio, who seems to have no great liking for the easily amused mob, lies down in the shade in front of the travelling theatre which has already been set up on the stage. The company arrives in a cart. Canio, the proprietor of the show, who is evidently a prime favourite with the villagers, secures silence by a vigorous pounding of the big drum; then, in a speech with all kind of comic underlinings, he invites them to the performance that evening at which they will have the pleasure of seeing Tonio spinning his web of intrigue, and above all the marital furies of Pagliaccio himself, and the fine snare he sets to get his revenge. The crowd accepts the invitation with naïve expressions of delight.

Tonio makes to assist Canio's pretty wife, Nedda, to alight

from the cart, but gets a box on the ear from the jealous husband for his pains, at which the crowd laughs once more. The
cart is taken off by another comedian of the company, Beppo; the
disgruntled Tonio also disappears, in pursuit of some boys who
have been making fun of him, muttering, as he goes, "He'll pay
for that, the scoundrel!" Canio is invited by some of the villagers
to drink with them at the tavern at the cross-roads. Beppo,
throwing down his whip, declares that he too will go with them:
Tonio, however, refuses Canio's call to him to come as well. He
will join them later, he says; at the moment he has to attend to the
donkey. One of the villagers humorously advises Canio to keep
his eyes open, for it seems to him that Tonio is remaining behind
to make love to Nedda. Canio frowns and at the same time smiles
at this. Such a game, he assures them, it would be better not to
play with him. Tonio, and not only Tonio but everyone else,
would do well to remember that the theatre and actual life are not
at all the same thing:

If up there—pointing to the booth—Pagliaccio happens to
surprise his wife with her lover, he just makes a humorous
speech and takes a thrashing, and the audience laughs and
applauds:

But, he goes on to say in a changed voice and to the accompaniment of a sinister new motive in the orchestra:

if Canio were to catch Nedda at her tricks in real life, the affair would have a very different ending! Then, recovering himself again, he reverts to his jocular tone of a minute before: "Such a game, believe me, is better not played with me!" Nedda, who has not taken her eyes off him all this time, is greatly perturbed. How much does he really know? she wonders. But surely Canio cannot suspect his Nedda? say the villagers. Of course not, he replies meaningly; he adores her! and he kisses her on the forehead as he leaves her.

The emotional atmosphere of the scene which opened so merrily has darkened sensibly by now. The tension is dissipated by the sound of bagpipes behind the scenes, summoning the faithful to vespers. After an ensemble in which they imitate the ding-dong of bells, and a parting reminder from Canio not to forget the coming performance, the chorus go off to church, leaving Nedda alone on the stage. She muses anxiously for a little while. Suppose the brutal Canio were to discover her guilty secret? Then, being young and romantic, she dismisses these gloomy thoughts and gives herself up, in a lilting ballatella, to the joy of contemplating the birds in their carefree flight through the sunlit air. The situation seems to have been created only to give the prima donna a chance to show what she can do, and the music, with its slender intellectual content, to have been written with the same object.

Nedda's solitude is broken in upon by Tonio, who has heard her song, and, being more of an amorist than a musical critic, has been enraptured by it. For Tonio, in spite of his uncouthness, or perhaps because of it, is in love with Nedda; for him she is the only escape open to him from a world of harsh and ugly reality into one of beautiful dreams. But Nedda has no intuition of the poetry, grotesque and abortive as it is, that lies at the core of the soul of the poor clown who is everyone's butt. She sees only the superficial absurdity of such a creature presuming to be in love.

and she makes the mistake of laughing at him, to the accompaniment of a figure of sprightly badinage in the orchestra:

The time and the place for him to talk to her like this, she tells him, will be this evening, when he can grimace to his clownlike heart's content in the comedy. He warns her not to go too far in her derision of him, but she is heartless in her merriment. She goads him into a passionate declaration of his love for her: he tries to kiss her, and she strikes him in the face with the whip that Beppo has left lying in front of the theatre. He goes off mad with rage, swearing that he will have his revenge.

A sensuous phrase in the orchestra:

announces the approach of Nedda's lover Silvio, a young peasant of the neighbourhood: he has left Canio drinking at the tavern and made his way stealthily by a roundabout way through the undergrowth. In a long duet he pours out his love and implores her to fly with him that very night, to which, after some resistance, she consents. They are lost to the world in a slow cadence in close-clinging sixths when Canio enters, accompanied by Tonio, who has seen the lovers together and has run to the tavern to fetch his master. Canio is just in time to hear Nedda promise to meet Silvio at midnight, and to see him escape over the wall at a warning cry from Nedda. Canio pushes Nedda roughly aside and pursues Silvio, but returns baffled. In a blind fury he demands the lover's name, which Nedda will not give him. He is only restrained from killing her there and then by Tonio and Beppo. The latter hurries Nedda into the theatre, while Tonio exhorts his master to be calm, if only for the better securing of his

revenge. The show must go on, he says: the people are already
beginning to assemble for it: the lover is certain to be there, and
is bound, in some way or other, to betray himself. At last he
leaves Canio, who, overcome with grief, launches into the
famous solo "Vesti la giubba". Pagliaccio, he mourns, is not a
man but only an actor, whom the people pay to amuse them: if
Harlequin has robbed him of his Columbine he must laugh
through his tears, and the public will applaud. His lament culminates in the agonised theme quoted as No. 2. His frame shaken
by sobs, he covers his face with his hands and disappears through
the curtain of his little theatre.

3

Between the first and the second act comes an orchestral
Intermezzo descriptive of the mournful meditations of Canio
before the rising of the curtain in his own theatre: it ends with an
expansive statement of the theme in the Prologue that had
accompanied Tonio's words about himself and his fellows being
not merely actors but human beings, of the same stuff as those
who laugh at them.

The second act is devoted to the feigned play which soon
becomes more real than life itself. In this comedy Canio becomes
Pagliaccio; Nedda is Columbine; Tonio is Taddeo; Beppo plays
Harlequin.

First of all we see the people thronging to see the play, and
Beppo arranging places for them, while Tonio is making a great
noise with the big drum. The villagers are first heard in a gay
chorus behind the scenes, exhorting each other to hurry, for the
play is about to begin. Gradually they take their seats: among
them is Silvio, who occupies a place at the front. Nedda, who is
going round the benches with a collecting-plate, manages to
exchange a few quiet words with him: Canio did not see him, she
says, and the plan for flight after the performance still holds good.

At last, after cries and appeals from the impatient audience, the
curtains of the booth are drawn aside. We see the sort of poor
attempt at a domestic interior that a small travelling company
would be likely to carry about—a little room with two side doors
and a window at the back: there is a table with two chairs, in one

of which Columbine is seated. The orchestra plays a pleasant minuet:

which accompanies Columbine's miming and soliloquising during the opening moments. She is very restless, getting up, walking about, then sitting down again; and she makes it clear to the audience that as her husband Pagliaccio will not be returning until late, she is eagerly expecting her lover. She gives a cry of joy as a guitar is heard preludising off-stage, and Harlequin sings, outside the window, a charming little serenade to his Columbine, who sits at the table once more in a flutter of expectation.

Taddeo, the grotesque servant of this humble establishment, now enters. He has been shopping, and he carries a basket containing his purchases. He falls on his knees before Columbine and makes love to her in the most clownish fashion. He knows she is pure as the driven snow, he says meaningly, while the orchestra gives out a suggestion of the skittish theme (No. 6) to which Nedda had derided Tonio's love-making in the first act. She snatches the basket from him, puts it on the table, then opens the window and gives a signal. The sprightly Harlequin jumps in, carrying a bottle which he deposits on the ground before he kicks Taddeo out. As he goes, Taddeo gives the lovers his mock blessing and assures them that he will keep watch and ward over them. The spectators are immensely amused by it all.

Columbine arranges knives, forks and spoons, and places on the table the fowl that Taddeo had brought in; while Harlequin picks up the bottle from the floor and deposits it beside the fowl. The pair express their naïve pleasure in each other's company in a dainty gavotte, and Harlequin gives Columbine a phial which she is to empty into Pagliaccio's evening drink: when the drug has done its beneficent work he and she will fly together. At that moment Taddeo rushes in with an air of mock terror, to tell them

that the husband has discovered everything, and, out of his mind
with rage, is looking for them both with a knife. Harlequin
manages to escape through the window just as Pagliaccio enters
through the door—in time to hear from Columbine exactly the
same parting words to Harlequin as Canio had heard Nedda
speak to her lover an hour ago: "Tonight, then! And for ever I
shall be thine!"

"The selfsame words!" says Canio to himself. Then, with
difficulty mastering his emotions, he becomes Pagliaccio again,
and, to the accompaniment of an expressive new theme in the
orchestra:

he begins to play his regulation part in the comedy. He accuses
Columbine of deceiving him. She pretends that no one has been
with her but Taddeo, whom she calls upon to be her witness: the
clown sarcastically assures Pagliaccio that his wife is veracity
itself. She laughs in Pagliaccio's face as he demands her lover's
name (No. 5). He can bear no more. The mask falls from him: "I
am Pagliaccio no more", he cries, "but a man wounded and
shamed, and thirsting for vengeance!" Columbine tries to keep
the comedy going, but Pagliaccio, as his grief and anger get the
upper hand of him, becomes more and more Canio; while the
more realistic his acting the more loudly the audience applauds.
At last Columbine in her turn also begins to change from Columbine to Nedda. If her husband is so tired of her, she says, with
feigned calmness, he can let her leave him, here and now. This
infuriates him still further: she shall remain, he shouts, and he
will have her lover's name.

With a great effort Columbine steers the play back into its
traditional comic vein; no one has been with her, she says with a
smile, to the music of the gavotte, but poor frightened, harmless
Harlequin. The rustic crowd bursts into a horse-laugh at this,
which is checked at the sight of Pagliaccio's frenzy, which is now
manifestly more than play-acting. Again he demands the name,

and again Columbine refuses it. An ensemble full of dramatic movement is built up. All take part in it—the two leading characters, Harlequin-Beppo, who appears at the back, frightened out of his wits and trying to run away before worse happens, Taddeo-Tonio holding him back, and the audience, realising at last the tragic turn the play has taken, trying to restrain Silvio, who has risen in his seat in uncontrollable excitement. As Nedda attempts to escape into the audience Canio stabs her. Silvio rushes at Canio, who turns on him and plunges the knife into his heart. The spectators seize Canio, who suddenly comes to himself. "The comedy is ended!" he cries out to them in a kind of stupor, as the knife falls from his hand and the orchestra gives out in a thunderous *fortissimo* the melody to which, at the end of the first act, he had sung the words, "Laugh, Pagliaccio, for the love that has been destroyed! Laugh for the grief that is poisoning your soul!"

WOZZECK

Alban Berg (1885-1935)

PRINCIPAL CHARACTERS

WOZZECK	*Baritone (and Speaking Voice)*
THE DRUM-MAJOR	*Heroic Tenor*
ANDRES	*Lyric Tenor (and Speaking Voice)*
THE CAPTAIN	*Buffo Tenor*
THE DOCTOR	*Buffo Bass*
MARIE	*Soprano*
MARGRET	*Contralto*

I

Until Berg's *Wozzeck* was launched in 1925 the literary world in general outside Germany knew little or nothing of Georg Büchner, on whose drama with the same title the opera is founded.[1] He was born on the 17th October 1813 at Goddelau, near Darmstadt, where his father was a doctor. The young Georg studied science, in particular anatomy and zoology, at Darmstadt, Strassburg and Giessen, with a view to adopting his father's profession. Becoming involved in the widespread political unrest of the period, he saw several of his young companions thrown into prison, and escaped a similar fate himself only by flying to Strassburg. There he continued to work hard not only at science but at philosophy and history, the epoch of the French Revolution having a special attraction for him. In Strassburg he wrote an essay "On the Nervous System of the Barbel" which brought him not only the dignity of a corresponding membership of the Strassburg Society for Natural Philosophy but a doctor's degree from the Philosophical Faculty of Zürich, in which latter town he settled in December 1836 as a teacher in the High School. On the

[1] He is not so much as mentioned in the latest edition of the Encyclopaedia Britannica, though there is an article there on his younger brother, Ludwig (1824-1899), the author of the *Force and Matter* (1855) that made something of a sensation in the scientific world of its own day

following 2nd February the first signs showed themselves of a disease that was probably typhus. Nineteen days later he was dead.

He had crowded a great deal of thinking and feeling into his life of little more than twenty-three years. In 1833 he had written *Danton's Death*, a remarkable drama dealing with the leading personalities of the Revolution. His other literary works consisted of a comedy, *Leonce and Lena*, the fragment of a psychological novel, *Lenz*,[1] and the drama *Wozzeck*. The world has seldom seen a more precocious talent. There is naturally a good deal that is merely young-mannish in some of his work, more especially in *Leonce and Lena*, where, in common with so many of his contemporaries, Büchner tries to philosophise in a style half-cynical, half-profound, imitated from some of Shakespeare's clowns. But there is also in all Büchner's work a knowledge of human nature quite astounding in a man of his years, an impatience with sacrosanct literary forms and subjects that lends him a peculiar interest today, and above all a sympathy with human suffering, especially that of the under-dog, that makes *Wozzeck* in particular one of the most moving documents of its genre and its period.

The boy was from the first in full revolt against the romanticism in which so many fine spirits at that time sought a refuge from the hard realities of life. The after-crop of the Napoleonic wars had been an exhaustion and a disillusionment that were already heralding, in the early 1830's, the attempts at a political revolution that came to a head everywhere towards the end of the 1840's. In Germany in particular the discontent was great: the people had rallied devotedly to the side of their princes in order to shake off the Napoleonic yoke, only to find, when victory had been achieved, that the princes, for the most part, made use of their new security only to forge fresh chains, material and spiritual, for their subjects. Büchner was one of those who felt that the time for romantic dreaming was past, but one also who

[1] i.e., Reinhold Lenz, the poet who in his early years was so closely associated with Goethe. He became mentally deranged some years before his death. The problems of his mind and fate evidently had a peculiar attraction for Büchner.

saw clearly that for the moment, as he wrote to his family in 1833, any attempt at open revolution was doomed to failure. And of course his conviction of the futility of action only deepened his sense of the curse that lay upon the majority of the human race. "I have been studying", he wrote to his fiancée in 1833, about the time he was engaged on *Danton's Death*, "the history of the Revolution. I felt utterly crushed under the horrible fatalism of history. I find in human nature a dreadful sameness, in human affairs a fatal force, that is in all of us and in none of us. The individual is merely foam on the wave, greatness a mere accident, the authority of genius a puppet show, a ludicrous struggle against an iron law which we can at most recognise, but to master which is impossible."

Like other highly-strung youths of the period—Berlioz and Flaubert, for instance—who had studied anatomy and practised in the dissecting room, Büchner felt at once a macabre contempt for the human body and mind and an ironic pity for them. Something of all this, of course, was merely a conscious distillation from Shakespeare in his Hamlet mood: it was fatally easy for the disillusioned youth of the romantic epoch, French and German, to strike a picturesque "Alas, poor Yorick!" attitude. But in Büchner, as *Wozzeck* was to show, the sense of burning pity for poor humanity finally submerged the ironic amusement over it. "People call me a scoffer", he says in one of his letters. "It is true that I often laugh,—never, however, at *what* a man is, but only *because* he is, which he cannot help in any way, and I laugh at myself, as sharing the same fate. . . . In a sense, indeed, I mock, not from disdain but from hatred. To hate is as permissible as to love, and I cherish hatred in the fullest measure against those who scorn. . . . Aristocracy is, at most, shameful contempt of the holy spirit in man: against it I direct its own weapons, pride against pride, mockery against mockery. . . . I hope I have always turned upon suffering, down-trodden creatures more glances of compassion than I have expended bitter words on the cold hearts of those in authority."

Evidently the world as he found it hurt his generous young heart grievously, but he could not bring himself, like so many of his contemporaries, to take refuge from it in a world of romantic make-believe: the evil inherent in the scheme of things, if it could not be overcome, should at any rate be courageously faced. "When I am told", he says in one of his letters, "that the poet must show the world not as it is but as it should be, I reply that I have no desire to improve on the good God, who assuredly has made the world as it must be. As for the so-called idealistic poets, my feeling is that for the most part they have created nothing but marionettes with sky-blue noses and affected pathos,—not creatures of flesh and blood whose joys and sorrows I can feel as my own, and whose actions inspire me with abhorrence or admiration. In a word, I lay much store by Goethe and Shakespeare, but very little by Schiller." The German romanticism that turned its gaze backwards to the idealised Middle Ages because it could find no foothold in the brutal present had no attraction for him, he said.

He raised the banner of revolt against not only the conventional literary subjects but the accepted forms of his epoch. One of the most salient features of *Danton's Death* and of *Wozzeck* is the rapid succession of scenes, some of them so short as to consist of only some half-dozen lines. This technique, which of course makes a modern stage production of either of the dramas a matter of some difficulty, he perhaps derived from Lenz. The classical drama being supposed to proceed on the assumption of the "unities" of time and place, many of the younger rebels against authority regarded it as a point of honour to flout these imaginary rules by presenting a dramatic action with the complete freedom, the absence of manufactured symmetries, that it would have in real life. The last scene but one of *Wozzeck*, for example, shows a few children playing in the street in front of the house door of the murdered Marie. Only some forty words in all are spoken: then the scene changes to the last scene of all, the dissecting-room of a hospital. There are present a doctor, a surgeon and a magistrate; the only words spoken are by the last-named, and they amount to no more than this—"A good murder, a real murder, a first-rate murder! As fine as anyone could wish for. It is a long time since we had one so fine!" Many technical difficulties of this kind, however, which are insoluble on the ordinary stage, can be overcome in opera, where the music can prolong the shortest of scenes to the full stretch of its emotional possibilities, or can supply, by means of orchestral prelude, postlude or interlude, what the poet has not given his characters sufficient time to say, or even what is better left unsaid in words. On the whole, Berg has been able to take over Büchner's text as it stands, with only a few omissions or slight adaptations, some of which will be noted in the course of our analysis of the opera.

The finer spirits of the early nineteenth century felt a burning sympathy with the appalling lot of the German poor. Heine, for instance, had sung in passionate accents the sorrows of the over-worked and starving Silesian weavers, sitting at their looms with their eyes filled with bitter tears, cursing the God who created them and to whom they pray in vain, cursing the King who extorts the last groschen from them in their misery and has them shot like dogs when they complain, cursing the "false fatherland where prosper only infamy and shame, where every flower is blighted in the bud, where rottenness and decay regale the worm, while we go on weaving, weaving—day and night weaving the old Germany's winding sheet, with a threefold curse woven into its threads." Büchner's Wozzeck is the German under-dog of the period in his most pitiable aspect. Officially he is Johann Franz Wozzeck, thirty years, seven months and twelve days old at the time of his death, militiaman and fusilier in the second regiment, second battalion, fourth company. Uneducated, uncomprehend-ing, he is the slave and the butt of everyone, not only of the Captain of his regiment, whose regimental servant he is, but of the Doctor, who laughs at him to his face, regards him merely as an interesting subject for scientific experiment, and uses him for demonstration purposes to the students. His one thin ray of sunshine in a dark world is the trull by whom he has had a child; and she is stolen from him by the boastful Drum-Major, who makes use of his physical superiority over the wretched Wozzeck to humiliate him in the eyes of the other soldiers. Over almost everyone and everything of first-line significance in the drama there broods the shadow of something like incipient madness: no one is wholly normal. It would have been impossible for any composer to treat such a subject in the traditional idiom of music: the attempt could in the nature of things only be made when many of the old conventions of opera had to some extent broken down.

2

Berg, who was the most gifted of Schönberg's associates and pupils, took about six years over the composition of *Wozzeck*. In any six years a fertile and vigorous mind is bound to outgrow its old self at various points; so it is not surprising to find indications in the final stages of the opera that the composer had outgrown the Berg of the first stages. It is useless to look in the work for a self-consistent idiom from the first page to the last: some parts of it represent a deliberate exploitation of the atonal theories of Schönberg in their most extreme form, while other parts are just a normal extension or subtilisation of the traditional German musical speech.

In his handling of the voices Berg has not always been conspicuously happy. In a foreword to the score he tells us that the vocal principle on which he has proceeded in certain episodes has been that of Schönberg in his *Pierrot Lunaire* and *Die glückliche Hand*. Though the notes are written in the usual way on lines and in spaces, they are not to be *sung* at these definite pitches. The business of the actor is merely to *suggest* the pitch while achieving what Berg calls "speech-melody"; he must convey neither the impression of singing nor that of the "realistically-natural" speech of everyday usage. We may grant the validity of a compromise of this sort in theory without being able to agree that so far it has worked out particularly well in practice. It is not merely that now and then the voices in *Wozzeck* do things that are both painful to the musical ear and provocative of irreverent laughter. A more serious hindrance to our whole-hearted acceptance of this would-be "speech-melody" is that it so often fails to do the very thing it sets out to do. It fails to carry conviction either as song, as speech, or as a fusion of the two; it is neither speech achieving melody nor song biting like speech, but a bastard by-product of speech and song, which neither captivates the ear nor commands the assent of the intellect. That a new compromise between song and speech will be effected in the opera of the future—or in certain portions of certain operas—can hardly be doubted: theory points in that direction, while Debussy has triumphantly demonstrated some possibilities of the genre in *Pelléas and Mélisande*. But the proof of the pudding will always be in the eating: if the concoction is not agreeable to the palate no amount of theorising will make us swallow very much of it.

Berg seems to have made the acquaintance of Büchner's drama for the first time in a Vienna production of May 1914, and to have resolved there and then to write an opera on the subject: a period of war service, however, made it impossible for him to proceed with the plan until the summer of 1917. The orchestral score was complete in every respect by April 1921. The piano arrangement (by Fritz Heinrich Klein) was published two years later. On the 11th June 1924 three extracts from the opera were given, under Hermann Scherchen, in concert form in Frankfurt-am-Main. The first stage performance of the complete opera took place at the Berlin Staatsoper, under Erich Kleiber, on the 14th December 1925.

The musical form of *Wozzeck* is original and peculiar. There is nothing eternally sacrosanct about any of the forms in which opera has so far realised itself, neither that of Monteverdi, nor that of Gluck, nor that of Mozart, nor that of Wagner, nor that of Debussy. Each of these forms was born of the general mentality of a particular epoch and the totality of the resources of music in that epoch; and their perfect validity for their own day inevitably makes them to some extent invalid for a later day. Once more, the proof of the pudding is in the eating: any form is good that makes it possible for the combined dramatic and musical conception to realise itself clearly and effectively. Wagner, for the purposes of opera, took over from instrumental music, especially that of Beethoven, the procedure we call symphonic development. There is not the slightest *a priori* reason why the opera composer of the future should not take over from instrumental music other devices, other forms, other textures. Berg has shown considerable originality and ingenuity in this respect. Practically every one of his fifteen scenes is cast into a recognised instrumental "form"— the suite, the passacaglia, the fugue, the rondo, sonata form, and so on. Fuller reference will be made to these in the course of the following exposition, though it is impossible in a book of this kind to analyse the musical texture in close technical detail.

The few musical quotations given here must not be looked upon as "motives" in the Wagnerian sense of that term, in spite of the fact that some of them crop up afresh in this scene or that. Finally, the best, if not the only, way for the plain man to approach *Wozzeck* for the first time in the theatre is to concentrate mainly on the drama and let the music, mostly atonal, take hold of him as and when it can.

3

Each of the three acts of the opera falls into five scenes. We see first the Captain's room in the early morning; he is sitting in front of a table, looking into a mirror as Wozzeck shaves him. From the outset we get the impression that practically everyone in the strange work is going to prove, in some way or other, to some degree or other, a trifle abnormal, if not half or wholly crazy. The Captain is philosophising after his own fashion, for in his vacant way he is a bit of a thinker: he has just made the remarkable discovery that Time is now an eternity, now only a moment, and he shudders when he reflects that the earth turns on its axis once in every twenty-four hours. From Wozzeck he gets, in answer to all his speculations, little more than a laconic "Jawohl, Herr Hauptmann!" This is even his resigned assent to the Captain's sly remark, made to test him, that the wind seems to be south-north. The Captain laughs at the man's simplicity, and proceeds to point out that Wozzeck has no morals. ("Moral", he condescends to explain, "means when a man has morality"). Wozzeck, it appears, has a child who has come into the world "without the blessing of the Church, as our highly respected garrison chaplain puts it." Wozzeck replies to this at what is for him unusual length. "Herr Hauptmann, the good God will not ask the poor little brat whether the Amen was said over it before it was made. The Lord said, 'Let little children come unto me'. We poor people! Money, money! What it is to have none! If I were a gentleman, and had a hat and a watch and an eyeglass and could speak properly, I would be virtuous all right! There must be something fine about virtue. But I am just a poor devil, and our sort are unlucky in this world and the next. No doubt if we got to heaven we would have to lend a hand with the thunder!" The Captain is a trifle discon-

certed by all this: Wozzeck is a decent fellow, he says, but he
thinks too much. A man should not think too much; it pulls him
down. The shaving finished, he dismisses Wozzeck, telling him
not to run as he generally does, but to go slowly, and exactly in
the middle of the street—"Slowly, remember, nice and slowly!"

The musical form of this scene is that of the suite—prelude,
pavane, gigue and gavotte with two "doubles". The opening
phrase of the opera (there is no overture):

recurs at intervals during the conversation, as does the theme of
the Captain, which is heard in the cor anglais, in the fourth bar,
immediately after No. 1:

Wozzeck's remark "We poor people!" is sung to a phrase used
a good deal in the course of the work:

T

Wir ar-me Leut!

After an orchestral interlude, which allows time for a change of
scene, we see Wozzeck and another soldier of the regiment,
Andres, cutting sticks in a copse: the time is the late afternoon of
the same day. The musical form of this short scene is described
by Berg as that of the rhapsody. Wozzeck's first remark, after
some chords in the brass that convey the uncanny atmosphere of
the milieu:

is, "This place is accursed!" His already slightly unhinged mind
sees strange lights streaking across the grass among the fungi:
he imagines a head trundling along the ground at night and turning into a hedgehog when some one picks it up. The stolid
Andres, who is not subject to these disordered whimsies, tries to
amuse himself and his companion by singing a simple little
hunting song which is couched musically in something resembling
a folk-idiom. (In this scene both men employ the "speech-
melody" from time to time, singing of the ordinary kind being
mostly reserved for more formal musical utterances such as
Andres' ditty).

The eeriness of the place and his own morbid fancies work
more and more upon Wozzeck. He babbles about the Freemasons,
stamps on the ground, cries out that a chasm is yawning and the
earth rocking beneath him, and sees strange shapes moving about.
At last his nerves snap; he staggers about blindly, imploring

Andres to fly with him. Andres tries to steady Wozzeck's ramb-
ling mind. When the rapidly sinking sun lights up the wood
harshly for a moment, Wozzeck sees in imagination a fire
mounting from earth to heaven, and hears the blaring of trombones and strange clashings and janglings around—all of which
is graphically illustrated in the orchestra. Andres, becoming, in
spite of his phlegm, a trifle unnerved himself by his companion's
fancies, assures him that what he hears is merely the drums
sounding at sunset in the barracks: he gathers up his sticks and
persuades Wozzeck to return to the town with him.

An impressive orchestral interlude, with hints of military music
in the background, prepares us for the following scene, which is
set in the humble room which Wozzeck occupies with Marie.
When the curtain rises we see her at the window, playing with
their little child. The regiment marches down the narrow street,
with the Drum-major at its head; and one of Marie's neighbours,
Margret, looking up, sees Marie lost, like herself, in admiration of
the Drum-major,—a fine figure of a man, they agree. He waves
his hand to Marie as they go by, and she returns his greeting.
Margret having commented maliciously on her neighbour's
evident interest in soldiers, the two women bandy reflections on
each other's virtue for a moment or two. The exchange of compliments ends with Marie shrieking an offensive epithet at her
neighbour and closing her window with a bang.

As a result of this closing of the window the military music
becomes inaudible inside the room. Marie takes her poor brat in
her arms and sings over it a lullaby which balances matters rather
happily between the German folk song and the new melodic and
harmonic idiom of the Schönberg school, as may be seen from the
"Eia popeia" refrain:

The child falls asleep, and Marie loses herself in dreams from
which she is roused by a knock at the window. It is Wozzeck. He

cannot come in, he tells her, for he is due at the barracks after having cut the sticks for the Major. From his confused speech she senses that all is not well with him: it appears that he has seen and heard strange things in the wood, and now he feels something sinister to be impending. In the hope of quietening him she holds out the child to him, but his thoughts are elsewhere and he does not look at it. He leaves hurriedly. Marie gazes anxiously at the sleeping child. "Ah, we poor people!" she moans as the room grows quite dark: "I cannot endure it!" And she runs to the door in terror.

After another brief orchestral interlude the curtain rises on the fourth scene. The time is the next day, and the setting the Doctor's study. This scene is constructed musically in passacaglia form—a series of twenty-one variations on a ground-bass given out by the 'cellos at the rising of the curtain:

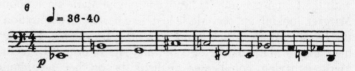

The Doctor is as mad as the rest of them; and Berg has told us that his object in choosing the passacaglia form for this scene was to stress the fact that the man is suffering from an *idée fixe*. Wozzeck, for him, is simply a subject for speculation and experiment. He has observed him coughing in the street, actually barking like a dog, in spite of his, the Doctor's, demonstration that the human diaphragm is controllable by the will. Wozzeck must eat nothing but beans till next week, when he can have a little mutton; for a revolution is taking place in the science of dietetics, and the Doctor tells off a few items on his fingers— white of egg, fats, carbon hydrates, oxyaldehydanhydride. Mixed up with it all are further fretful complaints about Wozzeck having coughed. From time to time the Doctor gains control of himself for a moment, only to lose it again as suddenly. Wozzeck tries to pacify him by pointing out that there is no going against nature. But as he proceeds he becomes more and more obsessed, more and more incoherent, talking of the world going so dark in front of a man that he has to feel his way about blindly with his hands, with everything slipping through his fingers like a cobweb; and yet, though all is dark, there is a red glow in the west, as it might be from a forge; and sometimes in the middle of the day, when the world seems to be going up in fire, he hears a fearful voice speaking to him.

"Wozzeck, you have an *aberratio*", says the Doctor; but before he can get any further with his scientific lucubrations Wozzeck breaks in on him with "And the fungi! Have you seen the rings they make on the earth—circular lines, figures? What do these mean?" The Doctor warns the man that he is shaping for a madhouse. "You are suffering from a fine fixed idea, a first-rate *aberratio mentalis partialis* of the second species, already well developed." Wozzeck, apparently neither seeing nor hearing him, groans "Oh Marie, Marie!", while the Doctor rubs his hands in ecstasy over the interesting case with which this poor fellow provides him. "Oh my theory! my fame!" he cries: "I shall be immortal! immortal! immortal!" And with each repetition of the word—which is always underlined by the trombones—his vocal line becomes more and more extravagantly absurd, till his megalomania culminates in a crazy trill:

Then, suddenly resuming his solemn professional manner, he goes up to Wozzeck and bids him let him see his tongue. Wozzeck obeys, and the curtain falls.

Berg now skips a couple of Büchner's scenes—those outside and inside a booth. The fifth scene, which opens with a flowing theme in flutes and violins (the marking is *andante affettuoso*):

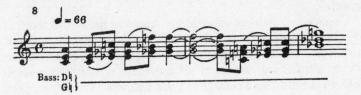

is set in the street in front of Marie's door. It is evening. Marie is admiring the Drum-major, who is posturing like a peacock before her. Never has she met a man who is so truly a man as he, she confesses; she is bursting with pride that he has condescended to take notice of her. But as he is now, he assures her, is nothing to what he is on Sunday parade, with his white gloves and his great plumes. It all ends with her flinging herself into his arms and disappearing with him through the open house door. As No. 8 recurs frequently in one form or another during this scene, the form may be described as that of the rondo.

4

The official explanation of the opening scene of the second act is that it is in sonata form, which, apparently, of all musical forms corresponds best to the interaction of the three characters. No. 3 plays a large part in the texture.

Once more we see Marie in her wretched room, the time, presumably, being the morning after. She is almost simultaneously engaged in admiring herself in a shabby little fragment of mirror, trying to get the child to sleep—now and then, for this purpose, she flashes the reflection from the glass across the wall—and envying the women who are better off than she though their mouths are no redder than hers. When Wozzeck enters she instinctively presses her hands to her ears. But he has caught the gleam of something in her hair, and she has to tell him what it is —merely a pair of ear-rings which, she assures him, she had found. Apparently he has his suspicions; but he masters himself and turns with his heart full of pity to the uneasily sleeping child, whose forehead is moist. "Wir arme Leut!" he ejaculates once more: "nothing under the sun but work: even in our sleep we sweat!" He gives Marie his scanty earnings and goes out, leaving her musing sadly on her wicked self and the evil there is in the world.

Common chords are exceedingly scarce in the atonal score of *Wozzeck*. When the poor fellow hands over his money to Marie, however, we hear in the orchestra a long-held chord in C major, which attracts our attention all the more strongly because it follows abruptly on a passage of great harmonic and contrapuntal complexity. Berg's somewhat naïve explanation of the intrusion of this obvious chord is that it symbolises as no other combination of notes could do the commonplace nature of money!

The usual orchestral interlude terminates in an upward harp glissando, which runs into the Captain's theme (No. 2) as the curtain rises. The Captain and the Doctor meet in a street. The latter is in a great hurry, and the Captain has much difficulty in getting him to stop for a chat. When he does so, he scares the life out of the Captain by telling him of the number of his patients who have died recently, some of them in agony. He runs an appraising professional eye over the Captain. Looking none too good, he says: bloated, neck too thick, threats of an *apoplexia cerebri* that will probably carry him off, though with luck it may paralyse him on one side only. He is certainly a most interesting medical case, and if it should happen that, by God's will, his tongue is partly paralysed, they will make experiments on him that will immortalise them. The next four weeks will probably decide. The Captain goes white with terror. Only four weeks! Already he sees the mourners wiping the tears from their eyes; at any rate they will be saying "He was a good man!" The passage in which the Doctor dwells gleefully on the possibility of the Captain having an apoplectic seizure:

is typical of Berg's vocal line at its most peculiar. The slither down from the high E to the low E flat, we learn from a note in the score, is intended to suggest the hee-haw of an ass.

Wozzeck appears, in a nervous hurry as usual. The precious pair detain him and make him the butt of their malicious humour.

The Captain introduces the subject of Wozzeck's profession of regimental barber, and asks him slyly if he has not found a hair from someone's beard in his plate—a sapper's beard, for example, or a corporal's, or—who knows?—a Drum-major's? Wozzeck has certainly a fine wife. Even if he does not find hairs in his soup, perhaps sometimes, as soon as he has turned the corner, they may be found on a certain pair of lips. Poor Wozzeck goes deadly pale. He is no match for these more educated men in innuendo and irony. All he can do is to say, "Herr Hauptmann, I am a poor creature! I have no one else in the world! If you are joking...", and then he wanders off into incoherencies. The Captain assures him that he means him no ill. The Doctor feels his pulse and pronounces it feeble and irregular—"optic muscles rigid", he continues professionally, "tense, eyes staring! Hm!" With a despairing cry Wozzeck tears himself loose from his tormen- tors and disappears. The Captain feels a trifle disconcerted: the Doctor merely remarks, "A phenomenon, this Wozzeck!" Then, seeing that the Captain is on the verge of another lapse into maudlin self-pity, he hurries away, with the other chasing him.

The musical form of this scene is that of a fantasia and fugue, three principal themes coming into play—that of the Captain (No. 2), one symbolising Wozzeck, and a third, derived from the passacaglia, which may be taken to represent the Doctor.

The next scene is once more the alley in which Wozzeck lives. Marie is standing outside her door. Wozzeck enters. He is visibly a stage nearer the mental breaking-point: he talks incoherently about sin, and Marie, and Marie's red mouth, and asks about "him", and whether "he" has stood there where he now stands. Marie replies that many people pass up and down, and she cannot forbid the street to anyone. For a moment she is terrified as she thinks he is going to strike her. "Better a knife in me than a hand on me", she says; "when I was ten years old my father did not dare that." She goes into the house. Come to himself again, Wozzeck repeats softly "Better a knife!... A man", he con- tinues below his breath, "is an abyss; his brain reels when he looks into it.... My head is swimming!" He goes slowly down the street.

In this scene, which corresponds in its musical form to the largo of a symphony, Berg employs only a chamber orchestra of one flute (also piccolo), one oboe, one cor anglais, two clarinets, a bass clarinet, one bassoon, a double bassoon, two horns and a solo string quintet.

A slow Ländler:

introduces the next scene, which takes place in a beer garden packed with soldiers, youths and girls, some of whom are dancing, others promenading. A few are tipsy and betray the fact in their conversation. A new dance is begun—a waltz:

in which Marie and the Drum-major, the former swimming in ecstasy, take part. They are watched by Wozzeck. Crazy with jealousy, he is on the point of rushing among the dancers when the waltz comes to an end and the couples leave the floor. He sits down again. Andres, the soldiers and some apprentices burst into a lusty song: and when this is over, Wozzeck starts a conversation with Andres the gloom and incoherence of which on Wozzeck's side soon bore Andres, who leaves him for more congenial company. One of the apprentices climbs on to a table and preaches a burlesque sermon in the best German pseudo-philosophical style; but he soon tails off into the drunken-maudlin, and is taken away by some of the others. While the company in general resume their singing and waltzing (No. 11 once more), a personage described as the Fool approaches the lonely and moody Wozzeck, and, whether by accident or by design, sets the poor man's brain whirring insanely again by telling him that he smells

blood. The figures on the dance floor, among whom are Marie
and the Drum-major, suddenly seem to Wozzeck to be going
round and round in a crimson sea.

The musical form of this scene is described as a scherzo with
two trios.

The transition to the fifth scene is made by way of a development of the waltz (No. 11). The new setting is the guard room of
the barracks. As the curtain rises we see the soldiers sleeping all
around with half-open mouths, and hear them snoring melodi-
cally and harmonically (in five parts) in the twelve-tone scale.
Wozzeck wakens Andres with his moaning. He cannot sleep;
if he closes his eyes he sees Marie dancing and hears the fiddles
playing, and a knife keeps flashing before him. "O Lord, lead us
not into temptation", he wails, as he tries to sleep again. But just
then the Drum-major enters, announced by a theme:

which becomes the principal factor in the rondo that follows.

The Drum-major, fatuously pleased with himself as usual,
begins to brag of his latest conquest. If they want to know the
name of the ardent beauty, let them ask Wozzeck. Taking a nip
from the flask he draws from his pocket he offers it to Wozzeck,
inviting him to drink with him. Wozzeck merely looks away and
whistles. Thereupon the Drum-major, losing his temper, hurls
himself savagely on the physically inferior Wozzeck, who is soon
beaten to the ground and nearly strangled. The vainglorious
Drum-major having left, after another swig from the flask,
Wozzeck, his face bleeding, raises himself and staggers to his
plank bed again. He sits down and stares into vacancy, while
Andres and the others, after a cynical comment or two, resume
their interrupted slumbers. The music ebbs away into silence as
the curtain falls.

The first scene of the third act presents us with seven variations
and a fugue on a theme: [1]

given out, as soon as the curtain rises, by various solo instruments
one after another.

Marie is sitting in her room at night, reading aloud from the
Bible, by the light of a candle, the story of the woman taken in
adultery, and bemoaning her own frailty. She thrusts the child
from her, saying, "The boy gives me a stab in the heart!", then
draws him to her tenderly again and tells him a little story: "Once
upon a time there was a poor child who had no father and no
mother . . . it was hungry and wept day and night. . . ." [2] She
breaks off, wondering why Wozzeck had not been to see her
yesterday or today; then she turns once more to the Bible and
reads out, "And she knelt before His feet and wept and kissed His
feet. . . ." She beats her miserable breast and cries, " Saviour, I
would anoint Thy feet; have pity on me and mine as Thou hadst

[1] The official description of the form of the third act is "Six Inventions",
distributed thus:

Scene 1. Invention on a Theme.
Scene 2. Invention on a Tone.
Scene 3. Invention on a Rhythm.
Scene 4. Invention on a Six-tone Chord.
      Invention on a Key. (Orchestral Interlude).
Scene 5. Invention on a Rhythm in Even Quavers. (Perpetuum mobile).

[2] This, the fifth variation on the theme, contrasts effectively with the
others by being quite tonal; it is as if Marie were taking pains to speak to the
child in a language simple enough for his undeveloped intelligence to understand.

pity on her!" The fugue commences with the words "And she knelt at His feet", which Marie gives out in a style that is at least as near to speech as to song:

though the vocal tones are sufficiently definite in pitch to offer themselves for imitation in the orchestra. A solo viola takes the subject up at the second bar, a solo violin at the third, and a solo double bass at the fourth. Marie's cry of "Saviour! I would anoint Thy feet..." which is also developed fugally, is " wholly sung", as the directions in the score put it.

The orchestral meditation on the theme of No. 14 dies away to a soft B natural deep down in the double basses; and this note, in one form or another, pervades in the most curious way most of the next scene. The curtain rises to show us a pond in a wood. It is growing dark. Wozzeck enters with Marie. She is anxious to get back to the town, and urges him to quicken his steps. But he makes her sit down beside him, sympathises with her for having walked so far, and assures her that her feet will not hurt her much longer. He likes the darkness and the quiet all round them. How long is it that they have known each other? he asks. "Three years at Whitsuntide", she replies. "And how long do you think it will last?" he continues. Her only answer to that is to leap to her feet with a feverish "I must go!" He forces her to sit down again, and his talk takes a sinister turn. He compliments her ironically on her goodness, her piety, her fidelity; then his mood changes suddenly and he speaks of the sweetness of her lips, for which he would give heaven itself. But soon his madness steals over him again. Marie shivers in the night air; whereupon he tells her that when the morning dew falls she will not feel the cold.

Silence falls on them both: the moon rises, and a long-held B natural persists like an obsession through all the harmonic changes in the orchestral tissue. "How red the moon is!" says Marie. For Wozzeck it is the symbol of blood. He draws a knife and plunges it into her throat, stoops for a moment over the body, ejaculates "Dead!", straightens himself nervously, and at last steals away in silence. The inexorable B natural is still sounding when the curtain falls.

A long crescendo on the B leads into a quick polka, played on an out-of-tune piano behind the scenes. The curtain rises on a room in a poor tavern, where a number of people, among them Margret, are dancing. Wozzeck is sitting at a table, feverishly urging the others to dance and dance again, as a means to make him forget his crime. Losing his self-control he ousts the piano music with a song of his own, and dances a few steps with Margret; then he draws her to his table, seats her on his knee, and embraces her. She sings for him a little song the burden of which is that long frocks and pointed shoes are not for serving-women. Something snaps in Wozzeck's brain. He leaps up, shouting "No! No shoes! One can go to hell barefoot! . . ." Margret sees blood on his hands, and her startled cry brings the others to the table. He stammers out that he has cut himself, an explanation which the others deride, as the blood is on his right hand and arm. At last, with a wild cry of "Am I a murderer?" he rushes out.

After a quick change of scene we see Wozzeck by the pond again in the moonlight. Terrified and remorseful, he has come straight from the tavern to search for the knife. He stumbles over Marie's body. What is that red necklace she is wearing? he asks crazily: was it, like the ear-rings, the price of her sin? He searches frantically for the knife, fearing it may betray him. At last he finds it and throws it into the pond. Just then the moon shows blood-red through the clouds, and he sees in it another witness and discloser of his crime. All nature seems to be proclaiming it! And the knife: where it fell will it not be found by some bather? And he plunges into the water, in part in search of the knife, in part to wash away the blood he feels to be still upon him. But the water itself turns to blood as he laves himself with it!

He gets out of his depth and drowns. His last choked cry is heard by the Doctor and the Captain, who enter just then and sense that someone is drowning, but are too terrified by the uncanniness of the spot, the red of the moon, and the grey of the clouds to think of doing anything to help. After the final groan from Wozzeck they hurry away; "Come, Doctor", says the Captain, tugging at his companion, "this is not good to hear!"

The orchestral interlude that follows, beginning with an *adagio* for strings:

is one of the finest sections of the whole work; it passes in review much of the material we have by now learned to associate with Wozzeck, so that it may be regarded, perhaps, as an elegy over him. (The *adagio* prelude is said to be derived from a symphony on which Berg was working in 1913-14). When at last the curtain rises for the short final scene we see again the street before Marie's house door. It is morning, and in the bright sunshine Wozzeck's tiny child is riding its hobby-horse while all the other children play about and sing an old rhyme:

Rin-gel, Rin-gel, Ro-senkranz, Rin - gelreih'n!

But a sudden end comes to both song and play as children come running in with the cry that something has happened to Marie. "Your mother is dead", says one of them to the child; but all he does is to ride his hobby-horse faster with a delighted "Hopp! Hopp! Hopp!" The older children all rush away to the pond to see the body; and after a moment's hesitation Marie's child follows them, still crying "Hopp!"

Büchner's final scene—the one in the dissecting room, already referred to—has not been used by Berg. For operatic purposes the scene of the children certainly makes an effective curtain: and yet one wishes that the composer had seen fit to show us Wozzeck on the dissecting table, with the orchestra, in a last and greatest effort, summing up the pitiful life and death of the poor fellow in a way that only music could achieve.

L'HEURE ESPAGNOLE
Ravel (1875-1937)

PRINCIPAL CHARACTERS

CONCEPCION	*Soprano*
GONZALVE	*Tenor*
TORQUEMADA	*Trial* [1]
RAMIRO	*Baritone-Martin* [1]
DON INIGO GOMEZ	*Buffo Bass*

I

L'Heure Espagnole was produced at the Paris Opéra-Comique on the 19th May 1911. The libretto, one of the most perfect things of its type ever written, is by Maurice Le Grand, who took the pseudonym of Franc-Nohain.

With some operas it is unnecessary for anyone who is listening to them on the gramophone or the radio, or merely studying them in the score, to have more than a general idea of what is going on on the stage at this moment or that. In the case of *L'Heure Espagnole*, however, it is difficult for anyone who has not seen a theatrical

---

[1] Antoine Trial was a very popular operatic tenor in Paris in the eighteenth century. "Trial" is now a term used to denote the high, somewhat thin and nasal tenor voice peculiarly fitted for certain comic parts in opera.

Jean Blaise Martin (1769-1837) was a French baritone famous in his day less for the quality of his acting than for a voice which was almost a tenor in its upper range and a bass in its lower.

It was the custom in the French provincial theatres of that epoch to define a rôle by the name of the actor or singer who had made a reputation for himself in it in Paris; each company had to have its own "Trial", its own "Martin", etc., or as near thereto as it could get. Some of these names are still in use in France as an epitome of the qualities of voice, appearance, style and so on required of a singer of a particular part. Thus Ellen, in *Lakmé*, figures in the list of *dramatis personae* not as a soprano but as a "dugazon". This name comes from a certain Louise Rosalie Dugazon (1735-1821). A "dugazon" part may be either a "jeune dugazon" or a "mère dugazon". It calls mostly for intelligent acting of the soubrette order rather than for brilliant singing.

performance of it to realise just how much of the fun depends on the neat stage-carpentry of the piece.

The action takes place in eighteenth century Toledo, in the shop of a middle-aged clock-maker, Torquemada, who is seen at his bench, with his back to us, when the curtain rises. On one side of the stage is the entrance from the street, on the other side a door leading to the living apartments. At the back is a large window looking on to the street; on either side of it stands a large "grand-father" clock. For later purposes of identification we shall call them A and B. A number of smaller clocks and automata of every variety are scattered about the place.

The work begins with a short orchestral introduction that is mostly based on the quiet theme heard in the wood wind in the opening bars:

While this is pursuing its tranquil way, all sorts of enchanting sounds are heard proceeding from the clocks and toys. Bells tinkle; pendulums tick; a cock crows shrilly; birds sing or squawk; an automaton plays a little solo; marionettes dance to the silvery music of a celesta. The whole thing is a miracle of scoring that defies verbal description. We seem to be in a fairyland of sweet, preposterous little noises; and through them all No. 1 goes on unhurried, unperturbed. Seemingly this Torquemada is the happiest of men, and his house and shop the happiest of places. He does not suspect what possibilities of danger to his marital security lurk in those two big clocks by the door.

He raises his head, the professional magnifying glass still in his eye, as the muleteer Ramiro enters. His figure, tall, well-knit, muscular, contrasts markedly with that of the fussy little clock-maker, whose whole appearance suggests more the bourgeois than the romantic, amiability rather than physical prowess. Ramiro, it appears, is in the government service: he and his mules

have to carry the town's post each day. For so responsible a job
the utmost punctuality is necessary; and unfortunately Ramiro's
watch—a huge affair which he produces from his fob and hands
over to Torquemada—has taken to going by fits and starts. It is
a cherished heirloom. Ramiro's uncle, a toreador at Barcelona,
had been saved, as the muleteer puts it, from the horns of death
by this very watch when a bull had charged him; "but if the
monster (*monstre*) was stopped by the watch (*montre*)", he goes
on to say in a gallant attempt at a punning antithesis, "it is the
montre that has now stopped." A Spanish rhythm in the orchestra,
reinforced by horn and trumpet fanfares and a good deal of
percussion:

brings the scene in the bull ring vividly before our eyes.

While Torquemada is examining the precious watch, the voice
of his young wife Concepcion is heard behind the scenes.
"Totor!" she calls loudly; and the placid watchmaker explains to
his customer that this is his spouse's "diminutif plein de charme"
of Torquemada.[1] An expressive little phrase in a solo 'cello:

seems to paint Concepcion as her husband sees her. Concepcion is
shocked to find her husband still in his shop. Has he forgotten,

---

[1] In both the vocal and the orchestral score the diminutive is given as
"Totor"; but in the Franc-Nohain text it is "Hector". "Totor" was perhaps
an improvement on the original that occurred to Ravel in the course of his
composition.

she asks him, that this is Thursday, the day of the week when he
has to go on his round of regulation of the municipal clocks? He
excuses himself on the ground that he is surrounded by so many
clocks all day long that he does not hear any of them telling him
the time. Why, Concepcion then asks him, has he not kept his
promise to let her have one of the two grandfather clocks for her
bedroom? A clock of that size, he protests, is not easy to cart
about. She looks at him meaningly, and comments sotto voce that
he certainly needs to avoid a prodigal expenditure of his physical
forces. He hastily collects his tools and goes out, asking the
muleteer to wait until he returns, when he will put his watch in
order for him.

Both Ramiro and Concepcion are a trifle embarrassed at the
turn events have taken. Ramiro, in an aside:

wonders what on earth he can talk to the señora about, because
conversation, especially with ladies, has never been his strong
suit. Concepcion, also in an aside, remarks bitterly that this is just
her luck—on the one day in the week when her husband is not at
home she has this nuisance of a customer on her hands! As her
dear Gonzalve may arrive any moment now, something, she sees,
will have to be done about it. So, pointing to one of the big
clocks, she asks the muleteer how many men he thinks would be
needed to remove it—two or three? At once he is in his element.
A thing like that is a bagatelle, he assures her, a nutshell, a bit of
straw that could be lifted with one finger. Does she want it
shifted to her room? Apologising for even thinking of troubling
him to such an extent, she explains that her room is on the first
floor. But he is delighted to oblige: deep down in every muleteer,

he says, is an amateur furniture remover; and a job like this will
be a little diversion for him while he is waiting for the clock-maker
to return. He picks up clock A with the utmost ease and slings it
over his shoulder. Concepcion gives him directions where to take
it—through the side door of the shop, across the lobby, and then
up the stairs; and they part on terms of mutual satisfaction.

Ramiro has no sooner disappeared than Gonzalve is heard
"off", singing an elaborate roulade. Being a poet, he naturally
lisps in numbers. Concepcion greets him with a rapturous cry;
but he is too much occupied with chanting the praises of so happy
a day to think of putting it to any other use—"At last", he
warbles, "at last has come the happy day (sing, ye harps!) when
my mistress is no longer the slave of a jealous husband":

En - fin re - vient   le jour si doux.

Har - pes, chan - tez, é - cla - tez, sal - ves!

and to a Spanish rhythm he works out an elaborate poetical
analogy between the enamel of the clock dials and the enamelled
hours of the garden of his joy:

"Yes, yes, dear one", says Concepcion; "but let us not waste the
fleeting hour in vain talk"; and to herself she murmurs, "The

muleteer may return any moment!" But the trouble with Gonzalve as a lover is that he is too much of a poet: he adores the music of his own words, and becomes lost in admiration of the literary images which every situation suggests to him. He is particularly pleased with that conceit of his of the enamel: he promises Concepcion that he will work it up into a sonnet and set it to music: the title will be "The Garden of the Hours". In vain does poor Concepcion beg him to "profit by this unique opportunity", and tells him how violently her heart had been beating in expectation of his coming. That only starts him off on a fresh series of images—her heart, indeed, is like a clock, throbbing as that does to a rhythm, and so on. And the more ardent she becomes, the more desperate at the passing of the valuable minutes, the more flowery does Gonzalve become, the more completely lost in plans for shaping a song out of this beautiful conceit, a sonnet out of that, a serenade out of a third.

He still has his head well up in the clouds when, to Concepcion's annoyance, the muleteer returns to announce complacently that the job upstairs is done, the clock in the place indicated by the lady. Obviously the man must be side-tracked somehow or other. A brilliant idea strikes her. With many apologies she explains to him that no sooner had he gone off with clock A than she realised that clock B would suit her room better. Professing himself delighted to oblige so courteous a señora, he is about to shoulder B when Concepcion asks him first to bring the other one back. Gonzalve, for his part, surveys the man of muscle disdainfully: "muleteers", he remarks, "have no conversation". Ramiro goes back to fetch clock A. To Gonzalve the incident merely suggests the theme for another poem—"Caprice de femme". But Concepcion puts a summary end to his poetising. She orders him to get into clock B without a moment's loss of time. He does not quite like the idea of being immured in "this box of cypress, or pine, or oak, or cedar, or whatever it is"; but after Concepcion has explained to him that there is no hope of a tête-à-tête with the muleteer coming in and out, while the man can be made to do something really useful by carting both the clock *and* Gonzalve into her room, he quite takes to the idea, merely, however, because it will be a sensation new to him, and one that

may be serviceable to him as a poet, to be carried across her
threshold like that, between two planks, for all the world, as he
puts it, as if he were in a coffin. Is it not, he asks her as he gets into
the clock, a proof on his part of a love stronger than death?
Though she does not quite take that view of the matter she
humours him in it, glad to see the affair promising to turn out
better than she could have hoped a few minutes before.

Just then a hearty voice greets her from outside the window;
and Concepcion has barely time to close the door of the clock on
Gonzalve before Don Inigo Gomez enters the shop. He is a rich
banker, heavy of build and with an adequate sense of his own
importance, as is indicated by the pompous theme in the horns
that accompanies his entrance.

He soon makes it clear to Conception that it is not her husband
he has come to see: was it not he, indeed, who had used his great
influence to obtain for the worthy Torquemada the job of regulat-
ing the town clocks once a week? If only, when her husband is
absent, Concepcion would be a little less inhuman to him! he
sighs as he tries to take her hand. She glances apprehensively at
the clock and urges Don Inigo to speak more softly, for clocks
have ears. Just as he approaches her again there comes into sight
in the doorway the tip of clock A, which Ramiro is returning.
Concepcion begs Don Inigo to excuse her: she has the furniture
removers in, she explains, pointing to the muleteer.

. "There you are", says Ramiro, depositing the clock in its
former place and making for the one (B) that contains Gonzalve.
Concepcion expresses the fear that this one may be rather too
heavy for him; but he flings it across his shoulder with the assurance that with objects of this kind it is a matter not of weight—
that is the merest trifle—but of bulk and balance; a think like this
clock, for instance, once you have it balanced, you can carry with
ease from roof to cellar; and he shows her how easy it is by tossing

the mass from one shoulder to the other and back again. Concepcion is lost in admiration of his strength. "This man has muscles of steel!" she says to herself; "but if he pitches Gonzalve about like that he will end by making him seasick!" However, she goes out with the muleteer, apologising to Don Inigo on the ground that the delicate mechanism of these clocks is easily deranged, especially the pendulum.

Don Inigo, who can take a hint as well as the next man, has a suspicion that he is being dismissed. Were he to consult only his dignity he would give up the pursuit and go; but he prefers to stay. In circumstances like these, he reflects, a lover generally conceals himself in a cupboard; but as there is no cupboard in the shop, a clock will have to do. Perhaps, he philosophises, it is his imposing mien that frightens poor little Concepcion; he will accordingly condescend to a little light humour on her account. With great difficulty he manages to squeeze himself into A, where he awaits her return. Hearing, indeed, what he takes to be her footsteps—they are really those of Ramiro—Don Inigo hastily closes the door of the clock. His complacent view of himself as "dans le fond un petit farceur" is expressed in a sober waltz-tune that runs all through this scene:

The muleteer, finding himself alone, indulges in a long soliloquy, to the accompaniment mostly of No. 4. This is a truly charming lady, he reflects. First of all she graciously permits him to oblige her in the little matter of carrying the clocks up and down, and now she has commissioned him to mind the shop until she returns. In his way he too, though a man of muscle rather than brain, and not at his best where words are concerned, is a bit of a philosopher. The machines in the shop remind him in their delicate mechanism, he says, of women, who also are complicated bits of machinery, though of another kind, and one less easy for a man like him to understand. Heaven forbid that he should take it on

himself to meddle with the feminine springs: the only talent that
has been bestowed on him, he muses sadly, is that of shifting
clocks. He has got thus far when Concepcion comes running in,
obviously not in the sweetest of moods. She can hardly speak for
vexation, she tells him. Let him think of her what he will; but she
cannot endure in her room a clock that doesn't go right: her
nerves really will not stand any more! Always the soul of comprehension where furniture removing is concerned, and always
ready to oblige so charming a señora, Ramiro goes off to do what
he has by now come to regard as his duty.

This gives Don Inigo his chance. Divesting himself of his
dignity, as he had promised himself he would do, and playing
down to the intellectual level, as he imagines, of Concepcion, he
opens the door of the clock a little and pipes "Cuckoo!" At first
she does not associate the cry with Don Inigo; she thinks it must
have come from the clock itself. She is flying into a worse temper
than before when she catches sight of the banker. He gallantly
declares that he would throw himself at her feet were there room
for him to do so:

But she is in no mood for gay badinage. She bids him come out;
but, as he very reasonably urges, why come out so soon from a
place into which it had given him so much trouble to get? Does
he make no appeal at all to her as a lover? He is not young, he
admits, not at all poetic—merely a great banker. But youth is not
always an asset; it often happens that a young man is inexperienced, easily thrown out of his stride in his love-making; poets
in particular are apt to be so intent on their dreams that they miss
reality when it is under their very noses. "If you only knew how
true that is!" she replies, with a world of feeling in her voice. He
is pointing out to her that a lover like himself presents "plus de
surface" when Ramiro appears once more, with clock B, and
Gonzalve inside it, on his shoulder. Concepcion hastily closes

the door of A on Don Inigo, and tells the muleteer where to
deposit B. Ramiro naturally thinks his next job must be to take
A up to Concepcion's room in its place. Don Inigo is quite
in favour of this, as he hints in an aside to Concepcion, opening
the door slightly and kissing her hand. Seeing no other way
out of the difficulty she gives the order to Ramiro to proceed.
But once more she expresses her concern at the burden she is
imposing on him; and once more, flinging the massive clock with
Don Inigo in it across his shoulder as though it were a feather,
he assures her that it is the merest bagatelle, a drop of water, a
grain of sand. Concepcion follows him admiringly with her
eyes: "this man is certainly gifted!" she says to herself as he
goes out.

She tears open the door of clock B, and, in a raging passion,
bids Gonzalve take himself off. But he is still nothing but the
poet, lost in his verbal fancies. He proposes, he says, to carve on
the clock his and her initials around a heart transfixed by arrows,
as ordinary lovers do on the bark of trees. He gets so involved in
his imagery that she cannot wait till he has finished. "Very
good", she says; "stay there if you choose, but don't expect me
to wait here and listen to your interminable verses. *Vous avez de
l'esprit, mais manquez d'à-propos*. I have had enough of you and
your pipings." And what that she flounces out.

Gonzalve cannot help feeling a little hurt, but, as he says, he
sees no reason to quit this "oaken envelope" in which fate has
seen fit to enclose him before he has worked out a poetic
comparison between himself and the woodland nymphs who
once found themselves in a similar situation in classical times:
"Impressions d'Hamadryade" would be a good title, he thinks:

But hearing Ramiro's footsteps he closes the clock door quickly,
remarking as he does so that crude people like this muleteer have
no feeling for the symbols of pagan antiquity.

Ramiro comes in again. He is more impressed than ever by the condescension of the charming lady of the house in allowing him to move the clocks about like this. And then the shop, how pleasant, how peaceful it is—nothing for him to do there but listen to the ticking of the pendulums and the tintinnabulation of the automata, without the slightest necessity for him either to speak or think. If he were not a muleteer he would like to be a clockmaker, spending his days in this particular shop, with this particular lady. His musings are interrupted by the entry of Concepcion. He guesses from her angry face that something in connection with the latest clock removal has displeased her. But she need not worry, he tells her; he will bring the thing back in a jiffy. And off he goes once more.

Concepcion now boils over. Was ever woman so unfortunate as she, with two lovers, one of whom *manque de tempérament* and the other *à ce point de nature?* And these men call themselves Spaniards! One of them can think of nothing but composing baroque verses, while the other, an even more grotesque object, has been unable to get more than half-way out of the clock! And soon her husband will return, and her day will be over, but not quite the day she had anticipated. Feeling she will go mad if she does not smash something she pounds on the clock containing Gonzalve; whereupon he opens the door, puts out his head for a moment, and murmurs "Impressions d'Hamadryade".

But just then the imperturbable Ramiro returns with the clock that holds the bulky Don Inigo. He puts it in its old place opposite the one containing Gonzalve, and, taking it for granted that there is another job for him to do, offers to carry the first clock upstairs again if the gracious lady wishes, or even the two together: and he begins to roll up his sleeves. "What serenity, what facility!" says Concepcion to herself. "And how he juggles with the clocks, lifts them, walks off with them, and always with a smile on his lips! Truly this man has biceps!" Suddenly she tells him to return to her room. "With which clock?" he asks. "*Sans horloge!*" she replies, and goes out once more, dutifully preceded by the muleteer.

Surmising that the course is now clear, Don Inigo opens his door, but at a call of "Cuckoo!" from a near-by clock he hurriedly closes it again. Then, cautiously putting his head out once more, he muses sadly on his unfortunate position. How pleasant it would be to be at home now in a large armchair, in his slippers, instead of in this tiresome box in which he cannot sit down and out of which he cannot get, and with no one in sight to help him. *"Cordon, s'il vous plaît! La porte! La porte!"* he calls, with a brave attempt at humour. He closes his door again as Gonzalve opens his. For Gonzalve has heard the cry, and realising that his solitude has been invaded he thinks it time to abandon what he describes, in the most flowery terms imaginable, as his hermitage. Looking out of the window, however, he sees Torquemada approaching, whereupon he makes for cover again, the prospect of explaining his presence there to the clock-maker having no charms for him. But in his perturbation he opens the wrong clock, and is astonished to find Don Inigo inside it. Thus both of them are in full view when Torquemada enters.

He is in the highest spirits. He greets Gonzalve and Don Inigo most courteously: if there is one thing more than another that pleases a clock-maker, he says, it is to find a numerous clientèle awaiting him when he returns. He hopes he has not kept them waiting too long. Gonzalve diplomatically praises his watches: Don Inigo explains that he had been so interested in the grandfather clock that he had got inside it for closer inspection of the wonderful mechanism. Torquemada finds this curiosity quite natural, and assures him he will be getting good value for his money—for of course he intends to buy the clock? "Certainly", says Don Inigo. Then, turning to Gonzalve, Torquemada asks him not to be envious of the other gentleman, for he himself can have the other clock at the same price—a genuine bargain. Gonzalve in turn has to agree, but he lets us know in an aside that though he has to do this to allay the man's suspicions, a poet finds these base commercial considerations disgusting.

All this being settled to everyone's satisfaction, Don Inigo asks Torquemada to help him out of the clock. The clockmaker, finding his own strength insufficient, calls in the aid of Gonzalve. The pair of them are still struggling vainly with their problem when Concepcion and Ramiro return. Forming a chain, the clock-maker, Gonzalve and Concepcion pull their hardest; but the chain breaks, leaving Don Inigo still in the clock. Thereupon Ramiro takes hold lightly of the banker and has him out in a jiffy, apparently without exerting himself in the least. Even Don Inigo is lost in admiration: while Concepcion agrees with him that the muleteer is a man of really remarkable strength.

There is only one operatic way to end up a story of this kind—with an ensemble in which everyone expresses his satisfaction with the turn events have taken. Torquemada apologises to his wife for having sold both the big clocks of which she was so fond; but Concepcion assures him that Ramiro, who passes her window every morning with his mules, will henceforth be as regular a chronometer as she could wish; and the clockmaker in his turn begs him to be sure to tell his wife the time each morning. Then all the characters line up at the footlights and address the audience. A financier, says Gonzalve politely, presenting Don Inigo: a poet, says the banker, turning to Gonzalve; an absurd husband, says Concepcion; a coquette, says Torquemada; all with a touch of Spain, adds Ramiro: "it is the Boccaccio moral—the time comes when the muleteer has his turn". The humorous quintet is sung to a habanera rhythm; and there is a particularly amusing moment when Gonzalve, Concepcion, Torquemada and Ramiro having in turn sung the line "Avec un peu d'Espagne autour", Don Inigo essays it, but finding the last note rather low for him leaves it to the sarrusophone to complete the phrase in his stead, which the instrument does on an even lower note than the ear has been led to expect.

L'Heure Espagnole is perhaps not everyone's opera. It is impossible in any language but French. It is better suited to a small, intimate theatre than to the large opera houses of our capital cities. It has to be taken imaginatively rather than realistically, for even the human characters have about them a touch of the charming unreality of the marionette milieu in which they are set, and which Ravel has described so enchantingly in his orchestra. He never over-stresses a point; indeed, for many spectators he perhaps under-stresses some of them. In an age that takes its pleasures heartily, if not, indeed, a trifle vulgarly, Ravel seems a reversion to the better-bred eighteenth century, when the aristocracy in every European country set the tone of social life. Lord

Chesterfield impressed it on his son that a gentleman, however vastly he may be amused, never permits himself to do more than smile: he himself, he said, had never been seen to laugh since he came to years of discretion. Ravel never laughs; nor does he wish the spectator to do more than smile at these puppets of his—a smile as thin-lipped and as discreet, if possible, as the composer's own.

The only real singing character in the opera is Gonzalve, who occasionally becomes almost lyrical. For the others, Ravel, in a prefatory note to his score, prescribes a speaking rather than a singing style—what he calls the quasi-parlando of Italian buffo recitative. The final quintet, of course, is in a different category.

BORIS GODOUNOV
Moussorgsky (1839-1881)

PRINCIPAL CHARACTERS

BORIS GODOUNOV	*Baritone*
FEODOR	*Mezzo-soprano*
XENIA	*Soprano*
THE NURSE	*Mezzo-soprano*
SHUISKY	*Tenor*
STCHELKALOV	*Baritone*
PIMEN	*Bass*
GREGORY (DMITRI)	*Tenor*
MARINA MNISCHEK	*Mezzo-soprano*
RANGONI	*Bass*
VARLAAM	*Bass*
MISSAIL	*Tenor*
THE HOSTESS	*Mezzo-soprano*
THE IDIOT	*Tenor*

I

When the Tsar Ivan the Terrible died, in 1584, he was succeeded by the pious Feodor, who was in turn succeeded in 1598 by his brother-in-law, an able and ambitious boyar of Tartar origin, Boris Godounov. Ivan had left behind him also a young son, Dmitri, by a non-legal marriage. This boy was murdered, in his ninth year, in 1591, and the instigator of the crime was believed in some quarters to have been Boris. The latter died in April 1605, after having named his young son Feodor as his successor. During the last year or two of Boris's life a claim to the throne of Russia had been put forward by an adventurer calling himself the genuine Dmitri—the child, he alleged, had escaped the assassins —but who seems to have been a renegade monk named Gregory (Grishka) Otrepiev. This pseudo-Dmitri found plenty of willing supporters of his pretensions in Russia, where neither the strict rule nor the Tartar origin of Boris was in his favour; and he was backed also by Russia's hereditary enemy, the King of Poland, and by the Pope of Rome, Gregory having prudently recognised the Roman Catholic as the one true church when he put forward his claim to the Muscovite throne. After the death of Boris, the pseudo-Dmitri advanced with his Polish allies on Moscow, where he had himself proclaimed Tsar, after having married Marina Mnischek, the daughter of a Polish magnate, the Voyevode of Sandomir. After a very short reign Dmitri was murdered in a popular uprising engineered by Prince Vassili Shuisky, who succeeded him as Tsar.

We have a contemporary account of most of these happenings in a report by a Dutch merchant then resident in Moscow, which was translated into English and published in London in 1607. The title of it is "The Reporte of a Bloudie and Terrible Massacre in the Citty of Mosco, with the fearefull and tragicall end of Deme- trius the last Duke, before him raigning at this present." From this we learn that after his death Dmitri was publicly condemned and his memory degraded by his successor. It was "alleadged that he had been a shauen and graduated monke, whose kinsmen, sisters and brothers were yet liuing, that is, his father in lawe, and his owne mother. . . ." These people took an oath that "his name was Gregorie . . . and that he was a Monke of this Cittie in the monasterie of the Castle: men say, that in his youth he was very diligent to reade and write, and delighted much to peruse and reade Histories and Chronicles, hauing sometimes serued in the Patriarkes Court, for a Singing man and a Musitian, euer carefully observing whatsoeuer might further his intentions. . . ."

We have also a contemporary portrait of Shuisky, which the reader will do well to keep in his mind when he is listening to the opera: it was drawn by a Scotch soldier, Captain Gilbert, who had been a member of Dmitri's foreign bodyguard. It shows us Shuisky very much as Pushkin and Moussorgsky have painted him, a cool, smooth, artfully dissembling intriguer, hiding his ambitions under a mask of modesty and humility. "The Nobles", says Gilbert, "cast lots foure times to receiue a Successor, as it were, by diuine sentence in lot-oracle: in euery of which times the lot fell vpon Suiskey . . . he modestly refusing and enforced by constancy of the various lot to accept that Scepter; whereof others

thinke him as ambitious, as was modest Boris before him. How-
euer, he hath left his name and memorie written in as blacke inke
as either Boris or Demetrius, if Reports bee true, which say that
he proued a wicked Prince, partly by poison, partly by the Tartars, making away all, whose bloud might by Nobilitie threaten
a probabilitie of their prouing his Corriuals." [1]

2

So much for the historical background of Pushkin's drama of
1825. The history of Moussorgsky's opera, which was based on
that work, is rather more complicated.

Building mainly upon Pushkin's play, with a little assistance
from ancient Russian chronicles, Moussorgsky wrote the music
of his opera between October 1868 and about May of the following year: the scoring was done between the summer and the mid-
December of 1869. The score that is known to most opera-goers
today by the title of *Boris Godounov* is an arrangement not of this
score of 1868, but a later one, by Rimsky-Korsakov. But between
the making of this and the original composition of the work a
good deal had happened, the full details of which have come to
light only during recent years.

Moussorgsky submitted his work to the Directorate of the
Imperial Theatres in Petersburg in the summer of 1870, but it was
rejected. Thereupon the composer made sundry alterations in,
abridgements of, and additions to, his score between about April
1871 and July 1872, when the orchestration of this second version
was completed. Three scenes from this version were given in the
Maryinski Theatre, Petersburg, on the 5th February 1873: a performance of the work as a whole—though with certain cuts—
followed on the 27th January 1874 in the same theatre. The vocal
score of this version was published about that time. This score
later became very scarce; but several of those who possessed a
copy of it kept up for many years a fire of criticism against
Rimsky-Korsakov for his "mutilations" of Moussorgsky's original. In the Rimsky-Korsakov score (first edition 1896, new
edition, with some restorations of matter previously omitted,

---

[1] The reader will find these and several other interesting contemporary
documents in Sonia E. Howe's book *The False Dmitri* (London, 1916).

1908), the order of the episodes in the last act is this: (1) the so-called Revolution Scene in the forest near Kromy, in which the people rise against their oppressors; (2) the triumphal entry of Gregory as Dmitri; (3) the lament of the Idiot; (4) the meeting of the Douma and the death of Boris. When the piano score of 1874 became generally available in a modern re-issue (about 1925), it was found that the "original" order of the closing scenes was (1) the death of Boris, (2) the Revolution Scene in the forest. The feeling was general that not only was this the authentic but it was the better ending: many admirers of the opera had come to regard the Russian folk as the true protagonists of it, and it was held to be most fitting that they should have the last word—to say nothing of historical accuracy. The case that had been slowly built up against Rimsky-Korsakov for so many years in certain quarters seemed now to be complete: the conclusion appeared obvious that the opera had been made to close with the death of Boris partly for the sake of the players of that important part, partly because the average audience does not like the "hero" of an opera to disappear before the very end has been reached.

In 1928, however, the *true* original score was published, i.e., the opera as it had been in Moussorgsky's manuscript of 1868-9: and it was now seen that, apart from sundry other differences between the various scores which need not be gone into here, the original settings of the last act were (a) the Square of the Cathedral of St. Basil in Moscow, where the disaffected people give vent to their grievances and the Idiot pours out his lament over Russia, (b) the Council Meeting in the Kremlin, at which Boris dies. (There was no Revolution Scene in the forest in this first version).[1]

We are thus confronted by some pretty problems. Putting the Rimsky-Korsakov version on one side for a moment, which of the other two has the right to be regarded as *the* "authentic" score,

[1] Some of the best things in *Boris Godounov* were originally written for an opera on the subject of Salammbô: Moussorgsky began work on this in 1863, but did not complete it. A list of passages from it that were incorporated in *Boris Godounov* will be found in Robert Godet's book, p. 144. (See *infra*, p. 601 note.)

U

with the best claim to performance today? Had the scheme of 1874 been the work of some unauthorised adaptor, the claim of that of 1868–9 would be beyond question. But the 1874 arrangement was after all, the composer's own. It is now held that Moussorgsky altered his score under semi-compulsion, in order to obtain a performance. To some extent that is true; but it is none the less true that the alterations are his own, and that some of them suggest strongly that between 1869 and 1872 he himself had come to take a different view of his subject from the one with which he had begun. A certain school of thought insists that the "true" Boris is the first one, which has the prior, if not the only, right to performance today. But the trouble is that each of the three scores, that of 1868–9, that of 1874, and that of Rimsky-Korsakov, has merits of its own and defects of its own. It is impossible to set forth in detail here all the divergencies between even Moussorgsky's own two scores. Each of them has certain qualities of dramatic construction or psychological characterisation which the other lacks, each of them has its special musical excellencies or shortcomings. Perhaps some day a kind of compromise or synthetic Boris Godounov will be constructed out of the two "original" scores—which, of course, will mean discarding certain pages in each of them, if only to keep the performance within reasonable time-limits. But there will still remain the problem of Rimsky-Korsakov's re-writing of some passages which he regarded as amateurish in their Moussorgskian form, and the further one of his scoring. The former problem is a technical one which mainly concerns musicians only; but the latter concerns the general public as well.

There can be no question that Rimsky-Korsakov's brilliant orchestration has played a large part in making the work the theatrical success it is. The faithful contend that Moussorgsky's own orchestration, even when it strikes the listener as a trifle colourless, should be retained purely and simply because it is Moussorgsky's, on the theory that it was in terms of colours such as these that he saw his characters and their milieu. But that again is in the last resort a question which, fortunately, does not call for detailed discussion here. The one fact that really concerns us in practice is that Boris Godounov is now inseparably associated, in the theatre, with Rimsky-Korsakov's arrangement and especially with Rimsky-Korsakov's orchestration. Whether the public could in time be induced to accept *in toto* one or other of the two actual Moussorgsky versions in place of the Rimsky-Korsakov one it is impossible to say. Certainly our experience goes to suggest that only a long series of performances could effect, by sheer repetition, this radical change in the public mentality; and as the public, by all appearances, will attend only an occasional performance of one of the "original" versions, regarding it merely as a historical curiosity, we seem to be penned within a vicious circle. As, therefore, the Rimsky-Korsakov version is the one which the average opera-goer will hear on ninety-nine occasions out of a hundred—though even this is cut to some extent in the ordinary performance—it is that version we shall analyse here.[1]

3

Moussorgsky had to compress and re-arrange Pushkin's play considerably, for the episodes of this are so many, and mostly so short, that an integral stage performance of it would involve no less than twenty-four changes of scene. The spectator must bear in mind that the action of the opera covers the space of some seven years. The opening scene, in which the populace is seen awaiting Boris's decision to accept or decline the throne of Russia, takes place in the early part of 1598: the next scene, that in Pimen's cell, belongs to 1603, the Polish scenes and Dmitri's march into Russia to 1604, and the last scene to 1605.

[1] I wish to make it clear beyond all possibility of misunderstanding that I am not taking this side or that in the matter. The problem of the three *Boris Godounovs*—for the Rimsky-Korsakov score certainly comes into the picture at times—is far too complicated a one for detailed discussion here. The reader who is interested in it can examine the scores for himself and read the specialist literature on the subject, beginning with Victor Belaiev's booklet *Musorgsky's 'Boris Godunov' and its new version* (Oxford University Press, 1928), and Robert Godet's *En Marge de Boris Godounof* (1926). Some of the differences between Moussorgsky's first and his second plan will be mentioned in the following analysis. The reader must decide for himself between these first and second thoughts of the composer. The problem for the theatres is a purely practical one.

Ivan the Terrible's little son Dmitri had been murdered in 1591, while Feodor was on the throne. Modern historians acquit Boris of that crime. But it seems to have been laid to his charge at a very early date, and by the time that Karamzin's History of Russia came to be written, in the early nineteenth century, it had acquired what may be called official sanction. Pushkin took the story over from Karamzin without any question, and it must of course be accepted as fact by the spectator of the opera, for the real tragedy of Boris—a "Russian Macbeth", as he has been described—is the haunting memory of his crime.

The Prologue takes place in the courtyard of the monastery of Novodievich, near Moscow. It is packed with people who have gathered, more or less by official command, to implore Boris Godounov to ascend the throne, now become vacant through the death of the Tsar Feodor. Moussorgsky took this scene over, in its essentials, from Pushkin's play, in which Boris is depicted as artfully making his acceptance of the throne more palatable to the people by a prolonged pretence of reluctance to assume in name an office which he had long exercised in fact. In Pushkin, what is going on in the mind of the as yet invisible Boris is made clear to us by the comments of the cynical, scheming Prince Shuisky; but this character does not function in the opera till later. In Moussorgsky, the leading character in the opening scene is the Russian people, which we see, in all its simplicity, being dragooned into expressing its free vote for Boris. The "national" atmosphere is defined at once in the phrase upon which the brief orchestral introduction is based:

I

Andante ♩ = 72

There is never anything conventional about Moussorgsky's choruses. They are not the ordinary choruses of opera, inserted to make an imposing mass effect at this or that climactic point of the action. They have a psychology of their own, which comes out both in the ensemble utterances and in the numerous little indi-

vidual comments that break through the main tissue every now
and then. When we first see the crowd in *Boris Godounov* they are
being hustled and browbeaten by the police to make them show
a trifle more ardour and spontaneity in their supplications to
Boris. They dutifully throw themselves on their knees and begin
to drone out the appeal demanded of them:

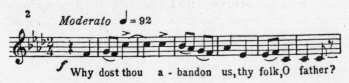

2   *Moderato* ♩ = 92

f Why dost thou a - bandon us, thy folk, O father?

and manage, in the end, to work themselves up to a pitch of
frenzy that satisfies even the constable who is busy with his cudgel
among them. But as soon as he has gone away they revert to their
former uncomprehending apathy, asking each other what it is all
about, dropping into gossip about their own little affairs, and
some of them, the women especially, coming near to scratching
each other's eyes out. When the police officer returns, however,
and threatens them again, they fall on their knees once more and
repeat their supplication to Boris (No. 2) for all the world as if
they meant it.

Stchelkalov, the Clerk of the Douma, enters, and, as in Pushkin, announces that Boris has still not yielded to the prayers
either of the Douma or the Patriarch. Stchelkalov has only some
thirty bars to sing, but Moussorgsky, with his curious faculty for
characterising people or situations that would appear insignificant
to most other musical dramatists, has made him not only a
personality in himself but the voice of a Russia too inarticulate to
find its own self-expression. "Woe to our Land!" he cries; "pray
ye to God that he may send comfort and help in this the hour of
its need, by enlightening the soul of the weary Boris!"

Just then there is heard in the distance a chorus of Pilgrims
singing a fervent appeal to heaven for protection for the Russia
that is so grievously tried, within and without. Soon the Pilgrims
enter, distributing amulets among the crowd, whom they exhort
to take up ikons and the holy emblems and go to meet the Tsar.
Their voices die away in the distance again as they enter the

monastery that stands on one side of the Square, there to make
their appeal to the widow of the deceased Tsar, the sister of Boris,
to add her entreaties to theirs. The curtain comes down slowly on
a strangely impressive scene.

We next see the courtyard of the Kremlin. In the background
is the Red Staircase which leads to the Tsar's apartments—the
Terem. In the space between the Cathedral of the Assumption and
that of the Archangels is a mass of kneeling people. The air is
pulsating with the clang of bells, great:

and small:

Boris has yielded, and the boyars are on their way in solemn
procession to the Cathedral of the Assumption. Shuisky, from the
steps of the Cathedral, cries, to the sound of trumpets, "Long live
the Tsar Boris Feodorovich!", and the people take up the cry in
their own way. Their choral melody:

continues through most of what immediately follows. The crowd is kept in line by the officials as the imposing procession moves on; and at last Boris himself appears.

As he does so the character of the music changes and the brilliant colour dies out of it. Boris, as in Pushkin, speaks to boyars and people of the sadness he now feels at having yielded to their prayers. His soul is filled with fear and foreboding for himself and for Russia. Invoking the blessing of heaven on him and it, he bids his people first kneel in prayer before the tombs of the great departed Tsars, then feast as his guests. Once more the procession passes on to the Cathedral, with the bells pealing out, the mob breaking ranks and the police restoring order, and the Homage Chorus (No. 5) preserving its own essential outlines at the same time that it fuses harmonically with the tones and overtones of the bells:

To shouts of "Glory to the Tsar!" Boris enters the Terem as the curtain falls.

4

When it rises again for the first act, the time, though not stated in the scores, is supposed to be some five years later. The venerable monk Pimen is seen writing by the light of a lamp in his cell in the monastery of the Miracle in Chudov; he is adding the final page to his chronicle of Russian history. A wandering figure in the bass accompanies graphically the slow passage of his pen across the parchment:

Some day, he muses as he halts in his labour for a moment, his record will come to light again before the eyes of some industrious monk, who will in his turn take up the task which he himself is about to lay down; and bending once more over his table he sets himself to write down the last sentences of his work.

Near him lies the young monk Gregory, asleep. He wakes with a cry: for the third time he has dreamed the same disturbing dream, which he now tells to Pimen. He had seen himself climbing the stairs of a tower, from the topmost height of which Moscow had appeared to him like an ant-hill: the squares below seethed with crowds who pointed up at him and broke into jeering laughter: overcome by shame and terror he had fallen headlong, and so awakened. The placid old monk bids him cool his young blood with prayer and fasting: even he, old and schooled by life as he is, sometimes dreams of wild happenings, battles and feasts and follies of all kinds, in which he had taken part in years gone by— for he had known the great Tsar Ivan the Terrible and his court in all their splendour, and sat at banquets and fought against Lithuanians under the walls of Kazan. Gregory envies him these rich experiences and his memories of them, and laments his own crabbed life as a poor monk. But Pimen recalls to him how many Tsars, weary of the world, had been glad at the last to exchange their vain pomp for the peace of the monastic life—among them the great Ivan himself, whom he had seen sitting in this very cell, shedding tears of remorse. His son, the gentle, pious Feodor, had transformed his palace into a cloister; when God had called him to Him his chamber was filled with sweet odours, and his face shone like the sun in its glory. But after that, God was wroth with Russia, and had sent it for its present Tsar a Tsar's assassin.

How old, asks Gregory, was the little Tsarevitch Dmitri when he was murdered? In Pushkin's play Pimen tells him the whole story; Moussorgsky omits most of it from his version of 1874. Pimen himself was in Uglich when it happened. He had been wakened by the tolling of an alarm bell. He followed the excited crowd to the palace where the body of the slaughtered boy lay. The mob had already captured and executed three suspected men, who, before they died, confessed their crime and named Boris as the instigator of it. The child was only seven years old. That was some twelve years ago, so that had he lived he would be the same

age as Gregory and would now be Tsar; and at this point we
hear in the orchestra the first quiet hint of a theme which will be
afterwards always associated with this Dmitri, and with Gregory
as the false Dmitri:

It is with this sad story, says Pimen, that he has closed his
chronicle, the continuation of which he commends to his young
companion.

The matin bell tolls, and the voices of monks are heard in
prayer outside. Pimen extinguishes his light and leaves the cell.
He is escorted as far as the door by Gregory, who pauses there,
however, to apostrophise Boris, whose crime, he says, will one
day meet with the general condemnation of men and the punishment of heaven.

The scene changes to an inn on the Lithuanian frontier. The
words of the Hostess's charming little song, wholly in the
Russian folk manner—"I have caught a drake"—were found by
Stassov in a collection of songs for children. The song is broken
in upon by voices outside; they are those of two wandering
monks, Varlaam and Missail, a couple of engaging sturdy rogues
and vagabonds who manage to combine piety with mendicancy
and both with deep drinking. The burden of their chant at the
moment is that if any rich believer shall be pleased to give—
through them—an alms for the building of a new church, God
will reward him a hundredfold.

The holy men enter with a blessing on the hostess and her
house. They are accompanied by Gregory, whom they have
fallen in with en route and about whom they are a trifle doubtful.
He is in secular clothes. All they have managed to learn about him
since he joined their company is that he is anxious to get to the
Lithuanian frontier; till then, as he now assures them once more
to a minor version of the Dmitri motive (No. 8), there will be no

U*

peace of mind for him. Recommending his own cheerful philosophy to the worried young man, Varlaam, having refreshed himself with the hostess's wine, launches into a lusty song about the fighting at Kazan, at which forty thousand Tartars were slain:

the text of which was another of Stassov's finds.

While the men of grace are getting drunker and drunker, Gregory takes the Hostess aside and asks her how far he is from the frontier. He can get there by nightfall, she tells him: but he will have difficulty in passing the guards, for it appears that some one has escaped from Moscow, and orders have come from the capital to detain and search all travellers. But there is another road into Lithuania besides the highway, details of which she gives the rather frightened Gregory. She has barely finished when a captain enters, accompanied by some guards, and interrogates the three men. Gregory does not seem to him to be worth bothering about, as his wallet is empty. In the oiliest of professional whines Varlaam protests that he and his pious brother in the Lord are also poor, for Christian folk, alas, are stingy nowadays. But the captain keeps looking at the old ruffian suspiciously: the fugitive from Moscow, he has been told, is a heretic monk, and Varlaam seems to him to fill that part of the bill to perfection. As the captain cannot read, and Varlaam thinks it prudent to deny that he has any learning himself, the warrant is handed to Gregory. "An unworthy monk", he reads out, "of the monastery of Chudov, Gregory Otrepiev, a heretic tempted by the devil, after trying to corrupt his holy brethren has fled towards the Lithuanian frontier, where, by order of the Tsar, he is to be arrested." "And hanged", adds the captain with gusto. Gregory says that there is nothing about hanging in the warrant; but the captain sagely remarks that the hanging is implied, for what is meant is not always put in writing. To oblige him, Gregory continues his reading with "to be arrested and hanged." Coming to the

description of the fugitive, he reads this out, looking meaningly
at Varlaam all the time, as "about fifty years old, of medium
height, baldish, grizzled, fat, red-nosed." The guards at once
fall on the sturdy monk, who, no doubt recalling his prowess at
Kazan, throws them off and threatens them with his clenched
fists. In presence of the danger that menaces him his scanty early
schooling most opportunely comes back to him; bit by bit he
manages to spell out the actual words of the warrant—"about
twenty years old, medium height, reddish hair, one arm shorter
than the other, a wart on his nose and another on his forehead."
He goes up to Gregory, takes a good look at him, and says
"You're the man!" But before any of them can lay hands on him,
Gregory, unsheathing a dagger, escapes through the window.

5

The second scene of the act is the Tsar's apartments in the
Kremlin. Xenia, Boris's daughter, is weeping over the portrait of
her dead lover, to whom she sings a moving little song. The young
Tsarevitch, Feodor, is poring over a large volume. The old
Nurse, who is busy with her needlework, tries to comfort and
distract the little Xenia by singing her a song in the folk-vein
about a gnat and other insects, the words of which were taken
from the collection of children's songs already mentioned, as were
those of the "hand-clapping game" that follows—in which, while
Feodor sings the tale of a hen, a pig and a calf and sundry other
farmyard fauna, he and the Nurse clap their hands on the first
beat of each bar. The song comes to a summary end as the Tsar
enters. He too tries, in grave and tender words, to comfort his
daughter in her sorrow, and then dismisses her and the Nurse.

The book which Feodor has been studying so eagerly is an
atlas of Russia, in which he now proudly points out to his father
all the leading features of the kingdom. Boris, after a word or two
of kindly encouragement, gives vent to the gloomy thoughts that
oppress him in a fine aria, "I have attained to highest power".
(In Pushkin this monologue occurs in an earlier and different
scene). It is six years, he muses, since he became Tsar; they have
been six years of care and calamity and disappointment. His
daughter has been bereaved of her lover: plague and famine have

devastated the land, and in spite of all he has done for his people they lay their misfortunes at his door: the Poles conspire against him: his nobles betray him. And worst of all, his crimes haunt him night and day; always he sees the bleeding body of the child he had murdered, his staring eyes, his hands raised in a plea for the mercy that was denied him. The realistic climax of the aria strikes terror through us, giving place to pity as the broken man murmurs, "O God, in Thy grace have mercy on me!"

From behind the scenes there comes a confused noise, the cause of which he sends Feodor to discover. A boyar, entering to announce that Prince Shuisky craves an audience, whispers in the Tsar's ear the bad news that has come from secret agents—that many of the boyars, among them Shuisky, are conspiring against the Tsar with his Polish and other enemies. Just then Feodor returns, and, apologising for troubling his father with his own trifling affairs when he has more weighty ones of his own to occupy him, tells him at considerable length the story of a tiff between his parrot and the old Nurse Nastasia. Boris congratulates him on the charming way he has explained the uproar he had been sent to investigate, adding, somewhat inconsequently, that "this is the fruit of learning, which gives wings to the mind", and expressing the hope that some day he may see his son rule Russia in his stead. Then Shuisky enters.

This scene is perhaps the weakest in the whole opera from the constructional point of view. There is no valid reason why Feodor should be present throughout Boris's long monologue, "I have attained to highest power", with its bitter self-communing and its confession of the crime of years ago. As we have seen, in Pushkin the magnificent monologue takes place much earlier —anterior, indeed, to the scene of Gregory and the friars at the frontier inn; and the Tsar is alone, as dramatic and psychological probability demands that he shall be, when he indulges in it. Why then does Moussorgsky keep the little Feodor on the stage all through this and much of the following scene? The only conclusion we can come to is that having the boy on his hands as a historical character he had to do something with him operatically. Xenia had had her little scene, and the Nurse—as also the Hostess at an earlier stage—had been allowed to sing at moderate

length. Obviously, then, the player of the part of Feodor would
also have to be given something or other to sing in addition to
his few lines in the "hand-clapping game", and this was the only
possible place for it in the whole opera; for the third act takes
place in Poland, and in the fourth, Feodor appears only when his
father is dying at a meeting of the Douma. Moussorgsky's
handling of the part of Feodor in this particular scene in the
second act nowhere makes sense. He gets the boy off the stage,
during the few words exchanged between the Tsar and the
messenger, under the pretext of sending him to discover the cause
of the uproar "off", which pretext in its turn becomes a pretext
for letting him explain it all in the song about the parrot. But
there may also have been at the back of Moussorgsky's mind the
vague idea that the boy ought not to be present—as he is in
Pushkin—when the messenger enters with the grave news of the
conspiracy of the boyars; for a little later, when Shuisky happens
to mention the names of the true and the false Dmitri, Boris
insists on the boy leaving them before he can learn any more.[1]
Feodor, apparently, must not know of the awkward report that
is spreading through the country that the Pretender is the real
Dmitri, falsely supposed to be dead, yet he is allowed to listen to
his father's confession of the murder of the child and to be a
witness of his soul-destroying remorse! In Pushkin, Feodor
remains in the room during both the report from the messenger
and the first part of the scene with Shuisky. The latter, at the
beginning of the interview, suggests that the boy be told to
withdraw, but Boris replies that "the Tsarevitch may learn what-

[1] Moussorgsky never improves matters by departing from Pushkin. In the
play, it is not until Shuisky's revelation that the Pretender who has appeared
in Poland claims to be the true Dmitri that Boris gives orders for the closing
of the Lithuanian frontier. The Tsar had issued no such orders when Gregory
had fled from the monastery. Why, indeed, should he do so? At that time he
knows nothing whatever of the monk. In Pushkin it is not the Tsar but the
Patriarch of the Church who, having heard of the flight of the renegade,
gives instructions for him to be captured and sent to do perpetual penance
somewhere: the Patriarch, indeed, expressly tells his informant (the Abbot of
the Chudov monastery) that there is no need to report the affair to Boris, in
spite of the fact that Gregory is known to have been babbling about his some
day being Tsar in Moscow.

ever Prince Shuisky knows." It is only later, when Shuisky mentions the danger to the throne in the current belief that Gregory is the Tsarevitch Dmitri, that Boris bids his son leave him. That makes sense, in Moussorgsky as in Pushkin; but it does not make sense in the opera to have a father anxious to keep from his son the terrible truth of his guilt in the matter of the murder of Dmitri, after he himself had laid it bare to him in an earlier scene!

The modern producer generally side-steps the absurdity of having Feodor present during the Tsar's agonised confession of his crime by getting the boy off the stage before Boris commences his monologue. But that Moussorgsky fully intended Feodor to be on the stage during the confession is proved by a letter of his to Stassov in 1871, in which he says, "The villainous Tsar Boris has now an arioso. . . . The words have been stitched together by my own exalted self. And since to watch and listen to the remorseful outburst of a villain for any length of time is both disgusting and depressing, a crowd of nursery-maids suddenly breaks into the room shrieking out some unintelligible gabble; the Tsar drives them out and sends his son to enquire what makes the women howl. In the boy's absence Prince Shuisky enters and whispers some secret information in Boris's ear. After he has been got rid of, the Tsarevitch returns, and the Tsar questions him"; after which comes the story of the parrot.[1] But in making these changes in his first plan (in 1871) Moussorgsky either failed to perceive the damage he was doing to the dramatic verisimilitude of the scene or was indifferent to it. We feel that he would have done better to keep more closely than he has done to Pushkin's scheme in this and one or two other places. Was he influenced to some extent in the present instance, one wonders, by the naïve desire to get in the song of the parrot by hook or by crook, having heard that it was in the reign of Boris that the first parrot came to Russia?

After this little excursion let us return to the point at which Shuisky enters.

Boris, who, from the reports of his spies, knows the Prince for the smooth, perfidious schemer that he is, begins to upbraid him for his hypocrisies and treasons. But Shuisky warns him that he

[1] Oscar von Riesemann, *Moussorgsky*, p. 189.

has grave news for him—a Pretender has appeared in Cracow, backed by the King of Poland, the nobles, and the Pope of Rome; and the danger to Boris lies in the fear that the Russian populace may accept this man as the true Dmitri. It is at this point that the agitated Tsar orders Feodor to withdraw—a command, as we have seen, which makes complete sense in the story as a whole as told by Pushkin, but makes something less than sense as Moussorgsky has seen fit to handle it. As soon as Feodor is out of hearing, Boris tells Shuisky to see that the Lithuanian frontier is closed at once. Then, his nerve already beginning to fail him, he asks the Prince whether he has ever heard of dead men rising from their graves to trouble Tsars who have been chosen by the voice of the people and anointed by the Patriarch. When he had heard of the death of the child, he says, it was Shuisky whom he had sent to Uglich to search the matter out. Will the Prince now swear that the body he saw was that of Dmitri? If he lies, he will meet with a punishment so dreadful that Ivan the Terrible would have shrunk from imposing it. Thereupon Shuisky tells him how for some days he had watched the body of the murdered child, laid out in the cathedral with the corpses of thirteen people who had been slaughtered by the mob; and while in these corruption had already set in, the body of the child was still whole, and his face as tranquil as if he were only sleeping.

The crafty Prince has thus poisoned Boris's soul while professing to heal it: he has certified that it was the body of the Tsarevitch himself which he had seen stretched out in the cathedral, with a deep gash in his throat, yet he has hinted that a miracle had happened and the child was not really dead. Boris dismisses Shuisky, who, as he goes, glances back maliciously at his victim. Boris is choking. An ominous chromatic figure in the orchestra:

hints at the storm raging in his brain. Moussorgsky now departs considerably from the Pushkin original. In the latter, Boris says, after a moment of weakness, "So this is why for thirteen years my dreams have been haunted by this murdered child!" Then he masters himself by a mighty effort. Who is this new enemy of his? he asks. A mere name, a shadow! He blows on the phantom and it vanishes! Not this shall wrest the succession from his son! He will go on his way cautiously, but without fear, heavy though his heart is. But in Moussorgsky he becomes the quintessence of all the Macbeths of life or literature. His guilty conscience pictures the murdered boy before him in the room, his throat dripping blood; the ghastly figure creeps towards him, quivering and groaning. "I am guiltless of thy murder!" cries Boris. "Not I! Not I! It was the people's will! O Lord my God, Thou who desirest not the sinner's death, show me Thy grace! Have mercy on the wretched Boris!" It is on this last broken cry of the crazed man that the curtain falls, after one of the most tremendous scenes in all opera. Moussorgsky has added curiously to the horror of the storm in the Tsar's brain by introducing the chiming of a big clock that stands on the left of the stage. That chiming clocks were probably first known in Russia in the reign of Boris was yet another discovery made by Stassov and Moussorgsky in the course of their researches in the Petersburg Public Library. Moussorgsky's genius for realism has enabled him to make the most moving psychological use of this effect.

6

The third act does not appear at all in the first score of the opera: it was added by Moussorgsky in 1871–2, presumably as a necessary step towards obtaining a performance, for one of the objections urged against the work as originally planned was that it contained no outstanding female rôle.

The actual Gregory, whom from this point onwards we shall for convenience' sake refer to as Dmitri, won the love of one Marina Mnischek, the daughter of a Polish notable, the Voyevode of Sandomir. The third act of the opera opens in Marina's apartment, where her maidens are amusing her with their songs as she sits before her mirror. Moussorgsky employs in this act the rhythms of the cracovienne (in 2/4 time), the mazurka, or the

polonaise (both in 3/4 time), to establish the Polish atmosphere.
The song of the girls in praise of Marina's beauty is of the
cracovienne type, while she herself answers them mostly in the
3/4 rhythm. She is not interested, she tells them:

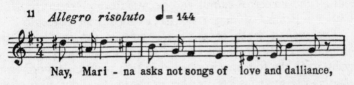

Nay, Mari - na asks not songs of love and dalliance,

in ditties of the conventional kind; her preference is for warrior
songs, tales of conquering heroes making the name of Poland
resound throughout the world. And when the maidens have been
dismissed she sings of the dullness of her life before this brilliant
adventurer from Russia came into it, this Dmitri, chosen by
heaven to punish Boris and take his throne from him. She is
ambitious for herself: she means both to persuade the Poles to
espouse his cause and to make him fall in love with her, for she
is weary of lovers of the ordinary sort. Already she sees herself, in
imagination, on the throne at Moscow, decked in jewels, a crowd
of admiring boyars at her feet. It must be confessed that these audacious sentiments lose much of their force in the stereotyped dance
rhythm in which Moussorgsky has seen fit to couch them.

She is interrupted by the entry of the Jesuit Rangoni, a
character of Moussorgsky's own invention. He laments the
poverty and neglect that have fallen to the lot of the Roman
Church in Poland, and exhorts Marina, if she should go to
Moscow, to make it her first duty to convert the Russian heretics
to the one true faith. She protests that a less exalted mission
would be more to her taste. But he insists. Her beauty, he says,
has bewitched this alien Pretender; she must now play her cards
in such a way as to enslave him utterly and then use him for the
Church's ends; nor need she be too scrupulous as to the means
she employs, so long as the purpose is attained. When she has
him in her toils, she is to extract an oath from him to work as the
Church directs. The proud, stubborn, self-seeking Marina turns
angrily on the Jesuit; but he cows her by asserting his claim, as
the messenger of heaven, to be the keeper of her soul.

There is nothing of all this in Pushkin—no character corresponding to Rangoni, indeed, though there are a few lines of
dialogue at one point between Dmitri and a Catholic priest, in
which the former promises that in two years' time "his people"
and all the Eastern Church will submit themselves to the Holy
Father in Rome.[1] Marina, of course, is a historical character.

The second scene of the act shows us the garden of the
Mnischek castle at Sandomir. It is moonlight, and Dmitri is
waiting by the fountain in obedience to a whispered word from
Marina. He sings his love for her in passionate terms. Out of the
shadow creeps the Jesuit Rangoni, accompanied by the oily,
snake-like motive:

which we have already learned to associate with him in the
preceding scene. He assures the young man that Marina is truly
in love with him, though she has to suffer much from those about
her at the court for having bestowed her affections on him.
Rangoni so works upon him that he loses what we may perhaps
call his inferiority complex as a conscious impostor and swears
that he will win Marina, make her his queen, and deal as they
deserve with the arrogant Polish nobles who despise him. The

[1] In Miss Howe's book will be found an English translation of the Pretender's letter of the 24th April 1604 to the Pope, written in Polish and
rendered into Latin by the Jesuit Sawicki. In this the false Dmitri, professing
to be anxious for the salvation not only of his own soul but that of all Mus-
covy, embraces "the immaculate and ancient doctrines of the Roman
Catholic and Apostolic Church", and declares himself willing, if God should
make his cause prosper, to use all his endeavours, when he has ascended his
"hereditary throne", to assist the Russians to see the light as he has been
fortunate enough to see it.

crafty Jesuit asks, as his own reward for his services, only to be
allowed to follow Dmitri wherever his fortunes may carry him,
as his spiritual counsellor and father. This Dmitri promises; then,
on the advice of the Jesuit, he conceals himself among the trees
as a number of guests pour out of the castle, Marina among them.
To the strain of a polonaise the Poles discuss the march on
Moscow that is in contemplation, or pay their compliments to
Marina.

At last they all re-enter the castle, and Dmitri, alone once more
in the garden, gives free vent to his hatred of the Jesuit, who, he
thinks, has deceived him with regard to Marina, for he has seen
her on the arm of an elderly Polish nobleman. The incident has
stung him to assert himself as, seemingly, he had never done
before. He will now, he declares, don his armour, mount his
steed, and lead his forces into battle for what he calls the throne
of his fathers. This resolution is symbolised by a bold motive in
the orchestra:

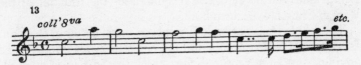

which will be used with fine effect in the last act.

At this point Marina enters. Dmitri pours out his heart to her,
but she at once gives him to understand that a return of his love
is impossible on her part unless and until she sees him enter
Moscow as Tsar; and once more we wish that Moussorgsky
could have found some better method of differentiating the two
characters musically than making Marina say everything she has
to say in a 3/4 rhythm that is too obviously labelled "genuine
Polish". He tries to bring her round to another way of thinking,
but she answers him only with irony and scorn: the upshot of it
all is that he can have her with Moscow but not without. In the
end she insults him beyond endurance, calling him just what he
is or has been, an impostor and a menial. This angers him; however mean his station may have been hitherto, he swears, he is the
rightful Tsar; and to the proud melody of No. 13 he tells her how
his cause is daily gaining strength in every quarter. On the

morrow he will march to Moscow; and then, when he is crowned
Tsar, he will look down on her in pride and contempt as she
crawls towards his throne, mocked by all.

Hereupon follows the "love-duet" proper, in which Marina
abandons the Polish dialect for a more international musical
idiom. She protests that it was only her great love for Dmitri
that had made her reproach him and seem to cross him as she had
done. She confesses that she loves him, and the scene ends with
their falling into each other's arms. As they do so we catch a
glimpse of the crafty Rangoni, who has been spying on them a
little distance away. It is the general practice of the theatres today
to omit Rangoni from the opera altogether, which is a great pity;
not only because without him there is no particular dramatic
point in bringing Marina into the story at all, but because the
spectator who has not made the Jesuit's acquaintance in the preceding scene misses entirely the subtle point of the downward-
gliding chromatic passage heard in the orchestra (No. 12) as
Dmitri and Marina embrace. It symbolises the triumph of the
Roman Church over them both.

The whole Polish episode is managed much better in Pushkin.
It is clear there that no one in high circles believes Dmitri to be
anything but an adventurer: they know that in Russia he is regarded merely as a renegade monk with a bad reputation, while
on his first entry into Poland he had been for a time a servant in
the house of Prince Vishnevetsky. In Pushkin's garden scene
Dmitri himself, annoyed by Marina's declaration that politics
and ambition count with her for more than love, admits frankly
that he is an impostor. For a moment Marina is shamed at the
discovery of how she has lowered herself, and stunned by the
blow to her ambitions. It is only when Dmitri's fighting spirit
revives, when he swears he will yet drive Boris from his throne
and then despise Marina, that something of respect for him is
reborn in her. But there is no love-making. She tells him frankly
that he can send for her when he is Tsar, but not before, and then
leaves him. After she has gone he says to himself that women are
craftier and more treacherous even than Tsars or Jesuits. He does
not trust her, and regrets having given her such a hold on him as
he has done by his confession. But at any rate his mind is at last

made up. He will waste no more time at the court of Poland: tomorrow he marches against Boris. All this makes sounder dramatic stuff than most of what Moussorgsky has given us in its place.   But, as we have seen, the third act did not exist at all in the first form of the opera. It was inserted mainly in order that the work should have a leading soprano as well as a leading tenor and a leading bass; and once she was admitted she was obviously marked out for a love-scene with the tenor.

7

But Moussorgsky's fourth act more than makes up for any shortcomings in the third.

The scene is a clearing in a wood, with the town walls of Kromy in the distance. A crowd of vagabonds rushes in, dragging with them a captured boyar, Kroutshov, bound hand and foot. They place him on a big fallen tree trunk in the middle of the stage, and there gag and plague and insult him, wreaking on this upholder of Boris the traditional hatred of the Russian peasantry and proletariat for their overlords. As it is not fitting, they say, that a boyar should be without a mistress and a cudgel, they install a toothless, mumbling, coughing old crone by him and put a whip in his hand, the while they sing a chorus in derision of him and of the Tsar and salute him with mock honours:

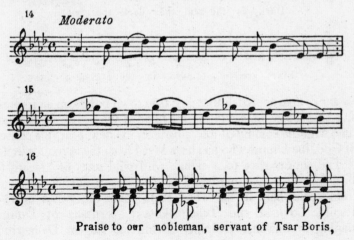

Praise to our   nobleman, servant of Tsar Boris,

Their orgy of malice is interrupted by the village Idiot, who is surrounded by a crowd of teasing boys. He is a pitiful figure, clothed in rags, with an iron saucepan on his head. Seating himself on a stone he sings a song which, perhaps, only Shakespeare among the poets could have matched for its pathos—a vacant, meaningless, yet heartbreaking song of cats crying in the moonlight, and he, the poor fool, praising God and hoping the weather will keep fine:

The boys torment the poor simpleton and rob him of his kopeck, whereupon he sets up a dismal howl.

Our attention is distracted from him by the voices of Varlaam and Missail behind the scene, singing of the evils that have descended on holy Russia because of the Tsar Boris:

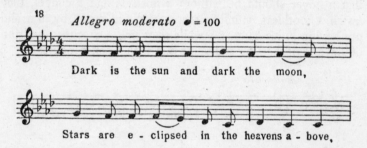

As the couple approach the stage the crowd builds up an impressive choral ensemble, voicing the hope of the people for a better time with the coming of their liberator, the new Tsar, the chosen of God, the Dmitri who had been saved from the assassin's knife.

The chorus rises to a climax with wild cries of "Death to Boris! Death to the murderer!" Then comes a sudden calm, and from somewhere in the wood there come the voices of two Jesuits, Lovitski and Tcherniakovski, partisans of Dmitri, singing in unison, "Domine, salvum fac Regem Demetrium

Moscoviae, Regem omnis Russiae". But Varlaam and Missail seem to resent this professional competition; they incite the mob against the Jesuits, who are dragged into the wood to be hanged.

Then martial music in the orchestra heralds the approach of Dmitri's troops. They are followed by Dmitri himself on horse-back. He is greeted with cries of joy by the crowd as he tells them that he, the lawful Tsarevitch of all the Russias, will protect them against Boris, and exhorts all who are for him to take part in his coming victory. This he sings to the accompaniment of the typical Dmitri motive (No. 8), which now receives a prouder form. He rides off to trumpet fanfares behind the scenes, followed by the crowd and by the two Jesuits—who, it turns out, have not been hanged after all—chanting a lusty "Deo Gloria!" The stage is at length empty except for the Idiot, who, still seated on the stone, laments prophetically the coming of woe unspeakable on the poor starving Russian folk. The curtain falls with a con-tinuous prolongation of his heartbreaking sobs in the orchestra:

Thus ends a scene that is unique in opera. And dramatically as well as musically it is almost wholly Moussorgsky's own inven-tion: even the moving figure of the Idiot, who appears for a moment in different circumstances in Pushkin, must really be placed to his credit.

The setting of the final scene is the reception hall in the Kremlin in Moscow. (In Pushkin the corresponding scene takes place after the defeat of the Pretender: it is not till later, after the death of Boris, that Dmitri attains his objective. This, of course, is in agreement with the historical facts).

A meeting of the Douma is in progress, and the boyars are arranging for a proclamation to be issued, branding the Pretender as a traitor and threatening with death all who support him. Shuisky, whom none of them trust, arrives late. He has disturbing news for them: recently, when leaving the presence of Boris, heavy at heart because he could see that all was not well with the Tsar, he had chanced to look back, and had seen him in a pitiable state—pale, trembling, wild-eyed, muttering strange fragments of phrases, seeing in his mind's eye the body of the murdered Tsarevitch, and shrinking back with a cry of "Avaunt!" Shuisky is still repeating this word when Boris himself enters and takes it up from him.

He is in a semi-cataleptic state, talking to himself for a while as if unaware that he is not alone. He is no murderer, he protests, and the lying Shuisky shall meet with atrocious punishment. Then, realising where he is and recovering himself somewhat, he seats himself on the throne, and begins to explain that he has summoned his boyars to counsel him in the difficult time that Russia is now passing through. But Shuisky craves permission to speak: outside, he says, is a pious old man who begs audience of the Tsar, for he has a weighty secret to impart to him. Boris orders him to be admitted: perhaps, he thinks, talk with one so good will ease his soul.

Pimen enters and plunges straight into his story. One evening, he says, an old shepherd, who had been blind from childhood, came to him and told him how he had heard a voice bidding him go to the Cathedral at Uglich and pray at the tomb of the Tsarevitch Dmitri, who is now a saint in heaven, able to work wonders. The shepherd had done so, and straightway his sight had been restored to him. Boris gives an agonised cry of "Help! Light! Air!" and collapses into the arms of some of the boyars. He bids them send for his son and bring the vestments to him. (It was the custom for the Tsars to prepare for death by being received into the Church and submitting to the tonsure).

The frightened little Feodor enters, and, left at length alone with him, Boris bids farewell to him and to the world. He counsels him to be firm and just when he becomes Tsar, trusting few, chastising traitors, defending the holy Russian Church and cherishing his sister Xenia. Upon his children, not upon himself, Boris invokes the protection of heaven. He takes Feodor in his arms and kisses him, then falls back exhausted. Outside are heard the solemn funeral bells and a chorus of church singers praying for the Tsar. "It is the mourners' wail!" says Boris: "give me the monk's robe; the Tsar goes to the cloister!" The boyars return in solemn procession, while the choristers sing of a little child who cried and struggled to be saved from death, and pleaded for mercy, but no mercy was granted him. With his last breath Boris starts up with a great cry of "I still am Tsar! Here"—pointing to his son—"is your new Tsar. Almighty God have mercy on me!" He presses his hand to his heart, sinks back in his chair, and dies.

This ending is Moussorgsky's own. In Pushkin it is the Patriarch of the Russian Church who tells the Tsar the story of the miracle of the shepherd. Boris shows some signs of agitation after hearing this, but makes no comment; and the situation is saved by Shuisky, who smoothly argues that a time of insurrection, such as the one they are then living in, is not the ideal time in which to test the truth of such tales, or, having tested them, to put them to profane use. He himself, he says, will publicly denounce the Pretender who presumably is the fountain head of all these rumours. In Pushkin's drama, as we have said, the death of Boris does not occur until much later. Boris, taken suddenly ill behind the scenes, is carried in by the boyars, is left alone with Feodor, and dies after giving his son a good deal of sound advice in statecraft on much the same lines as in Moussorgsky's final scene, but at greater length, and without any display of remorse or any hint of terror.

INDEX

626

INDEX

628

INDEX

MADE AND PRINTED BY OFFSET IN GREAT BRITAIN BY
WILLIAM CLOWES AND SONS LIMITED, LONDON AND BECCLES